BUYING DEFENCE AND SECURITY
IN EUROPE

Buying Defence and Security in Europe is the first critical evaluation of the EU Defence and Security Procurement Directive 2009/81/EC, which is now the basis for public and private entities buying armaments and sensitive goods and services in the EU. This instrument aims to ensure non-discrimination, competition and transparency in the security sectors. Part I provides a critical analysis of the economical, historical, political, military-strategic and legal contexts of the new EU Defence and Security Procurement Directive. Part II covers the main aspects of the Directive: its scope, procedures, security of supply and information, offsets and subcontracting and, finally, its review and remedies system. This book is an essential overview of a legislative milestone in the field.

MARTIN TRYBUS is Professor of European Law and Policy and Director of the Institute of European Law at the University of Birmingham. He has been involved in many studies of the OECD, the European Commission and the European Defence Agency on matters of public procurement and the European armaments market. He currently serves on the Procurement Review Board of the European Space Agency and is the legal expert on a team led by RAND Europe, providing advice and research for the European Commission on the transposition and implementation of the Defence and Security Procurement Directive.

BUYING DEFENCE
AND SECURITY IN EUROPE

The EU Defence and Security Procurement
Directive in Context

MARTIN TRYBUS

Professor of European Law and Policy
University of Birmingham

CAMBRIDGE
UNIVERSITY PRESS

CAMBRIDGE
UNIVERSITY PRESS

University Printing House, Cambridge CB2 8BS, United Kingdom

Cambridge University Press is part of the University of Cambridge.

It furthers the University's mission by disseminating knowledge in the pursuit of
education, learning and research at the highest international levels of excellence.

www.cambridge.org
Information on this title: www.cambridge.org/9781107002500

First published 2014

Printed in the United Kingdom by Clays, St Ives plc

A catalogue record for this publication is available from the British Library

Library of Congress Cataloguing in Publication data
Trybus, Martin, author.
Buying defence and security in Europe : the EU Defence and Security Procurement
Directive in context / Martin Trybus, Professor of European Law and Policy,
University of Birmingham.
pages   cm
Includes bibliographical references.
ISBN 978-1-107-00250-0
1. Defense contracts – European Union countries.   I. Title.
KJE5635.D45T75   2014
343.24'0156212–dc23
2014009751

ISBN 978-1-107-00250-0 Hardback

A Ana, Daniel y Thomas

CONTENTS

Acknowledgements   *page* xvi
Table of cases   xvii
Table of legislation and other instruments   xxx
Abbreviations   xliv

Introduction   1

PART I **The context of the Defence Directive**   15

1 The political and economic context of the Defence Directive Buyers,
   sellers, and national security   17
   1 Introduction   17
   2 The economic context   18
      2.1 Who is buying? Demand of defence and security goods and services in
           the EU   18
      2.2 Who is selling? The structure of the European defence and security
           market   21
           2.2.1 The European defence market: prime contractors   22
           2.2.2 The European security market: prime contractors   26
           2.2.3 Subcontractors   27
      2.3 Economic characteristics of defence procurement   27
           2.3.1 Buying European as a last resort: protectionism or buy
                  American   28
           2.3.2 Monopsony   31
           2.3.3 Monopolies   33
           2.3.4 Duplication   33
           2.3.5 High costs   35
           2.3.6 State ownership and control   37
           2.3.7 Inefficiency   38
   3 The political and military background   39
      3.1 Sovereignty and autarky   40

3.2   National security   41
   3.2.1   Security of supply   42
   3.2.2   Security of information   43
   3.2.3   The military security cost of non-Europe in
       defence   44
3.3   The pull and push towards deeper European defence and security
   integration   45
4   Technological and contractual characteristics of defence
  procurement   49
4.1   Research and development   50
   4.1.1   Off-the-shelf purchases   50
   4.1.2   Research and development procurement   51
4.2   Long life cycles   52
4.3   Collaboration   53
4.4   Offsets   54
4.5   Long supply chains   57
4.6   Public-private partnerships   57
4.7   Corruption   58
5   Conclusions   58

2   The legal base of the Defence Directive in EU Internal Market law:
  Prohibitions, exemptions and proportionality   61
1   Introduction   61
2   The EU Internal Market and defence and security procurement   62
2.1   The free movement of goods   63
2.2   The free movement of services and the freedom of
   establishment   67
2.3   The prohibition of discrimination on grounds of nationality   70
2.4   The public security exemption   70
   2.4.1   Public security   72
   2.4.2   The narrow interpretation: *Johnston, Sirdar, Kreil, and
       Dory*   73
   2.4.3   The proportionality test: *Campus Oil* and *Greek Petroleum
       Law*   76
      2.4.3.1   Proportionality   76
      2.4.3.2   *Campus Oil*   79
      2.4.3.3   *Greek Petroleum Law*   80
   2.4.4   Intensity of scrutiny – a real, specific and serious risk:
       Albore   81
3   Internal Market legal bases of the Defence Directive   82
4   Conclusions   83

3 Defence derogations from the Treaty: Articles 346 and
   347 TFEU   85

   1 Introduction   85
   2 The armaments exemption of Article 346(1) (b) TFEU   87
      2.1 The List of armaments according to Article 346(2)
          TFEU   88
          2.1.1 Armaments on the List   90
          2.1.2 Material not on the List   94
          2.1.3 Military use: the *Agusta* case law and *Finnish
                Turntables*   96
          2.1.4 Armaments intended for exports: *Fiocchi Munizioni*   103
      2.2 The effect of Article 346 (1)(b) TFEU   104
          2.2.1 Not necessary for national security: *Spanish Weapons* and
                beyond   108
                2.2.1.1 Intensity of scrutiny   110
                2.2.1.2 Proportionality   113
          2.2.2 Burden of proof   119
          2.2.3 Derogation on a case-by-case basis   120
          2.2.4 Procedural requirements and hard defence material intended
                for export   121
          2.2.5 When the review procedure under Article 348 TFEU is
                used   122
      2.3 The Commission's 2006 Interpretative Communication   125
      2.4 Summary: the interpretation of Article 346(1)(b) TFEU   127
   3 The secrecy exemption of Article 346 (1) (a) TFEU   128
      3.1 Abuse of Article 346(1)(a) TFEU   129
      3.2 Intensity of scrutiny: *German Military Exports*   131
   4 The crisis situations exemption in Article 347 TFEU   133
   5 Conclusions   134

4 The EU law and policy context beyond the Defence Directive:
   Intra-Community transfers, exports, standardisation, competition
   law, mergers, and State aid   136

   1 Introduction   136
   2 Trade in armaments and dual use goods   138
      2.1 Customs duties   139
      2.2 Intra-Community transfers   139
          2.2.1 Intra-Community transfers of armaments   140
                2.2.1.1 Situation before the ICT Directive   143
                2.2.1.2 Intra-Community transfers and
                        procurement   146
                2.2.1.3 The ICT Directive   147

2.2.2   Intra-Community transfer of dual-use goods: Regulation
        428/2009/EC   156
2.3   Defence exports   160
        2.3.1   Exports of dual-use goods   161
        2.3.2   Exports of armaments: Common Position
                2008/944/CFSP   163
3   Standardisation   166
4   Competition (anti-trust) law: Articles 101 and 102 TFEU   169
5   Merger control   172
6   State aid   176
        6.1   State aid practices in the defence sector   176
        6.2   Legality of State aid practices under the TFEU   181
7   Other activities   182
8   Conclusions   183

5   European armaments law and policy outside the EU
    Internal Market: EDA, OCCAR, Letter of Intent and NATO   185
    1   Introduction   185
    2   The European Defence Agency   186
        2.1   The organisational structure of the EDA   187
        2.2   The tasks of the EDA   189
                2.2.1   Development of policies   189
                        2.2.1.1   The EDA Procurement Code   191
                        2.2.1.2   Offsets and subcontracting   198
                        2.2.1.3   Enforcement and remedies   207
                        2.2.1.4   Compatibility of the EDA Procurement Code
                                  with the Defence Directive   209
                2.2.2   Evaluation of national capability
                        commitments   217
                2.2.3   Pooling and sharing   218
                2.2.4   Collaborative projects and joint research
                        programmes   218
        2.3   The EDA as part of the CSDP of the Treaty of Lisbon   221
    3   OCCAR   222
    4   Letter of Intent   225
        4.1   The LoI Framework Agreement Treaty   226
        4.2   Tasks   227
        4.3   Yet another framework   230
    5   Bilateral initiatives   231
    6   Overcoming the fragmentation of defence procurement
        frameworks   232
        6.1   Going the way of the WEAO: overcoming external
              fragmentation   233

6.2 Overcoming internal fragmentation 237

7 NATO Agencies 239

8 Conclusions 240

PART II **The contents of the Defence Directive** 243

6 Inside or outside the Defence Directive: Limitation of scope 245

1 Introduction 245

2 The personal scope of the Defence Directive: covered contracting entities 248

2.1 The abstract definition of contracting authorities 248

2.1.1 The State, regional or local authorities 249

2.1.1.1 Ministries of Defence and the armed forces 249

2.1.1.2 Contracting authorities other than Ministries of Defence and the armed forces 251

2.1.2 Bodies governed by public law 252

2.1.3 Utilities 253

2.1.4 Central purchasing bodies 255

2.1.4.1 Is the EDA a central purchasing body? 256

2.1.4.2 Are OCCAR and LOI central purchasing bodies? 258

2.2 The lack on an Annex IV for the Defence Directive 259

3 The material scope of the Directive: covered contracts 260

3.1 Military equipment 261

3.2 Sensitive contracts 263

3.3 Other included contracts 265

3.4 The Defence Directive and the other procurement Directives 266

4 The material scope of the Directive: excluded contracts 267

4.1 In-house contracts 268

4.2 The thresholds of the Defence Directive 269

4.3 Exceptions 272

4.3.1 Article 12 Defence Directive: contracts awarded under international rules 272

4.3.2 Article 13 Defence Directive: specific rules 276

4.3.2.1 Secrecy 278

4.3.2.2 Intelligence activities 281

4.3.2.3 Cooperative programmes 283

4.3.2.4 Contracts of forces deployed outside the territory of the Union 288

4.3.2.5 Government-to-government contracts 292

4.3.2.6 Contracts for R&D services 299

4.3.3   Article 11 Defence Directive: the safeguard clause?   301

4.4   The Defence Directive and the TFEU   303

4.5   The Defence Directive and the Public Sector Directive   305

4.6   The Defence Directive and the Utilities Directive   307

5   Transposition   307

6   Conclusions   308

7   Security through flexibility: The procurement procedures of the Defence Directive   310

1   Introduction   310

2   No open procedure   312

3   The restricted procedure   318

4   The (default) negotiated procedure with prior publication of a contract notice   322

5   Competitive dialogue   331

6   Negotiated procedure without prior publication of a contract notice   336

6.1   Situations *not* specific to the Defence Directive   338

6.2   Situations specific to the Defence Directive   341

6.2.1   Urgency resulting from a crisis   342

6.2.2   Armed forces deployed abroad   344

6.2.3   Research and development services   345

6.2.4   Summary   346

6.3   Control mechanism   347

7   Other procedures in the Defence Directive   347

7.1   Framework agreements   348

7.2   Electronic auctions   350

7.3   Dynamic purchasing systems   350

8   Cooperative programmes based on research and development (R&D)   351

8.1   European Space Agency   352

8.2   The Defence Directive   355

8.3   Public Sector Directive 2014/24/EU: innovation partnerships   355

9   Conclusions   356

8   Security of supply and security of information: Description in the specifications, contract conditions, qualification and award criteria   358

1   Introduction   358

1.1   Security of supply   359

1.2   Security of Information   361

2   Contract notice, technical specifications and contract conditions   362

2.1   Technical specifications   364

2.2 Contract performance conditions 366
   2.2.1 Security of supply 368
      2.2.1.1 Export, transfer and transit of goods associated with the contract 368
      2.2.1.2 Restrictions on disclosure, transfer or use 370
      2.2.1.3 Organisation of the supply chain 371
      2.2.1.4 Additional needs resulting from a crisis 373
      2.2.1.5 Maintenance, modernisation and adaptation 375
      2.2.1.6 Industrial changes 376
      2.2.1.7 Ceasing of production 376
      2.2.1.8 Conclusions on contract conditions concerning security of supply 377
   2.2.2 Security of information 379
      2.2.2.1 Commitment to safeguard confidentiality 379
      2.2.2.2 Information on subcontractors 380
   2.2.3 Description 381
2.3 National transposition 381
3 Qualification of bidders 382
   3.1 Exclusion of unsuitable candidates 383
      3.1.1 Professional conduct 384
      3.1.2 Grave professional misconduct 384
      3.1.3 Risks to the security of the Member State 386
   3.2 Economic and financial standing and technical and professional capacity 388
      3.2.1 Study and research facilities 389
      3.2.2 Geographical location of sources 390
      3.2.3 Classified information and security clearances 392
      3.2.4 Security of supply and information as technical capacity criteria 397
   3.3 Invitation to bid or negotiate: selection 398
   3.4 National transposition 400
4 Award criteria 400
5 Conclusions 403

9 Addressing the structure of the European defence industries: Substituting offsets with subcontracts? 406
1 Introduction 406
2 Offsets and subcontracts in defence procurement 406
3 Offsets in EU Internal Market law and the Defence Directive 410
   3.1 Offsets under the TFEU 411
   3.2 Offsets and the Defence Directive 418
   3.3 Commission Guidance Notes 422
   3.4 National laws of the Member States 425

4   The subcontracting regime of the Defence Directive   428
    4.1   Options for subcontracting   430
          4.1.1   Option A: the prime contractor is free to choose
                  subcontractors   431
          4.1.2   Option B: awarding subcontracts on the basis of competitive
                  procedures   432
          4.1.3   Option C: awarding minimum percentage of subcontracts
                  on the basis of competitive procedures   434
          4.1.4   Option D: requirement of minimal percentage to be
                  subcontracted and competition for subcontract beyond
                  the minimal percentage   436
    4.2   Subcontracting requirements in the prime contract award
          procedure   438
    4.3   Title III: rules applicable to subcontracting   440
          4.3.1   Scope   440
          4.3.2   Principles   441
          4.3.3   Thresholds and advertising   445
          4.3.4   Framework agreements   446
          4.3.5   Qualitative selection   447
          4.3.6   Exception clause   448
          4.3.7   Award criteria   450
          4.3.8   Subcontracts awarded by prime contractors
                  which are contracting authorities or entities   451
    4.4   The new Public Sector Directive 2014/24/EU   451
5   Conclusions   452

10 The 'hidden Remedies Directive': Review and remedies in the Defence
    Directive   455
    1   Introduction   455
    2   The need for review and remedies   456
        2.1   The "hidden" Remedies Directive   458
        2.2   Security derogations in the TFEU   460
    3   Adapting Public Sector Directive
        2004/18/EC   462
        3.1   Limitation   462
        3.2   Flexibility   464
        3.3   Description   465
        3.4   Substitution   466
    4   Adapting the Public Sector Remedies Directive   467
        4.1   Review bodies   468
        4.2   Security in the review bodies   471

4.3   Interlocutory proceedings   474
4.4   Ineffectiveness   477
5   Conclusions   481

Conclusions and recommendations   484

Bibliography   493
Index   503

ACKNOWLEDGEMENTS

I would like to thank a number of colleagues who supported the completion of this book by reading and providing feedback on several draft chapters: Andrew James (Manchester Business School) on chapter 1, Luke Butler (University of Bristol) and Luca Rubini (currently EUI Florence) on parts of chapter 4, Roberto Caranta (University of Turin) and Georgios Sampanis (University of Siegen) on chapter 6, Pedro Telles (University of Bangor) on chapter 7 and Michael Steinicke (University of Aarhus) on chapter 8. Moreover, I especially thank Tony Arnull (Birmingham Law School) for his feedback on chapters 3 and 10 and Baudouin Heuninckx (Belgian Air Force) for his feedback on chapters 5, 9 and 10. Baudouin and Luke also provided comments on my recommendations.

I have also benefited from seminar and conference events on European defence procurement which occurred during the completion of this book. This refers especially to the seven seminars on the Defence Directive at the European Institute of Public Administration (EIPA) in Maastricht between 2008 and 2012, but also to conferences organised by the Atlantic Council in Washington in 2010, the (United Kingdom) Procurement Lawyers Association (PLA) in London in 2011, the International Chamber of Commerce (ICC) in Paris in 2011, Forum Vergabe and the University of the Bundeswehr in Munich in 2012 and the Public Procurement Research Group of the University of Nottingham in 2013. These events gave me the opportunity to communicate with many colleagues, practitioners, the drafters of the Defence Directive and the drafters of some of the transposing legislation in the Member States.

Moreover, I benefited from discussions with Barbara Rupp, Bill Giles, Nicholas Pourbaix, Aris Georgopoulos, Bernardo Diniz de Ayala, Ciara Kennedy-Loest, Susie Smith, Michael Bowsher, Chris Yukins, Michael Walter, the participants of the event mentioned above, my PhD student Luke Butler, my LLM student Lucien Lagarde and the students on my public procurement and EU defence integration courses at the University of Birmingham. Finally, I want to thank Brina Počivalček (University of Ljubljana) for help with the compilation of the tables and bibliography. The title of this book was inspired by Christopher McCrudden, *Buying Social Justice* (2007).

Martin Trybus

TABLE OF CASES

European Court of Justice
Numerical

Case 26/62, *Van Gend en Loos* v. *Nederlandse Administratie der Belastingen* [1963] ECR 1, [1963] CMLR 105, 114

Case C-6/64, *Costa* v. *Ente Nazionale per l'Energia Elettrica* [1964] ECR 585, 216, 262

Case 24/68, *Commission* v. *Italy* ('Statistical Levy') [1969] ECR 193, [1971] CMLR 611, 64

Case 7/68, *Commission* v. *Italy* ('Arts Treasures') [1968] ECR 423, 63, 64

Case 13/68, *SpA Salgoil* v. *Italian Ministry of Foreign Trade* [1968] ECR 453, [1969] CMLR 181, at 192, 74, 79, 94, 117, 414

Joint Cases 2/69 and 3/69, *Sociaal Fonds for de Diamantarbeiders* v. *Brachfeld* ('Diamond Workers') [1969] ECR 211, 64

Case 2/73, *Geddo* v. *Ente Nazionale Risi* [1973] ECR 865, [1974] 1 CMLR 1, 65

Case 120/73, *Gebrüder Lorenz GmbH* v. *Germany* [1973] ECR 1471, 179

Case 8/74, *Procureur du Roi* v. *Dassonville* [1974] ECR 837, [1974] 2 CMLR 436, 65, 66, 141, 411, 412

Case 48/75, *Procureur du Roi* v. *Royer* [1976] ECR 497, 68

Case 77/77, *BP* v. *Commission* [1978] ECR 1513, [1978] 3 CMLR 174, 80

Case 120/78, *REWE – Zentrale AG* v. *Bundesmonopolverwaltung für Branntwein* ('Cassis de Dijon') [1979] ECR 649, [1979] 3 CMLR 494, 66, 413

Case 148/78, *Pubblico Ministero* v. *Ratti* [1979] ECR 1629, 214

Case 730/79, *Philip Morris Holland* v. *Commission* [1980] ECR 2671, [1981] CMLR 321, 23, 176

Case 50/80, *Dansk Supermarked A/S* v. *A/S Imerco* [1981] ECR 181, 67

Case 279/80, *Webb* [1981] ECR 3305, 69

Case 76/81, *Transporoute et Travaux SA* v. *Ministère des travaux publics* [1982] ECR 417, 271, 382, 443

Case 249/81, *Commission* v. *Ireland* ('Buy Irish') [1982] ECR 4005, 412

Joined Cases 177/82 and 178/82, *Jan van der Haar and Kaveka de Meern BV* [1984] ECR 1797, 67

Case 72/83, *Campus Oil Limited* v. *Minister for Industry and Energy*, [1984] ECR 2727, [1984] 3 CMLR 544, 73, 79–80, 81, 110, 111, 216, 391, 413, 416

Case 231/83, *Cullert* v. *Centre Leclerc* [1985] ECR I-306, [1985] 2 CMLR 524, 80

Case 103/84, *Commission* v. *Italy* [1986] ECR 1759, 412

Case 205/84, *Commission* v. *Germany* [1986] ECR 3755, 69

Case 222/84, *Marguerite Johnston* v. *Chief Constable of the Royal Ulster Constabulary* [1986] ECR 1651, [1986] 3 CMLR 240, 73–76, 79, 86, 93, 94, 97, 103, 105, 109, 117, 414, 468

Case 199/85, *Commission* v. *Italy* [1987] ECR 1039, 337

Case 263/85, *Commission* v. *Italy* [1991] ECR I-2457, 271, 443

Case 352/85, *Bond van de Adverteerders* v. *The Netherlands* [1988] ECR 2085, 69

Joined Cases 27/86 and 29/86, *CEI and Bellini* [1987] ECR 3347, 382

Case 302/86, *Commission* v. *Denmark* ('Danish Bottles') [1986] ECR 4607, 66

Case 29/87, *Dansk Denkavit Aps* v. *Danish Ministry of Agriculture* [1988] ECR 2965, 64

Case 31/87, *Gebroeders Beentjes BV* v. *The Netherlands* [1988] ECR 4635, 367

Case 45/87, *Commission* v. *Ireland* ('Dundalk') [1988] ECR 4929, 271, 365, 443

Case 187/87, *Cowan* v. *Trésor Public* [1989] ECR 195, 70

Case 307/87, *Commission* v. *Greece* [1989] ECR 461, 70

Case 3/88, *Commission* v. *Italy* ('Data Processing') [1989] ECR 4035; [1991] CMLR 115, 69, 271, 443

Case 21/88, *Du Pont de Nemours Italiana* v. *Unità Sanitara Locale di Carrara* [1990] ECR I-889, 271, 443

Case 347/88, *Commission* v. *Greece* ('Greek Petroleum Law') [1990] ECR I-4747, 80

Case 113/89, *Rush Portuguesa* v. *Office national d'immigration* [1990] ECR I-1417, 69, 443

Case 180/89, *Commission* v. *Italy* ('Italian Tourist Guides') [1991] ECR I-709, 69

Case 243/89, *Commission* v. *Denmark* ('Storebaelt') [1993] ECR I-3353, 67, 69, 271, 443

Case C-360/89, *Commission* v. *Italy* [1992] ECR I-3401, 271, 443

Case C-367/89, *Criminal Proceedings against Aimé Richardt and Les Accessoires Scientifiques SNC* [1991] ECR I-4645, 72, 86, 89, 140, 163

Joined Cases C-1/90 and C-176/90, *Aragonesa de Publicidad Exterior SA and Publivia SAE* v. *Departamento de Sanidad y Seguridad Social de la Generalidad de Cataluña* [1991] ECR I-4151, 67

Case C-159/90, *SPUC* v. *Grogan* [1991] ECR I-4685, 76

Case C-354/90, *Fédération Nationale du Commerce Extérieur des Produits Alimentaires and Syndicat Nationale des Négociants et Transformateurs de Saumon* v. *France* [1991] ECR I-5523, 179

Cases C-267 and C-268/91, *Criminal Proceedings against Bernard Keck and Daniel Mithouard* [1993] ECR I-6097, [1995] 1 CMLR 101, 66

Case C-272/91, *Commission* v. *Italy* ('Lottomatica') [1992] ECR I-3929, 271, 443

Case C-71/92, *Commission* v. *Spain* [1993] ECR I-5923, 337

Case C-389/92, *Ballast Nedam Group NV* v. *Belgian State* [1994] ECR I-1289, 337, 382

Case C-328/92, *Commission* v. *Spain* [1994] ECR I-1569, 337

Case C-324/93, *R.* v *Secretary of State for the Home Department Ex parte Evans Medical and Macfarlan Smith* ('Evans Medical') [1995] ECR I-563, 381

Case C-359/93, *Commission* v. *Netherlands* ('UNIX') [1995] ECR I-157, 67, 69, 365, 443

Case C-412/93, *Leclerc-Siplec* v. *TFI Publicité and M6 Publicité* [1995] ECR I-179, 67, 271

Case C-55/94, *Gebhard* v. *Consiglio dell'Ordine degli Avvocati e Precuratori di Milano* [1995] ECR I-4165, 68

Case C-70/94, *Fritz Werner Industrie-Ausrüstungen GmbH* v. *Germany* [1995] ECR I-3989, 72, 86, 94, 158, 163

Case C-83/94, *Criminal Proceedings against Peter Leifer and others* [1995] ECR I-3231, 72, 86, 114, 158, 163

Case C-87/94, *Commission* v. *Belgium* ('Walloon Buses') [1996] ECR I-2043, 271, 443

Case C-120/94 R, *Commission* v. *Greece* ('FYROM') [1996] ECR I-1513, 112, 113, 123, 124

Case C-3/95, *Reisebüro Broede* v. *Gerd Sanker* [1996] ECR I-6511, 412

Case C-120/95, *Decker* v. *Caisse de Maladie des Employés Privés* [1995] ECR I-1831, [1998] 2 CMLR 879, 66, 413

Case C-368/95, *Vereinigte Familiapress Zeitungsverlags- und Vertriebs GmbH* v. *Heinrich Bauer* ('Familiapress') [1997] 3 CMLR 1329, 66

Case C-44/96, *Mannesmann Anlagenbau Austria* v. *Strohal Rotationsdruck GmbH* [1998] ECR I-73, 246

Case C-323/96, *Commission* v. *Belgium* ('Vlaamse Raad') [1998] ECR I-5063, 246

Case C-360/96, *Gemeente Arnhem* v. *BFI Holding BV* [1998] ECR I-6821, 246

Case C-224/97, *Erich Ciola* v *Land Vorarlberg* [1999] ECR I-2530, 413

Case C-273/97, *Sirdar* v. *The Army Board* [1999] ECR I-7403, [1999] 3 CMLR 559, 73–76, 79, 97, 105, 113, 117, 127, 216

Case C-306/97, *Connemara Machine Turf Co Ltd* v. *Ciollte Teoranta* [1998] ECR I-8761, 246

Case C-414/97, *Commission* v. *Spain* ('Spanish Weapons') [1999] ECR I-5585, [2000] 2 CMLR 4, 97, 98, 100, 108–110, 111, 113, 115, 116, 117, 118, 119, 120, 121, 122, 125, 126, 127, 129, 130, 139, 142, 146, 163, 165, 166, 181, 210, 211, 213, 414, 415, 418

Case C-107/98, *Teckal Srl* v. *Comune de Viano* [1999] ECR I-8121, 246, 268, 269, 293, 300

Case C-225/98, *Commission* v. *France* ('Nord-Pas-de-Calais') [2000] ECR I-7445, 367, 382

Case C-275/98, *Unitron Scandinavia AS* v. *Ministeriet for Fødevarer, Landbrug of Fiskeri* [1999] ECR I-8291, 271, 443

Case C-285/98, *Kreil* v. *Germany* [2000] ECR I-69, 73–76, 79, 97, 105, 113, 117, 127

Case C-324/98, *Telaustria Verlags GmbH* v. *Telekom Austria AG* [2000] ECR I-10745, 271, 443

Case C-376/98, *Germany* v. *European Parliament and the Council* ('Tobacco Advertising') [2000] ECR I-8419, 83

Case C-380/98, *R. (on the application of Cambridge University)* v. *HM Treasury* [2000] ECR I-8035, 246

Case C-423/98, *Alfredo Albore* [2000] ECR I-5965, [1999] ECR I-5965, 74, 81–82, 86, 117

Case C-260/99, *Agorà Srl and Excelsior Snc di Pedrotti Bruna & C.* v. *Ente Autonomo Fiera Internazionale di Milano and Ciftat Soc. coop. arl.* [2001] ECR I-3605, 246

Case C-400/99, *Italy* v. *Commission* [2001] ECR I-7303, 179

C-470/99, *Universale Bau AG* v. *Entsorgunsbetriebe Simmering GmbH* [2002] ECR I-11617, 246, 271, 443

Case C-513/99, *Concordia Bus Finland Oy Ab* v. *Helsingin kaupunki and HKL Bussilikenne* [2002] ECR I-7213, 400, 401

Case C-59/00, *Bent Mousten Vestergaard* v. *Spøttrup Boligselskab* [2001] ECR I-9505, 67, 69, 443

Case C-280/00, *Altmark Trans GmbH* v. *Nahverkehrsgesellschaft Altmark GmbH* [2003] ECR I-774, 178

Case C-358/00, *Buchhändler Vereinigung GmbH* v. *Saur Verlag GmbH & Co und die Deutsche Bibliothek* [2002] ECR I-4685, 271, 443

Case C-373/00, *Adolf Truley* v. *Bestattung Wien* [2003] ECR I-1931, 246, 248

Case 186/01, *Alexander Dory* v. *Germany* [2003] ECR I-2479, 73–76, 79, 97, 113, 127

Case C-252/01, *Commission* v. *Belgium* ('Belgian Coastal Photography') [2003] ECR I-11859, 111, 216

Case C-448/01, *EVN AG and Wienstrom GmbH* v. *Austria* [2003] ECR I-14523, 401, 402

Case C-26/03, *Stadt Halle RPL Recyclingpark Lochau GmbH* v. *Arbeitsgemeinschaft Thermische Restabfall- und Energieverwertungsanlage TREA Leuna* [2005] ECR I-1, 268

Case C-84/03, *Commission* v. *Spain* [2005] ECR I-139, 268

Case C-231/03, *Consorzio Aziende Metano (Coname)* v. *Comune di Cingia de' Botti* [2005] ECR I-7287, 271, 443

Case C-234/03, *Contse SA, Vivisol Srl, Oxigen Salud SA* v. *Instituto Nacional de Gestion Sanitaria (Ingesa)* [2005] ECR I-9315, 271, 443

Case C-264/03, *Commission* v. *France* [2005] ECR I-8831, 271, 443

Case C-358/03, *Commission* v. *Austria* ('Parking Brixen') [2004] ECR I-12055, 271, 443

Case C-503/03, *Commission* v. *Spain* [2006] ECR I-1097, 75

Case C-535/03, *Commission* v. *Italy* [2006] ECR I-2689, 271, 443

Case C-490/04, *Commission* v. *Germany* [2007] ECR I-6095, 75

Case C-284/05, *Commission* v. *Finland* [2009] ECR I-11705, 74, 102, 109, 110, 115, 116, 118, 120, 122, 129, 139, 210, 415

Case C-294/05, *Commission* v. *Sweden* [2009] ECR I-11777, 74, 109, 110, 115, 116, 118, 120, 122, 129, 139, 210, 415

Case C-337/05, *Commission* v. *Italy* ('Agusta 1') [2008] ECR I-2173, 74, 75, 79, 96–103, 111, 116, 126, 127, 139, 142, 146, 163, 165, 181, 210, 263, 266, 415, 456, 489

Case 387/05, *Commission* v. *Italy* ('Agusta 2') [2009] ECR I-11831, 75, 79, 96–103, 116, 126, 127, 139, 142, 146, 163, 165, 181, 210, 263, 266, 415, 456, 489

Case C-409/05, *Commission* v. *Greece* [2009] ECR I-11859, 74, 109, 110, 115, 116, 118, 120, 122, 123, 129, 139, 210, 415

Case C-461/05, *Commission* v. *Denmark* [2009] ECR I-11887, 74, 109, 110, 115, 116, 118, 121, 122, 129, 139, 210, 415

Case C-38/06, *Commission* v. *Portugal* [2010] ECR I-1569, 74, 109, 110, 115, 116, 118, 120, 129, 139, 210, 415

Case C-157/06, *Commission* v. *Italy* [2008] ECR I-7313, 74, 96, 97, 98, 99, 121, 139, 210, 216, 263, 415, 456

Case C-239/06, *Commission* v. *Italy* [2009] ECR I-11913, 74, 109, 110, 115, 116, 118, 120, 122, 129, 139, 210, 415

Case C-532/06, *Emm. G. Lianakis AE and Others.* v. *Dimos Alexandroupolis and Others* ('Lianakis') [2008] ECR I-251, 382

Case C-141/07, *Commission* v. *Germany* [2008] ECR I-6935, 75

Case C-546/07, *Commission and Poland* v. *Germany* [2010] ECR I-00439, 75

Case C-317/08, *Rosalba Alassini* v. *Telecom Italia SpA*; Case C-318/08, *Filomena Califano* v. *Wind SpA*; Case C-319/08, *Lucia Anna Giorgia Iacono* v. *Telecom Italia SpA*; Case C-320/08, *Multiservice Srl* v. *Telecom Italia SpA* [2010] ECR I-2213, 468

Case C-279/09, *DEB Deutsche Energiehandels- und Beratungsgesellschaft mbH* v. *Germany* [2010] ECR I-13849, 468

C-364/10, *Hungary* v. *Slovak Republic*, Judgment of 16 October 2012, nyr, 456

Case C-615/10, *Insinööritoimisto InsTiimi Oy* ('Finnish Turntables'), judgment of 7 June 2012, nyr, 96–103, 122, 127, 210, 263, 266, 415, 489

Case C-465/11, *Forposta* v. *Poczta Polska*, judgment of 13 December 2012, nyr, 385

Alphabetical

Case C-260/99, *Agorà Srl and Excelsior Snc di Pedrotti Bruna & C.* v. *Ente Autonomo Fiera Internazionale di Milano and Ciftat Soc. coop. arl.* [2001] ECR I-3605, 246

Case C-337/05, ('Agusta 1') *Commission* v. *Italy* [2008] ECR I-2173, 74, 75, 79, 96–103, 111, 116, 126, 127, 139, 142, 146, 163, 165, 181, 210, 263, 266, 415, 456, 489

Case 387/05, ('Agusta 2') *Commission* v. *Italy* [2009] ECR I-11831, 75, 79, 96–103, 116, 126, 127, 139, 142, 146, 163, 165, 181, 210, 263, 266, 415, 456, 489

Case C-423/98, *Alfredo Albore* [2000] ECR I-5965, [1999] ECR I-5965, 74, 81–82, 86, 117

Case C-280/00, *Altmark Trans GmbH* v. *Nahverkehrsgesellschaft Altmark GmbH* [2003] ECR I-774, 178

Joined Cases C-1/90 and C-176/90, *Aragonesa de Publicidad Exterior SA and Publivia SAE* v. *Departamento de Sanidad y Seguridad Social de la Generalidad de Cataluña* [1991] ECR I-4151, 67

Case C-360/96, ('Arnhem') *Gemeente Arnhem* v. *BFI Holding BV* [1998] ECR I-6821, 246

Case 7/68, ('Arts Treasures') *Commission* v. *Italy* [1968] ECR 423, 63, 64

Case C-389/92, *Ballast Nedam Group NV* v. *Belgian State* [1994] ECR I-1289, 382

Case C-252/01, ('Belgian Coastal Photography') *Commission* v *Belgium* [2003] ECR I-11859, 111, 216

Case C-59/00, *Bent Mousten Vestergaard* v. *Spøttrup Boligselskab* [2001] ECR I-9505, 67, 69, 443

Case 352/85, *Bond van de Adverteerders* v. *The Netherlands* [1988] ECR 2085, 69

Case 77/77, *BP* v. *Commission* [1978] ECR 1513, [1978] 3 CMLR 174, 80

Case C-358/00, *Buchhändler Vereinigung GmbH* v. *Saur Verlag GmbH & Co und die Deutsche Bibliothek* [2002] ECR I-4685, 271, 443

Case 249/81, ('Buy Irish') *Commission* v. *Ireland* [1982] ECR 4005, 412

Case C-380/98, ('Cambridge University') *R. (on the application of Cambridge University)* v. *HM Treasury* [2000] ECR I-8035, 246

Case 72/83, *Campus Oil Limited* v. *Minister for Industry and Energy*, [1984]
    ECR 2727, [1984] 3 CMLR 544, 73, 79–80, 81, 110, 111, 216, 391, 413, 416
Case 120/78, ('Cassis de Dijon') *REWE – Zentrale AG* v.
    Bundesmonopolverwaltung für 11 *Branntwein* [1979] ECR 649, [1979] 3
    CMLR 494, 66, 413
Joined Cases 27/86 and 29/86, *CEI and Bellini* [1987] ECR 3347, 382
Case C-224/97, ('Ciola') *Erich Ciola* v *Land Vorarlberg* [1999] ECR I-2530, 413
Case C-546/07, *Commission and Poland* v. *Germany* [2010] ECR I-00439, 75
Case C-358/03, *Commission* v. *Austria* ('Parking Brixen') [2004] ECR I-12055,
    271, 443
Case C-87/94, *Commission* v. *Belgium* ('Walloon Buses') [1996] ECR I-2043,
    271, 443
Case C-323/96, *Commission* v. *Belgium* ('Vlaamse Raad') [1998]
    ECR I-5063, 246
Case C-252/01, *Commission* v. *Belgium* ('Belgian Coastal Photography') [2003]
    ECR I-11859, 216
Case 302/86, *Commission* v. *Denmark* ('Danish Bottles') [1986] ECR 4607, 66
Case C-243/89, *Commission* v. *Denmark* ('Storebaelt') [1993] ECR I-3353, 67,
    69, 271, 443
Case C-461/05, *Commission* v. *Denmark* [2009] ECR I-11887, 74, 109, 110, 115,
    116, 118, 121, 122, 129, 139, 210, 415
Case C-284/05, *Commission* v. *Finland* [2009] ECR I-11705, 74, 102, 109, 110,
    115, 116, 118, 120, 122, 129, 139, 210, 415
Case C-225/98, *Commission* v. *France* ('Nord-Pas-de-Calais') [2000] ECR
    I-7445, 367, 382
Case C-264/03, *Commission* v. *France* [2005] ECR I-8831, 271, 443
Case 205/84, *Commission* v. *Germany* [1986] ECR 3755, 69
Case C-490/04, *Commission* v. *Germany* [2007] ECR I-6095, 75
Case C-141/07, *Commission* v. *Germany* [2008] ECR I-6935, 75
Case 307/87, *Commission* v. *Greece* [1989] ECR 461, 70
Case C-347/88, *Commission* v. *Greece* ('Greek Petroleum Law') [1990] ECR
    I-4747, 80
Case C-120/94 R, *Commission* v. *Greece* ('FYROM') [1996] ECR I-1513, 112,
    113, 123, 124
Case C-409/05, *Commission* v. *Greece* [2009] ECR I-11859, 74, 109, 110, 115,
    116, 118, 120, 122, 123, 129, 139, 210, 415
Case 249/81, *Commission* v. *Ireland* ('Buy Irish') [1982] ECR 4005, 412
Case 45/87, *Commission* v. *Ireland* ('Dundalk') [1988] ECR 4929, 271,
    365, 443
Case 7/68, *Commission* v. *Italy* ('Arts Treasures') [1968] ECR 423, 63, 64
Case 24/68, *Commission* v. *Italy* ('Statistical Levy') [1969] ECR 12 193, [1971]
    CMLR 611, 64
Case 103/84, *Commission* v *Italy* [1986] ECR 1759, 412

Case 199/85, *Commission* v. *Italy* [1987] ECR 1039, 337
Case 263/85, *Commission* v. *Italy* [1991] ECR I-2457, 271, 443
Case 3/88, *Commission* v. *Italy* ('Data Processing') [1989] ECR 4035; [1991]
    CMLR 115, 69, 271, 443
Case C-180/89, *Commission* v. *Italy* ('Italian Tourist Guides') [1991]
    ECR I-709, 69
Case C-360/89, *Commission* v. *Italy* [1992] ECR I-3401, 271, 443
Case C-272/91, *Commission* v. *Italy* ('Lottomatica') [1992] ECR I-3929,
    271, 443
Case C-535/03, *Commission* v. *Italy* [2006] ECR I-2689, 271, 443
Case C-337/05, *Commission* v. *Italy* ('Agusta 1') [2008] ECR I-2173, 74, 75, 79,
    96–103, 111, 116, 126, 127, 139, 142, 146, 163, 165, 181, 210, 263, 266, 415,
    456, 489
Case C-387/05, *Commission* v. *Italy* ('Agusta 2') [2009] ECR I-11831, 75,
    79, 96–103, 116, 126, 127, 139, 142, 146, 163, 165, 181, 210, 263, 266, 415,
    456, 489
Case C-157/06, *Commission* v. *Italy* [2008] ECR I-7313, 74, 96, 97, 98, 99, 121,
    139, 210, 216, 263, 415, 456
Case C-239/06, *Commission* v. *Italy* [2009] ECR I-11913, 74, 109, 110, 115, 116,
    118, 120, 122, 129, 139, 210, 415
Case C-359/93, *Commission* v. *Netherlands* ('UNIX') [1995] ECR I-157, 67, 69,
    365, 443
Case C-38/06, *Commission* v. *Portugal* [2010] ECR I-1569, 74, 109, 110, 115,
    116, 118, 120, 129, 139, 210, 415
Case C-71/92, *Commission* v. *Spain* [1993] ECR I-5923, 337
Case C-328/92, *Commission* v. *Spain* [1994] ECR I-1569, 337
Case C-414/97, *Commission* v. *Spain* ('Spanish Weapons') [1999] ECR I-5585,
    [2000] 2 CMLR 4, 98, 100, 108–110, 111, 113, 115, 116, 117, 118, 119, 120,
    121, 122, 125, 126, 127, 129, 130, 139, 142, 146, 163, 165, 166, 181, 210, 211,
    213, 414, 415, 418
Case C-84/03, *Commission* v. *Spain* [2005] ECR I-139, 268
Case C-503/03, *Commission* v. *Spain* [2006] ECR I-1097, 75
Case C-294/05, *Commission* v. *Sweden* [2009] ECR I-11777, 74, 109, 110, 115,
    116, 118, 120, 122, 129, 139, 210, 415
Case C-513/99, *Concordia Bus Finland Oy Ab* v. *Helsingin kaupunki and HKL
    Bussilikenne* [2002] ECR I-7213, 400, 401
Case C-306/97, *Connemara Machine Turf Co Ltd* v. *Ciollte Teoranta* [1998]
    ECR I-8761, 246
Case C-231/03, *Consorzio Aziende Metano (Coname)* v. *Comune di Cingia de'
    Botti* [2005] ECR I-7287, 271, 443
Case C-234/03, *Contse SA, Vivisol Srl, Oxigen Salud SA* v. *Instituto Nacional de
    Gestion Sanitaria (Ingesa)* [2005] ECR I-9315, 271, 443

Case 6/64, *Costa v. Ente Nazionale per l'Energia Elettrica* [1964] 7 ECR 585, 216, 262

Case 187/87, *Cowan v. Trésor Public* [1989] ECR 195, 70

Case 231/83, *Cullert v. Centre Leclerc* [1985] ECR I-306, [1985] 2 CMLR 524, 80

Case 302/86, ('Danish Bottles') *Commission v. Denmark* ('Danish Bottles') [1986] ECR 4607, 66

Case 29/87, *Dansk Denkavit Aps v. Danish Ministry of Agriculture* [1988] ECR 2965, 64

Case 50/80, *Dansk Supermarked A/S v. A/S Imerco* [1981] ECR 181, 67

Case 8/74, ('Dassonville') *Procureur du Roi v. Dassonville* [1974] ECR 837, [1974] 2 CMLR 436, 65, 66, 141, 411, 412

Case C-3/88, ('Data Processing') *Commission v. Italy* [1989] ECR 4035; [1991] CMLR 115, 69, 271, 443

Case C-120/95, *Decker v. Caisse de Maladie des Employés Privés* [1995] ECR I-1831, [1998] 2 CMLR 879, 66, 413

Case C-279/09, *DEB Deutsche Energiehandels- und Beratungsgesellschaft mbH v. Germany* [2010] ECR I-13849, 468

Joint Cases 2/69 and 3/69, ('Diamond Workers') *Sociaal Fonds for de Diamantarbeiders v. Brachfeld* [1969] ECR 211, 64

Case C-186/01, ('Dory') *Alexander Dory v. Germany* [2003] ECR I-2479, 73–76, 79, 97, 113, 127

Case 21/88, *Du Pont de Nemours Italiana v. Unita Sanitara Locale di Carara* [1990] ECR I-889, 271, 443

Case 45/87, ('Dundalk') *Commission v. Ireland* [1988] ECR 4929, 271, 365, 443

Case C-324/93, ('Evans Medical') *R. v Secretary of State for the Home Department Ex parte Evans Medical and Macfarlan Smith* [1995] ECR I-563, 381, 400, 401, 402

Case C-448/01, *EVN AG and Wienstrom GmbH v. Austria* [2003] ECR I-14523, 401, 402

Case C-368/95, ('Familiapress') *Vereinigte Familiapress Zeitungsverlags- und Vertriebs GmbH v. Heinrich Bauer* [1997] 3 CMLR 1329, 66

Case C-354/90, *Fédération Nationale du Commerce Extérieur des Produits Alimentaires and Syndicat Nationale des Négociants et Transformateurs de Saumon v. France* [1991] ECR I-5523, 179

Case C-318/08, *Filomena Califano v. Wind SpA* [2010] ECR I-2213, 468

Case C-615/10, ('Finnish Turntables') *Insinööritoimisto InsTiimi Oy*, judgment of 7 June 2012, nyr, 96–103, 122, 127, 210, 263, 266, 415, 489

Case C-465/11, *Forposta v. Poczta Polska*, judgment of 13 December 2012, nyr, 385

Case C-120/94 R, ('FYROM') *Commission* v. *Greece* [1996] ECR I-1513, 112, 113, 123, 124

Case C-55/94, *Gebhard* v. *Consiglio dell'Ordine degli Avvocati e Precuratori di Milano* [1995] ECR I-4165, 68

Case 31/87, *Gebroeders Beentjes BV* v. *The Netherlands* [1988] ECR 4635, 367

Case 120/73, *Gebrüder Lorenz GmbH* v. *Germany* [1973] ECR 1471, 179

Case 2/73, *Geddo* v. *Ente Nazionale Risi* [1973] ECR 865, [1974] 1 CMLR 1, 65

Case C-376/98, *Germany* v. *European Parliament and the Council* ('Tobacco Advertising') [2000] ECR I-8419, 83

Case C-347/88, ('Greek Petroleum Law') *Commission* v. *Greece* [1990] ECR I-4747, 80

C-364/10, *Hungary* v. *Slovak Republic*, Judgment of 16 October 2012, nyr, 456

Case C-615/10, *Insinööritoimisto InsTiimi Oy*, ('Finnish Turntables') judgment of 7 June 2012, nyr, 96–103, 122, 127, 210, 263, 266, 415, 489

Case C-180/89, ('Italian Tourist Guides') *Commission* v. *Italy* [1991] ECR I-709, 69

Case C-400/99, *Italy* v. *Commission* [2001] ECR I-7303, 179

Case C-222/84, *Marguerite Johnston* v. *Chief Constable of the Royal Ulster Constabulary* [1986] ECR 1651, [1986] 3 CMLR 240, 73–76, 79, 86, 93, 94, 97, 103, 105, 109, 117, 414, 468

Cases C-267 and C-268/91, ('Keck') *Criminal Proceedings against Bernard Keck and Daniel Mithouard* [1993] ECR I-6097, [1995] 1 CMLR 101, 66

Case C-285/98, *Kreil* v. *Germany* [2000] ECR I-69, 73–76, 79, 97, 105, 113, 117, 127

Case C-412/93, *Leclerc-Siplec* v. *TFI Publicité and M6 Publicité* [1995] ECR I-179, 67, 271

Case C-83/94, ('Leifer') *Criminal Proceedings against Peter Leifer and others* [1995] ECR I-3231, 72, 86, 114, 158, 163

Case C-532/06, ('Lianakis') *Emm. G. Lianakis AE and Others. v. Dimos Alexandroupolis and Others ('Lianakis')* [2008] ECR I-251, 382

Case C-272/91, ('Lottomatica') *Commission* v. *Italy* [1992] ECR I-3929, 271, 443

Case C-319/08, *Lucia Anna Giorgia Iacono* v. *Telecom Italia SpA* [2010] ECR I-2213, 468

Case C-44/96, *Mannesmann Anlagenbau Austria* v. *Strohal Rotationsdruck GmbH* [1998] ECR I-73, 246

Case C-320/08, *Multiservice Srl* v. *Telecom Italia SpA* [2010] ECR I-2213, 468

Case C-225/98, ('Nord-Pas-de-Calais') *Commission* v. *France* [2000] ECR I-7445, 367, 382

Case C-358/03, ('Parking Brixen') *Commission* v. *Austria* [2004] ECR I-12055, 271, 443

Case 730/79, *Philip Morris Holland* v. *Commission* [1980] ECR 2671, [1981] CMLR 321, 23, 176

Case 148/78, *Pubblico Ministero* v. *Ratti* [1979] ECR 1629, 214

Case C-3/95, *Reisebüro Broede* v. *Gerd Sanker* [1996] ECR I-6511, 412

Case 120/78, *REWE – Zentrale AG* v. *Bundesmonopolverwaltung für Branntwein* ('Cassis de Dijon') [1979] ECR 649, [1979] 3 CMLR 494, 66, 413

Case C-367/89, ('Richardt') *Criminal Proceedings against Aimé Richardt and Les Accessoires Scientifiques SNC* [1991] ECR I-4645, 72, 86, 89, 140, 163

Case C-317/08, *Rosalba Alassini* v. *Telecom Italia SpA* [2010] ECR I-2213, 468

Case 48/75, *Procureur du Roi* v. *Royer* [1976] ECR 497, 68

Case C-113/89, *Rush Portuguesa* v. *Office national d'immigration* [1990] ECR I-1417, 69, 443

Case C-273/97, *Sirdar* v. *The Army Board* [1999] ECR I-7403, [1999] 3 CMLR 559, 73–76, 79, 97, 105, 113, 117, 127, 216

Joint Cases 2/69 and 3/69, *Sociaal Fonds for de Diamantarbeiders* v. *Brachfeld* ('Diamond Workers') [1969] ECR 211, 64

Case 13/68, *SpA Salgoil* v. *Italian Ministry of Foreign Trade* [1968] ECR 453, [1969] CMLR 181, at 192, 74, 79, 94, 117, 414

Case C-414/97, ('Spanish Weapons') *Commission v. Spain* [1999] ECR I-5585, [2000] 2 CMLR 4, 98, 100, 108–110, 111, 113, 115, 116, 117, 118, 119, 120, 121, 122, 125, 126, 127, 129, 130, 139, 142, 146, 163, 165, 166, 181, 210, 211, 213, 414, 415, 418

Case C-159/90, *SPUC* v. *Grogan* [1991] ECR I-4685, 76

Case C-26/03, *Stadt Halle RPL Recyclingpark Lochau GmbH* v. *Arbeitsgemeinschaft Thermische Restabfall- und Energieverwertungsanlage TREA Leuna* [2005] ECR I-1, 268

Case 24/68, ('Statistical Levy') *Commission v. Italy* [1969] ECR 12 193, [1971] CMLR 611, 64

Case C-243/89, ('Storebaelt') *Commission v. Denmark* [1993] ECR I-3353, 67, 69, 271, 443

Case C-107/98, *Teckal Srl* v. *Comune de Viano* [1999] ECR I-8121, 246, 268, 269, 293, 300

Case C-324/98, *Telaustria Verlags GmbH* v. *Telekom Austria AG* [2000] ECR I-10745, 271, 443

Case C-376/98, ('Tobacco Advertising') *Germany* v. *European Parliament and the Council* [2000] ECR I-8419, 83

Case 76/81, *Transporoute et Travaux SA* v. *Ministère des travaux publics* [1982] ECR 417, 271, 382, 443

Case C-373/00, *Adolf Truley* v. *Bestattung Wien* [2003] ECR I-1931, 246, 248

Case C-275/98, *Unitron Scandinavia AS* v. *Ministeriet for Fødevarer, Landbrug of Fiskeri* [1999] ECR I-8291, 271, 443

Case C-470/99, *Universale Bau AG* v. *Entsorgunsbetriebe Simmering GmbH*
[2002] ECR I-11617, 246, 271, 443
Case C-359/93, ('UNIX') *Commission* v. *Netherlands* [1995] ECR I-157, 67, 69,
365, 443
Case 33/74, *Van Binsbergen* v. *Bestuur van de Bedrijfsvereiniging
Metaalnijverheid* [1979] ECR 1299, 69
Joined Cases 177/82 and 178/82, *Jan van der Haar and Kaveka de Meern BV*
[1984] ECR 1797, 67
Case 26/62, *Van Gend en Loos* v. *Nederlandse Administratie der Belastingen*
[1963] ECR 1, [1963] CMLR 105, 114
Case C-368/95, *Vereinigte Familiapress Zeitungsverlags- und Vertriebs GmbH* v.
Heinrich Bauer ('Familiapress') [1997] 3 CMLR 1329, 66
Case C-323/96, ('Vlaamse Raad') *Commission* v. *Belgium* [1998]
ECR I-5063, 246
Case C-87/94, ('Walloon Buses') *Commission* v. *Belgium* [1996] ECR I-2043,
271, 443
Case 279/80, *Webb* [1981] ECR 3305, 69
Case C-70/94, ('Werner') *Fritz Werner Industrie-Ausrüstungen GmbH* v.
Germany [1995] ECR I-3989, 72, 86, 94, 158, 163

General Court (formerly Court of First Instance)

Case T-26/01, *Fiocchi Munizioni SpA* v. *Commission of the European
Communities* [2003] ECR II-3951, 79, 94, 95, 99, 103–104, 111, 121, 122, 125,
127, 216
Case T-258/06, *Germany* v. *Commission* [2010] ECR II-2027, 127, 442
Case T-411/06, *SOGELMA* v. *European Agency for Reconstruction* [2008] ECR
II-2771, 276

Commission Competition Cases

Case M.17, *Aérospatiale/MBB* [1992] 4 CMLR M70, 171, 174
Case M.086, *Thompson/Pilkington*, Decision of 23 October 1991,
unreported, 174
Case M.1438, *British Aerospace/GEC Marconi* (Dec. of 25 June 1999 and press
release IP/99/426 of 28 June 1999), 25
Case N 264/2002, *London Underground Public Private Partnership*, C (2002)
3578, [2002] OJ L-309/14, 178

International Court of Justice (ICJ)

Military and Paramilitary Activities in and against Nicaragua *(Nicaragua v
USA)*, Merits, 1986 ICJ-Reports 14, 116 16 paragraph 222 (June 27), 114, 115

National Courts

VG Koblenz, decision of 31 January 2005, 6 L 2617/04.KO (Germany), 461
OVG Koblenz, decision of 25 May 2005, 7 B 10356/05.OVG (Germany), 461
High Court, *Alstom Transport* v. *Eurostar International Limited and Siemens plc* [2010] EWHC 1828 (Ch) (England and Wales), 478

TABLE OF LEGISLATION AND OTHER INSTRUMENTS

European Union (formerly European Communities)

EU treaties

Charter on Fundamental Rights of the European Union 2000
Article 47 467, 472
Article 52(1) 472, 481
European Defence Community Treaty 1952
Annex I to Article 107 88
Annex II to Article 107 88
European Economic Community (EEC) Treaty (Rome) 1957
Article 30 29
Article 36 29, 105
Article 48 105
Article 66 105
Article 85 171
Article 86 171
Article 224 105
Article 223 88, 94, 106
European Community (EC) Treaty 1992 (amended Amsterdam 1997 and Nice 2000)
Article 6 70
Article 12 70
Article 28 66
Article 30 67
Article 45 105
Article 46 71
Article 47 7, 62, 63
Article 49
Article 55 7, 62, 83
Article 58 74
Article 95 7, 62, 83

Article 226 123
Article 227 123
Article 296 90, 94, 107, 111, 174, 489
Article 297 80, 105
Article 301 158
Treaty on the Functioning of the European Union (TFEU) 2009
Article 3 62
Article 4 62
Article 18 63, 70
Article 26 63, 83
Article 28 63
Article 29 64
Article 30 62, 64, 65, 77, 83
Article 34 7, 65–67, 69, 79, 130, 140, 141, 411, 412
Article 35 70
Article 36 66, 70, 71, 73, 75, 77, 79, 80, 85, 86, 95, 106, 110, 114, 139, 140, 160,
     166, 280, 304, 391, 413, 416
Article 43 83
Article 45 97, 106
Article 49 7, 63, 68, 69, 77, 83
Article 50 83
Article 51 97
Article 52 4, 7, 62, 72, 73, 75, 76, 77, 83, 106, 134, 135, 304
Article 53 62, 63, 83
Article 56 7, 62, 63, 67, 69, 71, 83, 412
Article 62 62, 63, 82
Article 65 74, 81, 97
Article 67 77
Article 72 62, 77, 83, 97
Article 101 169, 170
Article 102 170
Article 107 176, 179, 181, 182
Article 108 121, 122, 179
Article 114 7, 62, 82, 87, 123, 157
Article 207 159
Article 258 96, 100, 118, 122–5, 131, 132, 207, 210, 216, 222, 286, 297
Article 259 85, 118, 119, 123, 124, 456
Article 265 103
Article 267 483
Article 275 190
Article 288 127
Article 294 82, 83
Article 337 128

Article 346 1, 9, 12–14, 21, 41, 45, 48, 72, 73, 81, 83, 85, 87, 93, 102,
        103, 106, 107, 110, 113, 115, 118, 119, 121–5, 133, 135, 150, 156,
        171, 174, 181, 192, 194, 195, 200, 202, 205, 207, 209–13, 215, 216,
        220, 221, 226, 227, 238, 241, 245, 260, 266, 267, 278, 280, 303,
        308, 310, 322, 340, 347, 359, 361, 370, 398, 403, 405, 410, 414,
        417, 419, 420, 424, 426, 428–30, 444, 461, 467, 469, 477, 480,
        481, 484, 491
    (1)(a) 8, 76, 85, 87, 120, 128–31, 135, 278, 280, 304, 473
    (1)(b) 8, 73, 76, 85–9, 94, 101, 112, 114, 118–22, 125, 127–37, 139, 141,
        142, 146, 156, 157, 163, 165, 170, 173, 174, 180–2, 184, 209–11, 213, 221,
        261–3, 271, 291, 304, 305, 327, 374, 388, 391, 413–18, 427, 456, 460, 464,
        467
    (2) 88, 90, 94, 95, 99–101, 156, 181, 262, 489
Article 347 8, 73, 74, 76, 78, 81, 82, 85–7, 111, 119, 125, 131–4, 213, 342, 391
Article 348 85, 87, 100, 103, 115, 117–19, 122–5, 129–31, 135, 210, 347, 469
Treaty on European Union (TEU) Lisbon 2009
    Protocol 2 to Treaty of Lisbon 2009 on the Application of the Principles of
        Subsidiarity and Proportionality 78
    Preamble 78, 113
    Article 2 78, 113
    Article 4 121, 128, 132, 133, 146
    Article 5 78
    Article 6 467
    Article 16 188
    Article 24 190
    Article 29 163
    Article 40 209
    Article 42 80, 187, 189
    Article 45 187, 190–1, 209, 218–19
Statute of the Court of Justice of the European Union 2010

EU secondary instruments

Directives

Council Directive 70/150/EEC 65
Council Directive 89/665/EEC of 21 December 1989 on the coordination of the
    laws, regulations and administrative provisions relating to the application of
    review procedures to the award of public supply and public works contracts.
        Article 2 468, 476, 477, 479, 480
Council Directive 93/36/EC of 14 June 1993 coordinating procedures for the
    award of public supply contracts 96

Directive 2004/17/EC of the European Parliament and of the Council of 31
   March 2004 coordinating the procurement procedures of entities
   operating in the water, energy, transport and postal services sectors
   (Utilities Directive)
   Preamble 82
   Article 1 350, 356
   Article 2 253, 255, 462
   Article 10 441
   Article 16 271
   Article 22 307
   Article 30 254
   Article 37 431
   Article 38 367
   Article 40 339, 340
Directive 2004/18/EC of the European Parliament and of the Council on the
   coordination of procedures for the award of public works contracts,
   public supply contracts and public service contracts (Public Sector
   Directive)
   Preamble 441
   Article 1 247, 249, 251, 252, 256, 350
   Article 2 441
   Article 10 102, 261, 280, 290, 305–7
   Article 14 73, 279–81
   Article 15 273–6, 307
   Article 16 299
   Article 23 365
   Article 25 205, 429, 431, 466
   Article 28 300, 324, 336
   Article 29 129, 334
   Article 30 324, 326, 339
   Article 31 325, 338, 340–2, 345, 355
   Article 33 129, 348
   Article 35 364
   Article 37 129
   Article 38 321, 327
   Article 44 319, 321, 323, 332, 399
   Article 45 384–6, 388
   Article 48 389–91
   Article 58 129
   Article 64 129
   Article 69 129
   Article 75 129
   Annex III 249, 252

Annex IV 249–52
Annex V 250
Directive 2004/25/EC of the European Parliament and of the Council of 21
    April 2004 on take-over bids 172
Directive 2009/43/EC of the European Parliament and of the Council of 6 May
    2009 simplifying terms and conditions of transfers of defence-related
    products within the Community (ICT Directive)
Preamble 62
Recital 3 148
Recital 6 145, 148, 152
Recital 7 145, 152
Recital 13 50
Recital 17 76
Recital 21 150
Recital 26 151
Recital 34 152
Recital 35 153
Recital 55 50
Article 1 148
Article 3 148
Article 4 149, 150
Article 5 145, 150, 151
Article 6 145, 151
Article 7 150
Article 8 152
Article 9 151, 152, 162
Article 18 369
Defence Directive 2009/81/EC of the European Parliament and of the Council
    of 13 July 2009 on the coordination of procedures for the award of certain
    works contracts, supply contracts and service contracts by contracting
    authorities or entities in the fields of defence and security, and amending
    Directives 2004/17/EC and 2004/18/EC (Defence Directive)
Preamble 7, 62, 64, 83, 232, 274, 317, 464
Recital 4 245
Recital 5 245
Recital 9 245, 361, 379
Recital 10 93, 94, 102, 261–3
Recital 11 264
Recital 12 245, 265
Recital 13 283
Recital 16 86, 268
Recital 18 86
Recital 20 278

Recital 23 255-9
Recital 25 464
Recital 26 273, 274
Recital 27 279, 281, 282
Recital 29 289
Recital 30 298
Recital 41 367
Recital 42 393
Recital 43 394
Recital 44 389
Recital 45 419
Recital 47 325
Recital 48 335
Recital 53 343
Recital 54 343, 344
Recital 56 364
Recital 65 387
Recital 67 383, 386
Recital 68 392, 395, 396
Recital 69 400
Article 1 247, 248, 249, 253, 255, 256, 258, 259, 261, 263, 283, 289, 293
Article 2 260–5, 267, 278, 280, 289, 303–5, 342, 462
Article 4 420
Article 7 247, 379, 465
Article 8 247, 269, 307, 443, 445, 462
Article 11 247, 283, 292, 296, 301–3, 305
Article 12 224, 240, 247, 272–6, 286, 305, 307–9
Article 13 134, 213, 224, 247, 269, 272, 276–301, 304, 305, 307–9, 344, 345,
    346, 351, 353, 354, 463, 490
Article 18 365, 381, 465
Article 19 247
Article 20 247, 367, 420–1, 432–4
Article 21 247, 367, 430–1, 436, 438–40, 452
Article 22 379–81, 394, 429
Article 23 134, 147, 342, 343, 367–79, 402, 465
Article 25 325, 336, 337, 431
Article 26 323, 328, 332, 333, 421
Article 27 331–4
Article 28 287, 300, 325, 336–47, 374, 445
Article 29 348, 349, 447
Article 30 336, 364
Article 32 349
Article 33 311, 319, 321, 327, 342, 344

Article 38 319, 325, 332
Article 39 383–8, 398, 400, 403, 465
Article 42 380, 388–92, 394, 395, 399
Article 43 393
Article 46 398
Article 47 323, 400, 401, 420
Article 50 430, 440, 441, 466
Article 51 430, 440, 441, 442, 443, 466
Article 52 430, 440, 442, 443, 445, 446, 447, 450, 466
Article 53 372, 430, 440, 445, 447–9, 450, 466
Article 54 430, 466
Article 55 449
Article 60 475, 477, 478–81
Article 68 269, 392
Article 70 290, 307
Article 71 12, 290, 461
Article 73 255
Article 75 257
Title III 207, 390, 430, 432–4, 436, 439–41, 444, 445, 447–52
Title IV 3, 12, 13, 207, 455, 459–69, 473, 481–3, 488, 489
Annex III 365, 465
Council Directive 2013/16/EU of 13 May 2013 adopting certain directives in the
  field of procurement by reason of the accession of the Republic of Croatia 251
Directive 2014/24/EU of the European Parliament and the Council of 26
  February 2014 on public procurement and repealing Directive 2004/18/EC
  Recital 47 355
  Recital 49 355
  Article 1(3) 280
  Article 2 252, 256
  Article 4 270
  Article 9 274, 275
  Article 12 268
  Article 15 261, 279, 305, 306
  Article 16 290
  Article 18 441
  Article 24 261, 307
  Article 31 355, 356
  Article 33 447
  Article 37 347
  Article 46 451
  Article 48 331, 389, 390, 391
  Article 56 469–70, 471–3, 475, 476, 477
  Article 58 451

Article 59 451
Article 71(1) 424, 429, 431, 441, 451, 452
Article 72(3) 478
Annex I 250, 251, 252
Annex XII 389, 390
Directive 2014/25/EU of the European Parliament and of the Council of 26
    February 2014 on procurement by entities operating in the water, energy,
    transport and postal services sectors and repealing Directive 2004/17/EC 67,
    290, 298, 317
Article 4 253
Article 7–14 253
Article 24 290
Directive 2014/23/EU of the European Parliament and the Council of 26
    February 2014 on the award of concession contracts 3

Regulations

Council Regulation 4064/89/EEC of 21 December 1989 on the control of
    concentrations between undertakings 172
Council Regulation (EEC, Euratom) No. 1552/89 of 29 May 1989,
    implementing Decision 88/376/EEC, Euratom on the system of the
    Communities' own resources (OJ 1989 L155/1) as amended by Council
    Regulation (EC, Euratom) No. 1355/96 of 8 July 1996 (OJ 1996 L175/3)
        Article 2 109
        Articles 9–11 109
Council Regulation 3918/91/EEC of 19 December 1991 amending Regulation
    2603/69/EEC establishing common rules for exports 86
Council Regulation 2913/92/EEC of 12 October 1992 establishing the
    Community Customs Code
    Article 161 158
    Article 182 158
Council Regulation 3381/94/EC of 19 December 1994 setting up a Community
    regime for the control of exports of dual-use goods
    Article 2 157, 161
Council Regulation 1355/96/EC of 8 July 1996 amending Regulation 1552/89/
    EEC implementing Decision 88/376/EEC on the system of the Communities'
    own resources 109
Council Regulation 1150/2000/EC of 22 May 2000 implementing
    Decision 94/728/EC on the system of the Communities' own resources 109,
    118, 123
Council Regulation 1334/2000/EC of 22 June 2000 setting up a Community
    regime for the control of exports of dual use items and technology 158, 161
    Article 6 162

Council Regulation 1/2003/EC of 16 December 2002 on the implementation of the rules on competition laid down in Articles 81 and 82 of the Treaty 130, 169
Article 28 130
Council Regulation 139/2004/EC of 20 January 2004 on the control of concentrations between undertakings
Recital 19 174-5
Article 2 173
Article 21 175
Article 24 125
Article 25 172
Council Regulation 428/2009/EC of 5 May 2009 setting up a Community regime for the control of exports, transfer, brokering and transit of dual-use items (corrigendum of 27 August 2009) 158-9, 162
Article 1 158-9
Article 2 157
Article 22 158-9, 160
Annex I 159, 160
Annex IIIc 162
Annex IV 158-60
Commission Regulation 1177/2009/EC of 30 November 2009 amending Directives 2004/17/EC, 2004/18/EC and 2009/81/EC of the European Parliament and of the Council in respect of their application thresholds for the procedures for the award of contracts on the application thresholds of the procurement Directives
Article 3 270, 462
Commission Regulation 1251/2011/EC of 30 November 2011 amending Directives 2004/17/EC, 2004/18/EC, and 2009/81/EC of the European Parliament and of the Council in respect of their application thresholds for the procedures for the awards of contracts 269
Commission Regulation 1336/2013/EU of 13 December 2013 amending Directives 2004/17/EC, 2004/18/EC and 2009/81/EC of the European Parliament and the Council in respect of the application of thresholds for the procedures for the awards of contracts 269
Article 4 270, 462
Preamble 272

Decisions

Council Decision 255/58/EEC of 15 April 1958 defining the list of products (arms, munitions, and war material) to which the provisions of Article 223(1)(b) of the Treaty [now Article 346(1)(b) TFEU] apply 64, 89, 91-5, 99-102, 128, 211

Council Decision 88/376/EEC of 24 June 1988 on the system of the
Communities' own resources 109
Council Decision 94/728/EC of 31 October 1994 on the system of the
Communities' own resources 109
Council Decision 94/942/CFSP of 19 December 1994 on the joint action
adopted by the Council on the basis of Article J.3 of the Treaty on European
Union concerning the control of exports of dual-use goods 158
Council Decision 94/993/EEC of 22 December 1994 amending the
Protocol on the Statute of the Court of Justice of the European Community
119
Commission Decision 1999/763/EC of 17 March 1999 on the measures,
implemented and proposed, by the Federal State of Bremen, Germany, in
favour of Lürssen Maritime Beteiligungen GmbH & Co. KG 122, 181
Council Decision 2000/402/CFSP of 22 June 2000 repealing Decision 94/
942/CFSP on the joint action concerning the control of exports of dual-use
goods 158
Council Decision 2007/643/CFSP of 18 September 2007 on the financial
rules of the European Defence Agency and on the procurement rules and
rules on financial contributions from the operational budget of the
European Defence Agency 256
Council Decision 2011/411/CFSP of 12 July 2011 defining the statute, seat and
operational rules of the European Defence Agency and repealing Joint Action
2004/551/CFSP 186
Preamble 233, 235, 236
Article 1 187, 190, 209
Article 2 187, 189, 190
Article 5 189, 191, 209, 217–19, 234, 235
Article 7 187
Article 8 188
Article 9 188
Article 10 188–9
Article 11 189
Article 19 237
Article 20 237
Article 23 190
Article 24 234, 235
Article 25 234

Council Actions and Positions

Council Joint Action 2004/551/CFSP of 12 May 2004 on the establishment of
the European Defence Agency
Preamble 235

Article 1 186
Article 5 235
Article 25 235
Council Common Position 2008/944/CFSP of 8 December 2008 defining
common rules governing control of exports of military technology and
equipment 163, 228
Recital 15 164
Article 4 164
Article 8 164
Article 12 164

EU Communications

Commission Communication on the Challenges Facing the
European Defence-related Industry: A Contribution for Action at
European Level, COM (1996) 10 final 5, 12, 23, 27, 29, 37, 38, 40, 48, 53, 94,
137–40, 147, 148, 161, 163, 167, 176, 182, 183, 221
Commission Communication Implementing European Union Strategy on
Defence Related Industries, COM (1997) 583 final
Annex I: Draft Common Position on Framing a European
Armaments Policy 147, 183
Annex II: Action Plan for the defence-related industries 139, 182, 183
Commission Communication Industrial and Market Issues: Towards an EU
Defence Equipment Policy, COM (2003) 113 final 5, 48, 125, 137–40, 147,
157, 159, 161, 167–9, 172, 173, 181–3, 221
Commission Green Paper Defence Procurement, COM (2004) 608 final 5, 13,
48, 89, 105, 125, 127, 168, 183, 221, 254, 317, 428, 459
Commission Communication on the Results of the Consultation
Launched by the Green Paper on Defence Procurement and on the
Future Commission Initiatives, COM (2005) 626 final 5, 13, 23, 125, 211,
212, 221, 254, 316, 317, 327, 328, 428, 460
Commission Interpretative Communication on the Application of Article 296
of the Treaty in the Field of Defence Procurement, COM (2006) 779 final 5,
125, 126, 211, 414, 415, 489
Commission Communication on a Strategy for a Stronger and More
Competitive European Defence Industry, COM (2007) 764 final 2, 3, 22–25,
28, 106, 137, 141, 168, 169, 175, 177, 182, 183, 393
Commission Green Paper on the Modernisation of EU Public Procurement
Policy Towards a More Efficient European Procurement Market, COM
(2011) 15 final 328
Commission Proposal for a Directive of the European Parliament and of the
Council on Public Procurement, COM (2011) 896 final 5

Commission Report to the European Parliament and the Council on Transposition of Directive 2009/81/EC on Defence and Security Procurement, COM (2012) 565 final 6, 214, 262, 423

Commission Communication on a New Deal for European Defence: Towards a More Competitive and Efficient Defence and Security Sector, COM (2013) 542 final 2, 5, 19, 20, 23, 27, 28, 33, 34, 36, 37, 40, 48, 106, 137, 181, 183, 211, 286, 294, 357, 360, 362, 365, 453, 454, 491

European Defence Agency instruments

EDA Code of Conduct on Defence Procurement 2005 191–8, 429

EDA Code of Conduct on Offsets 2011 198–207, 411, 424, 426-7

EDA Code of Best Practice in the Supply Chain 2006 198, 205, 429

International treaties

Agreement on Trade Related Aspects of Intellectual Property Rights (TRIPS) 1995 WTO
Article 73 114, 134

European Convention on Human Rights (ECHR) 1953 (amended 2010)
Article 15 134

European Space Agency Procurement Regulations 2011 313, 352

Convention on the Establishment of the Organisation for Joint Armament Cooperation (Organisation Conjointe de Cooperation en matiere d'Armement, OCCAR) 2006
Article 5 223

Framework Agreement between the French Republic, the Federal Republic of Germany, the Italian Republic, the Kingdom of Spain, the Kingdom of Sweden, and the United Kingdom of Great Britain and Northern Ireland concerning Measures to Facilitate the Restructuring and Operation of the European Defence Industry, Farnborough, 27 July 2000 (Letter of Intent) 225–231

General Agreement on Tariffs and Trade (GATT) WTO 1948 (amended 1995)
Article XXI 114, 115

General Agreement on Trade in Services (GATS) WTO 1995
Article XIV 114, 134

Government Procurement Agreement (GPA) WTO 1996 (amended 2012)
Article VII 313
Article XVI 419, 420

North Atlantic Treaty (NATO) 1949
Article 42 46

Treaty of Amity, Economic Relations and Consular Rights Between the United States of America and Iran 1955

Article XX 134

United Nations Commission for International Trade Law (UNCITRAL) Model
  Law on Public Procurement 2012
  Article 27 313, 336, 351
  Article 28 313
  Article 30 336
  Article 34 336
Vienna Convention on the Law of Treaties 1969
  Article 31 114
  Article 32 114

National instruments

Bundesgesetz über die Vergabe von Aufträgen im Verteidigungs- und
  Sicherheitsbereich (BVergGVS) 2012 Austria
  § 23 317, 322, 331, 346
  § 25 341
  § 28 331, 334
  § 30 444, 446
  § 34 444, 446
  § 74 433, 435, 437
  § 112 347
  § 116 443, 451
  § 117 446, 451
  § 118 446, 451
  § 119 448, 451
  § 120 447, 451
  § 121 450, 451
  § 122 451
Code des tribunaux administratifs et des cours administratives d'appel (France)
  Article L22 471
  Article L23 471
Decree No. 558/A/04/03/RR of the Minister for the Interior of 11 July 2003
  authorising the derogation from the Community rules on public supply
  contracts in respect of the purchase of light helicopters for the use of police
  forces and the national fire service 2003 (Italy) 96
Defence and Security Public Contracts Regulations 2011 (DSPCR) United
  Kingdom
  Regulation 7 302, 346
  Regulation 16 341, 346, 381
  Regulation 27 331, 341, 346
  Regulation 37 432, 433, 441
  Regulation 42 446, 447

Regulation 44 448, 450
Regulation 48 347
European Union (Award of Contracts Relating to Defence and Security)
Regulations 2012 (ACRDSR) Republic of Ireland
Regulation 19 432, 433, 435, 437, 441
Regulation 27 341, 346
Regulation 40 347
Regulation 60 443, 446
Regulation 61 447
Regulation 62 448, 450
Federal Acquisition Regulation (FAR 14.101) USA 313
Gesetz gegen Wettbewerbsbeschränkungen (GWB) Germany
  § 104(1) 471
  § 105(2) 470
  § 110a 474
  § 116(3) 470
Vergabeverordnung für die Bereiche Verteidigung und Sicherheit (VSVgV)
2012 Germany
  § 1 346
  § 9 432, 433, 435, 437, 441
  § 11 317, 322, 331, 334
  § 12 341, 346
  § 13 331
  § 38 443, 451
  § 39 451
  § 40 448, 450, 451
  § 41 447, 451
  § 44 347

ABBREVIATIONS

ACRDSR	European Union (Award of Contracts Relating to Defence and Security) Regulations (Republic of Ireland) 2012
BAe	British Aerospace Systems
BDSV	German Defence Industries Association
BVergGVS	Austrian Defence and Security Procurement Law 2012
CEN	European Committee for Standardization
CENELC	European Committee for Electrotechnical Standardisation
CEPMA	Central Europe Pipeline Management Agency (NATO)
CERTIDER	Register for the Certified Defence-related Enterprises
CFSP	Common Foreign and Security Policy
CMLR	Common Market Law Reports
CoC	Code of Conduct
CSDP	Common Security and Defence Policy
CST	Common Staff Targets
DSPCR	United Kingdom Defence and Security Procurement Regulations 2012
EADS	European Aeronautic Defence and Space Company
EBB	European Bulletin Board
EC	European Community
ECAP	European Capabilities and Armaments Policy
ECDP	European Capabilities Development Plan
ECJ	European Court of Justice/Court of Justice of the EU
ECR	European Court Reports
EDA	European Defence Agency
EDEM	European Defence Equipment Market
EDIG	European Defence Industries Group
EDSTAR	European Defence Standards Reference System
EDTIB	European Defence Technological and Industrial Base
EEA	European Economic Area
EEC	European Economic Community
ESA	European Space Agency
ESDP	European Security and Defence Policy
ESS	European Security Strategy
ETSI	European Telecommunications Institute

EU	European Union
EUR	Euro
EUROPA	European Understanding of Research Organisation, Programmes and Activities
FA	Framework (Farnborough) Agreement (see LoI)
FAR	Federal Acquisition Regulations (USA)
FOI	Swedish Defence Research Institute
FYROM	Former Yugoslav Republic of Macedonia
GPL	Global Project Licence
GWB	German Competition Act
HMR	Harmonisation of Military Requirements
ICT	Intra-Community Transfers
IEPG	Independent European Programme Group
ISDEFE	Spanish Defence Research Institute
LoI	Letter of Intent
LTV	Long-Term Vision
NAHEMA	NATO Helicopter for the 1990s (NH90) Design and Development, Production and Logistics Management Agency
NAMA	NATO Airlift Management Agency
NAMSA	NATO Maintenance and Supply Agency
NATO	Northern Atlantic Treaty Organisation
NETMA	NATO Eurofighter and Tornado Management Agency
NSPA	NATO Support Agency
OCCAR	Organisation for Joint Armaments Procurement
OJ	Official Journal of the EU
PFI	Private Finance Initiative
PPP	Public–Private Partnership
PQQ	Pre-qualification Questionnaire
RAND	US National Defence Research Institute
R&D	Research and Development
R&T	Research and Technology
SIPRI	Stockholm International Peace Research Institute
SME	Small and Medium-sized Enterprises
TED	Tenders Electronic Daily
VAT	Value Added Tax
VgVVS	German Defence and Security Procurement Regulations 2012
WEAG	Western European Armaments Group
WEAO	Western European Armaments Organisation
WEU	Western European Union
WTO	World Trade Organisation

Introduction

Public procurement law regulates the acquisition of goods, services and works by public bodies from the private sector. Objectives of this regulation include the achievement of value for money, transparency, competition, non-discrimination and equal treatment of bidders. Some legal frameworks also aim to promote social and environmental objectives or to fight corruption. Procurement law, inter alia, requires the publication of contract opportunities, prescribes certain award procedures and criteria and provides a review and remedies system for aggrieved bidders. The main objective of EU public procurement regulation is to open the public procurement markets of the Member States, to ensure non-discrimination on grounds of nationality and thus to facilitate the EU Internal Market in public procurement. The EU legislator has passed a set of procurement Directives which had to be transposed into the national laws of the 28 Member States.

While the procurement of sensitive goods, works and services was covered by the legislation since the first procurement Directives of the 1970s, the acquisition of armaments had been left unregulated by a specific instrument at EU level until recently. Many legal, political, economic and historical reasons have been cited for this "gap" in specific regulation: national security, sovereignty in the core area of defence and industrial considerations. Thus while goods and services are subject to the Internal Market and had been covered by Public Sector Procurement Directive 2004/18/EC and its predecessors, in practice the extensive use of a number of derogations, most notably of what is now Article 346 TFEU, had taken most armaments and related services outside the EU's trade, competition and procurement rules. This resulted in 28 separate defence markets characterised by protectionism, inefficiencies and sometimes corruption, resulting in reduced levels of innovation and competitiveness, high prices and a lack of transparency. Overall, a widespread incomprehension or defiance of the then existing legal framework of defence procurement could be observed. For example, few of the relevant contracts were published in the Official Journal (OJ) of the EU. This does not necessarily mean that defence contracts were not subject to procurement regulation. Contracts were often published but in national or other media, not in the OJ. Contracts were awarded on the basis of prescribed procedures, but not on the basis of the

EU procurement Directives. Most importantly, these procedures only rarely resulted in the award of a contract to a bidder from another EU Member State.

This situation represented an extensive exclusion from the public procurement regime of the Internal Market in practice because the importance of the defence market to the European economy is considerable. According to 2012 figures of the European Defence Agency, the EU Member States spent €194 billion on defence in 2010. Their total procurement budget for armaments, civil goods, services and works, including operations and maintenance, was estimated at €86 billion[1] and the European defence industries have an annual turnover of €55 billion employing 400,000 people.[2]

Economists have argued that European integration in defence procurement would result in substantial economic benefits, most importantly for the taxpayer through lower equipment prices, for employment through the increased competitiveness of the European industries and for technology innovation as EU capabilities would be preserved.[3] The background to these economic benefits is that an integrated European defence market would allow for economies of scale and learning, greater competition and transparency. Legal analysts generally accept the benefits of European integration in public procurement, though some with certain reservations.[4] Legal writers on defence procurement also expect cost savings and an increased competiveness of the European

---

[1] Based on the 26 Member States then participating in the European Defence Agency. The figure is the overall €86 billion figure for procurement and research and development, including €9 billion for the latter, and including 22–23% of the overall €194 billion spent on operations and maintenance, see www.eda.europa.eu/docs/default-source/news/eu-us-defence-data-2011.pdf [accessed 28 March 2014]. The overall figure of €194 billion for 2010 is also confirmed in the recent Commission Communication "A New Deal for European Defence: Towards a More Competitive and Efficient Defence and Security Sector", COM (2013) 542 final, at 7.

[2] 2012 figures of the Commission Staff Working Document on Defence, SWD (2013) 279 final accompanying COM (2013) 542 final, at 32. Up to 960,000 additional indirect jobs are also mentioned citing the 2012 IndustriAll *Study on the Perspectives of the European Land Armaments Sector*, www.industriall-europe.eu/sectors/defence/2012/INFF_E3779_Final%20Report_v03-EN.pdf [accessed 28 March 2014]. 2007 figures of COM (2007) 764 final, 2 indicate a figure of 300,000; the Communication also points out that 20 years ago these figures were almost twice as high.

[3] See especially Keith Hartley, *The Economics of Defence Policy: A New Perspective* (Abingdon: Routledge, 2011); and "The Future of European Defence Policy: An Economic Perspective" (2003) 14 *Defence and Peace Economics* 107–115. See also the 2006 European Parliament Study, *The Costs of Non-Europe in the Area of Security and Defence* (2006) prepared by Hartmut Küchle of the Bonn International Centre for Conversion (BICC), Bonn, Germany, www.bicc.de/uploads/tx_bicctools/bicc_study_for_ep.pdf [accessed 1 November 2013].

[4] See the discussion in the English language public procurement law classics: Sue Arrowsmith, *The Law of Public and Utilities Procurement*, 2nd edn (London: Sweet & Maxwell, 2005), at 119–25; Peter Trepte, *Public Procurement in the EU: A Practitioner's Guide*, 2nd edn (Oxford University Press, 2007), at 3–5; Christopher Bovis, *EC Public Procurement: Case Law and Regulation* (Oxford University Press, 2006), ch. 1.

defence industries.[5] Moreover, some military experts expect strategic benefits through the increased interoperability of defence equipment in the context of the UN, NATO and the EU's Common Security and Defence Policy.[6] Finally, anti-corruption experts expect benefits from the transparency and review requirements of the relevant legislation.[7]

In 2009, after years of preparation and discussion, the Defence and Security Procurement Directive 2009/81/EC[8] (hereinafter "Defence Directive") entered into force. It forms part of a wider EU "defence package"[9] and aims to contribute to the establishment of an Internal Market for defence and security goods and services, complementing the EU arsenal of procurement Directives.[10] The Defence Directive regulates the procurement of armaments and other sensitive supplies, services and works by the defence ministries and other relevant contracting authorities and entities of the Member States. As in the other procurement Directives, this covers, inter alia, the precise definition of the goods and services, their publication in the OJ, procurement procedures, the qualification and rejection of bidders and award criteria. It also covers a review and remedies

---

[5] See especially Aris Georgopoulos, "European Defence Procurement Integration: Proposals for Action within the European Union", PhD Thesis, University of Nottingham (2004); Baudouin Heuninckx, "The Law of Collaborative Defence Procurement through International Organisations in the European Union", PhD Thesis, University of Nottingham and Belgian Military Academy (2011).

[6] See, for example, the welcome address by Jukka Juusti, European Defence Agency Armaments Director, SDR Conference, Tuusula (Finland), 17–18 November 2009, www.eda.europa.eu/docs/documents/Jukka_s_SDR_opening.pdf [accessed 1 November 2013].

[7] Mark Pyman, *Addressing Corruption and Building Integrity in Defence Establishments*, Transparency International Working Paper 02/2007 (Berlin, 2007), www.ethicsworld.org/publicsectorgovernance/PDF%20links/national_defence_and_corruption.pdf [accessed 1 November 2013]; Sanjeev Gupta, Luiz de Mello and Raju Sharan, *Corruption and Military Spending*, IMF Working Paper, February 2000, www.imf.org/external/pubs/ft/wp/2000/wp0023.pdf [accessed 1 November 2013].

[8] Directive 2009/81/EC of the European Parliament and of the Council of 13 July 2009 on the coordination of procedures for the award of certain works contracts, supply contracts and service contracts by contracting authorities or entities in the fields of defence and security, and amending Directives 2004/17/EC and 2004/18/EC, [2009] OJ L216/76.

[9] The EU Defence Package also consists of Directive 2009/43/EC simplifying terms and conditions of transfers of defence-related products within the Community [2009] OJ L146/1 and the Commission Communication "A Strategy for a Stronger and More Competitive European Defence Industry", COM (2007) 764 final. On the initial drafts: P. Koutrakos, "The Commission's 'Defence Package'" (2008) 33 *European Law Review* 1–2.

[10] Apart from the Defence Directive, in 2009 this "arsenal" consisted of Public Sector Directive 2004/18/EC (now replaced by Directive 2014/24/EU [2014] OJ L94/65), the Public Sector Procurement Remedies Directive 89/665/EEC [1989] OJ L395/33, the Utilities Procurement Directive 2004/17/EC [2004] OJ L134/1 (now replaced by Directive 2014/25/EU [2014] OJ L94/243), and the Utilities Procurement Remedies Directive 92/13/EEC [1992] OJ L76/14. Moreover the 2014 reforms added a new Directive 2014/23/EU on concessions [2014] OJ L94/1.

regime for aggrieved bidders in its Title IV, which for the public sector and utilities is regulated in separate Directives. The Directive is largely based on Public Sector Procurement Directive 2004/18/EC (hereinafter "Public Sector Directive"). However, the latter was adapted to take the specific characteristics of defence and security procurement, its complexity and in particular security of supply and security of information, into account. This was necessary to limit the use of the national security and secrecy and public security derogations in the TFEU, namely Articles 36, 52(1), and especially 346 TFEU, thereby keeping the majority of contracts "inside" the regime of the Defence Directive and the Treaty.

The author conducted extensive research on European defence procurement *before* the topic was subjected to regulation, resulting especially in his monograph *European Defence Procurement Law* (1999)[11] and parts of his monograph *European Union Law and Defence Integration* (2005).[12] This research showed the fragmentation of the European defence equipment market as a result of the legal framework, mainly the Internal Market rules and especially procurement regulation, but also competition law, State aid, merger regulation, intra-Community transfers and exports. It also showed that the Member States followed three different approaches to the national regulation of defence procurement – regulated, semi-regulated and non-regulated – without necessarily always following this regulation in practice. Moreover, the research showed that EU Internal Market law applies to the defence market and that thus the TFEU is an instrument of EU defence integration. The present book is built on this research but provides an analysis of EU defence procurement *after* the introduction of detailed defence and security specific regulation. The project evolved from the entering into force of the Defence Directive in 2009 to *after* its recent transposition in the Member States and *while* these national laws are starting to be implemented (applied) in practice. The book was completed in November 2013, two years after the transposition date, when the stakeholders already had been working in a legal context determined by the new national instruments. However, these dates also imply a limitation of the analysis possible at this stage. While the conception, introduction, substance and transposition of the Defence Directive can already be discussed, there is not yet sufficiently reliable data to analyse the implementation of the instrument in practice.

This book aims to address the crucial question to what extent the legal framework for the defence and security procurement has changed through the introduction and transposition of the Defence Directive. The methodology to answer this question is to provide a critical analysis of the provisions of the Defence Directive and other closely related instruments in their historical, economic,

---

[11] Martin Trybus, *European Defence Procurement Law: International and National Procurement Systems as Models for a Liberalised Defence Procurement Market in Europe* (The Hague: Kluwer Law International, 1999).

[12] Martin Trybus, *European Union Law and Defence Integration* (Oxford: Hart, 2005).

political and legal contexts. First, this requires a comparative analysis of the provisions of the Defence Directive with those of Public Sector Directive 2004/ 18/EC. The Defence Directive was based on Public Sector Directive 2004/18/EC; the latter was adapted to take national security considerations into account. Thus the comparison of the two Directives is the most important element of the analysis. The question of what has changed in the legal framework of defence and security procurement can to a large extent be answered by an analysis of these national security adaptations in the Defence Directive. However, beyond the comparison with the Public Sector Directive, the analysis will at times provide a comparison with other relevant sources, most importantly the Utilities Directive 2004/17/EC, the Procurement Remedies Directives 665/89/EEC and 92/13/EC, the former European Defence Agency Codes of Conduct for Procurement and the Supply Chain,[13] instruments of the Letter of Intent and the former Western European Armaments Group and NATO agencies.[14] The analysis will include a discussion of the impact of these instruments on the Defence Directive and vice versa. This is necessary to assess the change in the legal framework brought about by the Directive since these instruments form or formed part of that framework.

The analysis will not include a discussion of the new Public Sector Directive 2014/24/EU. First, at the time of writing the latter was still very much a "moving target".[15] Most importantly, the 2004 Public Sector Directive and not the future instrument was the "rock from which the legislator chiselled" the Defence Directive. However, at times reference is made to the new Directive and the new Utilities Directive 2014/25/EU to support an argument that a particular provision of the Defence Directive is specific to that instrument and not a feature of a general trend in EU procurement regulation. Moreover, in principle all the innovations of the new Public Sector Directive 2014/24/EU could be considered in a possible reform of the Defence Directive. However, this should be the subject of a separate publication and is therefore, apart from a few exceptions on procedures in chapter 7, not addressed in this book.

The necessary interpretation of the Defence Directive and the TFEU is also based on a number of relevant Communications (including the consultation of stakeholders before the Directive),[16] the 2007 Impact Assessment of the

---

[13] See ch. 5.   [14] See ch. 5.

[15] Directive 2014/24/EU of the European Parliament and of the Council of 26 February 2014 on public procurement and repealing Directive 2004/18/EC [2014] OJ L94/65 was officially published on 28 March 2014 when this book, completed in November 2013, was already at the proof stage. See, for the changing versions, "Proposal for a Directive of the European Parliament and of the Council on Public Procurement", COM (2011) 896 final (20/12/ 2011); Draft Report of the European Parliament of 3/5/2012, at www.europarl.europa. eu/document/activities/cont/201205/20120521ATT45494/20120521ATT45494EN.pdf; and quite different: Presidency compromise/consolidated version 24/7/2012, http://register. consilium.europa.eu/pdf/en/12/st12/st12878.en12.pdf [accessed 22 November 2013].

[16] COM (1996) 10 final, COM (1997) 583 final, COM (2003) 113 final, COM (2004) 608 final, COM (2005) 626 final, COM (2006) 779 final and COM (2013) 542 final.

Defence Directive,[17] a set of Commission "Guidance Notes" on several questions of the implementation of the Defence Directive,[18] relevant case law of the ECJ and academic literature. This will allow a perspective of the evolution of the Defence Directive until 2013, from the first proposals of the Commission in the 1990s, the evolving ECJ case law, the consultation with stakeholders of 2004 to 2006, the Proposal of 2007, the legislative process in Council and Parliament in 2008 to 2009 and the transposition from 2011 to mainly 2013.

Moreover, the analysis will include a discussion of the transposition of the Defence Directive in the Member States. In this context reference will be made to the 2012 Commission Transposition Report.[19] However, the analysis will also include relevant provisions of a selection of national laws and regulations of the Member States transposing the Defence Directive. The national laws discussed are the Austrian Federal Procurement Defence and Security Act 2011,[20] the German Competition Act as amended in December 2011[21] and the Defence and Security Procurement Regulation 2012,[22] the Irish European Union (Award of Contracts Relating to Defence and Security) Regulations 2012[23] and the United Kingdom Defence and Security Contracts Regulations 2011.[24] This selection of Member States includes civil law and common law jurisdictions, smaller and larger Member States and NATO and neutral states. This should provide an understanding of the Defence Directive in its various national "incarnations", which would be enhanced by but does not require a comprehensive discussion of the transposing laws and regulations of all the Member States. The inclusion of a comparative discussion of a selection of national laws transposing the Defence Directive enhances in some cases the understanding of its defence and security adaptations. Some but not all adaptations were transposed into the

---

[17] Commission Staff Working Document – Impact Assessment SEC (2007) 1593, http://ec. europa.eu/governance/impact/ia_carried_out/docs/ia_2007/sec_2007_1593_en.pdf [accessed 1 November 2013].

[18] On the topics field of application, exclusions, research and development, security of supply, security of information, subcontracting, and offsets, all are available at http://ec.europa.eu/ internal_market/publicprocurement/rules/defence_procurement/index_en.htm [accessed 22 November 2013].

[19] COM (2012) 565 final.

[20] Bundesgesetz über die Vergabe von Aufträgen im Verteidigungs- und Sicherheitsbereich (Bundesvergabegesetz Verteidigung und Sicherheit 2012 – BVergGVS 2012), BGBl. I Nr. 10/2012.

[21] Gesetz gegen Wettbewerbsbeschränkungen, of 15 July 2005, BGBl. I S. 2114; 2009 I S. 3850, as last amended by Art. 1 and Art. 4(2) of the Law of 5 December 2012, BGBl. I S. 2403.

[22] Vergabeordung für die Bereiche Verteidigung und Sicherheit – VSVgV, BGBl. I S.1509/2012.

[23] European Union (Award of Contracts Relating to Defence and Security) Regulations 2012, SI No. 62 of 2012.

[24] United Kingdom Defence and Security Public Contracts Regulations 2011, SI 2011/1848.

national laws. This suggests that not all adaptations were considered necessary, which allows an assessment of their significance.

The book is divided into two parts: Part I on the context of the Defence Directive and Part II on the rules of the Defence Directive itself. Part I is divided into five chapters. Chapter 1 discusses the economic, historical and political background of the Defence Directive, the specific factors of the defence and security sectors that influence defence procurement and its regulation. First, the structure and capacities of the European defence and security industries, both with regards to principal or prime contracts and the supply chain, will be explained. Moreover, special economic characteristics of the defence procurement context that differentiate it from other public sector and utilities procurement – and even security procurement under the Defence Directive – will be addressed. The discussion will distinguish between the armaments producing defence industries on the one hand and providers of non-military security goods and services on the other hand. Secondly, political and strategic factors, such as the different defence policies and ambitions of the EU Member States and the importance of sovereignty will be explained. This includes an introduction to the paramount objectives of national security and secrecy which feature throughout the book. Thirdly and finally, technological and contractual factors of defence procurement having an impact on its regulation, most importantly the long life cycles, the high costs, offsets and the importance of research and development are addressed.

Chapter 2 discusses the legal base of the Defence Directive in the EU Internal Market. Like all EU procurement Directives, the Defence Directive is a secondary EU law instrument with the purpose to amplify and give detail to the primary EU Internal Market regimes of the TFEU. Secondary EU law is legislation created by the relevant EU institutions within the limits authorised by legal bases in the primary TFEU. Directives are to be transposed into the national laws of the Member States, thereby harmonising these laws. The chapter will first discuss the foundations of the Defence Directive in the EU Internal Market regimes of the TFEU, namely the free movement of goods in Article 34 TFEU, the free movement of services in Article 56 TFEU and the freedom of establishment in Article 49 TFEU. This will include a discussion of the relevant regime-specific limitations to these freedoms in the public security dimensions of the derogations in Articles 36 and 52(1) TFEU. Moreover, this will include a discussion of the Internal Market legal bases for the Defence Directive in Articles 53(2), 62 and 114 TFEU.[25]

Chapter 3 discusses the specific national security derogations of the TFEU. As discussed in chapter 2, the Internal Market regimes of the TFEU on the free

---

[25] In the Preamble of the Defence Directive, before para. 1, still "Articles 47(2) and Article 55 and 95 [EC Treaty]" as the Directive dates from 13 July 2009 and the EC Treaty was replaced by the TFEU on 1 December 2009.

movement of goods and services apply to armaments and to other security goods and services, subject to narrowly defined and intensely scrutinised public security exemptions. However, with respect to armaments which are not the exclusive subject of the Defence Directive but at its core, and also with respect to secrecy concerns and crisis situations, an additional set of derogations may apply. This chapter will discuss these defence-specific exemptions in the Treaty relating to armaments in Article 346(1)(b), to secrecy in Article 346(1)(a) and to crisis situations in Article 347 TFEU. An understanding of the armaments exemption in Article 346(1)(b) TFEU will be particularly important since the main objective of the Defence Directive is to reduce the cases in which this exemption is used in practice to establish an Internal Market for armaments and other security-sensitive goods and services. Thus this provision is important for the understanding of all other chapters of the book and especially Part II: a book about the Defence Directive is necessarily a book about the armaments derogation in Article 346(1)(b) TFEU. It will be shown that compared to the public security exemptions from the Internal Market regimes of the Treaty discussed in chapter 2, the use of these exemptions can be subject to different pre-judicial and judicial review procedures and to a different standard of review. The purpose of this crucial chapter is to provide an understanding of the scope and interpretation of the fundamental derogation for the TFEU which determined the substance of the Defence Directive discussed in the chapters of Part II almost as much as its Internal Market objectives discussed in chapter 2. Moreover, more specifically it has to be understood as a provision limiting the scope of the Defence Directive discussed in chapter 6.

Chapter 4 discusses the EU Internal Market context of the Defence Directive beyond its legal base and limitations in the TFEU. This includes the secondary trade law regimes which partly amplify and harmonise the primary Internal Market regimes of the TFEU discussed in chapter 2 and partly regulate trade with third countries: customs duties, intra-Community transfers and defence exports. A special emphasis is put on intra-Community transfers, divided into transfers of armaments and dual-use goods due to the particular importance of the former leading to the relevant Intra-Community Transfers Directive being introduced in concert with the Defence Directive, as the second legally binding instrument of the EU "Defence Package". The regimes on intra-Community transfers, essentially regulating Member State licences of these transfers to other Member States, are also the focus of this chapter since they have a direct impact on the regulation and operation of the Defence Directive, especially with regards to the need for security of supply discussed in chapter 8. This is followed by sections on standardisation, competition (anti-trust) law, merger control and State aid. The chapter concludes with a very brief overview of other relevant Commission initiatives and policies.

Chapter 5 discusses European armaments law and policy beyond the EU Internal Market. European policy on armaments, not the only but the central object of the Defence Directive, is not exclusively regulated by the TFEU and the Defence Directive. First, defence procurement and other related issues are addressed as part of a European armaments policy, which is a crucial element of the emerging Common Security and Defence Policy (CSDP), which forms part of the Common Foreign and Security Policy (CFSP) of the EU. In 2005 a European Defence Agency (EDA) was established to manage those parts of the European armaments policy perceived to be outside the scope of the TFEU by the Member States. Until recently that included rules on procurement. Secondly, organisational structures outside the EU addressed the reorganisation and preservation of the European defence industrial base or parts of it as one of their tasks similar to EDA, complementing or competing with the Internal Market regimes and initiatives. The relevant frameworks are the Organisation for Joint-Armaments Procurement (OCCAR) and the Letter of Intent (LoI) which both only include EU Member States. Their initiatives do *not* include rules on defence procurement directed at the Member States. However, they affect various aspects of the Internal Market regime of which the Defence Directive is the most important part. Similar to the EDA regime, these initiatives complement or compete with some of those of the Commission. Furthermore, an understanding of the OCCAR and LoI activities is needed for the discussion of the scope of the Defence Directive in chapter 6: whatever is excluded from the scope of application of the Directive and TFEU can be addressed in frameworks outside the EU Internal Market. Part 6 will discuss how the fragmentation and overlap of these frameworks outlined in the previous parts of this chapter can be overcome. A short discussion of relevant agencies such as the NPSA, NETMA or NEHEMA which are parts of NATO and therefore not "European" organisations, and on some bilateral initiatives, will conclude this last chapter of Part I on the background of the Defence Directive.

Building on the discussion of the context of the instrument Part II of the book provides an analysis of the contents of the Defence Directive itself. Part II is subdivided into five chapters on scope, procedures, security of supply and information, offsets and subcontracting and review and remedies. The EU legislator used Public Sector Directive 2004/18/EC as the "rock from which they chiselled" the Defence Directive. In other words, the latter represents a Public Sector Directive adapted to the special needs of defence and security procurement. The purpose of the adaptations is to avoid Member States derogating from the procurement regime on the basis of Article 346 TFEU, but also Articles 36, 51, 52 and 62 TFEU explained in chapters 2 and 3. The Defence Directive is intended to accommodate most national security needs of the Member States to keep most of their procurement activities inside that Directive (and the TFEU). The most relevant adapted provisions are those on scope (chapter 6), procurement procedures and the situations in which they can be used (chapter 7), specifications and contract performance conditions (chapter 8), the qualification of bidders to ensure their reliability (chapter 8), award criteria determining the eventual contractor (chapter 8), offsets and subcontracting (chapter 9) and on review and remedies for aggrieved bidders (chapter 10). As the new instrument takes the specific needs of defence and security into account, recourse to security exemptions should be necessary in fewer situations than under the previous regime. As a consequence, procurement in the relevant areas and especially for armaments should no longer be conducted completely outside the rules of the Internal Market. Thus a Directive "tailored" for defence and security was created.[26] At the same time other objectives of EU public procurement law, such as non-discrimination on grounds of nationality, the equal treatment of bidders, competition, market access and transparency are promoted.

Chapter 6 addresses a crucial issue to be considered at the beginning of any analysis of procurement law, which is its scope or field of application, its coverage. In the context of the EU procurement Directives this concerns the questions of which contracting entities (personal scope) and which of their contracts (material scope) are covered. The latter aspect looks at the contract type, its value and at a number of exceptions. The earlier looks at the legal nature of the entity awarding the contract to a private sector economic operator. The extensive rules on procedures discussed in chapter 7; on specifications and contract conditions, qualification, selection and award criteria discussed in chapter 8; on offsets and subcontracts discussed in chapter 9; and finally on review and remedies discussed in chapter 10, only apply if the entity and contract are within the scope of the Defence Directive. Therefore it is necessary to commence Part II of this book with a discussion of the scope of the new instrument. It will be shown that the legislator adapted the rules on coverage through "limitation", through higher-value thresholds and most importantly additional and adapted exclusions from the material scope of the Directive.

Chapter 7 discusses the set of procurement procedures of the Defence Directive. Procurement procedures, also called methods of procurement, provide the contracting officer or committee with a legal framework for the acquisition process, from the publication of the contract to the conclusion or making of the eventual contract. It is this procurement phase *strictu sensu*, after the definition of the need and before the contract management or performance phase, which is affected by EU Internal Market law and regulated by the EU procurement

---

[26] As A. Georgopoulos, "Legislative Comment: The New Defence Procurement Directive Enters into Force" (2010) 19 *Public Procurement Law Review* NA1–3, at NA2 put it, "The new instrument is ... tailor-made for the specific characteristics of the sector." C. Kennedy-Loest and N. Pourbaix, "The New Defence Procurement Directive" (2010) 11 *ERA Forum* 399, at 403 called the objective "to create a procurement regime that would be 'fit for purpose' for the award of defence and security contracts". The Commission itself called it a "perfectly suited instrument" for defence, see Defence Procurement – Frequently Asked Questions, Brussels, 28 August 2009, Question 2: What are the main innovations of the Directive?: http://ec.europa.eu/internal_market/publicprocurement/docs/defence/faqs_28-08-09_en.pdf [accessed 23 September 2013].

Directives. Procedures range from those subject to a maximum of competition involving many bidders to those only involving a single-source. The more competition the less likely are barriers to the Internal Market. The procurement procedures of the Defence Directive are not specifically adapted to the needs of defence and security. However, an increased "flexibility" regarding the choice of the procedure to be used, in favour of the less competitive negotiated procedures, is intended to take the special demands of defence and security procurement into account. Thus the rules on the procedures (of Public Sector Directive 2004/18/EC) were adapted in the Defence Directive by increasing flexibility.

Chapter 8 addresses the accommodation of the needs for security of supply and information in the Defence Directive. After it is determined that a contracting entity and the respective contract are within the scope of the Defence Directive as discussed in chapter 6 and after the appropriate procedure has been chosen as discussed in the previous chapter 7, a number of requirements regarding the different stages of a procurement procedure have to be considered. First, there are rules on the precise description or definition of the good, service or work in question, the so-called (technical) specifications. Secondly, there are related rules on the rejection of bids that are not compliant with the contract requirements. Thirdly, there are rules on the qualification of the economic operators bidding for contracts, an issue of particular importance in defence and security procurement since the reliability of suppliers and providers is crucial for the security interests at stake. Fourthly, there are rules on the criteria that determine who is awarded the contract. Contract conditions are very closely connected to specifications. The rules of the Defence Directive were adapted to take the specific characteristics of the defence and security sectors into account. There are two crucial objectives motivating the adaptations: security of supply and security of information. It will be argued that the adaptations mainly took the form of "description" of particular security of supply and information requirements which are also legally possible under the Public Sector Directive. This description does not add substance but by expressly describing these requirements encourages their use and provides certainty on their legality.

Chapter 9 will discuss the crucial offset and subcontracting regimes of the Defence Directive. This will introduce a fourth technique the EU legislator used to adapt the rules of the original Public Sector Directive to defence and security requirements: substitution. However, it will be explained that, in contrast to the limitation (chapter 6), flexibility (chapter 7) and description (chapter 8) techniques of adaptation responding to the strategic defence and security needs of the contracting entities, substitution is mainly a response to the structure of the European defence industries. The chapter will first discuss the legality of offsets in Internal Market law. Secondly, the chapter will analyse the position of offsets under the regime of the Defence Directive. Finally, the subcontracting regime of the Defence Directive will be introduced. It will be argued that while not expressly mentioning offsets, the Defence Directive essentially offers its subcontracting regime in substitution for offsets, which are very difficult to justify under EU law.

Chapter 10 will discuss the review and remedies system of the Defence Directive for aggrieved bidders in the national courts and procurement review bodies of the Member States. Contrary to the public and utilities sectors where public procurement review and remedies are regulated in separate Public Sector and Utilities Remedies Directives respectively, the public procurement review and remedies system of the Defence Directive is covered in its Title IV, which is based on the Public Sector Remedies Directive, with certain adaptations. The general techniques the EU legislator used to adapt the substantive rules of the Public Sector Directive in the Defence Directive discussed in the previous four chapters will be referred to. This will, as in these other chapters, first, facilitate the understanding of the Defence Directive as a Public Sector Directive and Public Sector Remedies Directive adapted to defence and security requirements, a nature also applicable to the review and remedies system of Defence Directive. Thus the Defence Directive and more specifically its Title IV also represents a Public Sector Remedies Directive adapted to defence and security requirements. Moreover, some adaptations to the substantive parts of the Defence Directive will impact on the scope of the remedies system and the substantive problems featuring in review proceedings. Most importantly, the adaptations to the review and remedies system itself will be discussed. This will include an analysis of the rules on the relevant defence and security procurement review bodies of the Member States, the adaptations to the remedies which can be awarded by these public procurement review bodies and the compliance of these rules with human rights standards.

Before the introduction of the Defence Directive, Public Sector Directive 2004/18/EC applied to defence and security procurement "subject to Article [346] of the Treaty".[27] However, the Public Sector Directive was at times considered ill-suited for defence procurement thus not allowing Member States to procure inside Internal Market legislation,[28] perhaps encouraging reliance on Article 346 TFEU. The Defence Directive is intended to change that by providing a defence-specific instrument.[29] The consultation launched by the Commission's 2004

---

[27] See Art. 10 Public Sector Directive 2004/18/EC before and after its amendment through Art. 71 Defence Directive. See also Art. 15 of new Public Sector Directive 2014/24/EU.

[28] This has not always been the case; in COM (1996) 10 final, 17 the Commission argued that the civil regime should simply be extended to the military sector. For an analysis of the civil procurement regimes for the public sector and utilities (on the Directives before the Public Sector and Utilities Directives) as models for defence procurement regulation, see Trybus, *European Defence Procurement Law, supra* note 11, chs. 3 and 4 respectively.

[29] This was pointed out by the Commission's B. Schmitt and N. Spiegel (the drafters of the Defence Directive) in their presentation "The Specificities of the European Defence and Security Procurement Directive" at the seminar "European Defence Procurement and

Green Paper on Defence Procurement[30] had shown that "[a] majority of stake-holders found that a defence directive would be useful" but that it "could offer new, more flexible and more suitable rules for procurement of defence contracts, which are not covered by Article [346] and for which the existing Directive may be too rigid and inappropriate".[31] The consultation then led to an action plan which included both the 2006 Interpretative Communication on Article 346 TFEU discussed in chapter 3 and the Defence Directive itself. Both instruments aim to reduce the use of Article 346 TFEU in practice.

The Council passed the Defence Directive in 2009 with 26 Member States voting in favour and only Poland abstaining (Croatia only joined the EU in 2013). This suggests a clear political will of most governments to legislate against the excessive use of Article 346(1)(b) TFEU by their own contracting entities. This also shows that a national government representing a Member State in the Council on the one hand and the defence procurement authorities of that same Member State on the other hand can have different opinions and priorities. Moreover, it appears that in the course of the legislative process some Member States might have changed their mind. Initially France and Britain did not support an Interpretative Communication or a Directive, and other Member States were at best lukewarm.[32] However, it is submitted that the political will of a Member State, well considered and taking all arguments into account, is most convincingly expressed in the vote in the Council. In the end France and Britain both voted in favour of the Defence Directive, the EU Presidency of the latter being instrumental in getting it passed in Council. The European Parliament, especially through the work of its Internal Market and Consumer Protection Committee and its Rapporteur Alexander Count Lambsdorff, contributed considerably to the final substance of the Defence Directive. In particular the review and remedies regime in Title IV discussed in chapter 10 originated in Parliament. The European Parliament passed the instrument with a clear majority.

Other Defence Market Initiatives", at the EIPA, Maastricht, 15 November 2010. The Commission's Guidance Note *Field of Application, supra* note 17, 1–2 makes the same point in detail. It should be noted that throughout this book officials of the EU or national institutions are only cited from presentations they delivered to larger audiences at seminars and conferences, *never* from private conversations. References to conference papers are from notes of the author (on file) unless stated otherwise.

[30] COM (2004) 608 final.

[31] COM (2005) 626 final, 7; see also: A. Georgopoulos, "Commission's Communication on the Results of the Consultation Process on European Defence Procurement" (2006) 15 *Public Procurement Law Review* NA119.

[32] See J. Michel and J. Rivière (rapporteurs), *Rapport d'information sur les nouveaux défis de la construction de l'Europe de la défense*, Commission de la Défense Nationale et des Forces Armées, French National Assembly, No. 2531, 27 September 2005, 42 *et seq.* as cited by B. Heuninckx, "Lurking at the Boundaries: Applicability of EU Law to Defence and Security Procurement" (2010) 19 *Public Procurement Law Review* 91–118, at 91 footnote 3.

Although not always transposed by the August 2011 deadline,[33] by March 2013 all of the then EU Member States had transposed the Defence Directive[34] and from August 2011 to March 2013 872 contracts were awarded under the Defence Directive, representing a total of €1.77 billion.[35] Within the limits of the Defence Directive discussed in chapter 6 of this book, the governments of the EU Member States are now regulating the practice of their contracting entities through the EU rather than on a national basis, unless they invoked Article 346 TFEU. The Commission initiated the Directive and thus opted for legislation not instead of but in addition to the use of enforcement action against Member States.[36] It can be assumed that the Commission will regularly question why the new regime tailored for defence and security was not used, more than under the previous regime. However, it is hoped that it will become less necessary over time as the new rules get increasingly accepted and used in practice. The Commission had carefully considered, compared and finally dismissed alternative options to a separate Defence Directive, including the continuation of the status quo, regulation through the EDA, further clarifying Interpretative Communications and an amended Public Sector Directive.[37] All options considered, only a separate Defence Directive would offer the user-friendly, legally binding and visible instrument to change from the current separation of the EU into 28 separate national markets to an EU internal defence and security procurement market, ensuring value for money for the taxpayer, the best possible equipment and services for the armed forces and competitive European defence industries.

---

[33] Many Member States did not transpose the Defence Directive on time, see R. Williams, "Commission Takes Action on Implementation of Defence Procurement Rules" (2012) 21 *Public Procurement Law Review* NA223–4.

[34] According to the Commission Staff Working Document on Defence, SWD (2013) 279 final, at 43. While complete in the 28 EU Member States, in Norway – the only EEA Member State with an army, navy and air force – the new "Defense and Security Procurement Regulations" (known as "FOSA" in Norway) transposing the Defence Directive into Norwegian law, only entered into force in January 2014. Transposition is not complete in EEA Member State Iceland. See the Decision of the EEA Joint Committee No. 129/2013 of 14 June 2013 amending Annex XVI (Procurement) to the EEA Agreement, www.efta.int/media/documents/legal-texts/eea/other-legal-documents/adopted-joint-committee-decisions/2013%20-%20English/129-2013.pdf [accessed 22 November 2013].

[35] According to the Commission Staff Working Document on Defence, SWD (2013) 279 final, at 44–6. Similar figures were provided in http://export.gov/europeanunion/defenseprocurement/ [accessed 5 November 2013].

[36] The Commission can litigate in the ECJ against Member States violating EU law on the basis of Art. 258 TFEU and for violations of Arts. 346 and 347 TFEU also on the basis of Art. 348 TFEU. The intention to use these mechanisms more frequently once the transposition deadline for the new Directive has elapsed was expressed by K. Vierlich-Jürcke, "Specificities of the Defence Procurement Directive" at the seminar "European Defence and Security Procurement" at the EIPA, Maastricht, 19 January 2012.

[37] Commission Staff Working Document – Impact Assessment SEC (2007) 1593, *supra* note 17, at 32–44.

PART I

The context of the Defence Directive

The political and economic context of the Defence Directive

Buyers, sellers and national security

1 Introduction

The legal analysis of the Defence Directive provided in chapters 6 to 10 of this book cannot be seen in isolation. Therefore an extensive analysis of the broader legal context of the instrument, consisting of primary and secondary sources of EU law and other relevant instruments, will be provided in chapters 2 to 5. However, beyond this legal context, there are a number of specific factors of the defence and security sectors that influence defence procurement and its regulation. These can broadly be divided into economic, political/ military and technological factors. First, economic factors – most importantly the structure and capacities of the European defence and security industries, both with regards to principal or prime contracts and the supply chain – will be explained. Moreover, special economic characteristics of the defence procurement context that differentiate it from other public sector and utilities procurement – and even security procurement under the Defence Directive – will be addressed. The discussion will distinguish between the armaments-producing defence industries on the one hand and providers of non-military sensitive goods and services on the other hand. Secondly, political and strategic factors, such as the different defence policies and ambitions of the EU Member States and the importance of sovereignty will be explained. This includes an introduction to the paramount objectives of national security and secrecy which feature throughout the book. Thirdly and finally, technological and contractual factors of defence procurement, most importantly the long life cycles, the high costs, offsets and the importance of research and development are addressed.

The economic, political and technological factors are interconnected. Most importantly, national defence industrial capacities and high costs have an impact on defence policy. Similarly, an ambitious defence policy reinforcing sovereignty has an impact on investment in a national defence industrial base. However, it is explaining the impact of these economic, political and technological factors on the regulation of defence and security procurement which is the reason for this foundational chapter. Many of these factors will reappear in the various chapters of Parts I and II, their background and importance already introduced in this chapter.

2 The economic context

The discussion of the economic context of defence and security procurement can be subdivided into a description of the demand for defence and security goods and services in the EU Member States (section 2.1 below), an analysis of the structure of the European defence and security industries (section 2.2 below) and a number of economic characteristics that differentiate particularly defence procurement from other procurement (section 2.3 below).[1]

2.1 Who is buying? Demand of defence and security goods and services in the EU

The demand for goods and services covered by the Defence Directive needs to be differentiated between defence goods and services on the one hand and all other sensitive goods and services on the other hand. This is due to the numerous economic, political and technological factors discussed further in this chapter and the legal factors discussed throughout this book and in particular in chapter 3.[2] These factors differentiate the purchase of armaments, which are not exclusively but mostly conducted by ministries of defence, from other contracts, awarded by any contracting authority or entity. It is therefore helpful to differentiate between an "armaments market" (mainly but not exclusively ministries of defence) and a "security market" (all covered contracting entities).

The importance of the armaments market to the European economy is considerable. According to 2012 figures of the European Defence Agency (EDA), the EU Member States[3] spent €194 billion on defence in 2010. Their

---

[1] On points 2.2 and 2.3 with respect to defence procurement see M. Trybus, *European Defence Procurement Law: International and National Procurement Systems as Models for a Liberalised Defence Procurement Market in Europe* (The Hague: Kluwer Law International, 1999), ch. 1, at 7–10 and Aris Georgopoulos, "European Defence Procurement Integration: Proposals for Action within the European Union", PhD Thesis, University of Nottingham (2004), at 61–2 (on file); and more recently and extensively Baudouin Heuninckx, "The Law of Collaborative Defence Procurement through International Organisations in the European Union", PhD Thesis, University of Nottingham and the Belgian Royal Military Academy (2011), ch. 2, at 33–45 (on file).

[2] In particular the armaments exemption from EU Internal Market law in Art. 346(1)(b) TFEU, see 104–25.

[3] Denmark does not participate in the defence aspects of the Common Foreign and Security Policy (CFSP), including EDA.

total procurement budget for armaments, civil goods, services and works, including operations and maintenance, was estimated at €86 billion.[4] Defence expenditure in the then 27 EU Member States represented 1.6 per cent of GDP and 3.2 per cent of overall government expenditure.[5] Since the end of the Cold War in the late 1980s the defence budgets of the EU Member States have seen constant and in phases dramatic reductions. However, the degree of these reductions differs from Member State to Member State and there have been periods of stagnation and increase as well.[6] First, the general trend of defence budget reduction is mainly caused by the fact that the disappearance of the Soviet threat made large armed forces unnecessary and that public opinion expects a "peace dividend" in the form of smaller defence budgets. Secondly, the convergence criteria of the emerging European Monetary Union forced the Eurozone countries to cut expenditure, also in relation to their defence budgets.[7] Thirdly, the economic crisis since 2008 has accelerated that process of defence budget reduction. The United Kingdom, France, Spain, Belgium and Denmark will have double-digit defence budget cuts, while Greece and Bulgaria are facing reductions of their defence procurement of more than 30 per cent. This general trend is expected to continue with

[4] Based on the 26 EU Member States who participated in EDA at the time. The figure is the overall €86 billion figure for procurement and research and development, including €9 billion for the latter, and including 22–23% of the overall €194 billion which was spent on operations and maintenance, see www.eda.europa.eu/docs/default-source/news/eu-us-defence-data-2011.pdf [accessed 28 March 2014]. The overall figure of €194 billion for 2010 is also confirmed in the recent Commission Communication "A New Deal for European Defence: Towards a More Competitive and Efficient Defence and Security Sector", COM (2013) 542 final, at 7. This figure includes the procurement of "civilian" goods and services not covered by the Defence Directive but by Public Sector Directive 2004/18/EC, as will be further explained in chapter 6. Economists have highlighted the difficulties to provide reliable data on the defence market. Therefore the figures referred to in this chapter and throughout the book are to be treated with caution. However, they can give an approximate idea of the size of the market and market trends and that is sufficient for the purposes of this chapter – to provide the economic context of the legal analysis in the other chapters. On slightly older but more detailed figures see Commission Staff Working Document, *Annex to the Proposal for a Directive of the European Parliament and of the Council on the coordination of procedures for the award of certain public works contracts, public supply contracts and public service contracts in the fields of defence and security*, European Commission, Brussels, 2007, http://ec.europa.eu/internal_market/publicprocurement/docs/defence/impact_assessment_en.pdf [accessed 17 October 2013] hereinafter "Annex to the Proposal for the Defence Directive".

[5] Ibid.

[6] Stockholm International Peace Research Institute, SIPRI Military Expenditure Database with figures for 1988–2012, http://milexdata.sipri.org/files/?file=SIPRI+military +expenditure+database+1988-2012.xlsx [accessed in May 2013]. COM (2013) 542 final, at 7 reports an overall defence spending decline from €251 billion to €194 billion.

[7] Dominik Eisenhut, *Europäische Rüstungskooperation* (Baden-Baden: Nomos, 2010), at 38.

reductions of another $17 billion in Europe and the USA until 2015.[8] However, even with further budget cuts likely to continue, the EU "defence market" will continue to have a considerable multi-billion size.

The term "defence expenditure" refers to the procurement of the ministries of defence and their procurement of arms. As will be explained in more detail in chapter 6,[9] the personal scope of the Defence Directive covers contracting authorities and entities beyond these defence-specific bodies, including the police, prisons or even utilities. While the ministries of defence are responsible for territorial defence and military crisis management, the other contracting authorities and entities cover a wide range of public and private security threats, ranging from the combat of terrorism and organised crime to the protection of reservoirs or airport security. While often only a small part of the procurement activities of these bodies will be covered by the Defence Directive, the vast personal scope of the Defence Directive includes thousands of contracting authorities and entities in the EU and this adds up. There are only limited figures on the demand of this multitude of contracting bodies with regards to armaments and other sensitive goods and services, in other words on the "security market". However, it can safely be assumed that the large number of these bodies will have an annual demand adding significantly to the figures for defence expenditure provided above. A 2011 survey into the EU market for "goods and services to combat terrorism and organised crime", which covered the demand of various security bodies in the EU, provided a 0.48 per cent of GDP figure for 2007.[10] This equalled a procurement budget of €59 billion in the then 27 Member States.[11] While according to this survey these figures have increased considerably in the years following 2001,[12]

---

[8] Guy Anderson, "Major Defence Markets in an Era of Austerity – Trends and Mitigation Strategies", at the conference "Jane's Defence Industry", London, 17 October 2011. See in great detail: F. Stephen Larrabee et al., NATO and the Challenges of Austerity (Santa Monica, Arlington, Pittsburgh: RAND Corporation, 2012), www.rand.org/content/dam/rand/pubs/monographs/2012/RAND_MG1196.pdf [accessed 5 June 2013]. There is also a risk that by 2017 the EU "will have lost 12 per cent of its overall defence spending since the start of the economic crisis", according to a speech of European Council President Herman van Rompuy, "Defence in Europe – Pragmatically Forward", 21 March 2013, as cited in COM (2013) 542 final, at 35.

[9] At 251–6.

[10] Carlos Martí Sempere, A Survey of the European Security Market, Economics of Security Working Paper 43 (Berlin: Deutsches Institut für Wirtschaft (DIW), 2011), at 157, www.diw.de/documents/publikationen/73/diw_01.c.369424.de/diw_econsec0043.pdf [accessed 24 May 2013].

[11] Ibid., at 18. €66.5 billion according to Eurostat, Government expenditure function, Classification of the functions: 3 Public order and safety, figure for 2007, as cited by Sempere, A Survey of the European Security Market, supra note 10, at 13.

[12] In 2001 the figure for the 27 (2011) Member States was €44.7 billion, with an increase to 2002 of 15.2%, and increases of between 2.3% and 8.3% in the other years, see Sempere, A Survey of the European Security Market, supra note 10, at 13.

the impact of the economic crisis might lead to a reduction of this market as well. Nevertheless, there is no indication of this market shrinking to the extent that the defence market did since the end of the Cold War.

2.2 Who is selling? The structure of the European defence and security market

The discussion of the structure of the European defence and security market also needs to distinguish between the defence or armaments market on the one hand and the security market on the other hand. While, as will be explained in chapter 6, both markets are now subject to the Defence Directive, it is the defence or armaments market which has characteristics differentiating it from other "civilian" markets. In contrast, while the security sectors often operate in a similar national security context, the industrial and provider base does not differ significantly from other sectors. However, two factors have to be remembered to put this distinction between defence and security into perspective. First, many high-technology products can be used for both military and non-military purposes. Secondly, most of the European "defence" companies mentioned below produce military or dual-use goods as only one of several fields of activity, often also producing security and "civilian" products. The trans-European company EADS, for example, produces defence goods but also, most importantly, for space and aerospace. This makes it difficult to define "defence industries".[13] However, the Defence Directive was drafted on the background of Article 346 TFEU, which, as will be explained in great detail in chapter 3, does distinguish between armaments and other goods. This legal background makes it necessary to distinguish between defence

---

[13] The difficulties of defining a defence industrial sector have been identified by K. Hartley, "Arms Industry, Procurement and Industrial Policies" in Keith Hartley and Todd Sandler (eds.), *Handbook of Defence Economics*, 2 vols. (Amsterdam: North Holland, 2007), II, 1139, 1141 *et seq*. For Hartley the defence industries are all companies that (also) produce defence goods. In contrast, P. Dunne, "The Defence Industrial Base" in Keith Hartley and Todd Sandler (eds.), *Handbook of Defence Economics*, 2 vols. (Amsterdam: North Holland, 1995), I, 399, 402 *et seq*, emphasises the specific use of the goods. See some of the case law discussed in ch. 3 where these definitions became important. For an extensive related study see *Study on the Industrial Implications in Europe on the Blurring of Dividing Lines between Security and Defence: Final Report* (Institut des Relations Internationales et Strategiques, Instituto Affari Internazionali, and Manchester Institute of Innovation Research for the European Commission, 2010), http://ec.europa.eu/enterprise/sectors/defence/files/new_defsec_final_report_en.pdf [accessed 17 October 2013]. The difficulties of defining the defence industrial sector are also recognised by the Commission in the Annex to the Proposal for the Defence Directive, *supra* note 4, at 10.

industries and security industries, even when defence economists highlight the difficulties of defining the defence industries and the Defence Directive goes beyond the regulation of defence purchases.

2.2.1 The European defence market: prime contractors

The European defence industries have an annual turnover of €55 billion and employ 400,000 people.[14] They form part of a world market in which in 2010 the Top 100 defence producers, many of them based in Member States of the EU, sold goods and services for US$411.1 billion.[15] Seen as one market, the European defence industries have a wide range of capabilities, including all types of weapons for land, air and sea forces,[16] second only to the United States. Capacities include artillery,[17] defence electronics,[18] aircraft,[19]

---

[14] 2012 figures of the Commission Staff Working Document on Defence, SWD (2013) 279 final accompanying COM (2013) 542 final, at 32. Up to an additional 960,000 indirect jobs are also mentioned citing the 2012 IndustriAll *Study on the Perspectives of the European Land Armaments Sector*, www.industriall-europe.eu/sectors/defence/2012/INFF_E3779_Final%20Report_v03-EN.pdf [accessed 28 March 2014]. 2007 figures of the Communication from the Commission to the European Parliament, the Council, the European Economic and Social Committee and the Committee of the Regions, "A Strategy for a Stronger and More Competitive European Defence Industry", COM (2007) 764 final, at 2 indicate a figure of 300,000. The Communication also points out that 20 years ago these figures were almost twice as high. The 2010 *Study on the Impact of Emerging Defence Markets and Competitors on the Competitiveness of the European Defence Sector* (ECORYS, Teknologisk Institut, Cambridge Econometrics, CES Info, DEA Consult: for the European Commission), http://ec.europa.eu/enterprise/sectors/defence/files/study_defence_final_report_en.pdf [accessed 17 October 2013], hereinafter *"Emerging Defence Markets"*, has only older and higher figures. It can be assumed that the 2014 figures are lower.

[15] Stockholm International Peace Research Institute (SIPRI) in their 2011 Yearbook (released 27 February 2012), www.sipri.org/research/armaments/production/Top100/media/pressreleases/2013/AP_PR [accessed in May 2013], at 3. The Top 100 of arms producers contains many EU-based companies (with position in list where available): from the United Kingdom: BAe Systems (3), Rolls-Royce (17), Babcock (30), Serco (45), Qinetiq (56), GKN (72), Chemring (68), Ultra Electronics (90); from Italy: Finmeccanica (8), Agusta Westland, Fincantieri (63), Savio Cinven (93), Salex Galileo, Salex Communications, MDBA Italia; from France: Thales (11), Safran (15), DCNS (24), EADS Astrium, Nexter (66), Dassault (62); from Germany: Rheinmetall (26), Kraus-Maffei Wegmann (54), ThyssenKrupp (49), Diehl (60); from Spain: Navantia (55) and Indra (94); from Sweden: Saab (25); from the Netherlands: Thales Nederland; from Finland: Patria (87). The "multinationals": EADS (7), MDBA and Eurocopter are listed as EU companies. See www.sipri.org/research/armaments/production/Top100 [accessed in May 2013].

[16] See *inter alia* the listed capabilities on the SIPRI top 100 list, ibid.

[17] BAe, Finmeccanica, Rheinmetall, Nexter.

[18] BAe, EADS, Finmeccanica, Thales, Safran, SAAB, Rheinmetall, Salex Galileo, Ultra Electronics, Thales NL, Indra.

[19] BAe, EADS, Finmeccanica, CASA (EADS), Eurocopter (EADS), Agusta Westland, Alenia, Dassault, Patria.

missiles,[20] small arms and ammunition,[21] ships,[22] space,[23] military vehicles[24] and engines.[25]

However, seen separately, the national defence industrial capabilities of the EU Member States differ significantly. They can be subdivided into four broad groups.[26] First, France and the United Kingdom, nuclear powers with permanent seats in the UN Security Council, have the largest defence industries, matched by ambitious foreign policies. These include the use of their armed forces, as last seen 2011 in Libya. Britain cooperates militarily and industrially closer with the United States, whereas France has a stronger national and EU orientation.[27] Secondly, Germany, Italy, Sweden and increasingly Spain also have significant capacities.[28] Thirdly, Belgium, Finland, the Netherlands,

---

[20] BAe, EADS, Finmeccanica, Thales, MDBA, SAAB, Diehl, Thales Air Defence NL.

[21] BAe, Finmeccanica, Thales, Rheinmetall, Diehl, Nexter, Chemring, Patria.

[22] BAe, DCNS, Babcock, ThyssenKrupp, Navantia, Fincantieri.

[23] EADS Astrium, Thales.

[24] Finmeccanica, Thales, Rheinmetall, Kraus-Maffei-Wegmann, Nexter, Patria.

[25] Rolls-Royce, Avio-Cinven.

[26] Walker and Gummett categorised the European countries into five groups according to their defence industrial capabilities: Group 1: France and Britain; Group 2: Germany, Italy and Spain; Group 3: Belgium, Norway, Denmark and Switzerland; Group 4: Greece, Portugal and Turkey; with the *sui generis* group of Sweden in Group 5 (*sui generis* because while Sweden has a relatively small economy it has diverse defence industrial capabilities and counts as one of the "Big Six" in the EU), see Susan Walker and Philip Gummett, *Nationalism, Internationalism and the European Defence Market*, Chaillot Paper No. 9 (Paris: Institute for Security Studies of the Western European Union, 1993), at 12, and 20–3. Others divide into three or four groups: Andrew Cox and Keith Hartley, "The Costs of Non-Europe in Defence Procurement – Executive Summary", The Commission of the European Communities DG III, July 1992 (not published), at 11. The 2010 *Study on the Impact of Emerging Defence Markets and Competitors on the Competitiveness of the European Defence Sector, supra* note 14, implicitly divided the Member States into similar groups.

[27] All these features separate France and Britain from a group of Member States with otherwise comparable or larger size and economic weight – such as Italy or Germany – and put defence, including defence procurement, higher on the domestic political agenda.

[28] COM (2013) 542 final, at 49 also reports that 87% of European defence production is concentrated in six EU Member States: France, Germany, Italy, Spain, Sweden and the United Kingdom. The Commission in "The Challenges Facing the European Defence-related Industry: A Contribution for Action at European Level", COM (1996) 10 final, at 4 on the then 15 Member States: "About 90% of the EU total production of defence equipment is concentrated in some Member States: France, the United Kingdom, Germany, Italy, and Sweden." In the "Communication from the Commission to the Council and the European Parliament on the Results of the Consultation Launched by the Green Paper on Defence Procurement and on Future Commission Initiatives", COM (2005) 626 final, at 2 on the then 25 Member States: "85% of defence spending and 90% of the EU's industrial capabilities are concentrated in six major arms-producing countries", listing the United Kingdom, France, Germany, Italy, Spain, and Sweden in footnote 3. The 2010 *Study on the Impact of Emerging Defence Markets and Competitors on the*

Poland, the Czech Republic, Denmark and Romania have limited capacities, whereas, fourthly and finally, the other Member States have only very limited or no defence industries. None of these have defence policies comparable to those of France and Britain. Most Member States have to procure at least parts of their requirements abroad, not necessarily in the EU, but there are often capacities for subcontracting, as will be discussed further below. The fact that EU Member States differ in scale and scope of their economic power, and therefore in needs and possibilities for buying military equipment, is seen as an obstacle to market integration in itself.[29]

However, for the purposes of this book the EU Member States shall be divided into only two groups: the six Member States with considerable defence industrial capacities, namely Britain, France, Germany, Italy, Spain and Sweden on the one hand and the other Member States with limited or no defence industries on the other hand. This division into "Big Six" and "other" Member States is not entirely consistent. However, it is more or less[30] reflected in the membership of some of the structures discussed in chapter 5,[31] the attitudes to industrial policy and buying American discussed below and the position towards many aspects of the Defence Directive, which will be discussed throughout this book. The balance to be achieved between the strong industrial powers of the first group and the other Member States is a crucial problem.[32]

In all Member States with national defence industrial capacities, even in France and Britain, these capabilities are limited. No national defence industrial base is able to provide the full range of equipment needed by the armed forces, especially not at affordable prices. This has various consequences, including the drive to merge into larger defence companies especially in the

---

Competitiveness of the European Defence Sector, supra note 14, provides similar figures. See also COM (2007) 764 final, at 4.

[29] Pierre de Vestel, Defence Markets and Industries in Europe: Time for Political Decisions?, Chaillot Paper No. 21 (Paris: Institute of Security Studies of the Western European Union, 1995), at 71; Walker and Gummett, Nationalism, Internationalism and the European Defence Market, supra note 26, at 19; Andrew Cox, "The Future of European Defence Policy: The Case of a Centralised Procurement Agency" (1994) 3 Public Procurement Law Review 65, at 73. While these publications are dated, the point they make does not depend on recent data and is still valid.

[30] The grouping of some Member States might change. For example, Spain used to be a country with developing defence industries, like Greece or Portugal, while Belgium has limited capabilities but cooperates most notably in OCCAR, see ch. 5 at 22.

[31] Especially OCCAR and Letter of Intent, see ch. 5 at 225–37.

[32] Walker and Gummett, Nationalism, Internationalism and the European Defence Market, supra note 26, at 66; de Vestel, Defence Markets and Industries in Europe, supra note 29, at 71–3. While these publications are dated, the point they make does not depend on recent data and is still valid.

aerospace and electronics sectors, on a national[33] and also on a trans-European basis.[34] The limitations of national defence industrial capabilities have also led to collaborative projects to pool capabilities, as will be discussed further below. The fact that for many high-end pieces of equipment collaboration is necessary makes national competition for these items almost impossible and EU-wide competition very difficult. On the other hand, there are types of equipment, such as military vehicles and shipbuilding where there are sufficient if not excessive capacities for competition on an EU-wide basis, in some Member States even on a national basis. There have been much fewer mergers[35] as frequent State ownership, especially in the South, the reduced importance of technology and larger volumes (due to longer life cycles) reduce the pressure to consolidate.[36] Moreover, there have been political interventions stopping mergers.[37] Even for a major weapon system such as a fighter aircraft the EU still has several competitors: for fighter aircraft the collaborative Eurofighter/Typhoon, the Anglo-Swedish Gripen and the French Rafale. Thus while competition is difficult it is possible in large parts of the defence sector.

Apart from their overall competitiveness, another important question which will have a considerable impact on the future of the European defence industries is what type of equipment prime contractors will sell inside and outside the EU after the current generation of their products has become redundant. Thus the competitiveness of the European defence industries is not only determined by the size of the market and the number of competitors but also on the question whether they will have something competitive to sell in the future.

[33] BAe Systems is the product of a merger of British Aerospace with several other British companies which also acquired the defence parts of the US company General Electric (Marconi). The French Thales is the result of a merger of the French companies Alcatel, Dassault and Aerospatiale, as is the Italian company Finmeccanica. The French company Safran is the result of a merger of the French companies Snecma and Sagem.

[34] The European Aeronautic Defence and Space Company (EADS) is the product of a merger of the German DASA, the French Aerospatiale Matra and the Spanish CASA. Agusta Westland (helicopters) was formed by the Italian Agusta and the British Westland. The rocket and missile producer MBDA is the result of a merger of BAe Systems, EADS and Finmeccanica.

[35] COM (2007) 764 final, at 5. See also Tom Dodd, *European Defence Industrial and Armaments Cooperation* (London: House of Commons Library Research Paper 97/15, 1997) for the end of the last century.

[36] T. Guay and R. Callum, "The Transformation and Future Prospects of Europe's Defence Industries" (2002) 78 *International Affairs* 757, at 773; J. Anderson, *Cold War Dinosaurs or High-Tech Arms Providers? The West European Armaments Industry at the Turn of the Millennium*, Occasional Paper 23 (Paris: EU Institute of Security Studies, 2001), at 3 *et seq.* State aid and mergers are also discussed in more detail in ch. 4 at 172–6 (mergers) and 176–82 (state aid).

[37] Such as German Chancellor Merkel stopping the merger of BAe Systems and EADS in 2012.

2.2.2 The European security market: prime contractors

As explained in more detail in chapter 6,[38] not only military equipment is covered by the Defence Directive, but also all sensitive equipment, works, supplies, services directly related to armaments and sensitive equipment and finally works and services for specifically military purposes. This will include, for example, contracts regarding scanning equipment used at airports, the construction of an air force base or maintenance services for military equipment. The industrial and provider base for such a broad selection of goods and services varies considerably, depending on the category of good or service in question and on the size of the contract. For the more high-end technology products the industrial structure will be similar to the defence industries, with only a few providers in a few Member States being able to enter into such a contract. According to the 2011 DWI survey referred to above,[39] the Member States with most prime contractors for large security solutions with system integration capability and a relevant share in the market are France,[40] Germany,[41] the United Kingdom[42] and Sweden,[43] with some capability in Spain[44] and the Netherlands.[45] Noticeable about this list is the absence of Italy. Otherwise a division into a group of "Big Six" Member States with security industrial capability, comparable to the similar group in the defence sector, and a second group of Member States with only limited or no security industries appears appropriate. However, the inclusion of works in the material scope of the Defence Directive, for example, will lead to a prime contractor base for several "security contracts" in more Member States than the six listed above. Moreover, due to the niche character of many of these goods and services, these providers are not necessarily based in the same Member States as the armaments-producing companies. Furthermore, the high costs, long life cycles, heavy research and development and the other economic factors described further below will often apply to a lesser degree. Therefore, for many of the goods and services in question the industrial and service provider base will be more varied, more evenly spread across the Member States and will include more small and medium-size enterprises (SMEs). For these goods the numerous economic and political factors of the armaments sector apply to a much lesser extent and, depending on the individual contract, may not apply at all. Nevertheless, for these contracts

---

[38] At 263–6.

[39] Sempere, *A Survey of the European Security Market*, *supra* note 10, at 22–3.

[40] Thales Security Solutions, SAGEM Morpho and participation in Cassidian which is however classed as an EU company.

[41] Siemens Building Technologies, Giesecke and Devrient, Bosch Security Systems and Cassidian.

[42] G4S and Smith Detection (partly USA).

[43] Securitas Group, Niscayah, Gunnebo AB, Axis Comm. AB, Assa Abloy AB.

[44] Prosegur.   [45] Gemalto NV.

the security and secrecy considerations discussed below will have to be taken into account.

2.2.3 Subcontractors

Subcontracts are a feature in both the military defence sectors[46] and the non-military security sectors; as much as in contracts covered by the Utilities and Public Sector Directives. The more complex the contract, the more extensive the supply chain of subcontracts. While major companies will often also be subcontractors as well as prime contractors, subcontracting offers opportunities for SMEs that normally do not exist for prime contracting.[47] The European industrial and service capabilities at the subcontracting level are considerably more varied, extensive and evenly spread across all Member States than the defence industrial capabilities at the prime contract level described above. The provision of components of a major weapon system, which can be as simple an item as light bulbs, are simply markets that can be entered by more companies than the provision of the weapon system itself. In addition to the non-military security market described under the previous heading above which is now covered by the Defence Directive, the subcontracting market is also spread across all Member States of the EU and not just the "Big Six". Thus while for the prime contract level of armaments contracts, and to an extent security contracts, Member States can be divided into groups of those who have capabilities and those who do not, at the subcontracting level the industrial and services sectors of most Member States have relevant capabilities. As there are therefore opportunities for all Member States' economies at the subcontracting levels, the Defence Directive accommodates this in a specific subcontracting regime to be discussed in chapter 9.[48]

2.3 Economic characteristics of defence procurement

Economic characteristics of the defence sector impacting on the regulation of defence procurement are protectionism or buy American (section 2.3.1 below), monopsony (section 2.3.2 below), monopolies (section 2.3.3 below), duplication (section 2.3.4 below), the high costs of defence equipment (section 2.3.5 below), State ownership and control (section 2.3.6 below) and inefficiency (section 2.3.7

---

[46] See, for example, the British Cobham (47) and GKN (72) or the Italian Salex Galileo which are listed in the SIPRI Top 100, *supra* note 15, as providers of components for aircraft and defence electronics. According to COM (2013) 542 final, at 54, in the EU 1,320 defence-related SMEs "account for between 11 and 17 per cent of the EU's sales of defence equipment". Moreover, while the "Big Six" may boost 87% of the overall defence production in the EU, they "account for only 52 per cent of defence related SMEs".

[47] Already recognised in "The Challenges Facing the European Defence-related Industry: A Contribution for Action at European Level", COM (1996)10 final, at 4.

[48] At 428–52.

below). These characteristics apply normally to the armaments sector and not to the non-military security sectors. Moreover, they will normally apply to prime contractors, not necessarily to entire supply chains. In the context of the EU, monopsony, monopolies, duplication and inefficiency are the consequences of the fragmentation of the EU into 28 relatively closed national defence equipment markets. This is also due to the legal factors that will be discussed in chapters 2 and 3 and which the Defence Directive is intended to address. The high costs of defence equipment are a feature of defence equipment irrespective of the fragmentation of the EU markets, as a look at the United States reveals. However, EU market fragmentation leads to even higher costs, as will be discussed below.

2.3.1 Buying European as a last resort: protectionism or buy American

An important economic characteristic of defence procurement in Europe is the protectionism practised by the EU Member States with defence industrial capabilities. There is a traditional unwillingness to open defence markets to supplies from other Member States.[49] In 2005, for example, 80 per cent of defence equipment expenditure was spent on exclusively national procurement projects[50] and only 13 per cent on purchases from other Member States.[51] This tendency is not different to the behaviour of "civilian" procurement agencies

---

[49] More recent sources highlighting protectionism in the defence sector include: COM (2013) 542 final, at 41 and 53; COM (2007) 764 final, at 4 and the Annex to the Proposal for the Defence Directive, *supra* note 4, at 4. This was already highlighted in the 1980s, see Keith Hartley, "Public Procurement and Competitiveness: A Community Market for Military Hardware and Technology?" (1987) 25 *Journal of Common Market Studies* 237–47, at 238 and 242, and 1990s, see Cox, "The Future of European Defence Policy", *supra* note 29, at 65 and 68; Walker and Gummett, *Nationalism, Internationalism and the European Defence Market, supra* note 26, at 28; de Vestel, *Defence Markets and Industries in Europe, supra* note 29, at 26; Cox and Hartley, "The Costs of Non-Europe in Defence Procurement – Executive Summary", *supra* note 26, at 9; COM (1996) 10 final at 8.

[50] COM (2013) 542 final, at 41 and 54; Jean-Pierre Darnis, Giovanni Gasparini, Christoph Grams, Daniel Keohane, Fabio Liberti, Jean-Pierre Maulny, May-Britt Stumbaum, *Lessons Learned from European Defence Equipment Programmes*, Occasional Paper 69 (Paris: EU Institute of Security Studies, 2007), at 10. However, the expenditure on the collaborative projects of EU Member States discussed below by far exceeds the expenditure on these national programmes, as pointed out by Hartmut Küchle, *Rüstungsindustrie im Umbruch: Strategien deutscher Unternehmen und Ansätze einer europäischen Neuordnung* (Baden-Baden: Nomos, 2001), at 49.

[51] Commission Staff Working Document, Accompanying Document to the Proposal for a Directive of the European Parliament and of the Council on the Coordination of Procedures for the Award of Certain Public Works Contracts, Public Supply Contracts and Public Service Contracts in the Fields of Defence and Security Impact Assessment, SEC (2007) 1598 final Annex no. 13: Defence intra-community transfers and penetration rates, at 81.

and even utilities, especially before the introduction of the other procurement Directives. The protectionist tendency in the defence sector is even strengthened by economic and political developments as, for example, the defence budget cuts since the 1990s mentioned above. Protectionism is as much an economic as a political characteristic of defence procurement. Moreover, it is an important cause of the characteristics of monopsony, monopolies and duplication – and indirectly higher costs[52] and inefficiency as discussed below.

Protectionism is practised for a variety of reasons. Defence procurement is used as a means to reward friends and historic partners in the defence industries. Furthermore procurement agencies tend to stick to partners who, in the belief of these agencies, understand the basic needs of their armed forces best.[53] Protectionism in this area also involves all the problems that occur in public sector procurement, i.e. lack of market intelligence or cultural barriers.[54] In law and practice protectionism can take various forms. These range from direct awards, without following any legally binding procurement law involving publication or a procurement procedure, to less obvious practices such as technical specifications based on national standards or qualification based on security clearances only available to national suppliers. The Defence Directive is directed against this protectionism in the defence sector.

For EU Member States with only limited or no defence industries, protectionism only makes sense if there are any national capacities. However, if there is no capacity to protect, these Member States do not necessarily procure from EU Member States with defence capabilities. The dominant tendency in these Member States has been to buy from the United States.[55] In the 1990s Poland, for example, bought almost exclusively American.[56] The inefficiencies and high costs of many European products discussed below often do not compare well to the lower-cost and cutting-edge technology of their American competitors. Moreover, the acquisition of several EU-based defence companies

---

[52] For example for the 1980s Hartley, "Public Procurement and Competitiveness: A Community Market for Military Hardware and Technology?", *supra* note 49, at 240 cites United Kingdom official papers – Cmnd 9430-I, 1985, at 37 and HCP 399, 1986, at xii – suggesting that open and competitive markets could lead to cost savings of 20%, and for certain projects 35%.

[53] Cox, "The Future of European Defence Policy", *supra* note 29, at 84.

[54] See also Trybus, *European Defence Procurement Law*, *supra* note 1, at 7–8.

[55] COM (1996) 10 final, at 8 reports only 3–4% of the total procurement of major weapons systems in the then EU awarded to companies in other Member States; Eisenhut, *Europäische Rüstungskooperation*, *supra* note 7, at 69 footnote 236. According to COM (2003) 600 final, at 12 about a quarter of the defence contracts of the then 15 Member States were awarded to US companies.

[56] I. Anthony, "The United States: Arms Exports and Implications for Arms Production" in Herbert Wulf (ed.), *Arms Industry Limited* (Oxford University Press, 1993), 63, at 80 *et seq.*

has allowed US companies to improve their access to European markets.[57] A crucial question is what EU Member States without an industrial capacity can gain from an Internal Market in defence goods when this affects their ability to buy value for money from outside the EU in favour of less competitive products from other Member States. The concern in these Member States is being forced to subsidise the inefficient defence industries of their neighbours at the expense of their taxpayers and the quality of the equipment of their armed forces.[58] This concern has influenced the policy of the Member States on the integration of the European defence equipment market discussed below, and arguably, out of frustration with the opposition of the Member States with no or limited defence industrial capabilities, led the "Big Six" to develop structures excluding them discussed in chapter 5.[59]

As will be explained further in detail in chapter 2, the Defence Directive clearly has an Internal Market agenda directly aimed against protectionism. It is not directly aimed against the described buy-American policies, although it has raised American concerns to that effect.[60] However, as discussed in chapter 6,[61] the Directive leaves the choice on whether to open a procurement procedure to bidders from third countries such as the United States to the individual Member States. The Defence Directive only affects the decision on whether a procedure should be opened to bidders from other EU Member States. However, the fact that providers from all Member States have to be allowed to bid for a contract on the basis of the Defence Directive and that other barriers are addressed inside the Internal Market, for example licensing through the Intra-Community Transfers Directive discussed in chapter 4,[62] or outside the Internal Market through various EDA and Letter of Intent initiatives as discussed in chapter 5,[63] might give European competitors an advantage, depending on the circumstances of the individual contract. The third country and especially transatlantic dimension of the Defence Directive will not be analysed specifically in this book; this would require an entire

---

[57] Eisenhut, *Europäische Rüstungskooperation, supra* note 7, at 69 footnote 236 reports that General Dynamics bought the Spanish Santa Barbara, the Swiss MOWAG and the Austrian Steyr-Daimler-Puch. United Defence bought the Swedish BOFORS.

[58] On the concerns and motives of the smaller EU Member States with limited defence industries see Georgopoulos, PhD Thesis, *supra* note 1, especially ch. IV. Georgopoulos bases his discussion on Greece (ch. V) and Belgium (ch. VI).

[59] Especially OCCAR and Letter of Intent, see ch. 5 at 222–31.

[60] See on this topic the findings of Jeff P. Bialos, Catherine E. Fisher and Stuart L. Koehl, *Fortresses & Icebergs: The Evolution of the Transatlantic Defense Market and the Implications for U.S. National Security Policy,* 2 vols. (Baltimore and Washington DC: Centre for Transatlantic Relations, The Johns Hopkins University and the U.S. Department of Defense, 2009), I.

[61] At 295–8.   [62] At 139–60.   [63] At 186–222 (EDA) and 225–31 (LOI).

monograph at least.[64] However, deeper EU integration in defence procurement and trade primarily enhances the opportunities of goods and services originating in the EU. It is not too far-fetched that this might well happen at the expense of third-country providers.

2.3.2 Monopsony

The defence sector is characterised by monopsony.[65] This means that the mostly national producers of armaments often have only one prospective customer for their products: their government. This will normally be the national ministry of defence or another government agency buying armaments, such as ministries of the interior for the police, ministries of justice for prison services or border control agencies. Only the national government or – through exports – a foreign government will buy equipment. However, as will be explained in chapter 4[66] the sale to foreign governments is restricted through export control laws and the sale to private customers often prohibited by the national government or legislature. In countries with more restricted export practices such as Germany or the Netherlands, their own government is almost the only partner whereas in countries with a more open approach such as the United Kingdom, the government buys only half of the industrial output of the national industry whereas the other half is exported,[67] although this can vary from one year to another. Armament export policies may hinder liberalisation of defence procurement in Europe and therefore have to be harmonised. Otherwise defence industry firms and governments may be discouraged from working together because of uncertainties and lack of integration in this particular field. Different rules on exports give firms in Member States with more generous export rules an advantage. These aspects will be explained in chapter 4.[68] However, from an Internal Market as well as a third-country export point of view, the defence sector is limited to governments as the only customer in contrast to the "civil" sectors

---

[64] See the PhD thesis of Luke Butler, "Procurement Law as a Barrier to Transatlantic Defence Market Liberalisation", University of Birmingham (2013, on file).

[65] See the Annex to the Proposal for the Defence Directive, *supra* note 4, at 9. For the discussion of the US: David T. Day, "The Limits of Monopsony Pricing Power in the Markets for Defence Goods", *The Limits of Competition in Defense Acquisition*, Defense Acquisition University Research Symposium, September 2012; for the EU: *Emerging Defence Markets, supra* note 14, at 33; Cox and Hartley, "The Costs of Non-Europe in Defence Procurement – Executive Summary", *supra* note 26, at 3. The term "monopsony" describing a market in which there is only one buyer and many sellers was coined by Joan Robinson, *The Economics of Imperfect Competition* (London: Macmillan, 1933).

[66] At 160–6 and 139–60.

[67] See ch. VIII on the United Kingdom in Trybus, *European Defence Procurement Law, supra* note 1, for details.

[68] At 160–1.

where the government is usually only one of many customers, although always an important customer.

Monopsony has consequences on the relationship between the government buyers and the national defence industries depending on them for business and export licences. If considered a national defence company, possibly even a "national champion", the government will feel a responsibility for the industrial capability, employment, technical know-how and research and development such a company represents. This can have an effect on competition on defence procurement, especially when there is only one national provider, which, as outlined above, is often the case. The responsibility of the government for a defence industrial capability can lead to a tendency to often award contracts to the only national provider to keep that provider in business, for industrial policy reasons, national security reasons or both. Governments defend some of their industries as national champions motivated by national prestige and economic considerations. The effects of procurement decisions on employment are often especially visible to the electorate as large numbers of employees are made redundant, affecting whole regions and putting pressure on the respective governments so that even if they recognise the merits of open competition on economic grounds they may be politically unable to implement such open policies. The question of whether this is legally possibly under the TFEU and the Defence Directive will be discussed in other chapters of this book.[69] Moreover, monopsony may lead to intervention in the market ranging from various forms of State aid to State ownership, as will be explained in more detail below and in chapter 4.[70] This situation applies mainly to the "Big Six" defence industrial Member States.

However, the wider scope of the Defence Directive discussed in chapter 6 limits the importance of monopsony. First, one of the main objectives of the Directive is market integration and that will lead to defence companies having 28 or 32[71] potential customers instead of only one. Secondly, the inclusion of many contracting authorities and utilities in the personal scope and of small arms and ammunition in the material scope of the Directive leads to a multitude of buyers, for example a water utility company buying equipment for its security service. Thirdly, for many of the non-military security goods and services, monopsony does not apply at all. Similarly, for many large construction companies, for example, building army barracks is only one of many other contracts for various public and private customers.

---

[69] The TFEU will be discussed in chs. 2 and 3 whereas chs. 6–10 will deal with the Defence Directive.

[70] At 176–82.

[71] 28 Member States, since 1 July 2013 including Croatia as well as the EEA Member States Norway, Iceland and Liechtenstein, who also have to transpose the Directive, Switzerland being a special case.

2.3.3 Monopolies

The national armaments markets of the EU Member States are characterised by monopolies and duopolies.[72] With regards to armaments, the existence of often only one national provider in a national market and that market being closed to the Internal Market due to the protectionism discussed above, combined with the monopsony situation outlined above, can lead to a very close relationship between the contracting authority and that monopolist, in which competition would depend on breaking that monopoly by opening the market. This monopoly situation can only exist in the first group of "Big Six" Member States categorised above, which actually have the industrial capacity of a monopolist. For the other Member States there is no alternative to opening the markets. The same can be said for markets, for example for military vehicles in Germany, where there is more than one supplier but these suppliers have a dominant position because they are only a few. Monopolies and dominant positions could also develop due to the fact that the competition and State aid regimes of the EU did not always fully apply in practice, as will be further discussed in chapter 4. The Defence Directive does facilitate an Internal Market in defence procurement, within the limits discussed in chapter 6, thereby addressing monopsony and monopolies at the same time. Monopolies and oligopolies do not exist or not to the same extent as in the armaments market, in the non-military security markets and in the context of subcontracts.

2.3.4 Duplication

Especially in the group of the "Big Six" Member States[73] categorised above, the fragmentation of the EU defence equipment markets combined with monopsony and monopolies has led to duplication.[74] In other words, for many types of equipment there are many providers in the EU, in a market, which seen as a whole is only about 40 per cent the size of that of the United States, which often has fewer providers for each type of equipment. While, as discussed

---

[72] Keith Hartley, *The Economics of Defence Policy: A New Perspective* (Abingdon: Routledge, 2011), at 151–3; Hartley, "Public Procurement and Competitiveness: A Community Market for Military Hardware and Technology?", *supra* note 49, at 238; and Hartley, "The Future of European Defence Policy: An Economic Perspective" (2003) 14 *Defence and Peace Economics* 107–15, at 113.

[73] In this context one could speak of the "Big Four" since the mergers and acquisitions described for example in footnote 15 show that the land and marine systems capacities of Spain (Santa Barbara) and Sweden (Kockums, Hägglunds) are now part of companies from outside Spain and Sweden respectively. However, these companies do still produce in Spain and Sweden.

[74] Hartley, *The Economics of Defence Policy*, *supra* note 72, 133 and 151–3; "Public Procurement and Competitiveness: A Community Market for Military Hardware and Technology?", *supra* note 49, at 237, 238, 239; and "The Future of European Defence Policy", *supra* note 72, at 110. See also COM (2013) 542 final, at 41.

in chapter 4,[75] mergers both within the national markets and even across Member State borders have been occurring since the 1990s, the defence industrial base of the EU seen as a whole is not yet sufficiently consolidated. As explained above, there has been consolidation in the aerospace and electronics segments, leading to four and seven European providers respectively.[76] This compares to seven or eight providers for aircraft and 17 for electronics in the larger US market.[77] However, for other segments – especially military vehicles with seven[78] and land systems in general and for shipbuilding with seven[79] – there are still many providers. In contrast there are currently four providers of land systems[80] and six of marine systems[81] in the much larger US market. Duplication is particularly prominent in relation to research and development (R&D).[82]

Duplication has negative and positive consequences. On the one hand in order to have competition there needs to be more than one provider. Thus, depending on the type of equipment, a certain level of duplication is necessary to achieve the benefits of one of the competitive procedures under

---

[75] At 172–6.

[76] According to the SIPRI Top 100, *supra* note 15: BAe Systems, EADS, Thales and Finmeccanica for aircraft and BAe Systems, EADS, Thales, Safran, Ultra Electronics, Indra and Thales Nederland for electronics. On consolidation in the defence sector in general see also COM (2013) 542 final, at 48–53 also emphasising the need for "defence companies to reach a critical mass".

[77] According to the SIPRI Top 100, ibid: for aircraft: Lockheed Martin, Boeing, Northrop Grumman, United Technologies (incl. Sikorsky), Textron, Triumph Group and Hawker Beechcraft. For electronics: Lockheed Martin, Boeing, General Dynamics, Raytheon, Northrop Grumman, BAe Systems, L-3 Communications, United Technologies, Honeywell, ITT Exelis, Textron, Rockwell Collins, URS Group, Harris, SRA International, GenCorp and Flir Systems.

[78] Germany has the most extensive industrial base for land systems comprising Rheinmetall De Tec, Krauss Maffei Wegmann, Diehl and MAN. BAe is now the dominant provider of land systems in the United Kingdom after acquiring Alvis Vickers (Rolls-Royce) which had consolidated the British industries by acquiring smaller companies and also bought the Swedish provider Hägglunds. GIAT produces in France and Finmeccanica in Italy. See Eisenhut, *Europäische Rüstungskooperation, supra* note 7, at 50.

[79] After several mergers and acquisitions Thyssen Krupp Maritime Systems dominates the German, Swedish (Kockums) and Greek (Hellenic Shipyards) market. In the United Kingdom BAe Systems and Vosper Thornycraft provide marine systems. In France DCNS dominates the market and in Italy Fincantieri, in Spain Izar, and in the Netherlands Damen. See Eisenhut, *Europäische Rüstungskooperation, supra* note 7, at 51.

[80] According to the SIPRI Top 100, *supra* note 15: General Dynamics, Oshkosh Truck, Textron, Navistar, AM General and the Anglo-American BAe Systems, disregarding companies producing components and engines.

[81] According to the SIPRI Top 100, *supra* note 15: General Dynamics, Northrop Grumman, Hartington Ingalls Industries and the Anglo-American BAe Systems.

[82] Hartley, *The Economics of Defence Policy, supra* note 72, 133 and 151–3; "Public Procurement and Competitiveness", *supra* note 49, at 239.

the Defence Directive described in chapter 7. On the other hand, duplication is a result of the closed national markets leading to higher costs through a lack of economies of scale. Thus, inter alia, the European Security Strategy (ESS) aims to reduce duplication.[83]

The duplication in the European defence market needs to be differentiated from the duplication on the demand side. While there is only one Department of Defence procuring from the larger US defence market, the EU has 28 separate ministries of defence, armies, navies and air forces. There is no reliable published data on the costs of this duplication on the demand side but it can be assumed that this does come at a price.[84] As a response a centralised European defence agency has been discussed[85] and some of the structures discussed in chapter 5,[86] most importantly EDA and OCCAR, could eventually take on that role. However, the Defence Directive does not entail such a move and is mainly designed for the current multitude of contracting authorities.[87] Nevertheless, as will be discussed in chapter 6,[88] it could also be used by a centralised agency.

2.3.5 High costs

Defence equipment is very expensive and getting more expensive year by year.[89] Cox and Hartley estimate that the costs double every 7.25 years. Furthermore, the life cycle costs, such as maintenance and spare parts have to be taken into account. These may vary between 1.25 and 5 times the initial equipment costs.[90] For example, military aircraft cost around €100 million with the most expensive type reaching $2.4 billion per item,[91] a battle tank costs around

---

[83] European Security Strategy: *A Secure Europe in a Better World*, European Council, Brussels, 12 December 2003, www.consilium.europa.eu/uedocs/cmsUpload/78367.pdf [accessed 13 June 2013], at 13.

[84] Hartley, "The Future of European Defence Policy", *supra* note 72, at 109.

[85] Hartley, *The Economics of Defence Policy, supra* note 72, at 144; Cox, *supra* note 29.

[86] At 186–222 (EDA) and 222–5 (OCCAR).

[87] Hartley, *The Economics of Defence Policy, supra* note 72, at 144; and "The Future of European Defence Policy", *supra* note 72, at 112 suggests that a liberalised and competitive EU market could save 9% of costs, whereas a centralised agency could save 15%, combining both. This suggests considerable additional savings through addressing duplication on the demand side.

[88] At 255–9.

[89] Hartley, *The Economics of Defence Policy, supra* note 72, at 143. In "The Future of European Defence Policy", *supra* note 72, at 108 Hartley reports annual cost rises of 10%. The high costs are also recognised by the Commission in the Annex to the Proposal for the Defence Directive, *supra* note 4, at 9.

[90] Cox and Hartley, "The Costs of Non-Europe in Defence Procurement – Executive Summary", *supra* note 26, at 17.

[91] That was the B-2 Spirit, other very expensive examples include the F-22 Raptor costing $350 million, the G-17A Globemaster II costing $328 million or the P-8A Poseidon with a $290

€10–17 million,[92] submarines and aircraft carriers cost millions each.[93] These high costs have several consequences. First, the impact of each weapons programme on the national budget is considerable thereby making it also a political issue. Secondly, the high costs often give such a contract a high profile in the media, generating public attention. This is a feature shared with many other high-cost projects, which alone can lead to a degree of political interference that is rarer in other sectors. Thirdly, the amount of money made available for weapon systems makes them a major investment in the successful provider, his know-how and employment. Fourthly, the rising unit costs coincide with the shrinking defence procurement budgets discussed below, thereby leading to the purchase of fewer and fewer numbers of each piece of equipment by the individual national defence procurement authorities. This trend, coined the "defence economic problem" by Hartley,[94] is worsened by the fact that due to the fragmentation of the EU defence equipment markets, economies of scale are difficult if not impossible to achieve, making individual items even more expensive. The question is for how much longer the Member States can afford a meaningful air strike capacity or sea power on a national basis. Moreover, some equipment, such as aircraft, helicopters, electronics and missiles are characterised by learning economies and development costs are usually proportional to unit production costs for each type of equipment.[95] This shall be addressed in the context of the technological characteristics of defence procurement below.

Not all types of equipment or service covered by the Defence Directive are of the high-cost and cost-increase nature described above. There can be, for example, a contract to purchase small arms for the police or a utility security team for which prices are both relatively low and stable. Moreover, the construction of a sensitive army site, for example, might be of a very high value, but the prices for works contracts are not subject to the same increases as defence equipment. For most of these supply, services and works contracts,

---

million per item price tag. See www.time.com/time/photogallery/0,29307,1912203,00.html [accessed 13 June 2013].

[92] The Leopard 2 costs €10 million according to www.faz.net/aktuell/wirtschaft/ruestungsindustrie-qatar-will-angeblich-bis-zu-200-leopard-panzer-kaufen-11835934.html [accessed 13 June 2013]. In 2008 the Leclerc costs €17 million per unit according to www.marianne.net/Le-char-Leclerc-un-bide-a-113-millions-par-an_a184346.html [accessed on 13 June 2013].

[93] £7 billion for the two new carriers for the Royal Navy: www.bbc.co.uk/news/uk-13218582 [accessed 13 June 2013]. Around $2 billion for each submarine procured by the US Navy: http://tech.military.com/equipment/view/138675/ [accessed 13 June 2013].

[94] Hartley, "The Future of European Defence Policy", *supra* note 72, at 108. This dilemma is recognised by the Commission in COM (2013) 542 final, at 7: "Defence budgets are falling and the cost of modern capabilities is rising."

[95] Cox and Hartley, "The Costs of Non-Europe in Defence Procurement – Executive Summary", *supra* note 26: 1,000:1 for cheap missiles, 100:1 for combat aircraft.

some of them until recently covered by the Public Sector Directive, some security and secrecy measures will be needed but procurement can mostly be conducted like any "civil" procurement contract.

2.3.6 State ownership and control

Many EU Member States exercise considerable control over their national defence industries. First, some Member States still own at least parts of some of their defence companies, notably France, Portugal and Poland but also Germany.[96] Secondly, governments support their defence industries with various benefits, thereby distorting competition and affecting trade between Member States.[97] The financial instruments used to award aid are varied and include tax exemption, relief, deferral or cancellation; grants; advances repayable in the case of success; low interest rate or soft loans; guarantees; capital injection; non-monetary aid; provision of goods and services in preferential terms; and accelerated depreciation allowances.[98] The 2009 *EDA Study on State Ownership and Control*[99] provided a detailed picture of aid practices, dividing them into aid for R&D and innovation,[100] aid for industries in specific situations,[101] support for foreign sales[102] and other State

---

[96] COM (2013) 542 final, at 53; COM (1996) 10 final, at 5. In 2009 Member States with State-owned defence companies are Belgium with 1 (owned by the Walloon Region), Bulgaria with 4, the Czech Republic with 4, Finland with 1, France with 8, Germany with 6, Greece with 3, Hungary with 9, Italy with 3, Poland with 23(!), Portugal with 10, Romania with 3, the Slovak Republic with 8, Slovenia with 2 and Spain with 5: see Annex C to Carlos Martí Sempere *et al.*, *Level Playing Field for European Defence Industries: The Role of Ownership and Public Aid Practices* (Madrid: ISDEFE and Euskirchen: Fraunhofer Institut, for the European Defence Agency (EDA), Brussels, 13 March 2009), www.eda. europa.eu/docs/documents/Level_Playing_Field_Study.pdf [accessed 18 June 2013]. According to this study, at 18 the United Kingdom was the pioneer of privatisation and currently there are only 7 "golden shares", see below. There is no State ownership of defence industries in Austria, Sweden and the Netherlands. There are no defence industries in Cyprus, Ireland, Latvia, Lithuania, Luxembourg and Malta.

[97] "The Challenges Facing the Defence-related Industries", COM (1996) 10 final, at 22.

[98] *Level Playing Field for European Defence Industries*, *supra* note 96, at 26.

[99] Ibid., at 26–40.

[100] Ibid., at 28–30. These are further subdivided into aid for developing equipment for non-national armed forces (2.6.1.1.) and other aid for supporting equipment development (2.6.1.2.).

[101] Ibid., at 30–2. These are further subdivided into rescue aid (2.6.2.1.) and restructuring aid (2.6.2.2.).

[102] Ibid., at 33–7. The relevant practices are further subdivided into marketing assistance, public relations, display and operation by the armed forces of in-service materials, training of customer's operators and loan of personnel, export credit assistance, assistance to procurement project management and technical support services, rescheduling of deliveries to national armed forces, purchase of an undesired system by the armed forces to better support a foreign sale and tied aid.

aid.[103] While the extent to which these various forms of aid are used in practice varies between Member States and between the types of aid, the extent of State aid is far more considerable in this sector than in any other. Aid can originate in various ministries and public bodies and according to the 2009 *EDA Study on State Ownership and Control*, this is why the ministries of defence do not always have an overview of all the aid awarded. Finally, most Member States exercise control over some strategic defence companies, for example in the form of "golden shares" which allow them to intervene in management decisions, mergers or the relocation of assets. A recent prominent example for this intervention is the prevention of a merger between EADS and BAe Systems by the German government in 2012.[104] A precise analysis of State aid to the European defence industries goes beyond the aims of this book on defence procurement. However, since, as pointed out above, aid is extensive and varies between Member States, a "level playing field" is currently not established.[105] These and other differences in national defence industrial policies are particularly stark in the United Kingdom and France.[106] While London is keen to maintain a competitive market, Paris wants to play a constructive role in its defence industries.[107] This also affects the progress of liberalisation.[108] Thus chapter 4 will address this phenomenon in the context of a discussion of the EU Internal Market law regimes affecting the defence industries other than procurement regulation.[109]

2.3.7 Inefficiency

The dominant view of economists and policy-makers is that defence procurement in Europe is inefficient.[110] The costs of equipment and services are

---

[103] Ibid., at 37–40. These are further subdivided into employment aid, training aid, aid for SMEs, aid for risk capital investments in SMEs, regional aid and climate change and other environmental protection aid.

[104] "Germans Blamed for BAE-EADS Failure", www.ft.com/cms/s/0/aa352788-148c-11e2-aa93-00144feabdc0.html#axzz2WYoMuNSC [accessed 18 June 2013].

[105] This is ultimately the message of the 2009 EDA Study on *State Ownership and Control, supra* note 96, at 3: "[State aid has] a potential capability to provide selective advantages to undertakings that may affect trade conditions and therefore fair competition compromising the achievement of a level playing field in the [European Defence Equipment Market]."

[106] De Vestel, *Defence Markets and Industries in Europe, supra* note 29, at 62–73; Walker and Gummett, *Nationalism, Internationalism and the European Defence Market, supra* note 26, at 30; see in detail under "policy issues" in the respective country chs. VI–VIII on Germany, France and the United Kingdom in Trybus, *European Defence Procurement Law, supra* note 1, and on Belgium and Greece in Georgopoulos, Thesis, *supra* note 1.

[107] This is discussed further in ch. 4 at 176–82.

[108] See the respective country chs. VI–VIII Germany, France and the United Kingdom in Trybus, *European Defence Procurement Law, supra* note 1, and on Belgium and Greece in Georgopoulos, Thesis, *supra* note 1 for details.

[109] 136–84.

[110] Hartley, *The Economics of Defence Policy: A New Perspective, supra* note 72, 133. See also: COM (1996) 10 final, at 8.

higher than they could be, the completion of projects takes longer than it should and the quality of the goods and services is often below expectations. This situation can be and has been tolerated by public opinion and governments while there were lavish defence budgets and exports were not essential. However, expensive, overrun defence projects with disappointing end results are a frivolous luxury in times of economic crisis and therefore shrinking defence budgets, when defence has to stay affordable and exports are needed to achieve economies of scale and learning. Moreover, equipment which is late or wanting in any other way affects the efficiency of the armed forces and therefore compromises national security, as will be discussed further below. The economic analysis of whether and to what extent the Defence Package and especially the Defence Directive address the inefficiencies in the European defence markets is not the subject of this book. As outlined in the introduction, this book provides a legal analysis and this chapter merely puts this analysis into its economic context. However, while the special characteristics of defence procurement discussed above and below have to be taken into account when this problem of inefficiency is addressed, the argument that the principles governing the production and trade of non-military goods and services have facilitated an often highly efficient internal and export market is a strong one. Protectionism and market distortions always compromise competitiveness and therefore efficiency. Thus removing or reducing these factors should increase it.

3 The political and military background

Traditionally all Member States have perceived defence to be at the heart of national sovereignty. Moreover, defence procurement autarky has been seen as a matter of national security and pride for all countries with a significant defence industrial base. Defence and defence procurement are politically very sensitive as they are linked to aspects such as national security, employment and the political weight of a nation.[111] As discussed above, all these factors can lead to a close relationship between a State and its national defence industries and ultimately to protectionism preventing an EU Internal Market for armaments. However, this basic European paradigm has shifted since the early 1990s: EU Member States have started to integrate their defence policies, parts of the national defence industries were privatised and started to consolidate on a European basis and, finally, the rules of the Internal Market have started to be applied to the defence and security sectors, most notably through the Defence Directive. This section of the chapter will discuss the political and military background of defence and security procurement in

---

[111] See for the late 1990s Trybus, *European Defence Procurement Law, supra* note 1, at 10–12.

Europe determined by national sovereignty (section 3.1 below) and security (section 3.2 below). Secondly, the military costs of non-Europe in defence will be addressed. Finally, the evolving paradigm shift over the last two decades will be described and explained (section 3.4 below).

3.1 Sovereignty and autarky

A political characteristic of defence policy in general and defence procurement in particular, in Europe and elsewhere, is the special emphasis States put on sovereignty in this policy field.[112] In many cases the defence of the realm caused the very establishment of States. The necessity to defend a people and territory against attacks or to attack another people and territory was the fundamental reason and justification for the State. However, with respect to the EU Member States this emphasis on sovereignty is questionable. The majority of EU Member States are either "full" members of NATO or aligned to it.[113] Therefore, for some Member States for over 50 years, sovereignty over defence policy is intended and practised only in concert with the other members of that organisation, most importantly the United States. Moreover, the use of the armed forces is one of the areas of policy most regulated by international law, most importantly the UN Charter which only allows their use for self-defence or if authorised by the Security Council. Furthermore, many Member States have integrated their armed forces to varying degrees.[114] The CSDP of the EU discussed further below is geared towards further integration in the security and defence fields. If EU Member States use their military they almost always do so in concert with others. Finally, the control of national borders and monetary policy, for example, also used to be considered "at the heart of national sovereignty". However, in the first case for the Member States in the Schengen Zone and in the second case for the Member States in the Eurozone, sovereignty over these matters was finally transferred or at least limited. It is therefore submitted that sovereignty over defence matters is like sovereignty over any other matter of national policy: it will and can be transferred to EU or other structures if it suits the Member States and if the necessary political will can be generated. Defence is not a special policy field inappropriate for integration.

Sovereignty implies independence from anybody outside the nation. With respect to defence procurement this implies that a State can produce all its

---

[112] COM (1996) 10 final, at 9; Cox, "The Future of European Defence Policy", *supra* note 29, at 71–2; Walker and Gummett, *Nationalism, Internationalism and the European Defence Market*, *supra* note 26, at 29; de Vestel, *Defence Markets and Industries in Europe*, *supra* note 29, at 18. See also COM (2013) 542 final, at 8.

[113] Most importantly through the "Partnership for Peace". The only exceptions are the relatively small Cyprus and Malta.

[114] For example Eurocorps.

defence needs internally: defence autarky. This is also a national security concern, a notion to be discussed next below. However, autarky in defence procurement is no feasible policy option for most EU Member States due to the limitations of their defence industrial bases discussed above and available funds and the political difficulty to increase these funds at the expense of other policy areas, such as health and education. In view of the defence economics dilemma discussed above, in other words the rising prices for defence equipment and the current financial crisis this is unlikely to change in the foreseeable future. However, the aiming for defence autarky has a legacy[115] and touches on both economic and security concerns connected with defence industrial capacities. Governments of Member States with a defence industrial capability may place contracts with their national defence industries to keep technological capabilities, to preserve at least a certain level of autarky. In other words, such an award can be considered necessary for security reasons: to avoid sensitive dependencies on other countries and ensure security of supply. The question to what extent this is still possible shall be discussed especially in chapters 3 and 6.

A few considerations, however, put the objectives of sovereignty and defence autarky into perspective. First, defence equipment is never 100 per cent of a particular national origin. There are at least some foreign components in every piece of modern equipment. This is even more the case when the increasingly blurred borderline between armaments and many "civil" goods is taken into account. Thus 100 per cent defence autarky is an illusion for all EU Member States for this technological reason alone. Secondly, it is submitted that due to the limited funds and rising unit costs defence autarky is not a realistic policy option for any Member State. France or the United Kingdom might arguably still have the defence industrial capabilities and funds to go it alone but not the political will to do so at the expense of other parts of their budgets. If defence autarky is not an option, then partners have to be found. The most likely candidates are the United States and other EU Member States.

3.2 National security

National security is a crucial consideration for defence policy including defence procurement. As the word "national" indicates, this notion is defined on a national or Member State basis. In other words it is the national security of a Member State and not that of the EU as a whole which is considered. The concept features prominently in the armament exemption in Article 346 TFEU and other related exemptions discussed in chapter 3. It is also related to the general concept of "public security" which is accommodated in a number

---

[115] See, for example, on the French "Strategy of Means" discussed in ch. 6 on France in Trybus, *European Defence Procurement Law, supra* note 1.

of Internal Market exclusions discussed in chapter 2.[116] The common feature of these exemptions is that they can justify derogation from parts or all of EU Internal Market law. This shows that national security can be a barrier to trade if it is not adequately addressed in Internal Market legislation. Addressing security is particularly important for armaments but also, to a lesser extent, sensitive goods and services. National security implications of defence procurement decisions have to be taken into account throughout the procurement process, as well as before and afterwards. Situations in which national security considerations can become paramount are diverse, as the discussion in chapters 2 and 3 and other parts of this book will show. However, the two most important aspects of national security with implications for defence procurement are security of supply and security of information.

3.2.1 Security of supply

Security of supply is defined in the Commission's Guidance Note *Security of Supply* in "general terms" as

> a guarantee of supply of goods and services sufficient for a Member State to discharge its defence and security commitments in accordance with its foreign and security policy requirements.... This includes the ability of Member States to use their armed forces with appropriate national control and, if necessary, without third party constraints. Such a broad concept can cover a wide range of different industrial, technological, legal and political aspects.[117]

The basic concern behind the notion of security of supply is that both initially and during an often long life cycle of a contract, both in peace time and in time of crisis and war, a Member State needs to be sure that the goods, works and services it needs to operate its armed forces will be supplied and provided. This is essential for an efficient national defence policy and therefore national security. They need a "guarantee", "control" and "no third-party constraints". Otherwise the effective use of the armed forces can be compromised or completely undermined. Security of supply can be affected, inter alia, by unreliable economic operators, either as prime contractors or anywhere in the supply chain or by disrupted transport or other communications. These dangers can occur in both a domestic contract as well as a contract with a supplier from another Member State or a third country. However, they might well be more significant in a non-domestic context since the government has less control over the factors affecting security of supply, such as the management of economic operators or transport links. Moreover, additional threats to security of supply

---

[116] At 70–82.

[117] Commission's Guidance Note *Security of Supply*, http://ec.europa.eu/internal_market/publicprocurement/docs/defence/guide-sos_en.pdf [accessed on 14 June 2013], at 1.

exist in the non-domestic context. First, defence and security transfers are subject to licensing (authorisation) requirements of the national authorities in the country of production. This connects the accommodation of security-of-supply requirements in the Defence Directive to the other instrument of the "Defence Package", the Intra-Community Transfers Directive discussed in chapter 5.[118] However, many products or operators in the supply chain are third countries outside the EU. Secondly, defence and security transfers can be subject to other legal and political constraints affecting security of supply. Security of supply is part of both the traditional and the new paradigm of defence procurement discussed below. The difference is that in relation to contracts awarded to economic operators inside the EU, the concern should be addressed in the relevant instruments of the Internal Market, most notably the Defence Directive and the Intra-Community Transfers Directive,[119] and by instruments in the context of the other relevant frameworks discussed in chapter 5, most importantly the EDA and the Letter of Intent. The adaptation of the Defence Directive to security-of-supply requirements, especially with regards to specifications, qualification and award criteria is discussed in chapter 7. The Intra-Community Transfers Directive and other measures of the Defence Package are discussed in chapter 4.[120] At time of writing in 2014 it is too early to say whether developments like the Defence Package have sufficiently addressed security of supply to establish an Internal Market for defence goods. What can be said for certain is that the importance of this concept is evolving and that the measures taken are intended to reduce its importance in practice over time.

3.2.2 Security of information

The Commission's Guidance Note *Security of Information* makes clear that the notion referred in its title refers to "[t]he ability and the reliability of economic operators to protect classified information".[121] As security of information is concerned with the "ability and reliability of economic operators" it mainly affects the qualification and selection of tenderers. However, it also affects the rules on contract conditions and to a more limited extent on award criteria. Classified information is defined in Article 1(8) Defence Directive as

> any information or material, regardless of the form, nature or mode of transmission thereof, to which a certain level of security classification or

---

[118] At 147–60.

[119] Accommodating security of supply is clearly one of the main objectives of the Defence Directive, see Commission in the Annex to the Proposal for the Defence Directive, *supra* note 4, at 17–18, 22, 25–6, 27, 34, and 44–5.

[120] At 147–60 (ICT) and 182–3 (others).

[121] Commission's Guidance Note *Security of Information*, http://ec.europa.eu/internal_market/publicprocurement/docs/defence/guide-soi_en.pdf [accessed 16 October 2013], at 1.

protection has been attributed, and which, in the interests of national security and in accordance with the laws, regulations or administrative provisions in force in the Member State concerned, requires protection against any misappropriation, destruction, removal, disclosure, loss or access by any unauthorised individual, or any other type of compromise.

The Guidance Note rightly considers security of information to be a "particularly important feature" of the Defence Directive because of "the sensitive nature of many defence and security procurements".[122] The security of classified information needs to be safeguarded throughout the life cycle of the contract. However, as will be explained further in chapter 8,[123] in the absence of an EU security-of-information regime, the Member States decide on the information to be classified, on the level of confidentiality and grant the necessary security clearances, which are not automatically recognised by other Member States. In contrast to the licences for intra-Community transfers mentioned above, there is no EU Directive on this issue. This shall be further discussed in chapter 5 on approaches to address this problem outside the EU in the framework of the Letter of Intent and chapter 8 on the adaptation of the Defence Directive to security-of-information requirements.[124]

3.2.3 The military security cost of non-Europe in defence

The fragmentation of the EU into 28 national defence markets and procurement systems has often led to the 28 national armed forces of the Member States using technically entirely different and incompatible equipment. This is not much of a problem if 28 separate defence policies focus on the territorial defence of 28 separate and independent States. However, most Member States have been operating in concert with others in the context of the UN, NATO, formerly the WEU and now the EU through the CSDP, both for traditional territorial defence as well as for crisis management. This will be further explained under the next heading below. When detachments of various national armed forces operate in concert with others the question of the interoperability of the different national parts of such an operation is a crucial factor of their effectiveness. The effectiveness of armed forces is a national security issue, any lack or reduction of effectiveness compromises national security. An important element of that interoperability is the compatibility of the equipment used by the various parts of multinational forces or defence efforts. However, equipment is often not compatible. As a senior NATO commander in Afghanistan pointed out:

---

[122] Ibid.   [123] At 392–7.

[124] Accommodating security of information is clearly one of the main objectives of the Defence Directive, see Commission in the Annex to the Proposal for the Defence Directive, *supra* note 4, at 18–19, 27, 34, and 46–8.

I had to have nine different systems sitting on my desk just to communicate with all my units. All these different national systems are useless and it's unacceptable that we don't have a common operational network.[125]

It is therefore submitted that the fragmented structure of the EU defence market has led to considerable differences in the equipment used by the armed forces of the Member States which is often incompatible with the equipment of allies thereby compromising the interoperability and therefore effectiveness of forces acting in concert thus also compromising national security. An Internal Market with harmonised rules could contribute to the procurement of the same or at least compatible equipment enhancing the interoperability of joint missions and defence effort at least within the EU but also beyond. Therefore, as discussed further in chapter 3, the national security considerations which justify derogation from the Internal Market most importantly on the basis of Article 346 TFEU, have to be balanced with the effect of this derogation on the interoperability of national armed forces acting in concert. The more extensive the move from a national defence to a common defence in NATO or the EU, the stronger has to be the emphasis on the common "national" security of the respective defence alliance, "NATO security" or "EU security". A purely national security only makes sense when the defence is also organised on a purely national basis, which in the EU is not the case. This also has to be taken into account when evaluating if derogation from the Internal Market for national security reasons is actually justified.

3.3 The pull and push towards deeper European defence and security integration

The European and global geopolitical situation has been changing considerably over the last decades and these changes have had a profound impact on the armed forces of the EU Member States and the industries who supply them. The end of World War II made the United States and the Soviet Union leading nations of military alliances comprising their respective halves of Europe, with a few more or less neutral countries between these two opposing blocs. Within NATO and the Warsaw Pact, the United States and the Soviet Union respectively were also not the only but to varying degrees the dominant providers of armaments for the armed forces. On both sides the defence budgets, sizes of the armed forces and defence procurement activities reflected the perceived threat from the other side. In the NATO states, defence industrial collaboration was almost exclusively conducted on a transatlantic basis.[126]

---

[125] As cited by A. Menon, "Much Ado about Nothing: EU Defence Policy after the Lisbon Treaty" in Riccardo Alcaro and Erik Jones (eds.), *European Security and the Future of Transatlantic Relations* (Rome: Edizioni Nuova Cultura, 2011), 133, at 138.

[126] Eisenhut, *Europäische Rüstungskooperation, supra* note 7, at 29.

The dissolution of the Warsaw Pact and the Soviet Union changed that basic paradigm. First, a number of Warsaw Pact States, namely Poland, Hungary, East Germany, Czechoslovakia, Bulgaria and Romania – and even former Soviet Republics, namely Estonia, Latvia and Lithuania – reorganised and eventually made their way into NATO and the EU. As mentioned above, all European countries reduced their armed forces, defence budgets and armaments purchases. They no longer needed large armed forces to defend themselves in a major war against the "other side". What they need today are smaller forces for traditional territorial defence and readily deployable forces for international missions.

While the Warsaw Pact disappeared, both NATO and the EU went through a phase of enlargement and "change of mission". The enlarged NATO is still seen as the main defence organisation in Europe[127] but in addition it has taken on a new role as a crisis management organisation, most notably in Afghanistan.[128] At the same time the EU has extended its role beyond trade and developed a Common Foreign and Security Policy (CFSP) since Maastricht 1992 in several stages to a CSDP under the Treaty of Lisbon 2009.[129] This CSDP now includes, first, a crisis management component,[130] including permanent military structures[131] which have already led to sizable missions in Europe and beyond.[132] Secondly, it includes an automatic action commitment of all Member States in case of an armed attack on one of them.[133] Finally, and closest to the subject matter of this book, it includes an armaments policy including the permanent EDA[134] discussed in chapter 5.[135] While many of these initiatives are lagging behind, the EU is now also a defence organisation and there is clearly an ambition to develop this role further. The CFSP and CSDP are conducted separately from the Internal Market. This means that these "Second Pillar"[136]

---

[127] See the references to NATO in Art. 42(2) subpara. 2 and (7) subpara. 2 TEU (Lisbon).

[128] A possible competition between NATO and the EU is a problem in itself which cannot be further developed in this book. See H. Krieger, "Common European Defence: Competition or Compatibility with NATO?" in Martin Trybus and Nigel D. White (eds.), European Security Law (Oxford University Press, 2007), 174–97.

[129] See Erkki Aalto, "Towards a Common Defence? Legal Foundations after the Lisbon Treaty" in Martin Trybus and Luca Rubini (eds.), The Treaty of Lisbon and the Future of European Law and Policy (Cheltenham: Edward Elgar, 2012), 305.

[130] See Art. 43(1) TEU (Lisbon).

[131] Political and Security Committee, EU Military Committee, EU Military Staff.

[132] For an overview of the first missions see Frederick Naert, "ESDP in Practice: Increasingly Varied and Ambitious EU Security and Defence Operations" in Martin Trybus and Nigel D. White (eds.), European Security Law (Oxford University Press, 2007) 61–101.

[133] Art. 42(7) subpara. 1 TEU (Lisbon). See M. Trybus, "With or Without the EU Constitutional Treaty: Towards a Common Security and Defence Policy?" (2006) 31 European Law Review 145–66.

[134] Art. 42 (3) subpara. 2 and 45 TEU (Lisbon).   [135] At 186–222.

[136] The Treaty of Lisbon abolished the three-pillar structure; however, as explained further in ch. 5 at 221–2, the CFSP, while formally no longer the Second Pillar, is still a separate

policies are conducted under the control of the Council and the High Representative for the CFSP, and the roles of the Commission, European Parliament and ECJ are reduced to a minimum. This might be seen by some in these institutions as a threat to their policies and the "Defence Package", of which the Defence Directive forms the most important part, is at least in part a reaction to a concern over a delimitation of competencies over armament policy in the EU.

Political scientists such as Jones have argued that the developments of defence and security policies in the EU are the result of the end of the Cold War and a changed role of the United States as the only remaining superpower.[137] In this "unipolar" world the EU Member States see the remaining hegemon as a risk factor in international relations moving away from the security interests of Europe. This development triggered the European ambitions to develop autonomous military capabilities to be able to act without and if necessary against the will of the United States.[138] It also led to a move from defence industrial collaboration with the United States to predominantly European projects and to the CSDP outlined above. In contrast, functionalists such as Gabriel have explained the EU integration leap in security and defence as a spill-over from the successful economic integration process in areas connected to defence policy, such as trade in armaments, competition law or export control.[139] This will be discussed further in chapters 2 and 4. The regulation of these areas in the context of the Internal Market created pressure to also regulate defence and security within the EU. However, political will is still necessary, as Gabriel himself pointed out.[140]

Thus De Gucht and Keukeleire convincingly combine the two approaches and explain the EU defence integration leap with the political pull from a unipolar world order *and* the functionalist push from economic integration.[141] Two points need to be emphasised in the context of this combined explanation. First, apart from nuances in transatlantic relations and the progress of European economic integration, neither the pull nor the push towards deeper

---

intergovernmental framework dominated by the Member States in the Council, separate from the decision-making and legal principles of EU Internal Market and the TFEU.

[137] Seth Jones, *The Rise of European Security Cooperation* (Cambridge University Press, 2007), at 136 *et seq.* and "The Rise of European Defence" (2006) 121 *Political Science Quarterly* 245–95. The discussion of the political science background in the first part of this paragraph has benefited from Eisenhut, *Europäische Rüstungskooperation, supra* note 7, at 29–30.

[138] Eisenhut, *Europäische Rüstungskooperation, supra* note 7, at 29.

[139] J. M. Gabriel, "The Integration of European Security: A Functionalist Analysis" (1995) 50 *Aussenwirtschaft* 135–59, 135 *et seq.*

[140] Ibid., at 145.

[141] K. de Gucht and S. Keukeleire, "The European Security Architecture, the Role of the European Community in Shaping a New European Geopolitical Landscape" (1991) 6 *Studia Diplomatica* 29, at 30–1.

European defence integration are likely to weaken in the foreseeable future. Secondly, the Defence Directive is also a result of these basic parameters. Although part of the Internal Market, it forms an important part, arguably so far the most important part, of defence and security integration within the Internal Market.[142] In this context the Directive and the entire "Defence Package" are a special case, because, as will be explained in chapter 2, the EU/EC/EEC always had the competence to regulate the defence market, within the limits explained in chapter 3. Thus the Internal Market has now "occupied" a field which it had "owned" since 1957. However, it is argued that a plausible explanation for this only happening now is the political pull following the changes in the geopolitical situation and the functionalist push of half a century of economic integration, which is only really about 30 years in the specific area of public procurement regulation.[143] The push and pull arguably did not only move the EU legislator to produce the Defence Directive but also the Commission who produced various Communications since the 1990s[144] and even the ECJ in their interpretation of crucial provisions of EU law, most importantly Article 346 TFEU discussed in chapter 3.[145]

The move from Cold War to crisis management – in a UN, NATO or EU context – should have led to a transformation of the armed forces of the EU Member States from large territorial defence armies to smaller deployable and integrated forces. However, this happened only to a limited extent. The EU Member States currently have about 1.6 million-strong combined armed forces but only 100,000 men and women can be deployed world-wide.[146] This is not only partly due to the armed forces not being trained for these missions, but because they lack the necessary equipment. The most notable equipment gap is air transport capability where outside support in the form of

---

[142] On the contribution of EU Internal Market law to European defence integration see Martin Trybus, *European Union Law and Defence Integration* (Oxford: Hart, 2005), chs. 4–9.

[143] On the history of public procurement in the EU see Peter Trepte, *Public Procurement in the EU: A Practitioner's Guide*, 2nd edn (Oxford University Press, 2007), at 27–38.

[144] Most notably "The Challenges Facing the European Defence-related Industry: A Contribution for Action at European Level", COM (1996) 10 final; "Implementing European Union Strategy on Defence Related Industries", COM (1997) 583 final including the "Action Plan for the Defence-related Industries" which covers numerous internal market policies and their effect on the defence industries, including public procurement; "European Defence – Industrial and Market Issues: Towards an EU Defence Equipment Policy", COM (2003) 113 final, and then the Green Paper Defence Procurement, COM (2004) 608 final leading to the Defence Directive.

[145] See the case law following Case C-414/97, *Commission v. Spain* [1999] ECR I-5585, [2000] 2 CMLR 4 discussed in ch. 3, at 109–25.

[146] COM (2013) 542 final, at 8 provided the 1.6 million figure. Darnis *et al.*, *Lessons Learned from European Defence Equipment Programmes*, supra note 50, at 18, provided a 2 million figure and the figure of deployable troops.

leasing American, Russian or Ukrainian aircraft is needed.[147] Other gaps include communications, satellite surveillance and a mobile headquarters for out-of-area missions.[148] The considerable capability gaps of the European armed forces had two consequences. First, in the short and medium term the support of the US in critical areas will be necessary and the Berlin-Plus Agreement aims to ensure access to officially NATO but really US assets.[149] Secondly, the EU Member States have, especially through the EDA, formulated a number of headline goals to fill their capability gaps over time[150] and recently agreed on a framework for "pooling and sharing" their capabilities.[151]

4 Technological and contractual characteristics of defence procurement

There are a number of technological and contractual characteristics of defence procurement which have an impact on the regulation of defence procurement. These are the importance of research and development (section 4.1 below), long life cycles (section 4.2 below), collaboration (section 4.3 below), offsets (section 4.4 below), long supply chains (section 4.5 below), the increased involvement of the private sector (section 4.6 below) and corruption (section 4.7 below). Collaboration is particularly prominent in defence procurement but is also a feature of other sectors, most importantly aircraft and satellites. Offsets

---

[147] Trevor C. Salmon and Alistair J. K. Shepherd, *Toward a European Army: A Military Power in the Making?* (Boulder: Lynne Rienner Publishers, 2003), at 130 *et seq.*

[148] Kori Schake, *Constructive Duplication: Reducing EU Reliance on US Military Assets*, Working Paper (London: Centre of European Reform, 2002), at 19 *et seq.*

[149] The Berlin Plus agreement is a short title for a comprehensive package of agreements between NATO and the EU, based on conclusions of the 1999 NATO Washington Summit. It is comprised of the following major parts: NATO–EU Security Agreement; Assured Access to NATO Planning Capabilities for EU-led Crisis Management Operations (CMO); Availability of NATO Assets and Capabilities for EU-led CMO; Procedures for Release, Monitoring, Return and Recall of NATO Assets and Capabilities; Terms of Reference for DSACEUR and European Command Options for NATO; EU–NATO Consultation Arrangements in the Context of an EU-led CMO Making Use of NATO Assets and Capabilities; Arrangements for Coherent and Mutually Reinforcing Capability Requirements. All parts are tied together through the so-called "Framework Agreement", which consists essentially of an exchange of Letters between SG/HR and SG NATO, dated 17 March 2003. Since that day, the "Berlin Plus" package has been in effect and serves as the foundation for practical work between EU and NATO in that EU-led CMO makes use of NATO planning support or NATO capabilities and assets for the execution of any operations: www.europarl.europa.eu/meetdocs/2004_2009/documents/dv/berlinplus_/berlinplus_en.pdf [accessed on 14 June 2013].

[150] For a summary see CSDP: *Development of European Military Capabilities* (Brussels: Council, 2011), http://consilium.europa.eu/media/1222506/110106%20updated%20fact sheet%20capacites%20militaires%20-%20version%208_en.pdf [accessed 17 October 2013].

[151] See ch. 5 at 218.

almost only occur in defence procurement. Research and development can be part of any larger procurement project, including but not exclusively of security equipment, but it plays a particularly crucial role in developing new armaments. Long life cycles and long supply chains are a feature mainly of armaments but also occur in other sectors. Corruption occurs in all sectors but the situation is worst in construction and defence. All these technological and contractual features had to be addressed in the Defence Directive in addition to the national security concerns discussed above.

4.1 Research and development

Research and development (R&D) play an important role in the procurement of armaments.[152] Not least due to the monopsony situation outlined above, the private sector is normally not prepared to finance this R&D which therefore requires substantial public investment. R&D also contributes to the extremely long life cycles discussed below. Most defence equipment is of a highly techno-logical nature. First, this entails the fact that the more the equipment is technologically state of the art, the stronger the combat power of the armed forces using it. In 2003 the Iraqi armed forces with their 1980s equipment, for example, did not really stand a chance against the twenty-first-century state of the art equipment and training of the United States or the United Kingdom armed forces. Equipment wins wars. Secondly, this importance of being at the technological edge makes it necessary to replace equipment frequently and to be permanently involved in the R&D of new equipment. The procurement of supplies can therefore be divided into two main categories: off-the-shelf purchases and R&D procurement.

4.1.1 Off-the-shelf purchases

Off-the-shelf purchases concern the acquisition of equipment already in existence, without any R&D involved at time of procurement. This does not necessarily mean that the items have already been produced and are literally available "on the shelf" but merely that they can be produced almost immedi-ately. If this equipment can be classified as armaments, a category to be fully discussed in chapter 3,[153] then the usual national security and secrecy conside-rations discussed above apply but otherwise procurement according to the usual rules is possible, though adapted to security-of-supply and security-of-information concerns as discussed in chapter 8.

---

[152] This is recognised especially in Recitals 13 and 55 Defence Directive. Moreover, there is an entire Commission Guidance Note *Research and Development*, http://ec.europa.eu/internal_market/publicprocurement/docs/defence/guide-research_en.pdf [accessed 17 October 2013].

[153] At 88–104.

Most, but not necessarily all, of the armaments bought by procurement authorities and utilities other than those of the ministries of defence, such as the police, prisons and border control agencies, are off-the-shelf purchases. These would include small arms and ammunition and armoured vehicles. However, the complex tasks of these agencies will at times include projects involving R&D. Non-military security equipment used by the armed forces, security agencies and even utilities such as airports will normally be off-the-shelf. This does not mean that this equipment will not often require R&D. However, in contrast to the large armaments projects which require public investment in R&D, the R&D will normally be financed by the private companies selling the respective products. The private companies are prepared to accept the risks involved in such R&D because the monopsony situation described above does not apply to these products. As there are other potential customers, R&D does not necessarily have to be financed by the State. From the perspective of the contracting authorities and entities this gives these purchases an off-the-shelf character.

4.1.2 Research and development procurement

Procurement involving R&D is complex. The product does not already exist either as a blueprint or a product literally on the shelf. Crucial phases involving conception, research and development are necessary and are important elements of the procurement process. Normally there are a conception, a research, a development, a production and an introduction phase.[154] The complexity of this project cycle will have consequences on the procurement process. The procurement of other high-technology products, for example space products, will share many features with defence procurement. Due to the monopsony situation outlined above and the high costs and risks involved in R&D procurement, governments will have to bear most of the costs and a considerable share of the risk. Otherwise the defence industries will not cooperate with the government on such a project. Moreover, the defence industrial base for these most cost-intensive, long-term and risky R&D projects can often be even smaller than for "off-the shelf" contracts, at least with regards to prime contractors. This makes a competitive procurement procedure very difficult and, due to the small number of companies, often meaningless. The difficulties in these projects are aggravated by the fact that the high costs and limited defence industrial base will often make collaboration between several countries and their defence industrial bases, a feature of the defence sector further discussed below, inevitable. As each partner Member State seeks a "fair return" for their investment in the project for their national defence industries, a competitive and transparent procurement procedure becomes very difficult,

---

[154] See Trybus *European Defence Procurement Law, supra* note 1, at 26 for a more detailed overview of the phases.

at least at prime contract level. Taking the full supply chain into account, this becomes a possibility, although, again a difficult one. Introducing an element of competition by separating the R&D and production phases, by awarding separate contracts based on separate competitions for the R&D phase on the one hand and the production phase on the other hand, is also difficult. The defence industries are often only prepared to take their share of risks and costs involved in the R&D of a new piece of equipment if they get the production contract for that new product as well. All these problems will be discussed in chapter 6 on the scope of the Defence Directive and chapter 7 on procedures.[155]

Purchases covered by the Defence Directive made by contracting authorities and entities other than those of the ministries of defence will normally not fall into the category of R&D projects discussed in this section. Most will be off-the-shelf purchases. If they do involve R&D this will normally not involve the public investment and risk of military R&D. The relevant companies will conduct the necessary R&D as part of their private business activities. Collaboration, as discussed a little later, is also normally limited to military procurement.

4.2 Long life cycles

The life cycle of many defence products, from conception, feasibility, project definition through R&D, production and in-service support to disposal, can be extremely long. Depending on the product this can comprise decades and even over half a century. While the phases up to production will often be awarded to one consortium, although as discussed above the separation of R&D and production phases is a crucial issue in itself, parts of the in-service support and the disposal phases will often be subject to separate contracts to other economic operators. This is at least partly due to the long life cycle of military equipment: decades later the companies who produced the equipment in question might be no longer in business. Moreover, in-service support and disposal are detachable service contracts which can be – but do not have to be – part of the production contract. As with the R&D phase which can also be a separate service contract, the combination of the in-service contract for decades and the eventual disposal service contract with the production contract for the equipment can compromise competition. Thus in theory a maximum of competition can be achieved when those phases of the life cycle which can form detachable contracts are awarded as separate services and supplies contracts. This would also open additional opportunities for SMEs. However, the negative effect this might have on the willingness of industries to bid for only a separate part of the life cycle, especially a detached R&D service contract, might reduce competition. Overall certain phases will be detached from R&D

---

[155] At 245–309 and 310–57 respectively.

and production and addressed with a mixture of attached and separately awarded in-service and disposal contracts, and a mixture of in-house provision by the military itself and classic procurement. Many combinations are possible.

Non-military security products, including small arms for the police or screening equipment for airports, can also have long life cycles. However, the R&D at least will normally be covered by the economic operators. In-service support and disposal are often done in-house or by separate contractors.

4.3 Collaboration

Collaboration, such as the Eurofighter/Typhoon fighter aircraft, the Meteor air-to-air missile or the A400M transport aircraft, between two or more Member States is a regular occurrence for the development of new defence equipment in the EU.[156] This is a consequence of the limited industrial capacities even in the "Big Six" Member States categorised above. Moreover, this is a consequence of the high costs of defence equipment discussed above: often only the economies of scale achieved by the orders of several Member States and their combined public investment make a project financially possible. Traditionally these collaborative projects involved the United States and were organised on an ad hoc basis. Since the 1990s these projects became almost exclusively European, for the political reasons discussed above and because there was often no reciprocity of market and technological access to the disadvantage of the European partners.[157] Moreover, collaboration is increasingly conducted in the context of the more permanent structures discussed in chapter 5, such as OCCAR and EDA. Collaborative projects cover the most expensive, high-profile and technologically advanced defence projects. This has various consequences. First, the high costs both in relation to the R&D and the production phases incur a high level of public investment for which the investing government wants a return in the form of industrial participation of its national industry. This desire is reinforced by the high profile of these projects, including its employment implications, which put political pressure on the

---

[156] COM (1996) 10 final, at 8. Either through OCCAR, EDA or NATO logistics organisations (NPSA) and NATO production logistics organisations such as the Tornado Development Production and Logistics Management Agency (NETMA/NEFMO and NAMMO), or by using the so-called "lead national concept"; examples: Jaguar (lead national France), Bréguet Atlantique (lead nation France), BVRAAM/Meteor (lead national the United Kingdom), F-16 MNFP (lead nation USA), F-35 JSF/FJCA (lead nation USA). See the presentation by B. Heuninckx, "Collaborative Defence Procurement" at the seminar "European Defence and Security Procurement", European Institute of Public Administration (EIPA), Maastricht, 19 January 2012 (slide 12, on file).

[157] K. von Wogau and B. Rapp-Jung, "The Case for a European System Monitoring Foreign Investment in Defence and Security" (2008) 45 *Common Market Law Review* 47–68, at 55.

investing government for a "fair return". This will make it difficult to award such a contract on the basis of the competitive procurement procedures discussed in chapter 7, although not impossible, as will also be discussed. Moreover, the high-technology character of these projects brings with it all the problems of R&D procurement discussed above: the necessity of public investment in R&D and the difficulty in separating the R&D from the production phase.

In order to achieve economies of scale and to ensure a fair return for the investment of the Member States involved, these Member States will procure their needs with respect to the piece of equipment produced at the end of the project from the consortium involved in the project; in fact, a guarantee to that effect is required to convince the relevant defence industries to participate in the project in the first place. Thus with regards to the Member States participating in the collaborative project there will be direct awards rather than awards following a competitive procurement procedure. These combined difficulties and the lack of procurement regulation have led to unregulated ad hoc arrangements with mixed results. European collaborative defence projects are often inefficient, expensive and take more time than planned.[158] The cost increases in times of austerity and budget cuts and the time overruns when many military capability gaps have to be closed actually make a reform of European collaborative projects necessary. This could be conducted in the context of the Internal Market, for example, but not only through the Defence Directive, or through the structures discussed in chapter 5.

4.4 Offsets

Offsets[159] are a regular occurrence in defence procurement, whenever contracts are awarded to economic operators from a country other than that of the contracting entity. As part of the contract with the non-domestic economic operator, "compensation" for the taxpayer's money of the country awarding the contract is required from the economy of the country of the successful bidder. The German Defence and Security Industries Association *BDSV* provided the following definition of offsets:

> Offsets are understood to be some form of industrial compensation when buying defence technology products and/or relevant services, both in

---

[158] See on this topic B. Heuninckx, "A Primer on Collaborative Defence Procurement in Europe: Troubles, Achievements and Prospects" (2008) 17 *Public Procurement Law Review* 123–45 and in great detail his 2011 doctoral (PhD) thesis at the University of Nottingham, *supra* note 1 (on file).

[159] Related terms describing offsets are: industrial compensation, industrial cooperation, industrial and regional benefits, balances, *juste retour* (English: fair returns) or equilibrium.

transactions between national governments and between the industry and a national government . . . offset can be used as a synonym for any kind of compensation claimed.[160]

Offsets can take various forms but according to the 2008 EDA *Study on the Effects of Offsets on the Development of a European Defence Industry and Market*.[161] they can be divided into three main categories: direct (military) offsets, indirect military offsets and indirect civil offsets. Direct and indirect military offset requirements favour the defence industries of the awarding country, for example through the establishment of (job-creating) production sites in the awarding country, or through "sub-contracting, licensing, techno-logy transfer, investment and joint ventures between the seller and the purcha-sing country".[162] Direct military offsets only require compensation for the original defence procurement contract for which they are agreed. In contrast, indirect military offsets are independent from the performance of the original defence procurement contract but still require compensation in the form of contracts with the defence industries of the awarding state of the original contract. Finally, indirect offsets to the civilian industries (indirect civil offsets) are completely independent from both the original contract and the defence industrial sector of the awarding state. According to the 2007 figures of the 2008 *EDA Offsets Study* the overall distribution in the participating Member States according to type was: direct offsets: 40 per cent; indirect military offsets: 35 per cent; and civil indirect offsets: 25 per cent.[163] Georgopoulos has convincingly argued that due to the fact that modern defence systems contain technology which is used in both civil and military sectors, the distinction between indirect civil offsets and indirect military offsets will be especially difficult in practice.[164]

An offset arrangement is a contract separate from the initial procurement contract[165] but that separate contract is a condition for the latter.[166] The offset

---

[160] *Bundesverband der Deutschen Sicherheits- und Verteidigungsindustrie* (BDSV) at www.bdsv.eu/en/Issues/Offsets_compensation_benefits.htm [acessed on 16 October 2013].

[161] E. A. Erikson *et al.*, *Study on the Effects of Offsets on the Development of a European Defence Industry and Market* (Henley on Thames: SCS and Stockholm: FOI, for the EDA, Brussels, 2007), hereinafter *"EDA Offsets Study"* at 3.

[162] Ibid.

[163] According to the 2007 figures in the *EDA Offsets Study*, *supra* note 161, at 4,

[164] A. Georgopoulos, "Revisiting Offset Practices in European Defence Procurement: The European Defence Agency's Code of Conduct on Offsets" (2011) 20 *Public Procurement Law Review* 29–42.

[165] BDSV, *supra* note 160: "Offsetting consists of a defined obligation on the part of the supplier that is laid down as fringe benefits in an offset agreement which is associated with the supply contract, but is an independent agreement."

[166] "Offsets function as a condition of the sale of defence articles to the purchasing foreign government, whereby that foreign government or its economy recoups some portion of

can amount to more than 100 per cent of the value of the initial contract.[167] Offset practices vary considerably between EU Member States. Some Member States, notably France and Germany, do not require them at all; in others they are a legal requirement, for example as an award criterion.[168] This can mean that the offset contract has nothing to do with the subject matter of the original defence contract and that the qualification of the economic operator or the quality of the bid become minor considerations. Many Member States support considerable offset administrations, traditionally as part of their ministries for economy but more recently in their ministries of defence. This reorganisation is possibly motivated by the wish to hide the economic rather than defence rationale for offsets. However, it cannot be emphasised enough that offsets rarely serve national security but normally economic interests.[169] Offsets have been called "a strange animal" and "an idiosyncrasy of defence procurements".[170]

Normally the awarding defence procurement authority implements the offsets requirements through contractual obligations in the original defence procurement contract. These contractual obligations require offset contracts with the dedicated offsets administration of the awarding State and with the companies in the awarding State. The eventual contracts with the companies are regularly private law contracts and their compliance with the offset require-ments will be determined by a national offsets administration. Offset require-ments are also often considered as a sub-award criterion. Thus in procurement terms, offset requirements are contract performance conditions[171] or sub-award criteria.[172] In the first case a bidder not meeting the required offset conditions will be rejected and in the second case the chances of a bidder offering no or less attractive offsets will be reduced in comparison to a bidder who does offer them. The award of contracts on the basis of the EU public procurement Directives is affected twice. First, the award of the original contract imposing the offset requirements is directly affected by the contract

the acquisition's value." Source: Bureau of Industry & Security, U.S. Department of Commerce, 14 *Offsets in Defense Trade* (2009), at i.

[167] According to the 2007 figures of a 2008 EDA Study, *Study on the Effects of Offsets*, *supra* note 161, at 4, the underlying contract volume for offsets in the then 24 participating Member States was €4.2 billion. At an average offset percentage of 135% (!), this made an offset volume of €5.6 billion.

[168] France and Germany do not accept offsets as a matter of policy. The United Kingdom, Italy, Sweden and the Netherlands (net EU exporters with transatlantic imports) use indirect military offsets. Finland, Poland, Portugal, Greece and Spain (big importers some with some exports) use different kinds of offsets, mainly direct. The Member States without defence industries use indirect civil offsets. See the *EDA Study on Offsets*, *supra* note 161, at 4.

[169] D. Eisenhut, "Offsets in Defence Procurement: A Strange Animal – at the Brink of Extinction?" (2013) 38 *European Law Review* 393–403.

[170] Ibid., at 1.   [171] Discussed in ch. 9.   [172] Discussed in ch. 9.

performance conditions or sub-award criteria. Secondly, the award of the offsetting contract or contracts is affected because either that contract would otherwise be awarded to another bidder or not be awarded at all. The two sides of this double effect have to be evaluated separately. However, it is the effect on the original contract which is the main concern in the context of this discussion of offsets under the Defence Directive.

4.5 Long supply chains

There is often an extensive supply chain in armaments contracts, as discussed in the context of the structure of the European defence industrial base above.

4.6 Public–private partnerships

The national security and secrecy implications of defence have often prevented ministries of defence from having more extensive involvement with the private sector such as privatisation, outsourcing and contracting out, or public–private partnerships (PPP). Traditionally defence is organised on a public basis, with the State not only being the enabler and regulator but also the provider of defence. The procurement of equipment and some related services from the private sector was the major exception to this rule. In some Member States this has been changing since the 1990s, especially in the United Kingdom.[173] The decision on whether a certain service can be subjected to more private involvement – a naval base run as a PPP project, guarding services contracted out to a private security company, or even intelligence services provided by economic operators rather than in-house – will depend on the national security implications of each service, the mind set and attitudes of the contracting authority and the market. Moreover, it will differ from Member State to Member State. However, these practices lead to new public contracts that may have to be awarded on the basis of the Defence Directive. Therefore procurement legislation has to accommodate these practices, most notably in

---

[173] Keith Hartley, "The Economics of UK Procurement Policy", http://web.cenet.org.cn/upfile/53069.pdf [accessed 13 June 2013]; D. Parker and K. Hartley, "Transaction Costs, Relational Contracting and Public Private Partnerships: A Case Study of UK Defence" (2003) 9 *Journal of Purchasing and Supply Management* 97–108, "Military Outsourcing: UK Experience", http://web.cenet.org.cn/upfile/53057.pdf [accessed 13 June 2013]; K. Hartley. "The Economics of Military Outsourcing" (2002) 11 *Public Procurement Law Review* 287–97; K. Hartley, "The Economics of Military Outsourcing" (2004) 4 *Defence Studies* 199–200; J. E. Fredland, "Outsourcing Military Force: A Transaction Cost Analysis on the Roles of Military Companies" (2004) 15 *Defence and Peace Economics* 205–19; J. Brauer, "An Economic Perspective on Mercenaries, Military Companies, and the Privatisation of Force" (1999) 13 *Cambridge Review of International Affairs* 130–46; D. Shearer, "Private Military Force and Challenges for the Future" (1999) 13 *Cambridge Review of International Affairs* 80–94.

the rules on scope discussed in chapter 6 and the procurement procedures discussed in chapter 7. The rules on qualification need to address the possibility of private involvement, especially if such a contract is awarded to an economic operator in another Member State.

The private sector can be involved in the projects of relevant contracting authorities other than ministries of defence. Moreover, it will often be involved in the projects of utilities, for example when security checks at airports are subject to a contract with a private security company.

4.7 Corruption

The *Bribe Payer's Index* of Transparency International has rated the defence sector as one of the three most corrupt business sectors in the world.[174] There is no comparable data on security goods and services. Corruption also affects defence procurement in the EU, to varying degrees depending on the Member State. While corruption in procurement is a complex issue which cannot be comprehensively discussed in this chapter or book, it is clear that the lack of a transparent and enforceable procurement regime is a contributing factor. The procurement procedures and requirements especially with regards to transparency discussed in chapters 7 and 8 and the review and remedies system discussed in chapter 10 are not designed as anti-corruption instruments. However, it is a welcome side-effect of a legally binding and enforceable defence procurement regime based on transparency and competition that it makes corruption harder. While it is too early to evaluate the impact of the Defence Directive on corruption in defence and security procurement, it can safely be said that it is likely to lead to a reduction in corruption.

5 Conclusions

Even in times of financial crisis, shrinking defence budgets and capability gaps, the defence procurement of EU Member States is characterised by duplication and inefficiency. There are various reasons for this lamentable state of affairs, most importantly protectionism leading to market fragmentation, variations between Member States in State ownership and control, offsets and corruption.

---

[174] M. Pyman, *Addressing Corruption and Building Integrity in Defence Establishments*, Transparency International Working Paper 02/2007 (Berlin: Transparency International, 2007), www.transparency.org/publications/publications/working_papers/ wp_02_2007_integrity_in_defence; S. Gupta, L. de Mello and R. Sharan, *Corruption and Military Spending*, IMF Working Paper, February 2000, www.imf.org/external/pubs/ft/ wp/2000/wp0023.pdf; Control Risks Group, *International Business Attitudes to Corruption – Survey 2006* (New York: Simmons & Simmons, 2006), www.crg.com/pdf/ corruption_survey_2006_V3.pdf.

Economies of scale and learning cannot be achieved. There is no Internal Market for defence goods and services and considerable cost savings could be achieved if such a market could be introduced, ranging from 9 per cent if Member States only opened their markets to each other (11 per cent if it was also open to third countries) to 15 per cent if a centralised EU procurement agency procured from a liberalised market (17 per cent if that agency also bought from third countries).[175] Thus the "costs of non-Europe in defence" are substantial. The Defence Directive is only aiming at establishing an Internal Market for defence goods, in other words the least ambitious scenario with the lowest percentage of cost savings. However, the other scenarios require complex reciprocal agreements with third countries especially the United States or, in case of a centralised agency, are politically ambitious since they effectively require integrated EU armed forces.[176] The Defence Directive has more limited ambitions. It does not include a centralised procurement agency, but some of the structures discussed in chapter 5 might eventually develop into such an institution. The Directive addresses the crucial field of procurement and that will not suffice to establish an Internal Market. However, other elements of the "Defence Package" and beyond will also contribute to the achievement of that objective.

A contract covered by the Defence Directive can be a rather simple transaction where, for example, a police force, exclusively using public funds, buys off-the-shelf hand guns from a rather diverse and competitive market. A procurement Directive can regulate the award of such a contract. However, a contract of a ministry of defence pooling resources with other ministries of defence and possibly the private sector on a complex new weapon system involving research and development with a limited pool of prime contractors but a long and complex supply chain could also be subject to a procurement Directive, although as discussed in chapter 6 it is not covered by the Defence Directive.

Internal Market legislation such as the Defence Directive needs to take account of the special context of the defence sector. National security necessitates taking security of supply and security of information into account throughout the procurement process.[177] In addition the long life cycles, importance of R&D and prevalence of collaboration will require additional flexibility[178] or even limitations to the scope of the instrument.[179] Offsets will have to be addressed.[180] Moreover, the long supply chains require attention but they also offer opportunities for economic operators beyond the large

---

[175] Hartley, "The Future of European Defence Policy", *supra* note 72, at 112; and "Defence Industrial Policy in a Military Alliance" (2006) 43 *Journal of Peace Research* 473 *et seq.*

[176] Hartley, "The Future of European Defence Policy", *supra* note 72. Hartley calls it "politically impossible".

[177] See ch. 8.   [178] See ch. 7.   [179] See ch. 6.   [180] See ch. 9.

prime contractors mainly situated in the "Big Six" Member States.[181] Finally, a review and remedies system for aggrieved bidders, necessary to ensure the effective enforcement of the Defence Directive, would have to safeguard confidentiality and national security.[182]

The economic and political situation for the procurement of security goods and services other than armaments and related services is not comparable to that for armaments. The relevant contracting entities and the goods and services they may procure are diverse. It is not possible to write a list of the contracting entities as one could for defence[183] or of the relevant goods as exists for armaments.[184] The special conditions of the defence sector might apply in full or hardly at all. What will mostly apply are the security concerns and that led to the inclusion of these contracts in the field of application of the Defence Directive.

---

[181] Ibid.   [182] See ch. 10.   [183] See ch. 6 at 249–51.   [184] See ch. 3 at 90–1.

The legal base of the Defence Directive in EU Internal Market law

Prohibitions, exemptions and proportionality

1 Introduction

After the analysis of the economic and political context of the Defence Directive in chapter 1, its complex legal context needs to be discussed. This has to start with the Internal Market base of the Directive. Like all EU procurement Directives, the Defence Directive is a secondary EU law instrument. Its purpose is to amplify and give detail to the primary EU Internal Market regimes of the TFEU. Secondary EU law is legislation created by the relevant EU institutions, initiated by the Commission after extensive consultation with the relevant stakeholders, and passed by the Council representing the Member States and the directly elected European Parliament, within the limits authorised by legal bases in the primary TFEU. The primary EU Internal Market regimes created by the unanimous will of the Member State governments, and ratified by their elected national parliaments or through referenda, form the foundations and define the limitations of the Defence Directive. These primary foundations and limitations need to be discussed before the secondary Defence Directive itself can be analysed. Moreover, many individual provisions of the Directive discussed in chapters 6–10 cannot be fully understood without knowing their primary legal base.

The primary TFEU foundations of the Defence Directive include Treaty regimes other than the Internal Market. These include the competition (anti-trust) regime including merger control, the State aid (subsidies) regime and the (third-country) exports and intra-Community transfer of armaments and other security sensitive goods (the latter two are, strictly speaking, part of the Internal Market regimes). However, these regimes and their impact on the European defence market are complex and their discussion cannot all be accommodated in one chapter. Moreover, the Defence Directive is clearly an instrument to harmonise a part of the procurement dimension of the Internal Market. Therefore the non-Internal Market dimensions of the regulation of the European armaments market through the TFEU and other secondary instruments, and intra-Community transfers, shall be discussed in chapter 4 on the wider TFEU context of the Defence Directive. That chapter will follow chapter 3 on the defence-specific exemptions to the TFEU. The limitations of the EU Internal Market regimes enshrined in the armaments, secrecy and general defence exemption discussed in chapter 3 apply equally to the other relevant TFEU regimes since they represent limitations of the Treaty as a whole. Thus these defence exemptions will be discussed in chapter 3 immediately after the Internal Market foundations of EU procurement regulation in chapter 2 but before the wider legal context of the Defence Directive. Intra-Community transfers will also be discussed in chapter 4 since their discussion requires an understanding of the national security exemptions discussed in chapter 3.

This chapter will first discuss the foundations of the Defence Directive in the EU Internal Market regimes of the TFEU, namely the free movement of goods in Article 34 TFEU, the free movement of services in Article 56 TFEU and the freedom of establishment in Article 49 TFEU. This will include a discussion of the relevant regime-specific limitations to these freedoms in the public security dimensions of the derogations in Articles 36, 45(3), 52(1), 65(1)(b) and 72 TFEU. Moreover, this will include a discussion of the Internal Market legal bases for the Defence Directive in Article 53(2), 62 and 114 TFEU.[1] The chapter will show that the goods and services regulated by the Defence Directive are subject to the Internal Market regimes of the TFEU, subject to exceptional circumstances which allow derogation from the Treaty on a case-by-case basis, situations which are subject to judicial review by the ECJ and which need to be proportionate and proven by the Member State invoking them.

2 The EU Internal Market and defence and security procurement

The establishment of an Internal Market between the Member States of the EU is at the very core of European integration. The second indent of the Preambles of the TFEU (and the former EC Treaty) declares that the Member States are

> Resolved to ensure the economic and social progress of their countries by common action to eliminate the barriers which divide Europe . . .

The Internal Market is then stipulated partly as an area of exclusive EU competence in Article 3 TFEU[2] but mainly as an area of shared competence between the EU and the Member States in Article 4 TFEU.[3] Exclusive EU competence excludes any competence of the Member States. It represents a

---

[1] In the Preamble of the Defence Directive, before para. 1, still "Articles 47(2) and Article 55 and 95 [EC Treaty]" as the Directive dates from 13 July 2009 and the EC Treaty was replaced by the TFEU on 1 December 2009.

[2] Art. 3 TFEU reads: "1. The Union shall have exclusive competence in the following areas: (a) customs union; (b) the establishing of the competition rules necessary for the functioning of the internal market . . ."

[3] Art. 4 (2) TFEU reads: "Shared competence between the Union and the Member States applies in the following principal areas: (a) internal market . . ."

comprehensive transfer of sovereignty from the Member State to the Union.[4] Shared competence does not exclude the competence of the Member States. However, if the EU regulates an area of shared competence, Member State action on the same area is pre-empted. The Member States may still act if an area has not yet been regulated by the EU.[5] Thus as defence and security procurement is at least now regulated by the Defence Directive, if it was not already regulated by the Public Sector and Utilities Directives before that, Member State action on the same area (not transposing the Defence Directive) is pre-empted.

Moreover, the commitment to establish an Internal Market is reiterated in Article 26(3) TFEU which provides that:

> The internal market shall comprise an area without internal frontiers in which the free movement of goods, persons, services and capital is ensured in accordance with the provisions of this Treaty.

The Internal Market regimes of the TFEU most relevant to defence and security procurement and public procurement in general are the free movement of goods in Article 28 TFEU, the free movement of services in Article 56 TFEU and the freedom of establishment in Article 49 TFEU. Furthermore, the general prohibition of discrimination on grounds of nationality in Article 18 TFEU is to be mentioned. These Internal Market regimes and Article 18 TFEU essentially consist of prohibitions of protectionist behaviour directed at the Member States. In other words, the respective provisions of the Treaties ban Member States from practices raising barriers to trade for goods and services and the freedom of establishment. The Defence Directive is expressly based on these Internal Market regimes in the reference to the legal bases at the beginning of its Preamble. These legal bases were, at the time of enactment of the Directive: Article 47(2) EC (now 53(1) TFEU) on establishment, Article 55 EC (now 62 TFEU) on services and Article 95 EC (now 114 TFEU), the general Internal Market legal base. Again, the Defence Directive is a secondary EU law instrument to amplify and give detail to these regimes with respect to a specific aspect, the procurement of defence and security supplies, services and works.

2.1 The free movement of goods

At the core of the EU Internal Market is a free trade area for goods (Article 28 TFEU).[6] "Goods" were very widely defined by the ECJ in its *Arts Treasures*

---

[4] For a more detailed discussion see P. P. Craig, "The Lisbon Treaty: Process, Architecture, and Substance" (2008) 33 *European Law Review* 137, at 144.

[5] A comprehensive discussion of these listed Internal Market competences of the TFEU would go beyond the aim of this book. See ibid.

[6] On the free movement in general see Peter J. Oliver, *Oliver on Free Movement of Goods in the European Union*, 5th edn (Oxford: Hart, 2010); Paul Craig and Gráinne de Búrca, *EU*

judgment as "products which can be valued in money and which are capable of forming the subject of commercial transactions".[7] This definition clearly includes armaments: the items on the 1958 List of Armaments,[8] which shall be discussed in more detail in chapter 3, are all covered by the ECJ definition of a good since they are products which can be valued in money and can be the subject of commercial transactions. Moreover, the definition in *Arts Treasures* covers all other security goods. Procurement of whatever item is a commercial transaction and this requires the item in question to be valued in money.

The crucial provision of Article 30 TFEU prohibits all customs duties on imports and exports of goods between Member States and all charges having equivalent effect. The notion of "charges having equivalent effect to a customs duty" is also very widely defined.[9] Moreover, in contrast to most other Internal Market regimes, the prohibition is absolute: there are no derogations or mandatory requirements that could justify proportionate violations or allow taking a measure outside the scope of the prohibition (see below).[10] If the Internal Market is the core of European integration, then the free trade area for goods is at the centre of that core. A Common Customs Tariff in relation to goods from third countries outside the EU "upgrades" this free trade area to a customs union. According to Article 29 TFEU goods from third countries are treated like

---

Law: Text, Cases, and Materials, 5th edn (Oxford University Press, 2011), at 611–92 (hereinafter *EU Law*); J. Weiler, "From Dassonville to Keck and Beyond: An Evolutionary Reflection on the Text and Context of the Free Movement of Goods" in Paul Craig and Gráinne de Búrca (eds.), *The Evolution of EU Law* (Oxford University Press, 1999), at 349–76 (not included in the 2nd edn of 2011); Christine Barnard, *The Substantive Law of the EU*, 5th edn (Oxford University Press, 2010), at 33–192; Damian Chalmers, Gareth Davies and Giorgio Monti, *European Union Law*, 2nd edn (Cambridge University Press, 2010), at 744–82; Alan Dashwood *et al.*, *Wyatt and Dashwood's European Union Law*, 6th edn (Oxford: Hart, 2011), at 391–460; Jukka Snell, *Goods and Services in EC Law* (Oxford University Press, 2002).

[7] Case 7/68, *Commission v. Italy* ("Arts Treasures") [1968] ECR 423. This definition also applies to the important prohibition of quantitative restrictions and measures having equivalent effect discussed below.

[8] Decision defining the list of products (arms, munitions, and war material) to which the provisions of Art. 223(1)(b) of the Treaty (now Art. 346(1)(b) TFEU) apply (doc. 255/58). Minutes of 15 April 1958: doc. 368/58, as cited in the Preamble to the Defence Directive at L-216/77, *supra* note 1.

[9] The Court of Justice defined a charge having equivalent effect to a customs duty as: "any pecuniary charge, however small and whatever its designation and mode of application, which is imposed unilaterally on domestic or foreign goods by reason of the fact that they cross a frontier, and which is not a custom duty in the strict sense, constitutes a *charge having equivalent effect* . . . even if it is not imposed for the benefit of the State, is not discriminatory or protective in effect and if the product on which the charge is imposed is not in competition with any domestic product". See Case 24/68, *Commission v. Italy* ("Statistical Levy") [1969] ECR 193, [1971] CMLR 611; Joint Cases 2&3/69, *Sociaal Fonds for de Diamantarbeiders* v. *Brachfeld* ("Diamond Workers") [1969] ECR 211, [1969] CMLR 335; Case 29/87, *Dansk Denkavit Aps* v. *Danish Ministry of Agriculture* [1988] ECR 2965.

[10] See Craig and de Búrca, *EU Law*, *supra* note 6, ch. 18, at 611–30.

goods originating in a Member State once they are in free circulation. The prohibition of customs duties and charges having equivalent effect has no direct connection to the EU public procurement regime. However, the abolition of these charges eliminates barriers to trade and therefore also allows access to the public procurement markets of other Member States. It would obviously be difficult to offer the lowest price or be the economically most advantageous tender when you have to add 8 per cent or more for customs duties to your bid price in another Member State. Hence Article 30 TFEU is an essential prerequisite for a liberalised European procurement market including a liberalised European defence equipment market. Customs duties are also briefly discussed in chapter 4.

The most important Internal Market provision with respect to the procurement of goods (supplies) is Article 34 TFEU which reads:

> Quantitative restrictions on imports and all measures having equivalent effect shall be prohibited between Member States.

This prohibition is complemented by a similar provision for exports.[11] A "quantitative restriction" is defined as "any measure of a Member State that restraints the import, transit or export of a certain good [according to quantity or value]".[12] However, quantitative restrictions in the strict sense do not occur very often in practice. Member States are not that unsophisticated and not that openly opposed to the Internal Market. Thus the notion of "a measure having equivalent effect to a quantitative restriction" in Article 34 TFEU is crucial. It was given a very wide definition by the ECJ in the famous *Dassonville*[13] judgment:

> All trading rules enacted by Member States which are capable of hindering, directly or indirectly, actually or potentially, intra-Community trade . . .

Provided the EU has not introduced harmonising legislation on a particular good, the prohibition thus applies to all obstacles to the free movement of goods where they derive from rules regarding the characteristics of the good. These include rules regarding the form, size, weight, composition, labelling, packaging or presentation, provided the good in question was lawfully manufactured in

---

[11] Art. 35 TFEU reads: "Quantitative restrictions on exports, and all measures having equivalent effect, shall be prohibited between Member States."

[12] Case 2/73, *Geddo* v. *Ente Nazionale Risi* [1973] ECR 865, [1974] 1 CMLR 1.

[13] Case 8/74, *Procureur du Roi* v. *Dassonville* [1974] ECR 837, [1974] 2 CMLR 436. Commission and Council had aimed providing some clarity on the notion with an illustrative list in Arts. 1–3 Directive 70/50/EEC [1970] OJ Sp. ed. I-17 which included minimum or maximum prices specified for imported products and conditions in respect of packaging, composition, identification, size, weight etc. which only apply to foreign goods; limited publicity in respect of imported goods as compared with domestic products; and made it mandatory for importers of goods to have an agent in the importing Member State.

another Member State. This is the case even when the rules in question apply without distinction to both domestic and non-domestic goods.[14]

In the traditional understanding, a measure can be considered outside the field of application of the prohibition of Article 34 TFEU if it represents a proportionate response to an overriding public interest or mandatory requirement. This principle of mandatory requirements was established by the ECJ in its famous *Cassis* judgment and includes:

> the effectiveness of fiscal supervision, the protection of public health, the fairness of commercial transactions, and the defence of the consumer.[15]

Mandatory requirements are an open case law-based category to which the ECJ has been adding new concepts, most notably the protection of the environment,[16] the preservation of the variety of the media,[17] or a peril to the financial balance of the social security system.[18] The aim of the concept is to give Member States sufficient flexibility to respond to important public interests needs not foreseen in the Treaty which override the Internal Market without having to violate the Treaty. However, the use of these mandatory requirements or overriding public interest grounds is subject to the important principle of proportionality. This applies equally in the context of the derogations in Article 36 TFEU discussed below. The proportionate and therefore legal use of measures introduced to promote mandatory requirements can still raise barriers to trade in goods and thus threaten the functioning of the Internal Market. It is one of the tasks of secondary EU legislation in the form of Directives to harmonise these Member State rules and thus to lower or remove legal barriers to trade.

It appears from the jurisprudence of the ECJ that not only procurement laws and policies and wider practices but also independent decisions taken in the

---

[14] The wide definition of a "measure having equivalent effect to a quantitative restriction" in *Dassonville* led to an increasing tendency of traders to invoke Art. 34 TFEU as a means of challenging any rules whose effect is to limit their commercial freedom. This was the main reason for the controversial *Keck* judgment – Cases C-267 and C-268/91, *Criminal Proceedings against Bernard Keck and Daniel Mithouard* [1993] ECR I-6097, in which, while upholding the previous case law regarding rules concerning the characteristics of the goods, the Court of Justice ruled that "[c]ontrary to what has previously been decided . . . certain selling arrangements shall no longer be regarded as hindering State trade within the meaning of *Dassonville*". This introduced an important differentiation, whereby regulations concerning the characteristics of the goods are (still) covered by Art. 34 TFEU whereas regulations concerning certain selling arrangements are (no longer) covered by Art. 34 TFEU as long as they apply equally to all traders and have the same effect on imported and domestic goods.
[15] Case 120/78, *REWE – Zentrale AG v. Bundesmonopolverwaltung für Branntwein* ("Cassis de Dijon") [1979] ECR 649, [1979] 3 CMLR 494.
[16] Case 302/86, *Commission v. Denmark* ("Danish Bottles") [1986] ECR 4607.
[17] Case C-368/95, *Vereinigte Familiapress Zeitungsverlags- und Vertriebs GmbH v. Heinrich Bauer Verlag* ("Familiapress") [1997] 3 CMLR 1329.
[18] Case C-120/95, *Decker* [1995] ECR I-1831, [1998] 2 CMLR 879.

context of procurement activities can constitute a measure in the sense of Article 34 TFEU.[19] There is no *de minimis* rule whereby an act would be so insignificant that it would fall outside the prohibition.[20] Article 34 TFEU applies to all central, federal, regional and local authorities of the Member States and their emanations and all bodies governed by public law for which the Member States can be held responsible,[21] to the executive, legislative and judicial branches of government.[22] It is clear that it applies to the acts of contracting authorities subject to the procurement Directives 2004/17/EC (now replaced by Directive 2014/25/EU), 2004/18/EC (now replaced by Directive 2014/24/EU) and 2009/81/EC. It is not clear whether it also applies to private utilities operating on the basis of special or exclusive rights, but it appears that it does not apply to other private persons or entities.[23] Hence all public procurement-related laws and actions have to satisfy the requirements of the Treaty regime on the free movement of goods. The procurement of goods (supplies) is covered by Article 34 TFEU.

2.2 The free movement of services and the freedom of establishment

The TFEU takes a similar approach to the Internal Market regimes on the free movement of services in Article 56 TFEU[24] and the freedom of establishment in

[19] See Case C-243/89, *Commission* v. *Denmark* ("Storebaelt") [1993] ECR I-3353 where the contracting entity's requirement in the specifications to include national products and labour was held to be incompatible with Art. 28 EC (then Art. 30 EC and now Art. 34 TFEU); Case C-359/93, *Commission* v. *The Netherlands* ("UNIX") [1995] ECR I-157; Case C-59/00, *Bent Mousten Vestergaard* v. *Spøttrup Boligselskab* [2001] ECR I-9505. See also Sue Arrowsmith, *The Law of Public and Utilities Procurement*, 2nd edn (London: Sweet & Maxwell, 2005), at 185; Peter Trepte, *Public Procurement in the EU: A Practitioner's Guide* (Oxford University Press, 2007), at 8.

[20] Trepte, *Public Procurement in the EU*, *supra* note 19. On the discussion and arguments for a *de minimus* test in the context of the free movement of goods see Anthony Arnull, *The European Union and its Court of Justice*, 2nd edn (Oxford University Press, 2006), at 434–5 and 440–1. This was discussed by several Advocates General, for example Advocate General Jacobs in Case C-412/93, *Leclerc-Siplec* v. *TFI Publicité and M6 Publicité* [1995] ECR I-179. However, such a test would not apply to measures which discriminated against imports as they are prohibited by Art. 34 TFEU as such, even where their effect was only slight. See Arnull at 435. Thanks to Tony Arnull for discussing this point with me.

[21] Joined Cases C-1/90 and C-176/90, *Aragonesa de Publicidad Exterior SA and Publivia SAE* v. *Departamento de Sanidad y Seguridad Social de la Generalidad de Cataluña* [1991] ECR I-4151.

[22] For example, Case 50/80, *Dansk Supermarked A/S* v. *A/S Imerco* [1981] ECR 181.

[23] Joined Cases 177/82 and 178/82, *Jan van der Haar and Kaveka de Meern BV* [1984] ECR 1797. See Laurence Gormley, *Prohibiting Restrictions on Trade within the EEC* (Amsterdam: North-Holland, 1985), at 261.

[24] Art. 56 TFEU reads: "Within the framework of the provisions set out below, restrictions on freedom to provide services within the Community shall be prohibited in respect of nationals of Member States who are established in a State of the Community other than that of the person for whom the services are intended."

Article 49 TFEU.[25] The former protects the rights of nationals of the Member States to provide and receive commercial or professional services in another Member State on a temporary basis. It is often referred to as the freedom to provide services although this is not entirely accurate since the freedom also covers the reception of services and even correspondence services. Hence the service provider does not necessarily have to move from one Member State to another for the regime to apply. The individual or company does not permanently leave its Member State of origin to integrate into the economic framework of another Member State; that would come under establishment. Although involving the free movement of persons, the temporary nature of services makes them similar to goods. Therefore the ECJ has been developing principles, first developed for goods, for services also,[26] as will be explained further below.

The freedom of establishment protects the right of nationals of the Member States to establish themselves or an agency, branch or subsidiary in another Member State on a permanent basis. The self-employed individual or company integrates into the economic framework of another Member State, which involves a social dimension for the economic actors and their family members which is in many ways akin to the free movement of workers regime of the TFEU. Relevant secondary EU instruments, most importantly the Citizen's Directive 2004/38/EC,[27] therefore apply to both the regime on establishment and that on workers. However, it is the application and principles of the freedom to provide services and the freedom of establishment which are largely identical[28] and consequently many issues are regulated in the same provisions on the freedom of establishment to which the section on the free movement of services merely refers.[29]

---

[25] Art. 49 TFEU reads: "Within the framework of the provisions set out below, restrictions on the freedom of establishment of nationals of a Member State in the territory of another Member State shall be prohibited. Such prohibition shall also apply to restrictions on the setting-up of agencies, branches or subsidiaries by nationals of any Member State established in the territory of any Member State. Freedom of establishment shall include the right to take up and pursue activities as self-employed persons and to set up and manage undertakings, in particular companies or firms within the meaning of the second paragraph of Article 48, under the conditions laid down for its own nationals by the law of the country where such establishment is effected, subject to the provisions of the chapter relating to capital."

[26] See especially the book by Snell, *Goods and Services in EC Law, supra* note 6.

[27] [2004] OJ L229/35.

[28] On the common ground: Case 48/75, *Royer* [1976] ECR 497. On the differences: Case C-55/94, *Gebhard* v. *Consiglio dell'Ordine degli Avvocati e Precuratori di Milano* [1995] ECR I-4165.

[29] Art. 62 TFEU reads: "The provisions of Articles 51 to 54 shall apply to the matters covered by this Chapter."

Similar to the mandatory requirements or overriding public interest grounds of the *Cassis* jurisprudence in the context of the free movement of goods, the ECJ ruled that a measure can be considered outside the field of application of the prohibition of Articles 56 and 49 TFEU if it represents a proportionate response to an overriding public interest or imperative requirement. This applies, for example, in relation to professional rules justified by the common good[30] or consumer protection.[31]

Procurement laws and policies, wider practices and independent decisions taken in the context of procurement activities can constitute a measure prohibited by Article 56 TFEU.[32] Examples from the case law of the ECJ include a requirement for companies tendering for contracts involving certain data processing systems to be mainly or partly in Italian public ownership,[33] a contract clause for the use of Danish labour[34] or a French limitation on bringing a labour force from Portugal to perform a contract in France.[35]

Similar to Article 34 TFEU there is no *de minimis* rule whereby an act would be so insignificant that it would fall outside the prohibition. The rules on the free movement of services apply to all central, federal, regional and local authorities of the Member States and their emanations and all bodies governed by public law for which the Member States can be held responsible, to the executive, legislative and judicial branches of government. It clearly applies to the ministries of defence of the Member States and their procurement departments. As services share many similarities with goods, most importantly the location of the tenderer in another Member State than the contracting entity, these two

---

[30] Case 33/74, *Van Binsbergen* v. *Bestuur van de Bedrijfsvereiniging Metaalnijverheid* [1979] ECR 1299.

[31] Case C-180/89, *Commission* v. *Italy* ("Italian Tourist Guides") [1991] ECR I-709. Other imperative requirements are: the functioning of the justice system (Case 33/74, *Van Binsbergen*, *supra* note 30), interests of the workforce in good relations in the labour market (Case 279/80, *Webb* [1981] ECR 3305); interests of the holder of an insurance policy (Case 205/84, *Commission* v. *Germany* [1986] ECR 3755); conservation of the national historical and artistic heritage (Case C-180/89); social policy interests and the fight against fraud in the context of lotteries and gambling, protection of intellectual property rights, quality and pluralism of broadcasting (Case 352/85, *Bond van de Adverteerders* v. *Nederland* [1988] ECR 2085); coherence of domestic taxation systems, or the preservation of the good reputation of the national financial sector.

[32] See Case C-243/89, *Commission* v. *Denmark* ("Storebaelt"), *supra* note 19, where the contracting entity's requirement in the specifications to include national products and labour was held to be incompatible with what is now Art. 34 TFEU; Case C-359/93, *Commission* v. *The Netherlands* ("UNIX"), *supra* note 19; Case C-59/00, *Bent Mousten Vestergaard* v. *Spøttrup Boligselskab*, *supra* note 19. See also Arrowsmith, *The Law of Public and Utilities Procurement*, *supra* note 19, at 185; Trepte, *Public Procurement in the EU*, *supra* note 19, at 8.

[33] Case C-3/88, *Commission* v. *Italy* ("Re Data Processing") [1989] ECR 4035.

[34] Case C-243/89, *Commission* v. *Denmark* ("Storebaelt"), *supra* note 19.

[35] Case C-113/89, *Rush Portuguesa* v. *Office national d'immigration* [1990] ECR I-1417.

regimes are the most relevant for the public procurement of goods, services and works. The freedom of establishment is less likely to be affected by procurement decisions since violations of these rules normally happen independently from procurement procedures. However, as outlined above the regime is closely connected and partly overlaps with that on services.

2.3 The prohibition of discrimination on grounds of nationality

A general principle of prohibition of any discrimination on grounds of nationality is stipulated in Article 18 TFEU.[36] The principle is generally not applied independently[37] since it is also contained in the more specific free movement of regimes of the Treaty. The principle

> requires that persons in a situation governed by [Union] law be placed on a completely equal footing with nationals of the Member State.[38]

The principle only applies to nationals of the Member States of the EU and individuals and legal persons who are resident in them, not to nationals from third countries.

Since most public procurement decisions – regarding, for example, qualification, short-listing or contract award – are already covered by the regimes particularly on the free movement of goods and services outlined above, these more specific regimes will in most cases override the more general prohibition of the discrimination on grounds of nationality in Article 18 TFEU. Thus there is no need of Article 18 TFEU in the procurement context.[39]

2.4 The public security exemption

With regards to the free movement of goods, in contrast to the prohibition of customs duties and charges having equivalent effect outlined above, the prohibitions in Articles 34 and 35 TFEU are not absolute. Article 36 TFEU provides:

> The provisions of Articles 34 and 35 shall not preclude prohibitions or restrictions on imports, exports or goods in transit justified on grounds of public morality, public policy or public security; the protection of health and

---

[36] Art. 18 TFEU reads: "Within the scope of application of this Treaty, and without prejudice to any special provisions contained therein, any discrimination on grounds of nationality shall be prohibited."

[37] Case 307/87, *Commission* v. *Greece* [1989] ECR I-461.

[38] Case 187/87, *Cowan* v. *Trésor Public* [1989] ECR 195 at 219.

[39] Arrowsmith, *The Law of Public and Utilities Procurement, supra* note 19, at 218, also arguing against J. Winter, "Public Procurement in the E.C." (1991) 28 *Common Market Law Review* 741, at 762, that Art. 18 TFEU (then 12 and 6 EC respectively) does not apply to entities not covered by the free movement regimes.

life of humans, animals or plants; the protection of national treasures possessing artistic, historic or archaeological value; or the protection of industrial and commercial property. Such prohibitions or restrictions shall not, however, constitute a means of arbitrary discrimination or a disguised restriction on trade between Member States.

Therefore, in addition to the flexibility provided through the case law based concept of mandatory requirements discussed above, the Treaty itself stipulates a number of public interest grounds that can justify proportionate Member State measures derogating from the prohibition of quantitative restrictions and measures having equivalent effect. The derogation may even apply to measures that discriminate against goods originating in another Member State. The aim is to provide Member States with the flexibility to take necessary measures to protect a number of interests within their responsibility, which are so well known and crucial that they could already be directly accommodated in the text of the Treaty itself.

Similar to the public interest grounds that allow derogation from the free movement of goods according to Article 36 TFEU, Article 52 TFEU[40] provides a number of public interests grounds that can justify proportionate Member State measures derogating from the prohibition of restrictions of the free movement of services and the freedom of establishment. The list is shorter than that of Article 36 TFEU but includes public security. However, again similar to mandatory requirements and justifications in the free movement of goods regime, the Member State measures have to be proportionate.

Exceptions reflecting grounds justifying derogation in Article 36 and 52 TFEU are also part of the Public Sector, Utilities and Defence Procurement Directives.[41] These shall be discussed in more detail with regards to the Defence Directive in chapter 6.

The less relevant Treaty regimes on the free movement of workers, capital and payments, and the related provisions on the area of freedom, security and justice, also contain public security exemptions similar to Articles 36 and 52 TFEU. These are contained in Articles 45(3) TFEU for the free movement of workers,[42] 65(1)(b) TFEU for the free movement of capital and payments[43] and

---

[40] Art. 52 TFEU (ex 46 EC Treaty) reads: "1. The provisions of this Chapter and measures taken in pursuance thereof shall not prejudice the applicability of provisions laid down by law, regulation or administrative action providing for special treatment for foreign nationals on grounds of public policy, public security or public health. 2. The European Parliament and the Council shall, acting in accordance with the ordinary legislative procedure, issue directives for the coordination of the abovementioned provisions."

[41] See, for example, Art. 14 Public Sector Procurement Directive 2004/18/EC on secret contracts and contracts requiring special security measures.

[42] The relevant sections of Art. 45 (3) TFEU read: "It shall entail the right, subject to limitations justified on grounds of . . . public security . . ."

[43] The relevant sections of Art. 65 (1) (b) TFEU read: "1. The provisions of Article 56 shall be without prejudice to the right of Member States: . . . (b) to take all requisite measures to

72 TFEU for the area of freedom, security and justice.[44] They are mentioned here because many of the ECJ rulings discussed below refer to all the security exemptions, including the defence exemptions in Articles 346 and 347 TFEU discussed in chapter 3.

The main objective of the Defence Directive is to reduce Member States' recourse to Article 346 TFEU especially but also to the free movement public security exemptions in Articles 36 and 52 TFEU. As will be explained in more detail in chapter 6, the Directive is not limited to the procurement of armaments in the sense of Article 346 TFEU but includes other security goods and services as well. Therefore a good understanding of the interpretation of the latter exemptions is essential not only to understand the interpretation of the former, but also to understand the Treaty background of the non-armaments dimension of the Defence Directive. Both the free movement public security exclusions and the defence derogations represent exemptions accommodating security. The interpreting case law of the ECJ regarding the public security exemptions is "older" and thus more comprehensive and clear. The case law interpreting Article 346 TFEU developed later and on the basis of the interpretation of the public security exemptions.

2.4.1 Public security

For the purposes of this chapter the crucial public interest accommodated in Articles 36, 45(3), 52(1) and 65(1)(b) TFEU, is "public security". Public security is a wide concept covering all aspects of security, internal and external, as decided by the ECJ, inter alia, in *Richardt*, *Werner* and *Leifer*,[45] including the concept of national security. Schwarze defines public security as

> the entire field of rules, laid down by the sovereign authorities and incapable of being waived, which have been adopted in the interest of the political and social integrity of society.[46]

---

prevent infringements of national law and regulations, in particular in the field of taxation and the prudential supervision of financial institutions, or to lay down procedures for the declaration of capital movements for purposes of administrative or statistical information, or to take measures which are justified on grounds of public policy or public security."

[44] Art. 72 TFEU reads: "This title shall not affect the exercise of the responsibilities incumbent upon the Member States with regard to the maintenance of law and order and the safeguarding of internal security."

[45] Case C-367/89, *Criminal Proceedings against Aimé Richardt and Les Accessoires Scientifiques SNC* [1991] ECR I-4645, at para. 22; Case C-70/94, *Fritz Werner Industrie-Ausrüstungen GmbH* v. *Germany* [1995] ECR I-3989, at para. 25; Case C-83/94, *Criminal Proceedings against Peter Leifer and others* [1995] ECR I-3231, at para. 26.

[46] Jürgen Schwarze, *European Administrative Law* (London: Sweet & Maxwell, 1992), at 778, based on Wägbaur, in v. d. Groeben, v. Boeckh, Thiesing, Ehlermann (eds.), *Kommentar zum EWG Vertrag*, 3rd edn (Baden-Baden: Nomos, 1983), Art. 36, margin nos. 18 *et seq.*

This would cover all laws, regulations and individual decisions enacted to protect the integrity of a Member State. A situation causing a Member State to take such a measure is a situation posing a threat to its integrity. In contrast, the exemptions in Articles 346 and 347 TFEU discussed in chapter 3 relate to a narrower concept of security.[47] The latter concept could be called "national security" or "external military security",[48] although these expressions are not used in the Treaty itself.[49] On the basis of the definition of public security provided by Schwarze, "national security" could be defined as the entire field of rules which have been adopted to protect the territorial integrity, important strategic interests and political independence of a State. Articles 346 and 347 TFEU are special provisions superseding the wider public security provisions in Articles 36, 45(3), 52(1) and 65(1)(b) TFEU in most cases involving national security. For example, Article 36 TFEU only applies to material not covered by Article 346(1)(b) TFEU and only to situations not covered by Article 347 TFEU, as will be explained in more detail in the relevant chapter 3. Ultimately the "public security" exemptions from the free movement regimes of the Treaty cover only a small number of situations relating to the notions of national security and therefore defence. Thus it is mainly derogation on the basis of Article 346 TFEU and not on the basis on the public security exemptions which the Defence Directive aims to limit. However, as further explained in chapter 6, the Defence Directive also applies to sensitive non-military procurement and aimed to limit the use of the then applicable Article 14 Public Sector Directive 2004/18/EC "which is based on Articles [36 and 52(1) TFEU]"[50] – even if that is just an additional function.

2.4.2 The narrow interpretation: *Johnston, Sirdar, Kreil* and *Dory*

The leading judgment for the exemptions in Articles 36, 45(3), 52(1), 65(1)(b) and 72 TFEU, but also the security exemptions in general, including Article 346 and 347 TFEU, was *Johnston*.[51] The case concerned the prohibition against female officers of what is now the Police Service of Northern Ireland wearing firearms. This excluded women from a considerable part of police activities and was challenged under the EU Equal Treatment

---

[47] Advocate General Sir Gordon Slynn, Case 72/83, *Campus Oil Limited* v. *Minister for Industry and Energy* [1984] ECR 2727, at 2764, [1984] 3 CMLR 544, at 558.

[48] Ibid.

[49] The term "essential interests of … security" is used in Art. 346(1)(a) and (b) TFEU. Security is not mentioned explicitly in Art. 347 TFEU, but the situations described are situations affecting national security. For a more detailed discussion see ch. 3.

[50] Commission Staff Working Document – Impact Assessment SEC (2007) 1593, http://ec.europa.eu/governance/impact/ia_carried_out/docs/ia_2007/sec_2007_1593_en.pdf [accessed 1 November 2013], at 34.

[51] Case 222/84, *Marguerite Johnston* v. *Chief Constable of the Royal Ulster Constabulary* [1986] ECR 1651, [1986] 3 CMLR 240.

Directive.[52] The ECJ ruled that: "the only articles in which the Treaty provides for derogations applicable in situations which may involve public safety are ... Articles [36, 45, 52, 346 and 347 TFEU], which deal with exceptional and clearly defined cases. Because of their limited character", the Court ruled that

> these articles *do not lend themselves to a wide interpretation* and it is not possible to infer from them that there is inherent in the Treaty a general proviso covering all measures taken for reasons of public safety [emphasis added].[53]

Article 65(1)(b)[54] and 72 TFEU[55] were inserted into the Treaty after this judgment and need to be added to the list of exemptions set out in *Johnston*. The

---

[52] Directive 76/207/EEC on the implementation of the principle of equal treatment for men and women regards access to employment, vocational training, and promotion, and working conditions [1976] OJ L39/40. For a detailed discussion of this case see M. Trybus, "Sisters in Arms: Female Soldiers and Sex Equality in the Armed Forces" (2003) 9 *European Law Journal* 631–58 and Martin Trybus, *European Union Law and Defence Integration* (Oxford: Hart, 2005), at 266–9.

[53] Case 222/84, *Johnston, supra* note 51, at para. 26. See also Case 13/68, *SpA Salgoil* v. *Italian Ministry of Foreign Trade* [1968] ECR 453, at 463, [1969] CMLR 181, at 192 and Case 7/68, *Commission* v. *Italy* [1968] ECR 633, at 644.

[54] The Court, however, never mentioned Art. 65(1)(b) TFEU when it listed the security exemptions: Case C-285/98, *Kreil* v. *Germany* [2000] ECR I-69, at para. 16; Case C-414/97, *Commission* v. *Spain* [1999] ECR I-5585, [2000] 2 CMLR 4, at para. 21 (for a detailed discussion of this case see ch. 3); Case C-273/97, *Sirdar* v. *The Army Board* [1999] ECR I-7403, [1999] 3 CMLR 559, at para. 16 (for a more detailed discussion of Sirdar and Kreil see Trybus, "Sisters in Arms: Female Soldiers and Sex Equality in the Armed Forces", *supra* note 52, 631–58 and ch. 9 in Trybus, *European Union Law and Defence Integration, supra* note 52, at 262–90; P. Koutrakos, "Community Law and Equal Treatment in the Armed Forces" (2000) 25 *European Law Review* 433. In these cases the Court referred to the judgment in *Johnston*, which in 1986 could not take what is now Art. 65(1)(b) TFEU, which was adopted in 1994 (as Art. 73d and from 1999 Art. 58(1)(b) EC Treaty), into account. The fact that the Court did not add the provision to the list in *Kreil* or *Sirdar* appears to be an oversight. The advisory opinion of Advocate General Cosmas in Case C-423/98, *Alfredo Albore* [2000] ECR I-5965, at para. 47, seems to support this finding and the judgment ([1999] ECR I-5965, at para. 19) explicitly refers to what was then Art. 73d EC as one of the public security derogations to which the *Johnston* judgment applies. Art. 65(1)(b) TFEU, then Art. 58(1)(b) TFEU are also listed in the later cases of Case 186/01, *Alexander Dory* v. *Germany* [2003] ECR I-2479, at para. 31; Case C-337/05, *Commission* v. *Italy* ("Agusta") [2008] ECR I-2173, at para. 43 and Case C-157/06, *Commission* v. *Italy* [2008] ECR I-7313, at para. 23 (for a more detailed discussion of these cases see below). The provision is also listed in the relevant paragraphs in the judgments listed in the next footnote.

[55] The more recent 2009–10 enforcement cases all list both Art. 65(1)(b) and 72 TFEU. Case C-284/05, *Commission* v. *Finland* [2009] ECR I-11705, at para. 45; Case C-294/05, *Commission* v. *Sweden* [2009] ECR I-11777, at para. 43; Case C-372/05, *Commission* v. *Germany* [2009] ECR I-11801, at para. 68; Case C-409/05, *Commission* v. *Greece* [2009] ECR I-11859, at para. 50; Case C-461/05, *Commission* v. *Denmark* [2009] ECR I-11887, at para. 51; Case C-38/06, *Commission* v. *Portugal* [2010] ECR I-1569, at para. 62; Case

basic "*Johnston* principle" of a narrow interpretation of all the security exemptions was the basis of all other relevant public security and national security
judgments of the Court, including *Sirdar, Kreil, Dory, Commission* v. *Spain*, the
Agusta case law and the recent enforcement case law on military exports.[56]
Many of these cases will be discussed in more detail below and especially in
chapter 3. Therefore there is established case law on the narrow and strict
interpretation of the security exemptions, especially the most relevant, Article
36 TFEU on the free movement of goods and Article 52 TFEU on the free
movement of services.[57]

In *Johnston* the Court also gave a reason for this basic interpretation of the
security exemptions:

> If every provision of [EU] law were held to be subject of a general proviso,
> regardless of the specific requirements laid down by the provisions of the
> Treaty, this might impair the binding nature of [EU] law and its uniform
> application.[58]

This basic reasoning is also repeated in most of the relevant public and national
security judgments listed above.[59] Hence there is an underlying principle that
security exclusions from the Treaty are exhaustive and have to be interpreted
narrowly. There are no general and automatic national security exemptions
from the Treaty, as this would question the effectiveness of EU law. The TFEU
including the free movement regimes, their legally binding character, their
effectiveness and their uniform application would be undermined if a wide
interpretation of the exemptions allowed Member States to justify most of their
measures violating the prohibitions of the Treaty. The prohibitions would be
meaningless. Thus the rules of the Internal Market apply, unless a Member State
can invoke one of the exemptions allowing derogation from the Treaty on a
case-by-case basis. Another aspect of the *Johnston* principle is that it clarifies
through the exercise of this codified possibility in the Treaty that there is judicial
review and therefore scrutiny not just in the abstract text of the Treaty but in

---

C-239/06, *Commission* v. *Italy* [2009] ECR I-11913, at para. 46. Case C-186/01, *Alexander
Dory* v. *Germany, supra* note 54, also cites Art. 72 TFEU in para. 31. So do Case C-337/05,
Commission v. *Italy* ("Agusta"), *supra* note 54, at para. 43 and Case C-157/06, *Commission*
v. *Italy, supra* note 54, at para. 23.

[56] See the relevant paragraphs of these judgments cited in the previous two footnotes. See also
Case C-503/03, *Commission* v. *Spain* [2006] ECR I-1097, para. 45; Case C-490/04,
Commission v. *Germany* [2007] ECR I-6095, para. 86; and Case C-141/07, *Commission*
v. *Germany* [2008] ECR I-6935, para. 50 on the narrow interpretation of exceptions from
fundamental freedoms.

[57] For example, Case C-546/07, *Commission* v. *Germany* [2010] ECJ I-439, in para. 48: "It
follows from Article [52 TFEU], which must be interpreted strictly, that discriminatory
rules may be justified only on grounds of … public security …"; and Case C-490/04,
Commission v. *Germany* [2007] ECR I-6095, in para. 86 with a very similar wording.

[58] Case 222/84, *supra* note 51, para. 26.

[59] See the relevant paragraphs of these judgments cited in notes 54 and 55.

concrete practice. This is confirmed by the subsequent case law discussed below. These are the fundamental principles governing all the security type exemptions of the TFEU and the Directives. For the public security exemptions of the free movement regimes of the TFEU this means mainly that the notion of "public security" has to be interpreted strictly and therefore cannot include considerations remote to or outside of public security. For the national security derogations at the end of the Treaty the *Johnston* rule of narrow interpretation affects the material covered by Article 346(1)(b) TFEU and the situations covered by Articles 346(1)(a) and 347 TFEU. This shall be discussed in more detail in chapter 3. The limited character of the security exemptions through the combination of a narrow interpretation and the requirement of proportionality will become clearer when considering the subsequent case law.

2.4.3 The proportionality test: *Campus Oil* and *Greek Petroleum Law*

Articles 36, 45(3), 52(1), 65(1)(b) and 72 TFEU and the public interest grounds or mandatory requirements of the *Cassis* jurisprudence outlined above do not give a blank cheque to the Member States. Measures have to be proportionate to be legally justified under the Treaty. This is also reiterated in the Defence Directive which states in Recital 17 referring to these exemptions:

> the non-application of this Directive must be proportionate to the aims pursued and cause as little disturbance as possible to the free movement of goods and the freedom to provide services.

Thus an understanding of the principle of proportionality and its application to the public security exemptions is crucial also for the understanding of the precise scope of the Defence Directive.

2.4.3.1 Proportionality Proportionality requires, first, the suitability of the measure for the attainment of the desired objective; secondly, the necessity of the measure, meaning that there must not be a measure less restrictive to the Internal Market at the disposal of the Member State in question; and, thirdly, the proportionality *strictu sensu* of the measure, requiring a certain balance between the objective and the restriction.[60] The third stage of the proportionality test appears to be not always part of the scrutiny applied.[61] However, the ECJ will not reach this third stage if the case can be resolved at one of the two earlier stages or when no specific argument regarding the proportionality *strictu*

---

[60] Formulated by Advocate General van Gerwen in Case C-159/90, *SPUC* v. *Grogan* [1991] ECR I-4685 including the more controversial third element. Also in favour of the three-part test (based on the same test in German administrative law, see Craig and de Búrca, *EU Law*, *supra* note 6, at 545), Schwarze, *European Administrative Law*, *supra* note 46, at 712. On proportionality see the seminal article of G. de Búrca, "The Principle of Proportionality and its Application in EC Law" (1993) 13 *Yearbook of European Law* 105.

[61] Paul Craig, *EU Administrative Law*, 2nd edn (Oxford University Press, 2012), ch. 17.

sensu has been raised by the parties.[62] In some cases a strict differentiation between stage 2 and 3 will be warranted whereas in other cases these two stages are closely connected and the respective analysis appears blurred.[63] Only when the requirements of this three-part proportionality test are met can a balance be struck between the respective public interest ground and the Internal Market interests in the free movement regimes. This proportionality test is the standard of review applied by the ECJ in cases where a Member State measure in violation of Article 30, 45, 49, 56 or 67 TFEU might be justified by, inter alia, public security on the basis of Article 36, 45(3), 52(1), 65(1)(b) or 72 TFEU respectively.

The intensity of scrutiny may differ depending on the context, leaving a wider or narrower margin of discretion to the Member State. As de Búrca put it:

> the way the proportionality principle is applied by the Court of Justice covers a spectrum ranging from a very deferential approach, to quite a rigorous and searching examination of the justification for a measure.[64]

Considerations determining the position of a particular case on this "spectrum" of intensity are the competence of the EU and its limitations for the policy field in question (EU law aspect), the expertise and qualification of the Court in comparison to that of the challenged decision-maker (comparative expertise aspect) and, finally, the authority of a not democratically elected court of law to decide an issue rather than the legislature or the executive branches of government (division of powers aspect). The latter two aspects apply equally to any national court whereas the first aspect is specific to the ECJ, although similar considerations might apply in a national federal context. In other words, the ECJ will respect the Member States but apply more intensive scrutiny if a competence of the EU is at stake (EU law aspect); it will defer when it lacks the expertise but will apply a more intensive scrutiny if it feels it is equipped to make its own judgment (comparative expertise aspect); and it will not second-guess the discretion of the other branches of government but will interfere when the executive or legislature have exceeded their powers (division of powers aspect). These different degrees of intensity of the proportionality test provide the ECJ with a degree of flexibility to be applied in most if not all situations and contexts. In a security context, especially national security, the review will be more deferential.[65] The consequence is a less intensive review, normally leaving a relatively wide margin of discretion to the Member States. However, the matter can also be deemed non-justiciable. The burden of proof of the illegality

---

[62] Craig and de Búrca, *EU Law*, *supra* note 6, at 526.

[63] Ibid., at 526 puts this as follows: "in some cases the ECJ may ... in effect 'fold' stage three of the inquiry back into stage two".

[64] De Búrca, *supra* note 60, at 111.   [65] Ibid., at 112.

of the measure is put on the applicant.[66] This will be discussed in the context of the relevant case law below.

The proportionality test was "adopted" by the ECJ from German public law.[67] In German public law the requirement of proportionality of all State measures emanates from the rule-of-law principle enshrined in Article 20 of the Basic Law, the German federal constitution. State measures will regularly interfere with the basic rights of the individual and in order to be lawful and constitutional such a State measure must not be excessive or unnecessary but has to be proportionate in relation to its objectives.[68] The EU and all the other Member States are also founded on the rule of law as enshrined in the Preamble to the TEU (Lisbon)[69] and its Article 2.[70] Moreover, there is no doubt regarding the importance of the principle of proportionality being a requirement in and to be met by EU legislation and ECJ case law.[71] The position of proportionality as a general principle of EU law emanating from the rule of law as an EU value, now also enshrined in Article 5(4) TEU and a Protocol to the Treaty,[72] is crucial when interpreting Articles 346 and 347 TFEU, as will be explained in chapter 3.

The proportionality test is regularly applied to the use of a public security exemption by a Member State to justify a restriction of one of the free movement regimes.[73] There is normally strict scrutiny as the case will regularly involve a prima facie violation of a free movement regime which lies at the very core of what the EU is about.[74] The Court is one of the guardians of economic integration through the EU. Craig and de Búrca have identified four variables affecting the intensity of scrutiny in this context. First, scrutiny has tended to become more intensive over time.[75] Secondly, scrutiny intensifies in cases where the Court takes the justification only as a "front" for protectionism.[76] Thirdly, the nature of the subject matter is a determining factor when the Member States raise genuine concerns.[77] Fourthly, and finally, the ECJ often refers the actual application of the proportionality test back to the referring

---

[66] Ibid., at 112.

[67] Craig and de Búrca, *EU Law, supra* note 6, at 526 citing Schwarze, *European Administrative Law, supra* note 46, in what in the 1st rev. edn of 2006 is at 685–6.

[68] See Schwarze, *European Administrative Law, supra* note 46, at 685–6.

[69] The 4th paragraph of the Preamble to the TEU (Lisbon) says: "Confirming their attachment to ... the rule of law ..."

[70] Art. 2 TEU (Lisbon) reads: "The Union is founded on the values of ... the rule of law ... These rules are common to the Member States."

[71] Craig and de Búrca, *EU Law, supra* note 6, at 526.

[72] Protocol No. 2 (attached to the Treaty of Lisbon) on the Application of the Principles of Subsidiarity and Proportionality.

[73] See T. Tridimas, *The General Principles of EC Law*, 2nd edn (Oxford University Press, 2006), ch. 4; Craig, *EU Administrative Law, supra* note 61, ch. 18; Craig and de Búrca, *EU Law, supra* note 6, at 532.

[74] Craig and de Búrca, *EU Law, supra* note 6, at 532.

[75] See ibid., at 532 for the cases discussed as an example.   [76] Ibid., at 532.   [77] Ibid., at 532.

national court. This is, however, not to be misunderstood as an act of deference, as this will depend on the guidelines provided by the ECJ on the application of the proportionality test in a particular subject area.[78]

2.4.3.2 Campus Oil   The leading case on the public security exemption of the free movement of goods regime in Article 36 TFEU and the application of the proportionality test in this context is *Campus Oil*.[79] The case concerned an Irish law requiring companies dealing with oil products to buy 35 per cent of their requirements for crude oil from the only national refinery in the Republic. The reason for this requirement was to preserve a national refinery capacity. Article 34 TFEU (then 34 EEC Treaty) prohibited this Irish requirement: as a State measure which restricted intra-Community trade it represented a measure having equivalent effect to a quantitative restriction. Ireland invoked Article 36 TFEU (then 36 EEC Treaty) for reasons of public security. The Court applied the proportionality test in relation to the measure. It considered the Irish purchase requirement to be suitable and necessary because of the strategic importance of a national refining capacity and the connected importance of petroleum products for the functioning of the State. The Court also took the geographic isolation of Ireland and her status of neutrality into account. The judgment is probably the best example for a successful use of Article 36 TFEU in a security context and touches upon the narrower national security context, which will be explained in more detail in chapter 3.

Campus Oil suggests a wide margin of discretion left to the Member States for measures taken in the narrower national security context included in the notion of public security in Article 36 TFEU. However, it is submitted that the ruling cannot be interpreted as a general rule giving Member States a wide margin of discretion. Again, exclusions have to be interpreted narrowly.[80] Thus a unique national industrial or technological capability or the only provider of a particular service has to be in danger of going out of business without the measure in question. Without the respective provider, for example, the government and private companies would have to procure the good or service from outside the Member State. The capability has to be unique to a small country or it has to be the only provider in a certain region of a Member State with a large territory, such as France or Sweden. Therefore the exemption will only apply to a few markets. Furthermore, the capability has to be relevant to national security. As could be seen in *Campus Oil*, the only national provider for fuel, for example, will meet this requirement, as tanks, police cars and ambulances do

[78] Ibid.   [79] Case 72/83, *Campus Oil, supra* note 47.
[80] Case 222/84, *Johnston, supra* note 51, at para. 26. See also Case 13/68, *Salgoil, supra* note 53, at 192 and all the other judgments cited *supra* in notes 54 and 55, including *Kreil, Sirdar, Dory, Commission* v. *Spain*, the *Agusta* judgments and the 2009 and 2010 enforcement cases.

not roll without fuel. The only provider for boots, for example, will not meet this requirement, as soldiers or police officers can do without boots and wear shoes instead.[81] Therefore the exemption will only apply to a few goods and services. Moreover, the acceptance of economic means to implement security objectives by the Court in *Campus Oil* cannot necessarily be applied to other Member States. The Republic of Ireland is geographically isolated and it would be hard to deliver crucial supplies from other parts of the Union during a serious crisis,[82] except from Northern Ireland. Furthermore, unlike most other Member States, the Republic is neutral and in theory would have no allies in times of war.[83] A Member State in the heart of Europe who is also a member of NATO might find it harder to justify the implementation of security interests by economic means. Therefore the ruling can only apply to certain Member States. Finally, any reliance on this exemption will be subject to a strict proportionality test. This proportionality test will take the outlined considerations in relation to markets, products and neutrality into account. A justification based on Article 36 TFEU will probably not be accepted as necessary when the respective industrial capability is not crucial for defence or when a NATO ally in the vicinity can easily supply the products in question. Thus reliance on this situation is not likely to be accepted easily by the Court.

2.4.3.3 Greek Petroleum Law This interpretation of *Campus Oil* is confirmed by the judgment in *Greek Petroleum Law*,[84] concerning Greece, a Member State which has allies in NATO but also a unique national security

---

[81] In Case 231/83, *Cullert* v. *Centre Leclerc* [1985] ECR I-306, at 313, [1985] 2 CMLR 524, at 535 Advocate General Verloren van Themaat referred to paras. 34 and 47 of *Campus Oil* and pointed out: "reliance upon public security can be justified only in so far as the production capacity in question is necessary for the proper functioning of Irish public institutions and essential public services and even the survival of its inhabitants".

[82] See Advocate General Slynn in Case 72/83, *Campus Oil, supra* note 47, at 2764, and the arguments of the Irish Government, at 2735.

[83] See the arguments of the Irish National Petroleum Corporation Limited in Case 72/83, *Campus Oil,* ibid., at 2738, referring to "Austria, Barbados, Cyprus, Jamaica, New Zealand and Thailand which are in a geo-political and economic situation similar to that of Ireland" and who "all consider a domestic refining capacity to be an essential element of national security". Because of Art. 297 the principle of Community solidarity might be compromised in times of crisis or war. This principle requires Member States to help each other and is a foundation of the Union, see Case 77/77, *BP* v. *Commission* [1978] ECR 1513, [1978] 3 CMLR 174, at para. 15. Even that neutrality argument based argument could be challenged for 2013, since the 2009 Treaty of Lisbon brought the mutual defence clause of Art. 42(7) TEU, which obliges at least all Member States who are also NATO members to defend each other if attacked, including the neutral Member States, even though Ireland as a "neutral" Member State might not have to defend the others if they are attacked. See Trybus, *European Union Law and Defence Integration, supra* note 52, ch. 10.

[84] Case C-347/88, *Commission* v. *Greece* [1990] ECR I-4747.

situation with neighbouring Turkey. The facts of the case were almost identical to that of *Campus Oil* and the Court pointed out:

> Admittedly, in its judgment in [*Campus Oil*] the Court stated that a Member State which is totally or almost totally dependent on imports for its supplies of petroleum products may rely on grounds of public security within the meaning of Article 36 of the Treaty for the purpose of requiring importers to cover a certain proportion of their needs by purchases from a refinery situated in its territory at prices fixed by the competent ministry on the basis of the costs incurred in the operation of that refinery, if the production of the refinery cannot be freely disposed of at competitive prices on the market concerned.

However, the Court continued:

> it must be pointed out that Greece has not shown that if the State's rights with regard to the importation and marketing of petroleum products were not maintained in force, the public-sector refineries would be unable to dispose of their products on the market at competitive prices and thereby ensure their continued operation. Consequently, the argument relied upon in that regard by Greece must be dismissed.

This supports the limited interpretation of the seemingly wide *Campus Oil* approach provided above. Thus the Court is unlikely to issue another *Campus Oil* lightly. The narrow interpretation and strict proportionality requirement apply even where the security of supply of a strategically important commodity is concerned. However, it should be pointed out that this refers to goods other than armaments, since these are subject to a different derogation in Article 346 TFEU and thus, as discussed in chapter 3, a different interpretation, standard of review and case law.

2.4.4 Intensity of scrutiny – a real, specific and serious risk: *Albore*

The intensity of the scrutiny applied by the Court became particularly clear in *Albore*[85] which concerned an Italian law requiring non-Italians to acquire the consent of the local administration before buying property in certain areas of the country. These areas were classified as of military interest and included all the small islands of Italy. The law was challenged as representing discrimination on grounds of nationality. The Italian government justified the law by referring to what are now Articles 65(1)(b) and 347 TFEU. The Court pointed out that "a mere reference to the requirement of defence of the national territory, where the situation of the Member State concerned does not fall within the scope of Article [347 TFEU] cannot suffice" to justify a measure contrary to the Treaty.[86] "The position would be different only if it were demonstrated", said the Court, that to refrain from that measure contrary to the Treaty

---

[85] Case C-423/98, *supra* note 54.   [86] Case C-423/98, ibid., at para. 21.

would expose the military interest of the Member State concerned *to real, specific and serious risk* which would not be countered by less restrictive procedures.[87]

Thus a risk for the military interest ("specific") of the Member State has to actually exist ("real"), the risk has to be military-specific and the risk has to reach a certain level ("serious"), possibly excluding smaller risks. This represents a detailed three-limb suitability test as part of the proportionality test. Moreover, the measure has to be adequate ("which would not be countered by less restrictive procedures"). Thus in the context of the public security exemptions relating to military interests, the Court will apply a strict proportionality test including a specific three-limb suitability test. Furthermore, the Court emphasises the clear differentiation between the public security exemptions from the free movement regimes and defence exemptions from the Treaty as a whole, as indicated by the words "where the situation does not . . . fall within the scope of Article [347 TFEU]". This degree of scrutiny is appropriate for two reasons. First, in the context of the crucial free movement provisions all restricting measures have to be proportionate to ensure the functioning of the Internal Market. Secondly, the military interests of the Member States are sufficiently safeguarded by Articles 346 and 347 TFEU discussed in chapter 3. Thus there is no need to limit scrutiny in the context of the public security exemptions.[88]

3 Internal Market legal bases of the Defence Directive

According to the principle of conferred powers, the EU institutions can only enact secondary legislation when the Member States have authorised them to legislate in a particular field.[89] This requires a legal base in the Treaty. The legal bases for the Defence Directive are listed in the Preamble to Directive 2009/81/EC:

> Having regard to the [TFEU] and in particular Article [53 (1), and Articles 62 and 114] thereof, . . . Acting in accordance with the procedure laid down in Article [294] of the Treaty . . .

The other EU procurement Directives have exactly the same legal bases.[90] The crucial Article 114 TFEU provides:

[87] Case C-423/98, ibid., at para. 22.

[88] See M. Trybus, "The EC Treaty as an Instrument of European Defence Integration: Judicial Scrutiny of Defence and Security Exceptions" (2002) 39 *Common Market Law Review* 1347–72, at 1352–3.

[89] See Arts. 1(1) and 4(1) TEU.

[90] See the (beginnings of the) Preambles to Public Sector Directives 2004/18/EC and 2014/24/EU and the Utilities Directives 2004/17/EC and 2014/25/EU.

the following provisions shall apply for the achievement of the objectives set out in Article 26. The European Parliament and the Council shall, acting in accordance with the ordinary legislative procedure . . ., adopt a measure for the approximation of the provisions laid down by law, regulation or administrative action in Member States which have as their object the establishment and functioning of the internal market.

Article 114 TFEU is a residual provision which can only be used when there is no more specific legal base to attain the Internal Market, such as Articles 40, 50 and 53 TFEU.[91] With the exception of Article 53 TFEU, which is also expressly listed as a legal base for the Defence Directive, there is no more specific legal base in the Treaty. The legality of the use of Article 114 TFEU as a legal base for public procurement Directives is not controversial. No Member State or EU institution challenged the Defence Directive in an action for annulment for lack of legal base or for using the wrong legal base. Article 114 TFEU provides the institutions of the EU with a relatively wide legal base for Internal Market legislation, although the famous *Tobacco Advertising* judgment of the ECJ has shown that there are limits.[92] Moreover, the Preamble to the Defence Directive itself recognises that the defence exemptions and most importantly Article 346 TFEU, discussed in chapter 3, represent a limitation in this context. Again, the purpose of this legislation is to amplify and provide detail to the more general rules of the free movement regimes discussed above. A noticeable feature of Article 114 TFEU is that what is now called the ordinary legislative procedure in Article 294 TFEU allowing full "co-decision" of Council and European Parliament is used to enact legislation. This led to considerable amendments to the original Council text through the European Parliament, as will be explained where appropriate in the chapters of Part II of this book.

4 Conclusions

This chapter discussed the foundations of the Defence Directive in the EU free movement regimes of the TFEU, namely the free movement of goods in Article 30 TFEU, the free movement of services in Article 56 TFEU and the freedom of establishment in Article 49 TFEU. This included a discussion of the relevant regime-specific limitations to these freedoms in the public security dimensions of the derogations in Articles 36, 45(3), 52(1), 65(1)(b) and 72 TFEU. Moreover, this included a discussion of the Internal Market legal bases for the Defence Directive in Article 114 TFEU.[93] The chapter showed that the goods and

---

[91] See Craig and de Búrca, *EU Law*, *supra* note 6, at 590.

[92] Case C-376/98, *Germany* v. *European Parliament and the Council* [2000] ECR I-8419.

[93] In the Preamble of the Defence Directive, before para. 1, still "Articles 47 (2) and Article 55 and 95 [EC Treaty]" as the Directive dates from 13 July 2009 and the EC Treaty was replaced by the TFEU on 1 December 2009.

services regulated by the Defence Directive are subject to the free movement regimes of the TFEU, subject to exceptional circumstances which allow derogation from the Treaty on a case-by-case basis, situations which are subject to judicial review by the ECJ, and which need to be proportionate and proven by the Member State invoking them.

However, while the TFEU is clearly intended as an instrument of market integration including public procurement; it is not intended as an instrument of defence and security integration. First, this is clear from the lack of a legal base for such integration in the Treaty. Secondly, this is clear from a number of defence-specific exemptions in the TFEU which limit its market integrating function in areas where the Internal Market overlaps with the defence and national security interests of the Member States. As the Defence Directive covers exactly such an area, chapter 3 will provide an analysis of these defence-specific exemptions.

Defence derogations from the Treaty

Articles 346 and 347 TFEU

1 Introduction

As discussed in chapter 2, the Internal Market regimes of the TFEU on the free movement of goods and services apply to armaments and to other security goods and services, subject to narrowly defined and intensely scrutinised public security exemptions. However, with respect to armaments which are the central subject of this book, and also with respect to secrecy concerns and crisis situations, an additional set of derogations may apply. This chapter will discuss these defence-specific exemptions in the Treaty relating to armaments in Article 346(1)(b), to secrecy in Article 346(1)(a) and to crisis situations in Article 347 TFEU. This will include an analysis of the interpretation of these provisions provided by the ECJ, the European Commission, academia and Member State governments. A comprehensive understanding of the armaments exemption in Article 346(1)(b) TFEU will be particularly important since the main objective of the new Defence Directive is to reduce the cases in which this exemption is used in practice to establish an Internal Market for armaments and other security-sensitive goods and services.

The public security exemptions discussed in chapter 2 are superseded by the "national security" or "defence" exemptions in Articles 346 and 347 TFEU, containing specific derogations for armaments, secrecy and national security situations. The public security exemptions discussed in chapter 2, Article 36 TFEU for example, only apply to material not covered by Article 346(1)(b) TFEU and only to situations not covered by Article 347 TFEU. As will be explained in more detail below, a common feature of the national security exemptions is that in cases of "improper use" they can be subject to a special "enforcement" procedure under Article 348 TFEU.[1]

---

[1] Art. 348 TFEU reads: "[1] If measures taken in the circumstances referred to in Article 346 and 347 have the effect of distorting competition in the common market, the Commission shall, together with the State concerned, examine how these measures can be adjusted to the rules in the Treaty. [2] By way of derogation from the procedure laid down in Articles 258 and 259, the Commission or any Member State may bring the matter directly before the

Until the late 1990s the ECJ had shown a certain deference concerning Articles 346 and 347 TFEU. Even in *Johnston*, a judgment on all security exemptions, the Court considered it unnecessary to answer the specific question on Article 347 TFEU.[2] In *Aimé Richardt*[3] the Court, referring to *Johnston*, repeated the ruling on the narrow application of the exemptions in relation to Article 36 TFEU. However, following the Opinion of Advocate General Jacobs,[4] it considered it unnecessary to deal with Articles 346 and 347 TFEU. In *Werner*[5] and *Leifer*,[6] again, the Court, following the Opinion of Advocate General Jacobs,[7] considered it unnecessary to deal with the exemptions in the Treaty as there was a special provision in Article 11 (Export) Council-Regulation 2603/69/EEC.[8] In *Albore*[9] the Court, following the Opinion of Advocate General Cosmas, considered Article 347 TFEU not to apply to the case. Fortunately for the purposes of defence procurement, Article 346(1)(b) TFEU was the first and so far the only defence exemption that the Court dealt with specifically. The interpretation of this "armaments exemption" is obviously crucial for this book on the Directive on the procurement of armaments and other security products and services. Again, limiting the use of this exemption in practice is arguably the main operational or legal objective of the Defence Directive:

> The operational objective of the Commission is to limit the use of the exemption ... provided for in Article [346(1)(b) TFEU] to exceptional cases, in accordance with [Court of Justice] case law.[10]

A thorough understanding of the scope and limits of Article 346(1)(b) TFEU is a prerequisite for the understanding of the substantive rules of the Defence Directive discussed in Part II of this book, its unique scope, procedures, award

---

Court of Justice if it considers that another Member State is making improper use of the powers provided for in Articles 346 and 347. The Court shall give its ruling in camera."

[2] Case 222/84, *Marguerite Johnston* v. *Chief Constable of the Royal Ulster Constabulary* [1986] ECR 1651, [1986] 3 CMLR 240, at para. 60.

[3] Case C-367/89, *Criminal Proceedings against Aimé Richardt and Les Accessoires Scientifiques SNC* [1991] ECR I-4621.

[4] Case C-367/89, ibid., at para. 30.

[5] Case C-70/94, *Fritz Werner Industrie-Ausrüstungen GmbH* v. *Germany* [1995] ECR I-3189.

[6] Case C-83/94, *Criminal Proceedings against Peter Leifer and others* [1995] ECR I-3231.

[7] Cases C-83/94, ibid., and C-70/94, *supra* note 5, at para. 51.

[8] Regulation 2603/69/EEC [1969] OJ L324/25 as amended by Council-Regulation 3918/91/EEC [1991] OJ L372/3.

[9] Case C-423/98, *Alfredo Albore* v. *Italy* [2000] ECR I-5965.

[10] See Commission Staff Working Document, Annex to the Proposal for a Directive of the European Parliament and of the Council on the coordination of procedures for the award of certain public works contracts, public supply contracts and public services contracts in the field of defence and security, http://ec.europa.eu/internal_market/publicprocurement/docs/defence/impact_assessment_en.pdf [accessed 12 November 2013], at 3 and 31. See also Recitals 16–18 of the Defence Directive.

criteria and review mechanisms. Article 346 TFEU explains most of the differences to the rules of Public Sector Directive 2004/18/EC, which was the starting point when drafting the Defence Directive. Moreover, the armaments exemption limits the legal base for the Directive in Article 114 TFEU, as discussed at the end of chapter 2.

This chapter will discuss Article 346 TFEU followed by a brief discussion of the, for the purposes of this book, less important Article 347 TFEU. Article 346 TFEU consists of two national security exemptions: the armaments exemption in Article 346(1)(b) TFEU and the secrecy exemption in Article 346(1)(a) TFEU. It will be shown that compared to the public security exemptions from the Internal Market regimes of the Treaty discussed in chapter 2, the use of these exemptions can be subject to different pre-judicial and judicial review procedures and to a different standard of review. The exemptions in Article 346(1)(a) and 346(1)(b) TFEU are part of the sophisticated mechanism provided in the Treaty to balance the Internal Market and other interests of the Union with the national security interests of the Member States. This balancing mechanism allows its users, the Member States, the Commission and, if necessary, the ECJ to determine the borderline between the Internal Market and Member State competence in individual cases.

The purpose of this crucial chapter is to provide an understanding of the scope and interpretation of the fundamental derogation for the TFEU which determined the substance of the Defence Directive discussed in the chapters of Part II almost as much as its Internal Market objectives discussed in chapter 2. Moreover, it has to be understood as a provision limiting the scope of the Defence Directive discussed in chapter 6.

2 The armaments exemption of Article 346(1)(b) TFEU

The armaments exemption in Article 346(1)(b) TFEU[11] allows a Member State

> to take such measures as it considers necessary for the protection of the essential interests of its security which are connected with the production or trade in arms, munitions and war material.

The following sections of this chapter will discuss the interpretation of the various aspects of this exemption, starting with the notions of "arms, munitions, and war material" (section 2.1 below), the effect of the provision (section 2.2 below), its procedural requirements (section 2.3 below) and the special review procedure against its abuse in Article 348 TFEU (section 2.4 below).

---

[11] Ex Art. 296(1)(b) EC Treaty (Amsterdam and Nice) and ex Art. 223(1)(b) EEC/EC Treaty (Rome and Maastricht).

2.1 The list of armaments according to Article 346(2) TFEU

According to what was then Article 223(2) EEC[12] the Council had to draw a precise list of such "arms, munitions, and war material" to which what is now Article 346(1)(b) TFEU applies. The list has to be understood as an integral part of Article 346(1)(b) TFEU, detailing the words "arms, munitions, and war material" in the text of the Treaty provision. The legal status of this list is not clear. It is not one of the instruments defined in the Treaty and it is thus submitted that it is a *sui generis* instrument amplifying a notion of the TFEU. Inserting the list in Article 346(1)(b) TFEU itself would have made the provision very long, inadequately long for a founding treaty. Moreover, it might have prolonged the negotiations leading to the Treaties of Rome in 1957 as it might have led to disputes over individual items on the list. Hence it was adequate to move this question of detail to a later Council meeting in 1958. The difference between the list being stipulated in the Treaty itself, on the one hand, and being in a separate list to be decided on by the Council, on the other hand, is that in the earlier case amendments to the list could only have been decided by an Intergovernmental Conference. As the latter is the case, amendments are subject to a unanimous decision of the Council. Even in the European Defence Community Treaty[13] a similar list of armaments was stipulated in Annexes I and II to Article 107 of that Treaty rather than being included in the text of the Treaty itself.

[12] The current equivalent is Art. 346(2) TFEU which reads: "The Council may, acting unanimously on a proposal from the Commission, make changes to the list, which it drew up on 15 April 1958, of the products to which the provision of paragraph 1 (b) apply."

[13] Annex I to Art. 107 European Defence Community Treaty 1952: "1. *Weapons.* Small arms, machine guns, anti-tank weapons, artillery and mortars, anti-aircraft weapons and equipment for artificial fog, gas and flame-throwing. 2. *Ammunition and Rockets for all military purposes.* Ammunition for the above weapons, grenades, self-propelled missiles, torpedoes, mines and bombs of all types. 3. *Propellants and Explosives for Military Purposes.* The exemptions for civil use were listed. 4. *Armoured Equipment.* Tanks, armoured vehicles and armoured trains. 5. *All types of warship.* 6. *All types of military aircraft.* 7. *Atomic weapons.* 8. *Biological weapons.* 9. *Chemical Weapons.* 10. *Component parts only suitable for the construction of one of the items listed in groups 1, 2, 4, 5, 6 above.* 11. *Machines parts only suitable for the construction of one of the items listed in groups 1, 2, 4, 5, 6 above.*"

Annex II to Art. 107 EDC Treaty contained an additional list of atomic weapons; chemical weapons; biological weapons; long range missiles, guided missiles and influence mines; naval vessels other than minor defensive craft; and military aircraft. According to Art. 107(4)(a) and (b) EDC Treaty it was extremely difficult to obtain an export licence for any of these categories of weapons from the board of Commissioners. See Martin Trybus, *European Union Law and Defence Integration* (Oxford: Hart, 2005) at 39–42 on the defence economic regime of the EDC in general.

In 1958 the Council drew up this list of products to which Article 346(1)(b) TFEU applies.[14] There have been no amendments since then[15] and the list was often assumed outdated,[16] an assessment discussed further below. Products on this list are also called warlike or hard defence material, although these expressions are slightly misleading, as will be explained below. For a long time the list was not officially published[17] and the governments of the Member States had different attitudes regarding its confidentiality. Some governments and the Commission treated it as a confidential document. Other governments were happy to supply a copy to anybody interested. In the 1980s and 1990s it was produced in academic publications.[18] Hence it has been in the public domain. However, not everybody found it easy to get a copy. The problem with this half-secrecy was that governments could abuse Article 346(1)(b) TFEU by extending it to products which were not on the list. It is obviously difficult to argue against such a policy in practice without knowing the precise contents of the list.[19]

---

[14] Decision defining the list of products (arms, munitions and war material) to which the provisions of Art. 223(1)(b) – now Art. 296(1)(b) [under Lisbon Art. 346(1)(b)] – of the Treaty apply (doc. 255/58). Minutes of 15 April 1958: doc. 368/58 as cited in the Defence Directive in footnote 1 on [2009] OJ L216/77.

[15] Commission Answer to a Written Question 573/85 [1985] OJ C-269; Advocate General Jacobs in his Opinion in Case C-367/89, *Richardt, supra* note 3, at para. 30; P. Gilsdorf, "Les Reserves de sécurité du Traité CEE, à la lumière du Traité sur l'Union Europénne" (1994) *Revue du marché commun et l'Union europénne* 17, at 20.

[16] See, for example, the Commission's Green Paper on Defence Procurement, COM (2004) 608 final, at 7; Burkard Schmitt (ed.), *European Arms Cooperation: Core Documents*, Challiot Paper No. 59 (Paris: Institute of Security Studies of the European Union, 2003), at 10; Ramses A. Wessel, *The Foreign and Security Policy of the European Union: A Legal Institutional Perspective* (The Hague: Kluwer Law International, 1999), at 312; K. Eikenberg, "Article 296 (ex 223) E.C. and External Trade in Strategic Goods" (2000) 25 *European Law Review* 117, at 128; Wim F. van Eekelen, *The Parliamentary Dimension of Defence Procurement: Requirements, Production, Cooperation, and Acquisition*, Occasional Paper No. 5 (Geneva: Geneva Center for the Democratic Control of the Armed Forces, 2005), at 54: "list which by now is clearly obsolete".

[17] See Commission's Green Paper on Defence Procurement, ibid. Moreover the list cannot be found in the Official Journal of the EU (November 2013).

[18] See A. Courades Allebeck, "The European Community: From the EC to the European Union" in H. Wulf (ed.), *Arms Industry Limited* (Oxford University Press, 1993), at 214; Martin Trybus, *European Defence Procurement Law: International and National Procurement Systems as Models for a Liberalised Defence Procurement Market in Europe* (The Hague: Kluwer Law International, 1999), at 14–15 (footnote 41). It was also published in a publication of the Independent European Programme Group, the predecessor of the Western European Armaments Group of the Western European Union, called *Towards a Stronger Europe* (Brussels, 1987), today on www.assembly-weu.org/en/documents/sessions_ordinaires/rpt/2005/1917.php#P132_16717 [accessed 12 November 2013].

[19] See the thesis of Luke Butler, "Procurement Law as a Barrier to Transatlantic Defence Market Liberalisation", University of Birmingham (2014) (on file), ch. 2.

2.1.1 Armaments on the list

In 2001 in a written question a Member of the European Parliament asked the Council: "which products appear on the list of 15 April 1958 to which Article 296(1)(b) refers?"[20] In a reply the Council provided a version of the list:[21]

[List according to Article 346(2) TFEU]

1. Portable and automatic firearms, such as rifles, carbines, revolvers, pistols, sub-machine guns and machine guns, except for hunting weapons, pistols and other low calibre weapons of the calibre less than 7 mm.
2. Artillery, and smoke, gas and flame throwing weapons such as:
   (a) cannon, howitzers, mortars, artillery, anti-tank guns, rocket launchers, flame throwers, recoilless guns;
   (b) military smoke and gas guns.
3. Ammunition for the weapons at 1 and 2 above.
4. Bombs, torpedoes, rockets and guided missiles:
   (a) bombs, torpedoes, grenades, including smoke grenades, smoke bombs, rockets, mines, guided missiles, underwater grenades, incendiary bombs;
   (b) military apparatus and components specially designed for the handling, assembly, dismantling, firing or detection of the articles at (a) above.
5. Military fire control equipment:
   (a) firing computers and guidance systems in infra-red and other night guidance devices;
   (b) telemeters, position indicators, altimeters;
   (c) electronic tracking components, gyroscopic, optical and acoustic;
   (d) bomb sights and gun sights, periscopes for the equipment specified in this list.
6. Tanks and specialist fighting vehicles:
   (a) tanks;
   (b) military type vehicles, armed or armoured, including amphibious vehicles;
   (c) armoured cars;
   (d) half-tracked military vehicles;
   (e) military vehicles with tank bodies;
   (f) trailers specially designed for the transportation of the ammunition specified at paragraphs 3 and 4.
7. Toxic or radioactive agents:
   (a) toxic, biological or chemical agents and radioactive agents adapted for destructive use in war against persons, animals or crops;

---

[20] Written Question E-1324/01 by Bart Staes (Verts/ALE) to the Council, [2002] OJ C-364 E, 20 December 2001, at 85–6.

[21] For a more detailed discussion of this Council response see M. Trybus, "On the List According to Article 296 EC Treaty" (2003) 12 *Public Procurement Law Review* NA15–21.

    (b) military apparatus for the propagation, detection and identification of substances at paragraph (a) above;

    (c) counter-measures material related to paragraph (a) above.

8. Powders, explosives and liquid or solid propellants:

    (a) powders and liquid or solid propellants specially designed and constructed for use with the material at paragraphs 3, 4 and 7 above;

    (b) military explosives;

    (c) incendiary and freezing agents for military use.

9. Warships and their specialist equipment:

    (a) warships of all kinds;

    (b) equipment specially designed for laying, detecting and sweeping mines;

    (c) underwater cables.

10. Aircraft and equipment for military use.

11. Military electronic equipment.

12. Cameras specially designed for military use.

13. Other equipment and material.

14. Specialised parts and items of material included in this list insofar as they are of a military nature.

15. Machines, equipment and items exclusively designed for the study, manufacture, testing and control of arms, munitions and apparatus of an exclusively military nature included in this list.

Hence at least one version of the list has been easily accessible since then.[22] The Council published an "Extract of Council Decision 255/58 of 15 April 1958" on 26 November 2008.[23] According to the Commission's Guidance Note for the Defence Directive on *Field of Application* this is the relevant version:

> The 1958 list was translated in November 2008 into all languages of the EU and is publicly available since then.[24]

This suggests that the Council publication is the legally relevant version and implies that it is also the full version. However, the use of the term "extract" in the November 2008 Council publication suggests that this is not the full version. Moreover, it is submitted that the publication of an extract is no sufficient substitution for the publication in the OJ. The list is therefore still not

---

[22] Reply of 29 September 2001 to Written Question C-1324/01 of 4 May 2001 of Barts Staes (Verts) to the Council, [2001] OJ C-364E/85–6, see also at http://eur-lex.europa.eu/LexUriServ/LexUriServ.do?uri=OJ:C:2001:364E:0085:0086:EN:PDF [accessed 12 November 2013].

[23] Extract of the Council Decision 255/58 of 15 April 1958, document 14538/4/08 Rev 4, http://register.consilium.europa.eu/pdf/en/08/st14/st14538-re04.en08.pdf [accessed 12 November 2013].

[24] Commission Guidance Note *Field of Application*, at 4, footnote 11 with reference to the document cited in the previous footnote.

officially published.[25] Heuninckx therefore rightly calls this version "public but unpublished".[26]

There are a few comments to be made about these publicly available versions of the list.[27] First, the lists contained in the 2001 response and the 2008 extract are shorter and less detailed than those previously in the public domain.[28] There are more categories of weapons on the other lists. Moreover, categories such as warships (point 9), tanks (point 6) or firearms (point 1) are stipulated in more detail on these lists. An exception is artillery (category 2), which is more detailed on this list provided by the Council. Therefore the Council response and extract do not contain a complete version of the list. However, it is submitted that these variations do not amount to substantial differences. Most of the additional categories in previously accessible lists refer to spare parts and components of the main categories. Hence it is assumed that the list was not altered in substance. With regards to the 2001 response, the background to the variations might be a lack of meticulousness of the Council officials or *stagiaires* compiling the list for the response in Parliament. An indicator for this theory is that the category "aircraft and their devices for military purposes" in a previously published list "makes sense" whereas the related category 10 on the list provided in the parliamentary response "aircraft and equipment for military use" does not. The "equipment for military use" is meant to relate to "aircraft", hence the category should be named "aircraft and related equipment for military use". However, a look at the German[29] and French[30] versions of the list reveals that this is a case of a disputable English translation rather than a sloppy compilation of the list.[31] Another reason might be the intention not to go into too much detail in the context of a written answer given in the European Parliament. It cannot be assumed that the Council wanted to provide a tailored list.

Secondly, prima facie, category 13 on "other equipment and material" in the 2001 response represents an open category where the Council or the Member

---

[25] In April 2010 the United Kingdom Ministry of Defence published a similar version of the List, www.aof.mod.uk/aofcontent/tactical/toolkit/downloads/ecregs/ecregs_annd1.pdf [accessed in March 2011, no longer available on 12 November 2013].

[26] Baudouin Heuninckx, "The Law of Collaborative Defence Procurement through International Organisations in the European Union", PhD Thesis, University of Nottingham (2011), at 74, footnote 193 (on file).

[27] Most of the comments in this section were published before in Trybus, "On the List According to Article 296 EC Treaty", *supra* note 21.

[28] See *supra* note 17.

[29] "Luftfahrzeuge und *ihre* Ausrüstungen zu militärischen Zwecken [emphasis added]".

[30] "Aéronefs et *leurs* équipments à usage militaire [emphasis added]."

[31] As the list was drafted in 1958 it can be assumed that the German and French versions of this Council response are at least based on the original list. As the mainly English-speaking United Kingdom and the Republic of Ireland were not yet Member States of the European Communities, it is possible that the English version was specifically translated for the recent Council response.

States could add any type of product they could not think of when first compiling the list in 1958. This would undermine the exhaustive character of the list. This exhaustive character, however, is an essential part of the narrow interpretation of Article 346 TFEU. As explained in the context of the public security exemptions in chapter 2,[32] a narrow interpretation has to be applied to all exemptions from the Treaty as a wide interpretation could undermine the functioning of the Internal Market as a whole.[33] However, this first impression is only caused by the lack of detail of the list provided by the Council. On previously available versions of the list this category was just a heading for all kinds of material that could not be listed under other categories, such as parachutes or devices to cross waters.[34] The extract of the list published by the Council in 2008 differs from that in the answer to the written question of 2001 only in this point 13 "other equipment and material" (written question 2001, "other equipment" in the extract of 2008) where the detail in the form of subsections available in previously available versions of the list is provided.[35] Hence it is submitted that category 13 of the list provided by the Council in the 2001 response is not designed to undermine the exhaustive character of the list. The 2008 extract clarifies this.

Thirdly, the list is remarkably up-to-date for a document compiled in 1958. Most military equipment available to the armed forces of the Member States in 2004 is covered by one of the categories on this list. A stealth bomber, for example, is covered by category 10 "aircraft and equipment for military use". This shows that the categories are reasonably wide to accommodate technical progress in the military sector. The list is not outdated. Major changes were not and will not be necessary to take technological progress into account. This interpretation is confirmed by a reference to the list in Recital 10 to the Defence Directive:

> the list is generic and is to be interpreted in a broad way in the light of the evolving character of technology, procurement policies and military requirements which lead to the development of new types of equipment . . .

This does not contradict the narrow interpretation of the list advocated above. The list is exhaustive: material not stipulated in it is not covered by the

---

[32] At 73–6. [33] Case 222/84, *Johnston, supra* note 2, at para. 26.

[34] Parachutes and devices to cross waters appear to be out of place on a list of hard defence material. They seem to be dual-use material. As this type of dual-use material is on the list and all other material is not, this is another argument for the interpretation that only material on the list is covered by Art. 346(a)(b) TFEU. Dual-use material, with the exception of these two categories, is outside the ambit of the exception.

[35] Point 13: "Other equipment:
  (a) parachutes and parachuting equipment;
  (b) equipment for crossing watercourses specifically designed for military use;
  (c) electrically controlled searchlights for military use."

exemption.[36] Therefore Article 346(2) TFEU and the list it refers to are a limitation to Article 346(1)(b) TFEU.[37] An argument for this interpretation is that the wording of Article 346(2) TFEU clearly limits the application of Article 346(1)(b) TFEU to goods on the list. Moreover, the general rule from *Johnston* that exemptions need to be interpreted narrowly to protect the functioning of the Internal Market as a whole[38] requires the limitation of the provision to products stipulated on the list. The generic and broad interpretation in Recital 10 of the Defence Directive refers to items that are on the list, not to products that are not. The very concept of a list as part of an exemption indicates that it is exhaustive. Finally, Article 346(2) TFEU allows the Council to amend the list in case they consider it necessary to add another product. For such a case unanimity would be required.[39] A specific mentioning of the possible amendment of the list by the Council indicates its exhaustive character. A merely illustrative list does not need a special legal base for its amendment, as a piece of equipment would not have to be on the list in order to be covered.

2.1.2 Material not on the list

The crucial effect of the exhaustive character of the list is that "dual-use goods", materials that can be used for both military and civil purposes, are normally not on the list and therefore not covered by the exemption in Article 346(1)(b) TFEU.[40] This was also ruled by the General Court in the judgment of *Fiocchi*

---

[36] See Case T-26/01, *Fiocchi Munizioni SpA* v. *Commission of the European Communities* [2003] ECR II-3951, for details see below and Trybus, *European Law and Defence Integration, supra* note 17, at 249–50.

[37] Wessel, *supra* note 16, at 312.

[38] Case 222/84, *Johnston, supra* note 2, at para. 26. See also Case 13/68, *SpA Salgoil* v. *Italian Ministry of Foreign Trade* [1968] ECR 453, at 463, [1969] CMLR 181, at 192 and Case 7/68, *Commission* v. *Italy* [1968] ECR 633 at 644.

[39] Wessel, *supra* note 16, at 312.

[40] This was subject to debate. In Case C-70/94, *Werner, supra* note 5, the United Kingdom argued "that the list should not be regarded as exhaustive and that Article 223(1)(b) EC [now Article 296 (1) (b) EC] is capable of applying to products which were not included in that list". In contrast, France and Germany "considered that those provisions cannot be invoked in respect of products in 1958 pursuant to Article 223(2) EC [now Article 296(2) EC]", see the Opinion of Advocate General Jacobs, ibid., at para. 62. On the discussion on the applicability of Art. 296(1)(b) to dual-use goods see Eikenberg, *supra* note 16, at 125–8, who advocates that the provision does not apply to dual-use goods. See also the Commission in "The Challenges Facing the European Defence-related Industries: A Contribution for Action at European Level", COM (1996) 10 final, at 14; O. Lhoest, "La Production et la commerce des armes, et l'article 223 du traité constituant la Communauté européene" (1993) 26 *Revue belge de droit international* 176, at 184–5; Sue Arrowsmith, *The Law of Public and Utilities Procurement* (London: Sweet & Maxwell, 1996), at 858–9

Munizioni,[41] which is discussed further below. Examples of "dual-use goods", also sometimes referred to as "soft defence material", are transport aircraft, cross-country vehicles and tents.

It has been argued that the question of central significance was the criteria which determine the primary function of a product as either civil or military. Moreover, it has been argued that the absence of such criteria may result in an interpretative vacuum undermining the application of Internal Market law to the defence industries in practice.[42] However, it is suggested here that such criteria are not needed. The 1958 list according to Article 346(2) TFEU is exhaustive. The only criterion to differentiate hard defence material, to which Article 346(1)(b) TFEU applies, from any other material, to which it does not apply, is that 1958 list. Material not listed on the list is not covered by Article 346(1)(b) TFEU. Even the expression "hard defence material", understood as a legal category, is slightly misleading, although almost all of the material on the list is hard defence material. Due to the exhaustive character of the list, there could be a product that could clearly be classified as hard defence material but not on the 1958 list. Such a piece of hard defence material would not be covered by Article 346(1)(b) TFEU and could only be exempt through the public security exemption Article 36 TFEU discussed in chapter 2.[43] Similarly there could be a piece of civil or dual-use material on the list to which Article 346(1)(b) TFEU applied, such as "parachutes and devices to cross water" in category 13 of the list. Hence the only decisive factor is whether the product is on the list or not. The existence of the list does not leave room for an interpretative vacuum. A more accurate expression than "hard defence material" would be "material stipulated on the list according to Article 346(2) TFEU". However, as this is quite "a mouthful" the expression "hard defence material" shall be used in the remainder of this book.

---

and (2nd edn, 2005), at 243–4; Panos Koutrakos, *Trade, Foreign Policy, and Defence in EU Constitutional Law* (Oxford: Hart, 2001), at 184–6; and J.B. Wheaton, "Defence Procurement and the European Community: The Legal Provisions" (1992) 1 *Public Procurement Law Review* 432, at 434; W. Hummer, "Artikel 223" in Eberhard Grabitz and Meinrad Hilf (eds.), *Kommentar zum EWGV* (Munich: C. H. Beck Verlag, 1997) looseleaf, vol. II, Art. 223, at para. 12; Wessel, *supra* note 16; N. Emiliou, "Restrictions on Strategic Exports, Dual-use Goods and the Common Commercial Policy" (1997) 22 *European Law Review* 68, at 72.

[41] Case T-26/01, *Fiocchi Munizioni SpA* v. *Commission of the European Communities, supra* note 36, at para. 61.

[42] Koutrakos, *Trade, Foreign Policy, and Defence in EU Constitutional Law, supra* note 40, at 176 referring to Wheaton, "Defence Procurement and the European Community", *supra* note 40, at 434 and the approaches by various countries to distinguish military from dual-use products discussed by M. Bothe and T. Marauhn, "The Arms Trade: Comparative Aspects of Law" (1993) 26 *Revue belge de droit international* 20, at 27 *et seq.*

[43] At 70–82.

2.1.3 Military use: the *Agusta* case law and *Finnish Turntables*

Another related question of interpretation is whether it is sufficient for the application of Article 346(1)(b) TFEU for a relevant item to appear on the 1958 list, or whether additional requirements have to be met.

In 2008 the Court of Justice addressed this question in two Italian cases with a procurement context.[44] *Agusta*[45] concerned a consistent and long-standing Italian practice of directly awarding contracts for the purchase of Agusta and Agusta Bell helicopters for various military and civilian corps of the Italian State.[46] The fleets of the relevant corps are formed exclusively of such helicopters. None of them was purchased following a competitive tendering procedure at EU level. The Commission argued that the contracts should have been subject to a competitive procedure, in compliance with Article 6 of the old Supplies Directive 93/36/EC which was in force during the relevant period.[47] Italy argued, inter alia, that the supplies intended for the military corps are covered by the armaments exemption of Article 346(1)(b) TFEU and Article 3 Directive 93/36/EC. These exemptions applied because the helicopters in question were "dual-use items" serving both military and civilian purposes. After following the required pre-litigation procedure, the Commission brought actions under what is now Article 258 TFEU against Italy.

The second case, C-157/06, *Commission v. Italy*[48] concerned a ministerial decree requiring the direct award of helicopter contracts for certain units.[49] Hence a practice very similar to that in *Agusta* described above was required by decree. The adoption of this decree broadly coincided with the *Agusta* pre-litigation procedure.[50] Again, Italy put forward its "dual use"[51] and "technical specificity"[52] arguments.

---

[44] The following discussion of Cases C-337/05 and C-157/06 draws on the case note of the author in (2009) 46 *Common Market Law Review* 973–90.

[45] Case C-337/05, *Commission v. Italy* [2008] ECR I-2173.

[46] In *Agusta* these included the Corps of Fire Brigades, the Carabinieri, the Corpo Forestale dello Stato, the Coastguard, the Guardia di Finanza Revenue Guard Corps, the State Police and the Department of Civil Protection in the Presidency of the Council of Ministers.

[47] The then Public Supplies Directive 93/36/EC, [1993] OJ L199/1, now replaced by Directive 2004/18/EC of the European Parliament and the Council on the coordination of procedures for the award of public works contracts, public supply contracts and public service contracts, [2004] OJ L134/114.

[48] [2008] ECR I-7313.

[49] Decree No. 558/A/04/03/RR of the Minister for the Interior of 11 July 2003 authorising the derogation from the Community rules on public supply contracts in respect of the purchase of light helicopters for the use of police forces and the national fire service.

[50] P. McGowan, annotations on C-157/06 in (2009) 18 *Public Procurement Law Review* NA59, at NA61.

[51] Case C-157/06, *Commission v. Italy, supra* note 48, at para. 16.

[52] Case C-157/06, *Commission v. Italy*, ibid. at para. 18.

In *Agusta*, building on its previous case law on the matter discussed in chapter 2 and below in this chapter, the Court noted at the outset that the public security derogations Articles 36, 45, 52, 65, 72, 346 and 347 TFEU deal with exceptional and clearly defined cases. They cannot be interpreted as an inherent general exception excluding all measures taken for reasons of public security from Internal Market law.[53] They must be interpreted strictly.[54] The specific requirements of these provisions must be met. The recognition of the existence of a general exception without requirements would impair the binding nature of Internal Market law and its uniform application.[55] It is for the Member State which seeks to rely on those exceptions to furnish evidence that the exemptions in question do not go beyond the limits of such exceptional cases.[56]

The Court rejected the Italian argument based on the classification of the helicopters as dual-use items, serving both civilian and military purposes and therefore covered by Article 346(1)(b) TFEU. The products in question must be intended for specifically military purposes:

> It follows that the purchase of equipment, *the use of which for military purposes is hardly certain*, must necessarily comply with the rules governing the award of public contracts. The supply of helicopters to military corps for the purpose of civilian use must comply with those same rules [emphasis added].[57]

This interpretation is based on the clear wording of the provision. The Court then applied this interpretation to the case at hand. It was uncontested between the parties that the helicopters in question were certainly for civilian use and possibly for military use. Hence their military use was "hardly certain" in the sense of the interpretation and Article 346(1)(b) TFEU could not properly be invoked.[58] The judgment in C-157/06 "mirrored" that in the *Agusta* with regards to Article 346(1)(b) TFEU.[59]

As ruled by the ECJ in the *Johnston*[60] judgment discussed in chapter 2,[61] a wide interpretation of the security exemptions in the TFEU would undermine the

---

[53] Case C-337/05, *supra* note 45, at para. 43.

[54] Case C-157/06, *supra* note 48, at para. 23.

[55] Case C-337/05, *supra* note 45, at para. 43. Already established in: Case 222/84, *Johnston, supra* note 2, at para. 26; Case C-273/97, *Sirdar* v. *The Army Board* [1999] ECR I-7403, [1999] 3 CMLR 559, at para. 16; Case C-285/98, *Kreil* v. *Germany* [2000] ECR I-69, at para. 16; and Case 186/01, *Alexander Dory* v. *Germany* [2003] ECR I-2479, at para. 31, cited by the Court in C-337/05, *Agusta*.

[56] Case C-337/05, *supra* note 45, at para. 44 and C-156/06, *supra* note 48, at para. 23 citing Case C-414/97, *Commission* v. *Spain* [1999] ECR I-5585, [2000] 2 CMLR 4, at para. 22.

[57] Case C-337/05, ibid., at para. 47. Similar in Case C-157/06, ibid., at para. 26.

[58] Case C-337/05, *supra* note 45, at para. 49 and Case C-157/06, *supra* note 48, at paras. 26–8.

[59] McGowan, *supra* note 50, at NA61.   [60] Case 222/84, *supra* note 2.   [61] At 73–6.

functioning of the Internal Market by eroding its prohibitions. The narrow interpretation is therefore a logical and necessary consequence of the establishment of an Internal Market. In *Agusta* and also in Case C-157/06 the Court reiterates this principle with respect to the armaments exemption in Article 346(1)(b) TFEU, a provision it had somewhat neglected in the past. The judgment in *Spanish Weapons*[62] discussed below had been the only ruling specifically addressing this exemption before *Agusta* and C-157/06.[63] Together these three judgments show that the Court's deference with respect to the armaments exemption has limits.

The second part of Article 346(1)(b) TFEU limits the derogation:

> provided, however, that such measures do not alter the conditions of competition in the common market regarding products which are not intended for specifically military purposes.

It is this part of the derogation the Court's interpretation is based on.[64] It is intended to protect the Internal Market for civil goods when Member States derogate from the Treaty in relation to armaments. This recognises a feature of the relevant industries that already existed in the 1950s when the provision was drafted and is even more important today: defence and civil industries cannot always clearly be distinguished. This was discussed in chapter 1.[65] Many products have both defence and civil dimensions and most European companies producing armaments also manufacture civil products.[66] Hence measures taking armaments outside the field of application of Internal Market law may easily impact on civil goods. The second part of Article 346(1)(b) TFEU prohibits such an impact. However, alternative interpretations are possible. A wide *de minimus* interpretation to this part of the provision, whereby a measure applying to products not intended for military purposes could still be legal if it did not adversely affect competition in the market for such products, was outlined by Heuninckx.[67] However, in *Agusta* and

---

[62] Case C-414/97, *supra* note 56.

[63] See the overview of previous cases avoiding Art. 346(1)(b) TFEU in *supra* notes 2, 3, 5 and 6.

[64] Case C-337/05, *supra* note 45, at para. 47: "*It is clear from the wording of that provision* that the products in question must be intended for specifically military purposes. It follows that the purchase of equipment, *the use of which for military purposes is hardly certain*, must necessarily comply with the rules governing the award of public contracts [emphasis added]."

[65] At 21–2.

[66] See, for example, Arrowsmith, *The Law of Public and Utilities Procurement*, *supra* note 40, at para. 4.62.

[67] B. Heuninckx, "A Note on Case Commission v. Italy (Case-337/05) (Agusta Helicopters Case)" (2008) 17 *Public Procurement Law Review* NA187, at NA190. Heuninckx also gives a clarifying example: "This could for instance be the case if the effect of the procurement in question is negligible compared to the size of the market (e.g. procurement without

Case C-157/06 the Court provided a stricter interpretation.[68] Measures regarding products not intended for specifically military purposes cannot be justified on the basis of Article 346(1)(b) TFEU. The ECJ clarified the narrow interpretation of Article 346(1)(b) TFEU by establishing a "hardly certain" criterion, whereby material the military use of which is not certain is not within the scope of Article 346(1)(b) TFEU. However, the meaning of this criterion is not entirely clear and still leaves room for two alternative interpretations.

A contrario the "hardly certain" criterion could be interpreted as meaning that where the military use of a product is certain it would be covered by the exemption, irrespective of whether it is on the 1958 list of armaments. This would mean that dual-use products are a hybrid category where the degree of certainty of their military use determined their inclusion in the notion of "arms, munitions, and war material" in Article 346(1)(b) TFEU. The fact that the Court did not even mention the 1958 list in Agusta and Case C-157/06 supports this interpretation. The judges had to be aware of the list. It is specifically mentioned in the Opinion of Advocate General Mazák who submitted that "Article [346 TFEU] is applicable only to products that are enumerated on the list ..."[69] This had also been established by the General Court (then Court of First Instance) in Fiocchi Munizioni.[70] Hence, as argued above, the list is not an illustration but forms part of the Treaty provision. Moreover, according to the Advocate General, Article 346(1)(b) TFEU does not apply to dual-use goods.[71] A "degree of certainty" interpretation would make the proper application of Article 346(1)(b) TFEU very difficult or even impossible in practice, thereby facilitating abuse. Furthermore, this interpretation would ultimately be contra legem. With the 1958 list of armaments, which through Article 346(2) TFEU forms an integral part of Article 346(1)(b) TFEU, the Council as the competent "legislator" identified by the Treaty has defined the categories of equipment to which the armaments exemption applies. This was done in great detail. There is therefore no room for the Court to assume a hybrid category of dual-use goods beyond the list in the context of which the Court could rule on the certainty of their military use. Finally, this interpretation would be inconsistent with the narrow interpretation of Article 346(1)(b) TFEU as an exemption to expand its application beyond the 1958 list.

competition of one single civilian-type helicopter by the military of an EU Member State at the normal market price, when in the meantime 100 such helicopters are sold to airlines in the Common Market each year)." It should be pointed out, however, that Heuninckx is not himself advocating such an interpretation; he is merely discussing it as a possibility.

[68] Ibid.
[69] Case C-337/05, supra note 45, Opinion Advocate General Mazák, delivered on 10 July 2007, at para. 58.
[70] Case T-26/01, supra note 36, at para. 61.
[71] Case C-337/05, Opinion Advocate General Mazák, supra note 45 delivered on 10 July 2007, at para. 59.

Alternatively, the Court might have used the "hardly certain" criterion in the context of Item 10 on the 1958 list of armaments, which contains the category of "aircraft and equipment *for military use* [emphasis added]". Based on its wording, Item 10 actually requires a two-stage test. First, the material in question has to qualify as aircraft and, secondly, it has to be intended for military use. This two-stage test is not required for most other items on the list, such as tanks (Item 6a) or warships (Item 9a), arguably because these materials can only be used for warlike purposes, which makes their military use absolutely certain.[72] In contrast to the "certainty of military use" interpretation outlined above, the Court's "hardly certain" criterion would have been applied to the military use of an item on the 1958 list, in other words "inside" rather than "outside" the regime of the list. This interpretation would be consistent with the narrow interpretation of Article 346(1)(b) TFEU since it does not expand but rather limits its application beyond the list. Moreover, it makes sense since, in the context of aircraft in Item 10, their military use needs to be established for the list and thus Article 346(1)(b) TFEU to apply. The interpretation is also supported by a point in footnote 31 of the Advocate General's Opinion in which he argues that "products which appear on the list and are not intended for specifically military purposes do fall under [EU law]". Hence, at least for some of the products on the list, their military purpose needs to be established in addition to the fact that they are listed.

A strong argument against this interpretation is that the ECJ did not mention the 1958 list in its recent judgments, except the most recent of *Finnish Turntables* discussed below. This raises the question why, similar to *Spanish Weapons* discussed below, the list, which through Article 346(2) TFEU forms part of Article 346(1)(b) TFEU, was not mentioned. One reason could be that the list is still not officially published and at the time of the judgment was handled as a quasi-confidential document.[73] As discussed above, the Council published an extract of the list only later in the same year 2008.[74] Moreover, the judicial review of measures taken on the basis of Article 346(1)(b) TFEU should actually be conducted on the basis of Article 348 TFEU, which accommodates confidentiality, most notably through an *in camera* ruling. Similar to the scenario in *Spanish Weapons* discussed below, the analysis of Article 346(1)(b) TFEU had to be conducted in the context of Article 258 TFEU

[72] There are many categories on the list that could have non-military applications, or could influence the civil market: item 1 (small arms), item 3 (their ammunition), item 7.b (detection material for radiation does not depend on military or civilian applications), item 8.b (military explosives: many explosives are used by the military and in mining, etc.), 13.a (parachutes). Thanks to Baudouin Heuninckx (Belgian Air Force) for bringing these examples to my attention. The military use of these items would have to be determined as a second stage after determining that they are included on the 1958 list.

[73] See Trybus, *European Union Law and Defence Integration, supra* note 13, at 143–54.

[74] The judgment is of 8 April 2008 and the extract publication of November 2008.

proceedings. The Court might have been reluctant to mention a quasi-confidential list outside the Article 348 TFEU proceedings. As mentioned above and pointed out in the Opinion of Advocate General Mazák,[75] a version of the list can be found in the minutes of the European Parliament.[76] Hence it can hardly be considered confidential.[77] However, as pointed out above, this version did not entirely correspond to other versions.[78] The Court could have only applied a list-based analysis if there had been a publication of its official version. However, it can safely be assumed that the Court did have access to the official version of the list before its judgment, which supports the interpretation that the Court made a reference to the list with the "hardly certain" criterion without specifically mentioning it.[79]

The fact that the Court did not specifically mention the 1958 list in *Agusta* is regrettable because this compromises clarity. One commentator even suggested that the question whether dual-use goods could be covered by the exemption in Article 346(1)(b) TFEU was still open.[80] Since the list is an integral part of Article 346(1)(b) TFEU through Article 346(2) TFEU, however, the crucial question is not whether a certain item is considered hard defence, dual-use or civil material, but whether it is on the list or not. The important distinction is between listed and non-listed items. If the item is not on the list, the question whether Article 346(1)(b) TFEU applies is answered in the negative. This interpretation is reinforced by the fact that there are dual-use items on the list and that for listed items such as aircraft their military use needs to be determined in addition to the fact that they are listed, as outlined above. As the list is therefore so crucial for Article 346(1)(b) TFEU, the fact that the Court did not mention it is regrettable, if understandable due to the reasons discussed above. This also emphasises the rule-of-law and transparency arguments for the Council to finally allow the official publication of the 1958 list of armaments, which, for reasons that are not clear, in early 2014 still had not happened.

The most recent 2012 judgment of *Finnish Turntables*[81] finally contains clear references to the 1958 list of armaments. The ECJ started its Article 346(1)(b) TFEU analysis with the question whether the turntables acquired by the Finnish Defence Forces Technical Research Centre were covered by one of the items of the list. The Research Centre had not procured these turntables on the basis of the Public Sector Directive because it assumed they were excluded from the

---

[75] See footnote 29 of the Opinion, *supra* note 45.

[76] See Written Question E-1324/01 by Bart Staes (Verts/ALE), *supra* note 22.

[77] See also the publication of the list in academic publications, *supra* note 18.

[78] Trybus, "On the List According to Article 296 EC Treaty", *supra* note 21.

[79] See also the Advisory Opinion of Advocate General Mazák, at paras. 58–61.

[80] Annotations of Heuninckx, "A Note on Case Commission v Italy", *supra* note 67, at NA191.

[81] Case C-615/10, *Insinööritoimisto InsTiimi Oy* v. *Puolustusvoimat*, judgment of 7 June 2012, nyr.

Directive on the basis of its Article 10 and the Treaty on the basis of the armaments exemption. This "list-based" stage of the analysis, based on the 2008 version in the Council document mentioned above, resulted in the turntables being covered by points 15 read with points 11 and 14 of the list. Then the Court moved to the question of the effect of a listed item, although intended for specifically military purposes, also presenting "possibilities for essentially civilian applications". It ruled that such an item could justify derogation from the TFEU and Public Sector Directive applicable at the time

> only if that material, by virtue of its intrinsic characteristics, may be regarded as having been specially designed and developed, also as a result of substantial modifications, for such [military] purposes . . .

This latest judgment of the ECJ is significant because it is the first so clearly differentiating between a first stage of the analysis of Article 346(1)(b) TFEU in which it is considered whether the item in question is on the 1958 list of armaments and a second stage which considers whether the national security interests of the Member State justify derogation.[82] Moreover, the judgment builds on and further differentiates the *Agusta* case law discussed above by clarifying that material which is clearly intended for military purposes but which has also possibilities for essentially identical civilian purposes has to meet certain requirements to be considered covered by Article 346(1)(b) TFEU. The material in question has to be specifically designed and developed, inter alia, through "substantial modifications" for military purposes "by virtue of its intrinsic characteristics". This is a high threshold. Dual-use material covered by one of the items on the 1958 list of armaments needs to be specifically designed, developed and modified for military purposes. This rule is based on the strict interpretation of all derogations from the Treaty, including Article 346(1)(2) TFEU.[83] Inside the first list-based stage, *Finnish Turntables* introduces a two-part analysis of Article 346(1)(b) TFEU. Moreover, by providing a first stage of analysis based on the 1958 list of armaments it clarifies the importance of the list for the interpretation of the derogation, clarification that was missing from all previous cases including *Agusta*. First of all, an item has to come under one of the categories on the list to even be considered. Furthermore, the judgment clarifies the requirements for material intended for military purpose but with potential for civilian use to be considered under the armaments derogation. Finally, the ruling is the latest confirmation of the fact that the deference of the ECJ regarding Article 346 TFEU has limits.

According to its Recital 10, the Defence Directive is to apply to "military equipment" which "should be understood in particular as the product types

---

[82] Ibid., see para. 34 and then the analysis in the following paragraphs.

[83] Ibid., at para. 35 citing Case C-284/05, *Commission* v. *Finland* [2009] ECR I-11705, at para. 46 and the case law cited there.

included in the list". However, as will be explained in detail in chapter 6, the scope of the Directive will be wider. For the purposes of the interpretation of Article 346 TFEU, which is the subject of this chapter, the interpretation of the list discussed above is the relevant issue.

2.1.4 Armaments intended for exports: *Fiocchi Munizioni*

Again, all exemptions from the TFEU need to be interpreted narrowly.[84] In *Fiocchi Munizioni*[85] the General Court appears to have narrowed the scope of Article 346(1)(b) TFEU even further. The case concerned an Italian manufacturer of arms and munitions who had made a formal complaint to the Commission concerning subsidies Spain had granted to a Spanish State-owned undertaking producing arms, munitions and tanks. The Commission started bilateral communications with Spain on the issue within the context of Article 348 subparagraph 1 TFEU. Spain argued that the activities of the Spanish undertaking in question were covered by Article 346(1)(b) TFEU and recognised in Spanish law as being in the interest of the national defence of Spain and that its production was intended principally to provide for the requirements of the Spanish armed forces. Moreover, these activities were also subject to the Spanish law on State secrets. The Italian manufacturer brought an action for failure to act against the Commission under what is now Article 265 subparagraph 3 TFEU after the latter had not taken any action for over a year.[86] The Spanish manufacturer had successfully participated in invitations to tender in other Member States including Italy. The perception that this resulted in distortions of competition had motivated the Italian manufacturer to take action.

Apart from a couple of procedural points discussed below, the Court made a number of references to the argument of the applicant that the production of hard defence material intended for export rather than to satisfy domestic needs was outside the protection of essential security interests within the meaning of Article 346(1)(b) TFEU.[87] However, the Court did not establish this rule in *Fiocchi Munizioni*. An argument for this interpretation is that, based on the general rule that exemptions have to be interpreted narrowly, a Member State can only consider the production and trade of hard defence material intended for its own armed forces as necessary for the protection of its essential security interests. In the current geopolitical situation in Europe, the equipment of the

---

[84] Case 222/84, *Johnston, supra* note 2, at para. 26.

[85] Case T-26/01, *Fiocchi Munizioni SpA* v. *Commission of the European Communities, supra* note 36.

[86] Art. 265 subpara. 4 TFEU reads: "Any natural or legal person may, under the conditions laid down in the preceding paragraphs, complain to the Court of Justice that an institution of the Community has failed to address to that person any act other than a recommendation or an opinion."

[87] Case T-26/01, *supra* note 36, at para. 77 referring back to para. 8, see also para. 63.

armed forces of Germany, for example, cannot be an essential security interest of Spain.[88] However, it is submitted that Article 346(1)(b) TFEU covers measures concerning hard defence material intended for export. First, as mentioned above, the Court did not establish a rule excluding hard defence material intended for export from the application of the exemption in *Fiocchi Munizioni*. The impression that the Court considered this argument was partly due to the State aid context of this case, which will be discussed further in chapter 4.[89] Secondly, the Court did emphasise that Article 346(1)(b) TFEU has a general effect on the entire TFEU.[90] This means that, if successfully invoked, the provision allows derogation from the entire Treaty, without exception. Excluding measures regarding hard defence material intended for exports from the application of Article 346(1)(b) TFEU on a general basis would contradict this general nature of the provision. There is no segment in the wording of the exemption that suggests it being limited to hard defence material intended exclusively to satisfy domestic needs. Thirdly, the Court pointed out that the provision confers on the Member States a particularly wide discretion in assessing the needs of their security.[91] A Member State might consider a national defence industrial capability to be essential for its national security interests. That national defence industrial capability might not be economically viable, if dependent on the requirements of the armed forces of that Member State alone. Exports to other Member States might be necessary to keep that company in business. This general effect of the provision and the wide discretion of the Member States need to be differentiated from the necessity of such a measure and the judicial scrutiny applied to it by the EU courts. The former are strong arguments against a general exclusion of measures regarding hard defence material intended for export from the application of Article 346(1)(b) TFEU, not against such exclusion in an individual case. However, since this was not expressly settled in *Fiocchi Munizioni*, the generally strict interpretation of derogations from the TFEU might exclude listed armaments intended for export from the field of application of Article 346(1)(b) TFEU.

2.2 The effect of Article 346(1)(b) TFEU

There has been considerable disagreement as to the effect of Article 346(1)(b) TFEU. Voices in favour of a limited interpretation of Article 346(1)(b) TFEU argued that the exemption needed to be narrowly construed and was not automatic and categorical but must be expressly invoked by Member States

---

[88] However, in the 1930s, for example, France might have had a security interest in supplying arms to Czechoslovakia and Poland. Thanks to Anthony Arnull for pointing this out to me when commenting on an earlier version of this chapter.
[89] At 176–82.   [90] Case T-26/01, *supra* note 36, at para. 58.   [91] Ibid.

who wish to rely on it.[92] The TFEU applied to hard defence material unless a Member State could prove a situation justifying derogation. To use a "house" metaphor: armaments are inside the house (of the Internal Market) but there is a door (Article 346(1)(b) TFEU) through which the Member States can take some of them outside, provided certain conditions are met. The act of taking them out of the house through the door can be challenged in the ECJ.

Many Member States on the other hand have interpreted the provision as a general, categorical and automatic exemption of hard defence material from the application of the TFEU.[93] According to them they retained *unlimited* jurisdiction regarding these products and their national security concerns automatically overrule the objectives of the Internal Market. Using the "house" metaphor again, according to this interpretation armaments are always outside the house (of the Internal Market); thus there is no need to take them

---

[92] Most notably the Commission, see "The Challenges Facing the European Defence-related Industry", COM (96) 10 final, at 14 (following Arrowsmith, *The Law of Public and Utilities Procurement, supra* note 40, at 861–3); Green Paper Defence Procurement, COM (2004) 608 final, at 5. See also Answer to Written Question 1088/89 [1991] OJ C-130/2 as cited by Koutrakos, *Trade, Foreign Policy, and Defence in EU Constitutional Law, supra* note 40, at 176; Lhoest, "La Production et la commerce des armes", *supra* note 40, at 183, Eikenberg, "Article 296 (ex 223) E.C. and External Trade in Strategic Goods", *supra* note 16, at 119 and the references referred to in her footnote 8; Emiliou, "Restrictions on Strategic Exports, Dual-use Goods and the Common Commercial Policy", *supra* note 40, at 59.

[93] For example France: *La Notion de sécurité en droit européen*, ministère de la défense, secreteriat général pour l'administration, direction des affaires juridiques (DAJ), études juridiques No. 17 September 1999 at 7: "Cependant, une partie des Etats membres, et notament la France, on jusqu'ici considéré qu'en vertu de cette disposition [Art. 296(1)(b) EC (ex 223)] les règels du traité ne sont pas applicables au secteur de l'armement." This opinion has been put forward by the respective Member States in all cases referred to in this article. See the United Kingdom in Case 222/84, *Johnston, supra* note 2, at 1671: "The EEC Treaty itself leaves intact the power of the Member States to take such measures as they may consider necessary or expedient for the above mentioned purposes [safeguarding national security or for protecting public safety or public order] as is shown by the 'safeguard clauses' contained in Articles 36, 48, 66, 223 and 224 [now 36, 45, 52, 346 and 347]." According to Advocate General la Pergola's Opinion in Case C-285/98, *Sirdar, supra* note 56, at para. 10: "the French and Portuguese Governments submit that the activities of the armed forces are intimately linked to the concept of sovereignty, which the Member States have, in accordance with the Treaty, 'shared' only in certain areas other than defence. Defence, therefore, remains within their exclusive competence". At footnote 9 the Advocate General reports that "The French Government, in particular, takes the view that defence should be treated in the same way as the other functions traditionally reserved to States, such as justice, diplomacy, public finances and the police." In Case C-285/98, *Kreil, supra* note 56, at para. 12 it is stated: "According to it [the German Government], Community law does not in principle govern matters of defence, which form part of the field of common foreign and security policy and which remain within the Member State's sphere of sovereignty" and at para. 13 "the Italian and United Kingdom Governments, which presented oral argument, argue basically that decisions concerning the organisation and combat capacity of the armed forces do not fall within the scope of the Treaty".

outside. Article 346(1)(b) TFEU is not a door but a description of the where-abouts of armaments: outside the house.

The different interpretations are highly significant for both the regulation of defence procurement and for its practice. If the narrow interpretation as argued, inter alia, by the Commission applied, then armaments were "normally" inside the Internal Market, including the Public Sector Directive, subject to the possibility of derogation on a case-by-case basis. There would be no room for any abstract rules outside the framework of the Internal Market; the EU would have occupied the field. If the wider interpretation as practised by some Member States applied, then armaments were not only "normally" but always outside the EU Internal Market. Regulation could be introduced outside the Internal Market, including the frameworks discussed in chapter 5; the EU would *not* have occupied the field and would not have the competence to do so.

Due to the lack of an interpretation, the exemption was open to abuse and successfully used accordingly.[94] Abuse took mainly two forms. One was to extend the exclusion to goods that are not on the 1958 list. The other was to protect the national "hard defence" markets without justification, thereby leading to separate national markets for "arms, munitions, and war material" in practice. In the Communication "A Strategy for a Stronger and More Competitive European Defence Industry" the Commission reported that about 85 per cent of defence procurement was always exempt from the Treaty via Article 346 TFEU.[95] However, if the wide interpretation of the provision outlined above is correct, this situation was intended by the creators of the Treaties and is therefore perfectly legal under Internal Market law.

There are several reasons for the lack of an authoritative interpretation over several decades. First, the EEC Treaty was introduced in 1957 after the unsuccessful attempt to create the European Defence Community in 1954.[96] This initiative had failed because of opposition in some Member States caused by concerns about their sovereignty, especially in France. Therefore the EEC and EC Treaties were widely considered to completely exclude any notion of a common regime or policy on defence issues. Article 223(1)(b) EEC, now Article 346(1)(b) TFEU was considered a manifestation of this general exclusion.

---

[94] S. Mezzadri, *L'Ouverture des marchés de la défense: enjeux et modalités*, Occasional Paper No. 12 (Paris: Institute for Security Studies of the Western European Union, February 2000), at 5.

[95] COM (2007) 764 final. According to the 2013 Communication "A New Deal for European Defence: Towards a More Competitive and Efficient Defence and Security Sector", COM (2013) 542 final, at 41, from 2008 to 2010 contracts worth €4 billion were published on the Tenders Electronic Daily (TED) website of the OJ indicating procurement on the basis of Public Sector Directive 2004/18/EC. That is only around 1.5% of the total defence procurement expenditure in that period.

[96] See Trybus, *European Union Law and Defence Integration*, *supra* note 13, at 47–9.

Secondly, this historical background is connected to the decades of reluctance of the ECJ to interpret the exception. This reluctance facilitated abuse. Perhaps the Court did not want to jeopardise the acceptance of its judicial activism in other areas by avoiding this politically particularly sensitive provision. Moreover, courts of law, not only the ECJ, generally show a greater degree of deference in cases involving foreign affairs and defence and an armaments exemption is either a part of or very close to these policy fields. However, the provision was not at issue in many cases anyway. Thus there was probably also a reluctance of the Commission to bring an action in cases involving Article 346(1)(b) TFEU. This reluctance could have been motivated by the search for a "clear case". The Commission might have wanted a safe chance to win a precedent that provides a narrow interpretation to limit the application of the provision in practice. However, the enforcement cases discussed below and certain publications indicate that the Commission has been taking a more active approach to abuses of Article 346 TFEU over the last few years.

Finally, cases involving defence also involve secrecy. Therefore the Commission finds it difficult to detect and prove abuses in practice. Attempts to amend or abolish Article 346(1)(b) TFEU have not been successful.[97] The provision remained untouched in Maastricht, Amsterdam, Nice and Lisbon. The ill-fated 2004 Constitutional Treaty also contained this exclusion,[98] although the European Convention had discussed deletion.[99]

---

[97] Klepsch-Report, E. Klepsch, *European Armaments Procurement Co-operation* (Luxembourg, 1978); Greenwood-Report, D. Greenwood, *European Technological Co-operation and Defence Procurement* (Brussels, 1979); Tindemanns-Report, L. Tindemanns in A. Drown, *A Single European Arms Industry? European Defence Industries in the 1990s* (London, 1990), at 77–8. Aalto considers abolition impossible but amendment more feasible, see E. Aalto, "Interpretations of Article 296" in D. Keohane (ed.), *Towards a European Defence Market*, Chaillot Paper No. 13 (Paris: Institute for Security Studies, European Union, 2008), at 18.

[98] Art. III-436 of the Constitutional Treaty (version of 13 October 2004).

[99] See the "Contribution on 'European Defence'" made by Lamberto Dini, Brussels, 26 September 2002, in Jean-Yves Haine, *From Laeken to Copenhagen, European Defence: Core Documents*, Chaillot Paper No. 57 (Paris: Institute of Security Studies of the European Union, 2003), at 205: "It is also worth asking whether it would not be desirable to revise Article 296 of the European Community Treaty, which excludes armaments from the scope of the single market." The last half of the sentence reveals an understanding of the provision as an automatic exemption of armaments from the scope of the Treaty. See also Dominique de Villepin and Joschka Fischer, "Joint Proposal", Prague, 21 November 2002 in J.-Y. Haine, ibid., at 217: "La France et l'Allemagne proposent d'inscrire dans le Traité: les fonctions d'une politique européenne d'armement, dont la création progressive d'un marché européen d'armement, moyennant des procédures spécifiques, notamment d'une adaption de l'article 296 du TCE." However, the ministers did not specify how the provision should be adapted. See on more detail on the Constitutional Treaty: Trybus, *European Union Law and Defence Integration, supra* note 13, at 342–7.

Excluding certain types of material from the application of the Treaty is hard to justify. As discussed in chapter 1,[100] the example of the USA and her large and competitive defence equipment market shows that the benefits of an Internal Market, such as economies of scale and synergy effects, are especially prevalent in the defence sector. It is nebulous how the national security of Member States would *permanently* be compromised in an Internal Market for hard defence material. Most of them are allies in NATO, they cooperate in most major weapons development programmes and there is no piece of major defence equipment without foreign components. National security appears to be a mere excuse to protect non-competitive industries. However, extreme situations in which such an Internal Market could compromise the national security of a Member State are thinkable, for example limiting measures on extremely sensitive goods or during crisis situations. It is precisely this type of situation the national security derogations of the TFEU are intended for.

2.2.1 Not necessary for national security: *Spanish Weapons* and beyond

As discussed above, the ECJ and arguably the Commission avoided the armaments exemption for a long time. However, in a seminal judgment of 1999 the Court defined the application of Article 346(1)(b) TFEU in favour of a narrow interpretation. *Spanish Weapons*[101] involved a Spanish law exempting exports and intra-EU transfers of hard defence material from value-added tax (VAT). An EU Directive subjects all exports, imports and intra-EU transfers to VAT. During the eventual Court proceedings Spain submitted that its national legislation complied with EU law, in view in particular of what is now Article 346(1)(b) TFEU and that the Spanish law must be understood as having been adopted on the basis of that provision. Exemption from VAT constituted a necessary measure for the purposes of guaranteeing the achievement of the essential objectives of its overall strategic plan and, in particular, to ensure the effectiveness of the Spanish armed forces. However, this line of argument was not credible: it looked like Spain wanted to give its developing defence industries a boost by reducing the prices of its products by the VAT rate. For the Commission to take action in this case was possibly not only motivated by the availability of a clear case but also by the fact that the law in question affected the revenue of the Union.[102]

---

[100] At 29–30.

[101] Case C-414/97, *supra* note 56. See M. Trybus, "On the Application of the E.C.-Treaty to Armaments" (2000) 25 *European Law Review* 633–8; M. Trybus, "The Recent Judgment in Commission v. Spain and the Procurement of Hard Defence Material" (2000) 9 *Public Procurement Law Review* NA99–105.

[102] A share of VAT contributes to the budget of the EU institutions, in addition to Member State contributions, the income tax of the employees of the institutions, and third-country exports.

A similar factual background featured in the *Military Exports* cases of 2009 and 2010 when the ECJ ruled in a series of enforcement cases against a number of Member States.[103] These cases concerned the Union's own resources, a consideration which, as in the 1999 case, might explain the motivation of the Commission to bring these enforcement proceedings, at least in part. In these cases against Denmark, Finland, Germany, Greece, Italy, Portugal and Sweden the Member States had, in violation of the relevant secondary laws,[104] exempted imports of military material from customs duties and had refused to calculate and pay the resources of the EU component of the customs duties which were not collected because of that exemption. During the pre-litigation procedures the Member States relied on Article 346(1)(b) TFEU to justify the exemption of the exports of military materials from customs duties.

In *Spanish Weapons* the Court, not being able to avoid Article 346(1)(b) TFEU because it constituted the only substantive legal argument, referred to their ruling in *Johnston* discussed above and for the first time applied it directly to the exemption in Article 346(1)(b) TFEU. Thus they decided in favour of a limited interpretation advocated by the Commission and others. Returning to the "house" metaphor, armaments are inside the house and Article 346(1)(b) TFEU is a door through which Member States may take them outside under certain circumstances. On the basis of this general rule of a limited interpretation the Court considered that

> In the present case, . . . Spain has not demonstrated that the exemptions provided for by the Law [of 1987] are *necessary* for the protection of the essential interests of its security . . . It follows that the VAT exemptions are not *necessary* in order to achieve the objective of protecting the essential interests of the security of . . . Spain.[105]

The ECJ shuts the door in the face of Spain who may not take armaments outside the house. The judgment in *Spanish Weapons* is significant in that it confirms that the Court has the power to review the decision of a Member State to invoke Article 346(1)(b) TFEU, including a review of the justification. This was the first time this was done in relation to one of the national security

---

[103] Case C-284/05, *Commission v. Finland, supra* note 83; Case C-294/05, *Commission v. Sweden* [2009] ECR I-11777; Case 387/05, *Commission v. Italy* [2009] ECR I-11831; Case C-409/05, *Commission v. Greece* [2009] ECR I-11859; Case C-461/05, *Commission v. Denmark* [2009] ECR I-11887; Case C-38/06, *Commission v. Portugal* [2010] ECR I-1569; Case C-239/06, *Commission v. Italy* [2009] ECR I-11913.

[104] Arts. 2 and 9–11 of Council Regulation (EEC, Euratom) No. 1552/89 of 29 May 1989, implementing Decision 88/376/EEC, Euratom on the system of the Communities' own resources (OJ 1989 L155/1), as amended by Council Regulation (EC, Euratom) No. 1355/96 of 8 July 1996 (OJ 1996 L175/3; "Regulation No. 1552/89"), and the same articles of Council Regulation (Euratom, EC) No. 1150/2000 of 22 May 2000 implementing Decision 94/728/EC, Euratom on the system of the Communities' own resources (OJ 2000 L130/1).

[105] Case C-414/97, *supra* note 56, at para. 22, emphasis added.

derogations in Articles 346 and 347 TFEU. The Court rejected the use of a provision designed to protect the national security of the Member States. The ruling was possible and unavoidable as Spain provided such a clear and manifest case.

In the *Military Exports* case law of 2009 and 2010 introduced above, after reiterating the principles of the crucial paragraph 22 of *Spanish Weapons*, and after explaining that the Member States have the burden of proof that a situation justifying the use of Article 346 TFEU exists[106] and that the Member States in question had failed to produce that proof, the Court ruled:

> [Member State] has not shown that the conditions *necessary* for the application of Article [346 TFEU] are satisfied [emphasis added].[107]

While there are certain nuanced differences from the earlier case, it is submitted that these seven recent judgments confirm the crucial ruling of *Spanish Weapons*.

2.2.1.1 Intensity of scrutiny   The intensity of the scrutiny applied by the Court is a crucial issue. It is argued here that the use of the word "necessary"[108] in these 1999, 2009 and 2010 judgments amounts to scrutiny in the form of a proportionality test in relation to Article 346(1)(b) TFEU.[109] This does not necessarily mean that the Court applied the same level of scrutiny as it did in relation to Article 36 TFEU in *Campus Oil*,[110] discussed in chapter 2.[111] As pointed out by de Búrca, the proportionality test offers a "spectrum ranging from a very deferential approach, to quite a rigorous and searching examination of the justification for a measure".[112] In the context of all the exemptions designed to accommodate security, the Court applies the proportionality test to different degrees of intensity, leaving differently wide margins of discretion

---

[106] A question discussed in more detail below.

[107] Case C-284/05, *Commission* v. *Finland, supra* note 83, at para. 54; Case C-294/05, *Commission* v. *Sweden, supra* note 103, at para. 52; Case C-372/05, *Commission* v. *Germany, supra* note 103, at para. 77; Case C-387/05, *Commission* v. *Italy, supra* note 103, at para. 54; Case C-409/05, *Commission* v. *Greece, supra* note 103, at para. 59; Case C-461/05, *Commission* v. *Denmark, supra* note 103, at para. 60; Case C-38/06, *Commission* v. *Portugal, supra* note 103, at para. 71; Case C-239/06, *Commission* v. *Italy, supra* note 103, at para. 55.

[108] Case C-414/97, *supra* note 56, at para. 22, emphasis added. Advocate General Saggio also used the word in the same sense (at para. 12, referred to by the Court at para. 23).

[109] Other possible elements of scrutiny are legitimate expectations, non-discrimination and the emergent principle of transparency.

[110] Case 72/83, *Campus Oil Limited* v. *Minister for Industry and Energy* [1984] ECR 2727, at 2764, [1984] 3 CMLR 544.

[111] At 79–80.

[112] G. de Búrca, "The Principle of Proportionality and its Application in EC Law" (1993) 13 *Yearbook of European Law* 105 at 111.

to the Member States. In relation to the public security exemptions from the Internal Market regimes the test is applied strictly, leaving a relatively narrow margin of discretion to the Member States. However, *Campus Oil* and *Belgian Coastal Photography*[113] have shown that this public security margin is widened in situations close to national security and defence. This was discussed in chapter 2.[114] Article 347 TFEU is at the other end of the spectrum leaving a maximum margin of discretion to the Member States.[115] This will briefly be discussed below. Article 346(1)(b) TFEU is between these two extremes but closer to the latter provision. Since there can be a more deferential approach to proportionality as well as a more rigorous one, there is no need for an alterative test.[116]

As the exemption from VAT (*Spanish Weapons*) and the exemption from export duties (*Military Exports*) were manifestly unnecessary, the decisions do not support the assumption that a very strict scrutiny was applied. This scrutiny leaves a wide margin of political discretion to the governments of the Member States.[117] The question is whether they acted within the ambit of that discretion, whether they acted arbitrarily or in bad faith. What can be said for sure regarding the Court's scrutiny in the context of Article 346(1)(b) TFEU is that it will consider a measure disproportionate when (1) it is clearly unsuitable to promote national security and national security is put forward in bad faith; (2) when the Member State has arbitrarily chosen a measure which is more detrimental to the Internal Market than necessary; or (3) when the Member State has manifestly failed to balance the two. Neither *Spanish Weapons* nor *Military Exports* are authority for a deeper scrutiny as can be found in judgments where a public security exemption was invoked. It can be argued that due

---

[113] Case C-251/01, *Commission v. Belgium* [2003] ECR I-11859.   [114] At 76–82.

[115] See in detail: Trybus, *European Union Law and Defence Integration, supra* note 13, at 188–9.

[116] Aris Georgopoulos, suggests an alternative "manifest unsuitability test" in his PhD Thesis, "European Defence Procurement Integration: Proposals for Action within the European Union", University of Nottingham (2004), at 120–2. This alternative interpretation on the intensity of scrutiny applied by the Court was formulated before the 2006 Interpretative Communication, the 2008 *Agusta* case law and the recent *Military Exports* cases. Similarly, Panos Koutrakos suggests that the Court would only "seek to establish whether the argument put forward by the national Government is unreasonable", see *Trade Foreign Policy and Defence in EU Constitutional Law* (Oxford: Hart, 2011), at 189–91 and most recently in *The EU Common Foreign and Security Policy* (Oxford University Press, 2013), at 268.

[117] This was later confirmed by the Court of First Instance in Case T-26/01, *Fiocchi Munizioni SpA v. Commission of the European Communities, supra* note 36, at para. 58 where it was stated: "Article 296 (1) (b) EC confers on the Member States a particularly wide discretion in assessing the needs receiving such protection [measures taken for the protection of the essential interests of its security]."

to the subject matter of national security the level of intensity of the Court's scrutiny had and has to be "low" or "light".

First, intensity has to be "light" because the decision to exempt defence exports from VAT or other duties is a policy choice. In cases involving the restriction of individual rights, scrutiny will be rigorous, as proportionality is a necessary component of the recognition of such rights.[118] However, as was explained in the context of the discussion of proportionality in chapter 2,[119] policy choices are the reserve of the executive and legislative branches of government (division of powers dimension). In "certain specific policy contexts" including national security there is generally a higher degree of judicial deference[120] or "self restraint".[121]

Secondly, connected to the division of powers dimension just discussed, in the field of military security it is the government supported by the military staff which has the responsibility, training and expertise to take decisions (competence dimension). Their judgement cannot easily be substituted by a court of law.

Thirdly, in the constitutional system of the EU matters of defence and military security are primarily attributed to the Member States and not to the Union[122] ("federal" dimension). Thus, if the Court applied a proportionality test, it only considered the law in *Spanish Weapons* and the practices in *Military Exports* to be disproportionate because it represented a clearly unsuitable and manifestly inappropriate measure to ensure national security. In the context of Article 346(1)(b) TFEU a State measure will only be ruled out in clear and manifest cases where the measure is wholly unreasonable and disproportionate.[123] In less clearly established and manifest cases the Court is likely to be more cautious. However, it also needs to be emphasised that while defence and military security are clearly competences of the Member States, these Member States clearly conferred the regulation of the free movement of goods and

[118] Paul Craig and Gráinne de Búrca, *EU Law: Text, Cases, and Materials*, 5th edn (Oxford University Press, 2011), at 546.

[119] At 75–82.

[120] De Búrca, "The Principle of Proportionality and its Application in EC Law", *supra* note 112, at 111.

[121] Expression of N. Pourbaix, "The Future Scope of Application of Article 346 TFEU" (2011) 20 *Public Procurement Law Review* 1–8, at 4.

[122] De Búrca, "The Principle of Proportionality and its Application in EC Law", *supra* note 112, at 111.

[123] Advocate General Jacobs on Art. 347 TFEU in Case C-120/94 R, *Commission v. Greece (FYROM)* [1996] ECR I-1513, at para. 46. P. Koutrakos, "Is Article 297 EC 'A Reserve of Sovereignty'" (2000) 37 *Common Market Law Review* 1339; M. Trybus, "At the Borderline between Community and Member State Competence: The Triple-Exceptional Character of Article 297 EC" in T. Tridimas and P. Nebbia (eds.), *EU Law for the 21st Century: Rethinking the New Legal Order*, 2 vols. (Oxford: Hart, 2004), II, 137.

services to the EU. As discussed in chapter 2,[124] armaments are a military matter but they are also "goods" in the sense of the EU Internal Market.

2.2.1.2 Proportionality There are arguments for the assumption that a proportionality test was applied in *Spanish Weapons* and *Military Exports*. The term "necessary" implies a balance between the objective of a measure and its negative side effects. The use of this word in certain Treaty provisions led to the very establishment of the proportionality principle in EU law.[125] In *Spanish Weapons* the Court refers to the ruling in *Johnston* in which no differentiation between the security-type exemptions in the Treaty is made but only the public security exemptions from the Internal Market regimes were discussed.[126] In the cases of *Kreil* and *Sirdar* the Court applied the proportionality test in relation to the notion of public security, again without differentiating between the security-type exemptions of the Treaty.[127] In *Military Exports* the Court followed a similar line of argument including *Sirdar*, *Kreil* and *Dory*, which through *Spanish Weapons* leads more specifically to Article 346 TFEU.

Finally, as explained in chapter 2,[128] proportionality is a crucial aspect of the rule of law and the EU and all the Member States are founded on the rule of law as enshrined in the Preamble to the TEU (Lisbon) and its Article 2. Moreover, there is no doubt regarding the importance of the principle of proportionality being a requirement in and to be met by EU legislation and ECJ case law. Hence, it is argued, first, that if the ECJ has jurisdiction then there is no alternative to the application of the proportionality test and, secondly, that the flexibility of proportionality allows adapting the required standard of review to any exemption, policy field and situation.[129]

---

[124] At 63–4.

[125] Craig and de Búrca, *EU Law: Text, Cases, and Materials, supra* note 118, at 371–2.

[126] Case 222/84, *supra* note 2, at para. 26.

[127] Case C-273/97, *Kreil, supra* note 55, at para. 26, similar in Case C-285/98, *Sirdar, supra* note 55, at para. 25. However, the Court only said that no general exclusion of security-related matters could be deduced from these exemptions. This does not necessarily mean that there is no differentiation between the two groups of exemptions and that the proportionality test will be applied equally to the second group.

[128] At 76–9.

[129] Pourbaix, "The Future Scope of Application of Article 346 TFEU", *supra* note 121, at 7 argues that "[as] an important difference from the usual analysis of an exemption from the internal market rules, the [Court] has so far never applied a test of proportionality to a Member State's decision to reply on art. 346 TFEU. In other words, the [Court] has never gone so far as to consider whether a Member State's decision to exclude the application of the EU Treaties, in the basis of art. 346 TFEU, to a restrictive measure deemed necessary for the protection of that Member State's security interests was proportionate to the attainment of the security interests at stake, in the sense that no other, less restrictive measure would have been suitable to achieve that objective." This is not convincing. First, the proportionality test is not always applied in all its three parts. The second part of

However, there are possible arguments against the application of a proportionality test which need to be addressed. They relate to the wording, the *effet utile* and the special review procedure for Article 346(1)(b) TFEU.

2.2.1.2.1 The wording of the Treaty   First, Article 346(1)(b) TFEU allows a Member State to take measures "as *it* considers necessary for the essential interests of its security [emphasis added]". Thus, prima facie, the wording supports the "necessity" of the measure to be determined by the Member States alone.[130] It could be argued that if the Court were to decide otherwise, it would be against the wording of the Treaty and the words of a treaty always form the foundation of its interpretation.[131]

The comparison with the wording of the Internal Market derogations, such as Article 36 TFEU, is of no help since the word "justified" rather than the expression "necessary" is used in those provisions. However, the wording in Article XXI (b) of the General Agreement on Tariffs and Trade (GATT)[132] is similar to Article 346(1)(b) TFEU. The earlier served as a model for the latter. Moreover, the ECJ considers the GATT "to be relevant for the purpose of interpreting [an EU] instrument governing international trade".[133] In the famous *Nicaragua* case,[134] the International Court of Justice compared the wording of Article XXI GATT with that of Article XXI(d) of the 1956 US–Nicaragua Treaty of Friendship, Commerce and Navigation (hereafter "Friendship Treaty").[135] The Court emphasised that the latter provision speaks

---

necessity does not have to be applied to apply the proportionality test, the first part of "suitability" will often be sufficient. Secondly, even when the second part of "necessity" is applied, the Court does not always consider which alternative measures would have been at the disposal of the Member State. In the context of national security it will often not be appropriate for the Court to produce such alternatives. In *Commission* v. *Spain* the Court clearly used the word "necessity" repeatedly.

[130] Pourbaix considers this to be one of the possible interpretations and the interpretation that "may well prevail in future cases". This assessment is based on the special nature of defence and national security "lying at the heart of an EU Member State's sovereignty", see "The Future Scope of Application of Article 346 TFEU", *supra* note 121, at 7.

[131] In relation to the interpretation of the TFEU this principle was already established in *Van Gend en Loos* v. *Nederlandse Administratie der Belastingen* [1963] ECR 1, at 12, [1963] CMLR 105, at 129. For treaties in general see Arts. 31 and 32 of the 1969 Vienna Convention of the Law of Treaties, 1155 UNTS 331.

[132] Art. XXI GATT (also Art. XIV *bis* General Agreement on Trade in Services GATS and Art. 73 Agreement on Trade Related Aspects of Intellectual Property Rights TRIPS): "Nothing in this Agreement shall be construed . . . (b) to require any contracting party from taking any action which it considers necessary for the protection of its essential security interests . . ."

[133] Case C-83/94, *Leifer*, *supra* note 6, at para. 24.

[134] Military and Paramilitary Activities in and against Nicaragua (*Nicaragua* v. *USA*), Merits, 1986 ICJ-Reports 14, 116 para. 222 (27 June).

[135] Art. XXI of the Treaty of the Friendship Treaty: "1. The present Treaty shall not preclude the application of measures: . . . (d) necessary to fulfil the obligations of a Party for the

simply of "necessary" measures, not of those considered by the parties as such. This different wording means, *a contrario*, that the Court could scrutinise the necessity of the measure under the Friendship Treaty.

However, the decision still leaves room for the interpretation of Article XXI GATT as far as the justiciability of "necessity" is concerned. In *Nicaragua* the ICJ did not interpret Article XXI GATT but only the provision in the Friendship Treaty. The wording of the latter in contrast to the earlier supported its interpretation. However, it does not exclude the justiciability of measures taken under Article XXI GATT.[136] Thus the wording of Article XXI GATT, which is very similar to Article 346(1)(b) TFEU, does not exclude a court from reviewing "necessity". Moreover, in contrast to the GATT, Article 348 subparagraph 2 TFEU makes clear that there is at least some form of review to be exercised by the ECJ. Finally, the low intensity of the scrutiny suggested here would leave a wide margin of discretion to the Member States thereby respecting the wording of the Treaty. Thus, it is submitted that in the crucial paragraph 22 of *Spanish Weapons* the Court did not refer to the word "necessary" in Article 346(1)(b) TFEU.

In the recent 2009 and 2010 *Military Exports* cases against a number of Member States the ECJ used the word "necessary" with yet another angle. After reiterating the principles of the crucial paragraph 22 of *Spanish Weapons* and after explaining that the Member States have the burden of proof that a situation justifying the use of Article 346 TFEU exists[137] and that the Member States in question had failed to produce that proof, the Court ruled:

> [Member State] has not shown that the conditions *necessary* for the application of Article [346 TFEU] are satisfied [emphasis added].[138]

Here the word "necessary" appears to be used in the context of having to satisfy the burden of proof requirements of the exemption. However, in the following paragraph of each of the *Military Exports* judgments, the Court continues:

> In the light of those considerations, a Member State cannot be allowed to plead the increased cost of military material because of the application of

maintenance or restoration of international peace and security, or necessary to protect its essential security interest."

[136] C. Schloemann and S. Ohloff, "'Constitutionalisation' and Dispute Settlement in the WTO: National Security as an Issue of Competence" (1999) 93 *American Journal of International Law* 424, at 443 (footnote 104, last para.).

[137] A question discussed in more detail below.

[138] Case C-284/05, *Commission v. Finland*, *supra* note 83, at para. 54; Case C-294/05, *Commission v. Sweden*, *supra* note 103, at para. 52; Case C-372/05, *Commission v. Germany*, *supra* note 103, at para. 77; Case C-387/05, *Commission v. Italy*, *supra* note 103, at para. 54; Case C-409/05, *Commission v. Greece*, *supra* note 103, at para. 59; Case C-461/05, *Commission v. Denmark*, *supra* note 103, at para. 60; Case C-38/06, *Commission v. Portugal*, *supra* note 103, at para. 71; Case C-239/06, *Commission v. Italy*, *supra* note 103, at para. 55.

customs duties on imports of such material from third countries in order to avoid, at the expense of other Member States who collect and pay the customs duties on such imports, the obligations which the principle of joint financing of the Community budget imposes on it.[139]

This is connected to the burden-of-proof requirements but in essence a point of substance: the costs of military material cannot make the exemption from customs duties on imports *necessary*. Moreover, a few paragraphs back the same group of judgments also clarify the use of the word "necessary" in the paragraphs cited in footnote 138 of this chapter:

> As regards, more particularly, Article [346 TFEU], it must be observed that, *although* that Article refers to measures *which a Member State may consider necessary* for the protection of the essential interests of its security . . . , that Article *cannot* however be read in such a way as to confer on Member States a power to depart from the provisions of the Treaty *based on no more than reliance on those interests* [emphasis added].[140]

While this paragraph leads to the later burden-of-proof point cited above, it is expressly addresses necessity as a standard of review. If the Member States were allowed to derogate from the Treaty on the basis of Article 346 TFEU merely by relying on their national security interests, then the "necessity" would be determined by them alone and not by the ECJ in the context of judicial review. There would be no room for proportionality or any other tests to be applied by the Court. The use of the word necessary in *Spanish Weapons*, the *Agusta* case law and the 2009 and 2010 *Military Exports* cases would refer to "necessary" as considered by the Member States provided in Article 346(1)(b) TFEU. As based on these judgments mere reliance on national security interests is not allowed, there is and has been judicial review on whether a measure is "necessary" by the ECJ. This reinforces the point made above that the "necessary" in *Spanish Weapons* is not the "necessary" in Article 346(1)(b) TFEU.

---

[139] Case C-284/05, *Commission v. Finland, supra* note 83, at para. 55; Case C-294/05, *Commission v. Sweden, supra* note 103, at para. 53; Case C-372/05, *Commission v. Germany, supra* note 103, at para. 78; Case C-387/05, *Commission v. Italy, supra* note 103, at para. 55; Case C-409/05, *Commission v. Greece, supra* note 103, at para. 60; Case C-461/05, *Commission v. Denmark, supra* note 103, at para. 61; Case C-38/06, *Commission v. Portugal, supra* note 103, at para. 72; Case C-239/06, *Commission v. Italy, supra* note 103, at para. 56.

[140] Case C-284/05, *Commission v. Finland, supra* note 83, at para. 47; Case C-294/05, *Commission v. Sweden, supra* note 103, at para. 45; Case C-372/05, *Commission v. Germany, supra* note 103, at para. 70; Case C-387/05, *Commission v. Italy, supra* note 103, at para. 47; Case C-409/05, *Commission v. Greece, supra* note 103, at para. 52; Case C-461/05, *Commission v. Denmark, supra* note 103, at para. 53; Case C-38/06, *Commission v. Portugal, supra* note 103, at para. 64; Case C-239/06, *Commission v. Italy, supra* note 103, at para. 48.

2.2.1.2.2 Effet utile of Article 346 (and Article 347) TFEU Secondly, the inclusion of Articles 346 *et seq.* TFEU in addition to the Internal Market exemptions suggests that the creators of the Treaty wanted to include a separate set of derogations.[141] It could be argued that if proportionality applied, these circumstances could be dealt with in the context of the Internal Market exemptions discussed in chapter 2; Articles 346 and 347 TFEU would be superfluous. They would be deprived of their *effet utile*.[142] In other words, in order to safeguard the *effet utile* of the provisions the test applied by the Court in *Spanish Weapons* and *Military Exports* has to be interpreted as different to a proportionality test. However, first, the *effet utile* of the derogations in Articles 346 and 347 TFEU is taken into account by the low intensity of scrutiny suggested above. Secondly, even with the application of scrutiny, Articles 346 and 347 TFEU still form a second and separate set of derogations because Article 348 subparagraph 2 TFEU offers the possibility of subjecting the review of their use to a distinct procedure. Finally, Articles 346 and 347 TFEU apply to the Treaty as a whole, including but going beyond the Internal Market regimes which are subject to regime-specific public security exemptions, applying to relevant regimes on, inter alia, competition law and State aid which do not have regime-specific security exemptions.[143] The application of the defence exemptions to these latter regimes alone would constitute the *effet utile* and *raison d'être* of the provisions. They would not be superfluous and therefore there is no *effet utile* argument against the application of a proportionality test to their use.

2.2.1.2.3 The special review procedures of Article 348 subparagraph 2 TFEU Finally, the special procedure for reviewing abuse of Articles 346 *et seq.* TFEU in Article 348 subparagraph 2 TFEU could be interpreted as indicating that the creators of the Treaty wanted these exemptions to be subject to a different kind of scrutiny from the Internal Market exemptions. The judgments in *Johnston, Salgoil, Kreil* and *Sirdar* merely say that no exemption excludes security issues completely from the application of the Treaty. None of these cases involved Articles 346 *et seq.* TFEU directly. Thus they do not rule out a treatment of the defence exemptions different from that of the free movement public security exemptions.

However, it is submitted that the purpose of Article 348 subparagraph 2 TFEU is not to introduce a different level of scrutiny. First, the level of scrutiny,

---

[141] Advocate General Cosmas in Case C-423/98, *Alfredo Albore, supra* note 9, dealing with what is now Art. 347 TFEU.

[142] Pourbaix calls this the *raison d'être* of Art. 346 TFEU: "the insistence of the drafters of the Treaties to maintain the exclusion must mean that it does not simply duplicate arts 36, 52, and 62 TFEU, but should rather be viewed as a very exceptional measure, subject to its own regime", see "The Future Scope of Application of Article 346 TFEU", *supra* note 121, at 8.

[143] See on these Trybus, *European Union Law and Defence Integration, supra* note 13, ch. 8.

including the full proportionality test applied in the context of the free movement public security exemptions, was developed by the ECJ within the limits of the objectives and principles of the Treaties, not by the Member States as creators of the Treaties. In 1957 the then six Member States did not make any assumptions on the scrutiny to be applied by the Court and if they did they clearly did not include this in the text of the Treaty. This text, again, remained unchanged in Maastricht, Amsterdam, Nice and Lisbon with regards to all security exemptions.

Secondly, in *Spanish Weapons* the enforcement procedure in what is now Article 258 TFEU and not the special enforcement procedure in Article 348 subparagraph 2 TFEU was used. This was because the Spanish Government invoked Article 346(1)(b) TFEU only during the Court hearings and not during the pre-litigation procedure.[144] Thus it was simply too late. It is possible that the Commission would have initiated Article 348 subparagraph 2 TFEU proceedings, had Spain invoked the provision earlier on. However, the use of the word "may" in Article 348 subparagraph 2 TFEU indicates that the use of this procedure, rather than those of Articles 258 and 259 TFEU, is not obligatory in any case. Also during the litigation stages of the 2009 and 2010 *Military Exports* cases, the regular enforcement action of Article 258 TFEU was used.[145] Germany and Greece questioned the admissibility of the Article 258 TFEU enforcement actions because, as they had relied on Article 346 TFEU, the Commission could not bring an action on the basis of Article 258 TFEU but had to use the special procedure provided for in the second subparagraph of Article 348 TFEU. However, according to the Court, the Commission's objective in this action was to obtain a declaration of a failure to fulfil obligations under the relevant secondary law.[146] Article 348 TFEU is applicable only if the Commission alleges improper use of the powers provided for in Articles 346 and 347 TFEU.[147] This shall be discussed further below.

The major differences from the enforcement procedure in Article 258 TFEU are that there is another kind of pre-judicial stage in Article 348 TFEU proceedings and that the public is excluded. The former difference is partly due to the urgency of these situations and their political sensitivity. Thus the

---

[144] Case C-414/97, *supra* note 56, at para. 18.
[145] Case C-284/05, *Commission v. Finland, supra* note 83, at paras. 18–23; Case C-294/05, *Commission v. Sweden, supra* note 103, at paras. 18–26; Case C-372/05, *Commission v. Germany, supra* note 103, at paras. 18–27; Case C-387/05, *Commission v. Italy, supra* note 103, at paras. 18–27; Case C-409/05, *Commission v. Greece, supra* note 103, at paras. 18–22; Case C-461/05, *Commission v. Denmark, supra* note 103, at paras. 18–27; Case C-38/06, *Commission v. Portugal, supra* note 103, at paras. 18–25; Case C-239/06, *Commission v. Italy, supra* note 103, at paras. 18–28.
[146] Arts. 2 and 9–11 of Regulations 1552/89/EEC and 1150/2000/EC.
[147] Case C-372/05, *Commission v. Germany, supra* note 103, at paras. 28–35; Case C-409/05, *Commission v. Greece, supra* note 103, at paras. 23–8.

bilateral consultations according to Article 348 subparagraph 1 TFEU are less formalised than the pre-judicial part of Articles 258 and 259 TFEU proceedings.[148] There is no formal notification and no reasoned opinion. The procedure has a stronger diplomatic emphasis thereby taking account of the fact that the sovereignty of the Member States over defence and security issues was not transferred to the EU and that the latter does not have the capacity to shoulder this particular responsibility. In contrast to Article 346 TFEU, in the context of Article 347 TFEU the Member States also have the opportunity to put forward their arguments during the consultations.[149] Moreover the public is excluded from Article 348 subparagraph 2 TFEU proceedings in order to take the national security and secrecy interests of the Member States into account.[150] This suggests that exclusion of the public and the accommodation of the Member State responsibility for security and defence in a different pre-judicial stage, rather than the introduction of a different kind of scrutiny, are the purpose of Article 348 subparagraph 2 TFEU.

The general approach of the ECJ to subject measures taken under Article 346(1)(b) TFEU to scrutiny is welcomed. It reduces the possibilities of abuse, as Member States have to justify protective measures thereby possibly facilitating a liberalised market for defence products.[151] In theory, Member States, being aware of the possibility of scrutiny, might refrain from using the provision too easily. However, as discussed in the introduction to this book and above, before the introduction of the Defence Directive the possibility of judicial review was not a very powerful deterrent in practice. This was due to many factors, including a perceived lack of clarity of the interpretation of Article 346 TFEU and the scarcity of enforcement action against Member States in relevant cases.

2.2.2 Burden of proof

According to *Spanish Weapons* it is for the relevant Member State to prove a situation covered by Article 346(1)(b) TFEU:

> it is for the Member State which seeks to rely on those exemptions to furnish the evidence that the exemptions in question do not go beyond the limits of such cases.[152]

---

[148] Trybus, *European Union Law and Defence Integration, supra* note 13, ch. 4, at 132–4 on Art. 258 TFEU proceedings.

[149] Ibid., ch. 6, at 178–82.

[150] According to Art. 28 of the Statute of the Court of Justice of the European Community as amended by Council-Decision 94/993/EEC OJ [1994] L379/1 and the Treaty of Amsterdam, the Court can decide against Court hearings for serious reasons anyway. By derogation from Art. 34 of the Statute not all parts of the judgment have to be read in public.

[151] See also the later discussion of Art. 346(1)(a) TFEU below.

[152] Case C-414/97, *supra* note 56, at para. 22.

This ruling, putting the burden of proof on the Member States, was confirmed and phrased even more explicitly in *Military Exports* where the ECJ, after making the point discussed above that a mere reliance on the exemption is not enough ruled:

> Consequently it is for the Member State which seeks to take advantage of Article [346 TFEU] to prove that it is necessary to have recourse to that derogation in order to protect its essential security interests.[153]

It could be argued that the Court did not take the division of powers and federalism dimensions of Article 346(1)(b) TFEU discussed above sufficiently into account when establishing this evidence rule. In the constitutional framework of the EU the governments of the Member States are responsible for defence. They require flexibility to fulfil this responsibility in a sensitive policy field. Part of this flexibility is their wide margin of discretion. Putting the burden of proof for having acted within that margin of discretion on the Member States compromises their flexibility to an extent that might be considered as contradicting the very attribution of this flexibility. It could be argued that there is no reason why the Member State should have to prove the legality of its measures and there is no authority for this requirement in the Treaty. The burden of proof for bad faith or arbitrariness could be put on the Commission or other Member State challenging the legality of the measure. In order to safeguard the necessary flexibility there might be an argument for an evidentiary presumption in favour of the respective government including the benefit of any reasonable doubt.[154] In *Spanish Weapons* and *Military Exports* the Court might have gone too far on this point. This issue will be discussed again below in the context of the information privilege in Article 346(1)(a) TFEU.[155] Nevertheless the fact that the Member States carry the burden of proof is clearly established in this case law.

2.2.3 Derogation on a case-by-case basis

In *Spanish Weapons* the ECJ did not rule expressly that Article 346(1)(b) TFEU can only be invoked on a case-by-case basis. However, it is submitted that this

---

[153] Case C-284/05, *Commission v. Finland, supra* note 83, at para. 49; Case C-294/05, *Commission v. Sweden, supra* note 103, at para. 47; Case C-372/05, *Commission v. Germany, supra* note 103, at para. 72; Case C-387/05, *Commission v. Italy, supra* note 103, at para. 49; Case C-409/05, *Commission v. Greece, supra* note 103, at para. 54; Case C-461/05, *Commission v. Denmark, supra* note 103, at para. 55; Case C-38/06, *Commission v. Portugal, supra* note 103, at para. 66; Case C-239/06, *Commission v. Italy, supra* note 103, at para. 51.

[154] See the approach of the German *Bundesverfassungsgericht* in cases involving defence and foreign policy in Thomas M. Franck, *Political Questions/Juridical Answers: Does the Rule of Law Apply to Foreign Affairs?* (Princeton University Press, 1992), at 107–25.

[155] See below.

is how the derogation has to be understood. First, as will be discussed further below, in *Military Exports* the Court did rule expressly that the closely related secrecy exemption in Article 346(1)(a) TFEU can only be invoked on a case-by-case basis.[156] Moreover, in *German Military Exports* the Court ruled on the case-by-case nature of the exemption as a whole.[157] It can be argued that this includes Article 346(1)(b) TFEU, as will be discussed below. Secondly, the scrutiny applied to the use of the exemption in *Spanish Weapons* and *Military Exports*, including the burden of proof requirement discussed above, represent an analysis of the concrete situations of these cases which implies that the derogation can only be invoked on a case-by-case basis; otherwise this analysis would not make sense. In other words, since the burden of proof and the necessity of derogation can only be assessed for every individual case and situation, the exemption can only be used on a case-by-case basis. This would mean that a national code derogating from the Treaty as in Case C-157/06, *Commission* v. *Italy* discussed above, would not be legal under the Treaty as Article 346(1)(b) TFEU can only be used on a case-by-case basis, not on an abstract basis without reference to a concrete situation.[158]

2.2.4 Procedural requirements and hard defence material intended for export

There are a few procedural requirements for the use of Article 346(1)(b) TFEU. In *Fiocchi Munizioni*, introduced above, the General Court clarified a few of these points in relation to Articles 346(1)(b) and 348 TFEU. First, where a Member State considers it necessary to invoke the exemption in Article 346(1)(b) TFEU it does not have to notify the Commission in advance since the provision allows derogation from the rules on State aid. Neither can the Commission use the examination procedure laid down in Article 108 TFEU in this context.[159] Due to the use of Article 346 TFEU the Member State derogates from all obligations of the Treaty, including the detailed

---

[156] For example para. 76 of Case C-372/05, *Commission* v. *Germany*, *supra* note 103, reads: "In those circumstances, and in accordance with Article [4 (3) TEU (Lisbon)] which obliges Member States to facilitate the achievement of the Commission's task of ensuring compliance with the Treaty, Member States are obliged to make available to the Commission the documents necessary to permit inspection to ensure that the transfer of the [Union's] own resources is correct. However ... such an obligation does not mean that Member States may not, *on a case-by-case basis* and by way of exception, on the basis of Article [346 TFEU], either restrict the information sent to certain parts of a document or withhold it completely." See also point 168 of the Opinion of Advocate General Ruiz-Jarabo Colomer.

[157] Case C-372/05, *Commission* v. *Germany*, *supra* note 103.

[158] This was not expressly ruled in Case C-157/06, *Commission* v. *Italy*, *supra* note 48, as the use of Art. 346(1)(b) TFEU was rejected as the military use of the equipment in question was not certain.

[159] Case T-26/01, *supra* note 36, at para. 59.

obligations of its State aid regime, which will be discussed in more detail in chapter 4.

Secondly, the Court emphasised that two distinct and specific remedies are prescribed by the Treaty in relation to measures adopted by Member States on the basis of Article 346(1)(b) TFEU. These are the bilateral examinations according to Article 348 subparagraph 1 TFEU and court proceedings according to Article 348 subparagraph 2 TFEU. Within the context of bilateral examination it is within the discretion of the Commission to decide whether the invocation by the Member State concerned is prima facie credible. Contrary to the situation in the context of Article 108 TFEU, the Commission is under no obligation to adopt a decision concerning the measure at issue. Moreover, it has no power to address a final decision or directive to the Member State concerned.[160] In this context the Court also differentiated the facts of *Fiocchi Munizioni* from the facts behind Commission Decision 1999/763/EC of 17 March 1999 on the measures, implemented and proposed, by the Free and Hanseatic City of Bremen, Germany in favour of Lürssen Maritime Beteiligungen GmbH & Co. KK.[161] In the latter case the Commission had opened the procedure provided in Article 108(2) TFEU ending with a decision in the course of which Germany relied in her defence on the application of Article 346(1)(b) TFEU. By contrast, in *Fiocchi Munizioni* the Commission had opened bilateral examinations under Article 348 subparagraph 1 TFEU.

Fiocchi Munizioni represents a case decided on procedural grounds rather than an example for judicial scrutiny over Article 346(1)(b) TFEU. However, the case emphasised that once a Member State has invoked Article 346(1)(b) TFEU the Commission is confined to the special procedure in Article 348 TFEU and that it has discretion to decide whether the Member State's claim is credible or not.

2.2.5 When the review procedure under Article 348 TFEU is used

A related question is in which cases involving Article 346 TFEU the special review procedure in Article 348 TFEU, instead of regular procedures such as most importantly Article 258 TFEU, has to be used. In *Spanish Weapons* the regular enforcement procedure in Article 258 TFEU was used. No party invoked Article 348 TFEU, "not even the Court of its own motion".[162]

---

[160] Case T-26/01, ibid., at para. 74.   [161] [1999] OJ L301/8.

[162] Pointed out in the Opinion of Advocate General Ruiz-Jarabo Colomer in Case C-284/05, *Commission v. Finland, supra* note 83; Case C-294/05, *Commission v. Sweden, supra* note 103; Case C-372/05, *Commission v. Germany, supra* note 103; Case C-387/05, *Commission v. Italy, supra* note 103; Case C-409/05, *Commission v. Greece, supra* note 103; Case C-461/05, *Commission v. Denmark, supra* note 103; Case C-239/06, *Commission v. Italy, supra* note 103, at point 42.

Moreover, in over 50 years *FYROM*[163] was the only case in which the procedure in Article 348(2) TFEU was used at all.[164]

However, Article 348 TFEU was a contentious issue in some of the *Military Export* cases. During the litigation stages, Germany[165] and Greece[166] questioned the admissibility of the Article 258 TFEU enforcement action because, as they had relied on Article 346 TFEU, the Commission could not bring a regular enforcement action but had to use the special procedure provided in Article 348 subparagraph 2 TFEU. However, according to the Court, the objective of the Commission was to obtain a declaration of a failure to fulfil obligations under provisions of secondary law.[167] Article 348 TFEU is applicable only if the Commission alleges improper use of the powers provided for in Articles 346 and 347 TFEU.[168] Moreover, as pointed out in the Opinion of Advocate General Ruiz-Jarabo Colomer, the wording of Article 348 TFEU in any language[169] did not support the interpretation that the Commission is under an obligation to use the procedure: "the reference to that direct method of challenge is framed merely as a right".[170] Thus, as already argued by Hummer, the use of the word

---

[163] Case C-120/94, *Commission v. Greece* [1996] ECR I-1513. The case, which was not decided but removed from the register, concerned the unilateral measures adopted by Greece, which, according to the Commission, were intended to prohibit trade, via the port of Thessaloniki, in products originating in, coming from or destined for the former Yugoslav Republic of Macedonia (FYROM) and imports into Greece of products originating in or coming from FYROM. Greece had invoked Art. 347 TFEU, a provision that will be briefly discussed below.

[164] According to Opinion of Advocate General Ruiz-Jarabo Colomer in the *Military Export* cases, *supra* note 103, in footnote 26.

[165] Case C-372/05, *Commission v. Germany, supra* note 103, at para. 28.

[166] Case C-409/05, *Commission v. Greece, supra* note 103, at para. 23.

[167] Arts. 2 and 9–11 of Regulations 1552/89/EEC and 1150/2000/EC.

[168] Case C-372/05, *Commission v. Germany, supra* note 103, at para. 29; Case C-409/05, *Commission v. Greece, supra* note 103, at para. 25. In para. 24 of the latter judgment there was an additional procedural aspect considered by the Court: "It is evident that, while the Hellenic Republic refers to that objection of inadmissibility in its defence, the appropriate form of order is however only presented in the rejoinder, and consequently, in accordance with Article 42 of the Court's Rules of Procedure, that objection must be declared to be inadmissible since the applicant has been denied the opportunity to rebut it."

[169] The Spanish ("la Comisión o cualquier Estado miembro *podrá* recurrir directamente"), French ("la Commission ou tout État membre *peut* saisir directement la Cour de justice"), English ("the Commission or any Member State *may* bring the matter directly before the Court of Justice") and German ("*kann* die Kommission oder ein Mitgliedstaat den Gerichtshof unmittelbar anrufen"). See point 34 of the Opinion, *supra* note 103.

[170] In footnote 23 Advocate General Ruiz-Jarabo Colomer makes reference to Robert Bray (ed.), *Lenaerts, Arts, and Maselis, Procedural Law of the European Union*, 2nd edn (London: Sweet & Maxwell, 2006) at 141 and 142, who share his view with regard to the special procedure in Art. 114(9) TFEU. This should be applied to the special procedure referred to in Art. 348 subpara 2 TFEU, to which the authors refer under the heading "Relationship between Arts 226 and 227 of the EC Treaty [now 258 and 259 TFEU]. And

"may" in Article 348 subparagraph 1 TFEU indicates that the use of this procedure, rather than other procedures most importantly Articles 258 and 259 TFEU, is not obligatory in any case.[171] The subject matter of any legal proceedings, argued the Advocate General, is determined by the applicant and not by the claims of the defendant; if that were not so, an objection of inadmissibility would be capable of distorting the subject matter of a dispute.[172] The Commission was seeking a declaration of failure to fulfil obligations under Article 31 TFEU and a number of EU Internal Market regulations and decisions, but not under Article 346 TFEU. That provision had been relied on by Germany as one of the mainstays of its reasoning.[173] The choice of action by the applicant is not made subject to the arguments put forward by the defendant in the defence.[174]

Moreover, it is clear from the purpose of Article 348 TFEU and from a systematic interpretation of its two paragraphs that the Commission "may bring the matter directly before the Court of Justice" where it takes the view that there has been improper use of Article 346 TFEU and when "the conditions of competition in the common market" have been distorted.[175] The approach suggested by Advocate General Ruiz-Jarabo Colomer in the *Military Exports* cases and also Advocate General Jacobs in *FYROM*[176] supports the restriction of the remedy provided for in Article 348(2) TFEU to avoid "the collateral effects which [Articles 346 and 348 TFEU] may have on competition and on the economy".[177] As the *Military Export* cases clearly did not concern the distortion of competition, Article 348(2) TFEU was not available.[178]

Finally, according to the Advocate General, the procedure in Article 258 TFEU does not entail disadvantages to the Member States in comparison with that of Article 348 TFEU:

> it strengthens their rights of defence, beginning in the pre-litigation stage, which is absent from Article 348 TFEU ... the procedure under that provision is, rather, a summary procedure, since it limits the jurisdiction of the Court simply to determining whether the market and trade are functioning properly, thereby restricting the ability of the Member State concerned to defend itself.[179]

special procedures relating to the improper use of derogating provisions." According to the authors, "the opportunity afforded to the Commission by [Art. 114 TFEU] to bring a matter directly before the Court of Justice without incurring the delay of a pre-litigation procedure is intended to serve the [EU] interest of protecting in full the establishment of the internal market. However, this does not preclude the Commission from opting to bring proceedings under [Art. 258 TFEU] in the interest of the defendant Member State."

[171] Trybus, *European Union Law and Defence Integration, supra* note 13, at 156.
[172] Point 35.   [173] Point 36.   [174] Point 37.   [175] Point 38.
[176] Points 63–7 of the Opinion of Advocate General Jacobs in Case C-120/94, *Commission* v. *Greece* [1996] ECR I-1513, as cited by Advocate General Ruiz-Jarabo Colomer.
[177] Point 39.   [178] Point 40.   [179] Point 41.

However, there are also arguments against the interpretation that Article 348(2) TFEU is optional and that the Commission can choose to use other actions, most importantly the enforcement procedure in Article 258 TFEU. The word "may" could also simply mean that the Commission has the option but is not under an obligation to move from the pre-judicial stage in paragraph (1) to the judicial stage on paragraph (2) of Article 348 TFEU. The same option exists in the context of Article 258 TFEU. Moreover, Article 348 TFEU was only used once for Article 347 TFEU but its wording clearly stipulates that it is also to be used for Article 346 TFEU. The *effet utile* of Article 348 TFEU is not deleted but compromised when it is only an option. Nevertheless, the case law including *Fiocchi Munizioni* and *Military Exports* indicate that Article 348 TFEU is interpreted merely as an option.

2.3 The Commission's 2006 Interpretative Communication

Most importantly, the case of *Spanish Weapons* discussed above had already established most of the elements of the interpretation of Article 346(1)(b) TFEU by the end of 1999. However, it appears that this had no impact on defence procurement in practice. The case law was largely ignored by the Member States,[180] out of defiance, ignorance or difficulty in applying the derogation on the basis of this interpretation. To address this problem, the 2004 Green Paper on Defence Procurement suggested that the Commission should issue an Interpretative Communication to clarify the existing legal framework.[181] According to the consultation launched by the Green Paper, "a majority [of the stakeholders] considered an Interpretative Communication to be useful".[182]

The "Interpretative Communication on the Application of Article [346] of the Treaty in the Field of Defence Procurement" was finally issued on 7 December 2006[183] with the following objective:

> to prevent the possible misinterpretation and misuse of Article [346 TFEU] in the field of defence procurement.[184]

---

[180] Burkard Schmitt (Rapp.), *Defence Procurement in the European Union* (Paris: Institute for Security Studies of the European Union, 2005), at 17; H. Küchle, *The Cost of Non-Europe in the Area of Security and Defence* (European Parliament, 2006), Document DGExPo/B/PolDep/2005/13, at 42 *et seq.*; Heuninckx, Thesis (2011), *supra* note 26, at 76.

[181] COM (2004) 608 final, at 9. However, the Commission appears to have taken the decision to issue an Interpretative Communication already at least a year earlier, as expressed in the Communication "European Defence – Industrial and Market Issues: Towards an EU Defence Equipment Policy", COM (2003) 113 final, at 15: "There have been several important Court judgments in recent years that are relevant to this work – especially in helping to define the scope of Article [346]. The Commission will issue an Interpretative Communication by the end of 2003 on the implications of these judgments."

[182] COM (2005) 626 final, at 6.   [183] COM (2006) 779 final.   [184] Ibid., at 3.

The Interpretative Communication reiterates the relevant case law discussed above.[185] Hence, the exemption needs to be interpreted strictly.[186] It only refers to products identified in the 1958 list which "includes only equipment which is of purely military nature and purpose" (Section 3 "Field of Application").[187] Moreover, these goods are "not automatically exempted", as the conditions of Article 346 TFEU have to be met (Section 4 "Conditions of Application").[188] Furthermore, while the text of the provision gives Member States broad discretion and flexibility, there are limits. Referring to the crucial paragraph 22 of *Spanish Weapons*, the Commission argues:

> the particularly strong wording ("essential") limits possible exemptions to procurements which are of the highest importance for Member States' military capabilities.

While the intention of this sentence is to illustrate the conditions of application of Article 346 TFEU, the notion of "procurements which are of the highest importance for Member States military capabilities" would in itself require a definition to facilitate the correct interpretation of Article 346 TFEU, a definition which is not provided. However, the question is whether the Commission could provide such a definition. It is a gloss in the Treaty, which it is obviously ultimately for the ECJ to lay down. The Interpretative Communication then stresses that the exemption requires a case-by-case assessment "with great care" (Section 5 "How to apply Article [346 TFEU]").[189] The relevant contracting authorities have to evaluate in this context

> Which essential security interest is concerned? What is the connection between this security interest and the specific procurement decision? Why is the non-application of the Public Procurement Directive [2004/18/EC] in this specific case necessary for the protection of this essential security interest?

After the introduction of the Defence Directive, the reference to Directive 2004/18/EC would have to be replaced with a reference to the Defence Directive. The burden of proof for the existence of a situation justifying exemption lies with the respective Member State (Section 6 "The Role of the Commission").[190] In Section 6 the Commission also emphasises its role in enforcing the lawful use of Article 346 TFEU, suggesting a more active role in using the instruments of Articles 258 and 348 TFEU than in the past.[191] The *Agusta* and *Military Exports* case law discussed above could be interpreted as a manifestation of this more active role.

---

[185] Except the later *Agusta, Finnish Turntables*, and *Military Exports* judgments.
[186] Interpretative Communication COM (2006) 779 final, at 5.   [187] Ibid.
[188] Ibid., at 6.   [189] Ibid., at 6–7.   [190] Ibid., at 8–9.
[191] This is also the assessment of A. Georgopoulos, "The Commission's Interpretative Communication on the Application of Article 296 EC in the Field of Defence Procurement" (2007) 16 *Public Procurement Law Review* NA43–52, at NA52.

While not legally binding,[192] this Communication is a welcome contribution in clarifying the interpretation of Article 346 TFEU.[193] While the Commission provides some interesting details, for example on offsets,[194] the Interpretative Communication does not go beyond the relevant case law. Moreover, as since 2006 the *Agusta* and *Military Exports* case law added considerably to the Court's interpretation of Article 346 TFEU, the Interpretative Communication is no longer "state of the art". Its most important function at the moment is, as Georgopoulos explained, that it "provides an insight into the way that Commission approaches the scope of Art. [346 TFEU] and equally gives clues to the Commission's intentions".[195] In other words, it establishes how the Commission interprets the provision and contains a threat that it will use the instruments at its disposal to enforce this interpretation.

The Green Paper on Defence Procurement reveals that the Interpretative Communication was intended to complement the Defence Directive,[196] which was prepared at the same time. It preceded the latter but did not change Member States' misinterpretation of Article 346 TFEU, which arguably shows that the legally binding rules of the Defence Directive were necessary to achieve that change.

Additional relevant ECJ judgments, most notably the *Agusta*, *Military Exports* and *Finnish Turntables* and most importantly the EU "Defence Package" with the Defence Directive at its core, are important reference points for the now slightly dated 2006 Interpretative Communication. It is thus submitted that it has to be replaced by a state-of-the-art Communication which takes these references fully into account.

2.4 Summary: the interpretation of Article 346(1)(b) TFEU

On the basis of the case law of the ECJ, most importantly *Spanish Weapons*, *Agusta*, *Military Exports* and *Finnish Turntables*, but also *Sirdar*, *Kreil*, *Dory* and *Fiocchi Munizioni*, Article 346(1)(b) TFEU has to be interpreted narrowly.

---

[192] According to Art. 288 TFEU (ex 249 EC) only Regulations, Directives, and Decisions are legally binding. The fact that Interpretative Communications are not legally binding was also recently clarified by the General Court in T-258/06, *Germany* v. *Commission* [2010] ECR II-2027, at para. 162.

[193] This is also the assessment of Georgopoulos, "The Commission's Interpretative Communication on the Application of Article 296 EC in the Field of Defence Procurement", *supra* note 191, at NA47.

[194] Introduced in ch. 1 at 54–7 and discussed in detail in ch. 9.

[195] Georgopoulos, *supra* note 191, at NA52.

[196] COM (2004) 608 final, at 9–11: clarification and supplementation of the legal framework are presented as complementary not as alterative measures. See also the Interpretative Communication, at 9: "In parallel the Commission will continue its preparatory work on a possible procurement directive for military equipment to which Article [346 TFEU] does not apply."

The exemption applies only to armaments on the 1958 list (*Fiocchi Munizioni*) when they are clearly to be used for military purposes (*Agusta*). The exemption is not automatic or categorical (*Spanish Weapons*) but needs to be specifically invoked on a case-by-case basis (*Military Exports*). A situation justifying the use of the exemption has to be proven by the Member State in question (*Spanish Weapons* and *Military Exports*). The measure in question must not affect competition in markets other than listed armaments (*Military Exports*). The ECJ or General Court will scrutinise the legality of the measure by applying a proportionality test. Overall, the exemption of armaments from the TFEU is intended as the exception and inclusion in the Internal Market of the TFEU as a whole as the rule. To use the house metaphor again, armaments are normally inside the house of the Internal Market and Article 346(1)(b) TFEU is merely an emergency exit for exceptional circumstances. The exit is armed with an alarm and a porter will ask why the exit is used and might push the armaments back into the house. Well, the porter has often been very relaxed in the past but is unlikely to continue to be so in the future. This will be explained in more detail in Part II of this book. The situation of the European armaments market described in chapter 1 and the legal frameworks and practices analysed in chapter 5, however, deviate from the now dominant interpretation of Article 346(1)(b) TFEU.

3 The secrecy exemption of Article 346(1)(a) TFEU

Article 346 TFEU contains a second "defence" exemption. Article 346(1)(a) provides:

> no Member State shall be obliged to supply information the disclosure of which it considers contrary to the essential interests of its security.

This rule confers certain procedural privileges on the Member States in relation to national security and secrecy. It represents a possibility of derogation from the general obligation of Member States to supply information to the institutions of the Union according to secondary EU law provisions or Articles 337 TFEU[197] and 4(3) TEU.[198] Hence it only applies if there is an obligation under EU law to supply information. The Member States have a political

---

[197] Art. 337 TFEU reads: "The Commission may, within the limits and under the conditions laid down by the Council in accordance with the provisions of this Treaty, collect any information and carry out any checks required for the performance of the tasks entrusted to it."

[198] Art. 4 (3) TEU reads: "Pursuant to the principle of sincere cooperation, the Union and the Member States shall, in full mutual respect, assist each other in carrying out tasks which flow from the Treaties. Member States shall take all appropriate measures, whether general or particular, to ensure fulfilment of the obligations arising out of this Treaty or resulting from action taken by the institutions of the Union. Member States shall facilitate the achievement of the Union's tasks and refrain from any measure which could jeopardise the attainment of the Union's objectives."

discretion to decide whether their essential security interests are affected. The use of the provision is nevertheless subject to the scrutiny of the ECJ, especially through Article 348(2) TFEU, although this has never occurred. Moreover, it is subject to the bilateral communication between the Commission and a Member State provided in Article 348(1) TFEU if the Commission considers that necessary. The move to a narrow interpretation of Article 346(1)(b) TFEU, described above, however, might give a greater practical importance to this privilege in the future.

Procurement Directives involve many obligations to supply information to EU institutions, most importantly the obligation to publish contract notices and contract award notices in the Official Journal of the EU.[199] Not only because these obligations are connected to publication, which involves supplying information to anybody interested, the disclosure of this information may be considered contrary to the essential interests of the security of a Member State. Therefore the secrecy exemption in Article 346(1)(a) TFEU can be relevant in the procurement context. The Defence Directive aims to limit the need to invoke the secrecy exemption by adapting the rules of the Public Sector Directive to accommodate "security of information". This shall be discussed in detail in Part II of this book, especially in chapters 7 and 8.

3.1 Abuse of Article 346(1)(a) TFEU

There is a danger of abuse of Article 346(1)(a) TFEU. Member States could, for example, withhold the evidence necessary for the ECJ to scrutinise a measure taken on grounds of national security. According to *Spanish Weapons* and subsequent case law Member States are under the obligation to prove a situation covered by Article 346(1)(b) TFEU.[200] Thus the obligation to disclose the information needed to decide on the application of letter (b) might compromise the use of the privilege in letter (a), when the information in question is the only

---

[199] See, for example, in the context of Public Sector Directive 2004/18/EC: Chapter VI "Rules on Advertising and Transparency", Section 1 "Publication of Notices", Arts. 35–6 (Art. 37 "Non-mandatory Publication" does not contain an obligation), Art. 29(2) on the competitive dialogue, Art. 33(3) on dynamic purchasing systems, Art. 30(1) on negotiated procedures with prior publication of a contract notice, Arts. 58(1) and 64 on public works concessions, Art. 69(1) for design contests. There are also obligations to supply statistical information in Art. 75.

[200] Case C-414/97, *supra* note 56, at para. 22, discussed above. See also: Case C-284/05, *Commission* v. *Finland*, *supra* note 83, at para. 49; Case C-294/05, *Commission* v. *Sweden*, *supra* note 103, at para. 47; Case C-372/05, *Commission* v. *Germany*, *supra* note 103, at para. 72; Case C-387/05, *Commission* v. *Italy*, *supra* note 103, at para. 49; Case C-409/05, *Commission* v. *Greece*, *supra* note 103, at para. 54; Case C-461/05, *Commission* v. *Denmark*, *supra* note 103, at para. 55; Case C-38/06, *Commission* v. *Portugal*, *supra* note 103, at para. 66; Case C-239/06, *Commission* v. *Italy*, *supra* note 103, at para. 51.

proof available.[201] This problem is discussed below with regards to the disclosure of information in the ECJ in the context of Articles 348 or 258 TFEU proceedings. In the context of the pre-judicial stage of these proceedings this information would have to be disclosed to the Commission. However, it is argued here that the disclosure of sensitive information to the Commission should not be a serious problem. The experience of the Commission in handling professional secrecy under Article 28 Regulation 1/2003/EC in the context of competition cases suggests that the secrecy interests of the Member States could be safeguarded in the Commission.[202]

In the context of the GATT, it was argued that the exercise of a legitimate procedural right must not be used against a Member State.[203] Applied to the EU context this would mean that if a Member State refuses to disclose information under Article 346(1)(a) TFEU, the Court will accept the use of Articles 346(1)(b) or 347 TFEU in good faith. In such a case a Member State would not be required to prove the situation.

However, the exercise of the discretion under Article 346(1)(a) TFEU can be subjected to scrutiny of the Court under the *in camera* procedure of Article 348 subparagraph 2 TFEU. As the public is excluded from these proceedings, Member States are not able to use the privilege in Article 346(1)(a) TFEU in the context of these proceedings again to avoid having to supply information to the Court on the previous use of the same provision. If the use of Articles 346(1)(b) or 347 TFEU is the subject of these proceedings the respective Member State is not able to use the privilege either.[204]

First, the alternative view could make the review of the ECJ redundant. The narrow interpretation of Article 346(1)(b) TFEU in *Spanish Weapons*, for example, would be deprived of its practical effect if Member States could use their discretion to withhold information the Court needs to scrutinise a measure taken under that exemption. A Member State who abused letter (b) will not hesitate to abuse letter (a). Moreover, the Court allocated the burden of proof clearly on the Member States.

Secondly, the secrecy needs of the Member States are sufficiently accommodated in Article 348 subparagraph 2 TFEU proceedings, as the public is excluded. By derogation from Article 34 of the Statute of the Court, for example, secrecy also has to be taken into account when reading the judgment to the public. In any event it is only the operative part which is read out and in case of

---

[201] Arrowsmith, *The Law of Public and Utilities Procurement, supra* note 40, at 245.

[202] Thanks to Anthony Arnull for pointing this out to me when commenting on an earlier draft of this chapter.

[203] In relation to the similar provision of Art. XXI(a) GATT see Schloemann and Ohloff, "'Constitutionalisation' and Dispute Settlement in the WTO: National Security as an Issue of Competence", *supra* note 136, also referring to the statement of United States delegate Evans in the 1949 *Czechoslovakia* dispute, Doc. GATT/CP.3/38, at 9 (1949).

[204] See Arrowsmith, *The Law of Public and Utilities Procurement, supra* note 40, at 245–6.

an Article 348 TFEU judgment, which has never occurred, presumably not even that would be done.[205]

Finally, it is unlikely that a Member State will push it that far and abuse Article 346(1)(a) TFEU again in a case where the previous abuse of the same provision is the issue of Court proceedings. This would involve a political confrontation between Member States and institutions that does not occur very often in practice. Member States normally follow judgments of the ECJ and try to cooperate with the institutions of the Union.

To put the burden of proof on the Member States, similar to the position with respect to Article 346(1)(b) TFEU,[206] could compromise their wide discretion.[207] Moreover, it might be considered as not taking the nature of secrecy into account. On the other hand the Commission would find it difficult to supply the evidence for a disproportionate use of the provision. This would make its role under Article 348 paragraph 2 TFEU almost redundant and deprive the review procedure of its *effet utile* with regards to Article 346(1)(a) TFEU. However, it is clear that the former is to be used in the context of the latter. Furthermore, the evidence rules in relation to Article 346(1)(b) TFEU and Article 347 TFEU discussed above have to be taken into account, assuming a similar evidence rule for all defence exceptions. Thus Article 346(1)(a) TFEU cannot be used as a defence against the obligation to provide information to produce the necessary proof in Article 346 or 347 TFEU cases. Therefore it is submitted that the Member States carry the burden of proof for the use of Article 346(1)(a) TFEU as well. Article 348 TFEU accommodates secrecy concerns and it is precisely this conflict between the burden of proof on the Member States under Article 346 and 347 TFEU and their privilege under Article 346(1)(a) TFEU that required the insertion of the special procedure in the Treaty. However, as can be seen in *Spanish Weapons* and more clearly in *Military Exports*, it is not the special review procedure in Article 348 TFEU but the regular enforcement procedure in Article 258 TFEU that is used in practice.

3.2 Intensity of scrutiny: German Military Exports

Until very recently the standard of review in Article 346(1)(a) TFEU cases was unclear since there was no case law specifically dealing with the provision.[208] Thus, for the same reasons discussed in the context of Article 346(1)(b) TFEU above, it could only be assumed that the Court would apply a low-intensity proportionality test leaving wide discretion to the Member States. The Court

---

[205] Thanks to Anthony Arnull for discussing this point with me on the basis of an earlier draft of this chapter.

[206] See above.

[207] Arrowsmith, *The Law of Public and Utilities Procurement*, *supra* note 40, at 245.

[208] See the various possible interpretations outlined by Arrowsmith, ibid., at 245–6.

would only consider a measure disproportionate when a measure is outside the ambit of that discretion, when the Member State acted arbitrarily or in bad faith.[209]

In the recent *Military Export* cases some Member States argued that they did not have to supply the information the Commission would need to prove an infringement of the Treaty. In *German Military Exports*[210] the Article 258 TFEU enforcement action against Germany was claimed to be inadmissible by the latter because, due to the very nature of the action, the Commission was not capable of proving an infringement of the TFEU. As the Member States were under no obligation to provide the information requested by the Commission, the Commission did not have sufficient evidence relating to the imports at issue to enable it to prove any failure to fulfil Treaty obligations. Moreover, Germany claimed that it was entitled not to send the information requested by the Commission and that because the action was based, inter alia, on that failure the action was thus also not admissible in that respect. While these arguments did not refer specifically to Article 346(1)(b) TFEU but to Article 346 TFEU as a whole, they do refer to the provision as an exemption from the general obligation to provide information to EU institutions. The Court did not accept this line of argument. The application of the EU customs system requires the active involvement of EU and national officials "who are bound when necessary by an obligation of confidentiality, when dealing with sensitive data, which is capable of protecting the essential security interests of Member States".[211] Moreover, the Court ruled that

> the level of specificity to be attained in the declarations which Member States must periodically complete and send to the Commission is not such as to lead to damage to the interests of those States in respect of either security or confidentiality.[212]

Article 4(3) TEU, according to the Court, obliges Member States to make available to the Commission the documents necessary to permit inspection to ensure that the transfer of the EU own resources is correct. However, this obligation did not prevent the Member States,

> on a case-by-case basis and by way of exception, on the basis of Article [346 TFEU], [to] either restrict the information sent to certain parts of a document or withhold it completely.[213]

---

[209] See Trybus, *European Union Law and Defence Integration, supra* note 13, at 165.

[210] Case C-372/05, *Commission* v. *Germany, supra* note 103, at paras. 31 and 32.

[211] Ibid., at para. 74.

[212] Case C-372/05, *Commission* v. *Germany, supra* note 103, at para. 75.

[213] Ibid., at para. 76 and the Opinion of Advocate General Ruiz-Jarabo Colomer, at point 168, also cited by the Court.

Although this was not clearly spelt out in the judgment, it is submitted that this refers to the exemption from the obligation to supply information to EU institutions only in letter (a) of Article 346(1) TFEU rather than to the article as a whole. However, this also clarifies the interpretation and application of the exemption in Article 346(1)(b) TFEU. Apart from a relatively narrow field of application as an exemption from the obligation to provide information according to most importantly Article 4(3) TEU, the exemption not surprisingly shares many characteristics with its "sister" or "neighbour" derogation in Article 346(1)(b) TFEU. Most importantly, it is to be used as an exception and only on a case-by-case basis. This "case-by-case" notion had not even been as clearly spelt out for the armaments exemption as it was for the secrecy exemption in *German Military Exports*. As in the latter judgment the Court speaks about Article 346 TFEU as a whole, it could also be argued that it is authority for the "case-by-case" nature of the use of Article 346(1)(b) TFEU discussed above. The judgment is significant because it is the first ruling on Article 346(1)(a) TFEU and the Court did rule against the use of the exemption. It did not use the term "necessary". However, it did scrutinise the German argument quite thoroughly, looking at the safeguards of confidentiality in place and judging them to be sufficient to serve the secrecy requirements involved.

This confirms that like the exemption in its letter (b), Article 346(1)(a) TFEU is not automatic or categorical, has to be interpreted narrowly, can only be invoked as an exception and on a case-by-case basis, needs to be specifically invoked, the Member State has the burden of proof that a situation justifying its use exists and derogation will be scrutinised by the ECJ. The case law does not specifically rule on a proportionality test. However, based on the arguments submitted in the context of Article 346(1)(b) TFEU above (that all Member State derogations from the Treaty need to be proportionate) a proportionality test can be assumed.

4 The crisis situations exemption in Article 347 TFEU

The final defence exemption covers crisis situations. Article 347 TFEU provides for a special consultation procedure between Member States taking together the steps needed to prevent the functioning of the Internal Market being affected by measures, which a Member State may be called upon to take in a number of situations involving national security.[214] These situations apply:

1 "in the event of serious internal disturbances affecting the maintenance of law and order"

---

[214] The author has analysed this provision extensively: Trybus, *European Union Law and Defence Integration, supra* 13, ch. 6, at 167–95 and Trybus, "Borderline", *supra* note 123, 137.

2 "in the event of war"
3 "serious international tension constituting a threat to war"
4 "in order to carry out obligations it [the Member State] has accepted for the purpose of maintaining peace and international security".

The procurement link of Article 347 TFEU is very weak as it does not directly relate to goods or services.[215] Moreover, the practical relevance of Article 347 TFEU for defence procurement is limited. This is due to the fact that with Article 346(1)(b) TFEU, the Treaty provides an armaments-specific exemption, which will supersede the more general situation-based exemption in Article 347 TFEU. However, Article 347 TFEU could also be seen as the *lex specialis* to Article 346 as it applies only in extreme and therefore rare circumstances.[216] There are a number of provisions in the Defence Directive which appear to aim to limit the use of Article 347 TFEU rather than Article 346 TFEU in practice. These provisions deal with procurement in times of crisis or generally when troops are already deployed abroad[217] and will be discussed in more detail in chapter 6. Suffice it to say for the purposes of this chapter that also in the context of the extreme situations described in Article 347 TFEU, Article 346(1)(b) TFEU is the more specific exemption in relation to the listed armaments. The existence of such a situation would increase the margin of discretion left to the Member States and reduce the intensity of scrutiny applied by the ECJ, if the Commission or another Member State would bring proceedings at all. The same would apply in the context of the procurement of goods and services not appearing on the 1958 list of armaments during such a situation, to which the regime-specific exemptions in Articles 36 and 52(1) TFEU discussed in chapter 2[218] would be applied.

5 Conclusions

As explained in chapter 2, the TFEU applies to the procurement of goods and services, irrespective of the (additional) application of secondary EU law such as the Defence Directive or the Public Sector Directive. This prohibits all

---

[215] Art. 347 TFEU is a classical national security exemption, and it is not unusual in international treaties for this kind of situation to be covered by a special exemption, see Art. XXI(b)(iii) and (c) GATT, Art. XIV *bis* GATS, Art. 73 TRIPS, Art. 15(1) ECHR or Art. XX(1)(d) of the Treaty of Amity, Economic Relations and Consular Rights Between the United States of America and Iran 1955.

[216] Thanks to Anthony Arnull for discussing this point with me on the basis of an earlier draft of this chapter.

[217] See in the Defence Directive the exception in Art. 13(d), the security of supply provision in Art. 23(d) and (e), the case justifying the use of the negotiated procedure without publication of a contract notice in Art. 28(1)(c). The crisis relevance of the letters of Arts. 23 and 28 is more evident than that of Art. 13.

[218] At 70–82.

protectionist measures in defence procurement and requires it to be conducted transparently. However, in addition to the public security exemptions from the free movement regimes in Articles 36, 45(3), 52(1), 65(1)(b) and 72 TFEU, the defence exemptions in Articles 346 and 347 TFEU allow Member States to derogate from the TFEU. In contrast to the former, which only allow exemption from their specific regimes on goods, workers, services, establishment, capital and payments, and for the area of freedom, security and justice respectively, the latter allow derogation from the Treaty as a whole. Moreover, they are subject to the special review procedure in Article 348 subparagraph 2 TFEU. However, the armaments exemption in Article 346(1)(b) TFEU and the secrecy exemption in Article 346(1)(a) TFEU also have to be interpreted narrowly. They do not represent automatic exclusions but need to be justified, invoked and proven by the Member State that wishes to rely on them. The narrow interpretation is necessary to avoid these exemptions being used as loopholes that could potentially undermine the functioning of the Internal Market as a whole. In comparison to the first group of exemptions the Member States have a wider margin of discretion with regards to the measures they consider necessary concerning armaments and secrecy in the context of Article 346 TFEU.

The interpretation of Article 346(1)(b) TFEU in particular provided by the ECJ discussed above is essential to understand the Defence Directive. First, a narrow interpretation is required to make the very introduction of a Defence Directive worthwhile. If there was a categorical exemption of armaments from the Treaty the introduction of a Defence Directive with armaments at its core would not be useful. Secondly, as Article 346 TFEU is not abolished, the Defence Directive had to accommodate as many of the relevant national security concerns as possible to reduce the use of the armaments derogation in practice. This explains the adaptations to the rules of the Public Sector Directive in the Defence Directive. The latter is to take the national security concerns accommodated in Article 346 TFEU into account to an extent that would normally make derogation unnecessary. Unless one of its exemptions discussed in chapter 6 applies, the Defence Directive applies to the procurement of armaments, save in very exceptional national security situations.

4

The EU law and policy context beyond the Defence Directive

Intra-Community transfers, exports, standardisation, competition law, mergers and State aid

1 Introduction

The legal context of the Defence Directive goes beyond its legal base and limitations in the TFEU discussed in chapters 2 and 3. This "wider" legal context includes a number of economic regimes and policies of the TFEU as well as frameworks outside that Treaty and a comprehensive discussion of these regimes goes beyond the aims of this book. However, the new instrument cannot be understood without considering these complementary and possibly contradictory legal regimes impacting on the European defence and security market. The relevant initiatives will be discussed in their relation to the Defence Directive in the concluding chapters 4 and 5 of Part I of this book, before the chapters of Part II will analyse the Defence Directive itself.

This chapter will discuss the relevant regimes of the TFEU other than procurement discussed in Part II and their connection and direct or indirect impact on procurement regulation through the Defence Directive.[1] This discussion includes the other crucial element of the EU "Defence Package" introduced with the Defence Directive, the Intra-Community Transfers (ICT) Directive.[2] The regulation of intra-Community transfers in a second legally

---

[1] The author provided a chapter on most of the issues discussed in this chapter in his previous monographs: Martin Trybus, *European Defence Procurement Law: International and National Procurement Systems as Models for a Liberalised Defence Procurement Market in Europe* (The Hague: Kluwer Law International, 1999), ch. 4 and *European Union Law and Defence Integration* (Oxford: Hart, 2005), ch. 8; see also: "European Defence Procurement: Towards a Comprehensive Approach" (1998) 4 *European Public Law* 111–33 reprinted in Sue Arrowsmith and Keith Hartley (eds.), *Public Procurement*, 2 vols. (Edward Elgar: Cheltenham, 2002), II. Material from these publications has been used when compiling this chapter. However, the developments of the recent years and the material that has become available since the early years of the century have changed most of the context. This made it necessary to write an essentially new chapter on the area. Moreover, certain aspects were added to the discussion.

[2] Directive 2009/43/EC simplifying terms and conditions of transfers of defence-related products within the Community, OJ [2009] L-146/1. In the recent Commission Communication "A New Deal for European Defence: Towards a More Competitive and

136

binding Directive emphasises the importance of these transfers for European defence and security market. Moreover, the simultaneous introduction of the two Directives highlights their close connection. Due to its importance and this close connection to the Defence Directive, the ICT Directive will be the central object of analysis in this chapter. The third element of the "Defence Package", the Communication "A Strategy for a Stronger and More Competitive European Defence Industry",[3] does not provide comprehensive proposals for the EU laws and policies discussed in this chapter. However, the Commission had made comprehensive proposals regarding defence industrial and procurement issues before.[4] In its 2003 Communication "European Defence–Industrial and Market Issues: Towards an EU Defence Equipment Policy"[5] it had already identified standardisation, monitoring of defence-related industries, intra-Community transfers, competition rules (including merger control), export of dual-use goods and research as fields in which, in addition to the procurement rules, action is proposed.[6] However, it is argued that the export of "hard-defence material" to third countries has to be added to this list. All these regimes and policies are subject to the defence exemptions of the TFEU discussed in the previous chapter, most notably Article 346(1)(b) TFEU. A selection of these old "Community" regimes and initiatives shall be discussed in this chapter before looking in chapter 5 at relevant regimes and initiatives beyond EU Internal Market law, or what before the Treaty of Lisbon was known as the First Pillar.

Section 2 of this chapter will discuss the secondary trade law regimes which partly amplify and harmonise the primary Internal Market regimes of the TFEU discussed in chapter 2 and partly regulate trade with third countries: customs duties (section 2.1 below), intra-Community transfers (section 2.2 below) and defence exports (section 2.3 below). Special emphasis is put on intra-Community transfers, divided into transfers of armaments (section 2.2.1 below) and dual-use goods (section 2.2.2 below) due to the particular importance of the earlier leading to the relevant ICT Directive being introduced in concert with the Defence Directive. This is followed by sections on standardisation (section 3 below), competition (anti-trust) law (section 4 below), merger control (section 5 below) and State aid (section 6 below). The chapter concludes with a brief overview of other relevant Commission initiatives and policies (section 7 below), especially relating to research. It will be argued that the TFEU and relevant secondary EU law provide a relatively comprehensive

---

Efficient Defence and Security Sector", COM (2013) 542 final, at 8 this Directive and the Defence Directive are called the "cornerstone of the European defence market".

[3] COM (2007) 764 final.

[4] "European Defence – Industrial and Market Issues: Towards an EU Defence Equipment Policy", COM (2003) 113 final; "The Challenges facing the European Defence-related Industry", COM (1996) 10 final.

[5] COM (2003) 113 final. [6] Ibid., at 3–4.

legal framework for the European defence and security market of which the Defence Directive now forms the centrepiece.

2 Trade in armaments and dual-use goods

The legal and policy context of the European defence industries is determined to a large extent by the regulation of trade in armaments and dual-use goods.[7] This refers to all rules related to the control of the movement of defence-related products from one State to another, especially rules relating to licences for such movements. As discussed in chapter 1,[8] the small size of the national markets of the EU Member States makes "intra-Community transfers" and third-country exports of armament and dual-use goods relevant for the performance of the defence industrial base. In 2003 the overall value of intra-Community transfer licences was €8.9 billion and the value of third-country export licences was €19.4 billion.[9] The regulation of trade in armaments has a direct impact on competition in the defence industries.[10] A liberal regime is likely to increase sales thereby leading, inter alia, to economies of scale and learning as well as competitive prices. A restrictive regime will do the opposite. Therefore, the regulation of trade has an effect on the competitiveness of the defence industries comparable to the regimes on competition law, merger control and State aid and has to be discussed in the context of this chapter.

Trade in armaments and dual-use goods have to be divided into two separate but interrelated aspects. First, there are movements of arms and dual-use products between EU Member States. These are normally referred to as intra-Community transfers, although the European Community ceased to exist and was replaced by the EU with the entering into force of the TFEU on 1 December 2009. Thus these movements should be called "Intra-Union transfers". However, the most important instrument in this context was introduced before the entering into force of the Treaty of Lisbon and consequently called the "intra-Community Transfers Directive". Therefore this chapter will use this term. Intra-Community transfers will be discussed first (section 2.2 below). This regime is closely connected to the Internal Market regimes of the TFEU discussed in chapter 2 but also determined by the defence exemptions discussed in chapter 3. Secondly, there are movements of arms and dual-use goods from an EU Member State to a third country outside the EU. These are referred to as defence exports and will be discussed below after intra-Community transfers (section 2.3 below).

---

[7] COM (1996) 10 final, at 24.   [8] At 22–8.

[9] *Intra-Community Transfers of Defence Products* Study (Brussels: Unisys Belgium for the European Commission, 2005), www.edis.sk/ekes/en_3_final_report.pdf [accessed 29 October 2013], at 95. 6th Annual Report According to Operative Provision 8 of the European Union Code of Conduct on Arms Exports [2004] OJ C-316/1.

[10] COM (2003) 113 final.

2.1 Customs duties

Member States even impose customs duties on intra-Community transfers of armaments.[11] It is submitted that this practice cannot be reconciled with the narrow interpretation of Article 346(1)(b) TFEU after *Spanish Weapons*,[12] *Agusta*[13] and *Military Exports*[14] especially when considering the facts behind the judgments outlined in chapter 3.[15] A charge on armaments because they are crossing a border is not a proportionate measure in the interest of national security but a clear case of abuse of Article 346(1)(b) TFEU to protect national defence industries. In other words, it cannot be argued that customs duties could be necessary for the national security interest of a Member State.[16] Similarly the ECJ ruled against an exemption of armaments exports from VAT in *Spanish Weapons*.[17] In a relevant case the Court is likely to rule against customs duties on intra-Community transfers of armaments.[18]

2.2 Intra-Community transfers

The notion intra-Community transfer of arms and dual-use goods refers to trade in defence goods between the Member States of the EU. As explained in chapters 2 and 3[19] and above, the free movement of goods regime of the TFEU covers intra-Community transfers of such goods, within the limits of Articles 36 and 346(1)(b) TFEU. Intra-Community transfers affect public security in the sense of Article 36 TFEU and national security in the sense of Article 346(1)(b) TFEU. Therefore proportionate measures to safeguard these public interest grounds are compliant with the Treaty, even if that measure represents a

---

[11] COM (1996) 10 final: "it is in the interest of the European Union and the Community that certain imports of arms and equipment for the European armed forces should benefit from exemption from customs duties and a list of equipment suitable for exemption from such duties is therefore needed". See also "Implementing European Union Strategy on Defence-related Industries", COM (1997) 583 final, Annex II "Action Plan for the Defence-related Industry", at 5.

[12] Case C-414/97, *Commission v. Spain* [1999] ECR I-5585, [2000] 2 CMLR 4.

[13] Case C-337/05, *Commission v. Italy* [2008] ECR I-2173 and C-157/06, *Commission v. Italy* [2008] ECR I-7313.

[14] Case C-284/05, *Commission v. Finland* [2009] ECR I-11705; Case C-294/05, *Commission v. Sweden* [2009] ECR I-11777; Case 387/05, *Commission v. Italy* [2009] ECR I-11831; Case C-409/05, *Commission v. Greece* [2009] ECR I-11859; Case C-461/05, *Commission v. Denmark* [2009] ECR I-11887; Case C-38/06, *Commission v. Portugal* [2010] ECR I-1569; Case C-239/06, *Commission v. Italy* [2009] ECR I-11913 discussed in ch. 3 at 109–19.

[15] At 108–9.   [16] See also the Military Exports case law, *supra* note 14.

[17] *Supra* note 12.

[18] The fact that customs duties are not mentioned in COM (2003) 113 final, could be interpreted as an indication that customs duties no longer occur.

[19] Ch. 2 at 63–82 and ch. 3 at 87–128.

measure having equivalent effect to a quantitative restriction and is therefore covered by the prohibition of Article 34 TFEU.

The Member State measures in question normally take the form of often numerous and time-consuming national authorisation or licensing procedures. For intra-Community transfers of armaments these procedures take an average of two full months, without any guarantee of success.[20] These procedures are normally the same that apply to exports to third countries and take the form of individual *ex ante* licences for companies, import and export licences, checks on delivery and in some cases end-user certificates.[21] An important reason for this burdensome "red tape" is the desire of Member States to control the final destination of defence equipment, especially when this eventually involves third countries.[22] Many Member States do not want their strategic goods to end up in war zones or even hostile countries through another Member State, through so-called re-exports.[23] Such considerations can justify these controls on the basis of Article 36 TFEU for dual-use goods and on the basis of Article 346 TFEU for armaments.[24] Nevertheless, these procedures represent a considerable barrier to trade and contribute to the fragmentation of the European armaments market.[25]

2.2.1 Intra-Community transfers of armaments

According to the 2005 Study *Intra-Community Transfers of Defence Products*, there were 12,627 licence applications for conventional defence products delivery between the then 25 EU Member States in 2003, with an overall value of €8.9 billion. This is about 31.4 per cent of all transfers, with the remainder being exports to third countries.[26] Out of these only 15 licences were refused, all of them in the Baltic States.[27] There were no refusals anywhere else in the Union, including in the "Big Six" major defence-producing Member States identified in chapter 1.[28] Hence while licensing requirements exist it can be said that applications are almost never refused.

---

[20] UNISYS Study *Intra-Community Transfers of Defence Products, supra* note 9, at 59.

[21] COM (2003) 113 final.   [22] Ibid.

[23] In detail on the security motivation of Member States: Christian Mölling, "Options for an EU Regime on Intra-Community Transfers of Defence Goods" in David Keohane (ed.), *Towards a European Defence Market*, Chaillot Paper 113 (Paris: EU Institute of Security Studies, 2008), 51 at 63–5.

[24] Case C-367/89, *Criminal Proceedings against Aimé Richardt and Les Accessoires Scientifiques SNC* [1991] ECR I-4621.

[25] COM (1996) 10 final, at 19. The intra-Community trade in arms is only 3–4% of the overall armaments trade according to COM (1996) 10 final, at 8.

[26] UNISYS Study *Intra-Community Transfers of Defence Products, supra* note 9, at 95 reports that this percentage is in line with the turnover reported by large European enterprises: e.g. Thales reports a military turnover of 30% inside the EU and 70% outside (Interview D. L. August 2004).

[27] Ibid., at 94: six in each of Estonia and Latvia, and three in Lithuania.   [28] At 24.

The impact of licensing requirements on the Internal Market was convincingly summarised by the same 2005 Study:

> the very existence of specific licensing requirements on all countries under review is in itself an obstacle to intra-Community trade which is questionable with respect to the rules of the internal market . . . Overall the licensing requirements impose a significant administrative burden on companies and require long lead times – up to several months – in order to obtain transfer licences.[29]

An analysis of the indirect costs caused by the licensing requirements would go beyond the aim of this discussion of intra-Community transfers of armaments.[30] Suffice it to cite the estimated direct costs of €238 million for the 12,627 licences procedures of 2003 in the 2005 Study *Intra-Community Transfers of Defence Products*, of which €135.42 million have to be paid by the defence industries. In 1998 the European Defence Industries Group (EDIG) estimated their direct costs for export control measures at €107.1 million or 0.22 per cent of annual turnover of defence-related activities.[31] The 2007 Communication "A Strategy for a Stronger and More Competitive European Defence Industry" reports "red tape" costing industry €400 million per year.[32] These costs alone represent a Member State measure capable of directly and actually hindering intra-Union trade in the sense of the *Dassonville*[33] formula discussed in chapter 2.[34] Hence licensing requirements for the intra-Community transfer of armaments are generally measures having equivalent effect to a quantitative restriction in the sense of Article 34 TFEU.

With regards to armaments, Member States may invoke the armaments exemption in Article 346(1)(b) TFEU discussed in chapter 3 for most of these procedures, since for national security reasons trade in arms requires some form of control. Moreover, prima facie, licence requirements appear to be proportionate since they are the form of formal control the least detrimental to the Internal Market. In other words, there appear to be no measures less detrimental to the Internal Market which would safeguard the national security interest of the Member States equally well. However, the question of proportionality will depend on the details of the different licensing regimes in place.

---

[29] UNISYS Study *Intra-Community Transfers of Defence Products*, supra note 9, at 5. See also Mölling, "Options for an EU Regime on Intra-Community Transfers of Defence Goods", *supra* note 23, at 55, 61–2, and 68.

[30] See the discussion in ch. 1. UNISYS Study *Intra-Community Transfers of Defence Products*, *supra* note 9, at 112 estimates the indirect costs related to the obstacles to intra-Union transfers at €2.73 billion.

[31] As cited by the UNISYS Study *Intra-Community Transfers of Defence Products*, *supra* note 9, at 112.

[32] COM (2007) 764 final, at 4.

[33] Case 8/74, *Procureur du Roi* v. *Dassonville* [1974] ECR 837, [1974] 2 CMLR 436.

[34] 65–6.

With regards to the situation before the recent harmonisation efforts and after assessing all European Economic Area (EEA) countries and Switzerland, the *Intra-Community Transfers of Defence Products* Study comes to a clear assessment:

> Overall, the licensing requirements appear to be *out of proportion* with actual control needs, especially when we see that licence applications for intra-Community transfers are almost never rejected [emphasis added].[35]

This assessment is convincing. Hence the national licensing regimes are mostly disproportionate.[36] Moreover, it appears that most of these procedural requirements were introduced or continued under the assumption of an extensive interpretation of Article 346(1)(b) TFEU, according to which it is an almost automatic exemption of listed hard defence material from the application of the Treaty. There are no reports on Member States invoking the exemption to justify their licensing requirements. If Article 346(1)(b) TFEU was an automatic exemption, the lack of proportionality of the licensing requirements would not be a problem as all measures regarding armaments would be exempt from the Treaty. However, following the narrow interpretation of the armaments exemption clarified in *Spanish Weapons*,[37] *Agusta*[38] and the 2009 and 2010 *Military Exports* cases[39] discussed in chapter 3,[40] it needs to be specifically invoked for every single national procedural requirement. This could mean that there were disproportionate licensing requirements which cannot be justified by Article 346(1)(b) TFEU and thus are violating the Treaty. It is submitted that this clear legal situation after the judgments required a review and reform of these national procedures.[41]

As part of the 2007 "Defence Package" of which the Defence Directive is the main element, the EU also adopted Directive 2009/43/EC on the simplification of the terms and conditions pertaining to the transfer of defence-related products within the EU: the "Intra-Community Transfers (ICT) Directive". The deadline for the transposition of this Directive in the national laws of the Member States was 30 June 2011. However, these laws did not have to come into effect until 30 June 2012 thus allowing for a period of consultation for the transposition of the Directive. According to the Commission's 2012 "Report on

---

[35] *Supra* note 9, at 94; on p. 6 the Study reports: "In 2003, only 15 licences for intra-Community transfers were reported as rejected by the last annual Code of conduct [EDA] report, compared to 12627 that were granted."·

[36] Mölling, "Options for an EU Regime on Intra-Community Transfers of Defence Goods", *supra* note 23, at 52 also speaks of "disproportionate and costly burdens and obstacles". While it is not clear whether he is talking about proportionality in the sense of EU Internal Market law the use of the word clearly hints in that direction.

[37] *Supra* note 12.   [38] *Supra* note 13.   [39] *Supra* note 14.   [40] At 109–19.

[41] See also: UNISYS Study *Intra-Community Transfers of Defence Products*, *supra* note 9, at 7.

the Transposition of Directive 2009/43/EC"[42] 20 Member States had implemented by the deadline,[43] with Denmark having partially transposed, five Member States expecting to transpose in 2012[44] and Romania not having communicated transposition. The following pages will first describe the situation regarding intra-Community transfers before the transposition and implementation of the ICT Directive. This will include the impact of this "old" regime on defence procurement. This will be followed by a discussion of the rules and changes of the ICT Directive itself, including their likely impact on defence procurement. It will be explained that defence procurement and intra-Community transfers are two interrelated aspects of the liberalisation of the European defence equipment market which had to be addressed in legally binding instruments passed as part of one "Defence Package".

2.2.1.1 Situation before the ICT Directive   Before the introduction of the ICT Directive there was no general EU-wide transfer regime for armaments.[45] Each of the 28 Member States had their own national laws on licensing procedures for intra-Community transfers.[46] These laws varied considerably. Member States used different armaments lists,[47] often because "they have made their own modifications to them reflecting their national legislations and cultures".[48]

---

[42] "Report from the Commission to the European Parliament and the Council on Transposition of Directive 2009/43/EC Simplifying Terms and Conditions for Transfer of Defence-related Products within the EU", COM (2012) 359 final.

[43] Bulgaria, Czech Republic, Germany, Greece, Estonia, Ireland, Spain, France, Cyprus, Latvia, Lithuania, Hungary, Malta, the Netherlands, Austria, Poland, Slovenia, Slovakia, Sweden and United Kingdom: ibid., at 5 with details at 15–19.

[44] Belgium, Italy, Luxembourg, Poland, and Finland, see Transposition Report, *supra* note 42, at 5 and 15–19.

[45] See Mölling, "Options for an EU Regime on Intra-Community Transfers of Defence Goods", *supra* note 23, at 58.

[46] UNISYS Study *Intra-Community Transfers of Defence Products, supra* note 9, at 12.

[47] Ibid., at 9, lists: the 1958 list/Art. [346], the 1991 list/European embargos, the 1998 common list/Code of Conduct, the 2003 list/custom regulation [2003] OJ C-314/1, the Wassenaar list and individual lists referred to in the national legislation. At 10 it continues: "most of the Member States have either taken over the Wassenaar Munitions List or the European Common Military, with small additions, of their own. These additions create various small differences, which in turn create obstacles for the industry. A certain item may be licensable in one MS while not licensable in another MS. This implies difficulties for international companies, since they are required to verify with all of the 'ammunition' lists that are applicable to the particular export, import or transit action they would like to execute. This adds unnecessary complexity, which creates an unnecessary administrative burden for the industry." Note the use of the word "unnecessary" which implies a lack of proportionality which would question the possibility of justifying the licensing requirements through Art. 346(1)(b) TFEU. See also at 63.

[48] Mölling, "Options for an EU Regime on Intra-Community Transfers of Defence Goods", *supra* note 23, at 58.

Moreover, there were different kinds of licences, different criteria to be satisfied for the issuance of a licence if these criteria were listed at all, and different authorities in charge.[49] The discretion of the relevant authorities was often completely unfettered. According to the 2005 Study *Intra-Community Transfers of Defence Products*, the existence of many different laws is in itself "a serious burden for intra-Community transfers" as a lack of knowledge of both many traders and the administration is the result of a lack of a common information system, not to mention language problems.[50] This is then connected to the problem of differences in content related to the definition of material on the basis of different lists mentioned above, the validity of licences and the different steps of the procedure.[51] Moreover, in some Member States licences were subject to a fee. There were liberal regimes in which licences could be obtained for several years and restrictive regimes in which a licence was required for every single shipment. Renewals were often possible, but also varied with respect to the requirements which had to be fulfilled and with respect to their length of validity. Furthermore, the allocation of responsibility was not always clear, and more than one authority may have had to be involved.[52] This could require a set of additional licences.[53] The certification process for reliable defence exporters was also based on many different national practices in the Member States.[54]

Some or all of these characteristics often led to a lack of transparency, delays and inconsistent decisions. A crucial common principle of the national laws relating to intra-Community transfers before the implementation of the ICT Directive highlighted by the 2005 Study *Intra-Community Transfers of Defence Products*, however, was that intra-Community transfers and exports to third countries were subject to the same rules and practices.[55] In other words there were no national rules specifically adapted to take the obligations of the Member States under the rules of the Internal Market into account – it made no difference if the destination of the product was another Member State or not. No distinction was made between intra-Community transfers on the one hand and exports to third countries on the other hand. The situation was also criticised by the European defence industries.[56]

---

[49] See the discussion in Mölling, ibid.

[50] UNISYS Study *Intra-Community Transfers of Defence Products, supra* note 9, at 12 also at 59 and 64.

[51] Ibid., at 17–24 on the different procedures. See also: Mölling, "Options for an EU Regime on Intra-Community Transfers of Defence Goods", *supra* note 23, at 58.

[52] UNISYS Study *Intra-Community Transfers of Defence Products, supra* note 9, at 13 and 60–1.

[53] Ibid., at 15–16 with examples for such additional requirements, see also at 60–1.

[54] Mölling, "Options for an EU Regime on Intra-Community Transfers of Defence Goods", *supra* note 23, at 59.

[55] UNISYS Study *Intra-Community Transfers of Defence Products, supra* note 9, at 13.

[56] See the President of the European Defence Industries Group Corrado Antonini: "Political Harmonisation and Consolidation", EMP conference on the Future of the European

Three types of licences were in place for both the exports of armaments and dual-use products: individual, general and global.[57] An individual licence, as now defined in Article 7 ICT Directive, is a specific authorisation granted by a Member State to an individual supplier at its request, permitting one or several shipments to one recipient only. Before the transposition of the ICT Directive, individual licences were the most commonly used type of licence in the EU Member States.[58] The individual licence either expires by the usual time period of 12 months or is fulfilled by reaching a specified quantity. It is the most costly and onerous type of licence due to its limitations.

A general licence, as now defined in Article 5(1) ICT Directive, is a specific authorisation granted by a Member State to a supplier established on its territory to perform transfers of defence-related products to a category or categories of recipients located in another Member State. Before the transposition of the ICT Directive, Member States used these licences only in very limited circumstances. The United Kingdom is a prime example of this approach, using the "Open General Licence (OGEL)". At first, the United Kingdom had not really changed its Export Order 2008 in response to the Directive because the country provided for general licences anyway.[59] However, as explained below, the British instrument has since been amended. In contrast to an individual licence, a general licence authorises the transfer of a large quantity of goods to a number of designated recipients. Hence this type of licence is less expensive and onerous than the individual licence.

A global transfer licence, as now defined in Article 6(1) and (2) ICT Directive, is a specific authorisation, granted by a Member State in response to a request by a supplier, to transfer defence-related products or categories of defence-related products to authorised recipients or a category of recipients in one or more other Member States. Before the transposition of the ICT Directive, Member States issued global licences only for dual-use goods.[60] This type of licence was used for transfers for which otherwise a large number of individual licences would have been required. Similar to the individual licence, the global licence is only valid for a limited period but it is not limited with respect to quantity. This allows unforeseen shipments to be included and they can be used several times for

Defence Industry, Brussels, 10–11 December 2003 as cited in *Intra-Community Transfers of Defence Products*, *supra* note 9, at 80.

[57] Commission Staff Working Document, *Accompanying Document to the Proposal for a Directive of the European Parliament and of the Council on Simplifying Terms and Conditions of Transfers of Defence-related Products within the Community*, SEC (2007) 1593, 5 December 2007, http://eur-lex.europa.eu/LexUriServ/LexUriServ.do? uri=CELEX:52007SC1593:EN:HTML [accessed 29 October 2013] (hereinafter "ICT Commission Working Document"), at 4.

[58] Ibid., at 26 and 34.

[59] Thanks to Luke Butler for pointing this out to me when commenting on an earlier version of this chapter.

[60] ICT Commission Working Document, *supra* note 57, at 13.

similar transfers. The applicant may be required to provide the details of the recipients of the products every three months.

Rather than being the subject of EU legislation, until the ICT Directive, transfer licences had only been the subject of one serious initiative outside the Internal Market. The Letter of Intent (LoI), an organisational structure outside the EU discussed in more detail in chapter 5,[61] created a LoI Framework Agreement aimed at simplifying transfer licences. The LoI members are all EU Member States. EU Member States are not allowed to confer powers to organisations outside the EU when these powers have already been conferred to the EU. This would, inter alia, violate the loyalty clause in Article 4(3) TEU. The fact that the respective Member States have acted through the LoI is only possible on the basis of a wide interpretation of Article 346(1)(b) TFEU, which, as explained in chapter 3, has been rejected by the ECJ in *Spanish Weapons*,[62] *Agusta*[63] and *Military Exports*.[64] Member States cannot act when the EU has occupied the field. This now happened with respect to intra-Community transfers with the ICT Directive. Any framework outside this instrument can only be used after a successful invocation of Article 346(1)(b) TFEU. The Organisation for Joint Armaments Procurement (OCCAR), also an organisational structure outside the EU discussed further in chapter 5,[65] has not addressed licences and neither has the European Defence Agency.

2.2.1.2 Intra-Community transfers and procurement As security of supply,[66] a concept introduced in chapter 1,[67] is an important consideration in any defence procurement procedure, (1) transfer licence requirements for non-domestic goods as such and (2) their operation in practice have a direct impact on procurement. A contracting officer cannot take the grant of a required transfer licence for goods, including spare parts and components, from another Member State as a given. At least in theory it might be refused and delays are possible. This is to a large extent due to the fact that there is no general and reliable EU-wide transfer regime.[68] The same applies in case of imports from third countries outside the EU. It appears that the mere

---

[61] At 225–31.   [62] *Supra* note 12.   [63] *Supra* note 13.   [64] *Supra* note 14.

[65] At 222–5.

[66] The notion "security of supply" defines the ability of a defence authority or defence producer "to guarantee and to be guaranteed a supply of Defence Articles and Defence Services sufficient to meet its commitments in accordance with its foreign and security policy requirements (state actor) or its contract commitments (private actor) vis-à-vis another State or private actor". NATO definition cited in William Denk, presentation, "Security of Supply", US-Spain Defence Industry Cooperation Conference, Madrid, 16 July 2003, http://proceedings.ndia.org/3991/Denk.pdf [accessed 29 October 2013].

[67] At 42–3.

[68] Mölling, "Options for an EU Regime on Intra-Community Transfers of Defence Goods", *supra* note 23, at 55.

theoretical possibility of a licence being refused makes contracting officers inclined to award contracts for defence-related goods to domestic suppliers,[69] where such suppliers are available. The 2005 Study *Intra-Community Transfers of Defence Products* reports such an effect, despite the fact that licences are rarely refused in practice.[70] To a certain extent these security-of-supply considerations relating to transfer licensing requirements can be addressed in the regulation of defence procurement. This will be further discussed in chapter 8, as will be the consideration of security of supply in the procurement context generally.[71] Article 23(a) and (b) Defence Directive also allow taking into account restrictions of the ability of a tenderer to export, transfer or transport goods associated with the product.[72] Regulation specific to intra-Community transfers can address this effect by harmonising the rules and by making the application procedures for transfer licences as fast, efficient and uncomplicated as possible. Improvements in the licensing regimes might well help to overcome the negative effect they have on procurement decisions. However, in the light of the fact that licences are hardly ever refused, the attitude of many contracting officers is objectionable. If licences were not refused in practice even before the transposition of the ICT Directive, then licensing requirements cannot represent a threat to security of supply to which the exclusion of a non-domestic supplier from another Member State could be a proportionate response.

2.2.1.3 The ICT Directive The Commission and Member States have been working towards the simplification of intra-Community transfers for some time.[73]

---

[69] ICT Commission Staff Working Document, *supra* note 57, at 16. See also Mölling, "Options for an EU Regime on Intra-Community Transfers of Defence Goods", *supra* note 23, at 55 and 63.

[70] ICT Commission Staff Working Document, *supra* note 57, at 16; Mölling, "Options for an EU Regime on Intra-Community Transfers of Defence Goods", *supra* note 23, at 55 and 63.

[71] At 359–61 and throughout the chapter.   [72] See ch. 8 at 368–61.

[73] COM (1996) 10 final, at 19: "it implies especially, whenever possible, the simplification and rationalization of controls on intra-Community trade carried out by States"; COM (1997) 583 final, Annex I: Draft Common Position on Framing a European Armaments Policy, Art. 5: "the following measures will be adopted as soon as possible following the appropriate procedures: . . . a simplified system applicable to intra-Community transfers including exports and re-export guarantees, and monitoring and surveillance mechanisms", Annex II: Action Plan for the defence-related industries at 3: "the Commission will therefore propose to put in place a simplified licensing system applicable to the shipment of defence related products within the European Community. This system shall comprise guarantees for exports and re-exports as well as mechanisms for control and surveillance." This was planned for 1998, see the timetable on p. 10; COM (2003) 113 final. The UNISYS Study *Intra-Community Transfers of Defence Products*, *supra* note 9, was another initiative. After discussions of this study with the Member States, in 2006, a public debate was launched with the Consultation Paper on the intra-Community circulation of defence-related products. This was followed by an impact assessment study and then the proposal for a directive as part of the "Defence Package".

The ICT Directive, which entered into force on 30 June 2009,[74] aims to simplify the rules and procedures applicable to intra-Community transfers of defence products.[75] The Commission opted for a Directive rather than a Regulation as the earlier is more suited for Internal Market legislation, which requires detailed measures better enacted at national level. According to Recital 6 ICT Directive,

> This Directive only deals with rules and procedures as far as defence-related products are concerned, and, consequently, does not affect the policies of the Member States regarding the transfer of defence-related products.

The Directive does not refer to Member State competence in the field of intra-Community transfers in the actual definition of the scope of the Directive in its Article 1.[76] According to Article 1(2) ICT Directive, "[it] does not affect the discretion of Member States as regards policy on the export of defence-related products". Thus the Directive only applies to licensing. It does not affect Member State competence regarding their policies on transfers, while by regulating intra-Community transfers it does inevitably also regulate their policies which now have to comply with the details of the Directive. However, it does not expressly define the precise competence of the EU and the scope of the Directive regarding transfers in Article 1 itself, which only refers to exports. This indicates a lack of clear EU delimitation between Member State and EU competence in the field of transfers and is possibly a reflection of the fact that the extent of EU competence on exports is not quite clear. The EU Code on exports discussed below, for example, is very generic, not legally binding or very detailed and at the fringes of EU competence.[77]

2.2.1.3.1 Definition of transfer and objectives Arguably the most crucial innovation of the ICT Directive is contained in Article 3(2) which provides a definition of the notion "transfer" as

> any transmission or movement of a defence-related product from a supplier to a recipient in another Member State.

---

[74] Art. 18(1) ICT Directive.

[75] Recital 3 and 6 and Art. 18(1) ICT Directive. More specifically the objectives of the new regime are: to establish the free movement of defence goods within the EU; to ensure that national security and political interests of the Member States are considered, especially re-exports and security of supply; to simplify and harmonise licensing procedures; to organise a control traceability and transparency of transfers; to link the regime to the Code of Conduct on Exports and other international treaties; and to confirm safeguards options for Member States.

[76] Thanks to Luke Butler for pointing this out to me when commenting on an earlier version of this chapter.

[77] In developing the argument in this paragraph I benefited considerably from discussions with Luke Butler when he commented on an earlier draft of this chapter.

This definition introduces an important distinction between "transfers" and "exports", the latter now a separate term exclusively describing a transmission or movement of a defence-related product from a supplier to a recipient in a third country outside the EU. The distinction is important because it introduces a move away from treating transmissions to other Member States, on the one hand, and to third countries outside the EU, on the other hand, alike. The new Directive draws a qualitative distinction between the movement of defence-related goods between Member States and their export to third countries.[78] This addresses the main objective of the Directive: to avoid disproportionate control procedures for intra-Community transfers caused by them being treated the same as third-country exports.

An important objective of the ICT Directive is according to its Recital 29 the "progressive replacement of individual ex-ante control by general ex-post control". Nevertheless, the Directive still allows subjecting transfers to ex-ante control and provides that transfers require prior authorisation, subject to certain exceptions. However, according to Article 4(1)[79] Member States cannot ask for further authorisations for transits or for entering the territory of the recipient's Member State, save in some exceptional cases. According to Article 4(2) ICT Directive Member States may exempt transfers of defence-related products from the obligation of prior authorisation set out in that paragraph where:

(a) the supplier or the recipient is a governmental body or part of the armed forces; (b) supplies are made by the European Union, NATO, IAEA or other intergovernmental organisations for the performance of their tasks; (c) the transfer is necessary for the implementation of a cooperative armament programme between Member States; (d) the transfer is linked to humanitarian aid in the case of disaster or as a donation in an emergency; or (e) the transfer is necessary for or after repair, maintenance, exhibition or demonstration.

This is a crucial aspect since it allows the Member States by transposing or not transposing any of these exceptions to define the scope of the Directive.[80] According to the 2012 Commission Transposition Report some of the Member

---

[78] Luke Butler, "Procurement Law as a Barrier to Transatlantic Defence Market Liberalisation", PhD Thesis, University of Birmingham (2013), ch. 2.

[79] Art. 4(1) ICT Directive reads: "1. The transfer of defence-related products between Member States shall be subject to prior authorisation. No further authorisation by other Member States shall be required for passage through Member States or for entrance onto the territory of the Member State where the recipient of defence-related products is located, without prejudice to the application of provisions necessary on grounds of public security or public policy such as, *inter alia*, the safety of transport."

[80] H. Ingels, "The Intra-EU Defence Trade Directive: Positive Goals" in Alyson J. K. Bailes, Sara Depauw and Tomas Baum (eds.), *The EU Defence Market: Balancing Effectiveness with Responsibility* (Brussels: Flemish Peace Institute, 2011), 61 at 65.

States have used this possibility.[81] Out of the 20 Member States who had already fully implemented the ICT Directive in 2012, 12 had used the exception in letter (a) of Article 4(2), 11 the exception in letter (b) and (c), 12 the exception in letter (d) and 9 that in letter (e). Thus there seems a tendency to take advantage of the exceptions – but not everywhere.

2.2.1.3.2 Types of licences under the ICT Directive The ICT Directive still provides for individual, global and general licences. However, it aims to limit recourse to the currently most frequently used individual licences and to increase the use of global and general licences instead. The objective is to move from the most onerous to less onerous forms of licences. Under the ICT Directive, an individual licence should only be granted in a number of exceptional situations. According to Article 7 Directive 2009/43/EC this applies (a) to cases in which the application was limited to one transfer and (b) where an individual licence is necessary for the protection of the essential security interests of the Member State or on grounds of public policy. Moreover, this applies (c) where such a licence is necessary to comply with international obligations and commitments or (d) where a Member State has serious reason to believe that the supplier will not be able to comply with all the terms and conditions necessary to grant a global transfer licence. The list provided in Article 7 is exhaustive. These exceptions aim to address national security interests inside the ICT Directive thereby limiting the need for Member States to invoke Article 346 TFEU to derogate from the Directive and Treaty just to be able to insist on an individual licence. This is comparable to many of the adaptations in the Defence Directive discussed in Part II of this book. As with the Defence Directive, the aim is to keep the licensing regime inside the instrument and the Internal Market rather than insist on global and general licences in every single case. This flexible approach is appropriate to ensure the implementation of the regime in practice. Some of the exceptions can be revised or deleted in future revisions of the ICT Directive.

The ICT Directive clearly favours the use of general licences. These should be published (Recital 21),[82] which makes it unnecessary for the supplier to specifically apply for the licence. There are situations where a general licence is mandatory and situations where they are merely optional. According to Article 5(2) the mandatory situations apply (a) when the recipient is part of the armed forces of a Member State or a contracting authority in the field of defence or

---

[81] *Supra* note 42, at 6–7. Thanks to Luke Butler for drawing my attention to this point when commenting on an earlier version of this chapter.

[82] Recital 21 ICT Directive reads: "In order to facilitate transfers of defence-related products, general transfer licences should be published by Member States granting authorisation to transfer defence-related products to any undertaking fulfilling the terms and conditions defined in each general transfer licence."

(b) in cases where the recipient is certified in accordance with the ICT Directive. Moreover, this applies to (c) cases where the transfer is made for purposes of demonstration, evaluation and exhibition and (d) for cases where the transfer is made for the purpose of maintenance and repair, if the recipient is the original supplier.[83] The mandatory use of general licences reflects the reduced risk for national security in these situations, either because the recipient has already been checked or is unlikely to pose a risk. The existence of such a general licence will make a transfer more predictable and efficient and almost removes the licensing requirement as a barrier to the movement of the relevant defence-related products.

The use of general licences is optional under Article 5(3) ICT Directive for Member States participating in intergovernmental cooperative programmes concerning the development, production and use of one or more defence-related products, when such transfer to another participating Member State is necessary for the programme's execution. As mentioned above, the use of general licences was already the most common in connection with this kind of cooperative programme. As will be explained in more detail in chapter 6,[84] cooperative programmes are outside the scope of the Defence Directive, which would not exclude the voluntary use of the Directive. Hence neither Directive imposes mandatory rules on these programmes.[85]

For the ICT Directive global licences are the "second best" option. Whenever a general licence cannot be published, a global licence should be granted to individual companies, if they apply for it (Recital 26). According to Article 6(2) subparagraph 2 ICT Directive, a global licence should be granted for three years and may be renewed. During the preparation of the Directive a "global licences only" regime had been considered. However, it was feared that Member States would interpret global licences in such restrictive terms that they would remain too similar to individual licences.

2.2.1.3.3 Certification   The ICT Directive also for the first time establishes common certification requirements for the recipients of intra-Community transfers. According to Article 9(1) ICT Directive Member States must designate competent authorities to administer the certification of recipients on their territory. According to Article 9(2) the certification is to establish the reliability of the recipient, especially with regards to their capacity to observe exports limitations on products received from another Member State under an intra-Community transfer licence, on the basis of prescribed criteria.[86] The 2011

---

[83] See the 2012 Transposition Report, *supra* note 42, at 9.   [84] At 283–8.

[85] See the 2012 Transposition Report, *supra* note 42, at 9.

[86] These include: (1) proven experience, taking into account in particular the undertaking's record of compliance with export restrictions; (2) relevant defence industrial activity; (3) the appointment of a senior executive responsible for transfers and exports; (4) a written

Commission Recommendation of 11 January 2011 on the Certification of Defence Undertakings und Article 9 of Directive 2009/43/EC … simplifying terms and conditions of defence related products within the Community[87] provides common .certification guidelines for national authorities. The certificates must not be valid for more than three years and the authorities must monitor compliance every three years. According to Article 9(6) ICT Directive there is an obligation of mutual recognition of certificates issued on the basis of the Directive in another Member State. The competent authority may revoke the certification if the holder no longer satisfies the criteria or conditions, according to Article 9(7) ICT Directive.

The Register of the Certified Defence-related Enterprises (CERTIDER)[88] of the Commission's Directorate General Enterprise provides information about enterprises that are certified under the ICT Directive. CERTIDER contains a list of the competent national authorities of the Member States for certification, the list of certified enterprises, details about the certificates and links to relevant national legislation.

2.2.1.3.4 Export limitations   The export to a third country outside the EU after an intra-Community transfer of a defence-related good remains an important concern for many Member States. These concerns are addressed in the ICT Directive in the provisions on export limitations. The central provision of Article 11 provides:

> Member States shall ensure that recipients of defence-related products, when applying for an export licence, declare to their competent authorities, in cases where such products received under a transfer licence from another Member State have export limitations attached to them, that they have complied with the terms of those limitations, including, as the case may be, by having obtained the required consent from the originating Member State.

Article 8(1) ICT Directive requires Member States to ensure that suppliers inform recipients of the terms and conditions of transfer licences, including limitations regarding the end-use or export of the defence goods. Recipients have to declare to their national authorities that they have complied with the terms of any limitations including if required having obtained the consent

---

commitment that the undertaking will take all necessary steps to observe and enforce conditions relating to the end-use and export of any specific component or product received; (5) a written commitment that it will provide detailed information in response to requests and inquiries concerning the end-users or end-use of all products exported, transferred or received; and (6) a description of the undertaking's internal compliance programme or transfer and export management system: Art. 9(2)(a)–(f).

[87] [2011] OJ L11/62.

[88] http://ec.europa.eu/enterprise/sectors/defence/certider/ [accessed 29 October 2013].

of the supplier's Member State.[89] Article 11 ICT Directive concerns customs procedures to ensure a final check on exports and their conformity with relevant administrative formalities before leaving the EU. Member States have to provide rules on penalties for the provisions of false or incomplete information with regards to compliance with the export limitations attached to the export licence. The spirit of these rules is well summarised in Recital 34.[90]

2.2.1.3.5 Limitations of the ICT Directive A number of important limitations of the ICT Directive should be emphasised. First, the instrument does not affect the policies of the Member States relating to the transfer of defence-related products (Recital 6)[91] nor does it limit their discretion when deciding about licence applications (Recital 7) and certification. However, the latter limitation has to be seen in perspective as licence applications are hardly ever refused in practice. Moreover, while licensing and certification remain the prerogative of the Member States, the Directive introduces an agreed common set of rules and criteria.[92] After all, the objective of the ICT Directive is not to force Member States to grant licences which they would otherwise not have granted. The objective is rather to facilitate the simplification and acceleration of the licensing procedures.[93]

Secondly, provided compliance with the ICT Directive is ensured, it does not affect the possibility of Member States pursuing international cooperation or any other international obligations and commitments of the Member States (Recital 7).[94] This is also a reflection of the fact that international cooperation is accepted as a complementary vehicle for the liberalisation of the European defence equipment market. Moreover, as pointed out above, the use of global licences in the context of cooperative armaments programmes made the ICT Directive less necessary in this segment of the market than in others.

---

[89] See Recital 35 ICT Directive.

[90] Recital 34 reads: "In order to facilitate mutual confidence, recipients of transferred defence-related products should refrain from exporting those products where the transfer licence contains export limitations."

[91] Recital 6 (second sentence) reads: "This Directive only deals with rules and procedures as far as defence-related products are concerned, and, consequently, does not affect the policies of the Member States regarding the transfer of defence-related products."

[92] Mölling, "Options for an EU Regime on Intra-Community Transfers of Defence Goods", *supra* note 23, at 84.

[93] Recital 6 (first sentence) reads: "The relevant laws and regulations of Member States therefore need to be harmonised in such a way as to simplify the intra-Community transfer of defence-related products in order to ensure the proper functioning of the internal market."

[94] Recital 7 reads: "Harmonisation of the relevant laws and regulations of Member States should not prejudice the international obligations and commitments of the Member States nor their discretion as regards their policy on the export of defence-related products."

Nevertheless, the Directive has "Communitarised" and occupied a considerable part of the field, thereby reducing the scope for international cooperation in the field of intra-Community transfers.

Thirdly, the ICT Directive is still subject to the Treaty exemptions in Articles 36 and 346 TFEU. However, while this represents a limitation in theory, it is unlikely to have a considerable impact in practice. Again, licence applications are hardly ever refused even before the transposition of the new instrument into the national laws of the Member States. Again, simplification and acceleration are the objectives of the ICT Directive. Furthermore, Directives can never remove Treaty exemptions; that would require a Treaty amendment. They are designed to reduce the detrimental impact of the legitimate use of such exemptions on the Internal Market by Member States by accommodating the public interests enshrined in the exemptions, in this case public and national security.

The instrument only applies to goods listed in the Annex to the ICT Directive, which corresponds to the Common Military List of the European Union updated on 15 February 2010.[95] The 2012 Transposition Report considers this reference to the 2010 List as a problem.[96] Although the Annex to the ICT Directive

> should be identical at all times to the Common Military List of the EU, practice shows that the procedure for amendment of the Annex takes at least seven months. Consequently, it differs from the Common Military List of the EU during at least seven months of the year.[97]

The Commission Directive amending the Annex must be transposed by the Member States. Consequently national legislations transposing the Annex will never be identical to the 2010 Common Military List applying at that moment, unless the Member States transpose it without awaiting the amendment of the Annex. The resulting discrepancies

> lead to legal and administrative divergences for national authorities and defence-related undertakings within the EU and goes against the intention of the legislator for a strict correspondence between the Annex of the Directive and the Common Military List of the EU.[98]

The Commission suggested simplifying the procedure for aligning the Annex of the ICT Directive and the 2010 List.

As outlined above, according to the 2005 Study *Intra-Community Transfers of Defence Products* the Member States had previously relied on various lists and the introduction of an updated single point of reference represents an improvement to that situation. On the other hand this means that only a specific

---

[95] [2010] OJ C-69/19.   [96] *Supra* note 42, at 13.   [97] Ibid.   [98] Ibid.

type of goods can be transferred without an *ex-ante* individual licence, "components that are of a military nature but less sensitive regarding national security interests".[99] However, a start on moving away from individual licences has been made and it is not impossible that more goods will added to this category in the future.

According to the 2012 Transposition Report, 20 Member States had transposed the ICT Directive fully, one had transposed partially, six Member States expected transposition in 2012 and one had not communicated transposition.[100] The Member States discussed in Part II with respect to their transposition of the Defence Directive, namely Austria,[101] Germany,[102] Ireland[103] and the United Kingdom[104] had all transposed the ICT Directive.

Overall, the ICT Directive provided Internal Market harmonisation for defence products to allow Member States to take measures protecting their public and national security without a disproportionate impact on the free movement of defence goods. However, as Mölling pointed out, "the breakthrough ... will not depend on the Commission but on the Member States".[105] This depends not only on the transposition of the Directive and crucially on its implementation in practice. The regime has to be entrusted to the right institutions, trust needs to be established between Member States, the system needs to be kept simple and implementation has to happen step by step. Mölling does not expect an immediate impact on reducing red tape and saving costs:

> As progressive growth of trust is necessary, this time-consuming process may on the other hand consume the financial benefits of the process through the trickledown effect.[106]

---

[99] Mölling, "Options for an EU Regime on Intra-Community Transfers of Defence Goods", *supra* note 23, at 84.

[100] *Supra* note 42, at 15–19.

[101] Änderung des Kriegsmaterialgesetzes (KMG) vom 29.7.2011 (KMG), BGBl 72/2011.

[102] Gesetz zur Umsetzung der Richtlinie 2009/43/EG des Europäischen Parlaments und des Rates vom 6. Mai 2009 zur Vereinfachung der Bedingungen für die innergemeinschaftliche Verbringung von Verteidigungsgütern (AWGuaÄndV k.a.Abk.) G. v. 27.07.2011 BGBl. I S. 1595 (Nr. 41).

[103] European Communities (Intra-Community Transfers of Defence Related Products) Regulation 2011 S.I. No. 346 of 2011.

[104] Export Control Order 2008 already partially complied with the ICT Directive, see the 2012 Transposition Report, *supra* note 42, at 19. However transposition was only completed with the Export Control (Amendment) Order 2013, S.I. 2013 No. 428.

[105] Mölling, "Options for an EU Regime on Intra-Community Transfers of Defence Goods", *supra* note 23, at 84. See also Ingels, "The Intra-EU Defence Trade Directive: Positive Goals", *supra* note 80, at 65.

[106] Mölling, "Options for an EU Regime on Intra-Community Transfers of Defence Goods", *supra* note 23, at 87.

Ingels considers the ICT Directive "certainly not perfect" and highlights the extent to which its success depends on the cooperation of the Member States using it.[107] Thus the general licence depends on its scope which as highlighted above is to be defined by the Member States. The recognition of licences between Member States might meet language barriers and administrative cooperation needs to be strengthened to avoid any misunderstandings. Finally, the motivation to seek certification depends on the role of an economic operator in the supply chain and the licensing regime in the supplier's Member State. Certification does not make sense if the component in question is subject to a global or individual licence.[108] Ingels also predicts that the ICT Directive will enhance transparency since the Member States have to introduce harmonised licensing systems and the defence suppliers have to apply harmonised reporting requirements. The national licensing authorities have a considerable level of control since it is they who decide which economic operators will supply defence products in other Member States; they grant the licences.[109]

The success of the new regime can only be assessed after full transposition and implementation – use in practice – on a long-term basis. Hence a full assessment can only be made in a few years. However, a crucial decision has been made and that is that the regime is part of the Internal Market and not of an alternative framework outside of it. This indicates a "Communitarisation" of intra-Community transfers of armaments, similar to the "Communitarisation" of defence procurement through the Defence Directive. As both instruments represent long overdue harmonisation measures for the establishment of an Internal Market in defence goods, the ICT Directive and the Defence Directive are siblings of the same "Defence Package" family. Both aim to reduce the use of Article 346 TFEU in practice and both are designed to facilitate more movement of goods across intra-Community borders. However, the ICT Directive is the "little brother" since it only aims to move the emphasis to different licences, whereas the Defence Directive wants to change award procedures and decisions and legalise a formerly political process. However, little brothers are sometimes more successful than their elder siblings.

2.2.2 Intra-Community transfer of dual-use goods: Regulation 428/2009/EC

With regards to security goods and services which are not listed in the 1958 list of armaments according to Article 346(2) TFEU discussed in chapter 3,[110] and therefore not covered by Article 346(1)(b) TFEU, the

---

[107] Ingels, "The Intra-EU Defence Trade Directive: Positive Goals", *supra* note 80, at 65.
[108] Ibid. [109] Ibid. [110] At 88–94.

public security exemptions in Articles 36 and 52 TFEU may apply, again as discussed in chapter 2,[111] subject to proportionality and judicial review. In cases in which Member States are allowed to legally derogate from the Internal Market rules of the Treaty on the basis of these public security derogations, the EU legislator is empowered to introduce legislation based on Article 114 TFEU and other legal bases on the Internal Market with the aim of harmonising the national laws regulating these measures.[112] This is relevant with respect to dual-use goods. As mentioned in chapter 1, dual-use goods are goods, software and technologies likely to have both civilian and military uses.[113] According to Article 2(a) of the relevant Regulation 428/2009/EC, introduced in more detail below,

> "dual-use items" shall mean items, including software and technology, which can be used for both civil and military purposes, and shall include all goods which can be used for both non-explosive uses and assisting in any way in the manufacture of nuclear weapons or other nuclear explosive devices . . .

In chapter 3 it was argued that this is not a category relevant for the interpretation of Article 346(1)(b) TFEU, since this provision only applies to products on the 1958 list. In other words, "listed" or "not listed" are the only categories recognised by the armaments derogation.[114] However, the "dual-use" regime is relevant for the analysis in this book because, as explained in more detail in chapter 6,[115] such goods are also covered by the Defence Directive, which is not limited to armaments but includes other sensitive security supplies, works and services. Hence the export and intra-Community transfers of these goods has an effect on competition in procurement procedures for dual-use goods as suppliers and providers with more liberal regimes can achieve economies of scale and learning through foreign sales. The effect of export rules on procurement is indirect, whereas for intra-Community transfers of armaments and dual-use goods there is this indirect effect on competition and the more direct effect on procurement decisions as a security-of-supply concern. This more direct effect was explained in the context of the intra-Community transfers of armaments above. Due to lower security concerns, dual-use products are often separated from armaments and subjected to less restrictive control regimes.

---

[111] At 63–82.   [112] See ch. 2 at 82–3.
[113] COM (2003) 113 final, citing Regulation 1334/2000/EC, cited in the next footnote. Art. 2(a) Regulation 3381/94/EC [1994] OJ L367/1 denies dual-use products as "goods which can be used for both civil and military purposes".
[114] At 88–94.   [115] At 263–6.

In the EU the export,[116] brokering and transit of "dual-use goods" is regulated in Council Regulation 428/2009/EC,[117] which repealed the previous Dual-use Regulation 1334/2000/EC.[118] This description of the function of the Regulation in its Article 1 does not expressly include intra-Community transfers. However, as will be explained in the context of the discussion of its Article 22 and Annex IV below, the Regulation contains a limited intra-Community transfer regime for dual-use goods. There are clear similarities with the ICT Directive discussed above: both instruments operate on the basis of lists of the relevant goods and regulate the control mechanisms for goods to be transmitted. Moreover, as will be explained further below, both aim to move

---

[116] Art. 2(2) Regulation 428/2009/EC reads: "'export' shall mean: (i) an export procedure within the meaning of Article 161 of Regulation (EEC) No. 2913/92 (the Community Customs Code); (ii) a re-export within the meaning of Article 182 of that Code but not including items in transit; and (iii) transmission of software or technology by electronic media, including by fax, telephone, electronic mail or any other electronic means to a destination outside the European Community; it includes making available in an electronic form such software and technology to legal and natural persons and partnerships outside the Community. Export also applies to oral transmission of technology when the technology is described over the telephone . . ."

[117] Council Regulation (EC) No. 428/2009 of 5 May 2009 (+COR) setting up a Community regimes for the control of exports, transfer, brokering and transit of dual-use items (recast) (and corrigendum) [2009] OJ L134/1, which entered into force on 27 August 2009. (On the same date Council Regulation (EC) No. 1334/2000 of 22 June 2000 setting up a Community regime for the control of exports of dual-use items and technology was repealed.)

[118] Council Regulation 1334/2000/EC of 22 June 2000 setting up a Community regime for the control of exports of dual-use items and technology [2000] OJ L159/1 corrigendum: [2000] OJ L176/1. The Dual-use Regulation abolished the previous regime on the same matter. This was based on an inter-pillar approach whereby the regime was regulated in the Community Pillar Regulation 3381/94/EC [1994] OJ L367/1 and the Second Pillar Decision 94/942/CFSP [1994] OJ L367/8. Decision 2000/402/CFSP [2000] OJ L159/218 repealed Decision 94/942/CFSP. The latter incorporated the material scope and procedures of the earlier. The inter-pillar approach had been criticised because it relied on an obsolete distinction between trade and foreign policy and rendered the EU measure's *modus operandi* ineffective by excluding it from the legal framework of the EU. Economic sanctions are also imposed on the basis of an inter-pillar approach. Under Arts. 60 and 301 EC introduced by the Treaty of Maastricht, sanctions on third countries were to be imposed by means of a Council Regulation adopted by qualified majority and pursuant to a Common Position or Joint Action already adopted under Title V TEU. This formulised the combination of Community and non-Community measures under the European Political Co-operation before 1992. See Panos Koutrakos, *Trade, Foreign Policy and Defence in EU Constitutional Law: The Legal Regulation of Sanctions, Exports of Dual Use Goods and Armaments* (Oxford: Hart, 2001), in ch. 4. See also P. Koutrakos, "Inter-pillar Approaches to the European Security and Defence Policy – The Economic Aspects of Security" in Vincent Kronenberger (ed.), *The European Union and the International Legal Order: Discord or Harmony?* (The Hague: T. M. C. Asser Press, 2001), at 435. Economic sanctions are an instrument of foreign policy with security implications.

the emphasis of control mechanisms from more onerous and time-consuming controls to less bureaucratic ones.

However, there are of course also differences. Most importantly, Regulation 428/2009/EC is an external trade instrument and was therefore based on the relevant legal base of Article 207 TFEU.[119] It provides for legally binding common principles and rules for the national implementation and enforcement of dual-use export controls by the Member States (Article 1). Regulation 428/2009/EC comprises a common list of items subject to control (Annex I), which is directly derived from the consensus decisions taken in the international regimes mentioned above.[120] However, as mentioned above, Regulation 428/2009/EC also contains a limited intra-Community transfers regime for dual-use goods. Article 22(1) of Regulation 428/2009/EC reads:

> An authorisation shall be required for intra-Community transfers of dual-use items listed in Annex IV. Items listed in Part 2 of Annex IV shall not be covered by a general authorization.

Annex IV[121] is then subdivided into two parts. Part 1 lists items which can be subjected to a "national general authorisation" for intra-Community trade. Listed items include those relating to stealth technology, cryptography and MTCR technology (with exceptions). Intra-Community transfers of these goods require national authorisation, but this can take the form of the less onerous general authorisation, which is similar to the general licences of the ICT Directive discussed above. In contrast, Part 2 lists items where no such authorisation may be granted and include items of the Chemical Weapons Convention and NSG Technology. These items are more sensitive than those in Part 1 and require the most onerous type of authorisation, a national individual authorisation. The latter is similar to an individual licence in the context of the ICT Directive. There are a few other cases in which authorisation can be required by Member States in Article 22(2) Regulation 428/2009/EC. However, these cases relate to scenarios in which the item in question is transferred to another Member State for the purpose of transit to a third country. Hence these scenarios are close to the third-country export situation, the regulation of which is the main objective of this instrument.

A real intra-Community control regime for dual-use goods in the strict sense is only contained in Article 22(1) Regulation 428/2009/EC. It should be emphasised that this only concerns a small number of highly sensitive goods. Moreover the prescribed measures are proportionate and carefully differentiate between two categories of goods and the corresponding measures. However,

---

[119] The limited intra-Community transfer regime contained in the Regulation is as much an Internal Market instrument as the ICT Directive. Hence, it is submitted that this part and therefore the entire Regulation should have been based on Art. 114 TFEU as well.
[120] As pointed out by the Commission in COM (2003) 113 final.   [121] [2009] OJ L134/260.

in contrast to most (Annex I) dual-use goods where control measures can only be imposed on the basis of Article 36 TFEU on a case-by-case basis, Article 22(1) Regulation 428/2009/EC represents an abstract intra-Community control regime of these few goods. In contrast to intra-Community transfers of most dual-use goods which are not subject to any abstract controls, these "Annex IV" goods are subject to controls in a way similar to armaments under the ICT Directive. This can have a similar "security of supply" effect on the procurement of these goods. In other words, defence procurement authorities cannot take authorisation for granted and can only fully rely on security of supply as far as domestic products are concerned. Overall, however, with the exception of a small number of items and situations, dual-use goods can move freely in the EU, subject to Article 36 TFEU.

2.3 Defence exports

As mentioned in chapter 1, in addition to their economic importance outlined above, armaments and dual-use exports, in other words transmissions to third countries outside the EU, are a highly political issue in Europe. They are regarded as an important instrument of foreign and economic policy. On the one hand, governments encourage and control arms exports in order to exert influence in other regions of the world, generate external revenues, sustain internal capacity, maintain employment and keep production lines open to maintain capability for integrating weapons systems. On the other hand, the export of defence products is highly controversial as at least some governments and at least parts of the public and of the national parliaments are concerned about weapons ending up in the wrong hands, facilitating civil wars or support-ing oppressive regimes. In 2013 five EU Member States appear on the top ten list of arms exporters compiled by the Stockholm International Peace Research Institute (SIPRI), each with a comparable share of the global market: (3) Germany with 7 per cent, (4) France with 6 per cent, (6) the United Kingdom with 4 per cent, (7) Spain with 3 per cent and (8) Italy with 2 per cent.[122] Overall, in 2010 for example, EU Member States exported defence goods to third countries with a value of €5.46 billion.[123]

Differences in policy and practice have emerged between the governments of the Member States that may affect competition in the defence industries. Due to the fact that the major European arms producers have failed to realise the full potential of developing trade relations with other Member States, protectionism so far has made Europe only a limited market for Europe, and United States protectionism and the lack of competitive products

[122] www.sipri.org/yearbook/2013/05 [accessed 30 October 2013].
[123] Analysis of European Council data conducted by the author.

largely closes the US-American market for European producers.[124] The Third World and especially the Middle East have thus become the major export markets for Europe with all the problems this involves. These problems have led to an intensive arms control debate with Germany and the Netherlands on one side promoting a higher level of control and France and Britain on the other side supporting flexibility. These disparities also distort competition as producers in countries with a less strict regulation have a competitive advantage over countries with stricter rules, including in procurement procedures that might otherwise be open and competitive.

Member States participate in most international defence-related export control regimes. These include the Australia Group, the Missile Technology Control Regime, the Nuclear Suppliers' Group, the Wassenaar Arrangement[125] or, formerly, the Coordinating Committee on Multilateral Export Controls (COCOM).[126] These regimes are designed to prevent the transfer of strategic goods and technology to a region or country where the situation could become a cause of serious political, strategic or economic concern to the participating states. The regimes are not legally binding and contain common criteria for assessing destabilising weapons accumulations and notification procedures for all relevant exports. In the context of the EU the regulation of strategic goods has to be subdivided into the regimes on dual-use goods (section 2.3.1 below) and on armaments (section 2.3.2 below).

2.3.1 Exports of dual-use goods

As explained above, dual-use goods are goods, software and technologies likely to have both civilian and military uses.[127] Their relevance for the analysis in this book and their effect on procurement were discussed in the context of the intra-Community transfers of these products above. Control on

---

[124] The rather complex arms export problems with the United States and the resulting export deficit shall not be dealt with in this chapter, see COM (1996) 10 final, at 7.

[125] COM (2003) 113 final, at footnote 18: "The Australia Group controls exports and transhipments that could result in proliferation of chemical and biological weapons. The Missile Technology Control Regime aims at preventing proliferation of unmanned delivery systems for weapons of mass destruction by controlling exports of missiles and related technologies. The Nuclear Suppliers' Group controls transfers of nuclear-related dual-use equipment, material and technology in order to prevent civilian nuclear trade from contributing to nuclear weapons acquisition. The Wassenaar Arrangement controls transfers of conventional weapons and sensitive dual-use goods and technologies, primarily electronic products defined widely."

[126] Intended to regulate exports to the Soviet bloc and therefore in contrast to the other regimes an instrument for the Cold War, see P. d'Argent, "Les Enseignements du COCOM" (1993) 26 *Revue Belge de droit international* 500.

[127] COM (2003) 113 final, citing Regulation 1334/2000/EC, cited in the next footnote. Art. 2(a) Regulation 3381/94/EC [1994] OJ L367/1 denies dual-use products as "goods which can be used for both civil and military purposes".

the basis of the relevant Council Regulation 428/2009/EC, generally takes the form of "authorisations": individual, global and general.[128] All authorisations are valid throughout the EU. Two different groups of third countries outside the EU can be differentiated. Australia, Canada, the USA, Japan, Norway, New Zealand and Switzerland are subject to a "Community general export author-isation" set out in Annex II for a large number of products.[129] This means that this authorisation published in the Official Journal makes all other authorisations unnecessary. With regards to most dual-use goods exported to the safest countries and closest allies of the EU Member States, there is therefore only this EU general export authorisation. Most if not all EU Member States are similar to the listed third countries with regards to the security concerns (or the lack thereof) that exist with regards to security exports. Thus the "general licence" approach of the ICT Directive discussed above is inspired by this concept of Regulation 428/2009/EC or rather its predecessor Regulation 1334/2000/EC.

With regards to all other countries, exports authorisations are granted by competent authorities, a list of which is provided to the Commission, in the Member States. A "global export authorisation" is "granted to one specific exporter in respect of a type or category of dual-use item which may be valid for exports to one or more specified end users and/or in one or more specified third countries".[130] A "national general export authorisation" is granted "in accordance with Article 9(2) and defined by national legislation in conformity with Article 9 and Annex IIIc".[131] An "individual export authorisation" is "granted to one specific exporter for one end user or consignee in a third country and covering one or more dual-use items".[132] These authorisations closely resemble the licences under the ICT Directive.

Where a Member State considers that exports from another Member State might be detrimental to its essential national security interests, it can ask for the authorisation to be refused, cancelled, suspended, modified or revoked. In such cases non-binding consultations between the two Member States begin immediately and should terminate within ten days. In deciding whether to grant an authorisation, Member States must take into account their obligations as members of international non-proliferation regimes; EU, OSCE and UN positions; the EU Code of Conduct on Arms Exports (see below); and consid-erations about intended end-use and the risk of diversion. Member States may prohibit an export or impose an authorisation requirement for reasons of public security or human rights violations.

---

[128] Art. 6(2) Regulation 1334/2000/EC.
[129] The Czech Republic, Hungary and Poland are also listed but are, since 2004, Member States of the EU and therefore subject to the regime on intra-Community transfers of these goods.
[130] Art. 2(10).   [131] Art. 2(11).   [132] Art. 2(8).

In *Aimé Richardt*,[133] *Werner*[134] and *Leifer*[135] the ECJ suggested that the competence of the Member States for foreign policy be protected within the then Community legal system of external relations, which may also ensure the effectiveness of the Common Commercial Policy.[136] Chapter 3[137] discussed the narrow interpretation of Article 346(1)(b) TFEU, especially after *Spanish Weapons*,[138] *Agusta*[139] and the recent *Military Exports*[140] cases placing dual-use goods clearly outside the ambit of the armaments exemption and therefore inside the field of application of the TFEU.[141] As the TFEU covers this material, the export of dual-use goods can only be regulated under the TFEU. Therefore Regulation 428/2009/EC is to be welcomed as an instrument of secondary EU law complying with both the TFEU and the case law of the ECJ. Moreover, it signifies the acceptance of the Member States.

2.3.2 Exports of armaments: Common Position 2008/944/CFSP

The significance of Regulation 428/2009/EC is emphasised when compared to the legal nature of the export control regime for armaments. Common Position 2008/944/CFSP is based on what is now Article 29 TEU and defines common rules governing control of exports of military technology and equipment.[142] In contrast to its predecessor the Code of Conduct, Common Position 2008/944/CFSP is legally binding and constitutes a significantly updated and

---

[133] Case C-367/89, [1991] ECR I-4645.   [134] Case C-70/94, [1995] ECR I-3989.
[135] Case C-83/94, [1995] ECR I-3231.
[136] Trybus, *European Union Law and Defence Integration*, supra note 1, ch. 6, in particular at 122.
[137] At 104–85.   [138] *Supra* note 12.   [139] *Supra* note 13.   [140] *Supra* note 14.
[141] See also the Commission in COM (1996) 10 final, at 14; K. Eikenberg, "Article 296 (ex 223) E.C. and External Trade in Strategic Goods" (2000) 25 *European Law Review* 117, at 125–8; O. Lhoest, "La Production et la commerce des armes, et l'article 223 du traité constituant la Communauté européene" (1993) 26 *Revue belge de droit international* 176, at 184–5; N. Emiliou, "Restrictions on Strategic Exports, Dual-use Goods and the Common Commercial Policy" (1997) 22 *European Law Review* 68, at 72.
[142] Council Common Position 2008/944/CFSP of 8 December 2008 defining common rules governing control of exports of military technology and equipment [2008] OJ L335/99. The legal instrument chosen for the new Common Rules is a "Common Position", based on Art. 29 (ex Art. 15) TEU (Lisbon). Common Positions in the context of CFSP (Common Foreign and Security Policy) are designed to "define the approach of the Union". Art. 29 provides that Member States "shall ensure that their national policies conform to the Union Positions". In other words, Member States are required by the TEU (Lisbon) to comply with and uphold such positions which have been adopted unanimously at the Council level. They involve a commitment by the Union as a whole as well as by the individual Member States. The effectiveness of the Common Positions was to be reviewed in 2011. On the rather unclear results of this review see Council Conclusions on the Review of Council Common Position 2008/944/CFSP defining common rules governing control of exports of military technology and equipment, 3199th Foreign Affairs Council Meeting, Brussels, 19 November 2012, www.consilium.europa.eu/uedocs/cms_Data/docs/pressdata/EN/foraff/133569.pdf [accessed 30 October 2013].

upgraded instrument replacing the said Code of Conduct.[143] However, the Common Position is an instrument in the framework of the CFSP. This means that even after the entering into force of the Treaty of Lisbon, the roles of the Commission, the European Parliament and the ECJ are negligible and compliance can only be achieved by mutual "peer pressure" of the Member States.

Common Position 2008/944/CFSP sets minimum standards for the control of conventional arms exports from Member States to third countries and establishes an exchange and consultation mechanism. Annual Reports monitor the operative provisions of the instrument.[144] Its objective is to achieve greater transparency in arms transactions and to lead to a growing convergence of national export policies.

The material scope is not expressly defined and, similar to its predecessor,[145] does not as such contain a list of products it applies to. There is the "EU Common Military List" and the most recent version was adopted in 2013.[146] However, according to Article 12 Common Position 2008/944/CFSP, the EU Common Military List shall not replace the national lists but only serve as a reference point. Nevertheless, the Common List will streamline and shape the scope of the Common Position, even as a reference point. This will be reinforced by the other functions of the Common List, in the context of intra-Community transfers, as explained above, and as a basis of interpretation for EU arms embargos.

Eight revised criteria are to guide national export officials in the author-isation of armaments exports. A refusal to authorise an export is to be notified and justified through diplomatic channels.[147] The "no undercutting" rule covers the case where a Member State receives an application for an export licence for a product and country where this has been refused by another Member State. The Member State who received such an application has to consult with the other Member State. The earlier has to inform the latter about the granting of a licence in such a case and justify this decision.[148] An export licence must only be granted on the basis of reliable prior knowledge of end use, which will normally require a "thoroughly checked" end-user certificate or appropriate documentation and/or official authorisation issued by the country of final destination. Each Member State is required to circulate an annual report on

---

[143] Recital 15 Common Position 2008/944/CFSP.

[144] See, for example, the Fourteenth Annual Report According to Article 8(2) of Council Common Position 2008/944/CFSP Defining Common Rules Governing Control of Exports of Military Technology and Equipment, 14 December 2012 [2012] OJ C-386/1.

[145] Koutrakos, *Trade, Foreign Policy and Defence, supra* note 118, at 202.

[146] Common Military List of the European Union – equipment covered by Common Position 2008/044/CFSP defining common rules governing the control of exports of military technology and equipment [2013] OJ C-90/1.

[147] Art. 4(1) Common Position 2008/944/CFSP.   [148] Ibid.

exports of military equipment and technology to the other Member States. Moreover, as mentioned above, the publication of an EU annual report in the OJ is required.[149] Member States must also exchange experiences with third countries applying the criteria on their military technology and equipment export control policies and on the application of the criteria on a regular basis. The User's Guide to the European Code of Conduct on Exports of Military Equipment, drawn up and regularly updated by the Working Party on Conventional Arms Exports serves as guidance to assist Member States.[150]

However, even a Code of Conduct using the machinery of the CFSP had to be criticised as it assumes and requires an automatic exclusion of armaments from the TFEU. The narrow interpretation of Article 346(1)(b) TFEU, especially after *Spanish Weapons*,[151] *Agusta*[152] and *Military Exports*[153] discussed in chapter 3[154] places armaments inside the field of application of the Internal Market of the TFEU, unless a Member State can derogate from the TFEU on a case-by-case basis. Therefore an abstract Code can only be part of the Internal Market framework as the regulation of armaments exports is covered by the TFEU unless Article 346(1)(b) TFEU is successfully invoked. The foreign policy implications of arms exports might lead to frequently successful invocations of the armaments exemption. Thus even with an "EU Armaments Exports Regulation", which does not exist, the CFSP would still have a role to play. The solution could be partly based on the inter-pillar approach of the former dual-use export regime. Armaments exports would be covered by an Internal Market Regulation, which would provide a national security exemption based on Article 346(1)(b) TFEU. After the successful invocation of this exemption the individual arms export case would be "transferred" to the CFSP. The CFSP would have to provide a Code of Conduct using the CFSP machinery as a catch-up framework for these cases. Moreover, an additional international treaty based on this CFSP framework would allow third states to participate in the framework of such a Code. In extreme cases a Member State should be allowed to derogate from both frameworks and move to the Code of Conduct as a second catch-up framework. To summarise, the narrow interpretation of Article 346(1)(b) TFEU requires an "EU Arms Export Regulation" supplemented by a "CFSP Arms Export Common Position" for cases where the armaments exemption of the TFEU can be successfully invoked. This approach reflects the fragmentation of defence integration into two pillars which could potentially undermine its effectiveness. However, it is submitted that it would contribute to a more coherent arms export policy since fewer "solo attempts" by individual Member States would get through such a "filter system".

---

[149] See *supra* note 144.
[150] http://register.consilium.europa.eu/pdf/en/09/st09/st09241.en09.pdf [accessed 30 October 2013].
[151] *Supra* note 12.   [152] *Supra* note 13.   [153] *Supra* note 14.   [154] At 104–25.

Moreover, this would almost provide a single export regime for the Union, save for those cases where national security is invoked.

3 Standardisation

Standards operate in the defence market as in any other market. According to the definition of the Commission,

> standards are sets of voluntary technical and quality criteria for products, services and production processes. Nobody is obliged to use or apply them but they help businesses in working together which ultimately saves money for the consumer.[155]

Standards are essential for the functioning of the free movement of goods as they ensure that products comply with essential safety requirements – often required in harmonising Directives – which reduces or even eliminates the necessity of Member States to rely on public interest derogations such as Article 36 TFEU. The latter include public security as one relevant public interest. Standardisation is a progressive process, as Pelkmans wrote:

> it is the task of the competent (private) standardization organs, given technical progress, to formulate the technical specifications, on the basis of which industry needs to manufacture and market products complying with the fundamental requirements of the directives . . .[156]

Again, standards are not legally binding. But they can reverse the "burden of proof". If the Commission has published a standard in the OJ all Member States are obliged to accept products that have been produced in compliance with the standard. If the Member State objects to the product they have the burden of proof that the standard does not comply with the initial Directive. Goods may be produced according to specifications which deviate from the standards in which case the producer has to prove that the product meets the safety requirements of the Directive.[157] Pelkmans emphasised:

> Standards can have a market-creating effect or, in other words, the lack of a standard between adjoining countries can make the Euromarket (i.e. trade between Member States) impossible . . . Standards can also have an antici-patory effect. For instance, sufficient investment in product development, process technology and further innovations takes place in some products only when compatibility is ensured first.[158]

---

[155] Definition from the Commission's website, http://ec.europa.eu/enterprise/policies/european-standards/standardisation-policy/index_en.htm [accessed 30 October 2013].
[156] J. Pelkmans, "The New Approach to Technical Harmonisation and Standardization" (1987) 25 *Journal of Common Market Studies* 249, 252–3.
[157] Ibid.   [158] Ibid., at 260.

Organisations such as the European Committee for Standardization (CEN), the European Committee for Electrotechnical Standardisation (CENELEC) and the European Telecommunications Institute (ETSI) "ensure that that standardization processes take place in parallel with harmonization at [EU] level and are based on 'essential requirements'".[159]

For the public procurement process, standards are especially important when the specifications are drawn up for the open and restricted procedures discussed in chapter 7[160] as standards can be used for specifications as long as the words "or equivalent" are added. After all, standards are not legally binding and without the opportunity to meet the relevant safety concerns by alterative means they could be discriminatory or at least restrict market access. Standards can also be used for negotiated procedures for components that do not require innovation. Specifications and standards in relation to the Defence Directive will be discussed in more detail in chapter 8.[161]

Standards have an important military security dimension. Where the same national army or a coalition of national armies on a common mission or even in peacetime, uses equipment produced according to the same standards, the interoperability of that equipment and therefore the armies using it will enhance the effectiveness of these forces.[162] In contrast, equipment produced according to differing standards may well have a negative impact on interoperability and thus military effectiveness and thus security. The Commission has repeatedly emphasised the importance of standardisation for the establishment of a European armaments market. In their 1996 Communication "The Challenges Facing the European Defence-related Industry" they pointed out:

> Union-wide standardization policies are relevant to the defence-related industry in such key areas as information technology, telecommunications, power supply, laser technology, new materials, aerospace and quality systems and conformity assessment.[163]

However, the Communication also acknowledges that "civil standardization activity is proceeding faster than similar work organised for purely military purposes".[164] Moreover, the Communication encourages a greater convergence of civil and military use of standardisation and increased use of existing national, European and international standardisation bodies. In the 1997 "Communication Implementing European Union Strategy on Defence-related Industries"[165] and more specifically the "Action Plan for the Defence-related Industries" the rationalisation of the standards used by the national ministries of defence, encouraging the European defence industries to work towards a homogeneous system of standards, a regular exchange between NATO and

---

[159] Ibid., at 256.   [160] At 364–5.   [161] At 365–6.
[162] See also COM (2003) 113 final, at 13.   [163] COM (1996) 10 final, at 21.   [164] Ibid.
[165] COM (1997) 583 final.

European standardisation bodies and support for the European standardisation bodies are identified as steps forward.[166] In the 2003 Communication "European Defence – Industrial and Market Issues: Towards an EU Defence Equipment Policy"[167] a "Defence Standardization Handbook" with references to standards commonly used to support defence procurement contracts and guidelines for the best selection of such standards is envisaged. This was to be compiled in cooperation with the ministries of defence of the Member States and CEN by 2004, to be given formal status and be accompanied by "appropriate complementary measures to ensure the upkeep of the Handbook and its use" afterwards. However, the 2004 Green Paper on Defence Procurement[168] still laments that with respect to defence procurement, "technical specifications are often very detailed and based on widely differing standards". The 2007 Communication "A Strategy for a Stronger and More Competitive European Defence Industry" reports a similar situation and refers again to the Handbook:

> The Commission will *promote the use of common standards* to facilitate the opening up of defence markets. The Commission brought together stakeholders to develop a "Defence Standardisation Handbook" and is working with the EDA to encourage its use. *It calls on Member States to make full use of the Handbook in their defence procurement.*[169]

The Handbook, now the *European Defence Standards Reference System (EDSTAR),*[170]

> contain[s] references to "Best practice" standards and "standard-like" specifications. The "Best practice" standards are standards which have been selected by consensus by industry and governmental organisations to be the best applicable standards for defence purposes.[171]

A comprehensive analysis of EDSTAR would go beyond the aims of this chapter. Only a limited number of Member States actively participated in the different phases of its compilation, although this includes the Member States with a substantial defence industry.[172] It is not comprehensive but covers only certain products.[173] However, the progressive inclusion of more products is in the nature of the approach.

---

[166] Ibid., at 4–5.   [167] COM (2003) 113 final.   [168] COM (2004) 608 final, at 7.
[169] COM (2007) 764 final, at 7.
[170] www.eda.europa.eu/EDSTAR/home.aspx [accessed 30 October 2013].   [171] Ibid.
[172] Belgium, Finland, France, Germany, Italy, Norway, Poland, Spain, Sweden, Turkey and the United Kingdom.
[173] NBC detectors, energetic materials, fuels and lubricants, batteries packaging, electrical interfaces, electromagnetic environment, environmental engineering, armoured land vehicle technology (ALVT), ammunition, paints and coatings, fluid-handling systems, life-cycle management – service life management, life cycle management – technical documentation, quality of electric power supply/Portable electric power generators, terminology.

Several characteristics of the European policy on standardisation of defence goods can be identified. First, in line with the approach in the civil sectors, the standards are not legally binding, although their use has clear advantages for Member States and producers through the reversal of the burden of proof described above. Moreover, this approach can be reconciled with EU law requirements regarding technical specifications. Thus the fact that standards are not legally binding is not a disadvantage or shortcoming. Secondly, there are standards only for a limited number of goods, moreover standards are lacking for the most high-profile and security-intensive products, such as fighter aeroplanes and warships. This is connected to a third characteristic which is the progressive nature of the policy. More and more standards will be added, most notably to EDSTAR. More and more defence ministries will use these standards. More and more products will be produced according to these standards. Thus it will take years before the success of these initiatives can fully be assessed. The 2007 Communication "A Strategy for a Stronger and More Competitive European Defence Industry",[174] which together with the Defence Directive and the ICT Directive forms the EU "Defence Package", still sees the use of "non-harmonised standards" as an impediment to cooperation in R&D and production programmes[175] and promises to "promote the use of common standards" through the Handbook, the predecessor of the EDSTAR.[176] Thus with respect to standards, many actors, including the Commission and EDA, have a role to play without these roles being contradictory.

4 Competition (anti-trust) law: Articles 101 and 102 TFEU

EU competition or anti-trust law is regulated in Articles 101–6 TFEU and Regulation 1/2003/EC.[177] Article 101(1) TFEU prohibits agreements between undertakings, decisions by associations of undertakings and concerted practices which prevent, restrict or distort competition and which may affect trade between Member States. Competition law is extremely relevant to the defence industries. Many defence companies are large in size and turnover. Looking at each Member State separately there are many products which only a few firms can produce, and some for which there is only one single manufacturer.[178] For example, as mentioned in chapter 1,[179] for large combat aircraft, there are only three EU producers: the British-German-Italian-Spanish "Eurofighter/ Tyhoon", the French "Rafale" and the Swedish-British "Gripen".[180]

---

[174] COM (2007) 764 final.   [175] Ibid., at 4.   [176] COM (2007) 764 final, at 6.

[177] Council Regulation 1/2003/EC on the implementation of the rules on competition laid down in Arts. 81 and 82 of the Treaty [2003] OJ L1/1.

[178] See the overview of the French (ch. 6), German (ch. 7) and United Kingdom (ch. 8) defence industries in Trybus, *European Defence Procurement Law, supra* note 1, at 102–4, 140–1 and 174–5 respectively.

[179] At 25.   [180] Example from COM (2003) 113 final, at 11.

Furthermore, as outlined below, mergers are taking place on a national and increasingly on a European level, thereby leading to even fewer and even bigger companies. Where firms are large in size and few in number, there is a danger they may become involved in practices covered by Article 101 TFEU, which is not to imply that the provision applies only to the monopolies and oligopolies which, as discussed in chapter 1, are so typical for the European defence industries.

Various violations of Article 101 TFEU by defence industrial companies can be contemplated in a liberalised market as the case of *GEC-Siemens* v. *Plessey* has shown.[181] Infringements may occur where undertakings decide to divide the market according to products (Firm A for missiles, Firm B for tanks etc.) or according to territory (Firm A for Southern Europe, Firm B for Northern Europe etc.). In a nutshell, all kinds of anti-competitive practices happening in the civil sector are equally possible in the defence sector. Moreover, an Internal Market is likely to indirectly promote anti-competitive practices, as these practices would be made easier on a European-wide level. Thus, the application of Article 101 TFEU is clearly needed to deal with these kinds of problems.

Article 102 TFEU prohibits the abuse of a dominant position. It is designed to control the activities of undertakings enjoying an economic strength that makes them immune from the influence of the normal pressures of a competitive market. As with Article 101 TFEU, the application of Article 102 TFEU is increasingly needed to ensure the ultimate success of a liberalised defence market in achieving its ultimate objectives of value for money through competition. These could be negatively affected by the abuse of a dominant market position, in particular of the larger defence firms. As explained below, mergers are taking place, to some extent in response to market pressures, and mergers in the future may increase the prospect of undertakings obtaining a dominant position in the European market which they then might abuse. In many segments of the defence market – for example of fighter aircraft, missiles or warships – some national producers have a dominant position even without mergers with companies from other Member States. A liberalised defence procurement regime will further promote such mergers as they are a condition for achieving the policy objectives such as avoiding duplication, minimising defence budgets and building up competitiveness with countries outside the Union.

The armaments exemption of Article 346(1)(b) TFEU discussed in chapter 3, is crucial for the application of Articles 101 and 102 TFEU in the defence sector. While it is not entirely clear whether Article 346(1)(b) TFEU can only be invoked by Member States or also by private persons, for example companies

---

[181] See under the next heading below.

active in the defence industrial sector, the better view is that only Member States can invoke the armaments exemption.[182] Thus companies are subject to Articles 101 and 102 TFEU in the usual way, and are only exempt if a Member State authorised such an exemption. In other words, a defence company would need the protection of a Member State to benefit from Article 346(1)(b) TFEU. As explained in chapter 3,[183] the Member State in question needs to argue and justify invoking the exemption and prove that a situation affecting its national security actually exists, subject to the review of the ECJ. Thus, Articles 101 and 102 TFEU apply to the defence sector unless a Member State successfully invokes Article 346 TFEU.

There is an obvious interplay of the Defence Directive and EU competition law, both aiming at ensuring competition. The latter is directly aimed at the private defence and security industries. The former is directly aimed at defence and security contracting authorities and entities. Competition itself is the objective of competition (anti-trust) law, whereas with respect to public procurement law it is a means to the end of achieving value for money. Moreover, for the EU competition is also in itself an objective of the procurement regime, since it is connected to the crucial Internal Market objectives of facilitating market access and thus cross-border procurement. The two regimes meet when there is collusive behaviour between tenderers. EU anti-trust law directly prohibits such collusion and provides instruments to punish it, whereas public procurement law provides for additional and procurement-specific sanctions, such as disqualification and where applicable debarment from future contracts.

There have been cases where Member States do encourage the creation of monopolies and this may lead to distortions of competition or an abuse of a dominant position. France and Germany, for example, actually encouraged the creation of the Eurocopter S.A., which has now a monopoly for combat helicopters in both countries and they encouraged the creation of the national monopolies of Aérospatiale and MBB that existed before that merger. Moreover, the Commission is not necessarily opposed to such mergers. Encouraging monopolies, however, is not the same as encouraging infringements of competition law. This means that anti-competitive practices of undertakings that have monopolies encouraged by Member States may be subject to Articles 101 and 102 TFEU, unless the actual anti-competitive practices themselves are encouraged by Member States.[184]

---

[182] See the discussion of the Notice relating to a proceeding under Arts. 85 and 86 of the EEC Treaty (IV/33.018 *GEC-Siemens/Plessey*) [1990] OJ C-239/2 and the arguments for this interpretation in Trybus, *European Union Law and Defence Integration, supra* note 1, ch. 7, at 233–4.

[183] At 104–25.

[184] Even then there is no "unlimited unilateral derogation" from the Treaty as Art. 348 TFEU allows for judicial review over the exercise of the derogation in Art. 346 TFEU.

5 Merger control

EU competition law in the wider sense also includes the control of company mergers and take-overs. The Merger Regulation 139/2004/EC[185] deals with mergers, acquisitions and certain joint ventures between companies of a certain worldwide turnover in order to control the potential distortive impact of these transactions on the competition and the free movement of goods and services in the EU.[186] The Take-over Directive 2004/25/EC[187] regulates take-over bids with similar objectives. The disappearance of competitors through mergers and take-overs is detrimental to competition and thus can have an effect on procurement. In the extreme but possible case of only one remaining company able to supply a certain piece of equipment, the competitive procedures discussed in chapter 7 would no longer make sense, unless the procedure was opened to third-country companies.

As discussed in chapter 1,[188] mergers, take-overs and particularly joint ventures are increasingly common in the defence sector.[189] Moreover, a certain consolidation through mergers is considered necessary to preserve the European defence industrial base, as European companies are too small to be competitive and there are too many companies for many types of equipment. So far there have not been many full mergers between companies from different Member States. Instead Europe's defence companies have established project-specific joint ventures in particular business areas. Industrial cooperation of this kind offers advantages, such as economies of scale and learning effects in manufacturing. Moreover, wasteful duplication can be avoided. However, the components of the joint ventures are still run separately. Trans-border mergers involving a change of ownership still appear to be problematic.[190] This is mainly due to traditional attitudes in both the governments of the Member States and the defence companies themselves. As the defence industries have a strategic

---

[185] Council Regulation of 20 January 2004 on the Control of Concentrations between Undertakings [2004] OJ L24/1. According to its Art. 25(1) Merger Regulation 139/2004 repeals Council Regulation 4064/89/EEC [1989] OJ L395/1.

[186] For a more detailed discussion of the law of merger control and the defence industries see Trybus, *European Union Law and Defence Integration*, *supra* note 1, at 235–48.

[187] Directive 2004/25/EC of the European Parliament and of the Council of 21 April 2004 on take-over bids [2004] OJ L142/12–23.

[188] At 24–5.

[189] Carlos Marti Sempere *et al.*, *Level Playing Field for European Defence Industries: The Role of Ownership and Public Aid Practices* (Brussels: Ingeniería de Sistemas para la Defensa de España S. A. (ISDEFE) Madrid in association with the Fraunhofer Institut für Naturwissenschaftliche Trendanalysen Euskirchen for the European Defence Agency, 2009), www.eda.europa.eu/docs/documents/level_playing_field_study.pdf [accessed 30 October 2013], at 25 and the list of cases in Annex B to the Phase I Final Report (hereinafter "EDA 2009 Study on Public Ownership and Aid").

[190] COM (2003) 113 final.

significance and are part of the national defence effort, it is still often assumed that they cannot be owned or controlled by "foreigners". Nevertheless, these cooperation activities create dominant positions or even monopolies and it is very likely that full mergers will be established in the near future. Some European companies have already acquired others or established joint ventures or cross-border shareholdings not tied to a particular programme. Furthermore, there are numerous full mergers between companies from the same Member State.[191] It is a common view that future mergers will be necessary as part of a consolidation process to preserve the defence industrial base.[192] The trend towards more mergers is likely to continue and is increasingly encouraged by governments. There is a possibility that several pieces of equipment will be produced by "European companies", companies that are the result of cross-border mergers and take-overs. This could have an effect towards the establishment of a European defence procurement market. While security-of-supply considerations could still lead to the invocation of Article 346(1)(b) TFEU to award a relevant contract to a merged company which includes a "national component", the award would still include cross-border procurement due to the "non-national components" of the company.

The consolidation process through mergers can lead to a conflict between the EU interest of competition manifested in the Merger Regulation on the one hand and the survival of the defence industrial base and its strategic implications on the other hand.[193] The Commission can allow or prohibit mergers according to Article 8 Merger Regulation[194] and the application of the Merger Regulation to concentrations in the defence sector was made clear in the

---

[191] For example in the United Kingdom "GEC" bought the military vehicle and shipbuilder "VSEL" and in Italy "Finmeccanica" gained control of about 75% of the Italian defence industry through take-overs. Nevertheless, the European defence companies are consolidating at a much slower pace than their competitors from the United States.

[192] COM (1997) 583 final, at 24; W. Walker and S. Willet, "Restructuring the European Defence Industrial Base" (1993) *Journal of Defence Economics* 141, at 147 and 152; K. Hartley, "Public Procurement and Competitiveness" (1989) 3 *Journal of Common Market Studies* 237, at 241 and "Competition in Defence Contracting in the United Kingdom" (1992) 1 *Public Procurement Law Review* 440, at 441; J. Lovering, "Military Expenditure and the Restructuring of Capitalism: The Military Industry in Britain" (1990) 14 *Cambridge Journal of Economics* 453, at 458 and 460; implied in COM (2003) 113 final; for an alternative view see Hendrik Vredeling, *Towards a Stronger Europe* (Brussels: IEPG, 1986), at point 32: "In our view however, mergers are not the answer for the short term. They will do nothing to counteract the effects of the real barriers to free trading and co-operation which exist between European nations . . ."

[193] COM (1997) 583 final, at 24.

[194] Art. 2(1) Merger Regulation provides for a list of factors to be taken into account, including market structure, the company's economic power, sources of supply and entry barriers.

Eurocopter decision.[195] The Commission decided that the Regulation applies, but that the particular merger was compatible with the Internal Market.

The Merger Regulation is subject to defence and security exemptions. First, as clarified in its Recital 19,[196] it is subject to the armaments and secrecy exemptions in Article 346 TFEU discussed in chapter 3. The effect of Recital 19 depends on the interpretation of Article 346 TFEU. A merger in the defence sector, which is imposed or encouraged by a Member State, may escape the application of the Merger Regulation if the Member State or the Member States in question can successfully invoke Article 346(1)(b) TFEU. Member States have to specifically invoke the exemption and prove that a situation justifying its use actually exists, subject to review by the ECJ. It is submitted, that Article 346(1)(b) TFEU might allow a Member State to authorise a merger in the hard defence sector, even when the Commission has prohibited that merger. Moreover, the derogation might more generally be used to prevent EU Commission scrutiny on the impact of a merger on competition.[197] According to the 2009 *EDA Study on Public Ownership and Aid*, the use of Article 346 TFEU has been minimal in the context of the Merger Regulation.[198] However, the same study found that especially the larger Member States with a considerable defence industrial base have enacted limitations to certain mergers in the defence industries, especially in the form of prior authorisation or regarding the management of defence companies.[199] These limitations represent forms of State control of the defence industries that do not exist in other sectors.[200] They work directly, for example if such prior authorisation is denied. Moreover, they might work indirectly as they might deter mergers and take-overs. Ultimately defence companies cannot merge across borders

---

[195] Case 0.17, *Aérospatiale/MBB* [1992] 4 CMLR M70; see also Case M.086, *Thompson/ Pilkington*, Decision of 23 October 1991, unreported.

[196] Recital 19 of the Merger Regulation reads: "the exclusive application of this Regulation to concentrations with a Community dimension is without prejudice to Article 296 of the Treaty, and does not prevent the Member States from taking appropriate measures to protect legitimate interests other than those pursued by this Regulation, provided that such measures are compatible with the general principles and other provisions of Community law".

[197] *EDA Study on Public Ownership and Aid, supra* note 189, at 25.   [198] Ibid.

[199] Ibid., at 20–2. Out of the "Big Six", Germany, France, Sweden, Spain and the United Kingdom have such rules. Out of the other Member States, Belgium, the Czech Republic, Finland, Lithuania and Portugal also have such rules. Bulgaria, Estonia, Hungary, Ireland, Luxembourg and Slovenia do not have such rules. Italy has no specific rules: "Indirect constraints however may be used for preventing unacceptable foreign investment such as administrative authorizations for the production of arms. Investments in Finmeccanica and Fincantieri are regulated by firm's statutes."

[200] As their coverage in the *EDA Study on Public Ownership and Aid, supra* note 189, at 20–2 suggests.

as freely as other companies can. They need the consent and support of both respective governments.

Recital 19 also provides that legitimate interests can justify derogation from the Regulation, provided such Member State measures are "appropriate" and "compatible with the general principles and other provisions of [EU] law". The concept of legitimate interests allowing derogation is spelt out in detail in Article 21 Merger Regulation. According to Article 21(3) Merger Regulation, no Member State may apply its national competition legislation to any concentration with an EU dimension. However, according to Article 21(4) Merger Regulation, Member States may take appropriate measures to protect legitimate interests "other than those taken into consideration by this Regulation and compatible with the general principles and other provisions of [EU] law". Public security is one of these legitimate interests. It is submitted, that Article 24(4) Merger Regulation might allow a Member State to authorise a merger in the security sector, even when the Commission has prohibited that merger. Moreover, the derogation might more generally be used to prevent EU Commission scrutiny on the impact of a merger on competition.

With regards to the Take-over Directive, the 2009 *EDA Study on Public Ownership and Aid* found that there had been no hostile bids in the defence industries.[201] It argues that the most plausible reason is that there are only very limited chances of success for such bids, as Member States can use Article 346(1)(b) TFEU to prevent such a hostile bid, for example in case plans for the future of the company are unclear and fears exist that important defence industrial capabilities could be dismantled or lost at a later stage.[202] A hostile bid normally means that a take-over happens against the will of the management of the company to be taken over and thus against the will of the government behind it.

The Commission argues that the potential conflict between the EU interest in competition in the defence sector and the Member States interest in national security would be eliminated as a result of the establishment of an Internal Market for defence equipment.[203] The Communication "A Strategy for a Stronger and More Competitive European Defence Industry",[204] which together with the Defence Directive and the ICT Directive forms the EU "Defence Package", considers the "patchwork of national legislation on control of strategic assets" a factor preventing "consolidation, the removal of duplication and the development of more efficient industries".[205] While it suggests striking a "balance

---

[201] Ibid., at 26.   [202] Ibid.

[203] Ibid., at 26. "[a]s far as geographic markets remain, further concentration may aggravate monopolistic inefficiencies that can extend into civilian areas of business. On the other hand, if progress towards a common market for defence equipment is achieved, and provided that conditions of competition are preserved, business consolidation may contribute favourably to European competitiveness on a global market."

[204] COM (2007) 764 final.   [205] Ibid., at 7.

between freedom of investment and protection of security interests regarding control of material and other assets that are considered essential",[206] no proposals or details are provided. However, if this "patchwork" is detrimental to the Internal Market in defence goods, then an EU instrument harmonising these rules should be considered.

6 State aid

As discussed in chapter 1, parts of the European defence industries are publicly owned by the Member States in which they are registered.[207] This differs between Member States, with considerable State ownership in France and Poland on the one hand, for example, and a privatised defence industrial base in the United Kingdom on the other hand. Competition and trade can be affected as the respective Member State will want to ensure "that publicly owned companies benefit from their main acquisition programmes".[208] In other words, there is a presumption that a Member State who owns a defence company will normally award relevant contracts to that company. While the legality of such awards under the Defence Directive will have to be discussed in Part II of this book,[209] State ownership in the defence industries is not as such covered by any regime of the TFEU.

The governments of the Member States also provide various forms of support to their respective privately or partly publicly owned defence industries. This support can affect the TFEU regime on State aid[210] as defined in Articles 107–9 TFEU.[211] Public support constituting State aid may be in breach of Article 107 TFEU if the measure distorts or threatens competition and is capable of affecting trade between Member States.[212] Member States have to notify the Commission of plans to grant this kind of aid and the latter will only allow it if certain requirements are met. The Commission is of the opinion that these rules offer an appropriate framework for a European market for defence goods.[213]

6.1 State aid practices in the defence sector

EU Member State governments support their defence industries with various benefits, thereby distorting competition and affecting trade between Member States.[214] The financial instruments used to award aid are varied and include tax exemption, relief, deferral or cancellation; grants; advances repayable in

---

[206] Ibid., at 7.   [207] At 37–8.

[208] 2009 *EDA Study on Public Ownership and Aid, supra* note 189, at 52.   [209] Esp. ch. 7.

[210] For the most current work on the EU law of State aid see Kelyn Bacon (ed.), *European Union Law of State Aid*, 2nd edn (Oxford University Press, 2013).

[211] COM (1996) 10 final, at 22–4.

[212] Case 730/79, *Philip Morris Holland* v. *Commission* [1980] ECR 2671, at 2688.

[213] COM (1996) 10 final, at 22–4.   [214] Ibid., at 22.

the case of success; low interest rate or soft loans; guarantees; capital injection; non-monetary aid; provision of goods and services in preferential terms; and accelerated depreciation allowances.[215] The 2009 *EDA Study on State Ownership and Aid*[216] provided a detailed picture of aid practices, dividing them into aid for R&D and innovation,[217] aid for industries in specific situations,[218] support for foreign sales,[219] and other State aid.[220] While the extent to which these various forms of aid are used in practice varies between Member States and between the types of aid, the extent of State aid is far more considerable in this sector than in any other. Aid can originate in various ministries and public bodies and according to the 2009 *EDA Study* this is why the ministries of defence do not always have an overview of all the aid awarded, indicating a lack of transparency. The Commission has emphasised a need for transparency in State aid to the defence sector in their Communication "A Strategy for a Stronger and More Competitive European Defence Industry",[221] which is part of the 2007 "Defence Package". A precise analysis of State aid to the European defence industries goes beyond the aims of this book on defence and security procurement. However, since, as pointed out above, aid is extensive and varies between Member States, a "level playing field" is currently not established.[222]

The Court of First Instance has ruled that a contract award can be considered a State aid in the sense of the TFEU if it does not represent a "normal

---

[215] 2009 *EDA Study on Public Ownership and Aid, supra* note 189, at 26.

[216] Ibid. at 26–40.

[217] Ibid., at 28–30. These are further subdivided into aid for developing equipment for non-national armed forces (2.6.1.1.) and other aid for supporting equipment development (2.6.1.2.).

[218] Ibid., at 30–2. These are further subdivided into rescue aid (2.6.2.1.) and restructuring aid (2.6.2.2.).

[219] Ibid., at 33–7. The relevant practices are further subdivided into marketing assistance, public relations, display and operation by the armed forces of in-service materials, training of customer's operators and loan of personnel, export credit assistance, assistance to procurement project management and technical support services, rescheduling of deliveries to national armed forces, purchase of an undesired system by the armed forces to better support a foreign sale and tied aid.

[220] Ibid. 37–40. These are further subdivided into employment aid, training aid, aid for SMEs, aid for risk capital investments in SMEs, regional aid, and climate change and other environmental protection aid.

[221] COM (2007) 764 final, at 7.

[222] This is ultimately the message of the 2009 *EDA Study on Public Ownership and Aid, supra* note 189, at 3: "[State aid has] a potential capability to provide selective advantages to undertakings that may affect trade conditions and therefore fair competition compromising the achievement of a level playing field in the [European Defence Equipment Market]." This is also implied in COM (2007) 764 final, at 7.

commercial transaction".[223] Heuninckx argued that, in particular, it will not be a "normal commercial transaction" when the contracting authority has no actual need for the good or service procured or when the terms of that contract are in some way or other "excessively favourable to the contractor".[224] As the question of whether a measure represents State aid does not depend on its cause or aim but on its effect, it is perfectly possible that a defence contract is considered a State aid without the contracting authority's intention to grant such an aid.[225] Generally speaking, the Commission will assume a "normal commercial transaction" and thus no State aid in the sense of the TFEU when the contract is awarded following an "open, transparent and non-discriminatory procedure".[226] It is submitted that this does not require literally the use of the open procedure of the Public Sector and Utilities Directives discussed in chapter 7[227] but is equally satisfied when one of the other competitive procedures further discussed in chapter 7 are used. In other words, this would include the restricted procedure, the negotiated procedure with prior publication of a contract notice and competitive dialogue and exclude the negotiated procedure without prior publication of a contract notice.[228] This point is important because, as discussed in detail in chapter 7, the Defence Directive does not provide for the open procedure at all.[229] As Heuninckx argued, when the contract was not advertised, the bids were not examined in a transparent fashion, negotiations were conducted with one or a few individuals and, ultimately, the contract was not awarded to the lowest price or economically most advantageous tender, the Commission is likely to consider such a contract to constitute State aid in the sense of the TFEU which would require notification, even when these circumstances do not constitute conclusive evidence for such an aid.[230] Heuninckx points out:

---

[223] Case T-14/96, *Bretagne Angleterre Irlande (BAI)* v. *Commission* [1999] ECR II-139, at paras. 71–89.

[224] B. Heuninckx, "Defence Procurement: The Most Effective Way to Grant Illegal State Aid and Get Away With It, Or Is It?" (2009) 46 *Common Market Law Review* 141 (hereinafter "Illegal State Aid"), at 198.

[225] Ibid.

[226] Commission Case N 264/2002, *London Underground Public Private Partnership*, C (2002) 3578, [2002] OJ L309/14; Case C-280/00, *Altmark Trans GmbH* v. *Nahverkehrsgesellschaft Altmark GmbH* [2003] ECR I-774, at para. 93; Commission Decision 2000/513/EC of 8 September 1999 on aid granted by France to *Stardust Marine* (notified under document number C (1999) 3148) [2000] OJ L206/6, all as cited by Heuninckx, "Illegal State Aid", *supra* note 224, at 198.

[227] At 312–18.

[228] See Heuninckx, "Illegal State Aid", *supra* note 224, at 198, citing *London Underground PPP*, *supra* note 226, and further citations in his footnote 34.

[229] At 312–18.

[230] Heuninckx, "Illegal State Aid", *supra* note 224, at 198 citing Decision 2000/513/EC, *Stardust Marine*, *supra* note 226, at paras. 63–4.

This seems to describe a fairly extreme contract award process, likely to be in breach of the [TFEU] principles applicable to public procurement, but one that is not entirely impossible in the world of defence procurement.[231]

As mentioned above, the relevant ministry of defence will often not be aware that a defence contract constitutes State aid in the sense of the TFEU. Consequently it will not notify the Commission as required under the Treaty and the at least theoretical possibility arises, that a competitor of the company with which the contract in question was concluded brings proceedings in a national court. Heuninckx pointed out that such proceedings can lead to the annulment of the contract as the "standstill" period of Article 108(3) TFEU could have been breached.[232]

As pointed out above, the use of the negotiated procedure without prior publication of a contract notice might constitute State aid in the sense of Article 107 TFEU if it cannot be considered a "normal commercial transaction". In defence contracts there is normally no commercial market as a benchmark that would allow a comparison to determine whether the transaction was "normal".[233] Thus Heuninckx argues that an analysis of the pricing structure of the individual contract is needed to determine if it can be compared to a normal commercial transaction.[234] This pricing structure would have to avoid excessive prices and cross-subsidisation of the civil activities of the respective company. The "reasonableness of prices" has to be determined differently in firm or fixed price contracts, cost-plus contracts and target cost incentive contracts.[235] Because in most defence contracts the price cannot be determined in advance with reasonable

---

[231] Heuninckx, ibid.

[232] Case 120/73, *Gebrüder Lorenz GmbH* v. *Germany* [1973] ECR 1471; Case C-354/90, *Fédération Nationale du Commerce Extérieur des Produits Alimentaires and Syndicat Nationale des Négociants et Transformateurs de Saumon* v. *France* [1991] ECR I-5523; Case C-499/99, *Italy* v. *Commission* [2001] ECR I-7303; M. Ross, "State Aids and National Courts: Definitions and Other Problems – a Case of Premature Emancipation?" (2000) 37 *Common Market Law Review* 401; J. Hilger, "The Award of a Contract as State Aid within the meaning of Article 87(1) EC" (2003) 12 *Public Procurement Law Review* 109, at 127–9 as cited by Heuninckx, "Illegal State Aid", *supra* note 224, at 200.

[233] A. Georgopoulos, "The Commission's Green Paper on Defence Procurement" (2005) 14 *Public Procurement Law Review* NA34; Katia G. Vlachos, *Safeguarding European Competitiveness: Strategies for the Future European Arms Production and Procurement*, Occasional Paper No. 4 (Paris: WEU Institute of Security Studies, 1998), § 2.4; Stephanie Neumann, *Defence Industries and Dependency: Current and Future Trends in the Global Defence Sector* (Zurich: ISN, 2006), at 6; Burkard Schmitt, *Defence Procurement in the European Union: The Current Debate* (Paris: EU Institute of Security Studies, 2005), at 15; A. Doern, "The Interaction between EC Rules on Public Procurement and State Aid" (2004) 13 *Public Procurement Law Review* 97, at 123, as cited by Heuninckx, "Illegal State Aid", *supra* note 224, at 202.

[234] Heuninckx, "Illegal State Aid", *supra* note 224, at 202.   [235] Ibid.

certainty, fixed-price contracts[236] are more likely to constitute State aid when the costs overrun, which they frequently do.[237] If the costs agreed in the final price are "actually incurred and related to the performance of the contract" the reimbursement of the costs would not constitute cross-subsidisation. Thus a cost-plus contract[238] is not likely to constitute State aid.[239] Finally, provided efficient post-costing procedures are in place, target-cost incentive fee contracts[240] are the least likely to constitute illegal State aid in the sense of the TFEU.[241]

However, it needs to be emphasised that the question of the illegality of such practices as State aid would only arise in cases where the provision of Article 346(1)(b) TFEU discussed in chapter 3 could not successfully be invoked. After the transposition of the new Defence Directive such Article 346 TFEU cases should be less likely; reducing such cases is one of the main objectives of the Directive. This could mean that most defence contracts are awarded according to national law transposing the Directive. Based on the principles outlined above, this would mean that contracts awarded on the basis of the restricted procedure, negotiated procedure with prior publication of a contract notice or competitive dialogue would represent a "normal commercial transaction" and thus no State aid in the sense of the TFEU. Contracts awarded on the basis of the negotiated procedure without prior publication of a contract

---

[236] Ibid, at 198, at 204: "In firm or fixed price contracts, the price to be paid for the goods or services is agreed at the time of contract award and either does not vary (firm price) or varies only according to a Variation of Price (VOP) formula compensating variations in the prices of labour and materials (fixed price)."

[237] Allen Kaufmann, *In the Procurement Officer We Trust: Constitutional Norms, Air Force Procurement and Industrial Organisation 1938–1948* (Boston: MIT, 1998), at 21; Keith Hartley, *The Economics of UK Procurement Policy* (RMC Canada, 2002), at 449, as cited by Heuninckx, "Illegal State Aid", *supra* note 224, at 224.

[238] Heuninckx, "Illegal State Aid", *supra* note 224, at 204: "In *cost-plus* contracts, the contractor will be reimbursed for its actual justified costs for performing the contract, plus an agreed profit. This profit can be either a percentage of the actual costs (*cost plus percentage fee*), a fixed amount (*cost plus fixed fee*), or an amount that varies in inverse proportion to the costs (*costs plus incentive fee*)." According to Mark A. Lorell *et al.*, *Cheaper, Fast, Better? Commercial Approaches to Weapons Acquisition* (RAND, 2000), at 111 *et seq.* as cited by Heuninckx, "Illegal State Aid", *supra* note 224: "The use of cost-plus contracts in the defence sector, especially for research and development, is a direct consequence of the high cost uncertainties and lack of commercial outlet for defence products."

[239] Heuninckx, "Illegal State Aid", *supra* note 224, at 208.

[240] Ibid. at 204, also citing the UK Review Board for Government Contracts, *Report on the 2006 Annual Review of the Profit Formula for Non-Competitive Government Contracts* (London, 2006), at ix: "In target *cost incentive fee contracts*, a target cost for the contract is agreed at the time of the award and constitutes a ceiling. If the actual costs are lower than expected, the benefits will be shared between the contractor and the contracting authority according to an agreed formula, subject to a maximum price. If the actual costs are higher than expected, the contractor's profit will be lower (or even a loss), even though the contract could also include loss-sharing formulas."

[241] Heuninckx, "Illegal State Aid", *supra* note 224, at 209.

notice, contracts subject to one of the exemptions of the Directive discussed in chapter 6 and contracts still subject to Article 346 TFEU, unless subject to one of the exemptions of the State aid regime discussed below, may constitute State aid in the sense of the Treaty, unless the pricing structure of such a contract allows for a "normal commercial transaction". With respect to contracts subject to Article 346 TFEU, any practice would be justified by that provision.

According to the Commission all State aid to the defence industries are a reflection of the special characteristics of the defence sector and in particular to the close relationship with public authorities.[242] The arms trade between Member States is affected because the beneficiaries of this aid are competing with enterprises in other Member States even if they do not export (transfer) armaments to these States. Competition in defence procurement procedures is affected because companies who benefited from State aid are competing with companies who have to operate without such public support.[243]

6.2 Legality of State aid practices under the TFEU

Companies producing defence material on the list according to Article 346(2) TFEU discussed in chapter 3[244] are not automatically exempt from the State aid regime of the TFEU by virtue of Article 346(1)(b) TFEU. Based on the judgments *Spanish Weapons*,[245] *Agusta*[246] and *Military Exports*[247] discussed in chapter 3[248] and Commission Decision 1999/763/EC[249] the State aid regime of the TFEU applies to the defence material producing industries unless a Member State specifically invokes Article 346 TFEU on a case-by-case basis and subject to the review of the ECJ. According to the Commission, Article 346(1)(b) TFEU had not yet been applied to State aid in the defence industrial sector.[250]

There are a number of specific exceptions under Article 107(2) TFEU which apply automatically and some under Article 107(3) TFEU which may be granted at the discretion of the Commission. The most important exceptions potentially relevant to defence are Article 107(3)(b)[251] and

---

[242] COM (2003) 113 final. [243] Heuninckx, "Illegal State Aid", *supra* note 224, 141.
[244] At 88–94. [245] *Supra* note 12. [246] *Supra* note 13. [247] *Supra* note 14.
[248] At 108–25.
[249] Commission Decision 1999/763/EC of 17 March 1999 on the measures, implemented and proposed, by the Federal State of Bremen, Germany, in favour of Lürssen Maritime Beteiligungen GmbH & Co. KG [1999] OJ L301/8.
[250] Ibid. See also the discussion of State aid in COM (2013) 542 final, at 11.
[251] Art. 107(3)(b) TFEU provides for aid to promote the execution of a project of common European interest. The Commission came close to complaining about the fact that until March 2003 there has been no notification based on this provision (see COM (2003) 113 final). This strongly suggests that notifications would be available regarding State aid granted to major defence equipment projects such as the British-German-Italian-Spanish "Eurofighter/Typhoon" combat aircraft. The notion "*common* European interest [emphasis added]", however, would require the participation of defence companies

(c) TFEU.[252] The State aid regime of the TFEU also provides for a rule of reason that accommodates and allows aid in cases that are relevant to the defence industries. This enables Member States to support their defence industries even without invoking Article 346(1)(b) TFEU. There are, however, still problems here. One is the effect on the civil sector by aid awarded to the military sector, the problem of cross-subsidisation discussed in the context of pricing above. Many firms produce both military and civil materials, and aid to the military arm of a company may affect the civil sector, distorting competition also in the civil sector.[253] This interaction of civil and military sectors represents a major difficulty for the Commission to detect and prove violations of Article 107 TFEU in firms producing both civil and military goods.

Another problem is the case of dual-use goods, to be used both for military and civil purposes. Indirect distortions of competition in the civil sector are not, however, exempt from the State aid rules, by the national security exemption of Article 346(1)(b) TFEU. As discussed in chapter 3,[254] the armaments exemption clearly says: "such measures shall not, however, adversely affect the conditions of competition in the common market regarding products which are not intended for specifically military purposes".

7 Other activities

There are also a number of other relevant initiatives of the Commission. They include the monitoring of the defence industries,[255]

---

from at least two Member States. It is submitted that such a notification would not even require the project to contribute to the survival of the European defence industrial base or to be specifically designed to support the Common Security and Defence Policy or the European Capabilities Programme described in ch. 5, at 217–18. Another exception under Art. 107 TFEU is State aid to combat a general economic crisis (see COM (1985) 310 final, at 39–4). See also COM (2007) 764 final, at 9.

[252] Art. 107(3)(c) TFEU provides for aid for the economic development of certain areas and aid in the interest of the development of certain branches of industry. In relation to this sectorial aid the Commission is of the opinion that it can be permitted in relation to the so-called "sunset" industries, which have run into difficulties for external reason or are struggling, and "sunrise" industries, which are mainly new technological sectors with good future prospects. The former are to be supported by defined restructuring programmes like modernisation, the latter by any aid to facilitate their development, but marketing aid as well as aid for the expansion of capacity are in principle seen as inadmissible. On the other hand aid may be regularly permitted, subject to strict conditions, in case of serious difficulties making temporary restructuring aid necessary. See COM (1996) 10 final, at 22. See also COM (2007) 764 final, at 9.

[253] COM (1996) 10 final, at 22; COM (2003) 113 final.   [254] At 98–9.

[255] COM (2003) 113 final, at 13; See the "benchmarking" in COM (1997) 583 final, Annex II "Action Plan for the Defence-related Industries", at 9. The 2005 State Aid Action Plan features in COM (2007) 764 final, at 9.

taxation,[256] structural funds[257] and small and medium-sized enterprises (SMEs).[258] While the latter are relevant to procurement and shall be discussed in the context of subcontracting in chapter 9,[259] most of these policies are not comprehensive and are often very limited. Moreover they are often not consistently mentioned in the relevant Commission Communications, and mostly not subject to legally binding regulation. Therefore they are not discussed further in this chapter.

As explained in chapter 1,[260] research and development (R&D) play a major role in the defence sector. While the relevant Communications of the Commission have addressed their importance,[261] the role of the Internal Market and Commission competence in this area is rather limited and there is no TFEU regime on R&D for defence as such. R&D is conducted on a common basis in the frameworks outside the Internal Market which will be discussed in chapter 5. As discussed in chapter 6, R&D activities are also subject to derogation from the regime of the Defence Directive.[262]

8 Conclusions

In addition to the set of free movement rules discussed in chapter 2 and public procurement rules discussed in Part II of this book, an Internal Market for defence equipment also needs common rules on competition, merger control, exports, intra-Community transfers, standardisation and State aid. The issue of intra-Community transfers of armaments is addressed in a separate

---

[256] COM (1997) 583 final, Annex II "Action Plan for the Defence-related Industries", at 8 on both indirect and direct taxation. There is a limited tax regime in Arts. 110–13 TFEU mainly prohibiting discrimination on grounds of nationality in taxation. Taxation is not addressed in COM (2003) 113 final or COM (2004) 608 final or COM (2007) 764 final.

[257] COM (1997) 583 final, Annex II "Action Plan for the Defence-related Industries", at 7–8; COM (1996) 10 final, at 24–25. Structural funds are not addressed in COM (2003) 113 final or COM (2004) 608 final. They are briefly mentioned in COM (2007) 764 final, at 9.

[258] COM (1997) 583 final, Annex II "Action Plan for the Defence-related Industries", at 5. SMEs are not addressed in COM (2003) 113 final or COM (2004) 608 final. SMEs were the subject of an extensive *Study on the Competitiveness of European Small and Medium sized Enterprises (SMEs) in the Defence Sector* (European Economics, London for the European Commission, 2009), http://ec.europa.eu/enterprise/sectors/defence/files/2009-11-05_europe_economics_final_report_en.pdf [accessed 31 October 2013].

[259] At 428–32.   [260] At 50.

[261] See COM (2007) 764 final, at 8; COM (2003) 113 final, at 12; COM (1997) 583 final, Appendix to Annex I "Definition of Specific Characteristics of the Defence-related Sector", at 7, Annex II "Action Plan for the Defence-related Industries", at 4; COM (1996) 10 final, at 20–1; COM (2013) 542 final, at 16, and the accompanying Staff Working Document SWD (2013) 279 final, at 36–7.

[262] At 283–8 and 299–301.

ICT Directive introduced as part of the same "Defence Package" as the Defence Directive, but due to their differing transposition deadlines not really "in tandem". However, since 2012 both instruments had to be fully transposed and applied in practice. The ICT Directive is aimed at reducing the uncertainties and red tape of licensing and certification with respect to armament transfers within the Union and since the national laws transposing both applied, they have been working "in tandem" towards the free movement of armaments with the EU. EU regimes on intra-Community transfers of dual-use goods and for the export of armaments and dual-use goods to third countries outside the EU are also in place. Moreover, the Treaty regimes aimed at safeguarding competition with respect to collusive behaviour, abuses of a dominant position, merger control and State aid apply to the defence industries, subject to Article 346(1)(b) TFEU. They apply to the security industries anyway. In contrast to the specific regimes now existing with respect to defence procurement and the intra-Community transfers of armaments, no defence-specific regimes exist for these areas of competition law. Finally, a number of relevant areas such as taxation, SMEs, structural fund and monitoring of the defence industries are not (yet) subject to a comprehensive and legally binding regime, and might never be.

The effect of these regimes on defence procurement is partly direct and partly indirect. It is direct with respect to intra-Community transfers as a security-of-supply issue and with respect to standardisation. It is indirect with respect to exports and competition law since defence companies who operate within more relaxed national rules and are subject to more generous aid may have unfair advantages over their competitors.

5

European armaments law and policy outside the EU Internal Market

EDA, OCCAR, Letter of Intent and NATO

1 Introduction

The last three chapters discussed the EU Internal Market law relevant to defence and security procurement. The following five chapters will discuss the substantive rules of the Defence Directive itself. However, European policy on armaments, the central object of the instrument, is not exclusively regulated by the TFEU and the Defence Directive. Until the introduction of the latter, many stakeholders would even have seen it as anything but a matter for EU legislation. First, defence procurement and other related issues are addressed as part of a European armaments policy, which is a crucial element of the emerging Common Security and Defence Policy (CSDP), which forms part of the Common Foreign and Security Policy (CFSP) of the EU. In 2005 a European Defence Agency (EDA) was established to manage those parts of the European armaments policy perceived to be outside the scope of the TFEU by the Member States. Until recently that included rules on procurement. Since these regimes and initiatives complement or compete with some of those of the Internal Market, they will be outlined in the second part in this chapter, including their compatibility with the interpretation of the relevant TFEU provisions discussed in chapters 2 and 3. An understanding of these CFSP/CSDP/EDA activities is also needed for the discussion of the scope of the Defence Directive in chapter 6.

Secondly, organisational structures outside the EU addressed the reorganisation and preservation of the European defence industrial base or parts of it as one of their tasks similar to EDA, complementing or competing with the Internal Market regimes and initiatives. The relevant frameworks are the Organisation for Joint Armaments Procurement (OCCAR) and the Letter of Intent (LoI) which both include only EU Member States. These initiatives do *not* include rules on defence procurement directed at the Member States. However, they affect various aspects of the Internal Market regime of which the Defence Directive is the most important part. Similar to the EDA regime, these initiatives complement or compete with some of those of the Commission. Hence they will be outlined in sections 3 and 4 of this chapter, including their compatibility with the interpretation of the relevant TFEU provisions discussed in chapters 2 and 3. Furthermore, an understanding of the OCCAR and LoI activities is needed for the discussion of the scope of the Defence Directive in chapter 6: whatever is excluded from the scope of application of the Directive and TFEU can be addressed in frameworks outside the EU Internal Market. Section 5 will discuss bilateral initiatives. Section 6 will discuss how the fragmentation and overlap of these frameworks outlined in the previous parts of this chapter can be overcome. A short discussion of relevant agencies such as the NSPA, NETMA or NEHEMA which are parts of NATO and therefore not "European" organisations, will conclude this last chapter of Part I on the background of the Defence Directive.

2 The European Defence Agency[1]

With Joint Action 2004/551/CFSP of 12 May 2004[2] the Council established an agency in the field of defence capabilities development, research, acquisition and armaments in the then context of the Treaty of Nice. Together with an independent crisis-management capability and a mutual defence clause, this EDA is today one of the three main elements of the CSDP under the Treaty of Lisbon. Under that Treaty it is now regulated in Articles 42(3) and 45 TEU. Joint Action 2004/551/CFSP was replaced by Council Decision 2011/411/CFSP of 12 July 2011 defining the statute, the seat and operational rules of the EDA and repealing Joint Action 2004/551/CFSP (hereinafter "EDA Council Decision").[3] The 2011 EDA Council Decision contains only very limited changes compared to the 2004 Joint Action; even most article numbers remain the same. However, the move to a Council Decision was necessary after the entering into force of the Treaty of Lisbon to reflect the "new" instruments introduced by that Treaty.

The EDA started as a Franco-British initiative launched by President Chirac and Prime Minister Blair during their summit in Le Touquet in February 2003. Their proposal became an EU policy at the European Council meeting in Thessaloniki in June of the same year. The Convention on the Future of Europe then inserted provisions on the Agency in the failed Constitutional Treaty.[4] Under the Treaty of Lisbon the "European Capabilities and

---

[1] Parts of the EDA section are partly based on M. Trybus, "The New European Defence Agency: A Contribution to a Common European Security and Defence Policy or a Challenge to the Community *Acquis*?" (2006) 43 *Common Market Law Review* 667–703. However, the discussion is updated and significantly extended.

[2] Council Joint Action 2004/551/CFSP of 12 May 2004 on the establishment of the European Defence Agency, [2004] OJ L245/17. Art. 1(1) of the Joint Action read: "An Agency in the field of defence capabilities development, research, acquisition and armaments (the European Defence Agency), hereinafter referred to as 'the Agency', is hereby established."

[3] [2011] OJ L183/16.

[4] See on this development in more detail: M. Trybus, "With or Without the EU Constitutional Treaty: Towards a Common Security and Defence Policy?" (2006) 31 *European Law Review* 145–66.

Armaments Policy" (ECAP) is part of the CSDP and conducted by the EDA.[5] The activities of the Agency include developing defence capabilities, promoting defence research and technology, promoting armaments cooperation, creating a competitive European Defence Equipment Market (EDEM) and strengthening the European Defence Technological and Industrial Base (EDTIB).[6] Hence the EDA operates in an area concerned with the economic aspects of defence close to and potentially overlapping with subject matters regulated in the Internal Market. Article 2 EDA Council Decision stipulates that the mission of the Agency is "to support the Council and the Member States in their effort to improve the EU's defence capabilities in the field of crisis management and sustain the CSDP as it stands now and develops in the future". This wording could suggest a limitation to crisis management. However, a look at the functions and tasks of the Agency in Article 2(2) EDA Council Decision and Article 45 TEU (Lisbon) reveals a wide application, covering military capabilities of the Member States in general.

This part of the chapter on EDA will briefly discuss the organisational structure of the Agency, which is appropriate because it is argued further below that the EDA should eventually evolve into the only institutional structure for European armaments policy, apart from the institutions of the EU Internal Market. This is followed by a discussion of the EDA tasks, with an emphasis on its policies and more specifically the Code of Conduct on Defence Procurement and related instruments.

2.1 The organisational structure of the EDA

The Agency and its staff of 109 (2011)[7] are based in Brussels[8] and had an annual budget of some €30.5 million in 2013.[9] Its institutions are the Head of the Agency, the Steering Board and the Chief Executive and staff.

The High Representative for Foreign Affairs and Security Policy is the Head of the Agency, responsible for the overall organisation and functioning of the EDA and for the negotiation of administrative arrangements with third countries and other international organisations.[10] The combination of the offices of the High Representative with that of the Head of the Agency has been criticised. Keohane argued that the holder of all these offices would lack the time and the resources to lead the EDA effectively. Following the example of

---

[5] Arts. 42(3) subpara. 2 and 45 TEU (Lisbon).

[6] www.eda.europa.eu/ [accessed 18 October 2013].

[7] According to the EDA Financial Report 2011, published in June 2012, http://eda.europa. eu/docs/finance-documents/2011-financial-report.pdf?sfvrsn=0 [accessed 23 July 2013].

[8] See on more information on EDA, www.eda.europa.eu/home [accessed 23 July 2013]. Art. 1(5) EDA Council Decision: "The Agency shall have its seat in Brussels."

[9] www.eda.europa.eu/Aboutus/how-we-do-it/Finance [accessed 23 July 2013].

[10] Art. 7(1), (2) and (4) EDA Council Decision.

most national cabinets the Union should create a separate defence office or portfolio to give a face to the defence policy just as it created the office of the High Representative to give a face to the CFSP.[11] At least a Deputy High Representative for Security and Defence could be appointed, similar to the appointment of the deputy for counter-terrorism in March 2004 after the attacks in Madrid.[12] However, it is submitted, that the "double hat" of the High Representative – with substantial roles in both the CFSP and as Vice President and member of the Commission in the EU Internal Market – can help to "bridge" overlapping policies and initiatives and help to foster the coherence of, inter alia, EU policies on the defence market in general and defence procurement in particular.

A Steering Board, composed of one representative of each participating Member State and a representative of the European Commission without voting rights,[13] is the main decision-making body of the EDA.[14] Its responsibilities are the adoption of the general budget, the conclusion of administrative arrangements with third parties, the approval of the establishment of ad hoc projects with the EDA and ad hoc arrangements with third parties and the determination of the technical and financial arrangements concerning Member States' participation or withdrawal.[15] It convenes at least twice a year at the level of the Ministers of Defence of the Member States in meetings chaired by the Head of the Agency. Otherwise it convenes in various compositions, for example at the level of the National Capabilities Directors of the Member States. According to Article 9(2) EDA Council Decision, the Steering Board will take decisions by qualified majority of two-thirds of the votes of the participating Member States which shall be weighted in accordance with Article 16(4) and (5) TEU. However, it appears that decisions are almost always taken by unanimity.

The Steering Board also appoints the Chief Executive and his or her Deputy who act under the authority of the Head of the Agency and in accordance with the decisions of the Steering Board.[16] The Chief Executive is, inter alia, responsible for ensuring the EDA's annual work programme, staff matters, the oversight and coordination of the functional units and the preparation of the work of the Steering Board, including the preparation of the draft annual work programme and the draft annual general budget. Moreover he or (at the time of writing) she will ensure close cooperation with and provide information to Council bodies such as the Political and Security Committee and the EU Military

---

[11] David Keohane, "Europe's New Defence Agency", policy brief (Centre for European Reform, London, June 2004), at 6.

[12] Ibid.

[13] Art. 9(2) sentence 3 EDA Council Decision: "Only the representatives of the participating Member States shall take part in the vote."

[14] Art. 8(1) EDA Council Decision.   [15] Art. 9(1)(a)–(p) EDA Council Decision.

[16] Art. 10(1) EDA Council Decision.

Committee,[17] and most notably the day-to-day administration of the EDA.[18] She is empowered to enter into contracts and to recruit staff.[19] The Chief Executive is accountable to the Steering Board and is the legal representative of the Agency.[20] Staff consists of personnel recruited directly by the Agency, national experts seconded by participating Member States and seconded EU officials.[21]

2.2 The tasks of the EDA

The EDA tasks can be divided into three broad groups: the development of policies, the evaluation of national capability commitments and joint research programmes and project management. As defence procurement regulation is part of the development of policies task, the following discussion will emphasise this activity.

2.2.1 Development of policies

The Agency has a policy-making function. Article 42(3) subparagraph 2 TEU provides:

> Member States shall undertake progressively to improve their military capabilities. The [EDA] shall identify operational requirements, shall promote measures to satisfy those requirements, shall contribute to identifying and, where appropriate, implementing any measure needed to strengthen the industrial and technological base of the defence sector, shall participate in defining a European capabilities and armaments policy, and shall assist the Council in evaluating the improvement of military capabilities.

Article 2 EDA Council Decision then gives the EDA a broad mandate. It is "to participate in defining a European capabilities and armaments policy". Article 5 EDA Council Decision provides a list of detailed policies in the definition of which the Agency is to participate. These policies include capability objectives, defence industrial and technological policy, procurement policy and even policy in relation to operational needs. This indicates a comprehensive European Capabilities and Armaments Policy (ECAP), covering all relevant aspects including a European defence industrial policy. As far as the participation of the Council in the definition of an ECAP is concerned, there will be a stronger role for it than in the rather technical field of multilateral projects and joint defence research discussed below. The EDA will prepare the decisions of the Council. The tasks of the Agency are stipulated in more detail in the Preamble and Article 5 of the EDA Council Decision. However, these detailed tasks do not go beyond those stipulated in the TEU.

---

[17] On these institutions see Martin Trybus, *European Union Law and Defence Integration* (Oxford: Hart, 2005), at 109–11.

[18] Art. 10 (2) and (3) EDA Council Decision.   [19] Art. 10 (4) EDA Council Decision.

[20] Art. 10 (5) and (6) EDA Council Decision.   [21] Art. 11 EDA Council Decision.

The ECAP and the EDA as her institutional dimension are designed as intergovernmental instruments.[22] According to the Preamble and Articles 1(2) and 4 of the EDA Council Decision and Article 45(1) TEU, all activities are carried out "subject to the authority of the Council". Moreover, Article 2(2) EDA Council Decision and Article 42(3) subparagraph 2 TEU emphasise that the Agency is "to support the Council" or to "assist the Council". Hence the EDA will be supervised by the main intergovernmental institution of the EU. According to Article 45(2) sentence 3 TEU, the EDA is to liaise with the Commission where necessary. Article 23 of the EDA Council Decision clarifies that the Commission is a member without voting rights of the EDA Steering Board, the main decision-making body of the Agency, and participates in the programmes and projects of the Agency. Moreover, the EDA shall establish the necessary arrangements with the Commission,

> in particular with a view of exchanging expertise and advice in those areas where the activities of the Union have a bearing on the Agency's missions and where the activities of the Agency are relevant to those of the Union.

These arrangements indicate only a limited involvement of the supranational institution and only when that involvement is absolutely necessary. However, as outlined in chapter 4 of this book, the Commission has a substantial defence industrial and research policy. Thus these arrangements are needed to take the overlaps of the activities of the two institutions into account.

The European Parliament, which is not mentioned at all with regard to the EDA, neither in the EDA Joint Action nor the TEU, has only a limited role in the Agency and the CSDP in general.[23] Moreover, according to Article 24(1) subparagraph 2 sentence 6 TEU the jurisdiction of the ECJ over CFSP and CSDP matters is very limited.[24] Consequently, the Court is neither mentioned in the EDA Council Decision nor the EDA provisions of the TEU. Hence it could be said that the ECAP and EDA suffer from a democratic deficit and a rule-of-law or judicial review deficit. To summarise, the role of the supranational institutions – Parliament, Court and Commission – concerning the EDA

---

[22] The more intergovernmental character of the Agency has been emphasised repeatedly, see European Council Meeting at 20–21 March 2003 in Brussels, Antonio Missiroli, *From Copenhagen to Brussels, European Defence, Core Documents* (Paris: Institute for Security Studies of the European Union, 2004), at 70 (seen as the starting point of the EDA) and the Presidency Report on ESDP, European Council Meeting, Thessaloniki, 20 June 2003, Missiroli, ibid., 153, at 159.

[23] Art. 24(1) subpara. 2 sentence 5 TEU Lisbon: "The specific role of the European Parliament and of the Commission in this area is defined by the Treaties."

[24] Art. 24(1) subpara. 2 sentence 6 TEU Lisbon reads: "The Court of Justice of the European Union shall not have jurisdiction with respect to these provisions, with the exception of its jurisdiction to monitor compliance with Article 40 of this Treaty and to review the legality of certain decisions as provided for by the second paragraph of Article 275 of the Treaty on the Functioning of the European Union."

and the ECAP is very limited. While this is also the arrangement for the other aspects of the CSDP,[25] these deficits become problematic once the Agency produces binding rules or even non-binding codes of conduct. Any rules would be created without an involvement of the democratically elected Parliament and exempt from judicial review. This would not be the case if the ECAP and EDA were part of the TFEU or subject to parliamentary and judicial control under the TEU. The policy most relevant to the topic of this book is an EDA regime on various aspects of procurement directed at the harmonisation of the practices of the participating Member States consisting of rules on procurement procedures, security of supply, security of information, the supply chain and offsets.

2.2.1.1 The EDA Procurement Code   According to Article 5(3)(b) EDA Council Decision and Article 45(1)(b) TEU, EDA is involved in the harmonisation of procurement procedures with the objective of making the laws compatible. Thus there is a legal base for action towards the harmonisation of the national defence procurement regimes of the participating Member States. On 21 November 2005, the EDA Steering Board composed of the defence ministers of the then 24 Member States[26] participating in the Agency agreed on a "voluntary, non-binding, intergovernmental Code of Conduct for Defence Procurement (hereinafter 'EDA Procurement Code')[27] . . . on a reciprocal basis between those [Member States] subscribing to the regime".[28] It entered into force on 1 July 2006. In early 2013 there were 26 subscribing Member States, the EDA Member States, which are the Member States of the EU except Denmark, and (yet) without the participation of Romania and Croatia but with the participation of Norway.[29] This EDA Procurement Code was intended as part of a wider regime which also included the rules of security of supply and information, the supply chain and offsets discussed below.[30] The objective of the Code was to respond to

> the need for decisive progress towards [the] creation of an internationally competitive [EDEM], as a key means to strengthen the [EDTIB].[31]

Hence the Code was intended as a contribution to the establishment of a European armaments market. However, the Code was not intended as a challenge to the EU Internal Market of the TFEU and more specifically the

---

[25] See Trybus, *European Union Law and Defence Integration, supra* note 17, ch. 11, at 305–53.
[26] As pointed out above, Denmark does not participate.
[27] www.eda.europa.eu/docs/documents/code-of-conduct-on-defence-procurement.pdf?sfvrsn=0 [accessed 23 July 2013].
[28] EDA Procurement Code, at 1.
[29] www.eda.europa.eu/Otheractivities/Intergovernmentalregimedefenceprocurement/CoC/key facts [accessed in July 2011].
[30] See also *A Guide to the EDA's New Defence Equipment Market* (Brussels: EDA, 2006, on file).
[31] EDA Procurement Code, at 1.

procurement Directives but as an instrument to apply when the armaments exemption in Article 346 TFEU discussed in chapter 3 was invoked. Article 346 TFEU was the main reason for the regime, which was not intended to apply unless the derogation was invoked. This implies recognition by the EDA that Internal Market law applied when the exemption was not invoked.[32] The objective to "regulate" Article 346 TFEU national security situations necessarily led to the characteristics of the Code as (1) voluntary, (2) non-binding, (3) intergovernmental and (4) reciprocal. The voluntary nature of the Code was explained on page 2 as meaning that Member States who decided to follow the Code could change their mind and were "free to cancel their participation in the regime at any time". The non-binding nature of the Code was also explained on page 2 as meaning that "[n]o sanction is envisaged for any non-observance of this Code by any [subscribing] Member State". No enforceable obligations for the subscribing Member States were envisaged.[33] There would only be an element of "peer pressure" from the other Member States which is discussed in more detail below.

The voluntary and non-binding nature of the EDA Procurement Code had advantages and disadvantages. One advantage was that Member States must have found it easier to agree on an instrument that was not legally binding and which they could leave at any time. Another advantage was that the non-binding nature is likely to have helped to encourage application of competition in defence procurement[34] as Member States might have felt more comfortable to enter a more transparent and competitive regime knowing that they could "pull the emergency brake" at any time when, for example for unforeseen circumstances, the procurement did not progress in the way envisaged. However, Member States could also "cancel their participation" or "non-observ[e]" for any reason. The voluntary and non-binding nature of the Code was a consequence of its intergovernmental nature. In contrast, a supranational regime under the TFEU, such as the Defence Directive, is subject to the special nature of EU law, including the supremacy of EU law and its direct effect. Moreover, there is a different legislative procedure involving the Commission and European Parliament and it would be subject to judicial review by the ECJ. Finally, the reciprocal nature gave the Code some flexibility. The Member States, with the exception of Denmark and Romania, had subscribed to the Code, which put its reciprocal nature in perspective. However, it should also be pointed out that a subscribing Member State could decide not to apply the Code in some cases which could lead to other subscribing Member States

---

[32] I benefited from discussion with B. Heuninckx on this point when he commented on an earlier version of this chapter.

[33] A. Georgopoulos, "The European Defence Agency's Code of Conduct for Armaments Acquisitions: A Case of Paramnesia?" (2006) 15 *Public Procurement Law Review* 51, at 52.

[34] EDA Procurement Code, at 1.

deciding not to apply the Code to economic operators from that subscribing Member State, as there would have been no reciprocity.[35] While this will be discussed in detail in Part II of this book, it has to be pointed out here that the Code was voluntary where the Defence Directive is obligatory, non-binding where the Defence Directive is legally fully binding, intergovernmental where the Defence Directive is supranational and (in theory) reciprocal where the Defence Directive is universal and uniform.[36] These differences emphasise the significance of the step the EU Member States have taken in passing the Defence Directive: it is a more comprehensive, detailed, binding and uniform instrument than the EDA Procurement Code.

The following discussion of the EDA Procurement Code shall broadly follow the structure of that of the Defence Directive in Part II of this book, discussing the scope of the Code, its award procedures and criteria, offsets and subcontracting and enforcement and remedies. This will be followed by comparison of the Code with the Defence Directive. As explained further below, the EDA Procurement Code was suspended in 2013, to be replaced by a new regime in the future. However, the Code remains a crucial part of the context and thus understanding of the Defence Directive, as part of a regime covering similar issues, as an inspiration for parts of it and, most importantly, as a procurement instrument intended for cases in which Article 346 TFEU is invoked, a measure that the Defence Directive aims to avoid.

2.2.1.1.1 The scope of the EDA Procurement Code When looking at the scope of application of the EDA Procurement Code four important aspects need to be differentiated. First, the Code applied to

> The significant proportion of ... defence procurement [which] takes place outside EU internal market rules, on the basis of Article [346 TFEU].[37]

This means that many armaments contracts were covered.[38] Georgopoulos argued that the list of exempted goods and services discussed below show, *e contrario*, that most conventional hard defence contracts were covered by the Code.[39] This links the Code to the interpretation of Article 346 TFEU provided in chapter 3 of this book. The Code was to apply only "where the conditions for application of Art[icle 346 were] met".[40] While there was no differentiation in the Code between letter (a) and (b) of Article 346(1) TFEU,

---

[35] Thanks to B. Heuninckx for pointing this out to me when commenting on an earlier draft of this chapter.
[36] In contrast to the Code, the Defence Directive does apply to Denmark and Romania. It also applies to the EEA countries.
[37] EDA Procurement Code, at 1.
[38] Georgopoulos, "Code", *supra* note 33, at 52 and 53 argues that "most" armaments are covered.
[39] Ibid., at 53.   [40] EDA Procurement Code, at 1.

it can be assumed that this mainly, though not only, referred to contracts involving listed armaments. Moreover, the words "where the conditions ... are met" suggests a certain familiarity if not acceptance of the relevant case law of the ECJ.[41] This is a high threshold, since the derogation is not automatic and only applies in exceptional circumstances. It is not clear in what type of exceptional situations, involving national security justifying derogation from the TFEU on the basis of its Article 346, the use of a transparent and competitive regime of the EDA Procurement Code would nevertheless have been appropriate.[42] Suffice it say that based on the wording of the EDA Procurement Code there was no intention to regulate procurement activities which are subject to the TFEU.

Secondly, the Code was to apply to contracts above a threshold of €1 million. This threshold was not in line with those in the EU procurement Directives but originated from former intergovernmental regimes on defence procurement, most notably those of the Western European Armaments Organisation (WEAO) and Independent European Programme Group (IEPG)[43] discussed in section 6.1 below. This begs the question why a contract subject to Article 346 TFEU but below €1 million would be outside any regulation. However, due to the high costs of most military equipment discussed in chapter 1, there will not have been very many contracts that fell into that category, although such contracts exist, for example on munitions or equipment maintenance.

Thirdly, the EDA Procurement Code applied to the defence procurement authorities of the Member States, not to the EDA itself. This means that the Code had many of the same addressees as the Defence Directive, as discussed further in chapter 6.[44]

Fourthly, a number of exemptions applied. These can broadly be subdivided into three groups. As a first group, procurement of research and technology and collaborative procurements were exempt from the Code.[45] Rules for the procurement of collaborative projects were to be decided on an ad hoc and project-by-project basis by the participating Member States.[46] Again these exemptions continued the "*acquis*" of previous regimes of the IEPG and WEAO. As discussed in chapter 1, research and technology and collaborative procurements are politically sensitive areas which are also subject to exemptions

[41] See ch. 3, at 104–25.
[42] A question already asked by B. Heuninckx, "Towards a Coherent European Defence Procurement Regime? European Defence Agency and European Commission Initiatives" (2008) 17 *Public Procurement Law Review* 1–20, at 8.
[43] See Martin Trybus, *European Defence Procurement Law* (The Hague: Kluwer, 1999), at 18–20; Aris Georgopoulos, "European Defence Procurement Integration: Proposals for Action within the European Union", PhD thesis, University of Nottingham (2004), at 65–69; Georgopoulos, "Code", *supra* note 33, at 57–8.
[44] At 248–60.   [45] EDA Procurement Code, at 1.
[46] Georgopoulos, "Code", *supra* note 33, at 53.

from the Defence Directive, as will be discussed in chapter 6.[47] As a second group, certain types of equipment and services were exempt:

> procurements of nuclear weapons, and nuclear propulsion systems, chemical, bacteriological and radiological goods and services, and cryptographical equipment.[48]

Again these exemptions continued the "*acquis*" of previous regimes of the IEPG and WEAO. The position on these goods and services with respect to the Defence Directive will be discussed in chapter 6.[49] As a third group of exemptions, Member States could derogate from the regime in cases of

> pressing operational urgency; for follow-on work or supplementary goods and services; or for extraordinary and compelling reasons of national security.[50]

Pressing operational urgency, follow-on work and supplementary goods and services are quite frequently subject to special treatment in procurement regulation. However, under the Public Sector and Utilities Directives and the Defence Directive these situations do not necessarily allow derogation from the instrument as a whole, but rather allow the use of less competitive procedures within the regime. Moreover, the grounds for using them are limited to expressly stipulated situations. Nevertheless it is not unusual or surprising to exempt these situations from the Code. The position with respect to the Defence Directive will be discussed in detail in chapter 6[51] on the scope and chapter 7[52] on the procurement procedures of the Defence Directive.

The situation "extraordinary and compelling reasons of national security" did not go beyond the flexibility Member States already had due to the voluntary and non-binding nature of the EDA Procurement Code. Hence it was unnecessary but a welcome clarification.[53] Since the Code was intended for contracts subject to Article 346 TFEU and the notion "extraordinary and compelling reasons of national security" was intended to allow complete derogation even from that regime, it must be assumed that the reasons of national security were even more extraordinary and compelling than those that allow derogation from the TFEU under its Article 346, which is also intended for exceptional circumstances. In contrast to the first and second group of exemptions, the use of the third group of exemptions to derogate from the Code needed to be justified and notified to the EDA and was subject to monitoring and debate in the Steering Group.

---

[47] At 283–8 and 299–301. [48] EDA Procurement Code, at 1. [49] At 245–72.
[50] EDA Procurement Code, at 1. [51] At 288–92. [52] At 338–44.
[53] Thanks to B. Heuninckx for pointing out to me when commenting on an earlier draft of this chapter that it was a clarification.

2.2.1.1.2 Award procedures and criteria   Similar to the Public Sector Directive and the Defence Directive, the Code was based on the principles of fair and equal treatment of suppliers and transparency and equality of information.[54] As an innovation compared to previous initiatives,[55] contracts were to be published on a single internet portal.[56] There were rules on selection criteria, specifications and statements of requirements, award criteria and debriefing. Notifications of invitations to tender had to be posted on the EDA's European Bulletin Board (EBB), linked "to national websites or other directions to where full documentation [could] be obtained". Moreover,

> The notification [was to] briefly describe the requirement, the procedures and the timescales for the competition and the award criteria.

Furthermore, a brief "vade mecum" would also familiarise suppliers with national defence procurement authorities and procedures. This reinforces the point made above, that the national ministries of defence remained the main actors and that they continued to use their respective national procedures. However, this dominance of national ministries and procedures should have complied with the rather rudimentary requirement of the Code when the regime was used. Nevertheless, there were basic requirements for publication.

Specifications and statements of requirements were "formulated as far as possible in terms of function and performance". This was in line with the established regime of the EU procurement Directives, as clarified in the case law of the ECJ.[57] International standards rather than national standards or company-linked requirements would be included, wherever possible – in other words, wherever they existed. Selection criteria had to be transparent and objective and applied equally to all companies. "Security clearance, required know-how and previous experience" were listed as important examples. Award criteria had to be clarified from the beginning of the procedure, in the invitation to tender. "The most economically advantageous solution for the particular requirement" was to be the "fundamental criterion" for awards.[58] Considerations of "costs (both acquisition and life cycle), compliance, quality, security of supply, and offsets" were listed as important aspects of the "most economically advantageous solution".[59] The use of the term "inter alia" implies that this list of considerations was not exhaustive. The considerations of acquisition and life-cycle costs and quality are not

---

[54] EDA Procurement Code, at 2.
[55] On the Comprehensive Policy Document of the WEAG where contracts were published in the defence contracts bulletins of the participating Member States, see Trybus, *European Defence Procurement Law, supra* note 43, at 31–44.
[56] EDA Procurement Code, at 2. The European Bulletin Board EBB was at www.eda.europa. eu/ebbweb/ [accessed in January 2013, the website was no longer operational in July 2013, see below].
[57] See ch. 8 at 364–5.   [58] Ibid.   [59] EDA Procurement Code, at 2–3.

unusual and equally appear in Directives 2004/17/EC, 2004/18/EC, 2014/24/ EU, 2014/25/EU and 2009/81/EC.[60] The notion of "compliance" was not explained further in the Code and it is not entirely clear what was meant. However, most procurement laws including EU procurement law require the rejection of non-compliant tenders.[61] The listing of compliance as an award sub-criterion suggests a more relative concept, possibly used for negotiated procedures rather than open and restricted ones.

Offsets are specific to the defence procurement context. Security of supply, briefly introduced in chapter 1,[62] is an important notion in the Defence Directive also but not only as an award sub-criterion.[63] This will be discussed in detail in chapter 8.[64] It is actually important for any procurement contract. However, its prominence in the defence context is understandable as it is a national security consideration: if a product or service is not in place then this has implications for the deployability of the armed forces. The importance of security of supply was fleshed out elsewhere in the Code.[65] As the Code required strong mutual confidence and interdependence, the participating Member States were entitled to expect from each other that "dependable and competitive sources of supply" were maintained. It is submitted that this did not amount to an obligation to maintain existing industrial capabilities, although this section of the Code emphasised the roles of both governments and industries. However, it did represent an obligation to take the security of supply of other participating Member States into account when taking decisions affecting industrial capabilities, whatever that would mean in practice. The Code did not elaborate on this issue and remained rather vague, although it is submitted that it would have been difficult to be clearer – decisions on industrial capabilities involve both industries and governments and are difficult to regulate. Another aspect of security of supply was addressed to the participating Member States: "improving the predictability and dependability of . . . regulations and policies" especially "support efforts to simplify amongst them intra-Community transfers and transits of defence goods and technologies".[66] While this consideration is important for security of supply, it is submitted the notion did not amount to an EDA intra-Community transfers regime *en miniature*. This would have to be a bit more detailed, as discussed with respect to the respective EU Directive in chapter 4 of this book.[67] The EDA *Framework Arrangement for Security of Supply between subscribing Member States (sMS) in Circumstances of Operational Urgency* was decided

---

[60] See ch. 8 at 400–3.   [61] See ch. 8 at 364–6.   [62] At 42–3.
[63] See ch. 8, at 401–2.   [64] At 401–2.
[65] On offsets and security of supply see also: B. Heuninckx, "Security of Supply and Offsets in Defence Procurement: What's New in the EU" (2014) 23 *Public Procurement Law Review* 33–49.
[66] EDA Procurement Code, at 3–4.   [67] At 147–60.

on 20 September 2006[68] and addresses one important aspect of security supply with a regime providing consultation between the subscribing Member States, engagement with their respective industries and mutual administrative support.

The consideration of offsets, introduced in chapter 1,[69] is remarkable for several reasons. First, as will be discussed in chapter 9,[70] offsets are extremely difficult to justify under the TFEU and Defence Directive. Thus it is remarkable that they were included as an award sub-criterion as this implies that they were considered acceptable in the context of the EDA Procurement Code. Secondly, there was no order of importance in the award sub-criteria, which implies that offsets were just as important as price, quality and security of supply. Thus a practice very difficult to justify within the scope of the TFEU was considered as a factor contributing to the "economically most advantageous solution" in the context of the EDA Procurement Code. Offsets in the context of the Code will be discussed in more detail below. Nevertheless, it can be stated here that the inclusion and prominence of offsets as a consideration in the context of the award decision is one of the most important differences between the EDA Procurement Code and the Defence Directive.

2.2.1.2 Offsets and subcontracting Offsets and subcontracting, features of the defence market discussed in chapter 1[71] and in great detail in relation to the Defence Directive in chapter 9, are not only addressed in the EDA Procurement Code as such. There is also a separate 2011 *EDA Code of Conduct on Offsets* (hereinafter the "EDA Offsets Code")[72] and an *EDA Code of Best Practice in the Supply Chain* (hereinafter the "EDA Supply Chain Code").[73] However, together with the EDA Procurement Code, they are part of one more or less coherent intergovernmental EDA defence procurement regime.

2.2.1.2.1 Offsets The inclusion of offsets as an award sub-criterion in the EDA Procurement Code was discussed above. The EDA Offsets Code was passed in its current form in May 2011, replacing a previous version agreed in October 2008 which had entered into force on 1 July 2009 and following an EDA *Study on the Effects of Offsets on the Development of a European Defence Industry and Market* (hereinafter "EDA Offsets

---

[68] www.eda.europa.eu/SOSWeb/Libraries/Library/Framework_Arrangement_for_Security_of_ Supply_between_subscribing_Member_States.sflb.ashx [accessed 18 October 2013].

[69] At 54–7.   [70] At 410–22.   [71] At 54–7 and 16.

[72] www.eda.europa.eu/docs/default-source/documents/The_Code_of_Conduct_on_Offsets. pdf [accessed 27 August 2013].

[73] www.eda.europa.eu/docs/documents/EDA_Code_of_Best_Practice_in_the_Supply_Chain. pdf?sfvrsn=0 [accessed 27 August 2013].

Study").[74] The Code already acknowledges in the introduction that offsets are both economically and legally problematic:

> The [participating Member States] share the ultimate aim to create the market conditions, and develop an EDTIB in which offsets may no longer be needed. Nonetheless, the present structure of the EDTIB and our *early* open market efforts require, *in the short term, evolving* offsets, *compatible with EU law*, whilst *mitigating* any adverse impact they may have on cross-border competition [emphasis added].

Moreover, under the heading "Objectives and scope" the Code summarises:

> The Code of Conduct of Offsets sets out a framework for evolving offsets, whilst ensuring the right *balance* between developing the EDTIB and the need to achieve a *level playing field* in the European and global market [emphasis added].

Several remarks can be made about these citations summarising the "spirit" of the EDA Offsets Code. First, the adverse effect of offsets on an open defence market is recognised; they are almost treated as an unavoidable evil.[75] This implies that the Code is at least in part intended as an instrument *against* offsets by making them unnecessary. However, the very introduction of the EDA Offset Code could also be interpreted as implying that EDA and the participating Member States have given up on the prospect of a "perfect market" without offsets, at least in the short or medium term. Secondly, the Code is probably the first EU instrument to address offsets directly and it is therefore an "early" measure which might well evolve into something more substantial and effective in the future. The fact that this Code was amended in 2011 only three years after it was first introduced suggests a process of addressing offsets. The Code is meant as a measure for the short term not the long term. In the short term the state of offsets is meant to evolve, it is submitted, into a situation with fewer and less extensive offsets. Thirdly, the Code seems to assume that there are offsets that can be compatible with EU law. Based on the interpretation of the crucial Article 346(1)(b) TFEU provided in chapter 3 of this book and the opinion of the Commission in the 2011 Guidance Note *Offsets*[76] this opinion is very

---

[74] E. Anders Erikson *et al.*, *Study on the Effects of Offsets on the Development of a European Defence Industry and Market* (Henley on Thames: SCS; Brussels: FOI Stockholm for the European Defence Agency, 2007), www.eda.europa.eu/docs/documents/EDA_06-DIM-022_Study_on_the_effects_of_offsets_on_the_Development_of_a_European_Defence_Industry_and_Market.pdf [accessed 27 August 2013].

[75] EDA Offsets Code, at 2: "In a perfectly functioning market offsets would not exist. Nevertheless, we recognise that today's defence market is not perfect ... mitigate any adverse effects of offsets ..."

[76] http://ec.europa.eu/internal_market/publicprocurement/docs/defence/guide-offsets_en.pdf [accessed 23 July 2013].

controversial indeed. As discussed in great detail in chapter 9,[77] very few if any cases are conceivable in which offsets can be compatible with the TFEU or the procurement Directives, including the Defence Directive. They can only be legal under EU law if Article 346 TFEU can successfully be invoked, and that would be very difficult to do in order to justify an offset. This also shows the basic dilemma of the EDA and this Code: offsets are widespread and many formidable interests are affected. The practice can probably not be abolished overnight; it needs to be gradually phased out, if it can be done at all. Fourthly and connected to the third point, the Code aims to mitigate the effects of offsets to achieve a level playing field or cross-border competition with evolving or rather diminishing offsets.

Similar to the EDA Procurement Code, the EDA Offsets Code is (1) voluntary, (2) non-binding, (3) intergovernmental and (4) reciprocal.[78] Moreover, it is also meant to apply to products and services to which Article 346 TFEU applies. In contrast to the EDA Procurement Code it includes government-to-government off-the-shelf purchases and shall be applied to participating Member States as well as third countries.[79] These inclusions extend the application of the Code in comparison also with that of the Defence Directive which excludes such contracts, as will be discussed in chapter 6.[80] However, it is argued that a limitation or banning of offsets only with respect to participating Member States or EU Member States in general would not have made sense. Some companies from outside the EU, especially from the USA, are very strong in the EU market. Allowing them unfettered opportunities to offer offsets while at the same time phasing out or reducing the same possibility of companies from the EU would have put the latter at a disadvantage. This is a general dilemma when regulating rather than banning offsets – third countries need to be included.

The actual "guidelines" are intended to "help us progress towards closer convergence of offset policies and practices and to gradually reduce the use of offsets". The guidelines can be subdivided into two categories, those to achieve "increased transparency" on the one hand and those for the "evolving use of offsets" on the other hand.

The participating Member States have to provide each other with information on "offset practices and underpinning policies", information that needs to be regularly reviewed to ensure it is up to date. Secondly, the participating Member States have to provide the EDA with information on all the offset commitments, "whether parts of the procurement contract or otherwise". These measures will increase transparency for the Agency and its participating Member States, but do not contain any obligations towards companies or third countries.

With regards to the "evolving use of offsets" a number of guidelines can be considered as contributing to regulate them somewhat. First, offset

---

[77] At 54–7.   [78] EDA Offsets Code, at 2.   [79] Ibid.   [80] See ch. 6, at 292–9.

requirements need to be clearly stipulated in the contract notice, which also establishes a degree of transparency for everyone including, of course, not only the defence industries but also third countries. Secondly, it needs to be made clear from the outset if offsets are a "factor in the consideration of a company's bid during the procurement process". Thirdly,

> When used as a criterion for tender selection or award of contract, offsets will be *considered of a less significant weight* (or used as a *subsidiary criteri[on]* in case of offers with the same weigh[t]) in order to ensure that a procurement process is based on the best available and most economically advantageous solution for the particular requirement.

This demotes offsets, which are listed as a selection and award criterion in the EDA Procurement Code, to a second-class selection and award criterion. Fourthly, and this is an important limitation also based on the recommendations of the 2008 EDA Offsets Study, "offsets, both required and accepted, will not exceed the value of the procurement contract". This puts a 100 per cent limit on offset arrangements which is the most tangible rule of the EDA Offsets Code. Considering the often excessive percentages of military offset arrangements discussed in chapter 1,[81] the implementation of this rule in practice might well prove to be the most important contribution of this Code. Fifthly,

> The [subscribing] Member States will allow foreign suppliers providing offsets to select the most cost effective business opportunities within the purchasing country for the offset fulfilment, enabling fair and open competition within supply chains where it is efficient, practical and economically appropriate.

This guideline appears to provide for competition with regards to the industries of the purchasing country which benefit from the offset arrangement, both with regards to prime contractors and subcontractors. However, the reference to the supply chain refers to the fact that the industries of the purchasing country will often be involved as subcontractors for the contract itself or for other contracts. Moreover, the defence industries of a purchasing country can be rather small and limited, as was explained in chapter 1. Especially in the context of direct offsets, in other words offsets in the military field which are not explicitly discouraged by the EDA Offsets Code and might therefore increase, competition is difficult to achieve. If there are only one or two companies in the defence industrial sector of the Member State concerned and there is a direct offset requirement then it is clear that only those companies can benefit. If then the offset has to be integrated on a subcontractual basis into the original contract, there might be only one possible company left that can be integrated. In other words, competition might be difficult or impossible and the reservation "where

---

[81] At 54–7.

it is efficient, practical and economically appropriate" in the guideline is a crucial one in practice. Indirect offsets are illegal even when Article 346 TFEU is invoked. This mostly explains their absence from the EDA Offsets Code.[82] However, the limited defence industrial capabilities of many Member States are at least also part of the likely explanation for the fact that the EDA Offsets Code does not address or suggest limiting indirect offsets, or the possibility of offsetting military purchases with civil contracts. Many Member States do not have the defence industrial capability to meet a "direct offsets only" requirement. However, this situation also emphasises the disruptive effect of offsets on competition. Companies get contracts not on the basis of a competitive award procedure but to fulfil offset arrangements. One can imagine companies getting quite used to offset arrangements and getting expensive, slow, inefficient and difficult to deal with in the meantime. On the other hand the possibility of civil or indirect offsets should increase competition, not in general but when awarding offsets, because there is a more diverse industrial base. This could even be developed into an argument for indirect offsets as the better alternative to direct military offsets,[83] if not for the fact that all offsets are disruptive to competition and difficult to reconcile with the Internal Market and in the case of indirect offsets not even justifiable on the basis of Article 346 TFEU. Sixthly,

> The subscribing Member States will use, wherever practicable and on a voluntary basis, mutual abatements to reduce reciprocal offset commitments.

Mutual abatements are a practice whereby offsets are reduced. They can be agreed in advance, as a part of the offset proposal, applied at some stage during the fulfilment of existing offset obligations[84] or agreed as a memorandum of understanding in which offsets are mutually reduced or even cancelled.[85] This is obviously a significant technique serving the overall objective of the EDA Offsets Code to gradually reduce or even phase out offsets. However, according to the 2010 EDA in-house study *Abatements: A Pragmatic Offset Tool to Facilitate the Development of the European Defence Equipment Market*, only a number of the Member States and Norway use them.[86] Moreover, while also recognising the positive effects of abatements, the study also points out that "not all offset obligations can be abated and nations may require a limit on the percentage of the offset obligation to be fulfilled through ... abatement".[87]

---

[82] Thanks to B. Heuninckx for pointing this out to me when commenting on an earlier draft of this chapter.

[83] Ibid.

[84] See the EDA In-House Study, *Abatements: A Pragmatic Offset Tool to Facilitate the Development of the European Defence Equipment Market* (EDA, 2010, on file), at 11.

[85] See for the Memorandum of Understanding between the United Kingdom, the Netherlands, and Denmark, www.epicos.com/WARoot/News/Abatement_on_offsets_MoU_signed_between_Netherlands_.pdf [accessed 28 August 2013].

[86] EDA In-House Study *Abatements, supra* note 84, at 5.   [87] Ibid., at 6.

Abatement is only possible if there are defence prime contractors with offset obligations in both subscribing Member States.[88] Therefore its use is limited to Member States with industries able to be prime contractors.[89] Thus while abatements are clearly an important technique to achieve the objectives of the EDA Offsets Code, their use might well continue to be limited.

The EDA Offsets Code, while recognising the negative effects of offsets and aimed to reduce them, also contains positive statements. On page 3 it suggests:

> Offsets will be used to help develop industrial capabilities that are competent, competitive and capability driven. Therefore, offsets will help shape the aspired EDTIB of the future, notably by facilitating the development of globally competitive Centres of Excellence and avoiding unnecessary duplication.

This suggests that the EDA Offsets Code recognises offsets as a useful tool of industrial policy towards a competitive EDTIB providing the armed forces of the Member States with their requirements. The establishment of globally competitive centres of excellence and the avoidance of unnecessary duplication provide some clarification of what is meant by this statement. This suggests that everybody will get their fair share while at the same time rationalising the industries. While tools such as subcontracting, collaboration and industrial mergers are likely candidates to achieve such objectives, the use of offsets to this end is less clear. What is not expressly mentioned in the EDA Offset Code, probably because it is politically sensitive, is that if the prime contractor is from outside the EU then offsets can support the development of European defence industries which otherwise would not be involved in the programme.[90] In contrast, with an EU prime contractor offsets can have a negative impact on the competitiveness of the EDTIB. It is possible that companies who discontinue certain activities, for which another capacity already exists, will be offset with some other probably "exclusive" task. Avoiding duplication inside the Union obviously also has a negative effect on competition since competition requires at least two competitors, in other words competition requires at least some duplication. However, it appears that the competition would be ensured through global competition – and the EDA Offsets Code is to be applied equally to third countries. Nevertheless, the establishment of a defence market which includes third countries is a complex problem which is not sufficiently addressed in the EDA Offsets Code, let alone the EDA Procurement Code. Moreover, such a market would be a

---

[88] Thanks to B. Heuninckx for pointing this out to me when commenting on an earlier draft of this chapter.

[89] EDA In-House Study *Abatements*, *supra* note 84, at 5.

[90] Thanks to B. Heuninckx for pointing this out to me when commenting on an earlier draft of this chapter.

sensitive issue for some Member States.[91] The statement also speaks of "unnecessary" duplication, which suggests that some duplication is recognised as necessary, although this is not explained any further. This positive statement about offsets is also the first guideline, stipulated before all the limiting guidelines discussed above. However, it is submitted that this is not an indication of a predominantly positive message of the Code towards offsets. This merely recognises the considerable opposition against any type of limitation to offsets and could well be a diplomatic measure to ease the limiting guidelines through. The limiting guidelines would still lead to a reduction in offsets, which would present considerable progress. The guidelines continue with another "positive" statement:

> Offsets should, wherever possible, contribute to developing depth and diversity of the European defence-related supplier base, in particular by supporting the full involvement of SMEs and non-traditional suppliers in the EDTIB, fostering the industrial cooperation and help promote efficient and responsive lower tier suppliers in line with the principles of the [Code of Best Practice in the Supply Chain].

This connects offsets to another important aspect of defence procurement – subcontracting. This connection will be discussed in detail in the context of chapter 9,[92] as the Defence Directive essentially offers a subcontracting regime as a substitute for offsets. The connection between the two in the regime of the EDA requires a closer look at the EDA Supply Chain Code which specifically deals with subcontracting.

2.2.1.2.2 Subcontracts   The EDA Supply Chain Code was "to be read and implemented coherently with the Code of Conduct [on Procurement], of which [it] is an integral part".[93] Hence this Code shared the objectives, scope of application and characteristics of the EDA Procurement Code discussed above. Particular emphasis was put on the voluntary and non-legally binding nature of the Code, the application to cases where Article 346 TFEU is invoked and the precedence of national rules where they existed. The Code was

> established to promote the principles of the Code of Conduct on Defence Procurement in the supply chain thereby [e]ncouraging increased competition and fair opportunities for all suppliers, including of small and medium-sized enterprises (SMEs). The CoBPSC should enourage value to flow up the supply chain to the benefit of the [subscribing Member States] by adopting good practice down the supply chain.

---

[91] Thanks to B. Heuninckx for pointing this out to me when commenting on an earlier draft of this chapter.

[92] At 428–52.

[93] EDA Supply Chain Code, www.eda.europa.eu/docs/documents/EDA_Code_of_Best_Practice_ in_the_Supply_Chain.pdf?sfvrsn=0 [accessed 18 October 2013], at 1.

This suggests a policy towards competition in the supply chain on the one hand and a connected policy favouring SMEs on the other hand. Moreover, the EDA Supply Chain Code of Best Practice might have been extended later to "encompass all public procurements undertaken by the subscribing Member States".[94] This might have included contracts not subject to Article 346 TFEU, which, before the subcontracting regime introduced by the Defence Directive and discussed in chapter 9, would have been less problematic as there were only some very basic rules in the Public Sector Directive.[95]

The actual "principles" could be divided into core values, general principles, procurement-specific requirements and "dispute settlement" aspects. With regards to core values, the defence procurement agencies of the subscribing Member States and the suppliers were to ensure "fairness, honesty and openness, efficiency and effectiveness, and professionalism, maintaining the highest levels of integrity, impartiality and objectivity".[96] These core values could be called the "mission statement" of the EDA Supply Chain Code.

A general principle was that even under the Code prime contractors stayed "responsible ultimately for the selection and management of his supply chain".[97] Freedom of contract was ensured "except where mandated by law or customer requirement". This meant specifically that

> Buyers must be free to specify terms and performance requirements that meet their acquisition needs; however, those terms are to be clearly state[d] at the outset, drafted unambiguously and implemented in a balanced manner.[98]

The second part of this sentence already contained a procurement-related requirement. Nevertheless, there might have been situations where freedom of contract was not the general principle as

> Eventual direction from the contracting authorities of the relevant administrations of the [subscribing Member States] for a specific source of supply may result in a reassessment of risk sharing.[99]

The procurement-related principles mainly related to competition in subcontracting:

> The [Code] is to promote opportunities, where competition is efficient, practical and economically or technologically appropriate on a level playing-field basis for qualified and competent suppliers (both in-house and external), including SMEs, to participate in competitions. In the interests of both buyers and Suppliers numbers invited to tender could be limited to ensure optimum economy, whilst honouring (and testing, where appropriate) preferred supplier status and strategic alliances where

---

[94] Ibid., at para. 3. [95] Art. 25 Directive 2004/18/EC.
[96] EDA Supply Chain Code, at para. 8. [97] Ibid. [98] Ibid., at para. 9. [99] Ibid.

these exist. This will include the identification of contract and subcontract opportunities as soon as practicable by publication in the Contracts Bulletin of the relevant administrations of the [subscribing Member States], the Agency's Electronic Bulletin Board or the Suppliers websites as applicable.[100]

Hence the EDA Supply Chain Code favoured subcontracting on a competitive basis, but only when this was "efficient, practical and economically or technologically appropriate". This provision suggests that a competitive basis might not always have been "efficient, practical, and technologically appropriate", although the decision would have had to be taken on a case-by-case basis. Moreover, the decision about whether competition was appropriate stayed with the subscribing Member States. In addition, the Code allowed "honouring preferred supplier status and strategic alliances where these exist",[101] which allowed the abstract preference for a particular supplier in addition to the case-by-case derogation from the principle of competition outlined above. This possibility represented a significant deviation of the principle of competition, which, if used frequently, would have compromised the objectives of the Code.

If there was competition in the supply chain then the prime contractors should "make available the criteria for the evaluation of bids; to evaluate the bids objectively and to notify the outcome promptly to all bidders on the same day".[102] No specific award procedures were stipulated in the Code, but the procedures had to be clear, transparent and certain.[103] The economically most advantageous offer appears to have been the main award criterion but "it shall be taken into consideration that both Buyers and Suppliers need to take strategic sourcing decisions that are wider than individual contract or programme requirements".[104] Evaluation should also take into account "the approach undertaken or proposed for the selection of sources of supply (including, where appropriate, make or buy plans)".[105] It is not entirely clear whether this referred to tender evaluation at the prime contractor level, an interpretation supported by the wording of this paragraph, or at subcontractor level, an interpretation supported by the fact that the paragraph was part of the EDA Supply Chain Code. However, it can be assumed that this principle was meant to apply to both.

Since like the other Codes, the EDA Supply Chain Code was not legally enforceable, there was no review and remedies part as such. However, there was an obligation "within the bounds of commercial confidentiality, to debrief winners and losers, upon request, on the outcome of the bidding process and the reasons for not being so selected so as to facilitate better performance on future occasions".[106] Moreover, buyers at any level had to resolve any "difficulties or concerns of their supply chain" to which the Code applied.

---

[100] Ibid., at para. 11.   [101] Ibid.   [102] Ibid., at para. 12.   [103] Ibid., at para. 16.
[104] Ibid., at para. 13.   [105] Ibid., at para. 14.   [106] Ibid., at para. 12.

If such issues were not resolved, "they may be notified for transparency purposes to a Point of Contact of the relevant administration of the [subscribing Member State]".[107] Furthermore, there would have been a monitoring system based on information provided by prime contractors regarding the subcontracts they advertised "to assess the extent to which the [Code was] being applied".[108] This suggests an enforcement regime only based on peer pressure of the subscribing Member States: if a prime contractor in a subscribing Member State derogated from the EDA Supply Chain Code then there would be questions from that subscribing Member State "motivated" by the other subscribing Member States. While this was merely a diplomatic and intergovernmental enforcement mechanism which cannot be compared to the review and remedies system introduced by Title IV of the Defence Directive and discussed in chapter 10, it should not be underestimated. The involvement of the Point of Contact, the notification requirement, the monitoring mechanism and the fact that there was an assessment on the extent to which the Code was applied show a commitment of the subscribing Member States and also posed a threat to those thinking about not applying the Code. If such mechanisms were put in place they might well have been used.

As discussed in detail in chapter 9, Title III of the Defence Directive introduced a detailed subcontracting regime. As with the EDA Procurement Code, the EDA Supply Chain Code was voluntary where the Defence Directive is obligatory, non-binding where the Defence Directive is legally binding, intergovernmental where the Defence Directive is supranational and (in theory) reciprocal where the Defence Directive is universal and uniform.[109] Moreover, it could further be argued that in contrast to a "Code of Conduct" which suggests a stronger commitment of the Member States subscribing to it possibly resulting in peer pressure when its rules are violated, a "Code of Best Practice" suggests an even weaker binding force. Thus the Code had an important function when there was no binding subcontracting regime for defence contracts. Moreover, it was limited to cases where Article 346 TFEU applied. However, as with the rules of the EDA Procurement Code discussed above, it is not clear how in these extreme national security situations even non-binding best practice standards for the supply chain could be observed.

2.2.1.3 Enforcement and remedies As a framework outside the Internal Market, the EDA Procurement Code did not contain an enforcement and remedies system comparable to that under the TFEU (Commission enforcement against Member States according to Article 258 TFEU) and the Defence Directive (judicial review in the national courts of the Member States) discussed

---

[107] Ibid., at para. 15.   [108] Ibid., at para. 17.
[109] In contrast to the Code, the Defence Directive does apply to Denmark and Romania. It also applies to the EEA countries.

in chapter 10. There was no possibility of applying to a court to set aside procurement decisions, annul the contract or to award damages. The Code summarised: "[n]o sanction is envisaged for any non-observance of this Code by any [subscribing Member State]".[110] This was in line with the voluntary and non-legally binding nature of the Code discussed above. Moreover, this "no sanction" approach is the most important difference between the regime of the EDA Codes and that of the Defence Directive discussed in Part II of this book.

However, no public procurement system can work without some form of enforcement, without "teeth" to back up the substantive rules. The approach of the EDA Procurement Code was summarised as "the requirement to account to the other members of the regime", in the second part of the sentence summarising the "no sanction" principle.[111] Georgopoulos calls this "a form of institutionalised 'peer pressure' ... linked with ... the invocation of the exemptions"[112] from the Code discussed above. If a subscribing Member State invoked one of the exemptions to derogate from the Code it had to provide an explanation and had to "debate the circumstances in the EDA Steering Board".[113] Georgopoulos equates this requirement for an "explanation" with a requirement for a justification.[114] Hence the EDA, and more specifically its Steering Board, was the forum for this "enforcement mechanism".[115] Some more particulars were stipulated in the Code:

> Whilst no [subscribing Member State] will wish the EDA to assume the role of independent investigator of its affairs, we recognise that mutual visibility and reassurance about how each [subscribing Member State] is operating the Code will require an effective EDA monitoring system with regular reports to the Steering Board.[116]

Hence regular reports to the Steering Board introduced above were required. The subscribing Member States had to ensure that the relevant national civil servants were cooperative in providing this information to the Agency.[117] This would be in line with the peer-pressure approach of this mechanism which should have led to what Georgopoulos calls a "naming and shaming" of a subscribing Member State abusing the exemptions.[118]

While the EDA Procurement Code did not contain legally enforceable rules and no remedies system, it is submitted that the fact that derogation from the Code required an explanation or justification, had to be notified to the EDA and could be debated in the Steering Board represented progress when compared to

---

[110] EDA Procurement Code, at 2.   [111] Ibid.
[112] Georgopoulos, "Code", *supra* note 33, at 55.   [113] EDA Procurement Code, at 3.
[114] Georgopoulos, "Code", *supra* note 33, at 55.
[115] EDA Procurement Code, at 3: "The EDA will be the instrument to achieve this mutual transparency and accountability."
[116] Ibid.   [117] EDA Procurement Code, at 3.
[118] Georgopoulos, "Code", *supra* note 33, at 55.

the absence of any formalised pressure before the introduction of the Code. The mechanism, as Georgopoulos calls it, "provides some sort of a 'stick' to a regime which otherwise is 'toothless'".[119] The "stick" was the danger of having to defend a possibly abusive use of the exemptions in the Steering Board and thus perhaps even "retaliation" by other subscribing Member States, because abusive derogation would have challenged the reciprocity of the Code. Obviously this depended on the use of the mechanism in practice and the intensity of scrutiny applied to the derogations of subscribing Member States.

2.2.1.4 Compatibility of the EDA Procurement Code with the Defence Directive The relationship between the EDA Codes and the Defence Directive is addressed in the EDA Council Decision and the TEU. The EDA Council Decision and the Treaty of Lisbon TEU leave the *acquis communautaire* and all competences of the Commission and the other supranational institutions intact.[120] Thus the relationship between the two frameworks depends on the limits of the Internal Market. As discussed in chapter 3, the procurement of weapons is not automatically or categorically excluded from the application of the TFEU and all of the EU public procurement Directives. The TFEU and the Defence Directive apply to the procurement of armaments unless a Member State can successfully invoke Article 346(1)(b) TFEU. Therefore the EDA Codes could only apply where Article 346 TFEU was successfully invoked; it caught the exceptional cases where this could be done. However, in most scenarios, the specific national security and secrecy character of these cases would also necessitate and allow Member States to derogate from the Codes because their publication and other procedural requirements are impossible to reconcile with the urgency and security imperatives of such a scenario.[121] Nevertheless, the introduction of the EDA Codes on this legal background cannot be interpreted as meaning that the Codes were not intended to catch only the exceptional cases covered by Article 346 TFEU but as a basis for most or all armaments procurement in Europe.[122] The introduction of the EDA Codes cannot be interpreted as indicating that they were meant to be used instead of at least the formerly applicable EU Public Sector Directive and

---

[119] Ibid.

[120] This is emphasised in a reference to Art. 45 TEU and the reference "fully respecting the responsibilities of the European Union and its institutions" in the Preamble and Art. 1(2) and 5(1) of the EDA Council Decision. Art. 1(2) EDA Council Decision reads: "The Agency shall act under the Council's authority, in support of the CFSP and the CSDP, within the single institutional framework of the European Union, and without prejudice to the responsibilities of the EU institutions and the Council bodies. The Agency's mission shall be without prejudice to the competences of the Union, in full respect of Article 40 TEU."

[121] Heuninckx, "Towards", *supra* note 42, at 8.

[122] See Trybus, "EDA", *supra* note 1, where this interpretation is discussed.

the TFEU.[123] On the basis of the interpretation of Article 346 TFEU discussed in chapter 3, this would not be legally possible without amending that derogation. In the context of the current Treaty of Lisbon or the former Treaty of Nice which was in force when the Code was introduced, the regulation of all defence procurement as part of the CFSP, as a binding or non-binding Code, requires a wide interpretation of Article 346(1)(b) TFEU as an automatic and categorical exclusion of armaments from the TFEU. Moreover, it requires the exclusion to be abstract without reference to individual cases where the provision would apply. However, this abstract and categorical interpretation of the provision was clearly rejected by the ECJ in *Spanish Weapons*,[124] *Agusta*,[125] *Military Exports*[126] and *Finnish Turntables*[127] as discussed in chapter 3.[128] Member States can derogate from the Treaty on a case-by-case basis, subject to a low-intensity review of the ECJ expressly provided in Article 348 TFEU but also possible in the context of other proceedings, most notably Article 258 TFEU. Hence if it had been intended for all defence procurement, the Code would have been based on a misinterpretation of the TFEU and would have been a challenge to the defence procurement policy of the Internal Market. If this had been the case then by addressing defence procurement rules in the context of the more intergovernmental CSDP, the Member States would have assumed that the procurement of armaments was automatically excluded from the TFEU. They would have created an intergovernmental, voluntary and non-binding Code potentially overlapping with the supranational and binding Public Sector and later Defence Directive. However, it is argued below that the EDA Procurement Code and the other Codes were not intended as a challenge to the Internal Market but as a regime ensuring more transparency, competition and non-discrimination in cases in which Article 346 TFEU was rightfully or abusively applied.[129]

Nevertheless, there was a danger that the Code would develop into a threat to the *acquis communautaire*: Member States might have used it instead of the public procurement Directives. Heuninckx[130] has found interesting figures for

---

[123] This is also the interpretation of Georgopoulos, "Code", *supra* note 33, at 53.

[124] Case C-414/97, *Commission v. Spain* [1999] ECR I-5585, [2000] 2 CMLR 4.

[125] Case C-337/05, *Commission v. Italy* [2008] ECR I-2173 and C-157/06, *Commission v. Italy* [2008] ECR I-7313.

[126] Case C-284/05, *Commission v. Finland* [2009] ECR I-11705; Case C-294/05, *Commission v. Sweden* [2009] ECR I-11777; Case 387/05, *Commission v. Italy* [2009] ECR I-11831; Case C-409/05, *Commission v. Greece* [2009] ECR I-11859; Case C-461/05, *Commission v. Denmark* [2009] ECR I-11887; Case C-38/06, *Commission v. Portugal* [2010] ECR I-1569; Case C-239/06, *Commission v. Italy* [2009] ECR I-11913.

[127] Case C-615/10, *Insinööritoimisto InsTiimi Oy*, nyr, 7 June 2012.

[128] See ch. 3 at 104–25.

[129] I have benefited from discussions with B. Heuninckx on the points raised in this paragraph.

[130] B. Heuninckx, "The European Defence Agency Electronic Bulletin Board: A Survey after Two Years" (2009) 18 *Public Procurement Law Review* 43–66, at 62. See also the figures

the contracts published in the EBB for the two years from 2006 to 2008, when the Defence Directive had not been introduced yet. Based on the respective goods not being listed on the 1958 list or clearly not meeting the requirements of Article 346 TFEU,[131] the publication of 27.1 per cent of the contracts on the EBB was "unjustified or questionable". For the remaining 72.9 per cent of contracts he rightly questions whether the conditions of Article 346 TFEU were met when those contracts could still be published and subjected to a regime based on transparency and non-discrimination not too different from the Public Sector Directive.[132] The extreme national security situations allowing derogation from the Internal Market should actually also have prevented the use of the EDA regime. There appears to have been a danger that the EDA regime was used as an alternative to the Public Sector Directive during that period. Contracts published on the EBB since the deadline for the transposition of the Defence Directive suggest a similar danger for the latter.

Two considerations, however, put this danger into perspective. First, so far Article 346(1)(b) TFEU has not been properly applied by most national defence procurement authorities.[133] Therefore the Public Sector Directive did not cover the procurement of armaments in practice. Moreover, the Defence Directive which accommodates the interpretation of the Court in *Spanish Weapons* is still relatively new. Hence, there has been only limited experience of the instrument so far. The EDA Procurement Code reflected the essence of the EU public procurement Directives[134] and therefore arguably led to improved competitiveness and transparency in defence procurement thereby making an important contribution towards the creation of a European defence equipment market. In other words, the EDA Procurement Code was better than nothing, even when its use was based on an abuse of Article 346 TFEU. Secondly, the Commission provided the Commission Communication clarifying the existing legal framework only in late 2006[135] and introduced the Defence Directive only in 2009. The implementation of the latter was only to be completed in 2011 and, as indicated in the introduction to this book, often took longer. Therefore, until the introduction and transposition of the Defence Directive and before the publication of the Interpretative Communication there was no defence-specific

published in Commission Staff Working Document on Defence SWD (2013) 279 final accompanying COM (2013) 542 final, at 41.
[131] Heuninckx, "EEB", *supra* note 130, gives "blank cartridges for ceremonial use" as an example.
[132] Ibid., at 63.
[133] See the information on contracts published by the ministries of defence of the Member States in the Official Journal, COM (2005) 626 final, at 4.
[134] Georgopoulos, "Code", *supra* note 33, at 54: "the [CoC] draws clear parallels with the essence of the European public procurement legislation".
[135] "Interpretative Communication on the Application of Article [346] of the Treaty in the Field of Defence Procurement", COM (2006) 779 final, see ch. 3, at 125–7.

procurement instrument and no interpretative instrument to limit the extensive use of Article 346 TFEU.

In October 2004 the United Kingdom Government responded to the Green Paper discussed in the introduction to this book with a non-paper in which the EDA Procurement Code was suggested as a temporary solution to achieve more transparency for the period until the cumbersome process of agreeing on EU legislation on defence procurement could be completed.[136] This was also suggested by some of the stakeholders who participated in the consultation process leading to the December 2005 Communication of the Commission.[137] Hence until the Code was replaced by a binding Defence Directive and an Interpretative Communication leading to an increased use of Internal Market rules, it might have done more good than harm to the Internal Market as a temporary solution potentially providing equal treatment and transparency in contrast to the previous situation.

The EDA Procurement Code was a political move. While Article 346 TFEU was clearly abused by many Member States, the adoption of the EDA Procurement Code recognised this situation as largely unavoidable at that stage and attempted to provide more competition and transparency in a move towards progressively including defence procurement within the Internal Market. Thus, confirming the approach of the 2004 British non-paper discussed above, the Code was not a challenge to the Internal Market and the Public Sector Directive but an instrument to address the abuse of Article 346 TFEU in a politically pragmatic way, while awaiting a more suitable Internal Market instrument which was eventually introduced in the form of the Defence Directive. This interpretation of the EDA Procurement Code is also confirmed by the suspension of the Code in 2013 after all the Member States had transposed the Defence Directive, as discussed below. The pragmatic EDA "emergency" regime was removed as soon as the permanent Internal Market regime became fully applicable through comprehensive transposition in the Member States.

In their Communication issued after the creation of the EDA Procurement Code in December 2005[138] the Commission argued that the Code was complementary to their own initiatives and applied to a different segment of the defence market. According to the Commission the Code applied to cases where the conditions for the use of Article 346 TFEU are met.[139] Hence the Commission appears to assume that their own initiatives apply to cases where

---

[136] Indicated in the UK House of Lords, European Union, 9th Report, at point 61.

[137] Communication from the Commission to the Council and the European Parliament on the results of the consultation launched by the Green Paper on Defence Procurement and future Commission initiatives, COM (2005) 626, at 9. See also Heuninckx, "Towards", *supra* note 42, at 7–8.

[138] COM (2005) 626 final, at 8, 9, and 10.   [139] Ibid. at 10.

the conditions for the use of Article 346 TFEU are *not* met.[140] Again, according to the ECJ in *Spanish Weapons*, Member States can only derogate from the TFEU on the basis of Article 346(1)(b) TFEU for national security reasons, under certain strict conditions and on a case-by-case basis. The situations allowing them to derogate from the TFEU would also have allowed them to not apply the EDA Code, not only because the Code was not legally binding anyway, but also because no other subscribing Member State would have criticised this in a national security situation. However, a Member State could have taken the decision to derogate from the TFEU but not the Code. This would have improved the competitiveness, transparency and equal treatment in the context of such a contract. However, it appears that the Member States created a regime for armaments contracts situated between the application of the TFEU and exclusive Member State jurisdiction, which would have been unnecessary if Article 346(1)(b) TFEU was properly applied. Again, the EDA regime is a reaction to the extensive use of the armaments derogation before the Defence Directive, taking most armaments contracts outside the Internal Market.[141] It is better than no competition and transparency at all. However, as also highlighted by a survey conducted by Heuninckx,[142] some of the contracts advertised on the EBB were not necessarily Article 346 TFEU cases. Did contracting authorities almost automatically advertise armaments on the EBB instead of the OJ rather than making a case-by-case assessment, which they had to do on the basis of the interpretation of the derogation? This cannot be answered due to a lack of data, but if this was the case then the very existence of an EDA Procurement Code and EBB might have contributed to contracts not being subjected to the Internal Market. Moreover, the Commission could have made the excessive use of Article 346(1)(b) TFEU more difficult by using their powers under Articles 258 and 348 TFEU more extensively. Finally, the findings of this Communication might be already outdated since they mainly discuss the legal framework and practice under the old public procurement Directives, mainly considering them insufficiently suitable for the acquisition of armaments. As discussed in Part II of this book, the Defence Directive is more suitable for defence procurement than its predecessors.[143] Thus there is now less room for an EDA Procurement Code in its 2011 form, if any at all.

[140] Georgopoulos, "Code", *supra* note 33, at 53.
[141] According to the EDA, more than half of the defence procurement of the Member States was conducted outside the Internal Market before the introduction of the Code, see the EDA press releases, "EU Governments Agree Voluntary Code for Cross-Border Competition in Defence Equipment Market", Brussels, 21 November 2005 and "EDA Welcomes European Commission Move on Defence Procurement Rules", Brussels, 6 December 2005, as cited by Heuninckx, "Towards", *supra* note 42, at 6.
[142] Heuninckx, "EBB", *supra* note 130.
[143] On the old directives as an instrument of defence procurement see Trybus, *European Defence Procurement Law, supra* note 43, at 47–63.

At the time of writing in autumn 2013, the EDA Procurement Code was suspended. The EDA website refers to it with the following sentence:

> Due to the changes in the European Defence Equipment Market the EDA Steering Board tasked on 12 March 2013 the EDA to analyse the need for a possible new intergovernmental arrangement to replace the Code.[144]

Similarly it refers to the EDA Supply Chain Code with a similar sentence:

> On 12 March 2013 the EDA Steering Board tasked the EDA to commence the review of this Code.[145]

This review has not been completed. As the minutes of the Steering Board of that March 2013 meeting are not publicly available, it cannot be said for certain what exactly triggered this review. However, there are a number of indications that allow an interpretation of the notion "[d]ue to the changes in the European Defence Equipment Market". The Defence Directive entered into force in 2009 and had to be implemented by August 2011. As the October 2012 Commission Transposition Report[146] suggests, this did not happen by the deadline in all Member States, while at the time of writing transposition appears to be complete in all Member States.[147] Even Member States that were late with transposition often recognised the direct effect of the Defence Directive between the transposition deadline and the actual transposition of the instrument into national law.[148] Alternatively, they temporarily required the application of their "civil" procurement regime based on the Public Sector Directive.[149] Thus in

---

[144] www.eda.europa.eu/procurement-gateway/information/eda-codes-arrangements [accessed 23 July 2013]. This was still on the EDA website on 24 April 2014.

[145] Ibid.

[146] "Report from the Commission to the European Parliament and the Council on Transposition of Directive 2009/81/EC on Defence and Security Procurement", COM (2012) 565 final.

[147] A US Government source, http://export.gov/europeanunion/defenseprocurement/ [accessed 5 November 2013], reports complete transposition as of April 2013 – this is very close to the March 2013 meeting in which the suspension of the Code was decided, the EDA Steering Board might have known about a slightly earlier date of complete transposition in all Member States.

[148] This was the case in Belgium according to B. Heuninckx. The direct effect of Directives after their transposition deadline has passed is generally recognised in EU law anyway, without the need for Member States recognising that explicitly. See, inter alia, Case 148/78, *Pubblico Ministero* v. *Ratti* [1979] ECR 1629. However, for the contracting officers that clarification is useful and it also might help to prevent infringement proceedings against that Member State.

[149] This was the case in Germany: see Federal Ministry of Economy and Technology, 26 July 2011, Rundschreiben [English "Circular"] zur Anwendung der Richtlinie 2009/81/EG des europäischen Parlaments und des Rates vom 13. Juli 2009 über die Koordinierung der Verfahren zur Vergabe bestimmter Bau-, Liefer- und Dienstleistungsaufträge in den Bereichen Verteidigung und Sicherheit und zur Änderung der Richtlinien 2004/17/EG

March 2013 the EDA Steering Board had to react to the existence of a largely transposed Defence Directive. The "coexistence" of an EDA Procurement Code and Supply Chain Code with an Internal Market Public Sector Directive 2004/ 18/EC, the latter of which as many argued was not suitable for defence procurement, is a situation that can be defended by the EDA, the Member States and possibly even the Commission. The "coexistence" of an EDA Procurement Code and an Internal Market Defence Directive specifically drafted and adapted to defence and security cannot be so easily explained. As argued above, the EDA Code and the Defence Directive are frameworks directed at the abuse of Article 346 TFEU, the earlier offering a framework outside the Internal Market the latter offering a framework inside it. The continued coexistence of both instruments would suggest a constitutional turf war between CFSP and Internal Market institutions and contradictory policies of the Member States involved in the creation of both, let alone duplication and incoherence.[150] It is therefore submitted that the current review and likely replacement of the EDA Procurement Code is in effect a withdrawal of that Code in reaction to the (almost) complete transposition of the Defence Directive. This assessment is supported by the information published in the new "EDA Procurement Gateway" launched on the EDA website on 28 June 2013.[151] While the EBB has disappeared (!), the Procurement Gateway rather contains information on the EU procurement Directives,[152] the OJ platform for contract notices and other procurement notices "Tenders Electronic Daily" (TED)[153] and the case

und 2004/18/EG, www.bmwi.de/BMWi/Redaktion/PDF/I/interim-schreiben-anwendung-der-rl-2009-81-eg,property=pdf,bereich=bmwi,sprache=de,rwb=true.pdf [acccessed 24 July 2013, sent to the main federal ministries with procurement activities], at 3: "Unmittelbare Wirkung der Richtlinie mit Auswirkung auf Bestimmungen des GWB" [English: direct effect of the Directive with effects on provisions on the Competition Act]: "Um Vergabeverfahren europarechtskonform zu gestalten, sollten Auftraggeber ab dem 21. August 2011 bei der Vergabe verteidigungs- und sicherheitsrelevanter Aufträge das GWB-Vergaberecht entsprechend anwenden." (English: in order to conduct public procurement procedures in compliance with EU law, from 21 August 2011 contracting entities should apply the legally binding public procurement law in the GWB in analogy to defence and security contracts.)

[150] See also the Commission Staff Working Document – Impact Assessment SEC (2007) 1593, http://ec.europa.eu/governance/impact/ia_carried_out/docs/ia_2007/sec_2007_1593_en.pdf [accessed 1 November 2013], at 58 which warns: "the Commission will continue to participate in the various fora of the EDA, following especially the implementation of the Code of conduct in the light of the Interpretative communication on the application of Article [346] in the field of defence procurement".

[151] www.eda.europa.eu/info-hub/news/2013/06/28/european-defence-agency-launches-defence-procurement-gateway [accessed 24 July 2013].

[152] Directives 2004/17/EC, 2004/18/EC, 2009/81/EC and the Intra-Community Transfers Directive 2009/43/EC, www.eda.europa.eu/procurement-gateway/information/codeda-regulationaba [accessed 24 July 2013].

[153] Ibid.

law of the ECJ on the interpretation of Article 346 TFEU[154] discussed in chapter 3 and information on Article 258 TFEU infringement proceedings against Member States,[155] also discussed in chapter 10. While the EDA Procurement Code and the Supply Chain Code remain accessible,[156] there is now *no* EDA contract portal to publish any contracts and the reference to TED suggest that this is where ministries of defence are supposed to publish their contracts. The absence of the EBB transforms the Codes from instruments of soft law to documents of legal history. However, it is possible that the Code discussed above will be replaced by a modified instrument. Such an instrument would in all probability not suggest an alternative to the Defence Directive but would have a narrower focus on cases in which Article 346 TFEU can be successfully invoked. This would be limited to requirements that would still be possible in such a national security situation, such as information requirements of the other subscribing Member States and possibly the Commission or EDA. Moreover, it might only be the EDA Supply Chain Code which will be replaced. In contrast it appears unlikely that the Procurement Code will be reinstated in its current form. At the time of completing this book, in November 2013, there were discussions with the participating Member States on the future of the regime. Possible outcomes are either that there would be no new code, or that there would be a new code and adapted EBB applying when Article 346 TFEU is invoked, or there would be new "soft law" guidance applying to all defence procurement (even under the Directive).

The institutional structures of the EDA discussed above are adequate to facilitate the suspension and possible abolition or reform of the EDA procurement regime. The Head of the Agency has roles in both the CFSP and the Commission, the Commission is represented on the Steering Board even though they do not have voting rights and the staff of both EDA and the Commission are in permanent contact. These "bridges" between the two institutions should help to avoid or to contain any conflict between the regimes. They should facilitate the understanding that both EDA and Commission are working towards the same objective of a competitive and transparent European defence equipment market rather than just fighting over the competence to regulate it.

---

[154] Listing: "Case 6/64 Costa v Ente Nazionale per l'Energia Elettrica (ENEL); Case 72/83 Campus Oil Ltd v Ministry for Industry and Energy; Case C-252/01 Commission v Belgium; Case T-26/01 Fiocchi munizioni SpA v Commission; Case C-337/05 Commission v Italy; Case C-157/06 Commission v Italy; Case C-273/97 Sirdar v The Army Board; Case C-414/97 Commission v Spain; Case C-615/10 Finland v European Commission".

[155] www.eda.europa.eu/procurement-gateway/information/codeda-regulationaba/eu-infringment-cases-and-rulings [accessed 24 July 2013].

[156] www.eda.europa.eu/procurement-gateway/information/eda-codes-arrangements [accessed 24 July 2013].

2.2.2 Evaluation of national capability commitments

According to Articles 5(3)(a) EDA Council Decision and 45(1)(a) TEU the Agency evaluates observance of the capability commitments given by the Member States. This indicates the role of an oversight authority for capability commitments which does not overlap with any area of the TFEU or a function of the Commission. The precise limits of this function are not clearly spelt out. This lack of precision is not surprising since capability commitments are a highly political issue.[157] In 2006 the Agency issued a long-term vision (LTV) report for European defence capabilities and capacity needs[158] in which three key issues for the development of European defence capabilities were identified. These were (1) interoperability; (2) rapid acquisition, especially the faster exploitation of new technologies; and (3) an industrial policy addressing the steady decline of the EDIB by increasing investment, consolidating the EDIB and targeting strategic industrial capabilities to be preserved. On this basis the EDA developed in 2008 a European Capabilities Development Plan (ECDP) with the aims of making the long-term vision capability guidance of the LTV more specific, identifying priorities for capability development and bringing out opportunities to pool resources and to cooperate. Based on this ECDP the EDA Steering Board subsequently agreed on 12 defence capabilities on which action should be taken. The ECDP "is a living document that will require regular updates".[159] While the participating Member States will also have to meet the requirements of the Plan on a national level, there is also a substantial role for collaborative programmes, which in 2008 led to the approval of the European Armaments Cooperation Strategy.[160]

As Heuninckx pointed out, the ECDP is no supranational defence equipment or capability plan aiming at replacing national defence plans and programmes.[161] This also raises the question of what the EDA would do in case a Member State repeatedly failed to meet its capability commitments. It cannot initiate infringement proceedings against the Member State the way the Commission can under Articles 258 or 348 TFEU. The ECDP only aims to support the national decision-making processes of the Member States. It was

---

[157] B. Heuninckx, "The European Defence Agency Capability Development Plan and the European Armaments Cooperation Strategy: Two Steps in the Right Direction" (2009) 18 *Public Procurement Law Review* NA136–43.

[158] EDA, *An Initial Long-Term Vision for European Defence Capability and Capacity Needs*, 3 October 2006, http://ue.eu.int/ueDocs/cms_Data/docs/pressdata/EN/reports/91135.pdf [accessed 25 October 2013].

[159] EDA, Background Note – European Capability Development Plan, http://consilium. europa.eu/uedocs/cmsUpload/080708-CDP_Press_Background_brief%20.pdf [accessed 25 October 2013].

[160] EDA, *European Armaments Cooperation Strategy*, 15 October 2008, www.eda.europa.eu/ docs/news/European_Armaments_Cooperation_Strategy.pdf [accessed 25 October 2013].

[161] Heuninckx, "Capability Development Plan", *supra* note 157, at NA140.

probably too early for the participating Member States to commit to a supra-national planning process. However, also in view of the lack of success of similar intergovernmental approaches in the past,[162] a supranational approach should be considered in the future[163] to ensure the enforceability and effectiveness to the Plan. As pointed out above, this oversight function of EDA does not overlap with the Internal Market or any competences of the Commission. However, it forms an important part of the context of the Defence Directive since at least with respect to the national and non-collaborative aspects of the Plan, the envisaged capability increases will often have to be met by applying the Defence Directive.

2.2.3 Pooling and sharing

Pooling and sharing is a practice related to capability development. In November 2012 the EDA adopted a Code of Conduct on Pooling and Sharing[164] to create a systematic approach to this practice. It is argued that pooling and sharing as understood in the context of this Code comprises essentially two approaches: (1) "the expansion of national programmes to other Member States"[165] and (2) "the joint use of existing capabilities by Member States".[166] The earlier is relevant for defence procurement since it should lead to more collaboration involving R&D which, as explained in chapter 6[167] would be exempt from the Defence Directive. The Code comprises a number of actions aimed at mainstreaming the practice in the planning and decision-making processes of the subscribing Member States. These actions are to be implemented on a national and voluntary basis, in line with defence policies of Member States.[168] Thus this is also an intergovernmental regime. Overall, it is argued that there is no conflict with the TFEU.

2.2.4 Collaborative projects and joint research programmes

According to Article 5(3)(c) EDA Council Decision and 45(1)(c) TEU, the Agency will be in charge of multilateral projects. Multinational collaborative programmes such as the British-German-Italian-Spanish "Eurofighter/ Typhoon" could be conducted by the EDA. Even though the EDA has the

---

[162] The Western European Armaments Group (WEAG) discussed further below was such an intergovernmental approach, see Assembly of the WEU, Arms Cooperation in Europe: WEAG and EU activities – reply to the annual report of the Council, Document Number A/1800, 4 December 2002, at http://assembly–weu.itnetwork.fr/en/documents/sessions_ ordinaires/rpt/2002/1800.html as cited by Heuninckx, "Capability Development Plan", *supra* note 157, at NA142.

[163] Heuninckx, "Capability Development Plan", *supra* note 157, at NA142.

[164] EDA Pooling and Sharing Code, www.eda.europa.eu/docs/news/code-of-conduct.pdf [accessed 25 October 2013].

[165] Ibid., at point 3.   [166] Ibid., at point 5.   [167] At 283–8.

[168] EDA Pooling and Sharing Code, at point 1.

legal capacity to do that, it does not consider that this is its core business for now and that it is structured to perform this task. EDA prefers to delegate this task to OCCAR,[169] which is discussed below.

According to Article 5(3)(d) and 45(1)(d) TEU, the Agency will be in charge of joint research programmes. This refers to projects where a group of Member States decides to approach the research and development (R&D) of a certain piece of equipment on a common basis.[170] Such a project may also concern research only. In such a case the common programme would normally replace individual Member State programmes. However, there is no rule preventing a Member State from continuing or starting a similar project on a national basis. Nevertheless, in times of tight defence budgets this is unlikely. The EDA could have the role of a practical coordinator and manager for joint projects. This task is not mentioned in Article 45 TEU and it is submitted that this indicates that this rather technical matter was not considered controversial or important enough for the Treaty. It is mentioned in Article 5(3) EDA Joint Action. Moreover, the Member States decide on their participation in an individual joint research programme on an ad hoc basis anyway. No Member State is forced to participate.

As mentioned in chapter 4,[171] there is a TFEU research policy and the Commission has a growing annual civil research budget which in 2013 was just below €11 billion.[172] Some of the projects, for example the Galileo satellite navigation system, could perform military tasks. Moreover, the Commission has a substantial security research programme, directed against terrorism, organised crime and natural disasters.[173] While this is not a competing programme against that of the EDA, which is primarily military in nature, there are potential overlaps which need to be addressed in liaising with the Commission.

After the suspension of the EDA Procurement and Supply Chain Codes discussed above, collaborative procurement programmes involving R&D are potentially one of the most important issues with regards to the relationship of EDA procurement-related activities and those pursued in the context of the Internal Market. This is not only due to the technological, financial, economic and military importance of these projects discussed in chapter 1.[174] This is also due to the fact that while with the Defence Directive the Internal Market

---

[169] Baudouin Heuninckx, "The Law of Collaborative Defence Procurement Through International Organisations in the European Union", PhD Thesis, University of Nottingham (2011), at 178.

[170] EDA, *A European Defence Research and Technology Strategy* (2008), www.eda.europa.eu/docs/documents/edrt_strategy.pdf [accessed 25 October 2013].

[171] At 183.

[172] http://ec.europa.eu/research/fp7/index_en.cfm?pg=budget [accessed 28 August 2013].

[173] http://ec.europa.eu/enterprise/policies/security/ [accessed 28 August 2013].

[174] At 53–4.

has asserted its jurisdiction over defence procurement within the limits of Article 346 TFEU, it has explicitly excluded collaborative projects involving R&D in Article 13(c) Defence Directive. This suggests a division of competences between the Internal Market and CFSP "pillars" of the EU through the Defence Directive which will be discussed in detail in chapter 6.[175] Suffice it to say in the context of this chapter that the EDA was left a considerable part of defence procurement. However, it needs to be pointed out that, as discussed under the next heading below, the EDA does not currently see itself as a procurement agency but as a policy-maker.[176] Thus this important function is a potential and currently not an actual one.[177]

A special procurement regime exists for purchases conducted by EDA as a contracting entity. This includes the EDA Procurement Regulations[178] and the EDA R&T Projects User Guide. The EDA Procurement Rules and Rules for Financial Contributions for the Operational Budget of the European Defence Agency are broadly in compliance with the Public Sector Directive 2004/18/EC in relation to the provisions regulating procurement covered by that Directive but not (yet) in compliance with the Defence Directive in relation to contracts covered by that instrument. This shall be discussed in more detail in chapter 6.[179] The Rules were approved by the Steering Board on 14 December 2006 and have not been amended since then, although this might already be on the way. The non-legally binding but crucial *EDA R&T Projects User Guide*[180] covers R&D projects in which more than one contributing Member State (except Denmark), which can include Norway or Switzerland, collaborate on an ad hoc basis. This guide is not in compliance with the rules of the procurement Directives but subject to the principle of fair returns discussed in chapter 1.[181] In other words, companies situated in the "Contributing Member [States]" have to receive a share of the project contracts which more or less equals that of their financial contribution. However, as explained in detail in chapter 6, this type of collaborative R&D contract is expressly excluded from the field of application of the Defence Directive. Nevertheless, unless Article 346 TFEU can be invoked by the Member States involved, the TFEU and its procurement principles would still apply, preventing practices commonly used in collaborative projects, such as the principle of fair returns, from being applied.

---

[175] At 286–8.   [176] EDA, *European Armaments Cooperation Strategy, supra* note 160.
[177] Thanks to B. Heuninckx for discussing this point with me when commenting on an earlier draft of this chapter. See also his article on security of supply and offsets, *supra* note 65.
[178] www.eda.europa.eu/docs/documents/EDA_Procurement_Rules_and_Rules_on_Financial_Contributions.pdf [accessed 29 August 2013].
[179] At 286–8.   [180] www.eda.europa.eu/RandTUserGuide [accessed 29 August 2013].
[181] At 53–4.

2.3 The EDA as part of the CSDP of the Treaty of Lisbon

The EDA is the institutional dimension of the ECAP which forms part of the intergovernmental CSDP and CFSP. The establishment of the Agency as part of what used to be called the "Second Pillar of the TEU" gives this part of European armaments cooperation a strong intergovernmental character. Details concerning this intergovernmental character were discussed in the context of the tasks of the EDA above. There are a number of remarks to be made about this approach. First, so far there has been an intergovernmental tradition of European armaments cooperation and the establishment of the EDA only continues this tradition. Only the failed EDC Treaty of 1952 envisaged a supranational European armaments policy, where procurement was to be conducted by an independent Board of Commissioners.[182] Secondly, the establishment of a supranational agency does not appear to be politically feasible at the moment and an intergovernmental EDA is better than no agency at all. Thirdly, especially with regards to the control of capability commitments, the intergovernmental approach might be the most appropriate.

However, the establishment of an EDA in the context of the CFSP is problematic. First, it is doubtful whether an intergovernmental agency will be sufficient to address the current problems of capability shortfalls and fragmentation. There will be no binding decisions and no binding legal framework. In the past this approach has not always been successful.[183] Secondly, especially with the EDA Procurement Code, the Member States reacted to the extensive and often abusive use of Article 346 TFEU by creating an EDA regime as part of the intergovernmental CFSP and CSDP. In other words, a regime outside the Internal Market was created for contracts which, perhaps not always but at least often, should have been awarded inside it. However, as explained in chapter 3, the supranational TFEU does apply to the types of goods the EDA is supposed to be dealing with, unless one of the Member States can successfully invoke Article 346(1)(b) TFEU. This does not preclude the introduction of intergovernmental elements, but the application of the TFEU cannot be ignored. In its communications "The Challenges Facing the European Defence-related Industry",[184] "Implementing the European Union Strategy on Defence-related Industries",[185] "Towards an EU Defence Equipment Policy",[186] the Green Paper on Defence Procurement[187] and the Communication of December 2005,[188] the Commission discussed the role of what at the time was still called "Community" law in the area of armaments without making concrete proposals

---

[182] See Trybus, *European Union Law and Defence Integration*, *supra* note 17, at 39–42.
[183] For an overview of past initiatives see Trybus, *European Defence Procurement Law*, *supra* note 43, ch. 1, at 18–20.
[184] COM (1996) 10 final.   [185] COM (1997) 583 final.   [186] COM (2003) 113 final.
[187] COM (2004) 608 final.   [188] COM (2005) 626 final.

yet. Nevertheless, for many of the policy fields EDA is intended to cover, the TFEU represents an alternative model with clear advantages over the current intergovernmental approach. For example, the Commission has a long experience in public procurement regulation and policy. While this Internal Market or "Community" regulation and policy cannot be considered a complete success, the binding TFEU and EU Public Sector, Utilities and Defence Directives have established a viable legal framework for the operation of the Internal Market in their respective sectors. The Commission can enforce these Directives, if necessary through the ECJ under Article 258 TFEU. The intergovernmental EDA has yet to develop a comparable experience and a viable alternative to EU Internal Market law sufficient to lead to the establishment of a European defence equipment market. All other intergovernmental initiatives failed to match up to the record of EU Internal Market law, although the EDA has made considerable progress and relatively fast.

3 OCCAR[189]

The Organisation for Joint Armaments Cooperation (hereinafter OCCAR[190]) was created in 1996 by France, Germany, Italy and the United Kingdom. In 2014 Spain and Belgium were also Member States.[191] The organisation was developed from the earlier Franco-German armaments cooperation structure as a result of their dissatisfaction with the lack of progress to establish a European armaments agency within the WEU.[192] The OCCAR's purpose is that of a management organisation for joint programmes involving two or more Member States but also of purely national programmes assigned

---

[189] This discussion is based on a section in M. Trybus, "Defence Procurement: The New Public Sector Directive and Beyond" (2004) 13 *Public Procurement Law Review* 198–210, at 207–9. On OCCAR see also: Aris Georgopoulos, "European Armaments Policy: A Sine Qua Non for Security and Defence?" in Martin Trybus and Nigel White (eds.), *European Security Law* (Oxford University Press, 2007), 198–222, at 209–12; and very detailed: Heuninckx, Thesis, *supra* note 169, at 158–96.

[190] The abbreviation is based on the French name: *Organisme conjointe de coopération en matière d'armement*.

[191] www.occar.int/185 [accessed 24 April 2014]: "At this moment six nations are Member States of OCCAR: Belgium, France, Germany, The United Kingdom, Italy and Spain." Belgium joined in 2003 and Spain in 2005, see Georgopoulos, "European Armaments Policy", *supra* note 189, at 209. "The OCCAR community consists however out of 12 Nations as Finland, Sweden, Poland, Luxembourg, the Netherlands and Turkey are also participating to one or more OCCAR Programmes", see www.occar.int/185 [accessed 26 July 2013].

[192] *Defence Trade: European Initiatives to Integrate the Defence Market*, Report to the Secretary of Defence (Washington DC: United States General Accounting Office, October 1997), at 7.

to it. The OCCAR Convention[193] (hereinafter OCCAR) was signed in 1998. The ratification process was completed in December 2000 and OCCAR attained legal status in 2001. According to Article 8 OCCAR, the organisation can cover a large range of activities and may become a fully fledged armaments agency. OCCAR is based in Bonn and manages several programmes.[194]

According to Article 8 OCCAR, the organisation shall fulfil the following tasks

and such other functions as the Member States may assign to it:
(a) management of current and future co-operative programmes, which may include configuration control and in-service support, as well as research activities;
(b) management of those national programmes of Member States that are assigned to it;
(c) preparation of common technical specifications for the development and procurement of jointly defined equipment;
(d) co-ordination and planning of joint research activities as well as, in co-operation with military staffs, studies of technical solutions to meet future operational requirements;
(e) co-ordination of national decisions concerning the common industrial base and common technologies;
(f) co-ordination of both capital investments and the use of test facilities.

Two of these functions are important as part of the context of the Defence Directive: the management of collaborative projects involving R&D in Article 8(a) OCCAR, on the one hand, and the management of national programmes of Member States assigned to it in Article 8(b) OCCAR, on the other hand.

With regards to the management of collaborative programmes, as a basic rule, the OCCAR "Member States renounce the analytical calculation of industrial *juste retour* or fair returns on a programme-by-programme basis, and replace it by the pursuit of an overall multi-programme [and] multi-year balance."[195] As mentioned in chapter 1, the principle of fair returns, if applied in a strict sense, impedes competition in procurement because the defence industry of the Member State that contributes a certain percentage to a project is entitled to an equal share of the contract. Therefore, this move away from strict fair returns is to be welcomed. However, even the "balance" approach will

---

[193] Convention on the Establishment of the Organisation for Joint Armaments Co-operation OCCAR, printed in Burkard Schmitt, *European Armaments Cooperation: Core Documents*, Chaillot Paper No. 59 (Paris: Institute for Security Studies of the European Union, 2003), at 45–59, see also www.occar.int/media/raw/OCCAR_Convention.pdf [accessed 26 July 2013].

[194] See, for example, the Franco-German "Tiger" attack helicopter, the Franco-Italian Future Surface-to-Air Missile Family, the Belgian-British-French-German-Spanish-Turkish A400M transport aircraft. The latter involves non-OCCAR members.

[195] Art. 5 OCCAR.

restrict competition and will not contribute to a liberalised defence procurement market in Europe with respect to the procurement activities of OCCAR. Moreover, the "balance approach" already implies a certain preference for the industries of the OCCAR Member States rather than openness to the EU as a whole, as clearly spelt out in Article 24(4) OCCAR.

Article 13(c) Defence Directive on "contracts awarded in the framework of a cooperative programme based on [R&D], conducted jointly by at least two Member States for the development of a new product and, where applicable, the later phases of all or part of the life-cycle of this product" excludes collaborative projects involving R&D from the scope of the Directive. While this exclusion is to be discussed in detail in chapter 6,[196] it can be stated that this type of activity can be conducted by OCCAR on the basis of the OCCAR rules without violating the Defence Directive.

The OCCAR is an important part of the context of the Defence Directive. It is one of several initiatives of EU Member States towards a European armaments policy outside the EU and more importantly outside the EU Internal Market. Whereas "civilian" public and utilities procurement regulation is characterised by an interplay of EU Internal Market law and the national laws of the Member States, defence procurement is also affected by the CFSP through the EDA, as outlined above and by separate international organisations such as the OCCAR. This is likely to have an effect on the coherence and therefore effectiveness of the approach to establish an EDEM. Coherence will depend on whether the activities are complementary or competing or even contradictory. This will also depend on how the various organisational structures, for example the EU and the OCCAR, have addressed their relationship and therefore the distribution of tasks. With regards to the Defence Directive this will be discussed in chapter 6. What is important for the purposes of this chapter is, first, that OCCAR does not establish or aim to establish a liberalised armaments market between its member nations,[197] neither on an intergovernmental basis as EDA nor on a supranational basis as the Defence Directive. OCCAR is an agency procuring on the basis of its own rules and these rules are not intended to affect the procurement activities of the contracting authorities and entities of the Member States. Thus with respect to the Defence Directive OCCAR does not represent a competing framework but a potential contracting authority covered by the Defence Directive. Secondly, the exclusion in Article 13(c) Defence Directive expressly leaves an important task of OCCAR and an important part[198] of defence procurement unregulated by its rules. While this can be criticised for reasons to be discussed in chapter 6, this exclusion addresses the relationship between the EU Internal Market defence procurement regime and the

---

[196] At 283–8.   [197] Georgopoulos, "European Armaments Policy", *supra* note 189, at 210.
[198] See the overview over the OCCAR's multi-million and since 2004 billion € expenditure in Heuninckx, Thesis, *supra* note 169, at 160.

OCCAR regime. This avoids contradictions and allows the regime to complement rather than to compromise each other. However, as explained in more detail in chapter 6,[199] a Member State might want to assign a project to the OCCAR with the intention of avoiding having to comply with the Defence Directive.

In contrast to the EDA, OCCAR is, however, with the exception of Belgium, a club of a limited number of EU Member States with defence industrial capabilities, and is also a result of the frustration of these countries with the lack of progress in the relevant EU framework at the time, most importantly the Council's POLARM and the WEU initiatives discussed below. It was felt that more could be achieved in a smaller group of States with more common ground than in the EU or WEU as a whole. With the foundation of the EDA there is a certain level of overlap and duplication with that structure rather than with the EU Internal Market. However, in the medium term a transfer of the activities of OCCAR to the EDA, which did not exist when the earlier was founded, should be considered to ensure the coherence of the EU defence procurement regime and to avoid a duplication of efforts. As outlined above, this is not the view of the EDA itself though.

4 Letter of Intent[200]

The Letter of Intent (LoI) is another framework affecting the regulation of the defence industries and trade in armaments in Europe. The initial LoI was signed in July 1998 by the defence ministers of France, Germany, Italy, Spain, Sweden and the United Kingdom.[201] It is therefore clearly a framework of the EU Member States with the most extensive defence industrial capabilities identified in chapter 1. According to Point 1.1 LoI: "The Participants desire to establish a cooperative framework to facilitate the restructuring of European defence industry."[202] The six areas of (common) interest identified in the initial LoI were security of supply, export procedures, protection of classified information, R&D, exchange of technical information and standardisation of military requirements.

---

[199] At 283–8. See also at 273–4 on Art. 12(a) Defence Directive.

[200] The author wishes to express his gratitude to Ms Brina Pocivalsek (University of Ljubljana, Slovenia), the Institute of European Law (University of Birmingham) Leonardo da Vinci Research Assistant for the summer of 2013, for her help with the research on this section. The information collected is based on material published by the LoI organisation.

[201] www.defensa.gob.es/Galerias/politica/armamento-material/ficheros/DGM-Letter-intent-ingles.pdf or http://archives.sipri.org/contents/expcon/loisign.html [accessed 4 September 2013].

[202] See also the very similar Art. 1(a) of the Framework Agreement outlined below.

4.1 The LoI Framework Agreement Treaty

The 1998 LoI initiative led to negotiations which resulted in legally binding commitments aiming at the integration of trade in defence articles and services among these six LoI States.[203] The LoI *Framework Agreement Treaty (FA)*, *officially the Framework Agreement Concerning Measures to Facilitate the Restructuring and Operation of the European Defence Industry*[204] was signed in 2000 during the Farnborough Air Show by the defence ministers of the six LoI nations. The six areas of interest identified in the 1998 document reappear in legally binding form: security of supply,[205] export procedures,[206] protection of classified information,[207] R&D,[208] exchange of technical information[209] and standardisation of military requirements.[210] However, these areas are developed further; most significantly the area of export procedures now includes transfers between the six nations, and a seventh area – namely on the protection of commercially sensitive information[211] – was added. All of these areas relate to national security and could therefore be subject to one of the relevant exemptions in the TFEU, most importantly Article 346 TFEU. However, the interpretation of this derogation does not categorically exclude these areas from Internal Market law and most of them are also addressed there, most notably in the Defence Directive itself.

The FA is an international and intergovernmental treaty outside the framework of the EU. There is no office, secretariat or budget and the LoI framework relies on the six nations to agree and deliver its work programmes. Each nation in turn chairs the "Executive Committee" for a year. It meets two or three times a year to review progress on current activities and agree new priorities and activities and is responsible for providing regular reports to the relevant national authorities. The Agreement itself only creates a framework for the six nations to cooperate in the field of armaments, sets principles and policies governing cooperation between them and can lead to specific measures in a number of areas designed to help industrial and equipment cooperation. Further technical and administrative details are recorded in subsidiary arrangements under the FA.

---

[203] http://archives.sipri.org/contents/expcon/indrest02.html [accessed 4 September 2013]. The initial LoI of 1998 was not legally binding, see Point 1.21.1 LoI 1998: "The Participants have determined that this LoI … does not represent as legally binding commitment between them under international law."

[204] Ibid.

[205] http://archives.sipri.org/contents/expcon/indrest03.html [accessed 26 July 2013].

[206] http://archives.sipri.org/contents/expcon/indrest04.html [accessed 26 July 2013].

[207] http://archives.sipri.org/contents/expcon/indrest05.html [accessed 26 July 2013].

[208] http://archives.sipri.org/contents/expcon/indrest06.html [accessed 26 July 2013].

[209] http://archives.sipri.org/contents/expcon/indrest07.html [accessed 26 July 2013].

[210] http://archives.sipri.org/contents/expcon/indrest08.html [accessed 26 July 2013].

[211] http://archives.sipri.org/contents/expcon/indrest09.html [accessed 26 July 2013].

4.2 Tasks

Six specialist subcommittees were established under the FA to facilitate the restructuring of the defence industrial base.[212]

Subcommittee 1 on security of supply focuses on, first, establishing procedures for consultation among the nations in case of the formation of Transnational Defence Companies (TDC) or significant changes of defence companies on which another LoI nation relies for its supplies. Moreover, it aims to facilitate the opening of defence equipment markets. This includes developing a system to facilitate the prioritisation, allocation, acceleration or expansion of production of defence articles to meet the requirements of the LoI nations. Nations should not unnecessarily hinder the supply of defence material to other LoI nations and should work together on providing supplies from national stocks. A LoI Code of Conduct could be used by all EDA-participating Member States or even formally transferred to the EDA. The parties have signed an Implementing Arrangement on Security of Supply and are currently developing a code of practice on defence industry restructuring which establishes procedures for industries to inform governments in advance of any industrial restructuring process located in their territories that implies the abandonment, transfer or relocation of part or whole of key strategic activities. Industry representatives from all six nations were invited to subscribe to this code on a voluntary basis. These arrangements are directed at areas regulated by EU Internal Market law, especially on merger control and intra-Community transfers, mentioned in chapter 4,[213] and on security of supply as addressed in the Defence Directive, discussed in chapter 8. On the one hand, they complement rather than compromise these Internal Market regimes as they are directed at reducing a national security concern that can allow Member States to derogate from these regimes on the basis of Article 346 TFEU. By reducing security-of-supply concerns, they reduce the necessity for the Member States participating in the LoI to derogate from the Treaty. On the other hand, since not all EU Member States participate in the framework, they could develop into discrimination against non-LoI Member States of the EU.[214] Overall, a transfer of this regime to the EDA or Internal Market should be considered to avoid this discrimination.

Subcommittee 2 on export procedures and transfers aims to, first, simplify transfers of defence articles and defence services between LoI nations, in the course of joint development and production programmes and with regards to transfers for each other's national military requirements. Secondly, it aims to

---

[212] The following description of the subcommittees is based on material of the LoI itself.
[213] At 147–60 and 172–6.
[214] Thanks to B. Heuninckx for pointing this out to me when commenting on an earlier draft of this chapter.

increase cooperation in exports, to ensure that the exports of equipment produced in cooperation will be responsibly managed in accordance with each participating State's international obligations and commitments in the export control area, especially the criteria of the Council Common Position 2008/994/CFSP defining common rules governing control of exports of military technology and equipment,[215] to develop lists of permitted export destinations for jointly produced military goods on a consensual, project-by-project basis. The parties have signed an Implementing Arrangement on Export Procedures. As directed by the FA, this subcommittee established the Global Project Licences (GPLs)[216] to facilitate the transfer of the components, subsystems and systems required for cooperative armament programmes. For the Member States outside the Agreement, the principles of Council Common Position 2008/994/ CFSP are the basis, along with their national legislation and other relevant international commitments. These arrangements are directed at areas regulated by EU Internal Market law, especially on intra-Community transfers and exports to third countries, discussed in chapter 4.[217] The LoI transfers regime was one model for the drafting of the Intra-Community Transfers Directive. Thus it could be said that this regime is already transferred to the EU Internal Market to an extent.

Subcommittee 3 on security of information is reviewing the effectiveness of provisions regarding personal and facility security clearances and access to classified information. It aims to reduce the time to grant those clearances and access and to facilitate transfer of classified information. The objective is to adapt procedures relating to security clearances, transmission of classified information and visits and to facilitate industrial cooperation without undermining the security of classified information and material.[218] These arrangements are directed at areas regulated by EU Internal Market law, specifically the Defence Directive, discussed in chapter 8. However, as also discussed in chapter 8,[219] there is no Internal Market regime on security clearances. Therefore it can be said that this LoI regime complements the Internal Market with respect to its participating Member States. However, there is a danger of discrimination for Member States not part of LoI and the introduction of an EDA or Internal Market regime avoiding such discrimination would be preferable.

The task of the Group of Research Directors is to foster coordination of joint research activities to increase the advanced knowledge base and thus encourage technological development and innovation; exchange information on defence-related R&T programmes, strategies and policies; develop a

[215] OJ [2008] L-335/99.
[216] www.gov.uk/global-project-licence [access on 29 July 2013].
[217] At 147–60 and 163–6.
[218] Security Annex of the Framework Agreement, http://archives.sipri.org/contents/expcon/indannex.html [accessed on 29 July 2013].
[219] At 392–7.

common understanding of what technologies are needed with the objective of establishing a coordinated approach to fulfil those needs; and analyse the information exchanged to make best use of resources. Research and technology coordination of joint research activities will be fostered to increase the advanced knowledge base and thus encourage technological development and innovation. The Group was also instrumental in establishing the security-of-information clauses enshrined within the EUROPA Research and Technology Memorandum of Understanding. As mentioned above and discussed in detail in chapter 6,[220] collaborative programmes based on R&D and R&D services are excluded from the scope of the Defence Directive. This means that these programmes can be addressed and even regulated outside the Directive. Moreover, based on the wording of the relevant Article 28 FA, it appears that the LoI only addresses research and technology rather than R&D.[221] However, while this mostly avoids a conflict with EU Internal Market law, there is an overlap with the most important activities of the EDA discussed above.[222] Nevertheless, the LoI is not intended as a third European defence procurement agency. The framework is no agency and lacks legal personality. The LoI Group of Research Directors is rather intended as a forum to facilitate information exchange and analysis regarding collaborative research and technology, not with collaborative programmes aiming at developing new equipment. Moreover, the LoI was initiated before the EDA came into existence. Hence it was not intended as an alternative to the latter but to the EU structures that existed before, or the lack thereof. Both the LoI and the OCCAR discussed above are initiatives of the EU Member States with the most comprehensive defence industries and defence investment identified in chapter 1.[223] They are therefore also the most likely to be involved in collaborative programmes. The continued existence of LoI and OCCAR more than seven years after the foundation of the EDA suggests that separate frameworks of the larger EU defence industrial Member State are still wanted. They provide the LoI Member States with a stick when progress is delayed in an EDA requiring the unanimity of 27 Member States.

The Subcommittee on Treatment of Technical Information aims at harmonising the contracting processes for the disclosure, transfer, use and ownership of technical information to facilitate the restructuring and subsequent operation of the European defence industry, harmonising Intellectual Property Rights for defence contracts.[224] This crucial issue is not addressed as a harmonising issue

---

[220] At 283–8 and 299–301.

[221] Thanks to B. Heuninkcx for pointing this out to me when commenting on an earlier version of this chapter.

[222] See the EDA *Research and Technology Strategy*, *supra* note 170. [223] At 24.

[224] Implementing arrangement concerning technical information, www.defensa.gob.es/ Galerias/politica/armamento-material/ficheros/DGM-Convenio-aplicacion-transferencia-info-tecnica-ingles.pdf [accessed 4 September 2013].

in the Defence Directive and could therefore even complement it with regards to the Member States participating in the LoI. However, there is also a danger of discrimination against non-LoI Member States and therefore an EDA or Internal Market regime would be preferable.

The Subcommittee on Harmonisation of Military Requirements aims to facilitate better equipment cooperation through the development of a methodology for identifying potential candidates for cooperative equipment programmes. This led to the establishment of a Harmonisation of Military Requirements (HMR) Board. There is a process to harmonise military requirements, including the definition of Common Staff Targets (CST). This area of activity does not overlap with EU Internal Market law as such. The development of a methodology for identifying potential candidates for cooperative equipment programmes is outside the scope of the Defence Directive due to the exclusion of collaborative programmes involving R&D. However, it appears to at least partially overlap with the capability oversight function of the EDA described above.

4.3 Yet another framework

The existence, policies and activities of yet another institutional and legal structure aiming to regulate or otherwise harmonise the laws and policies relevant for the defence industries of some but not all EU Member States implies the dangers of duplication and inconsistency. Some activities are similar and potentially overlap with those of the EU Internal Market, some with those of the EDA, and some with both. The initial LoI had addressed this problem: the work of other frameworks had to be taken into account.[225] Such a requirement is absent in the eventual FA. Most importantly, the difference in membership of the LoI on the one hand and the EU on the other hand are problematic. Even if policies and activities complemented each other, the LoI would only affect the LoI nations and not the EU as a whole. According to the LoI most tasks under the FA are completed or near completion, except in politically sensitive or legally complex areas, such as security of supply.[226] The LoI itself recognises the changes since the LoI and FA were signed, most importantly the Treaty of Lisbon CSDP, the creation of the EDA and the Defence Package. Moreover, the LoI organisation is slowly but progressively collaborating with the EDA on common projects. However, most of the issues the LoI is dealing with should be

---

[225] See Point 2.4 LoI 1998: "The Executive Committee and its Working Groups, will have due regard to any similar work being carried out in other fora in order to avoid different evaluations of the same problem and to establish, where possible, a consistent and common position."

[226] Presentation of Mr Werner Frank, Chairman of the Executive Committee, LoI, "Measures Adopted within the Letter of Intent framework to Strengthen EDTIB", Seminar, Madrid, 8 March 2010, slide 10, www.defensa.gob.es/dgamue2010/PresentacionesSeminario2/Werner_Frank_Speech.pdf [accessed 25 October 2013].

discussed in the context of the EU Internal Market and the EDA where all Member States can participate rather than in an exclusive club outside the EU. It is submitted that as a forum of cooperation and discussion the LoI does duplicate the existing EU structures.

Nevertheless, the LoI framework could also be a positive contribution to European defence procurement integration. It was started more than a decade before the Directives of the EU Defence Package entered into force and eight years before EDA was founded. Therefore it was not intended to challenge these EU initiatives but as an alternative to the EU and WEU structures in existence in 1998 and 2000. Whatever work has been done in the LoI context could be transferred to the EDA and EU Internal Market. It appears that this already happened especially in the context of the Intra-Community Transfers Directive discussed in chapter 4,[227] which was to a large extent based on the model of pre-existing LoI instruments. Similar transfers of the LoI *acquis* should be considered. For some of the LoI areas a transfer to the intergovernmental EDA, with the possibility to transfer it to the EU Internal Market later, might be more realistic than a straight transfer to the Internal Market.

5 Bilateral initiatives

Armaments cooperation in Europe also has a history of bilateral initiatives. Belgium, for example, participates, inter alia, in the Belgian-Dutch cooperation in a joint navy, the Belgian-Dutch joint support of the NH90 helicopter and the Belgian-Luxembourg cooperation in the procurement and support of transport aircraft.[228] The OCCAR discussed above was developed from the Franco-German armaments cooperation structure. The move from bilateral to multi-lateral and, if possible, inclusive structures such as the EDA, the LoI and the OCCAR is to be welcomed in the interest of coherence and to avoid the wasteful duplication of efforts. A possible exception could be the cooperation of France and the United Kingdom, who, as discussed in chapter 1, are the most militarily ambitious Member States, with nuclear weapons and permanent seats in the UN Security Council. Their 2010 Defence Treaty[229] was signed when all the other initiatives, including the Defence Directive, already existed, initiatives in all of which both countries participate. The Defence Treaty envisages defence industrial cooperation in various areas overlapping with Internal Market, EDA and LoI initiatives, including common purchases of particularly expensive equipment, most importantly an aircraft carrier. However, the 2010 Defence

---

[227] At 147–60.

[228] Thanks to B. Heuninckx for providing me with this list when commenting on an earlier draft of this chapter.

[229] English text: (2011) Cm. 8174, www.official-documents.gov.uk/document/cm81/8174/ 8174.pdf [accessed 12 September 2013].

Treaty does not challenge the existing frameworks. Paragraph 4 of the Preamble and Articles 8(4), 10(2) and 13 emphasise that the Defence Treaty is intended to be compliant with other treaties and Article 10(2), especially, emphasises that the EU law applicable to procurement procedures applies also in the context of the Defence Treaty. Moreover, the Defence Treaty arguably reinforces the principles of the TFEU and the Defence Directive, as Article 8(2) provides: "Each Party undertakes not to hinder legitimate access to its markets and to its Government contracts in the field of defence and security." However, this does not add anything to the obligations under the TFEU and Defence Directive between the two EU Member States. There is French uneasiness about the exclusive character of the Treaty and it is currently not clear whether it will ever create a meaningful framework.[230] While it is recognised that the two Member States have characteristics and ambitions that distinguish them from all other Member States, it is not quite clear why they had to add yet another framework to the European armaments architecture. Participation in the Internal Market, the EDA, the OCCAR, the LoI and the Defence Treaty could be interpreted either as an attempt to fragment efforts or as testimony to the importance of defence and defence industrial policy in France and Britain. The area where there is room for a separate framework is nuclear weapons which are arguably too sensitive for any other framework and which only the two parties to the 2010 Treaty possess.

6 Overcoming the fragmentation of defence procurement frameworks

More than one institutional and legal structure aiming at regulating or otherwise harmonising the laws and policies relevant for the defence industries of some, most or all EU Member States exist in Europe. This implies the dangers of duplication and inconsistency: the duplication of efforts wasting funds and political energy, mutual undermining and a lack of clarity on the applicable regime.[231] While this applies also to an extent to the initiatives aiming at the management of programmes, such as EDA and OCCAR and the NATO agencies discussed below, it is the plurality of initiatives aiming at harmonising the laws and policies of the EU Member States, such as the Defence Directive, the former EDA Procurement Code and LoI initiatives which are most relevant for the analysis in this chapter.

The fragmentation of the relevant frameworks has an external and an internal dimension. First, external to the EU, OCCAR is a European defence procurement agency for collaborative projects in addition to the EDA and the

---

[230] I have benefited from discussions with my LLM student Lucien Lagarde, who wrote a 2012 University of Birmingham LLM dissertation on the 2010 Anglo-French Defence Treaty.

[231] Georgopoulos, "European Armaments Policy", *supra* note 189, at 200.

LoI organisation is active in areas partly overlapping with both EDA and relevant Internal Market activities. It is submitted that the transfer of the OCCAR and LoI *acquis* to the EDA would overcome external fragmentation. The flexibility of the EDA framework can help to accommodate the concerns of the OCCAR and LoI Member States to make such a transfer possible. This flexibility could also accommodate any concerns of France and the United Kingdom which led to their 2010 Treaty, possibly excluding nuclear deterrents. Secondly, more importantly, there is an internal EU overlap of at least parts of the EDA activities with those of the Internal Market. It will be argued that this fragmentation can be overcome with a clear delimitation of competences, which arguably already exists, and respect of both the EDA and the Commission for this delimitation, which arguably also exists. Thus overcoming the current fragmentation of the European defence procurement landscape or architecture is feasible.[232]

6.1 Going the way of the WEAO: overcoming external fragmentation

The establishment of the EDA could contribute to overcoming the external fragmentation of European defence integration with regards to armaments. OCCAR and LoI could be dissolved and their external *acquis* incorporated into the EDA. The Agency was intended to replace the OCCAR, the WEAG/WEAO and the LoI. The latter are to be transferred to the earlier.[233] The external frameworks are addressed in the Preamble,[234]

---

[232] See also: Antonio Missiroli, *CFSP, Flexibility and Defence*, Chaillot Paper No. 38 (Paris: Institute for Security Studies of the Western European Union, 2000), at 37.

[233] With respect to OCCAR and WEAG/WEAO this clearly spelled out in the Conclusions of the General Affairs and External Relations Council in Brussels on 17 November 2003, Antonio Missiroli, *From Copenhagen to Brussels, supra* note 22, 256 at 263 with respect to OCCAR and at 264. At 266 it says: "The Agency should establish close working relations with existing arrangements/groupings/organisations, such as L.o.I., OCCAR, WEAG/WEAO, including the R&T mechanism of EUROPA [Memorandum of Understanding], with a view to incorporate them or assimilate their principles and practices in due course, as appropriate." The United Kingdom–Italy Summit on 21 February in Rome, Missiroli, ibid., at 42 concluded: "[We should create an] agency which would incorporate, at the appropriate time, existing bodies such as WEAG/WEAO, OCCAR, and LOI". The progressive enlargement of OCCAR suggested at the Franco-German Summit on the occasion of the 40th Anniversary of the Elysée Treaty on 22 January 2003 in Paris, Missiroli, ibid., at 23 and the Franco-British Summit on 4 February 2003 in Le Touquet, Missiroli, ibid., at 39, are aiming in the same direction.

[234] Recital 5 EDA Council Decision reads: "The Agency should develop close working relations with existing arrangements, groupings and organisations, such as those established under [LoI FA], as well as [OCCAR] and the European Space Agency (ESA)." Section 8 of the Preamble to the EDA Joint Action read: "The Agency should develop close working relations with existing arrangements, groupings and organisations such as [LoI], [OCCAR] and [WEAG/WEAO], with a view to assimilation or

Article $5(3)(c)(v)^{235}$ and Article 24(2) EDA Council Decision in a way which implies their eventual assimilation into the new EDA structure. Article 24(2) is particularly clear on this point:

> 2. The Agency shall develop close working relations with the relevant elements of OCCAR and with those established under the LoI Framework Agreement, *with a view to incorporating those elements or assimilating their principles and practices in due course*, as appropriate and by mutual agreement.[236]

As a first and important step in that direction of assimilation or incorporation, the activities of one of the previous European armaments organisations, the WEAG and WEAO were transferred to the EDA.

In 1996 the ministers of defence of the Western European Armaments Group (WEAG),[237] the armaments policy part of the then WEU, had established the Western European Armaments Organisation (WEAO) by signing the WEAO Charter[238] and the European Understanding of Research Organisation, Programmes and Activities (EUROPA). According to Article 1 of the WEAO Charter, the aim of the organisation was to assist in promoting and enhancing European armaments cooperation, strengthening the European defence technology base and creating a European defence equipment market, in accordance with the policies agreed by the WEAG. The executive body of the WEAO, the Research Cell was co-located with the WEU Secretariat and the Armaments Secretariat of the WEAG in Brussels and was considered a possible precursor for a later armaments agency, since Article 7 of the 1997 WEAO Charter provided for a broad range of possible activities. These were defence research and technology activities, procurement of defence equipment, studies, management of assets and facilities and other functions to carry out the aim of the organisation. The WEAO and WEAG are particularly interesting for the purposes of this chapter since it was the predecessor of the EDA in most of its current and recent main functions, which included a non-binding and

---

incorporation of relevant principles and practices as appropriate." This reflects the slightly different European defence procurement architecture at the time.

[235] Art. 5(3)(c)(v) EDA Council Decision reads: "preparing, at the request of Member States, programmes to be managed by OCCAR or through other arrangements, as appropriate. . .".

[236] Art. 25(2) EDA Joint Action read: "The Agency shall develop close working relations with the relevant elements of OCCAR, the [LoI FA], and WEAG/WEAO with a view to incorporate those elements or assimilate their principles and practices in due course, as appropriate and by mutual agreement." This reflects the slightly different European defence procurement architecture at the time.

[237] Austria, Belgium, the Czech Republic, Denmark, Finland, France, Germany, Greece, Hungary, Italy, Luxembourg, the Netherlands, Norway, Poland, Portugal, Spain, Sweden, Turkey and the United Kingdom were full members of the WEAG.

[238] WEAO Charter, printed in Burkard Schmitt, *European Armaments Cooperation: Core Documents*, Chaillot Paper No. 59 (Paris: Institute for Security Studies of the European Union, 2003), at 11–22.

intergovernmental defence procurement regime based on principles and publication of contracts in national defence contracts bulletins,[239] originating in the 1970s with the Independent European Programme Group. The WEAO was an integral part of the WEU and shared that body's fate. The latter featured prominently in the Maastricht and Amsterdam versions of the TEU but was deleted from the Nice and Lisbon versions. It can be said that all the WEU functions were transferred to the EU. The WEU was disbanded. The WEAO ceased to exist on 23 May 2005. Consequently, while the Preamble, Articles 5(3.4.2.) and 25(2) and (6) EDA Joint Action still address the relationship of EDA to the WEAG/WEAO, these references had disappeared from the later Recital 5 of the Preamble and Articles 5(3)(c)(v) and 24(2) of the EDA Council Decision.

However, it is important that the assimilation of OCCAR and LoI also happens in the not too distant future. Since the LoI is a forum of the defence-producing countries representing their common interests which contrast those of the defence-consumer countries, which it excludes, this might not be so easy. The case of OCCAR is a bit more complex since, apart from big defence industrial countries, Belgium is also a member and especially Turkey, the Netherlands, Luxembourg and Poland participate in OCCAR programmes.[240] It is unlikely that these countries can simply be forced to follow the interests of the larger EU defence industrial Member States. However, assuming that the creation of EDA will eventually lead to the assimilation of all other armaments initiatives, it is to be welcomed. The flexibility of the EDA framework could accommodate the different interests of the defence-producing Member EU States on the one hand and the other Member States on the other hand. Article 46(2) TEU (Lisbon) provides:

> The Agency shall be open to all Member States wishing to be part of it . . .
> That decision should take account of the level of effective participation in
> the Agency's activities. Specific groups shall be set up within the Agency
> bringing together Member States engaged in joint projects.

This provision suggests that the EDA is construed as a flexible framework. No Member State is obliged to participate. Two main levels of flexibility need to be differentiated.

First, there is flexibility regarding participation in the Agency. This is also expressed in the definition of "participating Member States" as EU Member States who participate in the Agency in Article 3 EDA Joint Action. When there are participating Member States there have to be non-participating Member

---

[239] On this regime see ch. 2 of Trybus, *European Defence Procurement Law, supra* note 43, at 31–44.

[240] I benefited from discussing this point with B. Heuninckx when he commented on an earlier draft of this chapter.

States. Thus neither the TEU nor the EDA Joint Action envisages all Member States to participate in the Agency. This is also confirmed by Article 1(3) and (4) EDA Joint Action which differentiates between Member States who wish to participate immediately on the one hand and those who wish to participate after its adoption or withdraw from it on the other hand. Thus the basic institutional platform of the EDA is designed as a flexible framework. Since – with the exception of Denmark[241] – all Member States are participating in the Agency under the EDA Council Decision, no differentiation is to be foreseen with regards to this level of flexibility in practice. Nevertheless, the possibility of withdrawing from the EDA makes it a flexible framework in theory and might have encouraged almost universal participation.

Secondly, there is flexibility regarding participation in the individual programmes and projects conducted within this basic institutional framework. This is also expressed in the definition of "contributing Member States" as EU Member States contributing to a particular project or programme in Article 3 EDA Joint Action. The groups of Member States cooperating in a particular project, for example a new fighter aircraft or tank, are always formed on a one-off and ad hoc basis. This follows the tradition of European collaborative projects, also conducted within OCCAR, which under the TEU and EDA Council Decision are to be conducted in the framework of the EDA. Theoretically, a Member State could decide never to participate in a procurement project. Nevertheless, depending on the project, Member States participating in individual projects will often have to make long-term commitments regarding such a project.[242] Given the one-off and ad hoc character of procurement projects, however, it could be said that this area is covered by informal flexibility as well as a form of more permanent cooperation. This finding is confirmed, inter alia, by the Preamble and Chapter IV of the EDA Council Decision.[243] This form of ad hoc flexibility regarding individual projects is necessary and only reflects normal practice in collaborative projects. Some Member States, such as Luxembourg, Malta or Estonia might want to participate in only a few projects whereas other Member States such as the United

---

[241] The last paragraph of the Preamble to the EDA Council Decision reads: "In accordance with Article 5 of Protocol (No 22) on the position of Denmark, annexed to the TEU and to the TFEU, Denmark does not participate in the elaboration and implementation of decisions and actions of the Union which have defence implications. Denmark will therefore not be bound by this Decision ..." Chapter IV is on "Ad Hoc Projects or Programmes and Associated Budgets".

[242] This depends on the individual project: some projects are only for a couple of years. Thanks to B. Heuninckx for pointing this out to me when commenting on an earlier draft of this chapter.

[243] Para. (18) of the Preamble to the EDA Council Decision reads: "The Agency, while being open to participation by all Member States, should also provide for the possibility of specific groups of Member States establishing ad hoc projects or programmes."

Kingdom or France might wish to participate in most common projects. The Agency needs to accommodate the different sizes of the Member States, of their armed forces, their defence budgets and their defence industrial capabilities discussed in chapter 1.[244] This second dimension of flexibility can be differentiated further. On the one hand there are collaborative projects where the participation of all Member States of the EDA is presumed and Member States not wishing to participate will inform the Chief Executive accordingly (Category A).[245] This means also that participating Member States do not have a choice with which other Member States they cooperate in a Category A project.[246] On the other hand there are collaborative projects where the participation of all Member States of the EDA is not presumed. Here the Member States wishing to collaborate inform the Steering Board and the other Member States can decide whether they wish to participate (Category B).[247] The participation of additional Member States is subject to the agreement of the initially participating Member States, which gives the latter a choice regarding the former.[248] The Steering Board may also decide within one month not to allow the project under the auspices of the Agency. This represents a balance between the large defence-producing countries and the smaller defence-consumer countries with respect to pre-arranged collaborative projects. While the former can bring such projects under the remit of the EDA, the latter may block this, for example if they feel they have been locked out. However, it needs to be pointed out that the second dimension of flexibility does not apply to the control of capability commitments: once a Member State has decided to sign up to the basic institutional platform of the Agency, they participate in this function. All Member States with the exception of Denmark have decided to do so.

This flexibility accommodated the transfer of the WEAO *acquis* to the EDA and may accommodate that of the OCCAR, since both were mainly frameworks for collaborative projects. Flexibility is less useful for the transfer of many parts of the *acquis* of the LoI, especially in relation to technical information or the harmonisation of military requirements.

6.2 Overcoming internal fragmentation

A crucial issue for the overall context of the Defence Directive is the EU internal fragmentation of armaments policy initiatives between the Internal Market of which the Defence Package is the most important part and the initiatives of the

---

[244] At 22–5.   [245] Art. 19 EDA Council Decision.
[246] Thanks to B. Heuninckx for pointing this out to me when commenting on an earlier draft of this chapter.
[247] Art. 20 EDA Council Decision.
[248] Thanks to B. Heuninckx for pointing this out to me when commenting on an earlier draft of this chapter.

EDA. Again, fragmentation implies the dangers of duplication, overlaps and contradictions leading to incoherence and waste of energy and finance. This could lead to both frameworks compromising each other. The continued coexistence of two defence procurement regimes, Defence Directive and EDA Procurement Code, would have been a prime example for this danger of duplication and mutual undermining. If Member States continued to use the EDA Procurement Code even years after the introduction and transposition of the Defence Directive, as they did until the suspension of the regime in 2013,[249] then this compromises the Defence Directive.[250] However, the problem was not the coexistence of both regimes but the extensive use and abuse of Article 346 TFEU leading to the contract being subjected to the EDA Code rather than the Defence Directive. The two frameworks could complement rather than compromise each other. For defence procurement this would require a clear delimitation of competences on the basis of the narrow interpretation of Article 346 TFEU discussed in chapter 3 and of the exclusions of the Defence Directive discussed in chapter 6. This would subject many contracts to the regime of the Defence Directive, certainly most of the contracts which until March 2013 were advertised on the EDA's EBB. Contracts to which Article 346 TFEU applies or which are subject to the exclusions in the Defence Directive, most importantly collaborative projects involving R&D, can fall under a regime of the EDA. However, as outlined above it is doubtful whether the extreme situations in which Article 346 TFEU can apply make these contracts an adequate subject of regulation at all. In particular, the EDA Procurement Code was not adequate for these contracts: advertising, competitive and time-consuming procedures and transparent qualification and award criteria are difficult to reconcile with extreme national security situations, hence the derogation of Article 346 TFEU. Thus there is not much room for an instrument to replace the now suspended EDA Procurement Code. A procurement regime for collaborative projects is equally difficult but not impossible, as, inter alia, the ESA Procurement Regulations and the relevant rules of OCCAR and even the EDA itself show.[251]

The division between Internal Market initiatives on the one hand and the EDA initiatives on the other hand is also a division between what used to be the First (supranational) and the Second (intergovernmental) Pillars until the Treaty of Nice and continues to be governed by different legal principles and decision-making procedures under the Treaty of Lisbon.[252] Therefore as long as

---

[249] As shown by the number of contracts still advertised on the EBB portal of the EDA until March 2013.

[250] Which would require most of the contracts advertised on the EBB to be published in the OJ/TED.

[251] See also Heuninckx, Thesis, *supra* note 169.

[252] See Erkki Aalto, "Towards a Common Defence? Legal Foundations after the Lisbon Treaty" in Martin Trybus and Luca Rubini (eds.), *The Treaty of Lisbon and the Future of European Law and Policy* (Cheltenham: Edward Elgar, 2012), at 305.

this division in EU law continues, the defence industries, which have both economic and national security dimensions, will be affected and regulated by both the EU Internal Market framework and the still largely separate CFSP and CSDP framework. Only a fundamental constitutional change – which cannot be envisaged in the short or medium term – could change that. In the meantime the institutions governing the two frameworks can complement rather than compromise each other by respecting the delimitation of their competences and by coordinating their initiatives. The representation of the Commission in the EDA Steering Board facilitates this coordination. The suspension of the EDA procurement regime in March 2013 indicates respect for the limits of its competences. Moreover, the existence of the intergovernmental and flexible EDA can help to overcome external fragmentation, as outlined above.

7 NATO agencies

Several NATO agencies – such as the NATO Eurofighter and Tornado Management Agency (NETMA) or the NATO Helicopter for the 1990s (NH90) Design and Development, Production and Logistics Management Agency (NAHEMA) – deal with defence procurement. The NATO Support Agency (NSPA) is discussed here as an example for these agencies and their role for the European armaments market.

The NSPA is the integrated logistics and services provider agency of NATO. It combines three former NATO agencies: the Maintenance and Supply Agency (NAMSA), the Central Europe Pipeline Management Agency (CEPMA) and the NATO Airlift Management Agency (NAMA) which were merged on 1 July 2012. The NSPA is a subsidiary body of NATO with the task to provide individual or collective support to NATO itself and its Member States.[253] As a NATO body, NSPA includes third countries[254] but excludes a number of EU Member States.[255] Neither the NSPA nor its predecessors aim to regulate the defence procurement of its member States as the Defence Directive does and the EDA Procurement Code did for EU Member States. However, procurement for the benefit of one or more of its member States, which include EU Member States,[256] is one of its tasks.[257] Subject to certain conditions, goods and services are procured through an international competitive bidding process on the basis of the NSPO Procurement Regulations which entered into force in

---

[253] On the former NAMSO in detail: Heuninckx, Thesis, *supra* note 169, at 197–234.

[254] Canada, Norway, Iceland, Turkey and the USA.

[255] Austria, Cyprus, Finland, Ireland, Malta and Sweden.

[256] Belgium, Bulgaria, Croatia, Czech Republic, Denmark, Estonia, France, Germany, Greece, Hungary, Italy, Latvia, Lithuania, Luxembourg, Netherlands, Poland, Portugal, Romania, Slovakia, Slovenia, Spain, United Kingdom.

[257] Arts. 4(c) and 5 NAMSO Charter.

2013.[258] Member States will normally task NSPA with procurement for them in groups, as "support partnerships" or "support conferences".[259] However, it is also possible that individual member States ask NSPA to do procurement for them.[260] There is therefore a danger that an EU Member State or a group of them tasks NSPA with the procurement of a good or service which would otherwise have been procured by themselves on the basis of the Defence Directive, possibly with the intention of avoiding the application of the latter. The extent to which this is legally possible will be discussed in chapter 6 in the context of the relevant exclusion in Article 12(a) Defence Directive.[261]

8 Conclusions

Organisational structures beyond the EU Internal Market address aspects of the European armaments market or actually conduct defence procurement. The procurement activities of some of these structures, most notably the NATO agencies which include third countries outside the EU, are subject to exclusions from the Defence Directive, as explained in chapter 6. Collaborative projects involving R&D are equally excluded. This allows for structures outside the EU, most notably the OCCAR, to conduct most of their procurement outside the Directive. The EDA, an agency forming part of the CFSP/CSDP of the EU, and the LoI, a framework outside the EU but exclusively consisting of EU Member States, are not acting as defence procurement agencies but as policy-makers in defence procurement and related policy fields. In contrast to the inclusive EDA, the LoI and the OCCAR consist of only limited numbers of EU Member States. This multitude and, arguably, congestion of multilateral structures and policies, partly overlapping and not always including all Member States, implies the dangers of incoherence, in particular that funds and effort are wasted on duplicate projects which partly contradict and even compromise each other. However, this problem could be addressed by a process of rationalisation and clear delimitation of competences. Structures other than the EDA, most notably the OCCAR, should be transferred to the inclusive and EU-integral EDA. Moreover, the *acquis* of the LoI should be transferred to the EDA or EU Internal Market frameworks. The delimitation of competences between the EDA and the Internal Market is the crucial issue to ensure the internal coherence of EU policies on the armaments market. It has to be based on the correct interpretation and application of the national security exemptions and most

---

[258] Regulations approved by the NSPO Agency Supervisory Board on 26 June 2013, AC/338-D(2013)0048-REV1 dated 30 May 2013, AC/338-D(2013)0048-REV1-ADD1 dated 16 June 2013 and AC/338-R(2013)0003, Item 7, www.nspa.nato.int/pdf/procurement/NR-4200_e.pdf [accessed on 6 September 2013].

[259] www.nspa.nato.int/en/organization/NSPA/customers.htm [accessed 6 September 2013].

[260] Ibid.   [261] At 273–4.

notably of Article 346 TFEU discussed in chapter 3 and the specific exemptions of secondary EU law, most notably those of the Defence Directive discussed in chapter 6. The recent suspension of the EDA Procurement and Supply Chain Codes suggests that this delimitation of competences is respected. The advent of the Defence Directive has already started to rock the convoluted European defence procurement architecture described in this chapter. It might – and, it is argued, should – lead to an architecture in which, apart from the NATO agencies, only the EU Internal Market and the EDA, the latter ideally as an integral part of the former, remain.

PART II

The contents of the Defence Directive

Inside or outside the Defence Directive

Limitation of scope

1 Introduction

The EU legislator used Public Sector Directive 2004/18/EC as the rock from which they chiselled the Defence and Security Procurement Directive 2009/81/EC (Defence Directive). In other words, the latter represents a Public Sector Directive adapted to the special needs of defence and security procurement. The purpose of the adaptations is to avoid Member States derogating from the procurement regime on the basis of Article 346 TFEU,[1] but also Articles 36, 51, 52 and 62 TFEU.[2] These Treaty provisions were explained in chapters 2 and 3. The Defence Directive is intended to accommodate most national security needs of the Member States to keep most of their procurement activities inside that Directive (and the TFEU). The most relevant adapted provisions are those on scope (this chapter), procurement procedures and the situations in which they can be used (chapter 7), on the qualification of bidders to ensure their reliability (chapter 8), on award criteria determining the eventual contractor (chapter 8), on contract performance conditions (chapter 8), on offsets and subcontracting (chapter 9) and on review and remedies for aggrieved bidders (chapter 10). As the new instrument takes the specific needs of defence and security into account, recourse to security exemptions should be necessary in fewer situations than under the previous regime. As a consequence, procurement in the relevant areas and especially for armaments should no longer be conducted completely outside the rules of the Internal Market. Thus a Directive "tailored" for defence and security was created.[3] At the same time other

---

[1] See Recitals 4, 5, 9 and 12 of the Defence Directive. Recital 4 reads: "One prerequisite for the creation of a European defence equipment market is the establishment of an appropriate legislative framework. In the field of procurement, this involves the coordination of procedures for the award of contracts to meet the security requirements of Member States and the obligations arising from the Treaty."

[2] N. Pourbaix, "The Future Scope of Application of Article 346 TFEU" (2011) 20 *Public Procurement Law Review* 1–8.

[3] As A. Georgopoulos put it, in "Legislative Comment: The new Defence Procurement Directive Enters into Force" (2010) 19 *Public Procurement Law Review* NA1–3, at NA2,

objectives of EU public procurement law discussed in chapter 2, such as non-discrimination on grounds of nationality, the equal treatment of bidders, competition, market access and transparency, are promoted. Whether this legislative balancing act was successful depends on whether the adaptations to the defence and security environment are suitable to "keep these contracts inside the Directive". A comprehensive assessment is only imaginable in a few years' time when a procurement practice inside or outside the new instrument can be detected, if the required empirical data will ever be available. However, a legal analysis is already possible now and will be conducted in Part II of this book.

A crucial issue to be considered at the beginning of any analysis of procurement law is its scope or field of application, its coverage. In the context of the EU procurement Directives this concerns the questions of which contracting entities (personal scope, see section 2 below) and which of their contracts (material scope, see section 3 below) are covered. The latter aspect looks at the contract type, its value and at a number of exceptions.[4] The former looks at the legal nature of the entity awarding the contract to a private sector economic operator. The extensive rules on procedures (discussed in chapter 7); on specifications and contract performance conditions, qualification, selection and award criteria (discussed in chapter 8); on offsets and subcontracts (discussed in chapter 9); and finally on review and remedies (discussed in chapter 1) only apply if the entity and contract are within the scope of the Defence Directive. Therefore it is necessary to commence Part II of this book with a discussion of the scope of the new instrument.

"The new instrument is ... tailor-made for the specific characteristics of the sector." C. Kennedy-Loest and N. Pourbaix, "The New Defence Procurement Directive" (2010) 11 *ERA Forum* 399, at 403 called the objective "to create a procurement regime that would be 'fit for purpose' for the award of defence and security contracts". The Commission itself called it a "perfectly suited instrument" for defence, see Defence procurement – Frequently Asked Questions, Brussels, 28 August 2009, Question 2: What are the main innovations of the Directive?, http://ec.europa.eu/internal_market/publicprocurement/docs/defence/faqs_28-08-09_en.pdf [accessed 23 September 2013].

[4] On scope and coverage of the "civilian" Public Sector Directive 2004/18/EC see Peter A. Trepte, *Public Procurement in the EU: A Practitioner's Guide*, 2nd edn (Oxford University Press, 2007), at 89–127 (scope), 257–70 (thresholds), 239–56 (exceptions); Christopher Bovis, *EC Public Procurement: Case Law and Regulation* (Oxford University Press, 2006), at 203–6 and 334–96, 208–12 (thresholds), 206–8 (exceptions); R. Noguellou, "Scope and Coverage of the EU Procurement Directives" in Martin Trybus, Roberto Caranta and Gunilla Edelstam (eds.), *EU Law of Public Contracts* (Brussels: Bruylant, 2014), ch. 1, at 15–36. Scope of coverage is also frequently an issue on ECJ judgments, see inter alia: Case C-44/96, *Mannesmann* [1998] ECR I-73; Case 45/87, *Dundalk* [1987] ECR 4929; Case C-470/89, *Universale-Bau* [2002] ECR I-11617; Case C-373/00, *Truley* [2003] ECR I-1931; Case C-380/98, *Cambridge University* [2000] ECR I-8035; Case C-323/96, *Vlaamse Raad* [1998] ECR I-5063; Case C-306/96, *Connemara* [1998] ECR I-8716; Case C-360/96, *Arnhem* [1998] ECR I-6821; Case C-260/99, *Agora* [2001] ECR I-3605; Case C-107/98, *Teckal* [1999] ECR I-8121.

The rules on the scope of the Defence Directive are contained in its Chapter II ("Scope"), in Articles 7–19. Moreover, there are special rules for services contracts in Chapter II (Articles 20–2) and parts of the definitions in Article 1 Defence Directive which are relevant for the determination of the scope of the instrument. A Commission Guidance Note, *Field of Application*,[5] which, as mentioned in the introduction to this book,[6] is one of six Guidance Notes on various aspects of the Defence Directive intended to support the implementation of the Directive, deals specifically with scope. Moreover, a further Guidance Note, *Defence-Specific Exclusions*,[7] deals with one particular aspect of scope. However, it should be re-emphasised here that in contrast to the rules of the Directive, these Guidance Notes are not legally binding. Nevertheless, since they express the interpretation of the initiator of the Directive and were written by the same expert officials who drafted the Defence Directive, they should be taken into account as important guidance when interpreting the instrument. They are likely to be taken into account by the ECJ when interpreting the relevant provisions on scope and more importantly by the relevant contracting entities in practice. However, as the Defence Directive and its specific exclusions are still relatively new at time of writing in November 2013, there is no case law on their interpretation yet. This makes the Commission's Guidance Notes and the available case law on the Treaty derogations discussed in chapters 2 and 3 so particularly valuable for their interpretation today.

If an entity or contract falls outside the personal and material scope of a procurement instrument, the scope of other legal frameworks needs to be considered. For the purposes of the Defence Directive these other frameworks could be the Public Sector Directive 2004/18/EC (see section 4.5 below) and its successor Directive 2014/24/EU, the Utilities Directive 2004/17/EC (see section 4.6 below) and its successor Directive 2014/25/EU,[8] or the rules of the TFEU directly (see section 4.4 below), for contracts which are still inside the Internal Market discussed in chapter 2. This would include national rules of the Member States which might still have to comply with the TFEU. It could also be the rules of the European Defence Agency (EDA)[9] or the Organisation for Joint Armaments Procurement (OCCAR) discussed in chapter 5 and below in sections 4.3.1 and 4.3.2.3. Furthermore, it could be the rules of other international organisations such as NATO or the World Bank Group as will be discussed in section 4.3.1 below.

---

[5] http://ec.europa.eu/internal_market/publicprocurement/docs/defence/guide-scope_en.pdf [accessed 23 September 2013].

[6] At 6.

[7] http://ec.europa.eu/internal_market/publicprocurement/docs/defence/guide-exclusions_en.pdf [accessed 23 September 2013].

[8] Guidance Note *Field of Application, supra* note 5, at 1.

[9] Formerly also the EDA Code of Conduct for Defence Procurement intended for the Member States or a future code replacing it. Now only the rules intended for the procurement activities of the Agency itself, see ch. 5, at 191–8.

Finally, it is possible that the procurement of a contract is excluded from any legal framework, excluded from primary and secondary EU Internal Market law and any international and national rules, and can be awarded merely on the basis of economic, political, military or other considerations.

This chapter will look first at the personal scope (section 2 below) and then at the material scope (sections 3 and 4 below) of the Defence Directive. In the context of the latter it will first discuss the contracts covered by the Directive (section 3 below). Then it will discuss thresholds (section 4.2 below), the exceptions of the Directive (section 4.3 below), the exceptions of the TFEU (section 4.4 below) and the scope of the Defence Directive in relation to the scope of the Public Sector and Utilities Directives (sections 4.5 and 4.6 below). It will be shown that not only a considerable but the larger part of the contracts of the relevant contracting entities is *not* covered by the new Directive. In other words, not all the contracts of the ministries of defence of the Member States will have to be conducted on the basis of the national laws transposing the Defence Directive. On the other hand the contracts of many other contracting entities, including utilities will be included in the scope of the new instrument. The Defence Directive is not a "ministry of defence" instrument. The discussion of the material scope in section 3 below will show one of the techniques the EU legislator has used to adapt the rules of the Public Sector Directive in the Defence Directive:[10] limitation.

2 The personal scope of the Defence Directive: covered contracting entities

The personal scope of a Directive addresses the question of *who* is covered, in this case by the Defence Directive. To which contracting authorities and entities does the instrument apply? Procurement laws, including the EU Directives, normally contain abstract definitions (section 2.1 below) of the covered entities as well as lists of entities to which they apply (section 2.2 below).[11]

2.1 The abstract definition of contracting authorities

The abstract definition for the covered contracting entities for the Defence Directive is contained in its Article 1(17),[12] which defines contracting entities as

contracting authorities as referred to in Article 1(9) [Public Sector Directive].

---

[10] The others being flexibility (ch. 7), descriptiveness (ch. 8) and substitution (ch. 9).

[11] See, for example, Art. 1(9) Public Sector Directive and Art. 2 Utilities Directive discussed below.

[12] Art. 1(2) Defence Directive defines the notion of contract with reference to Art. 1(2)(a) of Public Sector Directive 2004/18/EC, which defines a contract as "between one or more economic operators and one or more contracting authorities and having as their object the execution of works, the supply of products or the provision of services within the meaning of this Directive". Directive 2004/18/EC has been replaced by Directive 2014/24/EU. The following discussion refers to the 2004 Directive to which the Defence Directive refers.

Thus the definition of a contracting entity in the context of the Defence Directive depends on that in the Public Sector Directive, which in its Article 1(9) defines a contracting authority as

> the State, regional or local authorities, bodies governed by public law, associations formed by one or several of such authorities or one or several of such bodies governed by public law.

Therefore the personal scope of the Defence Directive covers all contracting entities covered by the Public Sector Directive. There is a common concept of personal scope, though not an equal concept of scope, since, as will be explained further below, the personal scope of the Utilities Directive is also covered by the Defence Directive.

2.1.1 The State, regional or local authorities

The personal scope of the Defence Directive covers "the State, regional or local authorities" according to Article 1(9) Public Sector Directive in conjunction with Article 1(17) Defence Directive. A list of central government authorities is provided in Annex IV Public Sector Directive, which will be further discussed in section 2.2 below. It should be pointed out that in the context of the Directives the lists are not as helpful as they seem since they do not eliminate all uncertainty for listed entities. They are merely illustrative, non-dispositive and non-exhaustive.[13]

2.1.1.1 Ministries of defence and the armed forces   The abstract notion of "the State" in Article 1(9) Public Sector Directive already includes the ministries of defence and the armed forces of the Member States. However, in addition the list of authorities in the relevant Annex IV to the Public Sector Directive contains expressly or impliedly all the ministries of defence and related defence procurement agencies of the Member States.[14] As an instrument that entered into force shortly before ten new Member States joined the EU on 1 May 2004

---

[13] B. Heuninckx, "Lurking at the Boundaries: Applicability of EU Law to Defence and Security Procurement" (2010) 19 *Public Procurement Law Review* 91–118, at 95 explains: "[The list in Annex III of Directive 2004/18/EC] is not dispositive, and so merely illustrative in the sense that entities listed are not in fact covered if they do not properly fall within the definition and that entities not listed but falling within the definition are covered, and determining if a body meets the definition of body governed by public law must be done case by case." See also Case C-283/00, *Commission* v. *Spain* [2003] ECR I-11697, at para. 77; Case C-373/00, *Truley* [2003] ECR I-1931, at para. 44 as cited by Heuninckx, ibid., in footnote 25.

[14] It is interesting that in Annex IV, of the 15 Member States in 2004, Germany, Italy, Portugal and Finland exclude military goods from the procurement activities of their respective ministries or forces, whereas the references for the entities of the other Member States do not contain such a reservation.

and before the 2007 and 2013 accessions, the original text of the Public Sector Directive covers 15 Member States.

For Belgium Annex IV lists "the State",[15] for Denmark the "Ministry of Defence", for Germany the "Federal Ministry of Defence (no military goods)", for Greece "Army General Staff, Navy General Staff, Air Force General Staff (non-warlike materials covered by Annex V)", for Spain the "Ministry of Defence", for France the "Ministry of Defence (non-warlike materials)", for Ireland the "Department of Defence", for Italy the "Ministry of Defence (non-warlike materials)", for Luxembourg the "Ministry of Foreign Affairs, Foreign Trade, Cooperation and Defence: Army", for the Netherlands the "Ministry of Defence", for Austria the "Federal Ministry of Defence", for Portugal the "Ministry of Defence (non-warlike material covered by Annex V)", for Finland the "Ministry of Defence – Finnish Defence Forces (non-warlike materials)", for Sweden the "Defence Materiél Administration and the Swedish Defence Forces" and for the United Kingdom the "Ministry of Defence and the Defence Procurement Agency". These entities are expressly mentioned here to emphasise that while the Defence Directive itself does not list and therefore directly "address" them (as in "you are covered"), the ministries of defence are clearly addressed by the legislation, they are "called by name". They are clearly covered by the Directive. As indicated below, this could be clearer, but it is sufficiently clear and thus it is submitted that a clarifying judgment of the ECJ on this matter of the inclusion of the ministries of defence and the armed forces is not needed.

The consolidated version of the Public Sector Directive for 1 January 2012 and Annex I to Directive 2014/24/EU[16] includes some clarifications[17] and the relevant ministries of the Member States which joined the EU in 2004 and 2007. This refers namely to Bulgaria,[18] the Czech

---

[15] The amended version of Public Sector Directive 2004/18/EC from 1 January 2012 now expressly lists for Belgium the "Ministère de la Défense/Ministerie van Landesvertediging" (Ministry of Defence), http://eur-lex.europa.eu/LexUriServ/LexUriServ.do?uri=CONSLEG: 2004L0018:20120101:EN:PDF [accessed 23 September 2013]. See Annex I to Directive 2014/24/EU.

[16] Ibid.

[17] *Supra* note 15. For Belgium it expressly lists the "Ministère de la Défense/Ministerie van Landesvertediging", for Denmark it now lists 5 relevant institutions. For Luxembourg a ministry responsible for defence is no longer listed because this no longer appears in the name of the relevant Ministry of Foreign Affairs and Immigration: www.mae.lu/en/Site-MAE/Defense [accessed 23 September 2013]. For Italy the addition "(non-warlike materials)" was removed after the entry for the Ministry of Defence. For the United Kingdom the entry "Defence Procurement Agency" was replaced by "Defence Equipment and Support" to reflect the restructuring of the relevant parts of the Ministry of Defence. See also Annex I to Directive 2014/24/EU.

[18] The Ministry of Defence of the Republic of Bulgaria is mentioned, *supra* note 15, at 119: Министерство на отбраната. Thanks to Stoyan Panov, PhD student and Postgraduate Teaching Assistant at the University of Birmingham for his help on this footnote.

Republic,[19] Estonia,[20] Cyprus,[21] Latvia,[22] Lithuania,[23] Hungary,[24] Poland,[25] Romania,[26] Slovenia[27] and Slovakia.[28] No ministry of defence is listed for Malta since defence comes under the responsibilities of the Ministry for Home Affairs and National Security.[29] Finally, Council Directive 2013/16/EU of 13 May 2013 Adapting Certain Directives in the Field of Public Procurement, by Reason of the Accession of the Republic of Croatia[30] adapts Annex IV to the latest EU accession.[31] As the occasional changes of ministerial responsibilities and titles (Luxembourg) as well the rebranding and reorganisation of agencies (United Kingdom) show, personal scope based on a listing by name in the text of the Directive is not advisable. If the allocation of responsibilities within an individual Member State government or the name of a procurement agency can change, then an abstract definition together with only illustrative lists in annexes is the better legislative technique as it allows for flexibility without substantially changing the personal scope when a rebranding or reorganisation of contracting entities occurs.

2.1.1.2 Contracting authorities other than ministries of defence and the armed forces   The abstract definition of "the State, regional or local authorities" in Article 1(9) Public Sector Directive and the list in Annex IV also

---

[19] Ministerstvo obrany (Ministry of Defence), *supra* note 15. Thanks to Stoyan Panov, for his help on this footnote.

[20] Kaitseministeerium (Ministry of Defence), *supra* note 15.

[21] Υπουργείο Άμυνας (Ministry of Defence). Thanks to Aris Georgopoulos (University of Nottingham) for this translation.

[22] Aizsardzības ministrija un tās padotībā esošās iestādes (Ministry of Defence), *supra* note 15.

[23] Institutions under the *Krašto apsaugos ministerijos* [Ministry of National Defence], *supra* note 15.

[24] Honvédelmi Minisztérium (Ministry of Defence), *supra* note 15.

[25] Ministerstwo Obrony Narodowej (Ministry of National Defence), *supra* note 15. Thanks to Stoyan Panov, for his help on this footnote.

[26] *Ministerul Apărării* (Ministry of Defence). Other central agencies though can be considered as military procurement agencies.

[27] *Ministrstvo za obrambo* (Defence Ministry) and *General štab Slovenske vojske* (General staff of the Slovenian army). Thanks to the (Birmingham) Institute of European Law research assistant Ms Nina Boč for the translation.

[28] Ministerstvo obrany Slovenskej republiky (Ministry of Defence of the Republic of Slovakia), *supra* note 15. Thanks to Stoyan Panov, for his help on this footnote.

[29] See the Maltese government website: http://gov.mt/en/Government/Government%20of% 20Malta/Ministries%20and%20Entities/Pages/Home-Affairs-and-National-Security.aspx [accessed 23 September 2013].

[30] [2013] OJ L158/184.

[31] No ministry of defence is listed but it can be assumed that the listed "Government of the Republic of Croatia", "Offices of the Government of the Republic of Croatia" or "Ministries" (*supra* note 15), cover the ministry of defence. In Annex I to Directive 2014/24/EU the "Ministarstvo obrane" is expressly listed.

includes many other authorities which cannot be classified as defence procurement agencies.[32] This ranges from entities with a security-relevant function
such as the police authorities on the national, regional and local levels; coast-
guards; border security agencies; or prison services.[33] Moreover, this includes
authorities which do not have a security function per se, such as ministries of
culture or universities. Furthermore, it needs to be re-emphasised that the lists
in both Annex III and Annex IV of Directive 2004/18/EC or Annex I of the new
Directive 2014/24/EU are merely illustrative anyway. The abstract definition
brings them all within the personal scope of the Defence Directive, even if they
were "forgotten" in the Annexes or did not even exist when the Annexes were
compiled. The personal scope of the Defence Directive includes that of the
Public Sector Directive and, as will be explained below, the Utilities Directive.
Hence it is additionally the material scope discussed below which ultimately
determines whether a contract is covered by the new Directive. Thus, again, the
Defence Directive is clearly not a ministry of defence Directive. It is not even
just a public sector Directive. Covered are all contracting entities already
covered by the Public Sector and Utilities Directives. This also means that the
extensive body of case law of the ECJ on the scope of the other two Directives[34]
is fully relevant to the personal scope of the Defence Directive.

2.1.2 Bodies governed by public law

Article 1(9) Public Sector Directive 2004/18/EC (Article 2(1) Directive 2014/24/
EU) also includes "bodies governed by public law" in the personal scope of the
Defence Directive. This concept of "bodies governed by public law" is further
defined in the second sentence of Article 1(9) and also clarified by a non-exhaustive
list in Annex III to the 2004 Public Sector Directive, which, again, through Article 1
(17) Defence Directive also applies to the latter. The Commission Guidance Note
Field of Application summarises the definition of a body governed by public law as

> a body established for the specific purpose of meeting needs in the general
> interest not having an industrial or commercial character that has legal
> personality and is closely dependent on the State, regional or local author-
> ities or other bodies governed by public law.[35]

This is supported by a reference to Article 1(9) and by a number of illustrative
examples: "science, research and development establishments, or police

---

[32] The Defence Directive applies to all relevant authorities at the national, regional and
municipal levels beyond ministries of defence when procuring relevant goods and
services. This could be relevant for police authorities, border control agencies or prison
services.

[33] The Commission Guidance Note *Field of Application, supra* note 5, at 3 lists "science,
research and development agencies, emergency services, or police forces".

[34] See the judgments *supra* note 4.

[35] Guidance Note *Field of Application, supra* note 5, at 3.

forces".[36] All such bodies, including universities or development agencies, can thus be relevant for the Defence Directive if they are awarding a relevant contract.

2.1.3 Utilities

Through the reference to Article 2 Utilities Directive 2004/17/EC (Article 4 Utilities Directive 2014/25 EU) in Article 1(17) Defence Directive, public and private utilities are also included in the personal scope of the new Directive.[37] Article 2 defines utilities for the purposes of the scope of the Directive. This includes public undertakings pursuing activities in the sectors referred to in Articles 3–7 Utilities Directive 2004/17/EC (Article 7–14 Utilities Directive 2014/25 EU). According to the Guidance Note *Field of Application* this includes, inter alia, "the supply of gas, heat, electricity and water, transport services and postal services, as well as the provision of ports and airports".[38] In Article 2(1)(d) of the 2004 Utilities Directive, public undertakings are defined as

> undertakings over which contracting authorities exercise directly or indirectly a dominant influence by virtue of ownership, financial participation or of the rules governing such undertakings.[39]

Moreover, this includes private undertakings "that perform sectoral activities" of the kind listed above "and operate on the basis of special or exclusive rights granted by a Member State".[40] Thus, for example, public and private ports and airports with their extensive security procedures are included in the personal scope of the Defence Directive.[41] The Defence Directive can also be a utilities Directive. However, as explained in the context of the Public Sector Directive, the question of whether the Utilities or Public Sector Directives are to be applied will ultimately depend on the material scope of the Directive, in other words on the contract. This will be discussed in detail in section 3 below.

The legal link between the Utilities Directive and the Defence Directive established by Article 1(17) Defence Directive might have unintended consequences.[42] The inclusion of utilities in the personal scope of the Defence Directive was not envisaged in the first drafts but inserted rather late during

---

[36] Ibid.

[37] This could be relevant to any utility when procuring relevant goods and services, even in the water or energy sectors, but is most likely to be relevant for example for airport security.

[38] Guidance Note *Field of Application, supra* note 5, at 3.   [39] See also ibid.

[40] Ibid., at 3.

[41] Ibid. Also listed as examples are "operators of networks for the distribution of gas, heat, electricity or water and public transportation networks".

[42] As reported by the Commission's N. Spiegel, "Directive 2009/81/EC: Defence Specificities" at the seminar "The European Defence and Security Procurement Directive and the Challenges for its Implementation", European Institute of Public Administration (EIPA), Maastricht, 21 June 2010 (notes of the author, on file).

the second half of 2008.[43] According to one of the drafters of the Defence Directive, this rush led to doubtful results and in retrospect he is not sure whether it was a good idea to include these authorities.[44] First, as this was never covered by any kind of impact assessment the likely impact cannot be estimated.[45] Legislating without impact assessment and additionally without consultation is not good legislative practice and certainly not a habit of the Commission. Secondly, those introducing the extension of the personal scope to the Defence Directive to utilities appear not to have been aware of the fact that although the Defence Directive is flexible, a "Public Sector Directive light", the Utilities Directive is also a more flexible and "lighter version" of the Public Sector Directive.[46] Many utilities rather than finding some of their relevant contracts covered by a more flexible regime might find themselves in the stricter regime of the Defence Directive. For example, Article 30 Utilities Directive 2004/17/EC provides for a procedure whereby "a given activity is directly exposed to competition" and therefore can be taken out of the material scope (see below) of the Utilities Directive.[47] However, such an activity, although taken out of the Utilities Directive through its Article 30, would not at the same time be taken out of the Defence Directive. While the Utilities Directive intends exclusion from its flexible regime, the stricter regime of the Defence Directive might still apply. The French Presidency proposals had envisaged that the Article 30 exemption would "break through" to the Defence Directive, would exempt the activity from the Defence Directive at the same time as the Utilities Directive. However, this was deleted in later versions and in August 2008 the sections on security of supply and information discussed in chapter 8 were more important. The Commission explained this by the special structure of the defence and security markets which did not justify exemption for these contracting entities.[48] Thus the regime of the Defence Directive is less flexible than that of the Utilities Directive and the benefit of this reduction in flexibility is not convincing and the result of the questionable inclusion of the utilities in the personal scope of the Defence Directive, which should be reconsidered. The United Kingdom had opposed the inclusion of utilities in the personal scope of

---

[43] Spiegel, ibid. Consequently the Commission Staff Working Document – Impact Assessment SEC (2007) 1593, http://ec.europa.eu/governance/impact/ia_carried_out/docs/ia_2007/sec_2007_1593_en.pdf [accessed 1 November 2013] does not address the inclusion of utilities in the scope of the Directive.

[44] Spiegel (June 2010), *supra* note 42 (notes of the author and slide 7, on file).

[45] Spiegel, ibid. and the Commission Staff Working Document, *supra* note 43, which does not consider the inclusion of utilities. Neither did COM (2004) 608 final or COM (2005) 626 final.

[46] Spiegel (June 2010), *supra* note 42 (notes of the author and slide 7, on file).

[47] The most obvious example according to Spiegel, ibid.

[48] Michael Fruhmann and Hanno Liebmann, *Bundesvergabegesetz Verteidigung und Sicherheit 2012* (Vienna: Manz, 2012), at 51.

the Directives.[49] One of the drafters of the Defence Directive wonders whether the impact will be very significant but nevertheless assumes that this might become an issue to be looked at during the review of the Defence Directive.[50] Utilities should be subjected to the regime specifically adapted to their context and not to an adapted Public Sector Directive. The necessary defence and security adaptations can be inserted into the relevant provisions of the Utilities Directive. Overall it is submitted that utilities should be removed from the field of application of the Defence Directive and subjected to an adapted regime of the Utilities Directive instead.

2.1.4 Central purchasing bodies

As summarised by the relevant Recital 23 of the Defence Directive, "centralised purchasing techniques help to increase competition and streamline purchasing". This positive position towards centralised purchasing leads to a similar position on central purchasing bodies in Recital 23:

> Consequently, Member States should be allowed to provide that contracting authorities/entities may purchase goods, works and/or services through a central purchasing body. Provision should therefore be made for a Community definition of central purchasing bodies and of the conditions under which, in accordance with the principles of non-discrimination and equal treatment, contracting authorities/entities purchasing works, supplies and/or services through a central purchasing body may be deemed to have complied with this Directive. A contracting authority/entity which is bound to apply this Directive should in any event be eligible to act as a central purchasing body.

Continuing this line of thought, Article 1(18) Defence Directive then provides this definition of central purchasing bodies and includes them in the personal scope of the Directive. It provides:

> "Central purchasing body" means a contracting authority/entity as referred to in Article 1(9) of Directive 2004/18/EC and Article 2(1)(a) of Directive 2004/17/EC, *or a European public body*, which:
> – acquires supplies and/or services intended for contracting authorities/ entities, or,
> – awards contracts or concludes framework agreements for works, supplies or services intended for contracting authorities/entities
>
> [emphasis added]

---

[49] Spiegel (June 2010), *supra* note 42 (notes of the author and slide 7, on file).

[50] Ibid. (notes of the author and slide 7, on file). According to Art. 73(3) Defence Directive the Commission has to report on whether the objectives of the Directive have been met by 21 August 2016.

Thus, building on the concept of the contracting authorities and entities discussed above, central purchasing bodies which are themselves meeting the definitions as contracting authorities and entities and conduct procurement procedures for and on behalf of other contracting authorities and entities are also covered by the Defence Directive. This is in line with the similar arrangements in Article 1(10) Public Sector Directive 2004/18/EC (Article 2(16) Directive 2014/24/EU) and Article 1(8) Utilities Directive 2004/17/EC (Article 2(10) Directive 2014/25/EU) which also include central purchasing bodies.

2.1.4.1 Is the EDA a central purchasing body?   The noticeable difference to the other directives in the Defence Directive is the inclusion of "a European public body" which, first, includes any relevant body to be founded in the future. Moreover, it includes the already existing European Defence Agency (EDA) discussed in chapter 5. This inclusion of the EDA is confirmed by the last sentence of Recital 23 of the Defence Directive which provides:

> At the same time, Member States should also be free to designate European public bodies not subject to this Directive, such as the [EDA], as central purchasing bodies, provided that such bodies apply procurement rules compliant with all the provisions of this Directive to those purchases.

According to one of the drafters of the Defence Directive this notion of a "European public body" is

> more or less tailor-made for the EDA, because it is not an agency but an intergovernmental body which has to follow the Directives when purchasing; [now EDA is also covered] when they would act as a central purchasing body.[51]

While the differences between the notions of an "agency" and an "intergovernmental body" and the significance of these differences are not quite clear, it is clear that the rules were made for the EDA. It should be emphasised again that Article 1(18) Defence Directive includes the EDA as a (central) purchasing agency itself, not in its capacity as the creator of the former soft law Code of Conduct on Defence Procurement discussed in chapter 5. The rules that are currently in place are Council Decision 2007/643/CFSP of 18 September 2007 on the financial rules of the [EDA] and on the procurement rules and rules on financial contributions from the operational budget of the [EDA].[52] As the 2007 date – well before the completion of the legislative process of the Defence Directive – already indicates, this does not represent the transposition of the Defence Directive. There is currently no information on this transposition. As discussed in chapter 5, the current Council Decision provides rules on contracts

---

[51] Spiegel (June 2010), *supra* note 42 (notes of the author, on file).
[52] [2007] OJ L269/1, Annex at 16–36.

covered by the Public Sector Directive requiring them to be published in the OJ and on contracts not covered by the Public Sector Directive. The rules on contracts covered by the Public Sector Directive are in compliance with the latter and the rules on contracts outside the Public Sector Directive are largely in compliance with the principles of the TFEU. It should also be emphasised that, as clarified by the passage of Recital 23 of the Defence Directive, "Member States *should also be free* to designate European public bodies *not subject to this Directive* [emphasis added]": first, that the Member States are not under an obligation to designate the EDA as a central purchasing body; secondly, this passage of Recital 23 clarifies that the EDA is not covered by the Defence Directive unless the Member States designate the central purchasing function to it. This complies with Article 75 Defence Directive, which clarifies that, as with all Directives, the instrument is addressed to the Member States. Thus it could be argued that the Defence Directive is not addressed to any EU body such as the EDA. However, first, this interpretation would contradict the clear wording of the Defence Directive which clearly includes "a European body" acting as a central purchasing agency. Hence one might only be able to argue against the EDA being included in the personal coverage of the Defence Directive if this wording was not there.

Secondly, with central purchasing through the EDA the Member States substitute their own procurement activities in more or less the same way as contracting authorities substitute their own purchasing activities with that of a central purchasing agency. Thus the same logic applies and leads to inclusion in the personal coverage of the Directive, unless it is expressly excluded, which is not the case; on the contrary, provided the EDA has been designated as a central purchasing body.

Thirdly, the application if not of the precise wording but of the principles of the EU procurement Directives to EU institutions, notably the Commission and its agencies and the European Parliament, has been clarified by the ECJ.[53] Thus it is not an anomaly. Subjecting an EU body, even a body acting within the CFSP and CSDP, to even the full scope of a Directive, is only one step further.

At time of writing it is not clear whether the EDA has ever been designated as a central purchasing body in the way envisaged in Recital 23 Defence Directive. It is probably too early. Moreover, as pointed out in chapter 5, the EDA is currently not a central procurement agency for the EU. This might change in the future, especially when the functions of OCCAR, discussed under the next heading below, would be transferred to the EDA, which is currently not even structured for that purpose. The significance of the possibility of designating the EDA as a central purchasing body is also not just a question of the personal scope of the Defence Directive. This will also depend on the material scope

---

[53] See on these rules Hans-Joachim Priess, "Contract Passed by EU Institutions" in Trybus, Caranta, Edelstam (eds.), *EU Law of Public Contracts, supra* note 4, 417–42.

discussed below. Many contracts might be below the thresholds or subject to one of the many exemptions discussed in section 4 of this chapter.

2.1.4.2 Are OCCAR and LoI central purchasing bodies? The LoI organ-isation discussed in chapter 5 is currently not aiming to be or to develop into a purchasing agency.[54] The OCCAR also discussed in chapter 5 is a different matter. The OCCAR is not expressly mentioned in Recital 23 Defence Directive. Only EU Member States are members of OCCAR.[55] Since it is therefore a European intergovernmental body it could, prima facie, be considered a "European public body" in the sense of Recital 23 and Article 1(18) Defence Directive. Moreover, the passage "*such as* the European Defence Agency [emphasis added]" in Recital 23 suggests that the notion of a "European public body" is not necessarily limited to the EDA. Furthermore, the benefits of central purchasing outlined above can be achieved by any defence procurement organ-isation, especially by European organisations that can also already contribute some experience to such a function. Finally, as already mentioned above, the Member States substitute their own procurement activities with that of OCCAR in very much the same way as contracting authorities covered by the Directives substitute their procurement with that of a central purchasing body. Allowing Member States to avoid the personal scope of the Directives by designating an organisation outside the EU to substitute what would otherwise be their indi-vidual procurement activity or perhaps could and should be that of EDA, could develop into a loophole of the Directives. This danger is, however, limited. This is due to the fact that not only the personal scope of the Defence Directive but also its material scope needs to be taken into account. Many if not most of the activities of OCCAR are in the area of the development of new equipment which is subject to a number of exemptions discussed in section 4 below.

A number of arguments against the assumption that OCCAR is intended as a possible central purchasing body have to be considered. First, in contrast to the EDA, OCCAR is not expressly mentioned in Recital 23. If a particular body is mentioned and another is not then it could be assumed that this suggests the inclusion of the earlier and the exclusion of the former. On the other hand, the EU legislator cannot include an organisation outside the EU in the personal scope of a Directive. Yet the Recital and Article 1(18) Defence Directive do not include the EDA in the personal scope of the Directive; they merely allow for the possibility of the EDA being designated as a central purchasing body if the Member States should wish to do so. Since then the additional designation of a body as a central purchasing body by the Member States is needed in addition to

---

[54] At 225–31.

[55] Belgium, France, Germany, Italy, Spain, and United Kingdom are members, the OCCAR community consists of Finland, the Netherlands, Luxembourg, Poland and Turkey, see www.occar-ea.org/185 [accessed 23 September 2013]. See ch. 5 at 222–5.

this being envisaged in the Defence Directive; there is no encroachment on the law of another international organisation if OCCAR would be designated as a central purchasing body under Article 1(18) Defence Directive. Thus the wording of Article 1(18) and Recital 23 Defence Directive does not exclude the possibility of OCCAR or LoI being designated as a central purchasing body, even when the EDA appears to be the more appropriate body as a structure open to all Member States.

2.2 The lack of an Annex for the Defence Directive

The Defence Directive itself does not have an Annex listing the entities covered by its personal scope. It merely refers back to that of the Public Sector Directive. The references to the other Directives and the lack of an annex to the Defence Directive listing the relevant contracting authorities appear unnecessarily confusing and a bit messy. The paragraphs on "personal scope" in the Guidance Note *Field of Application* do not add anything helpful either.[56] Providing all the necessary definitions in the Defence Directive itself, including an annex to the Defence Directive, would have been more in line with its objective to provide a visible and clear instrument for the ministries of defence and other relevant security agencies.[57] The Directive should strive as much as possible to be a self-contained regime. An annex would have been helpful in facilitating the message of the Defence Directive as a tailored defence and security framework. However, the Member States could address this complication in the transposition process, an opportunity not always used: neither Austria, Germany, Ireland nor the United Kingdom introduced a list.[58] On the other hand, the reference technique has been hailed as a "very coherent approach"[59] as the type of contract will be the only differentiating factor between Defence Directive on the one hand and Utilities Directive and Public Sector Directive on the other hand – any relevant

---

[56] *Supra* note 5, at 3.

[57] See the Commission Staff Working Document, *supra* note 43, at 36 and 40.

[58] The definitions of contracting authorities and entities are contained in the following provisions, which do not contain annexes, listing entities: Austria: § 4 Bundesgesetz über die Vergabe von Aufträgen im Verteidigungs- und Sicherheitsbereich (Bundesvergabegesetz Verteidigung und Sicherheit 2012 – BVergGVS 2012, BGBl. I Nr. 10/2012); Germany, § 1(1) Vergabeverordnung Verteidigung und Sicherheit vom 12. Juli 2012 [VgVVS] (BGBl. I S. 1509), die durch Artikel 8 des Gesetzes vom 25. Juli 2013 (BGBl. I S. 2722) geändert worden ist, in connection with § 98 Gesetz gegen Wettbewerbsbeschränkungen in der Fassung der Bekanntmachung vom 26. Juni 2013 (BGBl. I S.1750), das durch Artikel 2 Absatz 78 des Gesetzes vom 7. August 2013 (BGBl. I S. 3154) geändert worden ist; Republic of Ireland: Regulation 3(1) European Union (Award of Contracts Relating to Defence and Security) Regulations 2012 [ACRDSR] S.I. No. 62 of 2012; United Kingdom: Regulation 4 United Kingdom Defence and Security Contracts Regulations [DSPCR] 2011, S.I. 2011 No. 1848.

[59] Heuninckx, "Lurking at the Boundaries", *supra* note 13, at 98.

contract of an entity to which the latter two instruments apply would be covered.[60] However, it is submitted here that the Defence Directive should aim to be a self-contained regime and that it should therefore have its own definitions and its own annex listing contracting authorities. This would be easier when, as suggested above, utilities would be removed from the scope of the Defence Directive.

The procurement laws of the Member States investigated in this book have all implemented the rules on personal scope.[61] Thus the slightly "messy" approach of defining personal scope in the Defence Directive has been transposed to many national laws. However, while in Austria and the United Kingdom this has led to the same kind of cross-referencing to the public sector and utilities instruments as in the Defence Directive,[62] Regulation 3 of the Irish Regulations repeats these definitions rather than cross-referencing them. This remedies the messy approach of the Directive rather than transposing it. In Germany, the traditional hierarchy of the "higher" GWB and the "lower" VgVVS led to a single provision on personal scope applicable to all procurement regulations in § 98 GWB anyway. In particular, the Irish example shows how the transposition of a Directive may address some of its shortcomings.

Due to the crucial material scope of the Defence Directive discussed under the next heading below, its personal scope is less important than it could have been. The Commission had considered basing applications only on the "nature of the contracting authority" and "not the type of equipment procured".[63] Such a "Defence Sector Directive" would have required the inclusion of rules on goods and services not subject to Article 346 TFEU and the other security derogations, probably repeating those of the Public Sector Directive. Alternatively the same rules would have been applied, without that being justified by security requirements and leading to legal uncertainty.[64] The Commission did not therefore follow this approach.

3 The material scope of the Directive: covered contracts

With respect to the types of contract covered, Article 2 Defence Directive is the basic provision on scope:

> Subject to Articles [36, 51, 52, 62 and 346] of the Treaty, this Directive shall apply to contracts awarded in the fields of defence and security for:
> (a) the supply of military equipment, including any parts, components and/or subassemblies thereof

---

[60] This would include, for example, the procurement of hand guns for the security guards of Severn Trent Water or the French railways SNCF.

[61] See the reference in *supra* note 58.   [62] Ibid.

[63] See the Commission Staff Working Document, *supra* note 43, at 33.   [64] Ibid.

(b) the supply of sensitive equipment, including any parts, components and/or subassemblies thereof;

(c) works, supplies and services directly related to the equipment referred to in points (a) and (b) for any and all elements of its life cycle;

(d) works and services for specifically military purposes or sensitive works and sensitive services.[65]

Not surprisingly the Directive applies to military equipment (section 3.1 below). However, not only military equipment is covered by the Defence Directive, but also all sensitive equipment, works and services (section 3.2 below); works, supplies and services directly related to military and sensitive equipment (section 3.3 below); and finally works and services for specifically military purposes (section 3.4 below). This broader material scope of the Defence Directive means that the new instrument will apply to many procurement contracts previously clearly covered by the Public Sector Directive. In other words, this does not only concern armaments on the 1958 list but also works and services not subject to Article 346(1)(b) TFEU. The procurement of these goods, services and works are now to be conducted under the Defence Directive. This also necessitated a change of the "ministries of defence provision" in Article 10 Public Sector Directive 2004/18/EC (Article 15 Directive 2014/24/EU) mentioned in chapter 3 and briefly discussed in section 4.5 below.[66] As criticised above, the Defence Directive now also covers goods, services and works previously covered by the 2004 Utilities Directive. This necessitated the insertion of a new Article 22(a) (Article 24 Directive 2014/25/EU) into the latter.

3.1 Military Equipment

The Defence Directive applies to military equipment on the basis of its Article 2(a). Military equipment is further defined in Article 1(6) Defence Directive as equipment specifically designed or adapted for military purposes and intended for the use of an arm, munitions or war material,[67] which according to Recital 10 Defence Directive is a reference to the 1958 list of armaments discussed in chapter 3.[68] This is emphasised again in the 2012 Transposition Report of the Commission:

---

[65] Guidance Note *Field of Application*, *supra* note 5, at 3: "The terms 'contracts', 'works contracts', 'supply contracts' and 'service contracts' are defined in Article 1 (2), (3), (4) and (5) of the Directive."

[66] See At 305–7.

[67] T. Briggs, "The New Defence Procurement Directive" (2009) 18 *Public Procurement Law Review* NA129, at NA131.

[68] See Recital 10 Defence Directive: "For the purposes of this Directive, military equipment should be understood in particular as the product types included in the list of arms, munitions and war material adopted by the Council in its Decision 255/58 of 15 April 1958, and Member States may limit themselves to this list only when transposing this

Some Member States use specific national lists to define the field of application of the directive in the area of defence. In principle, these lists constitute legitimate references for the interpretation of Article 2 *provided they reflect the list of 1958* [emphasis added].[69]

Thus the material scope of the Defence Directive with regards to armaments defined in its Article 2(a) is identical to that of Article 346(1)(b) TFEU. The 1958 list of armaments is the only legitimate reference.[70] Different definitions of the term "military equipment" for EU primary and EU secondary law would compromise legal certainty.[71] The Commission, which had considered defining the material scope on the basis of a specific list, rejected this option for the same reason.[72] Furthermore, it is submitted that the "supremacy" of primary Internal Market law over secondary Internal Market law excludes any other interpretation. Similarly, the 1958 list prevails over any CFSP instrument due to the competence of the Council as an EU Internal Market institution to compile the list on the basis of Article 346(2) TFEU. Thus the Common Military List to which the Council Common Position 2008/994/CFSP[73] for Arms Exports applies can be useful for the definition of armaments as far as it complies with the 1958 List of Armaments. Finally, due to the supremacy of EU Internal Market law over the national laws of the Member States[74] the 1958 list prevails over any national list.

Directive. This list includes only equipment which is designed, developed and produced for specifically military purposes. However, the list is generic and is to be interpreted in a broad way in the light of the evolving character of technology, procurement policies and military requirements which lead to the development of new types of equipment, for instance on the basis of the Common Military List of the Union. For the purposes of this Directive, military equipment should also cover products which, although initially designed for civilian use, are later adapted to military purposes to be used as arms, munitions or war material." See also the Guidance Note *Field of Application, supra* note 5, at 4. The expression "in particular" in Recital 10, ibid., is interpreted as "not exclusively" and the word "types" as "not simply products".

69 "Report from the Commission to the European Parliament and the Council on Transposition of Directive 2009/81/EC on Defence and Security Procurement", COM (2012) 565 final, at 4–5. Moreover: "It will be subject to further detailed assessment, whether this is the case."

70 I benefited from comments provided by Mr Georgios K. Sampanis (PhD candidate at the University of Siegen, Germany) on the basis of an earlier draft of this chapter and from his paper "Defining the Field of Application of the Defence and Security Directive as an Indication of its (In)Effectiveness" at the conference "Public Procurement: Global Revolution VI", 26 June 2013 in Nottingham (on file). See also Pourbaix, "The Future Scope of Application of Article 346 TFEU", *supra* note 2, at 3.

71 Sampanis, "Defining the Field of Application", *supra* note 70.

72 See the Commission Staff Working Document, *supra* note 43, at 42: "this would create problems of interpretation and implementation".

73 [2008] OJ L335/19. Formerly the EU Code of Conduct on Arms Exports [2006] OJ C-66/1, see ch. 4 at 163–6.

74 Case 6/64, *Costa* v. *ENEL* [1964] ECR 585.

Moreover, as discussed further below, the entire interpretation of Article 346(1)(b) TFEU provided in chapter 3[75] applies. As clarified most recently in *Finnish Turntables*,[76] this includes an analysis starting with a first stage based on one of the items on the list. While a product that is not covered by one of the listed items cannot be subject to Article 346(1)(b) TFEU and thus Article 2(a) Defence Directive, there is a broad and flexible approach to the interpretation of listed items which is justified by the age and generic character of the 1958 list mentioned above.[77] However, this generic and broad interpretation also reiterated in Recital 10 Defence Directive refers to items that are on the list, not to products that are not. Consequently, "dual-use products" are not covered by Article 2(a) Defence Directive.[78] On the contrary, based on the *Agusta*[79] and *Finnish Turntables*[80] case law discussed in chapter 3, it is essential for listed equipment with possible civil uses to be specifically designed or adapted for military purposes.[81]

3.2 Sensitive contracts

Article 2(2) subjects "sensitive contracts" to the scope of the Directive. These are defined in Article 1(7) Defence Directive as

> 7. "Sensitive equipment", "sensitive works" and "sensitive services" means equipment, works and services for security purposes, involving, requiring and/or containing classified information . . .

---

[75] At 104–25.

[76] Case C-615/10, *Insinööritoimisto InsTiimi Oy* v. *Puolustusvoimat*, judgment of 7 June 2012, nyr.

[77] Commission Guidance Note *Field of Application, supra* note 5, at 4: "Such flexibility seems appropriate, in particular since the list is rather generic and over 50 years old. It may therefore be the case, for example, that military equipment is not explicitly mentioned in the list simply because it did not exist in 1958 when the list was drawn up (e.g. IT soft- and hardware)."

[78] Transposition Report, *supra* note 69, at 5.

[79] Cases C-337/05, *Commission* v. *Italy* [2008] ECR I-2173 and C-157/06, *Commission* v. *Italy* [2008] ECR I-7313.

[80] Case C-615/10, *Insinööritoimisto InsTiimi Oy* v. *Puolustusvoimat*, judgment of 7 June 2012, nyr.

[81] Guidance Note *Field of Application, supra* note 5, at 4 and 5. With regards to equipment specifically adapted for military purposes an example is provided: "This can be the case, for example, for a 'militarised' version of a helicopter which was initially developed for the civil market. However, to qualify as 'military equipment' in the meaning of this Directive, the helicopter would have to have distinguishable military technical features (weapon systems, avionics, etc.) enabling it to carry out missions that are clearly military (e.g. armed reconnaissance, fire support, air-to-air combat)." This example is clearly taken from the Agusta case law briefly discussed above, see *supra* note 75 and more extensively in ch. 3 at 96–101.

There are two requirements therefore for a contract to qualify as sensitive: (1) the contract is intended for a specific security purpose and (2) involves classified information.

The required security purpose can be of a military or non-military nature. Recital 11 Defence Directive assumes such a security purpose when

> military and non-military forces cooperate to fulfil the same missions

or when

> the purpose of the procurement is to protect the security of the Union and/or the Member States on their own territory or beyond it, against serious threats from non-military and/or non-governmental actors.

The Guidance Note *Field of Application* provides examples: "border protection, police activities and crisis management missions" or "police, customs services, civil protection".[82] However, there is no single EU notion of security because this would be difficult in view of changing geopolitical contexts and the difficulty in separating the defence and security areas, as discussed in chapter 1.[83] Fruhmann and Liebmann suggest a wide definition, covering numerous actors and areas and ensuring that all "grey zones" between defence and security are covered by the scope of the Defence Directive.[84]

The requirement that classified information needs to be "involved, required or used",[85] does not require a minimum level of classification. Article 2(8) Defence Directive defines classified information as "any information or material, regardless of the form, nature or mode of transmission thereof, to which a certain level of security classification or protection has been attributed".[86] Neither the Directive itself nor the Guidance Note *Field of Application* provide specific examples in respect of sensitive procurement. The wording of the provision does not suggest that the equipment has to be conceptualised or adapted for security purposes.[87]

The notion of "sensitive equipment" in Article 2(b) is broader than the term military equipment in Article 2(a). It is not limited by a list, the definition of a list, or the object of the contract. In contrast to military equipment which has to have a military purpose, sensitive equipment needs to have a security purpose and relate to confidential information. Any type of equipment can be considered as sensitive equipment if these two conditions are met.

---

[82] *Supra* note 5, at 6.   [83] At 21–2.   [84] *Supra* note 48, at 35–6.   [85] Ibid., at 36.

[86] Heuninckx, "Lurking at the Boundaries", *supra* note 13, at 100 refers to Council Decision 2001/264/EC adopting the Council's security regulations OJ [2001] L-101/1.

[87] Fruhmann and Liebmann, *Bundesvergabegesetz Verteidigung und Sicherheit 2012, supra* note 48, at 36.

3.3 Other included contracts

According to its Article 2(c) the Defence Directive applies to "works, supplies and services directly related to the equipment referred to in points (a) and (b) for any and all elements of its life cycle". The works, supplies and services are limited to those directly related to military equipment and sensitive contracts. The Guidance Note *Field of Application* has provided a number of examples for supplies, services and works directly related to military equipment.[88] Contracts "for any and all elements of [the] life cycle" are covered. Recital 12 Defence Directive includes:

> research and development, industrial development, production, repair, modernisation, modification, maintenance, logistics, training, testing, withdrawal and disposal. These stages include, for example, studies, evaluation, storage, transport, integration, servicing, dismantling, destruction and all other services following the initial design.

While this long list suggests a wide approach to the definition of these contracts, it actually represents a limitation. The crucial limitation to these categories of contracts is contained in the notion "directly related", which is to be interpreted restrictively[89] and requires "a close connection between the works, services or supplies in question and the military equipment".[90] The direct connection may result "from the purpose or the condition of use" and "the connection must be so close that the works, services or supplies may not be put to a meaningful use without the military equipment to which it is related".[91] The same interpretation applies to works, supplies and services directly related to sensitive equipment.[92] Overall, the "directly related" requirement significantly limits the contracts included by Article 2(c) Defence Directive. It is possible that difficulties in interpreting the "directly related" requirement might lead to a couple of disputes, even though the Commission attempted to provide a more detailed interpretation including examples in the Guidance Note *Field of Application*. It is submitted that the Commission could not have done more.

According to its Article 2(d), the Defence Directive applies to "works and services for specifically military purposes or sensitive works and sensitive services". With regards to military purposes the Guidance Note *Field of*

---

[88] Supplies directly related to military equipment: "special tools, machines necessary for production and maintenance of such equipment, additional equipment – special suits, helmets, for pilots of combat aircraft". Services directly related to military equipment: "overhaul and repair of military aircraft, tanks, warships, etc." and works directly related to military equipment: "construction of test facilities for military equipment": Guidance Note *Field of Application, supra* note 5, at 5.

[89] Fruhmann and Liebmann, *Bundesvergabegesetz Verteidigung und Sicherheit 2012, supra* note 48, at 3.

[90] Ibid.   [91] Guidance Note *Field of Application, supra* note 5, at 5.   [92] Ibid., at 7.

Application refers to "services and works which are not directly related to military equipment but have a specific military purpose".[93] The purpose assigned at the beginning of the award procedure is decisive and without the presence of a specific military purpose the other procurement Directives apply.[94] With regards to sensitive works and sensitive services the principles on sensitive equipment discussed in section 3.2 above apply.[95] The crucial requirement here is that of a "specifically military purpose" which limits the category significantly and is arguably based on the case law of the ECJ in *Agusta*[96] and *Finnish Turntables*[97] discussed in chapter 3.[98] This would include an air-raid shelter but exclude an officers' casino. With regards to sensitive works and services, the security purpose and confidentiality requirements discussed in section 3.2 above will apply and limit the scope of the category.

3.4 The Defence Directive and the other procurement Directives

The rules on material scope clarify that the Public Sector Directive still applies to the procurement of many types of supplies, services and works by the ministries of defence and other relevant contracting entities of the Member States, such as office equipment, uniforms, medical equipment, the construction of barracks or cleaning services. In other words, the Defence Directive covers some but certainly not all purchases previously covered by the Public Sector Directive. Ministries of defence, for example, have to follow either the Defence Directive or the Public Sector Directive, depending on the type of good, service or work they wish to procure,[99] unless they need to derogate from the former on the basis of Article 346 TFEU.[100]

---

[93] Guidance Note *Field of Application, supra* note 5, at 6. An example for a relevant service is the transport of troops and an example for a relevant work is the construction for a runway or air-raid and fall-out shelters. Ibid.

[94] Ibid. with reference to the first Agusta Case C-337/05, *Commission v. Italy, supra* note 79.

[95] The Guidance Note *Field of Application, supra* note 5, at 6–7 discusses sensitive equipment, services and works together in one section.

[96] Case C-337/05, *Commission v. Italy, supra* note 79.

[97] Case C-615/10, *Insinööritoimisto InsTiimi Oy* v. *Puolustusvoimat*, judgment of 7 June 2012, nyr.

[98] At 96–103.

[99] B. Heuninckx, "The EU Defence and Security Procurement Directive: Trick or Treat?" (2011) 20 *Public Procurement Law Review* 9–28, at 11: "When the Defence and Security Directive applies, the Public Sector Directive does not apply"; see also: Briggs, *supra* note 67, at NA130.

[100] In the United Kingdom, for example, before the implementation of the Defence Directive about 12% of the contracts were subject to the Public Contracts Regulations 2006 (based on the 2004 Public Sector Directive), 12% to Art. 346 TFEU and other exemptions and 76% below the value thresholds of the Public Sector Directive (see below). After the

Finally, related to the discussion in section 2.1 above, the inclusion of sensitive equipment makes the new instrument relevant beyond the ministries of defence, also including other entities procuring these goods, including the police, prisons, border agencies and civilian intelligence services.[101] Moreover, as indicated above, it includes relevant contracts of utilities. In other words, this shows again that the Defence Directive is not only a "ministry of defence Directive". This also partly explains the reference to the security exemptions in what are now Articles 36, 51, 52 and 62 TFEU discussed in chapter 2 in addition to Article 346 TFEU discussed in chapter 3. While other security entities also buy certain armaments, the new Directive is not just an "armaments Directive". It addresses also the security concerns accommodated in the other (Internal Market) security exemptions of the Treaty – and these are relevant beyond the ministries of defence.

The Member States discussed in this book have all transposed the rules on the covered contracts in Article 2 Defence Directive almost word for word.[102] No changes to the wording outlined above were introduced as part of that transposition.

4 The material scope of the Directive: excluded contracts

Article 2 Defence Directive already contains a crucial exemption limiting the scope of the new Directive as it is subject to Articles 36, 51, 52, 62 and 346 TFEU. This means that Member States can still derogate from the instrument for reasons of national and public security. The interpretation of these provisions has been discussed in chapters 2[103] and 3.[104] The Directive cannot change the Treaty and it merely expressly integrates the Treaty derogations into the Defence Directive.[105] These derogations would have applied anyway. However, the difference from the previous situation is that the Defence Directive is designed to take the public and national security concerns of the Member States into account. This is intended to significantly limit the necessity for

transposition, 2% will be subject to the Public Contracts Regulations 2006, 4% exempt, 15% will be subject to the Defence and Security Contracts Regulations 2011 and 79% below the threshold values of Public Sector Directive and Defence Directive. See D. Kiltie (Ministry of Defence), "Implementing and Applying Directive 2009/81/EC in the UK" at the seminar "European Defence and Security Procurement", European Institute of Public Administration (EIPA), Maastricht, 20 January 2012 (notes of the author, on file).

[101] According to the Commission's N. Spiegel (2010), *supra* note 42, this inclusion of "homeland security" was decided rather late (second half of 2008) and was extremely contested.

[102] Austria in § 1(1) BVergGVS, Germany in § 99(7) GWB, Ireland in Regulation 4 ACRDSR, the United Kingdom in Regulation 6 DSPCR.

[103] At 63–82. [104] At 87–135.

[105] See the Commission Guidance Note *Field of Application*, *supra* note 5, at 1.

Member States to use the Treaty security derogations to exceptional circumstances. The Directive does not take away the possibility for derogation, but it is designed to address security concerns to a degree that makes it unnecessary to use the exemptions.[106] The interpretation of the Treaty derogation in the context of the exclusions of the Defence Directive is discussed further in section 4.3 below.

4.1 In-house contracts

A certain category of contracts, separate from the thresholds and the exceptions discussed under the next headings below, needs to be discussed in the context of the material scope of the Defence Directive: the so-called "in house" contracts. Similar to the Public Sector Directive 2004/18/EC (but see Article 12 Directive 2014/24/EU), these are not mentioned in the Defence Directive itself. The concept was developed by the ECJ in *Teckal*[107] in the context of the Public Sector Directive and is based on the definition of "contracting authority" discussed above. If (1) the contracting authority exercises a certain level of control over the entity it procures from and (2) the latter is economically dependent on the earlier, the contract will be considered "in-house", therefore not as public procurement, and thus as outside the field of application of the Directive. This applies when the contract would be concluded within the same contracting authority but also when the entities are legally distinct, provided the contracting authority exercises a level of control over the other entity which is comparable to the level of control it exercises over its own departments. With regard to economic dependence, "this criterion is only met if the activities of the in-house entity are devoted principally to the

---

[106] Ibid. at 2 summarises a situation in which derogation from the Defence Directive would still be possible: "there may still be contracts which, for example, necessitate such extremely demanding requirements in terms of security of supply, or which are so confidential and/or important for national sovereignty, that even the specific provisions of Directive 2009/81/EC would not be sufficient to safeguard a Member State's essential security interests ... In these cases, the Member State concerned must ensure and, if necessary, be able to demonstrate that the concrete measure taken is objectively suitable for the protection of the essential security interest identified and that, in qualitative and quantitative terms, it does not go beyond what is strictly necessary for that purpose." See also Recital 16 of the Defence Directive.

[107] The leading case is Case C-107/98, *Teckal Srl* v. *Comune de Viano, supra* note 4, especially at paras. 49–50. See also: Case C-26/03, *Stadt Halle* [2006] CMLR 39, at para. 48; Case C-84/03, *Commission* v. *Spain* [2005] ECR I-139, at para. 40; R. Caranta, "The In-House Providing: The Law as it Stands in the EU" in M. Comba and S. Treumer (eds.), *The In-house Providing in European Law* (Copenhagen: Djøf Publishing, 2010), at 13–52; K. Weltzien, "Avoiding the Procurement Rules by Awarding Contracts to an In-house Entity – Scope of the Procurement Directives in the Classical Sector" (2005) 14 *Public Procurement Law Review* 237.

contracting authority. Any other activities should only be of marginal signifi-cance.[108] Heuninckx refers in this context to the national depots of Member States for the maintenance of their military equipment, for example the four depots performing aircraft maintenance for the *Armée de l'Aire* owned by the French Ministry of Defence.[109] However, it would have to be examined as well whether services rendered to entities other than the French Air Force are of marginal significance.[110] In contrast, a contract awarded by one contracting authority to another without that level of control is not considered in-house. This is different to the defence and security-specific government-to-government exclusion in Article 13(f) Defence Directive discussed in section 4.3.2.5 below, where the two authorities are two different governments and already legally distinct for that reason. The in-house exemption represents an interesting aspect of the scope of the Defence Directive because ministries of defence could in theory preserve an entirely national defence industry by making them controlled and economically dependent departments in the sense of the *Teckal* requirements. As discussed in chapter 1 this was a phenomenon in the past, especially in France, and to a limited extent this is and will be a feature. However, a large-scale nationalisation of the European defence industries is unlikely and the in-house exemption is therefore of limited importance in the context of the Defence Directive.

4.2 The thresholds of the Defence Directive

Similar to the other procurement Directives, the Defence Directive is only applicable above certain contract value thresholds. Article 8 Defence Directive as amended[111] provides:

> This Directive shall apply to contracts which have a value excluding value-added tax (VAT) estimated to be no less than the following thresholds:

[108] Commission Staff Working Paper concerning the application of EU public procurement law to relations between contracting authorities, SEC (2011) 1169 fin, at 11. Thanks to Georgios Sampanis for pointing this out to me when commenting on an earlier version of this chapter.

[109] Heuninckx, "Lurking at the Boundaries", *supra* note 13, at 101.

[110] See www.spacewar.com/reports/Snecma_Signs_Partnership_Agreement_With_French_Military_Aircraft_MRO_Arm_999.htm [accessed 26 September 2013]. Thanks to Georgios Sampanis for pointing this out to me.

[111] See Commission Regulation 1336/2013/EU of 13 December 2013 amending Directives 2004/17/EC, 2004/18/EC and 2009/81/EC of the European Parliament and of the Council in respect of the application thresholds for the procedures for the awards of contracts, OJ [2013] L-335/17. See the old thresholds in Commission Regulation 1251/2011/EU of 30 November 2011 amending Directives 2004/17/EC, 2004/18/EC, and 2009/81/EC of the European Parliament and of the Council in respect of their application thresholds for the procedures for the awards of contracts, OJ [2011] L-319/43. The legal base for this Regulation with respect to the Defence Directive is Art. 68 of the latter.

(a) EUR 414 000 for supply and service contracts;
(b) EUR 5 186 000 for works contracts.

Value thresholds are not only set by the Directive itself but revised and adapted on a biannual basis. The current figures are valid from 1 January 2012 until 31 December 2015.[112] Thresholds represent a limitation of scope and an exemption, because they clarify that the Directive does *not* apply to contracts with a value below the thresholds.

The threshold for works contracts is meant to be the same as that in the old or new Public Sector Directive. In contrast, the value thresholds for supplies and services are considerably higher with respect to central government (€134,000) and other contracting entities (€207,000).[113] The values of many of the most visible contracts, such as fighter aeroplanes or battleships, are well above these thresholds. However, many of the relevant contracts will cover the resupply of parts, repairs, training, accessories, smaller weapon systems or ammunition which are frequently below these thresholds.[114] Therefore the difference in thresholds matters: a relevant purchase with a contract value between €134,000 and €414,000 is now outside the scope of both the Defence Directive and the old or new Public Sector Directive, whereas in the past it would have been covered by the 2004 Public Sector Directive. This results in a number of contracts which used to be covered by secondary Internal Market law now being outside such regulation altogether.[115]

However, a number of considerations put the different thresholds in perspective. First, while the 2004 Public Sector Directive applied in theory, it was often not applied in practice. Secondly, €414,000 is below the €1 million threshold of the former EDA Code of Conduct discussed in chapter 5, which some Member

---

[112] See Art. 4 of Regulation 1336/2013/EU and Art. 4 Directive 2014/24/EU. Before 2012, in accordance with the then Art. 3 of Regulation 1177/2009/EC on the application thresholds of the procurement Directives, the following changes were incorporated in respect of the original wording of the Defence Directive: Art. 8(a) was amended so that the threshold in Euros for supplies and services contracts was modified from €412,000 to €387,000; Art. 8 (b) was amended so that the threshold in Euros for works contracts was modified from €5,150,000 to €4,845,000. Hence in 2011 the thresholds were actually increased to €400,000 for supplies and services and €5,000,000 for works. Similarly in 2013 they were increased again to €414,000 and €5,186,000 respectively.

[113] See also Briggs, "The New Defence Procurement Directive", *supra* note 67, at NA132 with respect to the similar situation under the 2009 thresholds.

[114] I have benefited from discussions with B. Heuninckx on this point of the type of contracts to be covered by the Defence Directive. See also the figures in the next footnote below.

[115] So D. Kiltie (Ministry of Defence) in his 2012 presentation, *supra* note 100, expects a slightly higher percentage of United Kingdom Ministry of Defence contracts to be below the thresholds: 79% rather than 76%. Considering that with France the United Kingdom has one of the largest procurement budgets in the EU, it can be assumed that in many Member States this percentage is similar or even higher.

States had suggested during the consultation for the Defence Directive.[116] Thus, the legislator's intention is to move many contracts from the non-binding former EDA Code with a higher threshold to a binding Directive with a lower threshold. Thirdly, while the Defence Directive does not apply below its thresholds, the TFEU, which imposes a number of requirements such as non-discrimination and transparency, does apply.[117] There is no *de minimus* rule for the Internal Market.[118] It is necessary to advertise many of these contracts, but not in the OJ, and to follow non-discriminatory procedures, but not necessarily those of the Defence Directive. Overall, contracts between below €414,000 or €1 million are important for the Internal Market regime not only because of their number but also because they are normally too small to affect the essential security interests of the Member States in the sense of Article 346(1)(b) TFEU.[119] The thresholds appear based on those of the Utilities Directive 2004/17/EC or new 2014/25/EU in its Article 16, which might be a consequence of the unfortunate last-minute inclusion of utilities in the personal scope of the Defence Directive.

[116] See the Commission Staff Working Document, *supra* note 43, at 43.

[117] Case law on the application of the Treaty: Case 76/81, *Transporoute et Travaux SA v. Ministère des travaux publics* [1982] ECR 417; Case 263/85, *Commission v. Italy* [1991] ECR I-2457; Case 45/87, *Commission v. Ireland* ("Dundalk") [1988] ECR 4929; Case C-3/88, *Commission v. Italy* ("Re Data Processing") [1989] ECR 4035, [1991] CMLR 115; Case C-21/88, *Du Pont de Nemours Italiana v. Unita Sanitara Locale No. 2 di Carrara* [1990] ECR 889; Case C-243/89, *Commission v. Denmark* ("Storebaelt"); C-360/89, *Commission v. Italy* [1992] ECR I-3401; Case C-272/91, *Commission v. Italy* ("Lottomatica") [1992] ECR I-3929; Case C-87/94, *Commission v. Belgium* ("Walloon Buses") [1996] ECR I-2043; Case C-275/98, *Unitron Scandinavia* [1999] ECR I-8291; Case C-324/98, *Telaustria* [2000] ECR I-10745; Case C-470/99, *Universale Bau AG* [2002] ECR I-11617; Case C-358/00, *Buchhändler Vereinigung* [2002] ECR I-4685; Case C-231/03, *Coname* [2005] ECR I-7287; Case C-234/03, *Contse and others* [2005] ECR I-9315; Case C-264/03, *Commission v. France* [2005] ECR I-8831; Case C-358/03, *Parking Brixen* [2004] ECR I-12055; Case C-535/03, *Commission v. Italy* [2006] ECR I-2689. Other relevant material: "Commission Interpretative Communication on the Community Law Applicable to Contracts Not or Not Fully Subject to the Provisions of the Public Procurement Directives", 1 August 2006, OJ [2006] C-179/02; and "Commission Interpretative Communication of Concessions under Community Law", 29 April 2000, OJ [2000] C-121/2.

[118] For the crucial Art. 34 TFEU: Trepte, *Public Procurement in the EU*, *supra* note 4, at 8. On the discussion and arguments for a *de minimus* test in the context of the free movement of goods see A. Arnull, *The European Union and its Court of Justice*, 2nd edn (Oxford University Press, 2006), at 434–5 and 440–1. This was discussed by several Advocates General, for example Advocate General Jacobs in Case C-412/93, *Leclerc-Siplec v. TF1 Publicité and M6 Publicité* [1995] ECR I-179. However, such a test would not apply to measures which discriminated against imports as they are prohibited by Art. 34 TFEU as such, even where their effect was only slight, see Arnull, ibid., at 435.

[119] See B. Heuninckx, "Towards a Coherent Defence Procurement Regime? European Defence Agency and European Commission Initiatives" (2008) 17 *Public Procurement Law Review* 1–20, at 18 regarding a contract slightly above €1 million.

Otherwise different thresholds would have been necessary for public bodies and utilities. However Sentence 2 of Point (3) of the Preamble Regulation 1336/2013/EU provides that "the thresholds laid down by Directive 2009/81/EC should be aligned to the revised thresholds laid down in Article 16 of Directive 2004/17/EC". This suggests that at least in 2013–14 the use of the thresholds of the Utilities Directive for the Defence Directive is intentional. In 2007 the Commission had intended to use the thresholds of the Public Sector Directive, also for the sake of SMEs.[120] However, for contracting authorities the higher thresholds represents an additional and possibly welcome limitation of the Defence Directive.

4.3 Exceptions

Apart from the thresholds; the listed goods, services and works; and the Treaty security exceptions, Section 3 of Title II of the Defence Directive and especially Articles 12 and 13 Defence Directive contain a number of specific exclusions which limit its scope even further. These can be subdivided into exceptions that also feature in the other Directives (section 4.3.1 below), exceptions specific to the Defence Directive (section 4.3.2 below), the safeguard clause in Article 11 (section 4.3.3 below), provisions in the Public Sector and Utilities Directives regulating their respective relationship with the Defence Directive (sections 4.4 and 4.5 below) and the still relevant exemptions from the TFEU (section 4.6 below). It was the intention of the Commission to "limit the number of explicit exclusions to a minimum".[121]

4.3.1 Article 12 Defence Directive: contracts awarded under international rules

Article 12 Defence Directive contains a set of three exceptions for contracts awarded under international rules:

Contracts awarded pursuant to international rules

This Directive shall not apply to contracts governed by:
(a) specific procedural rules pursuant to an international agreement or arrangement concluded between one or more Member States and one or more third countries;
(b) specific procedural rules pursuant to a concluded international agreement or arrangement relating to the stationing of troops and concerning the undertakings of a Member State or a third country;
(c) specific procedural rules of an international organisation purchasing for its purposes, or to contracts which must be awarded by a Member State in accordance with those rules.

The relevant Recital 26 to the Defence Directive does not add anything to the wording of this provision. Article 12 Defence Directive ultimately regulates "the law of conflicts" with other international rules, such as the World Bank

---

[120] See the Commission Staff Working Document, *supra* note 43, at 43.   [121] Ibid.

Guidelines[122] or those of the NATO agencies discussed in chapter 5,[123] or more generally situations in which a third country is involved.[124]

Article 12(a) Defence Directive on "specific procedural rules pursuant to an international agreement or arrangement concluded between one or more Member States and one or more third countries" is similar but still different from Article 15(a) Public Sector Directive 2004/18/EC (see Article 19 Directive 2014/24/EU). The Commission's Guidance Note *Defence and Security-specific Exclusions* describes it as "very generic".[125] There is "no restriction as to the subject matter of the agreement/arrangement, which can therefore concern any defence or security related issue".[126] The basis of the rules does not have to be an international treaty: a memorandum of understanding, which is the usual instrument, is sufficient.[127] The exemption applies only to agreements or arrangements between States and governments, not to other legal persons such as public or private undertakings.[128] The most relevant limitation of the exemption in letter (a) is that at least one EU Member State or government and at least one third state or government needs to be a party to the arrangements or agreement. This clearly excludes the structures of EDA, OCCAR and LoI discussed in chapter 5 or any other arrangement which only includes EU Member States. On the other hand the inclusion of only one third country, for example Turkey, could bring an arrangement under letter (a). Individual projects of OCCAR for example could therefore be excluded if they include a third country and the legal basis would be a relevant arrangement. However, a

---

[122] As the World Bank Group would finance a particular project, they could and would insist on the use of their own rules. See most importantly Guidelines: Procurement of Goods, Works, and Non-Consulting Services under [International Bank for Reconstruction and Development IBRD] Loans and [International Development Agency IDA] Credits & Grants, January 2011, http://web.worldbank.org/WBSITE/EXTERNAL/PROJECTS/PROCUREMENT/0,,contentMDK:20060840~menuPK:93977~pagePK:84269~piPK:6000 1558~theSitePK:84266,00.html [accessed 1 October 2013].

[123] See especially NATO's NSPA discussed in ch. 5 at 239–40. Most NSPA procurement includes third countries such as the USA, Canada and Turkey. During the seminar "European Defence and Security Procurement", at the European Institute of Public Administration (EIPA), in Maastricht, 19–20 January 2012, B. Heuninckx also convincingly argued that this exemption refers to organisations such as NSPA's predecessor NAMSA, but not OCCAR (notes of the author, on file).

[124] "Third country" is understood as a country that is not a Member State of the EU. See in more detail on the corresponding provision in the 2004 Public Sector Directive: Martin Trybus, *European Union Law and Defence Integration* (Oxford: Hart, 2005), at 222–6.

[125] *Supra* note 7, at 3.   [126] Ibid.

[127] This was clarified by the Commission's B. Schmitt and N. Spiegel (the drafters of the Defence Directive) in their presentation "The Specificities of the European Defence and Security Procurement Directive" at the seminar "European Defence Procurement and Other Defence Market Initiatives", at the EIPA, Maastricht, 15 November 2010 (notes of the author, on file).

[128] Commission Guidance Note *Defence and Security-specific Exclusions*, *supra* note 7, at 3.

separate agreement or arrangement which includes that third country would be required. Letter (a) of Article 12 is wider than its letter (c) discussed below, as the procurement does not have to be for the own purposes of the arrangement but can be for the benefit of its Member States.[129]

Article 12(b) Defence Directive concerns "specific procedural rules pursuant to a concluded international agreement or arrangement relating to the stationing of troops and concerning the undertakings of a Member State or a third country".[130] Letter (b), an exception which has been taken over without modification from Article 15 Public Sector Directive 2004/18/EC, is actually redundant after the end of the Cold War. This is also stated in the Commission's Guidance Note *Defence and Security-specific Exclusions*.[131] However, some Member States wanted to include the provision without giving any reasons.[132] Obviously, the adoption of a provision which is redundant is recognised by the legislator as such and without providing justifications cannot pass as good legislation. If a provision is redundant and there is no reason for it then it should not be adopted. Exemptions are exceptions to the rule; they compromise the consistency of the legal instrument and should therefore be kept to a minimum, as was indeed the intention of the Commission.[133]

Letter (b) includes troops of Member States in another Member State, troops of a third country in a Member State and troops for a Member State in a third country, as also clarified by Recital 26 Defence Directive.[134] The best example is the US, British, French, Belgian, Canadian and Dutch forces that used to be or still are stationed in Germany.[135] As the author has argued before with respect to what became Article 15(b) Public Sector Directive 2004/18/EC, it is understandable why the procurement of for example US troops stationed in a Member State like Germany are excluded from the Directives as they are not contracting entities of a Member State.[136] Third-country troops are already outside the personal scope of the Directives, hence the exemption is not even necessary with respect to

---

[129] Heuninckx, "Lurking at the Boundaries", *supra* note 13, at 110.

[130] See also Recital 26 of the Preamble to the Defence Directive.

[131] *Supra* note 7, at 3: "Dating from the Cold War, the provision is probably of little relevance today, particularly since Article 12(a) already covers all international agreements and arrangements between Member States and third countries. However, the much narrower Article 12(b) may become of practical relevance in cases where an agreement or arrangement relating to the stationing of troops is concluded between Member States only."

[132] Schmitt and Spiegel (European Commission, November 2010), *supra* note 127. Art. 9 Directive 2014/24/EU no longer includes this redundant provision.

[133] See the Commission Staff Working Document, *supra* note 43, at 43.

[134] Guidance Note *Defence and Security-specific Exclusions*, *supra* note 7, at 3: "According to Recital 26, the provision concerns not only the stationing of troops from a Member State in a third country, or the stationing of troops from a third country in a Member State, but also the stationing of troops from a Member State in another Member State, be it for a limited or unlimited period of time."

[135] Trybus, *European Union Law and Defence Integration*, *supra* note 124, at 226.   [136] Ibid.

these troops. The rationale for excluding the troops of Member States stationed in a third country and in particular of Member State troops stationed in another Member State is less clear. According to the Guidance Note *Defence and Security-specific Exclusions* the Commission considers the "Member State to Member State" constellation to be the most relevant case of the exemption.[137] It is submitted that there is actually no obvious justification in excluding Member State troops stationed in another Member State while at the same time Member State troops that stay within their own borders are included. Is this the result of a cut-and-paste operation from the 2004 Public Sector Directive? Was this overlooked or rushed through? Are there any unexpressed motives behind this exclusion? Overall, since the exemption is redundant, unnecessary with respect to third-country troops and its objectives are unclear, if indeed there are any, it should be reconsidered as part of the next revision of the Defence Directive. Article 9 Directive 2014/24/EU no longer includes this exemption.

Article 12(c) Defence Directive on "specific procedural rules of an international organisation purchasing for its purposes, or to contracts which must be awarded by a Member State in accordance with those rules" ultimately regulates "the law of conflicts" with the procurement rules of other international organisations, such as especially NATO rules. This exemption is inspired by Article 15(c) Public Sector Directive 2004/18/EC,[138] and the initial Draft Proposal for the Defence Directive simply replicated the latter. However, the wording in the final version of the Defence Directive is different. The exemption is narrower since only purchases for the organisation's own purposes are covered.[139] This is clearly spelt out in the Commission's Guidance Note *Defence and Security-specific Exclusions*:

> 7. Purchases made by an international organisation in its own name and for its own purposes are outside the scope of the Directive. However, by referring explicitly to "*specific procedural rules of an international organisation purchasing for its purposes*", the provision points to the fact that purchases made by an international organisation for the purpose of its members or of third parties may not be excluded from the Directive.[140]

This clear limitation is then emphasised by providing examples for what is *not* included in the scope of the exemption:

> This may be the case when an international organisation acts only as an intermediary on behalf of one of its members (with the procurement

---

[137] Guidance Note *Defence and Security-specific Exclusions, supra* note 7, at 3: "Article 12(b) may become of practical relevance in cases where an agreement or arrangement relating to the stationing of troops is concluded between Member States only."

[138] Art. 15(c) Public Sector Directive 2004/18/EC reads: "(c) pursuant to the particular procedure of an international organisation". See also Art. 9 Directive 2014/24/EU.

[139] See also: Heuninckx, "Lurking at the Boundaries", *supra* note 13, at 109.

[140] At 4, emphasis taken from the original.

contract concluded between the member and the supplier), or when the organisation simply resells to one of its members supplies, works or services (which it procured from economic operators at the request of that member). In any case, Member States may not use contract awards via international organisations for the purpose of circumventing the provisions of the Directive (Article 11).[141]

Therefore it is argued that the practical relevance of letter (c) is limited. This is because only a few international organisations procure defence and security equipment for their own purposes,[142] according to the Guidance Note *Defence and Security-specific Exclusions* "NATO is the most prominent example."[143] The organisations discussed in chapter 5, such as EDA and OCCAR, which at least potentially buy defence and security equipment, do so for their Member States, not for their own purposes. This is expressly excluded in the second citation from the Guidance Note provided above. Letter (c) would therefore not apply. This also makes the Article 15(c) Public Sector Directive 2004/18/EC discussion[144] and case law[145] – about what exactly constitutes an international organisation for the purposes of the exemption and if third countries need to be parties to it[146] – largely irrelevant for Article 12(c) Defence Directive. The latter is narrower in scope.

Article 12 excludes certain contracts from the application of the Defence Directive which previously had also been excluded from the 2004 Public Sector Directive, even though the exemptions are not exactly the same. Hence it does not represent a change from the previous regime; it merely inserts a relevant set of exclusions into the new Directive.

4.3.2 Article 13 Defence Directive: specific rules

Article 13 Defence Directive on "specific rules" is more interesting since it adds a number of exceptions[147] to those taken over and modified from the Public

---

[141] Ibid. On Art. 11 Defence Directive see the discussion below.   [142] Ibid.

[143] *Supra* note 7, at 4. Heuninckx, "Lurking at the Boundaries", *supra* note 13, in footnote 122 gives a specific example with "the procurement for the benefit of the E-3A Airborne Warning and Control Systems (AWACS) aircraft (modified Boeing 707–320B) owned by NATO that are managed by the [former] NATO Airborne Early Warning and Control Programme Management Organisation (NAPMO): see NATO Public Diplomacy Division, NATO Handbook (2006), ch. 34."

[144] Heuninckx, ibid., at 106–7.

[145] See, for example, Case T-411/06, *SOGELMA* v. *European Agency for Reconstruction* [2008] ECR II-2771, at para. 115.

[146] For a requirement that third countries need to be parties to it: Trybus, *European Union Law and Defence Integration*, *supra* note 124, at 225–6; A. Georgopoulos, "European Defence Procurement Integration", PhD Thesis, Nottingham (2004), at 92. Against such a requirement: B. Heuninckx, "Defence Procurement in the EU: Time to Listen to the Wake-up Calls" (2006) 7 *Business Law International* 208.

[147] Heuninckx, "Lurking at the Boundaries", *supra* note 13, at 111 calls this "a fairly large number of specific exceptions".

Sector Directive. Additional exceptions do of course limit the field of application when compared with the latter, and limit it further with each additional exemption. According to the Commission's Guidance Note *Defence and Security-specific Exclusions* the additional exemptions were "newly created in order to accommodate the specific situation in the defence and security sectors".[148] Article 13 reads:

> This Directive shall not apply to the following:
> (a) contracts for which the application of the rules of this Directive would oblige a Member State to supply information the disclosure of which it considers contrary to the essential interests of its security;
> (b) contracts for the purposes of intelligence activities;
> (c) contracts awarded in the framework of a cooperative programme based on research and development, conducted jointly by at least two Member States for the development of a new product and, where applicable, the later phases of all or part of the life-cycle of this product. Upon the conclusion of such a cooperative programme between Member States only, Member States shall indicate to the Commission the share of research and development expenditure relative to the overall cost of the programme, the cost-sharing agreement as well as the intended share of purchases per Member State, if any;
> (d) contracts awarded in a third country, including for civil purchases, carried out when forces are deployed outside the territory of the Union where operational needs require them to be concluded with economic operators located in the area of operations;
> (e) service contracts for the acquisition or rental, under whatever financial arrangements, of land, existing buildings or other immovable property, or concerning rights in respect thereof;
> (f) contracts awarded by a government to another government relating to:
>   (i) the supply of military equipment or sensitive equipment,
>   (ii) works and services directly linked to such equipment, or
>   (iii) works and services specifically for military purposes, or sensitive works and sensitive services;
> (g) arbitration and conciliation services;
> (h) financial services, with the exception of insurance services;
> (i) employment contracts;
> (j) research and development services other than those where the benefits accrue exclusively to the contracting authority/entity for its use in the conduct of its own affairs, on condition that the service provided is wholly remunerated by the contracting authority/entity.

Exclusions (e) and (g)–(j) are not specific to the Defence Directive, they are also contained in the Utilities and Public Sector Directives, whereas exclusions (a)–(d) and (f) are specific to the Defence Directive. These additional

---

[148] *Supra* note 7, at 1.

exemptions are the most important aspect of adapting the rules of the Public Sector Directive through limitation. It is these additional exemptions which shall be discussed in the following section of this chapter.

4.3.2.1 Secrecy Exclusion (a) on "contracts for which the application of the rules of this Directive would oblige a Member State to supply information the disclosure of which it considers contrary to the essential interests of its security" is a reflection of the Treaty exemption in Article 346(1)(a) TFEU.[149] The latter exemption was discussed in chapter 3.[150] This could cover especially cases which are so sensitive that the very existence of the contract is a secret.[151]

Contracts determined by a situation covered by Article 346(1)(a) TFEU are actually already excluded from the Directive through the reference to Article 346 TFEU in Article 2 Defence Directive discussed above.[152] However, the Commission's Guidance Note *Defence and Security-specific Exclusions* identifies a main difference between the exemptions in the Treaty and the Directive. The earlier only refers to the "right not to disclose information but not [to] further measures possibly related to such non-disclosure", whereas "Article 13(a), by contrast, explicitly establishes a link between non-disclosure of information and non-application of the Directive."[153] In other words, Article 13(a) is more specific and clear. The Guidance Note therefore sees Article 13(a) to be "particularly important" for contracts outside the military context to which Article 346(1)(a) TFEU does not apply.[154] Neither the allegation that Article 13(a) Defence Directive is more specific and clear than Article 346(1)(a) TFEU nor the alleged connection to non-military security contracts, further developed below, are sufficiently explained or convincing. Moreover, the concept of "non-military security contracts" is not clear. Based on the examples of the Guidance Note discussed in the next paragraph below, this would refer to entities other than the defence procurement authorities. However, based on the wording of Article 13(a) it also applies to non-armaments contracts of the latter. These would already be exempt from the Directive through its Article 2.

---

[149] Guidance Note *Defence and Security-specific Exclusions, supra* note 7, at 4. Art. 346(1)(a) TFEU reads:

1. The provisions of the Treaties shall not preclude the application of the following rules:
   (a) no Member State shall be obliged to supply information the disclosure of which it considers contrary to the essential interests of its security . . .

[150] At 128–33.

[151] Heuninckx, "Lurking at the Boundaries", *supra* note 13, at 112, Trybus, *European Union Law and Defence Integration, supra* note 124, at 214, referring to the similar but not equal Art. 14 Public Sector Directive 2004/18/EC, see below.

[152] See also the second subparagraph of Recital 20 to the Defence Directive, also referred to by Heuninckx, "Lurking at the Boundaries", *supra* note 13.

[153] *Supra* note 7, at 5.   [154] Ibid.

According to Recital 27 Defence Directive, Article 13(a) would apply to "contracts which are so sensitive that it would be inappropriate to apply this Directive, despite its specificity", also providing a number of examples.[155] The Guidance Note considers this list of examples as indicative that "Article 13(a) was introduced essentially to allow for the explicit exclusion of highly confidential non-military security contracts."[156] However, sensitive procurement might be conducted in other areas and the list is not exhaustive but merely illustrative.[157] Hence the "secrecy exemption" covers situations in which security and secrecy considerations would be compromised by advertising contracts or by complying with other transparency requirements.

The Commission's Guidance Note *Defence and Security-specific Exclusions* also contains a number of warnings not to apply too wide an interpretation. The list of examples in Recital 27 "is only indicative and refers to 'certain purchases'". Thus the exclusion does not automatically cover all purchases in the listed areas.[158] Moreover, a strict interpretation applies to the exemption, the burden of proof lies with the contracting authority, and the principle of proportionality applies. However, these are the general principles to be applied to exemptions from primary and secondary EU Internal Market law discussed in chapters 2 and 3.

It could be questioned whether Article 13(a) Defence Directive is a defence and security-specific exemption. First, as mentioned above, there are other "non-specific" exemptions in Article 13; letters (e) and (g)–(j) are not specific to the Defence Directive, they are also contained in the Utilities and Public Sector Directives. Thus Article 13 is not the location of the "defence and security-specific" exclusions. Secondly, based on the interpretation of the Guidance Note *Defence and Security-specific Exclusions* and the examples in Recital 27 discussed above, Article 13(a) is not defence-specific, as opposed to security-specific, since it is intended for non-military contracts.

Thirdly, a similar exemption is contained in Article 14 Public Sector Directive 2004/18/EC.[159] This provision has been discussed in the literature.[160]

---

[155] See also Guidance Note *Defence and Security-specific Exclusions, supra* note 7, at 5, point 9. Examples provided in Recital 27 Defence Directive are: "particularly sensitive purchases which require an extremely high level of confidentiality, such as, for example, certain purchases intended for border protection or combating terrorism or organised crime, purchases related to encryption or purchases intended specifically for covert activities or other equally sensitive activities carried out by police and security forces".

[156] Ibid.   [157] *Supra* note 7, at 5.

[158] Guidance Note *Defence and Security-specific Exclusions*, ibid., at 5, point 9.

[159] Art. 14 Public Sector Directive 2004/18/EC secret contracts and contracts requiring special security measures. See Trybus, *European Union Law and Defence Integration, supra* note 124, at 213–21 and especially 214–16. See also Art. 15(2) subpara. 2 Directive 2014/24/EU.

[160] Sue Arrowsmith, *The Law of Public and Utilities Procurement*, 2nd edn (London: Sweet & Maxwell, 2005) at 152; Trybus, *European Law and Defence Integration, supra* note 124, at 214–16.

The author argued previously that since Article 10 Public Sector Directive 2004/18/ EC (see Article 1(3) Directive 2014/24/EU) already excluded contracts covered by Article 346 TFEU as a whole, including Article 346(1)(a) TFEU, Article 14 Public Sector Directive 2004/18/EC must have another equivalent in the TFEU. This equivalent was identified as the public security exemptions from the Treaty discussed in chapter 2, most importantly Article 36 TFEU.[161] While Article 2 Defence Directive also refers to Article 346 TFEU, a similar connection of its Article 13(a) to the public security exemptions in the Treaty cannot be assumed. First, as explained above, the Guidance Note *Defence and Security-specific Exclusions* clearly describes the connection between Article 13(a) Defence Directive and Article 346(1)(a) TFEU. Secondly, in contrast to the Public Sector Directive, the Defence Directive contains a considerable number of specific provisions, relating, inter alia, to qualification and other stages of the procurement process discussed in chapter 8, which aim to address and accommodate the type of secrecy concern that can be addressed and accommodated in an Internal Market instrument. As with harmonising secondary Internal Market law in general, the Defence Directive aims to bridge the gap between Internal Market objectives and the legitimate concerns of the Member States regarding, inter alia, public security. Thus, in contrast to the Public Sector Directive, it is the aim of the Defence Directive to address "Article 36 TFEU" secrecy concerns inside the Directive. In other words, the intention of the legislator was to accommodate many of the relevant secrecy considerations in the substantive rules of the Defence Directive, thereby reducing the necessity of using Article 346(1)(a) TFEU. Article 13(a) is (only) needed in the Defence Directive for extreme cases in which even this specific Directive does not sufficiently accommodate security-of-information requirements.[162] Thus a specific exemption reflecting the secrecy dimension of public security exemptions such as Article 36 TFEU rather than Article 346(1)(a) TFEU would be against the purpose of the Defence Directive. Therefore Article 13(a) Defence Directive is not the equivalent to the first alternative of Article 14 Public Sector Directive 2004/18/EC but an exemption specific to the Defence Directive.

However, it is submitted that as Article 2 Defence Directive already refers to Article 346 TFEU as a whole, Article 13(a) Defence Directive is actually not necessary. The drafters of the Directive reported the inclusion of Article 13(a) is *also* a "gesture" to the Member States and to the "security community".[163] As the substance of the provision does not add any value and does not reduce the scope of the Directive it could be argued that it is *only* a gesture and from a legal perspective is superfluous and should be deleted.

---

[161] Trybus, *European Union Law and Defence Integration, supra* note 124, at 214–16.
[162] Case C-615/10, *Insinööritoimisto InsTiimi Oy* v. *Puolustusvoimat*, judgment of 7 June 2012, nyr.
[163] Schmitt and Spiegel, "The Specificities of the European Defence and Security Procurement Directive", *supra* note 127.

4.3.2.2 Intelligence activities   Exclusion (b) on "contracts for the purposes of intelligence activities" is connected to exclusion (a). Both letters (a) and (b) are addressed in the same Recital 27.[164] However, the secret nature of intelligence activities made it necessary in the opinion of the legislator to exclude them from the new Directive. The Guidance Note *Defence and Security-specific Exclusions* calls it "a tailor-made exclusion for a specific category of highly-sensitive contracts".[165] It is not unusual for intelligence activities to be contracted out, especially in the USA,[166] and it seems understandable that the very nature of these activities cannot easily be reconciled with the requirement of a Directive based on, inter alia, the principle of transparency, also encompassing publication requirements.[167] Intelligence activities were probably already excluded from the 2004 Public Sector Directive[168] by its Article 14. The express introduction of a specific exclusion in the Defence Directive, however, represents a welcome clarification.[169]

The exclusion covers contracts procured by intelligence services "for the purposes of their intelligence activities" as well as contracts of other contracting authorities to intelligence services for specific supplies, works or services.[170] The latter variation would cover the contract of a non-intelligence service to an intelligence service. This would not be covered by the in-house exemption

---

[164] Recital 27 reads: "In the fields of defence and security, some contracts are so sensitive that it would be inappropriate to apply this Directive, despite its specificity. That is the case for procurements provided by intelligence services, or procurements for all types of intelligence activities, including counter-intelligence activities, as defined by Member States. It is also the case for other particularly sensitive purchases which require an extremely high level of confidentiality, such as, for example, certain purchases intended for border protection or combating terrorism or organised crime, purchases related to encryption or purchases intended specifically for covert activities or other equally sensitive activities carried out by police and security forces."

[165] *Supra* note 7, at 5.

[166] See on this issue (in the USA) the contribution of S. Chesterman, "The Privatization of Intelligence", *EJIL Talk!* (2009), www.ejiltalk.org/privatization_of_intel/ [accessed 1 October 2013] with further references and the response of this author: www.ejiltalk.org/a-response-to-simon-chesterman-%E2%80%9Cwe-can%E2%80%99t-spy%E2%80%A6if-we-can%E2%80%99t-buy%E2%80%9D/ [accessed 1 October 2013]. When discussing an earlier draft of this chapter B. Heuninckx pointed out that paying informants is also a kind of services contract and that likewise, leasing spy-satellite time for intelligence/observation purposes is also an outsourcing very often applied in Europe (most such satellites are owned by a small number of States).

[167] Heuninckx, "Lurking at the Boundaries", *supra* note 13, at 112. The Guidance Note *Defence and Security-specific Exclusions*, *supra* note 7, at 5 puts this in the following words: "This provision is based on the assumption that contracts related to intelligence are by definition too sensitive to be awarded in a transparent and competitive procedure."

[168] Heuninckx, "Lurking at the Boundaries", *supra* note 13.   [169] Ibid., at 112.

[170] Guidance Note *Defence and Security-specific Exclusions*, *supra* note 7, at 5, the protection of government IT networks is given as an example.

discussed above, since that other contracting authority, which could be a regional government or a municipality, will normally not exercise any kind of control over the intelligence service and the latter would not be financially dependent on the former.[171] The intelligence service might then have to procure the goods, service or works from the private sector. Whether these purchases from the private sector would still be covered by Article 13(b) is not clear, since they would not procure "for the purposes of *their* intelligence activities [emphasis added]" but for the purposes of the other contracting authority. However, the Guidance Note *Defence and Security-specific Exclusions* highlighted the sensitive nature of "contracts related to intelligence", before also referring to these contracts of other contracting authorities. This suggests a wide interpretation of the exclusion bringing the purchases from the private sector by intelligence services resulting from contracts of other contracting authorities within its scope. Otherwise the sensitivity of these contracts would not be accommodated in the sense intended by the legislator. The inclusion of contracts of other contracting authorities to intelligence services would not make practical sense if the resulting purchases then had to be procured transparently on the basis of the Defence Directive.

Article 13(b) excludes "activities", not entire intelligence agencies or services.[172] The drafters of the Directive and Guidance Notes argued that there is a risk of vagueness when speaking of "services" rather than of "activities".[173] The definition of the notion is left to the Member States,[174] since there is no "single, commonly agreed definition of intelligence and the way intelligence activities are organised differs between Member States".[175] This leads to a relatively wide notion of intelligence activities, the personal scope of which includes the intelligence services, "no matter whether the service or agency concerned is in charge of a specific intelligence function (military, security, criminal or external intelligence) or specialised in the collection of information from certain sources", and other contracting authorities awarding contracts to intelligence services. Not all purchases of intelligence services are excluded by Article 13(b), only those related to "core tasks".[176]

---

[171]   However, this kind of control might occasionally be exercised by a regional government. The German States (*Länder*), for example, do have intelligence services (*Verfasungsschutz*) in addition to the intelligence services on the Federal level (*Bundesnachrichtendienst, Verfassungsschutz, Militärischer Abschirmdienst*).

[172]   K. Vierlich-Jürcke (European Commission), "Specificities of the Defence Procurement Directive" at the seminar "European Defence and Security Procurement" at the EIPA, Maastricht, 19 January 2012 (slide 15, on file).

[173]   Schmitt and Spiegel, "The Specificities of the European Defence and Security Procurement Directive", *supra* note 127.

[174]   Recital 27 of the Defence Directive.

[175]   Guidance Note *Defence and Security-specific Exclusions, supra* note 7, at 5.

[176]   Fruhmann and Liebmann, *Bundesvergabegesetz Verteidigung und Sicherheit 2012, supra* note 48, at 66.

As with all the exclusions discussed in this section of the chapter, there is a danger of abuse, especially but not only with respect to contracts of other contracting authorities to intelligence services. The Guidance Note *Defence and Security-specific Exclusions* issues its general warning by referring to the safeguard clause in Article 11 Defence Directive discussed in section 4.3.3 below and by reiterating the strict interpretation of the exclusion. This is elaborated as "the exclusion must be confined to contracts of the type described in the provision and cannot be applied by way of analogy".[177] However, this only refers to the principles of the interpretation of derogations and exclusions discussed in chapter 2 and 3; it does not add any substance.

4.3.2.3 Cooperative programmes   Exclusion (c) on "contracts awarded in the framework of a cooperative programme based on research and development [R&D], conducted jointly by at least two Member States for the development of a new product and, where applicable, the later phases of all or part of the life-cycle of this product" refers to the large collaborative programmes, such as the "Eurofighter/Typhoon" aircraft between two or more Member States which are a regular occurrence for the development of new equipment.[178]

First, as the "decisive criterion",[179] the programme must involve the development of a new product, which requires it to be based on R&D as defined in Article 1(27)[180] and explained in Recital 13 Defence Directive.[181] Off-the-shelf

---

[177] Guidance Note *Defence and Security-specific Exclusions, supra* note 7, at 6.

[178] Either through OCCAR, EDA or NATO's NSPA discussed in ch. 5 or by using the so-called "lead nation concept", examples: Jaguar (lead nation France), Bréguet Atlantique (lead nation France), BVRAAM/Meteor (lead national the United Kingdom), F-16 MNFP (lead nation USA), F-35 JSF/FJCA (lead nation USA). See the presentation by B. Heuninckx, "Collaborative Defence Procurement" at the seminar "European Defence and Security Procurement", European Institute of Public Administration (EIPA), Maastricht, 19 January 2012 (slide 12, on file).

[179] Guidance Note *Defence and Security-specific Exclusions, supra* note 7, at 6. The word "new" is the only word in the main text of the Guidance Note written both in bold and in italics.

[180] Art. 1(27) Defence Directive reads: "'Research and development' means all activities comprising fundamental research, applied research and experimental development, where the latter may include the realisation of technological demonstrators, i.e., devices that demonstrate the performance of a new concept or a new technology in a relevant or representative environment ..."

[181] Recital 13 Defence Directive reads: "For the purposes of this Directive, research and development should cover fundamental research, applied research and experimental development. Fundamental research consists in experimental or theoretical work undertaken mainly with a view to acquiring new knowledge regarding the underlying foundation of phenomena and observable facts, without any particular application or use in view. Applied research also consists of original work undertaken with a view to acquiring new knowledge. However, it is directed primarily towards a particular practical end or objective. Experimental development consists in work based on existing

procurement of existing products does not meet this requirement.[182] An R&D phase is required, although the words "where applicable" in Article 13(c) indicate that later phases of its life cycle may be included, naming production and maintenance as examples.[183] The exclusion will apply to contracts related to such later phases as long as they are awarded "in the framework of the cooperative programme".[184] Moreover, the exemption will apply to contracts of Member States who join an existing cooperative programme after the completion of the R&D phase for later phases of the life cycle of a product.[185] However, this requires that such Member States become "fully fledged" members of the programme, based on a formal agreement with the original Member States which implies the specific rights and obligations reserved for members of that programme. Moreover, the requirement for notifying the Commission, discussed below, applies to the "new" Member State.[186]

The programme has to include at least two Member States, although programmes with third-country participation are also covered by Article 13(c).[187] The Guidance Note *Defence and Security-specific Exclusions* implies, however, that in such a scenario with third-country cooperation, there still have to be at least two EU Member States in addition to the third country. This interpretation is also in line with the rationale of the exclusion which is to "acknowledge . . . the particular importance of cooperative programmes for the strengthening of Europe's military capabilities and the establishment of a truly European . . . Defence Technological and Industrial Base".[188] Moreover, the wording "at least two Member States" in the Directive is quite clear. The Guidance Note also emphasises that the terms "conducted jointly" and "cooperative programme" are interpreted as a requirement of a "genuine cooperative concept",[189]

knowledge obtained from research and/or practical experience with a view to initiating the manufacture of new materials, products or devices, establishing new processes, systems and services or considerably improving those that already exist. Experimental development may include the realisation of technological demonstrators, i.e. devices demonstrating the performance of a new concept or a new technology in a relevant or representative environment. Research and development does not include the making and qualification of pre-production prototypes, tools and industrial engineering, industrial design or manufacture."

[182] See ch. 1, at 50–1 for definitions.
[183] Ibid. and Schmitt and Spiegel, "The Specificities of the European Defence and Security Procurement Directive", *supra* note 127 (slide 12, on file); Spiegel, "Directive 2009/81/EC: Defence Specificities", *supra* note 42 (slide 11, on file).
[184] Guidance Note *Defence and Security-specific Exclusions*, *supra* note 7, at 7. However, the para. continues: "By contrast, a Member State which participates in the research and development phase but decides to make its purchases for the later phases of the programme separately (i.e. outside of the cooperative framework and via a national contracting authority) will have to apply the Directive for the award of these contracts."
[185] Ibid., at 8.   [186] Ibid.   [187] Ibid., at 7.   [188] Ibid., at 6.
[189] Ibid., at 7. The words "genuine cooperative concept" is one of the few underlined words and expressions in the Guidance Note.

excluding the mere procurement of equipment and requiring "in particular the proportional sharing of technical and financial risk and opportunities, participation in the management of and the decision-making on the programme".

The new nature of a product in question and the cooperative nature of a programme covered by the exclusion are subject to a specific control mechanism. Article 13(c) Defence Directive provides:

> Upon the conclusion of such a cooperative programme between Member States only, Member States shall indicate to the Commission the share of [R&D] expenditure relative to the overall cost of the programme, the cost-sharing agreement as well as the intended share of purchases per Member State, if any.

Thus the Commission must be informed by Member States of a cooperative programme at the very earliest stage, but this notification is unnecessary if one or several third countries are involved in the programme.[190] This information requirement did not feature in the initial drafts of the Defence Directive but was introduced by the European Parliament to allow verification that the exemption is not abused by Member States.[191] There is no detail on the type of information that needs to be provided to the Commission in the Directive, but the Guidance Note *Defence and Security-specific Exclusions* suggests that the provision implies that the information must prove that the programme concerns the development of a new product within the meaning discussed above, and that "the participation of Member States is more than just a symbolic contribution to a national programme".[192]

Three features of this control mechanism require some further comment: the very existence of such a requirement, the consequences of non-compliance with the requirement or of not meeting the conditions of Article 13(c) and the fact that programmes involving third countries are exempt. The existence of the requirement shows a concern of the legislator, most importantly the European Parliament, about the potential abuse of the exemption. The Commission is also concerned about abuse: as the Guidance Note *Defence and Security-specific Exclusions* puts it: "to ensure that the exclusion remains limited to genuinely cooperative programmes".[193] No comparable control mechanisms exist for the other exemptions. Thus there appears to be a concern that in particular this exemption could develop into a major loophole if not carefully policed. While it

---

[190] Ibid.
[191] B. Giles, "R&D in the Defence Directive", presentation at the "C5 Forum on EU Defence and Security Procurement", 18 November 2009 as cited by Heuninckx, "Lurking at the Boundaries", *supra* note 13, in his footnote 136.
[192] Guidance Note *Defence and Security-specific Exclusions*, *supra* note 7, at 7.
[193] Ibid.

remains unclear how the Commission would verify abuse since no minimum R&D amount is required in the exemption, the information requirement might well allow the detection of the most obvious cases of abuse.[194] The consequences of non-compliance or of not meeting the conditions of Article 13(c) Defence Directive are that the Member State in question would be in violation of its obligations under the Directive and could be subjected to enforcement action by the Commission under Article 258 TFEU. This could lead to a judgment of the ECJ and the information requirements could facilitate these actions as the Commission receives the necessary information. The fact that programmes involving third countries are exempt from the information requirement is also a reflection of the fact that the international agreements exemption in Article 12 Defence Directive discussed above already excludes such a programme[195] and, in contrast to Article 13(c) Defence Directive, the earlier exemption is not subject to an information requirement.

Article 13(c) Defence Directive also regulates the delimitation of activities between the EU Internal Market and the activities of the intergovernmental EDA and OCCAR[196] discussed in chapter 5. Especially the activities of the latter are mainly situated in the collaborative projects covered by this exemption. The exemption leaves these projects to frameworks outside the EU Internal Market[197] and is significant since it relates to the financially, strategically, militarily, industrially and politically most important large projects of crucial new high-technology equipment. Thus an important part of defence procurement is outside the Defence Directive. Moreover, it has been argued that the collaborative programmes exemption in Article 13(c) and the international agreements exemption in Article 12(a) Defence Directive will drive Member States to more collaborative procurement to avoid compliance with

---

[194] Heuninckx, "Lurking at the Boundaries", *supra* note 13, at 111.

[195] See also Heuninckx, ibid.

[196] On relevant activities of OCCAR see www.occar-ea.org/programmes [accessed 1 October 2013].

[197] See also Recital 28 Defence Directive: "Member States often conduct cooperative programmes to develop new defence equipment together. Such programmes are particularly important because they help to develop new technologies and bear the high research and development costs of complex weapon systems. Some of these programmes are managed by international organisations, namely the *Organisation conjointe de coopération en matière d'armement* (OCCAR) and NATO (via specific agencies), or by agencies of the Union, such as the European Defence Agency, which then award contracts on behalf of Member States. *This Directive should not apply to such contracts*. For other such cooperative programmes, contracts are awarded by contracting authorities/entities of one Member State also on behalf of one or more other Member States. In these cases too, this Directive should not apply [second emphasis added]." See also COM (2013) 542 final, at 10 highlighting again that the rules of the Defence Directive would not be "appropriate" for collaborative programmes.

the new Directive.[198] This is potentially problematic due to the complicated management of these programmes and the legal uncertainty into which most of them develop.[199] However, collaboration can increase the cost-effectiveness of defence programmes.[200] This was discussed in chapter 1.[201] Moreover, while not being part of the Internal Market, these projects have an alternative "European dimension" as joint endeavours of more than one Member State. R&D is also the subject of a situation that according to Article 28(2)(a) Defence Directive allows the use of the negotiated procedure without publication, as discussed in chapter 7.[202] It was initially not intended as an exemption but Member States were "quite insistent" on also including an exclusion.[203] Hence their inclusion would have been difficult and politically sensitive.[204] Article 28(2)(b) Defence Directive now only applies to services other than those subject to the exception in Article 13 Defence Directive. The negotiated procedure without prior publication of a contract note allows a maximum of flexibility and comes very close to exclusion. Moreover, the invention of an entirely new procedure or the adaptation of an existing one for these projects could have been considered, an issue to be discussed in chapter 7.[205] From an Internal Market point of view, the more radical approach of excluding the important collaborative programmes based on R&D is of doubtful necessity. The Article 28 Defence Directive route would have allowed keeping these programmes inside the Directive while at the same time allowing for the necessary flexibility. The United Kingdom Ministry of Defence, for example, has to follow the Defence Directive while the EDA and OCCAR do not. This might have to be revisited in a future revision of the Directive. However, it also needs to be considered whether exclusion represents a pragmatic approach, since inclusion would have required addressing a multitude of problems, such as the applicability of EU law to international

---

[198] J. Robinson, "To What Extent Will Contracts Remain outside the Defence Procurement Regime", presentation at the "C5 Forum on EU Defence & Security Procurement", 17 November 2009; B. Giles, "R&D in the Defence Directive" at the same event, 18 November 2009 as cited by Heuninckx, "Lurking at the Boundaries", *supra* note 13, in his footnote 133.

[199] Heuninckx, "Lurking at the Boundaries", *supra* note 13, at 111. In detail: B. Heuninckx, "A Primer to Collaborative Procurement in Europe: Troubles, Achievements and Prospects" (2008) 17 *Public Procurement Law Review* 123–45.

[200] Heuninckx, "Lurking at the Boundaries", *supra* note 13, at 111.   [201] At 53–4.

[202] At 345–6.

[203] Schmitt and Spiegel, "The Specificities of the European Defence and Security Procurement Directive", *supra* note 127.

[204] See on this topic Heuninckx, "A Primer on Collaborative Defence Procurement in Europe", *supra* note 199 and in great detail his 2011 doctoral (PhD) thesis at the University of Nottingham, "The Law of Collaborative Defence Procurement Through International Organisations in the European Union" (on file).

[205] At 351–6.

organisations.[206] OCCAR, for example, is a separate international organisation with a separate legal personality. Moreover, regulation in the Defence Directive might have met opposition of at least some Member States and have derailed or delayed the legislation as a whole.[207] Nevertheless, leaving these projects entirely without regulation is not satisfactory, because of the negative effects on the establishment of an Internal Market for defence goods in an important segment of the market. A Code of Conduct, possibly through the EDA, could be at least a temporary solution to start addressing this problem.

4.3.2.4 Contracts of forces deployed outside the territory of the Union   The exclusion in Article 13(d) on "contracts awarded in a third country, including for civil purchases, carried out when forces are deployed outside the territory of the Union where operational needs require them to be concluded with economic operators located in the area of operations" is a reflection of the peace-keeping dimension of defence policy, on a national basis, as part of the relatively new CSDP of the EU, or other frameworks such as NATO or the UN.[208] While this policy is clearly outside the scope of the EU Internal Market, the procurement of goods and services to carry them out are not. However, there are also various political, practical and military reasons to allow troops on peacekeeping or similar missions to procure some of their needs in the country where they are deployed. There might be, for example, major logistical problems in procuring goods and services "back home", possibly thousands of kilometers away. This exception accommodates these reasons and is intended for basic commodities such as water and food, which, however, might often be below the thresholds anyway.[209]

   The exemption is subject to a number of limitations which are elaborated in the Guidance Note *Defence and Security-specific Exclusions*. First, the personal scope of the exemption is limited. Although the specific operations in question may be "civil, military, or civil-military in nature", the forces in question must only be deployed on a temporary basis.[210] Moreover, the personal scope of the exemption is limited to forces that are actually already deployed,[211] not, for example, for forces waiting to be deployed or recently returned from such a deployment. Finally, that deployment has to be outside the EU.

---

[206] See the PhD thesis of Heuninckx, *supra* note 204, in great detail on these problems.

[207] Thanks to B. Heuninckx for bringing this point to my attention.

[208] Guidance Note *Defence and Security-specific Exclusions*, *supra* note 7 at 8: "tailor-made for crisis operations outside the EU"; Schmitt and Spiegel, "The Specificities of the European Defence and Security Procurement Directive", *supra* note 127: "it is tailor-made for crisis operations" (notes of the author, on file).

[209] Schmitt and Spiegel, "The Specificities of the European Defence and Security Procurement Directive", *supra* note 127 (notes of the author, on file). Moreover, if above the threshold, they would be subject to the Public Sector Directive, see below.

[210] Guidance Note *Defence and Security-specific Exclusions*, *supra* note 7, at 8.   [211] Ibid.

Secondly, the material scope of the exemption is limited. While the term "operational needs" is not defined in Article 13(d) or Recital 29 of the Directive,[212] according to the Guidance Note a narrow interpretation of the term is suggested by the use of the words "needs" and "require" in Article 13(d) and "imposed by" and "requirements" in Recital 29 of the Directive, which limits the material scope to "requirements arising out of the operation itself".[213] Only the conduct of the operation itself necessitates exemption from the requirements of the Defence Directive and purchases from local economic operators. Examples are provided in the Guidance Note:

> This can be the case, for example, when the award of contracts to EU suppliers would overstretch supply lines and imply disproportional transportation costs and delays, or when the involvement of EU suppliers would require additional security measures which weaken the military capabilities of the troops on the ground.[214]

Civil purchases are expressly included in the material scope of the exemption. In fact, the drafters of the Directive suggested that it is intended for basic commodities such as water and food,[215] which are civil rather than defence and security goods. Civil purchases are defined in Article 1(28) as "contracts not subject to Article 2 covering the procurement of non-military products, works and services for logistical purposes". A contract "not subject to Article 2" Defence Directive, which defines the material scope of the latter, is outside the Defence Directive. According to the Guidance Note, the notion "for logistical purposes" implies a limitation.[216] Again, all relevant purchases must be "directly connected to the conduct of [the relevant] operations".[217] Many of such purchases would be subject to Article 2 Defence Directive, especially letters (c) and (d) and therefore within the material scope of the Defence

---

[212] Recital 29 Defence Directive reads: "In the event that armed forces or security forces from Member States conduct operations beyond the borders of the Union, and when imposed by operational requirements, authorisation should be given to contracting authorities/entities deployed in the field of operations not to apply the rules of this Directive when they award contracts to economic operators located in the area of operations, including with respect to civilian purchases directly connected to the conduct of those operations."

[213] Guidance Note *Defence and Security-specific Exclusions, supra* note 7, at 9, para. 22.

[214] Ibid.

[215] Schmitt and Spiegel, "The Specificities of the European Defence and Security Procurement Directive", *supra* note 127 (notes of the author, on file).

[216] Guidance Note *Defence and Security-specific Exclusions, supra* note 7, at 8, para. 21. Examples are also provided: "storage, transport, distribution, maintenance and disposition of materiel; transport of personnel; acquisition or construction, maintenance, operation and disposition of facilities; acquisition or provision of services, medical and health service support; food and water supply, etc.".

[217] Recital 29 and Guidance Note *Defence and Security-specific Exclusions, supra* note 7, at 8, para. 21.

Directive. However, "purely civil purchases"[218] subject to the Public Sector Directive could be concerned as well. This inclusion of civil purchases in Article 13(d) Defence Directive effectively makes it an exception from both the Defence Directive and the Public Sector Directive.[219] Theoretically, in the unlikely event of an entity covered by the Utilities Directive being part of a force deployed outside the EU, the civil purchases of such a utility would also be exempt by Article 13(d) Defence Directive. Cleaning services for the British troops in Afghanistan, for example, would actually be covered by the Public Sector Directive but are exempt from it through Article 13(d) Defence Directive.[220] Heuninckx detected a contradiction in this inclusion of civil purchases in the material scope of the exemption and the scope of the Defence Directive which, as discussed above, is limited to defence and security goods and related services.[221] While he accepts that makes "a lot of practical sense", he also considers an exemption in one Directive which extends to another Directive without amending the latter as legally not entirely correct. Sampanis pointed out that this is rather a problem of lawmaking since one legal instrument can always be affected by another instrument of equal legal status.[222] This author concurs with this assessment. The Defence Directive is not a ministry of defence or armed forces Directive. Amendments to both the Public Sector Directive and the Defence Directive were required. An exemption similar to Article 13(d) Defence Directive was contained in Article 10 Public Sector Directive 2004/18/EC as amended by Article 71 Defence Directive, as discussed in section 4.5 below, and is now contained in Article 16(1)(b) of the new Public Sector Directive 2014/24/EU. These provisions exempted or exempt contracts excluded from the Defence Directive on the basis of, inter alia, Article 13 Defence Directive also from Directive 2014/24/EU. Thus these provisions also exempted or exempt the civil purchases of forces deployed outside the EU from the material scope of the old and new Public Sector Directives respectively.[223] However, an amendment of the Defence Directive is still needed: the words "including for civil purchases" should be deleted from the text of its Article 13(d).

The inclusion of civil purchases in the material scope of Article 13(d) Defence Directive might be less problematic in practice. As the drafters of the

---

[218] Ibid.   [219] Heuninckx, "Lurking at the Boundaries", *supra* note 13, at 112.
[220] See the similar example provided by Heuninckx, ibid.   [221] Heuninckx, ibid.
[222] When commenting on an earlier draft of this chapter.
[223] Such an exemption was also needed for the Utilities Directive to cover the unlikely event of the involvement of a utility. The Guidance Note *Defence and Security-specific Exclusions*, *supra* note 7, at 8, para. 20, for example, not only refers to contracting authorities but also to contracting entities, the latter term being normally used for utilities. Such an exemption existed in Art. 22(a) Utilities Directive 2004/17/EC as amended by Art. 70 Defence Directive and now exists in Art. 24(1)(b) Utilities Directive 2014/25/EU.

Directive suggested, many of the basic commodities the exclusion is intended for might often be below the thresholds anyway.[224] They would therefore already be outside the field of application of all three substantive procurement Directives.

The application in practice of Article 13(d) to the core subject of the Defence Directive, which is military and security equipment and related services, is doubtful. Even when deployed in operations outside the EU, most EU armed forces will use equipment purchased at home and then shipped or flown to the area of operations. The British forces deployed in Afghanistan at the time of writing, for example, will use their rifles, tanks, helicopters etc. procured by the Ministry of Defence back home in the United Kingdom, even if they were specifically procured for peacekeeping operations generally or for the Afghanistan mission in particular. Purchases of military equipment from the local Afghan market, even of ammunition, are unlikely.[225] Therefore it is submitted that in practice it is goods and services within the scope of the Public Sector Directive rather than the Defence Directive for which the exemption in Article 13(d) is most relevant. Consequently, this point supports the amendment of the Public Sector Directive which, as explained above, occurred in the new Directive 2014/24/EU.[226]

On the basis of the wording of the Directive, the contracts of forces deployed abroad exempt through Article 13(d) Defence Directive would still be subject to the basic requirements of the TFEU. However, it is submitted that due to the security-sensitive special situation Article 13(d) aims to accommodate and its strict personal, material and geographical limitations, contracts covered by Article 13(d) Defence Directive would regularly represent a proportionate use of the exemptions in Article 346(1)(b) or 36 TFEU and could therefore be taken outside the field of application of the Treaty as well.

Thirdly, the geographical scope of the exemption is limited. The term "area of operations" in which the relevant economic operators are located is defined

---

[224] Schmitt and Spiegel, "The Specificities of the European Defence and Security Procurement Directive", *supra* note 127 (notes of the author, on file).

[225] For military security reasons, political reasons and because there is no defence industrial capacity in Afghanistan.

[226] This appears to be subject to the ongoing (at time of writing) reform of the Public Sector Directive, see "Proposal for a Directive of the European Parliament and of the Council on Public Procurement" in the Presidency compromise/consolidated version 24 July 2013 at http://register.consilium.europa.eu/pdf/en/12/st12/st12878.en12.pdf [accessed 13 November 2013], Art. 14: "1. Subject to Article 346 of the Treaty on the Functioning of the European Union, this Directive shall apply to the awarding of public contracts and to design contests organised in the fields of defence and security, with the exception of the following contracts: (a) contracts falling within the scope of Directive 2009/81/EC; (b) *contracts to which Directive 2009/81/EC does not apply pursuant to Articles 8, 12 and 13 thereof* [emphasis added]."

in the Commission statement annexed to the minutes of the Council adopting the Defence Directive as

> for the purposes of this Directive, as being the third country(ies) in which a defence or security operation is being undertaken, together with those third countries in the surrounding geographic zone.[227]

This implies a geographical limitation, which is, however, to be understood as possibly being outside the country of deployment and even extending "beyond bordering countries, but should be limited to the geographical neighbourhood in order to limit the risk of abuse".[228] Overall, the motivation of the exemption to take account of the conditions of military and security operations will limit its geographical scope, which is also limited with respect to economic operators. The latter have to be "located in the area of operations". This does not prevent that operator being a subsidiary of a company situated in the EU or a third country. However, the Guidance Note *Defence and Security-specific Exclusions* warns that the contract awarded to a local subsidiary in the area of operations cannot be executed by its mother company outside that area as this would amount to a circumvention of the Directive prohibited by its Article 11 discussed below and would impact on the Internal Market.

As discussed in chapter 1, since the end of the Cold War the focus of military activities of the EU Member States has been shifting from traditional territorial defence to peacekeeping operations, also in the context of the CSDP. While these troops are deployed abroad, their operational needs make it necessary to award contracts to economic operators in the area of operations rather than in the EU. Thus exemption from the Defence Directive is the only viable option and has received a positive response.[229] Whether a large contract of British troops deployed in Afghanistan, for example, should be awarded to a local operator without any form of competitive and perhaps even transparent procedure is another question. However, this affects issues of value for money, probity and transparency in the Afghan (and perhaps Pakistani) market, outside the Internal Market.

4.3.2.5 Government-to-government contracts   The exclusion in Article 13(f) Defence Directive of "contracts awarded by a government to another government relating to: (i) the supply of military equipment or sensitive equipment, (ii) works and services directly linked to such equipment, or (iii) works and services specifically for military purposes, or sensitive works and sensitive services" refers to a common practice of the government of one country "procuring" military

---

[227] As cited in the Guidance Note *Defence and Security-specific Exclusions*, *supra* note 7, at 9, para. 23.
[228] Ibid.   [229] Heuninckx, "Lurking at the Boundaries", *supra* note 13, at 112.

supplies, works and services from another country's government.[230] Contracts between two governments are not public procurement, since they do not involve purchases from a private operator. They concern services which are provided by the selling government, goods which have already been procured by the latter or services linked to such goods. Therefore the exclusion is actually not necessary since these goods and services are outside the very notion of public procurement. This exclusion is related but different to the exemption of "in-house" contracts established by ECJ case law and discussed in section 4.1 above. In both exclusions there is no private sector economic operator. The latter concerns purchases within the same contracting authority or from entities over which it exercises a level of control comparable to the level of control it exercises over its own departments and which are financially dependent on it. This is quite different from Article 13(f) Defence Directive involving two governments which by definition are separate and do not exercise control over and are financially dependent on each other, at least never to the level required for the in-house exemptions.

According to the Guidance Note *Defence and Security-specific Exclusions*, the notion "government" is that defined in Article 1(9) Defence Directive discussed above.[231] This includes the national (central) governments of the Member States and third countries and "a regional or local government entity having its own legal personality".[232] However, the exemption does not apply to "[c]ontracts concluded by, or on behalf of, other contracting authorities/ entities, such as bodies governed by public law or public undertakings".[233] The "personal scope" of this exemption is therefore limited and excludes all utilities and bodies governed by public law. This is in line with an exemption addressing an already existing practice between governments with regards to defence and security contracts.

In contrast, the "material scope" of the exemption is rather wide. With regard to services contracts, a "broad range of very different purchases" is included.[234] As far as supply contracts are concerned, "the exemption is primarily intended for sales of equipment which is delivered from existing stocks, such as used

---

[230] The Public Sector Directive does generally apply to contracts awarded by one contracting authority to another contracting authority, unless the latter is controlled by the former and the latter is financially dependent on the earlier and the contract is therefore in-house, see especially C-107/98, *Teckal*, *supra* note 4. In detail: M. Comba and S. Treumer (eds.), *The In-House Providing in European Law* (Copenhagen: Djøf, 2010).

[231] Guidance Note *Defence and Security-specific Exclusions*, *supra* note 7, at 10, para. 25.

[232] Ibid.

[233] Guidance Note *Defence and Security-specific Exclusions*, *supra* note 7, at 10, para. 25.

[234] Ibid. provides an example: "The government of Member State A may, for example, decide for operational reasons to conclude a contract with the government of Member State B on the training of its pilots by the air force of Member State B. Such a service contract would be covered by the exemption."

equipment or stocks that are surplus to requirements".[235] Thus the exemption will apply to supplies purchased by one government for its own purposes which later prove to be an excess of requirements or no longer suitable for the purposes of the armed forces so that they can be sold. At the beginning of the legislative process, the exemption was intended to be limited to this surplus equipment. However, in its current wording it includes new items.[236] This is confirmed by the Guidance Note *Defence and Security-specific Exclusions*:

> However, the exemption is not restricted to such operations and applies to all contracts for the supply of military or sensitive equipment, including, in principle, even purchases of new material.

There is a danger of abuse when the selling government is purchasing from the private sector with the intention of selling to another government.[237] However, this danger is put into perspective in the Guidance Note *Defence and Security-specific Exclusions* which points out, with regard to the purchase of new material, that

> it should be borne in mind that the exclusion only covers the contract between the two governments, and not any related contracts concluded between the selling government and an economic operator. Therefore, if Member State A purchases new military equipment from the government of Member State B, the latter must ensure to procure the material in question in accordance with the contract award rules set out in Directive 2009/81/EC. It may do so by using framework agreements, for example, or options included in existing supply contracts awarded under the rules of the Directive.[238]

In other words, when a Member State government is buying from the private sector with the intention of selling the items to another Member State government, these new items need to be procured on the basis of the Defence Directive. It is submitted first, that the Article 13(f) exclusion actually includes two distinct "exemptions": a government-to-government surplus procurement exemption on the one hand and a government-to-government new equipment procurement exemption. The first "surplus exemption" is a classic exemption, since it simply excludes these purchases from the application of the Directive. However, since such an activity does not include a private operator it is, strictly speaking,

---

[235] Guidance Note *Defence and Security-specific Exclusions, supra* note 7, at 10, para. 26.

[236] Schmitt and Spiegel, "The Specificities of the European Defence and Security Procurement Directive", *supra* note 127 (notes of the author, on file).

[237] As Vierlich-Jürcke, "Specificities of the Defence Procurement Directive", *supra* note 172, emphasised: "[it] cannot be used to circumvent the directive" (slide 16, on file). The Commission also expressed its concern about the possible abuse of the government-to-government sales exemption recently in COM (2013) 542 final, at 10.

[238] Guidance Note *Defence and Security-specific Exclusions, supra* note 7, at 10, para. 26.

not public procurement anyway. It would therefore not require an express exemption from the Defence Directive. This would nevertheless require some clarification on what exactly is meant by surplus, especially on how long the equipment in question has been stored by the selling government. This would be crucial for the distinction between surplus and new equipment. New equipment "wrongly labelled" as surplus equipment could become a danger to the Internal Market and the objectives of the Defence Directive as it does not expressly have to be procured by the selling government on the basis of the Directive. Even the question of whether the equipment was procured before or after the deadline for the transposition of the Defence Directive could become an issue here, as equipment procured before the deadline is less likely to be procured on the basis of transparent and non-discriminatory procedures.

The second "new equipment exemption" is, strictly speaking, not a classic exemption either, since the original procurement of the equipment from the selling government still has to be conducted on the basis of the Defence Directive. It is only the purchase of the buying government from the selling government of equipment already procured on the basis of the Defence Directive which is exempt from the instrument. Thus there is neither a plus nor a minus in procurement based on the Directive, since the award of the original contract must adhere to the instrument. A problem may arise if, while in possession of the selling government, the value of the equipment in question rises above the thresholds, while during its procurement it was valued below the thresholds and therefore not procured on the basis of the Directive. It is submitted, in line with the general requirement to interpret exemptions narrowly and the understanding that equipment above the thresholds has to be procured on the basis of the Directive at some stage, that in such a case, where the original contract was below the thresholds and the "selling-on contract" is above the thresholds, the new equipment version of Article 13(f) Defence Directive cannot apply.

However, the above considerations apply only when both the selling and the buying government are EU Member States and the sale takes place within the Internal Market. An additional problem arises when the selling government is that of a country outside the EU. The Guidance Note *Defence and Security-specific Exclusions* addresses this issue as follows:

> If a Member State purchases new military equipment from the government of a third country, it must do so with due regard to its obligation under Article 11 not to use such contracts for the purpose of circumventing the provisions of the Directive. This is particularly relevant in situations where market conditions are such that competition within the Internal Market would be possible.[239]

---

[239] Ibid.

First, this refers to the general "safeguard clause" in Article 11 Defence Directive discussed under the next heading below, which prohibits the use of its exemptions to circumvent the instrument. Thus a warning is issued.

Secondly, it is submitted that sales of surplus equipment from the government of a third country to the government of an EU Member State is not the main problem. This is supported by the fact that this citation from the Guidance Note *Defence and Security-specific Exclusions* refers specifically to the purchase of new equipment. Thus it is sales of new equipment which is problematic. After all, it would be difficult if not impossible to require the government of a third country, such as the USA, Australia or Turkey, to have procured their new equipment to be sold to an EU Member State government on the basis of the Defence Directive, the way that a Member State government would be required in the same situation. In this context it is not entirely clear what the above citation in paragraph 26 of the Guidance Note on third-country government involvement contributes to the interpretation of Article 13(f) Defence Directive. It is submitted that it at least suggests a narrow interpretation of the exemption with respect to the purchase of new equipment from the government of a third country. This is supported by the safeguard clause in Article 11 Defence Directive discussed below, which is anyway only a confirmation of well-established case law of the ECJ on exemptions from Internal Market law.[240] If a Member State government can avoid the application of the Defence Directive, and the complications of including both Member State and third-country operators in a procurement procedure,[241] simply by purchasing from a third-country government, then Article 13(f) Defence Directive could develop into exactly the kind of loophole undermining the entire framework which the Court has never allowed. The Guidance Note also appears to require a primacy of the Internal Market, in other words procurement on the basis of the Defence Directive, over the government-to-government purchase from a third country. This does not necessarily exclude third-country operators, since the Directive neither requires nor prohibits opening a procurement contract to third countries.

However, two situations need to be differentiated. First, in practice there is equipment, such as missiles or spare parts for existing equipment, which may only be procured on a government-to-government basis, in particular the so-called Foreign Military Sales (FMS) from the US government which are required by US law. In these situations there is no alternative to the third-country equipment in the EU. Thus requiring government-to-government purchases of new items to be covered by the Directive would cut the supply

---

[240] On this case law see ch. 2 at 63–82 and ch. 3 at 104–25.   [241] To be discussed in ch. 7.

chain for these goods. Moreover, as pointed out above, including government-to-government procurement from a third country in the scope of the Defence Directive would oblige the supplying third-country government to comply with the Directive and that does not appear to be realistic or sensible. It is submitted that Article 13(f) is to be interpreted as clearly excluding the purchase of new equipment from a third-country government from the scope of the Directive when there is no alternative and therefore no competition for that equipment in the EU.

Secondly, however, the citation from paragraph 26 of Guidance Note *Defence and Security-specific Exclusions* could be interpreted as meaning that Article 13(f) Defence Directive cannot be used for purchases of new equipment when there are providers and therefore competition for that equipment in the EU and it could therefore be purchased on the basis of the Defence Directive *in the EU*. In other words, only when new equipment cannot be bought in the EU can that purchase from a third-country government be exempt through Article 13(f) Defence Directive. First, the reference to Article 11 Defence Directive contains a warning not to abuse the government-to-government exemption and this entails the risk of Commission enforcement through Article 258 TFEU or private litigation in national courts. Secondly, the objectives of Directive 2009/81/EC as a whole include competition and the free movement of goods and services in the Internal Market. Thirdly, and connected to the second point, exemptions in EU law, such as the government-to-government exemption, have to be interpreted narrowly. It would require a very wide interpretation of the government-to-government exemption, and considerable compromising of the competition and free movement objectives of the Directive, to allow a direct purchase for example from the US through a government-to-government contract when the product or service could be procured in the EU, when there is competition in the Internal Market. However, ultimately the interpretation of Article 13(f) Defence Directive as not being applicable to government-to-government purchases of a Member State from a third country when there is competition for the relevant piece of equipment in the EU is not entirely clear from the wording of the Directive and the Guidance Note *Defence and Security-specific Exclusions*. Clarification is needed.

The third variation of a third-country government buying from the government of an EU Member State is neither addressed in the Directive nor in the Guidance Note *Defence and Security-specific Exclusions*. This is surprising since this is common practice for defence exports to third countries. The interesting question impacting on the defence exports of such a Member State is whether it needs to follow the Defence Directive when purchasing new equipment from the private sector for such a government-to-government arrangement. In the context of the two constellations addressed in the Guidance Note, it emphasises that when the selling government is procuring the goods it later wants to sell to another government, it needs to follow the competitive rules of the Directive.[242] This indicates that this requirement might also apply to the "Member State government to third-country government" constellation. However, the case could be made that due to these purchases being intended for export, they are outside the Internal Market and the Directive. Nevertheless, this is not expressly addressed in the Directive or Guidance Note. Since this is unclear it might be advisable for the selling government to publish a contract award notice in the OJ to limit the remedy of ineffectiveness discussed in chapter 10[243] and point out that this is an Article 13(f) case.

The Public Sector Directives 2004/18/EC and 2014/24/EU do not contain an exemption comparable to Article 13(f) Defence Directive; neither do the Utilities Directives 2004/17/EC and 2014/25/EU, which do not involve "governments" anyway. Hence the government-to-government exemption is defence-specific, which is supported by Recital 30 of the Defence Directive:

> Given the specificity of the defence and security sector, purchases of equipment as well as works and services by one government from another should be excluded from the scope of this Directive.
>
> [emphasis added]

It is submitted that the mere reference to the specificity of the defence sector is a weak argument for the exclusion of government-to-government contracts. This exclusion is acceptable for surplus equipment, since this is a special feature of the defence sector. "Exclusion" is also acceptable with respect to the sale of new equipment from one EU Member State government to another, since the original procurement needs to be conducted on the basis of the Directive and the requirements of the Internal Market are thus satisfied. However, the exclusion of the sale of new equipment from a third-country government to an EU Member State government or vice-versa cannot simply be justified by the "specificity" of the defence sector. After all, the same argument could also justify the offsets discussed in chapter 9 or generally the absence of an Internal Market for defence goods in practice, discussed in Part I of this book. Moreover, the latter might at least be justified by more pronounced national security and secrecy needs. At the beginning of the legislative process the exemption was to be limited to surplus items, excluding new equipment.[244] Moreover, the

---

[242] Guidance Note *Defence and Security-specific Exclusions*, *supra* note 7, at 10, at para. 26: "it should be borne in mind that the exclusion only covers the contract between the two governments, and not any related contracts concluded between the selling government and an economic operator. Therefore, if Member State A purchases new military equipment from the government of Member State B, the latter must ensure to procure the material in question in accordance with the contract award rules set out in Directive 2009/81/EC."

[243] At 477–81.

[244] Schmitt and Spiegel, "The Specificities of the European Defence and Security Procurement Directive", *supra* note 127 (notes of the author, on file).

Guidance Note *Defence and Security-specific Exclusions* explains that it is "primarily intended for sales of equipment which is delivered from existing stocks".[245] On the other hand, as discussed above, the exclusion of third-country government-to-government purchases of new items takes account of the reality of defence trade; these purchases are often only possible through the third-country government. The exclusion of a government-to-government purchase from a third country when there is competition in the Internal Market for the product in question is less convincing. The practice over the next few years will show if the inclusion of new equipment from third countries will develop into the loophole it has the potential to be. This will have to be closely observed. If this proves to be the case, the Commission would have a strong argument to propose a change of the text of the Directive, by adding the words "delivered from existing stocks" to Article 13(f) "(i) the supply of military equipment or sensitive equipment" or to expressly exclude government-to-government purchase from a third country when there is competition in the Internal Market for the product in question from the scope of Article 13(f). Alternatively they could change the wording of the Guidance Notes.[246]

4.3.2.6 Contracts for R&D services   Article 13(j) Defence Directive on "[R&D] services other than those where the benefits accrue exclusively to the contracting authority/entity for its use in the conduct of its own affairs, on condition that the service provided is wholly remunerated by the contracting authority/entity" is, strictly speaking, not a defence and security-specific exclusion. According to the Guidance Note *R&D*, its "(somewhat unwieldy) wording" is "almost identical" to Article 16(f) Public Sector Directive 2004/18/EC.[247] However, as with the definition of R&D in its Article 1(5), the Defence Directive provides more detail; it could be argued that legal certainty is increased in comparison to the old Public Sector Directive.[248] As explained in chapter 1, R&D is of particular importance in the defence and also security sectors and the exclusion is part of Article 13, it shall be discussed in this context. A number of limitations apply to the exclusion. First, it applies only to service contracts.[249] This would not

---

[245] Guidance Note *Defence and Security-specific Exclusions, supra* note 7, at 10, para. 26.

[246] For example by changing Guidance Note *Defence and Security-specific Exclusions, supra* note 7, at 10, para. 26, from "primarily intended for sales which is delivered from existing stocks" to "exclusively intended . . .".

[247] http://ec.europa.eu/internal_market/publicprocurement/docs/defence/guide-research_ en.pdf [accessed 2 October 2013], at 3.

[248] P. Le Louarn, "Perspective on the Implementation of the New Procurement Rules", presentation at the "C5 Forum on EU Defence & Security Procurement", 19 November 2009, as cited by Heuninckx, "Lurking at the Boundaries", *supra* note 13, footnote 149.

[249] Guidance Note *R&D, supra* note 247, at 4.

include a research-related supply contract,[250] which might be awarded on the basis of the negotiated procedure without prior publication of a contract notice if the requirements on Article 28(2)(b) Defence Directive are met, as will be explained in chapter 7.[251] Secondly, the exclusion applies only to activities co-financed by both the contracting entity and the contractor, not to services funded by and benefiting the contracting entity only.[252] In the latter case, however, the contract might be awarded on the basis of the negotiated procedure without prior publication of a contract notice, as will be discussed in chapter 7.

There is concern, especially in industrial circles, that the R&D phase of a defence procurement project would be detached and separated from the production phase, with the earlier being awarded outside the scope of the Defence Directive and the latter on the basis of the Directive. This is feared to lead to a reduction of both efficiency and the amount of defence R&D investment.[253] It is clear that the exclusion of R&D services on the basis of Article 13(f) cannot be extended to the production phase following this R&D. Heuninckx argues that these concerns are at least partially unfounded. Either, in order to ensure best value for money, contracts including both R&D and production phases should be awarded as one contract on the basis of the Defence Directive,[254] or, if the production phase was detached from the R&D phase and put out to tender, the contract would be awarded either to the contractor of the R&D contract or to another tenderer offering an economically more advantageous product.[255] The defence industries understandably fear "losing" the production phase after the R&D phase. However, the fear of tenderers not being awarded a contract is a necessary component of competition to meet its value-for-money objectives: namely, increasing quality and moving prices down. Good procurement

---

[250] The Guidance Note *R&D*, ibid., provides some guidance on differentiating a research-services contract from a research-related supply contract, at 4: "According to Article 1 (5) of the Directive, '*a contract having as its object both products and services shall be considered to be a "service contract" if the value of the services in question exceeds that of the products covered by the contract'*. If, on the other hand, the value of the products (e.g. a demonstrator) exceeds that of the research services, the contract has to be considered as a supplies contract. The value of the products and services thus determines the nature of the contract, and the choice of the rules to be applied." Moreover, in footnote 4 the Guidance Note adds: "Unlike in the case of a mixed contract for both works and services, in the present case the determination is based solely on a comparison of the respected values of products and services; it does not depend on an objective analysis of the main purpose of the contract. See judgments of 11 May 2006 in Case C-340/04 Carbotermo, paragraph 31, and of 1 July 1999 in Case C-107/98 Teckal, paragraph 38."

[251] At 345–6.   [252] See Recital 34 Defence Directive.

[253] P. Braghini, "To What Extent Will Contracts Remain outside the Defence Procurement Regime" and B. Giles, "R&D in the Defence Directive", presentations at the "C5 Forum on EU Defence & Security Procurement", on 17 and 18 November 2009 respectively, as cited by Heuninckx, "Lurking at the Boundaries", *supra* note 13, footnote 150.

[254] Heuninckx, "Lurking at the Boundaries", *supra* note 13 at 113.   [255] Ibid., at 113.

legislation embraces and facilitates this fear; it is, prima facie, not a problem but desirable for the taxpayer and the military or other end-user of the product.[256]

However, it is submitted that this fear of the defence industries may become a problem when the fear described above reaches a level at which it reduces competition for a detached R&D phase contract[257] or even leaves the contracting entity without any partner in the market. However, if such a scenario is likely, the R&D phase should not be decoupled and taken outside the Directive on the basis of the exclusion in Article 13(f). In such a case the R&D as well as the production phases of the contract should be awarded as *one* contract on the basis of the Directive. In the extreme case that such an "undetached" contract would not generate any interest on the market, equally extreme measures are available. The first possible measure would be to open such a contract to third-country competition. The second and arguably very extreme measure would be to research, develop and produce the product through an "in-house" capacity, outside the field of application of the Directive as explained in section 3.1 above. However, these more extreme measures might not even be necessary as the Defence Directive offers other possibilities. First, it contains more exclusions, for example the collaborative programmes exclusion which will apply to many programmes with a R&D phase. Secondly, the use of less competitive procedures, most notably the negotiated procedure without prior publication of a contract notice discussed in chapter 7, could be used in many of these cases. All these possibilities of flexibility provided in the Defence Directive, it is argued, will not make it necessary to pull the emergency brakes of Articles 346 or 36 or 52 TFEU and thus allow conducting the procurement inside the Directive and the TFEU.

4.3.3 Article 11 Defence Directive: the safeguard clause?

Article 11 Defence Directive contains a provision which the Guidance Notes describe as a "general safeguard clause":[258]

> None of the rules, procedures, programmes, agreements, arrangements or contracts referred to in this section may be used for the purpose of circumventing the provisions of this Directive.

Neither the Public Sector Directive, the Utilities Directive nor the initial Draft of the Defence Directive contain such a clause. This raises the question of the precise function and motivation of this provision. The Guidance Note *Defence and Security-specific Exclusions* describes Article 11 as

---

[256] Ibid.

[257] Which might still be awarded on the basis of a competitive procedure *not* based on the Defence Directive.

[258] See Guidance Note *R&D*, *supra* note 247, at 4, point 12 and Guidance Note *Security of Information*, http://ec.europa.eu/internal_market/publicprocurement/docs/defence/guide-soi_en.pdf [accessed 2 October 2013], at 11, point 26.

an explicit reminder of the ECJ case law prohibiting the use of legal structures that are exempt from EU public procurement rules with the principal aim of avoiding transparent and competitive contract award procedures without objective reasons.[259]

It continues to emphasise that such exceptions must be strictly interpreted:

> This means that exclusions from the scope of the Directive provided under Articles 12 and 13 must be confined to contracts of the type described in these provisions.[260]

Contracting authorities bear the burden of proof that the contract is subject to one of the stipulated exclusions.[261] On the basis of these explanations in the Guidance Notes it can be said that Article 11 Defence Directive has merely a declaratory effect. It does not add any substance to the legal framework. This might be the reason why some Member States, for example the United Kingdom,[262] Ireland[263] or Germany,[264] have not transposed Article 11 Defence Directive. Austria transposed the provision.[265] Strict interpretation, safeguarding against avoiding the framework and closing loopholes are long-established principles for the use and interpretation of exceptions in EU Internal Market law, as was discussed in chapters 2 and 3. However, Article 11 may still serve a useful function as a warning to contracting officers to abuse

---

[259] Guidance Note *Defence and Security-specific Exclusions, supra* note 7, at 1, point 2, para. 1 citing judgment of 9 June 2009 in Case C-480/06, *Commission* v. *Germany*, para. 48. On this logic, if the agreement etc., exempt from EU procurement rules do apply transparent and competitive contract award procedures, and those procedures are used on the basis of objective reasons, they will prima facie be compatible with EU law.

[260] Guidance Note *Defence and Security-specific Exclusions, supra* note 7, at 1, point 2, para. 2; Guidance Note *Security of Information, supra* note 258, at 11, point 26, and Guidance Note *R&D, supra* note 247, at 4, para. 12, all citing judgment of 13 December 2007 in Case C-337/06, *Bayerischer Rundfunk*, para. 64.

[261] Guidance Note *Defence and Security-specific Exclusions, supra* note 7, at 1, point 2. The Guidance Note at 1-2, point 2, para. 3 also encourages contracting authorities/entities intending to rely on one of the exceptions, thereby possibly awarding the contract without advertising (at least in the OJ of the EU), to consider publishing a voluntary *ex ante* notice under Arts. 60(4) and 64 of the Directive. By publishing such a notice, the contracting authority/entity formally announces and justifies its decision to award a contract without prior publication of a contract notice in the OJEU. If the contracting authority/entity has published such an *ex ante* notice and observed a standstill period of 10 days following its publication, the contract cannot be considered ineffective by application of Art. 6(1) of the Directive. This will be discussed further in ch. 10 at 477–81. Importantly, it must be observed that the exercise of such an option would be at the discretion of the contracting authority/entity. The contracting authority/entity will have to weigh up in advance the likelihood that the contract would otherwise be deemed ineffective under Art. 60(1) were it not to publish a voluntary *ex ante* notice.

[262] See Regulation 7 DSPCR.   [263] Regulation 9 ACRDSR.   [264] § 100(c) GWB.

[265] § 2(3) BVergGVS.

the set of exclusions as loopholes. This might be necessary considering that the list of exceptions is longer than in the Public Sector and Utilities Directives. Moreover, while Article 11 itself does not cover the exceptions in the TFEU, which will be discussed under the next heading below, the same case law-based principles apply to them.

Article 11 is not entirely clear. What exactly is meant by "used" for the purpose of "circumventing" the provisions of the Directive? Butler assumes that this omission may be indicative of a general uncertainty about the precise relationship between the international obligations and the EU law obligations of the Member States in the field of defence procurement, instead opting for a general declaratory statement designed to warn against rather than regulate potential conflicts.[266]

4.4 The Defence Directive and the TFEU

Article 2 Defence Directive contains what could be described as exclusions limiting the scope of the Directive as it is subject to Articles 36, 51, 52, 62 and 346 TFEU. This was explained above. Member States can derogate from the new instrument for reasons of national and public security. The Directive thus integrates these Treaty exclusions into the Directive.[267] The interpretation of Articles 36, 51, 52 and 62 TFEU was discussed in detail in chapter 2[268] and the interpretation of Article 346 TFEU was discussed in chapter 3.[269]

The difference from the pre-2009/81/EC situation is that now there is a Defence Directive specifically designed to take the public and national security concerns of the Member States into account. This taking into account of these concerns is done by adapting the procurement procedures discussed in chapter 7; the qualification, selection and award criteria discussed in chapter 8; the review and remedies system discussed in chapter 10; and by introducing the subcontracting regime discussed in chapter 9. These adaptations are intended to significantly reduce the necessity for Member States to use the Treaty security exemptions to exceptional circumstances. The exemptions from the Directive discussed in sections 3.1 and 3.2 above have a different objective since, by definition, they do not aim to keep the relevant contracts inside the instrument; on the contrary, they categorically exclude these contracts.

---

[266] Luke Butler, "Public Contract Law as a Barrier to and an Instrument for Transatlantic Trade Liberalisation", Thesis, University of Birmingham (2013), ch. 3. The Guidance Note *Field of Application, supra* note 5, at 1 specifically refers to the obligation of EU Member States under Art. 4(3) TEU to ensure that "Member States may not assume obligations under international law that might affect EU rules or alter their scope." This suggests that it is likely that Art. 11 is designed to reinforce this obligation. However, it may be questioned why this obligation is not rendered explicit in Art. 11 itself.

[267] See the Commission Guidance Note *Field of Application, supra* note 5, at 1.

[268] At 63–82.   [269] At 104–25.

Moreover, in contrast to the Treaty derogations, the exemptions from the Directive do not allow proportionate derogation on a case-by-case basis like the Treaty exemptions but are categorical and absolute. Thus while both the Treaty security derogations and the exclusions from the Defence Directive are exemptions that can lead to the same result, taking a contract outside the scope of the Directive, they operate differently in practice. Moreover, while in the context of the former the ECJ will rule on the interpretation of the derogation and on whether it could be invoked in a particular case, scrutiny in the context of the exemptions from the Directive will be limited to its interpretation; there is no room for a proportionality test. An exemption to this categorical nature of the exclusions of the Defence Directive is the secrecy exclusion in its Article 13(a) since, as explained above, it is based on the derogations in Article 36 and 346(1)(a) TFEU and therefore shares the nature of the latter: a proportionality test is to be applied.[270] However, apart from Article 13(a), it might be helpful to speak about different notions of exemption: of "exclusions" as far as Articles 12 and 13(b)–(j) Defence Directive and "derogations" as far as Articles 36, 51, 52, 62 and 346 TFEU (Article 2 Defence Directive) are concerned.

If the derogations referred to in Article 2 Defence Directive apply in an individual case, they will allow derogation from the Directive and the TFEU. In contrast, the exclusions in Articles 12 and 13 Defence Directive do not lead to derogation from the Treaty. The Treaty derogations still have to be decided on a case-by-case basis. This is important since if the TFEU still applies, its principles of non-discrimination and transparency would have to be respected in the procurement procedure. However, a contract subject to the secrecy exemption in Article 13(a) and the intelligence services exemption in Article 13(b) Defence Directive will normally allow derogation on the basis of Article 346(1)(a), 36 or 52(1) TFEU. Contracts of forces deployed outside the territory of the Union subject to Article 13(d) could allow derogation under any of the derogations including Article 346(1)(b) TFEU. Contracts subject to the cooperative programmes exception in Article 13(c) and the government-to-government exemption in Article 13(f) Defence Directive with respect to new equipment are more likely to be still covered by the TFEU. However, derogation from the Treaty is not automatic in case one of the categorical exclusions from the Defence Directive applies, since the earlier still depend on proportionality to be assessed on a case-by-case basis. As pointed out by Arrowsmith with respect to the application of the exclusions of the old Public Sector Directive, they do not allow derogation from EU primary law to the same extent as the Treaty derogations.[271] What is crucial is that, in comparison to the difficult derogations of the TFEU, the categorical exclusions of the Defence Directive provide a "user-friendly" or "easy" way to avoid the application of the Directive. This is

---

[270] I benefited from discussions with Georgios Sampanis on this point.
[271] Arrowsmith, *The Law of Public and Utilities Procurement*, *supra* note 160, at para. 9.94.

in line with the overall approach and objective of the Defence Directive which is to limit the use of the primary security derogation and especially Article 346(1)(b) TFEU – which through its Article 2 are also part of the Directive – in practice. Apart from the adaptations to be discussed in the following four chapters, the provision of the secondary exclusions makes it unnecessary to use the more difficult Treaty derogations in cases covered by the exclusions of the Defence Directive.

4.5 The Defence Directive and the Public Sector Directive

With the exception of contracts subject to the exemptions in the TFEU and the Public Sector Directive and below its thresholds, the Defence Directive now applies to many contracts to which previously the Public Sector Directive applied. The same can be said to a more limited extent about the Utilities Directive, which will be discussed under the next heading below. The relationship between the Public Sector Directive[272] and the Defence Directive is regulated in Article 10 Public Sector Directive 2004/18/EC (Article 15 Directive 2014/24/EU), which was amended by Article 71 Defence Directive and read as follows:

> Article 10
> **Contracts in the fields of defence and security**
> Subject to Article [346] of the Treaty, this Directive shall apply to public contracts awarded in the fields of defence and security, with the exception of contracts to which Directive 2009/81/EC of the European Parliament and of the Council of 13 July 2009 on the coordination of procedures for the award of certain works contracts, supply contracts and service contracts by contracting authorities or entities in the fields of defence and security . . . applies.
> This Directive shall not apply to contracts to which Directive 2009/81/EC does not apply pursuant to Articles 8, 12 and 13 thereof.

This provision clarifies that the Defence Directive is *lex specialis* to the Public Sector Directive for defence procurement authorities. It is, however, also *lex specialis* for all other contracting authorities. The notion of "public contracts awarded in the fields of defence and security" in Articles 10 Directive 2004/18/ EC and 15 Directive 2014/24/EU differs from the notion of "public contracts awarded by contracting authorities in the field of defence" in the previous version. It is submitted that this is a consequence of the fact that, as discussed above, the personal scope of the Defence Directive goes beyond "contracting authorities in the field of defence". Thus despite its wording which suggests a wider meaning, the notion "public contracts awarded in the fields of defence

---

[272] Before the amendment Art. 10 Public Sector Directive 2004/18/EC read: "Defence procurement. This Directive shall apply to public contracts awarded by contracting authorities in the field of defence, subject to Article [346] of the Treaty." Art. 15 of the new Directive is differently organised and slightly different in wording but does not differ from Art. 10 of the old Directive in substance.

and security" is based on the personal scope of the Defence Directive. In addition to the defence procurement authorities of the Member States also previously subject to Article 10 Public Sector Directive 2004/18/EC, this personal scope includes the other security authorities, such as police, prisons or border guards. Through its Article 10 these entities are still subject to the old and new Public Sector Directive for contracts not covered by the material scope of the Defence Directive, subject to the exemptions and thresholds of the old and new Public Sector Directive.

Subject to exemptions and thresholds, contracts now within the scope of the Defence Directive used to be covered by the old Public Sector Directive. The amended Article 10 of the latter is a consequence of the transfer from the latter to the former. As discussed in chapter 1,[273] it was to a large extent the perceived unsuitability of the old Public Sector Directive for defence and security contracts, also expressed during the consultation process, which led to the adoption of the Defence Directive. However, regulating the relationship between the Defence Directive and the Public Sector Directive is not the only function of Article 10. The provision also clarifies that contracts not covered by the Defence Directive, above the thresholds of the Public Sector Directive, and not subject to one of its exemptions, are still subject to the latter.[274] This means that ministries of defence and other relevant authorities still have to apply the national legislation transposing the Public Sector Directive for relevant contracts. It would apply, for example, for the purchase of food, medical equipment or uniforms, cleaning services or to the construction of a new ministry of defence building. This is another important dimension of the fact that the Defence Directive is not a "ministries of defence Directive"; these authorities are still subject to other EU rules. In view of clarity this is perhaps not an ideal situation. However, 2004/18/EC (2014/24/EU) and 2009/81/EC are only Directives, instruments of indirect legislation that require national transposition. Therefore the Member States were free to address the possible lack of clarity by introducing a "ministry of defence code" which complies with both Directives and the Treaty while at the same time ensuring the compliance of their other relevant legislation. However, this does not appear to be a transposition approach used very often. Neither Austria, Germany, Ireland nor the United Kingdom introduced such an instrument.

The second paragraph of Article 10 Public Sector Directive 2004/18/EC (Article 15 Directive 2014/24/EU) – according to which it shall not apply to contracts to which the Defence Directive does not apply pursuant to its exemptions Articles 8, 12 and 13 – makes the Defence Directive thresholds and exclusions discussed

---

[273] At 12–13.

[274] See the Commission's Guidance Note *Field of Application*, *supra* note 5, at 1: "Contracts awarded by contracting authorities and entities in these [defence and security] fields which are not covered by [the Defence Directive] will in principle continue to be subject to [the Utilities Directive] and [the Public Sector Directive]." See also Heuninckx, "Lurking at the Boundaries", *supra* note 13, at 95.

above equally applicable to relevant contracts that have to be awarded on the basis of the Public Sector Directive.[275] With regards to Article 8 Defence Directive, this means that the higher thresholds of the Defence Directive also apply to a "civil" contract awarded "in the field of defence and security". The motive of this adaptation of the scope of the Public Sector Directive is not clear. With regards to Article 12 Defence Directive, there is no difference, since, as discussed above, this provision largely corresponds to Article 15 Public Sector Directive 2004/18/EC. The same can be said about the exclusions in Article 13(e) and (g)–(j), which are not specific to the Defence Directive. With regards to the exclusions in Article 13(a)–(d) and (f), which are specific to the Defence Directive, the amended Article 10 Public Sector Directive 2004/18/EC, now Article 16 Directive 2014/24/EU, may make a difference. However, this ultimately concerns the scope of the Public Sector Directive and not of the Defence Directive, which is the subject of this book.

4.6 The Defence Directive and the Utilities Directive

The at least in part slightly unusual and perhaps surprising inclusion of utilities in the personal scope of the Defence Directive discussed above led to a new Article 22(a) in the Utilities Directive 2004/17/EC (Article 24 Directive 2014/25/EU), introduced by Article 70 of the Defence Directive:

> Article 22a
> **Contracts in the fields of defence and security**
> This Directive shall not apply to contracts to which [the Defence Directive] applies, nor to contracts to which that Directive does not apply pursuant to Articles 8, 12 and 13 thereof.

Since the Defence Directive now applies to some contracts before its introduction subject to the Utilities Directive, the latter now needs a provision similar to Article 10 Public Sector Directive 2004/18/EC. The discussion regarding Articles 8, 12 and 13 of the Defence Directive under the previous heading above equally applies to Article 22(a) Utilities Directive 2004/17/EC.

5 Transposition

The Member States investigated in this book have all implemented the rules on scope and coverage of the Defence Directive: Austria in §§ 1–2 and 4–9 BVergGVS; Ireland in Regulations 4–6 and 8–9 (ACRDSR); and the United Kingdom in Regulations 4 and 6–7 DSPCR. In Germany § 100(c) was added to the GWB to transpose some of the defence-specific exclusions discussed above in section 4.3.2, while the other exemptions had already been transposed in § 100 GWB to comply with the 2004 Public Sector Directive or were inserted

---

[275] See also Heuninckx, ibid.

into that provision to transpose the Defence Directive. The substance of these national laws does not differ from Article 12 and 13 Defence Directive. However, this was to be expected. As discussed in section 4.5 above, the Defence Directive, which provides the relevant contracting entities with desirable flexibility, is *lex specialis* to the Public Sector Directive, which is less flexible. Thus national legislators were neither able nor willing to deviate from the precise scope of the Defence Directive when transposing it.

6 Conclusions

The Defence Directive applies to a considerable part but not all of the defence and security procurement of the Member States. On the one hand it applies not only to armaments, but also to related services, security works and services. Moreover, it applies not only to ministries of defence but to any public body or utility procuring relevant goods, services or works. On the other hand, a large part of these goods, services and works are outside the scope of the instrument. First, while the overall aim of the Defence Directive is to limit the use of Article 346 and the public security exemptions in the TFEU, these remain in force and can be invoked to take contracts outside the Directive and the Internal Market on a case-by-case basis. Secondly, a set of value thresholds excludes a number of contracts that should not be underestimated, without any need of justification as far as the Directive is concerned. Thirdly, a long list of exclusions exempt a significant part of the European armaments market from the scope of the Defence Directive.[276] The exemption of large collaborative projects in particular represents a significant limitation. The ministries of defence can abandon their habit of "jumping straight on Article 346 TFEU" without looking at all the other exclusions.[277] This is intended as it is in line with reducing the use of the Article 346 TFEU. However, the share of defence contracts actually subject to the Defence Directive might be only around 10 per cent[278] and the more significant impact of the new instrument might be felt in security markets rather than in

---

[276] Heuninckx, "Trick or Treat?" *supra* note 99, at 13: "the exemptions from applicability of the Directive are many"; "Lurking at the Boundaries", *supra* note 13, at 110: "The Defence and Security Directive also lists a fairly large number of specific exemptions." See also: Briggs, "The New Defence Procurement Directive", *supra* note 67, NA132–3.

[277] As reported in the presentation of M. Walter (EADS-HQ), "Auswirkungen des 'Defence Package' aus Bietersicht" at the conference "Vergabe von Leistungen im Verteidigungs- und Sicherheitsbereich", of the Forum Vergabe e.V., the University of the German Federal Armed Forces Munich, and the Kanzlei (law firm) Orth Kluth Rechtsanwälte, 15 February 2012, in Munich (notes of the author, on file).

[278] This would still be contracts worth €8–9 billion per year. Based on the 26 Member States participating in EDA the 2012 figures indicate a figure of €86 billion for procurement and research and development, including €9 billion for the latter, and including 22–3% of the overall €194 spent on operations and maintenance, see www.eda.europa.eu/News/12-01-25/EU_and_US_government_Defence_spending [accessed 4 October 2013].

defence procurement.[279] This might have been the price to overcome the opposition of the defence establishments of Member States with reservations against the Defence Directive as well as of EDA and OCCAR. However, scope will have to be discussed in the context of a possible revision of the new Directive. This should include an Annex to the Defence Directive listing relevant contracting authorities, taking utilities out of the scope of the Defence Directive, the deletion of redundant exclusions such as Article 12(b) and a re-evaluation of the exclusion of cooperative programmes involving R&D in Article 13(c) and the inclusion of new products in the government-to-government exclusion in Article 13(f).

The comparison with the Public Sector Directive reveals that the rules on the material scope of the Defence Directive, especially the defence-specific exemptions but also the adaptation of the other exemptions, have been adapted to take defence and security into account. The scope was adapted through its limitation.

---

[279] See the figures of Kiltie (2012), *supra* note 100 (slide 34, on file) for the United Kingdom. The police, border agencies or utilities such as airports will be able to take advantage of the thresholds but not of many of the exclusions. This might well make the Defence Directive more important to them than to the ministries of defence.

7

Security through flexibility

The procurement procedures of the Defence Directive

1 Introduction

After the discussion of the scope of application of the Defence Directive provided in chapter 6, the actual legal requirements of the instrument for contracts within that scope have to be addressed. Chapters 7–10 provide a discussion of these requirements. Chapter 7 analyses the set of procurement procedures or methods of the Directive. Chapter 8 will cover the rules on specifications, qualification and award criteria adapted to the requirement of security of supply and security of information. Chapter 9 addresses the Directive's regime on offsets and subcontracting. Finally, chapter 10 discusses the review and remedies system of the Defence Directive. Throughout these chapters the discussion will focus on those provisions of the Defence Directive where the rules of the 2004 Public Sector Directive were adapted to take defence and security requirements into account. The adequate adaptation of these provisions is decisive for the suitability of the Defence Directive for defence and security procurement within its field of application. This will determine whether the Directive can reduce the use of Article 346 TFEU and the other Treaty exemptions discussed in chapters 2 and 3 and thus ensure that the relevant contracts are awarded on the basis of the Directive and inside the Internal Market. It is submitted that the suitability of the Defence Directive for defence and security procurement will also be important to establish EU Internal Market law as the locus of the regulation of defence and security procurement, rather than one or more of the legal frameworks discussed in chapter 5.[1] Finally, a suitable Defence Directive might develop into a cornerstone to which other EU Internal Market law instruments in the areas discussed in chapter 4[2] could be added to complete an Internal Market for defence and security goods and services.

---

[1] EDA, OCCAR, LoI or bilateral frameworks such as the 2010 Franco-British Defence Treaty. See ch. 5, at 186–222 and *passim*.

[2] At 136–84.

This chapter discusses the set of procurement procedures of the Defence Directive. Procurement procedures, also called methods of procurement,[3] provide the contracting officer or committee with a legal framework for the acquisition process, from the publication of the contract to the conclusion or making of the eventual contract.[4] It is this procurement phase *strictu sensu*, after the definition of the need and before the contract management or performance phase, which is affected by EU Internal Market law and regulated by the EU procurement Directives.[5] Procedures range from those with maximum competition to single-source. The more competition the less likely are barriers to the Internal Market. The procurement procedures of the Defence Directive are not specifically adapted to the needs of defence and security. However, an increased flexibility regarding the choice of the procedure to be used, in favour of the less competitive negotiated procedures, is intended to take the special demands of defence and security procurement into account.

The old Public Sector and Utilities Directives provide for five main types of procurement procedure: the open procedure (section 2 below), the restricted procedure (section 3 below), the negotiated procedure with prior publication of a contract notice (section 4 below), the competitive dialogue (section 5 below) and the negotiated without publication of a contract notice (section 6 below). Moreover, there are "accelerated versions" of the restricted procedure and the negotiated procedure with publication.[6] The essence of these rules is that urgency situations allow a reduction of the time limits. Hence these are restricted and negotiated procedures with publication but with shorter time limits. Their use is limited through the urgency requirement. Finally there

---

[3] Sue Arrowsmith, John Linarelli and Don Wallace Jr, *Regulating Public Procurement* (The Hague: Kluwer Law International, 2000), at 459.

[4] On the similar procedures in the old Public Sector Directive and the old Utilities Directive see Peter Trepte, *Public Procurement in the EU*, 2nd edn (Oxford University Press, 2007), at 373–84, 271–89 and 462–80 (open and restricted procedures), at 384–401 (negotiated procedures); Christopher Bovis, *EC Public Procurement: Case Law and Regulation* (Oxford University Press, 2006), at 233–8 and 426–9, 263–5 and 429–42, 212–18 (open and restricted procedures), at 243–8 and 417–26 (negotiated procedures); and Julio González García, "Classic Procedures" (ch. 3 on the Public Sector Directive), at 59–80, Francois Lichère, "New Award Procedures" (ch. 4 also on the Public Sector Directive), at 81–104, and Simone Torricelli, "Utilities Procurement" (ch. 9), at 223–47, in Martin Trybus, Roberto Caranta and Gunilla Edelstam (eds.), *EU Public Contract Law* (Brussels: Bruylant, 2014).

[5] There is, however, an evolving effect of EU Internal Market law on the contract management phase of public procurement contracts, after the conclusion or making of the contract, see Mario Comba, "The Effect of EU Law on Contract Management" in Trybus, Caranta and Edelstam (eds.), *EU Law of Public Contracts, supra* note 4, at 317–37. Nevertheless, this chapter shall focus on the classical understanding of EU Internal Market law affecting the procurement phase from publication to conclusion.

[6] See Art. 33(7) Defence Directive (or Art. 38(8) Public Sector Directive 2004/18 EC which is exactly the same).

are the "special procedures" (section 7 below), namely framework agreements (section 7.1 below), dynamic purchasing systems (section 7.2 below) and electronic auctions (section 7.3 below). The Defence Directive provides all of these procedures also found in the other Directives with the notable exception of the open procedure. The analysis concludes with a discussion of procedures or methods which, in addition to the open procedure, have not been provided in the Defence Directive (section 8 below). This will very briefly cover procurement methods found in other legal frameworks and the new Public Sector Directive 2014/24/EU.[7] As in chapter 6 on scope, the analysis will include a discussion of the transposing legislations in Austria,[8] Germany,[9] the Republic of Ireland[10] and the United Kingdom.[11] It will be argued that while the EU legislator could have provided more flexibility through a bigger choice of procedures, a selection of methods based on the negotiated procedure with prior publication of a contract notice as the default procedure is a defensible approach to accommodate the requirements of defence and security procurement. Moreover, it could also be argued that too many choices lead to a confusing "paradox of choice". Thus in some situations it is preferable to have less choice;[12] too much flexibility can have disadvantages.

2 No open procedure

The open procedure allows for a maximum of competition and transparency. Based on a detailed (technical) description or specifications of the good, service or work to be procured, all economic operators, subject to qualification,[13] can bid for the contract. Under the Public Sector Directive, for example, a contract notice is published in the Official Journal of the EU (OJ) and interested operators have 52 days to submit their bid, or 30 days when a prior information notice announcing the upcoming contract was published before the contract notice.[14] Both the qualification of all bidders and all the submitted tenders themselves will be evaluated by the contracting authority. Communication

---

[7] [2014] OJ L4/65.

[8] Bundesgesetz über die Vergabe von Aufträgen im Verteidigungs- und Sicherheitsbereich (Bundesvergabegesetz Verteidigung und Sicherheit 2012 – BVergGVS 2012), BGBl. I Nr. 10/2012.

[9] Vergabeverordung für die Bereiche Verteidigung und Sicherheit – VSVgV, BGBl. I S.1509/2012.

[10] European Union (Award of Contracts Relating to Defence and Security) Regulations 2012, S.I. No. 62 of 2012 (hereinafter ACRDSR).

[11] United Kingdom Defence and Security Public Contracts Regulations 2011, SI 2011/1848 (hereinafter DSPCR).

[12] Thanks to Pedro Telles for pointing this out to me when commenting on an earlier draft of this chapter.

[13] Discussed in ch. 8, at 382–400.

[14] See Art. 38(2) and (4) Public Sector Directive 2004/18/EC.

between the bidders and the contracting authority is only allowed for the purpose of clarification or supplementing the contents of the bids or the requirement of the contracting authority and when the principles of non-discrimination and equal treatment of all bidders are respected.[15] Other negotiations between the contracting authority and the bidders are prohibited and the contract is awarded on the basis of the written or electronic bids containing the price and other terms for the supply of the good, service or work.[16] This considerable limitation of communication between the authority and the bidder is possible because the bid is based on a response to the detailed specifications of the contracting authority. After all, both a contract notice and a bid represent communication between the contracting authority and the bidder. Therefore the finalisation of detailed specifications, which make negotiations unnecessary, must be possible. Non-compliant bids must be rejected. All compliant bids of all qualified bidders will be evaluated at the award stage. The Public Sector and Utilities Directives provide for the open procedure and most procurement laws include a procedure more or less resembling the open procedure of the Directives. These can be called "open tendering" or just "tendering",[17] "open competitive tendering"[18] or "sealed bidding".[19] In the Public Supplies, Public Works and Public Services Directives – in the versions preceding the reforms of the early 1990s, which preceded the 2004 and 2014 Public Sector Directives – the open procedure was the only freely available procedure.[20] Not only had the use of the negotiated procedures to be justified on the basis of one of the respective grounds stipulated in these pre-1993 Directives, but even that of the restricted procedure. The open procedure was the default procedure of these old public sector Directives. This only changed with the reform of these Directives in the early 1990s.[21] It

---

[15] Trepte, *Public Procurement in the EU, supra* note 4, at 376.

[16] Arrowsmith, Linarelli and Wallace, *Regulating Public Procurement, supra* note 3, at 463.

[17] See, inter alia, Arts. 27 and 28 of the United Nations Commission for International Trade Law (UNCITRAL) Model Law on Public Procurement 2011, www.uncitral.org/pdf/english/texts/procurem/ml-procurement-2011/ML_Public_Procurement_A_66_17_E.pdf [accessed 9 October 2013], Official Records of the General Assembly, Sixty-sixth Session, Supplement No. 17 (A/66/17), annex I, according to which "open tendering" is even the default procedure. See also Art. VII(3)(a) Government Procurement Agreement (GPA) of the World Trade Organisation (WTO), www.wto.org/english/docs_e/legal_e/gpr-94_01_e.htm [accessed 9 October 2013].

[18] See Art. 13(1) ESA (European Space Agency) Procurement Regulations ESA/C (2011)72 Annex I.

[19] US Federal Acquisition Regulation (FAR 14.101) as cited by Arrowsmith, Linarelli, and Wallace, *Regulating Public Procurement, supra* note 3, at 463.

[20] See Martin Trybus, *European Defence Procurement Law: International and National Procurement Systems as Models for a Liberalised Defence Procurement Market in Europe* (The Hague: Kluwer Law International, 1999), at 50–1.

[21] Ibid., at 50.

can be argued that the open procedure is the "original" or "mother" procedure of most procurement laws. It is often called the "normal" procedure under the EU Directives or other laws.[22]

The open procedure has clear advantages in allowing a maximum of competition: any bidder interested in participating may do so. The contracting authority has no discretion in selecting operators for tender, a discretion which can be abused to favour certain operators.[23] The high degree of competition is aimed at achieving value for money by putting pressure on the bidders to lower their prices and offer better quality and conditions. It is also aimed at overcoming protectionism and barriers to trade as the EU-wide publication, time limits and other requirements aim to overcome these barriers and discrimination on grounds of nationality. The objective is that every bidder means every bidder, irrespective of in which EU Member State the bidder is based. There is also a maximum of transparency as not only the contract notice and the contract award notice but also the detailed specifications are publically available. Negotiations which by nature lack transparency are not allowed. The high level of transparency, the absence of negotiations and the reduced discretion of the contracting officer or committee, especially when combined with the lowest price award criterion,[24] also make a manipulation of the procurement procedure due to protectionism, corruption, other forms of favouritism or collusive behaviour particularly difficult,[25] though not impossible. This explains the presence and importance of this procedure in many procurement regimes, including the EU procurement Directives.

However, the open procedure also has a number of disadvantages. In a large market an open procedure can lead to many bids and considerable costs can be associated with evaluating a large number of them.[26] In particular for complex contracts evaluation costs are high and, as explained in chapter 1,[27] many defence and security contracts are complex. When high evaluations costs are to be expected, the costs can easily outweigh the benefits.[28] A large number of unqualified or non-compliant bids can lead to wasted procurement costs. Moreover, the desired competition might not be achieved because economic operators are not willing to risk the participation costs without a good chance

---

[22] Bovis, EC Public Procurement, supra note 4, at 234. Arrowsmith, The Law of Public and Utilities Procurement, 2nd edn (London: Sweet & Maxwell, 2005), at 423: "the normal method".

[23] Arrowsmith, The Law of Public and Utilities Procurement, supra note 22, at 422.

[24] See the discussion of award criteria in ch. 8, at 400–3.

[25] Arrowsmith, The Law of Public and Utilities Procurement, supra note 22, at 422.

[26] Trepte, Public Procurement in the EU, supra note 4, at 376; Arrowsmith, The Law of Public and Utilities Procurement, supra note 22.

[27] At 49–58.

[28] Arrowsmith, The Law of Public and Utilities Procurement, supra note 22, at 422.

of winning the contract.[29] However, this can be minimised by good practice as too many bids are often provoked by specifications that are too broad.[30]

The benefits of an open procedure are also doubtful when the number of potential bidders in the market is limited.[31] As discussed in chapter 1,[32] this limited number of potential bidders is a feature of large parts of the defence and security sectors. Moreover, the costs will often outweigh the benefits when the risk of corruption, discrimination or collusive behaviour is low.[33] However, as mentioned in chapter 1,[34] the risk of corruption and discrimination is not low in the defence sector. Moreover, the defence markets of most EU Member States are closed to each other due to protectionism and so there is discrimination on grounds of nationality. Therefore, with respect to corruption and discrimination, it is submitted that the cost of an open procedure might not necessarily always outweigh the benefits of facilitating probity and non-discrimination.

Thus, in situations in which it is possible to finalise detailed specifications for the good, service or work in question and in which negotiations between contracting authority and bidders are not necessary, a pre-selection, as in the restricted procedure discussed under the next heading below, might be preferable to avoid the costs associated with the evaluation of a large number of bids. On the other hand, the more detailed the pre-selection, the higher the transaction costs for both the supplier who is required to complete the relevant paperwork and the contracting authority that needs to process it.[35] In most Member States the open procedure is the preferred procedure of local authorities (municipalities) who procure in more local and therefore smaller markets, whereas central governments which procure in a more national and EU-wide – and therefore larger – market, prefer the restricted procedure.[36] The United Kingdom is the only Member State where the restricted procedure is used more often than the open procedure.[37] As discussed in chapter 1,[38] in the defence sector and to a certain extent also the non-military security sectors, industrial

---

[29] Arrowsmith, ibid.

[30] Thanks to Pedro Telles for pointing this out to me when commenting on an earlier version of this chapter.

[31] Arrowsmith, *The Law of Public and Utilities Procurement*, supra note 22, at 422.

[32] At 21–7.

[33] Arrowsmith, *The Law of Public and Utilities Procurement*, supra note 22, at 423.

[34] At 58.

[35] Thanks to Pedro Telles for pointing this out to me when commenting on an earlier version of this chapter.

[36] Jan Heijboer and Jan Telgen, "Choosing the Open or the Restricted Procedure: A *Big* Deal or a Big *Deal*?" (2002) 2 *Journal of Public Procurement* 197.

[37] Pedro Telles, "Award Criteria in the United Kingdom" in François Lichère and Roberto Caranta (eds.), *Award Criteria* (Copenhagen: Djøf Publishing, 2013), at 249.

[38] At 21–7.

and service capabilities are often very limited.[39] For some contracts there are only a few providers in the EU market as a whole. For these contracts for especially the most complex military equipment, the costs associated with having to evaluate a large number of bids are unlikely to become an argument against the use of the open procedure. Thus it could be questioned why the open procedure was considered unsuitable for the Defence Directive. For example, if there are only three suppliers in a specific market, what would be the added value of using the more complex restricted procedure when the minimum number of bidders selected to submit full tenders would be three anyway? It could be argued that it would be preferable to save the time and effort associated with the selection stage of the restricted procedure and use it to evaluate full tenders.[40] On the other hand, the potential bidders having the required capacity will often not only be very few in number but also well known to the contracting authority, making the use of the open procedure with its strict time limits unnecessary for that reason. However, it cannot be excluded that for certain contracts, for example ammunition or equipment maintenance services, there is a large number of potential bidders of which some are not known to all contracting authorities.

Moreover, the two central features of the open procedure, namely the requirement to finalise detailed specifications at the beginning of the procedure and the prohibition of negotiations, make it unsuitable for contracts in which the first is not possible and the second is (therefore) required. The same can be said about the restricted procedure.[41] Thus the open procedure is unsuitable for most complex contracts which require innovative input from the bidders and intensive communication between the contracting authority and the bidders. The open procedure is considered by many Member States and contracting authorities only suitable for simple off-the-shelf procurement.[42] However, while as mentioned above most defence contracts and many security contracts will not be off-the-shelf procurement, some relevant contracts, such as for certain ammunition or equipment maintenance contracts could be described as such.

Finally, the high level of transparency can be a disadvantage when security of information has to be taken into account. This was highlighted by some of the stakeholders in the consultation[43] following the 2005 Commission

---

[39] See also B. Heuninckx, "The EU Defence and Security Procurement Directive: Trick or Treat?" (2011) 20 *Public Procurement Law Review* 9, at 14.

[40] Thanks to Pedro Telles for pointing this out to me when commenting on an earlier version of this chapter.

[41] Ibid.

[42] H. Gordon, S. Rimmer and S. Arrowsmith, "The Economic Impact of the European Union Regime on Public Procurement: Lessons for the WTO" in the "Public Procurement: Global Revolution I" Conference, Aberystwyth, 11–12 September 1997.

[43] "Communication from the Commission to the Council and the European Parliament on the Results of the Consultation Launched by the Green Paper on Defence Procurement and on the Future Commission Initiatives", COM (2005) 626 final, at 5.

Communication "Green Paper on Defence Procurement".[44] However, while some stakeholders expressed this reservation towards "open tendering procedures" and considered the negotiated procedure to be "the only appropriate procedure", there was no explicit argument not to provide an open procedure as one of several procedures in a future Defence Directive.[45] On the other hand, the position that the negotiated procedure is the only appropriate procedure could be interpreted as a statement against including an open procedure, and against including a restricted procedure, although this is not absolutely clear from the text of the 2005 Communication.

Thus in contrast to Public Sector Directives 2004/18/EC and 2014/24/EU and Utilities Directive 2004/17/EC and 2014/25/EU, the Defence Directive does not provide the open procedure at all.[46] The open procedure is not mentioned in the provisions or Recitals of the Directive or the Commission's Guidance Notes. It is only briefly mentioned in the consultation leading to the Defence Directive.[47] Heuninckx assumes that the legislator might have considered defence and security contracts as too complex for the open procedure.[48] Furthermore, it can be assumed that at least some Member States argued strongly against its inclusion.[49]

The four national legislators discussed in this book have not included the open procedures in their instruments transposing the Defence Directive. § 11(1) of the German VSVgV, § 23(1) of the Austrian BVergGVS, Part 6 (Regulations 23–30) of the Irish ACRDSR and Part 3 (Regulations 14–22) United Kingdom DSPCR do not include the open procedure. To a large extent this is only the consequence of a compliant transposition of provisions of the Directive into national law which were voted on by the governments of these Member States in the Council a few years before. However, it is argued that the inclusion of an open procedure based on that in the Public Sector and Utilities Directives in the national instruments transposing the Defence Directive would not have violated the Directive or Treaty. It is always possible to add procedures that provide more competition and transparency than those in the Directive, especially when there is a free choice between that procedure and the restricted

---

[44] COM (2004) 608 final.   [45] COM (2005) 626 final.

[46] Art. 25 Defence Directive "choice of procedures" does not mention the open procedure, nor is it mentioned anywhere else in the provisions of the Directive or its preamble. See also Heuninckx, "Trick or Treat?", *supra* note 39, at 14. Ciara Kennedy-Loest and Nicholas Pourbaix, "The New Defence Procurement Directive" (2010) 11 *ERA Forum* 399, at 403, call this "Perhaps unsurprisingly …"

[47] See *supra* note 43.   [48] Heuninckx, "Trick or Treat?", *supra* note 39, at 14.

[49] D. Kiltie (Ministry of Defence), "Implementing and Applying Directive 2009/81/EC in the UK" at the seminar "European Defence and Security Procurement", European Institute of Public Administration (EIPA), Maastricht, 20 January 2012, said he was happy about the open procedure not being included because otherwise he might be required to use it (notes of the author, on file).

procedure and the negotiated procedure with prior publication of a contract notice, as outlined below. However, some voices also indicate that the exclusion of the open procedure is welcome in national governments and their ministries of defence since they do not want to end up being required to use it in practice.[50] If provided in the national legislation there might be pressure to use it in practice.

The lack of the open procedure in the Defence Directive is not entirely convincing.[51] There are contracts, in a market of mostly limited industrial capacities, where the limitation of competition through shortlisting in a restricted procedure is simply unnecessary. The complexity of contracts is mainly an argument against the use of the open procedure when many potential tenders would have to be assessed.[52] For example, for the acquisition of ammunition, for which technical specifications are standardised and the number of suppliers is limited, the open procedure is currently routinely used.[53] Since the number of bidders would often be limited and these bidders would know that, they would consider their bid costs a worthwhile risk rather than discouraging the competition the open procedure aims to achieve. Moreover, it is the most competitive and transparent procedure in the other EU procurement Directives and most procurement regimes. As explained below, there is a free choice between the restricted procedure and the negotiated procedure with prior publication of a contract notice. The open procedure could have been added to this choice of freely available procedures thereby increasing the flexibility of the Defence Directive. It is submitted that the legislator should have given the open procedure a chance and see whether this option is used in practice.[54]

3 The restricted procedure

The Defence Directive provides the restricted procedure, which shares many features with the open procedure discussed above. Under both the Public Sector

---

[50] Kiltie, ibid.

[51] Heuninckx, "Trick or Treat?", *supra* note 39, at 14: "this might seem strange".

[52] Ibid.

[53] According to B. Heuninckx when commenting on an early draft of the author's article, "The Tailor-made EU Defence and Security Procurement Directive: Limitation, Flexibility, Description, and Substitution" (2013) 39 *European Law Review* 3–29.

[54] K. Vierlich-Jürcke (European Commission), "Specificities of the Defence Procurement Directive" at the seminar "European Defence and Security Procurement" at the EIPA, Maastricht, 19 January 2012, said that she was having "second thoughts" about not including the open procedure (notes of the author, on file). The Commission's B. Schmitt and N. Spiegel (the drafters of the Defence Directive) in their presentation "The Specificities of the European Defence and Security Procurement Directive" at the seminar "European Defence Procurement and Other Defence Market Initiatives", at the EIPA, Maastricht, 15 November 2010 (notes of the author, on file), said something similar.

Directive and the Defence Directive, as in the open procedure, detailed specifications have to be finalised and a contract notice is published in the OJ. Economic operators interested in the contract have normally 37 days from the day the contract notice is published to send a "request to participate".[55] This request to participate is not a full tender but simply a document which expresses the wish to participate and contains information about the economic operator. This will be followed by a shortlisting or selection process based on objective and regulated criteria and only the shortlisted operators, a minimum of five in the Public Sector Directive[56] and three in the Defence Directive,[57] will be invited to tender. Economic operators who did not request to participate may not be invited to bid and neither are those who do not have the required qualification.[58] Both the open and the restricted procedures include selection and checking of qualification. However, in the former it is simply a "pass or fail" exercise whereas in the latter it amounts to a separate stage.[59] After selection, the selected operators have 40 days from the date on which the invitation to tender was sent to send their tenders.[60] Non-compliant bids and unqualified bidders have to be rejected. The contract will be awarded to one of the qualified bidders who submitted a compliant bid on the basis of the established award criteria.[61] Similar to the open procedure, the restricted procedure requires finalised technical specifications[62] when the contract is advertised and negotiations between contracting entity and bidders are prohibited.

The restricted procedure shares many of the advantages of the open procedure without sharing some of its disadvantages. There is a relatively high degree of competition and transparency since in the first stage all interested economic operators may send a request to participate. This has similar effects on competition, transparency, probity and non-discrimination as the actual tender in the open procedure. The danger of the costs of the procedure outweighing the benefits due to a large number of tenders having to be evaluated is addressed. At the first stage a theoretically unlimited number of requests to participate rather than full tenders have to be evaluated. In contrast to the latter, the former do not amount to full tenders. However, this does not mean that the necessary

---

[55] Art. 38(3)(a) Public Sector Directive. This time limit is the same according to Art. 33(2) subpara. 1 Defence Directive.

[56] Art. 44 (3) subpara. 2 Public Sector Directive 2004/18/EC.

[57] Art. 38(3) Defence Directive.

[58] Art. 44(3) subpara. 3 Public Sector Directive 2004/18/EC. This rule is the same according to Art. 38(4) Defence Directive.

[59] I benefited from discussions with Pedro Telles when he commented on an earlier draft of this chapter.

[60] Art. 38(3)(b) Public Sector Directive 2004/18/EC. This time limit is the same according to Art. 33(2) subpara. 2 Defence Directive.

[61] Specifications, qualification and award criteria are discussed in ch. 8.

[62] On specifications see ch. 8 at 364–5.

documents are only a few pages long. In practice pre-qualification question-naires tend to be very extensive and detailed precisely because bidders have to be shortlisted "from best to worst".[63] Nevertheless, economic operators are less likely to shy away from participating due to too much competition as at this stage the relevant effort and costs will be rather limited. Moreover, they are likely to stay in the procedure and submit a full tender when they have been selected and invited to do so. This will be even more the case under the Defence Directive where only three rather than five operators have to be invited to bid. The costs for handling these three full tenders will be smaller compared to the requirements of the open procedure.

The restricted procedure also has a number of disadvantages. First, similar to the open procedure, detailed technical specifications must be finalised at the beginning of the procedure and negotiations are prohibited. This makes the restricted procedure unsuitable when technical specifications cannot be fina-lised and negotiations are necessary. A disadvantage which might be crucial in some cases is that the period to send requests to participate of 37 days and the period to submit the tender of 40 days add up to 77 days. This is rather long, although the comparison with the shorter 52 days in the open procedure under the Public Sector Directive does not apply in the context of the Defence Directive, where the open procedure is not available anyway. With respect to the negotiated procedures and the competitive dialogue, 40 days will normally not be sufficient and the restricted procedure might therefore, depending on the individual case, be a shorter option. The selection process before the actual invitation to bid to three or five economic operators requires a certain degree of discretion on the part of the contracting officer or committee. Moreover, trans-parency is not as easily accommodated in this process as in the open procedure where public tender openings or sealed bidding techniques can be used. These can be used for the eventual tender stage but not the possibly equally important selection stage. The necessary discretion and reduced transparency make manipulating the selection process for protectionist or corrupt motives easier. Furthermore, the restricted procedure has often higher transaction costs since a detailed pre-qualification questionnaire (PQQ) needs to be filled in by all interested economic operators and afterwards a full tender still has to be submitted in case the supplier has been shortlisted. The contracting entity has to process the detailed PQQs *and* the detailed tenders.[64] Finally, there is also a higher risk of litigation when economic operators are excluded at the selection stage. This might also partly explain why, as discussed above, the restricted procedure is so popular in the United Kingdom where public procurement

---

[63] Thanks to Pedro Telles for pointing this out to me when commenting on an earlier version of this chapter.

[64] Ibid.

review proceedings are expensive and rare,[65] whereas the restricted procedure is less used in the south of the EU,[66] where access to courts is cheap and easy and aggrieved tenderers are considerably more litigious.

The reason for the smaller number of economic operators to be invited to tender under the Defence Directive – three, in comparison to five under the Public Sector Directive – is not quite clear. This might be due to the smaller number of bidders in many segments of the defence and security market discussed in chapter 1.[67] A minimum number of five might prove a high threshold in the context of some contracts. This high threshold might then represent a valid reason against the use of the restricted procedure and for the use of the negotiated procedure with prior publication of a contract notice. For this latter procedure even under the Public Sector Directive the minimum number of operators who will be invited to negotiate is three.[68] In contrast to the Public Sector Directive, the use of the latter procedure is free under the Defence Directive thereby making any justification unnecessary. Thus the legislator addressed the free use of the negotiated procedure with publication of a contract notice when reducing the minimum number of operators to be invited to bid in the restricted procedure to three. The increased flexibility of the restricted procedure will make it more attractive and therefore might lead to its increased use in practice when negotiations are not really necessary and contracting officers prefer a more regulated procedure.

There is also an accelerated version of the restricted procedure. This applies according to Article 33(7) Defence Directive where urgency renders the minimum time limits laid down in Article 33(2) impracticable. This leads to a reduction of the time to submit a request to participate from 37 to 15 days, 10 days if the notice was sent by electronic means, and of the time limit for receipt of tenders from 40 to 10 days from the date of the invitation to tender. The basic stages of the restricted procedure outlined above, however, do not change in this accelerated version. This possibility of acceleration exists in addition to the shorter time limits when a prior information notice was sent according to Article 33(3) Defence Directive. The accelerated version of the restricted procedure also exists with exactly the same wording in Article 38(7) Public Sector Directive 2004/18/EC. Different degrees of urgency exist and are accommodated in the Defence Directive. The degree of urgency allowing the use of the accelerated restricted procedure, which is not free to use but must be justified by that degree

---

[65] See M. Trybus, "An Overview of the United Kingdom Public Procurement Review and Remedies System with an Emphasis on England and Wales" in Steen Treumer and François Lichère (eds.), *Enforcement of the EU Public Procurement Rules* (Copenhagen: Djøf Publishing, 2011), at 201–34. See also ch. 10.

[66] Thanks to Pedro Telles for pointing this out to me when commenting on an earlier version of this chapter.

[67] At 21–7.   [68] Art. 44(3) Public Sector Directive.

of urgency, is different from the degree of urgency allowing the use of the negotiated procedure without prior publication of a contract notice discussed below. The accelerated version of the restricted procedure extends the suitability of that procedure to relevant urgency situations, which might well occur in defence and security procurement. Consequently it might be used more often as urgency is accommodated.

The four national legislators discussed in this book have all included the restricted procedure in their instruments transposing the Defence Directive. § 11(1) of the German VSVgV, § 23(1) of the Austrian BVergGVS, Regulation 23 of the Irish ACRDSR and Regulation 17 UK DSPCR do provide for the restricted procedure. This is not surprising since it was necessary to transpose this most competitive of the procedures in the Defence Directive to comply with its requirements. However, the other, less competitive procedures also had to be implemented to ensure legislation that is flexible enough to reduce cases in which Member States derogate from the Treaty, especially on the basis of Article 346 TFEU.

The free use of the negotiated procedure with prior publication of a contract notice discussed under the next heading below makes that procedure the default procedure under the Defence Directive, a position held by the open and restricted procedures in the Public Sector Directive. This reduces the importance of the restricted procedure in the Defence Directive in comparison with the Public Sector Directive. In contrast, the old and new Utilities Directives also allow the free use of the negotiated procedure with prior publication of a contract notice. Also in this aspect the Defence Directive follows the more flexible approach of the Utilities Directive.[69] Due to the absence of an open procedure in the Defence Directive, the restricted procedure is the only procedure in which operators tender on the basis of a detailed set of technical specifications. Moreover, it is not the only procedure contracting authorities are free to use. This shifts the emphasis of the procurement regime from tendering to negotiations. This shall be discussed in more detail under the next heading below.

4 The (default) negotiated procedure with prior publication of a contract notice

Similar to the 2004 and 2014 Public Sector and Utilities Directives, the Defence Directive provides for the negotiated procedure with prior publication of a contract notice. As in the restricted procedure discussed under the previous heading, a contract notice is published in the OJ and interested economic operators have 37 days after the date on which the contract notice was sent to

---

[69] The Defence Directive *also* adopted the higher thresholds of the 2004 Utilities Directive, see ch. 6 at 269–72.

send a request to participate to the contracting authority or entity.[70] There is also a shortlisting process as in the restricted procedure, which is based on objective and regulated criteria and only the shortlisted operators, a minimum of three,[71] will be invited to bid. Economic operators who did not request to participate may not be invited to bid and neither are those who do not have the required technical and professional capacity.[72] However, this is where the similarities to the restricted procedure end. First, in the negotiated procedures there are no finalised and detailed specifications at the beginning of the procurement process, only much broader defined requirements. Moreover, the selection of three operators in the first stage will be followed not by bids but by negotiations with the shortlisted operators, followed by a best and final offer. Article 26(1) Defence Directive summarises this crucial stage of the procedure as follows:

> In negotiated procedures with publication of a contract notice, contracting authorities/entities shall negotiate with tenderers the tenders submitted by them in order to adapt them to the requirements they have set in the contract notice, the contract documents and supporting documents, if any, and to seek out the best tender in accordance with Article 47.

Thus the crucial differences to both the open and restricted procedures discussed above are the absence of detailed technical specifications at the beginning of the procedure and not only the permission but the importance of negotiations. In fact the precise description of the product, service or work to be procured will only emerge – to a degree of detail compared to technical specifications – in the course of the negotiations. The intellectual input of the bidders is required and facilitated during the negotiations; receiving that input is a crucial objective of this procedure. The negotiations will lead to the adaptations to the initial requirements referred to in Article 26(1) Defence Directive. Offering the product, service or work best meeting the requirements of the contracting authority is as important – if not more so – as offering the best quality, contract conditions and price.

This is a very flexible procedure as there are only very few rules on how negotiations should be conducted by the authority. Both formal tendering procedure and informal discussions are possible. However, according to Article 26(3) Defence Directive the equal treatment of all tenderers needs to be ensured and, in particular, information has to be distributed in a non-discriminatory manner to avoid unfair advantages for bidders with more information than others. According to Article 26(4) Defence Directive, the negotiated procedure may be conducted in successive stages "in order to reduce the number of tenders to be

---

[70] Art. 33(2) Defence Directive.   [71] Art. 38(3) Defence Directive.
[72] Art. 44(3) subpara. 3 Public Sector Directive. This rule is the same according to Art. 38(4) Defence Directive.

negotiated by applying the award criteria set out in the contract notice or the contract documents". In this case the contract notice or the contract documents must indicate the use of this option. Both paragraphs also feature in the Public Sector Directive with precisely the same wording.[73] This scarcity of rules on how the procedure should be conducted represents the most important aspect of the flexibility of the negotiated procedure with prior publication. Negotiations are possible and will often but not always be what is done in practice. Arrowsmith reports that in the United Kingdom one or more tender phases might be integrated into negotiated procedures.[74] It should be emphasised that, while – and because – the Defence Directive and the other procurement Directives contain only very few rules on how negotiations should be conducted, there is room for national procedures to be more specific and prescribe certain stages and procedures.

As a crucial difference from the Public Sector Directive 2004/18/EC, which in its Article 30 limits the use of the negotiated procedure with prior publication of a contract notice to expressly stipulated situations or grounds, the Defence Directive allows its free use without the need to justify it. This follows the example of the Utilities Directive which is generally more flexible than the Public Sector Directive. In 1999, based on the predecessor of the current Utilities Directive 2004/17/EC, Directive 93/38/EEC, the present author had suggested the use of the utilities regime as model for defence procurement, and specifically the free use of the negotiated procedure with prior publication of a contract notice,[75] although the competitive dialogue discussed under section 5 below was not part of the Directives at the time. This is an example of where the EU legislator used the old Utilities Directive rather than the old Public Sector Directive as the model for the Defence Directive.[76]

The assessment of the negotiated procedure with prior publication of a contract notice as the ideal procedure for defence and security procurement was based on the special characteristics and necessities of the military sector, also described in chapter 1 of this book.[77] The Commission considered the need to negotiate as the "rule for the procurement of defence and sensitive security equipment".[78] The open and negotiated procedures were considered "too rigid" for the Defence Directive.[79] They were suitable for the procurement of "civil

---

[73] Art. 30(3) and (4) Public Sector Directive 2004/18/EC.

[74] Arrowsmith, *The Law of Public and Utilities Procurement*, *supra* note 22, at 593.

[75] Trybus, *European Defence Procurement Law*, *supra* note 20, at 77.

[76] Another example is the use of the thresholds of the Utilities Directive discussed in ch. 6 at 269–72.

[77] At 41–4. Trybus, *European Defence Procurement Law*, *supra* note 20, at 76.

[78] Commission Staff Working Document – Impact Assessment SEC (2007) 1593, http://ec. europa.eu/governance/impact/ia_carried_out/docs/ia_2007/sec_2007_1593_en.pdf [accessed 1 November 2013], at 17.

[79] Ibid.

supplies, works and services" but not for "defence and sensitive non-military security procurement" which "is different by its very nature" and required flexibility.[80] Apart from accommodating flexibility and thereby responding to the complexity of defence and security procurement, the negotiated procedure with prior publication of a contract notice also allows striking a balance between the military interests of secrecy and national security and the interest of competition.[81] The complex national security requirements, including most importantly security of supply and information,[82] and the necessity of input of economic operators into the finalisation of the specifications based on pre-defined broad requirements, require the possibility of negotiations. This will be explained further below. The accommodation of national security in the form of security of supply and information through the flexibility of negotiations has to be understood both separately and in addition to the accommodation of these requirements throughout the procurement procedure, from technical specifications (where applicable) to qualification and award criteria. This will be discussed in detail in chapter 8. While this procedure is also provided in the Public Sector Directive, it is its free availability in the Defence Directive, without having to justify its use, which constitutes its increased flexibility in comparison to the Public Sector Directive. The motivation for this flexibility in the Defence Directive is summarised along similar lines in its Recital 47:

> The contracts covered by this Directive are characterised by specific requirements in terms of complexity, security of information or security of supply. Extensive negotiation is often required to satisfy these requirements when awarding contracts. As a result, the contracting authorities/entities may use the negotiated procedure with the publication of a contract notice, as well as the restricted procedure, for contracts covered by this Directive.

First, this clarifies the free use of the negotiated procedure with prior publication of a contract notice. This is also expressly stipulated in Article 25 subparagraph 2 Defence Directive which reads:

> Contracting authorities/entities may choose to award contracts by applying the restricted procedure or the negotiated procedure with publication of a contract notice.[83]

The cases justifying the use of the negotiated procedure *without* publication of a contract notice are listed in Article 28 Defence Directive in a manner comparable to Article 31 Public Sector Directive 2004/18/EC. They will be discussed further below. A similar list of cases justifying the use of the negotiated procedure

---

[80] Commission Staff Working Document, *supra* note 78, at 15.
[81] Trybus, *European Defence Procurement Law*, *supra* note 20, at 76.
[82] See on these concepts and how they are accommodated otherwise in the procurement procedures in ch. 8.
[83] For comparison see Art. 28 Public Sector Directive 2004/18/EC.

with prior publication of a contract notice does exist in Article 30 Public Sector Directive 2004/18/EC but is missing from the Defence Directive, also implying that the use of this procedure does not have to be justified in the same way as in the Public Sector Directive.

Secondly, this explains the motivation for the free use of the negotiated procedure with prior publication of a contract notice with the special character-istics of defence and security, and specifically three of them. The complexity discussed in chapter 1,[84] including the technical complexity, prominent research and development phases, long life cycles or complicated supply chains, is one of the reasons. Moreover, the requirements of security of supply and security of information which led to significant adaptations to the rules on technical specifications, contracts conditions, qualification and award criteria discussed in the following chapter 8 and even the review and remedies system discussed in chapter 10, also led to this increase in flexibility which is the free use of the negotiated procedure without publication of a contract notice. The case for complexity to explain this increase in flexibility is quite strong. Detailed technical requirements being finalised at the beginning of the procedure are a crucial feature of the restricted procedure and the complexity of many contracts will make that impossible, thereby making this procedure unsuitable for these contracts. Similarly, the complexity makes negotiations, prohibited under the restricted procedure, a necessity.

Moreover, security of information is accommodated by the reduced trans-parency of the negotiated procedure with publication of a contract notice compared to the restricted procedure. The precise features of the product, service or good will only be known to the contracting authority and the small number of bidders selected for negotiations, if not only to the authority and the successful bidder. Information about many requirements, problems or even shortcomings of the contracting authority might emanate during the negotia-tions but it will only become known to those involved in the negotiations. In contrast, both requirements and problems of the contracting authority are much more visible in open or restricted procedures.

Security of supply is much less obvious as a motivation for the use of the negotiated procedure with prior publication of a contract notice. However, as discussed in more detail in chapter 8,[85] security-of-supply requirements are often the subject of complex contract arrangements which can be addressed in a negotiated procedure, while in the restricted procedure these have to be stipu-lated in the technical specifications at the beginning of the procedure. Thus the flexibility of freely available negotiations may well accommodate the precise definition and agreement of security-of-supply requirements in the contract.

Similar to the restricted procedure discussed above, there is also an accel-erated version of the negotiated procedure with prior publication of a contract

---

[84] At 49–58.   [85] At 359–61 and 368–79.

notice. This applies according to Article 33(7) Defence Directive where urgency renders impracticable the minimum time limits laid down in Article 33(2). This leads to a reduction of the time to submit a request to participate from 37 to 15 days, 10 days if the notice was sent by electronic means, and of the time limit for receipt of tenders from 40 to 10 days from the date of the invitation to tender. The basic stages of the negotiated procedure with prior publication of a contract notice outlined above, however, do not change in this accelerated version. This possibility of acceleration exists in addition to the shorter time limits when a prior information notice was sent according to Article 33(3) Defence Directive. The accelerated version of the negotiated procedure with prior publication of a contract notice also exists with exactly the same wording in Article 38(7) Public Sector Directive 2004/18/EC. Different degrees of urgency exist and are accommodated in the Defence Directive. The degree of urgency allowing the use of the accelerated negotiated procedure with prior publication of a contract notice, which is not free to use but must be justified by that degree of urgency, is different from the degree of urgency allowing the use of the negotiated procedure without prior publication of a contract notice discussed below. As pointed out in the context of the accelerated restricted procedure above, accelerated procedures accommodate urgency and are there-fore an important feature of the flexibility of the Directive which enhances its suitability of the defence and security context where such urgency occurs. This reduces the need to derogate from the regime of the instrument.

Thus the negotiated procedure *with* prior call for tender is not *de jure* but *de facto* the default procedure of the Defence Directive.[86] In other words, this is the procedure the legislator considers to be most suitable for defence and security procurement. This was also a result of the consultation with stakeholders the Commission conducted in preparation of the Defence Directive which was published in 2005.[87] The negotiated procedure with prior publication of a contract notice allows taking the special characteristics of the military and security sectors into account even though this procedure is often considered to allow for a lower level of competition and transparency than the open and restricted procedures.[88] It is clearly less detrimental to competition and trans-parency than the use of the negotiated procedure without prior publication of a contract notice, which is discussed in section 6 below. Most importantly it is less detrimental to the Internal Market and transparency than the exemption of a contract from the regime of the Defence Directive through Article 346(1)(b)

[86] Heuninckx, "Trick or Treat?", *supra* note 39, at 14: "the 'standard' procedure". The differentiation of *de facto* and *de jure* is also an expression of B. Heuninckx, communicated to the author when discussing a draft of the author's article "The Tailor-made EU Defence and Security Procurement Directive", *supra* note 53.

[87] COM (2005) 626 final, at 7.

[88] Trybus, *European Defence Procurement Law, supra* note 20, at 77.

TFEU or one of the other security exemptions, which is still possible if the conditions for its use are met. The Defence Directive must be, as the stakeholders put it in the consultation, "flexible enough to become a credible alternative to national procedures"[89] which would be used after invoking the armaments exemption or another security-derogation. Every step towards more flexibility, including the free use of the negotiated procedure with prior publication of a contract notice, contributes to this quality of the Defence Directive as an alternative to derogation.

However, flexibility can be taken too far and thus the free use of the negotiated procedure with prior publication of a contract notice procedure can also be criticised.[90] With the goodwill and professionalism of the relevant procurement personnel, non-discriminatory, fair and transparent competition is perfectly possible in the context of negotiated procedures with publication of a contract notice.[91] However, due to the dangers of their abuse and genuinely incorrect application,[92] this flexibility has to be really necessary. This cannot simply be assumed for all defence and security contracts in all Member States and will depend on the context and circumstances of each individual case. It could be argued that a longer list of circumstances justifying the negotiated procedure with prior publication of a contract notice would have been an alternative approach to achieve more flexibility than in the Public Sector Directive.[93] However, four considerations put this criticism into perspective. First, the 2011 Commission Green Paper on the Modernisation of EU Public Procurement Policy suggested that in future the negotiated procedure with competition might no longer be limited to certain situations within the scope of the Public Sector Directive either,[94] although in the end the new Public Sector Directive 2014/24/EU again limits the use of what is now called the competitive procedure with negotiation to prescribed situations.[95] Nevertheless, it is quite possible that in future the negotiated procedure with competition will be freely available, not only as already now within the scopes of the Utilities Directive and the Defence

---

[89] COM (2005) 626 final, at 7.

[90] And this is also an opinion expressed by some stakeholders, see COM (2005) 626 final, at 8. However, this was a minority view.

[91] Transparency is ensured, inter alia, by the publication of the contract notice and the requirements to be set in that notice (Art. 26(1) Defence Directive). Equal treatment and non-discrimination are expressly required, inter alia, in Art. 26(2) Defence Directive. Art. 26(3) Defence Directive contains one of the references to the award criteria which have to be applied in negotiated procedures with competition.

[92] Due to these dangers negotiated procedures are more risky for tenderers but also more susceptible to legal challenges (founded or not). See also Trepte, *Public Procurement in the EU, supra* note 4, at 384 in footnote 44.

[93] Trybus, *European Defence Procurement Law, supra* note 20, at 77.

[94] European Commission Green Paper on the Modernisation of EU Public Procurement Policy, COM (2011) 15 final, at 15–16.

[95] See Art. 26(4) Directive 2014/24/EU.

Directive, but also the Public Sector Directive. Hence the Defence Directive, perhaps not intentionally, is following a possible general trend in the legislation.

Secondly, as argued by Trepte, the negotiated procedure with prior publication of a contract notice is a competitive procedure and not necessarily less competitive than an open or restricted procedure.[96] This applied in particular to contracts involving some form of public–private partnership (PPP) such as those under the United Kingdom Private Finance Initiative (PFI), which, as explained by Arrowsmith, often involve several tendering stages.[97] Trepte argues with reference to the 2004 Public Sector Directive and its predecessors, that the assumption that the negotiated procedure even with prior publication of a contract notice was less competitive than the restricted procedure was connected to the "EC regulator's instinctive distrust of any procedure which suggests a lack of transparency and which appears to allow discussions between purchasers and economic operators."[98] The lack of rules on how to conduct negotiations before the 2004 reform of the procurement Directives, so Trepte says, "reinforced the misleading impression given that the negotiated procedure . . . was merely a licence given for private discussions between a purchaser and his preferred candidate".[99] This author agrees with Trepte in that a negotiated procedure with prior publication of a contract notice can be as competitive as a restricted or open procedure, especially when looking at the United Kingdom context with its PPP experience. However, the United Kingdom procurement system is also characterised by a relatively low level of corruption and a relatively high level of professionalism of procurement officers. This good starting position to conduct negotiations characterised by competition, fairness, professionalism and probity is not given in all of the 27 other Member States. However, negotiations are not problematic only due to a lack of goodwill or professionalism but because of deficits in training and skills amongst procuring officers.[100] Moreover, issues such as regulator capture[101] or information asymmetries in favour of the tenderers even cast doubts on the success of the PPP/PFI experience in the United Kingdom.[102] Procurement is often not a career path, people fall into procurement roles or worse some procurement gets added to their role. In local authorities the situation is even more obvious. Furthermore, reviews in Scotland and Wales in 2006 and 2012 highlighted the lack of skills

---

[96] Trepte, *Public Procurement in the EU, supra* note 4, at 384.
[97] Arrowsmith, *The Law of Public and Utilities Procurement, supra* note 22, at 593.
[98] Trepte, *Public Procurement in the EU, supra* note 4, at 384.   [99] Ibid.
[100] Thanks to Pedro Telles for pointing this out to me when commenting on an earlier version of this chapter.
[101] Regulator capture describes a situation in which the public entity that is supposed to supervise the implementation/performance of the contract may not be able to do so due to being influenced by the private operator. Thanks to Pedro Telles for discussing this point with me.
[102] Ibid.

and training as one of the most pressing issues in the profession.[103] One of the typical skill shortages currently found in procurement officers is in negotiation techniques. This also appears to be the situation in the defence sector. Furthermore, even if the level of procurement skills and training is particularly good in the United Kingdom and, as outlined above, serious doubts are in order about such an assessment, the EU has to legislate for all Member States. In many Member States the levels of training, skills, probity and professionalism are problematic. Moreover, it is the mission of the EU legislator to overcome discrimination and market barriers in public procurement and in many national contexts that will be easier when the restricted or open procedure is used. As discussed in chapter 1,[104] this concern for competition, probity and market access also applies to the defence sector of many Member States.

Thirdly, at least with regards to armaments procurement, the Commission's claim that the list of grounds that would have limited the use of the negotiated procedure with prior publication of a contract notice in the Defence Directive would have been "endless" rings true.[105] Security of supply, security of information, system integration, interoperability needs, specification of performance and customisation[106] are some of the examples. Thus it would have been difficult to include all the necessary grounds and situations in the Directive thereby setting clear and objective conditions for the use of the procedure. This might have undermined the main objective of the instrument to provide a suitably flexible set of rules to move most defence and security into the Directive and Internal Market.

Fourthly, this is the first time for many Member States and their defence contracting authorities in which they will follow binding procurement rules. All other contracting authorities and entities have already had decades of experience in using binding procurement rules and could slowly adapt to them since the introduction of the first procurement Directives in the 1970s. This requires a certain degree of flexibility to ensure the successful implementation of the Directive. Whether this is sufficient will only be shown after some years of practice.[107] However, the flexibility offered by the Defence Directive is in this respect considerable. Overall, provided there is a certain level of training and skills among procurement officers, it is submitted that the negotiated

---

[103] John F. McClelland, *Review of Public Procurement in Scotland: Report and Recommendations* (Edinburgh: Scottish Executive, 2006), www.scotland.gov.uk/Resource/Doc/96269/0023302. pdf [accessed 15 October 2013]; John F. McClelland, *Maximising the Impact of Welsh Procurement Policy* (Cardiff: Welsh Government, 2012), http://wales.gov.uk/about/cabinet/cabinetstatements/2012/mclellandfinalreport/?lang=en [accessed 15 October 2013]. With regards to the defence sector this emerged for example from a series of articles on defence procurement law and practice in the United Kingdom in *The Times* in December 2011.

[104] At 33–5 and 58.   [105] Commission Working Document, *supra* note 78, at 49.

[106] Ibid.

[107] For the United Kingdom, Kiltie (Ministry of Defence, 2012), *supra* note 49, considers this procedure the most suitable for defence procurement (notes of the author, on file).

procedure with prior publication of a contract notice is a suitable procedure for defence procurement.

The four national legislators discussed in this book have all included the free use of the negotiated procedure with prior publication of a contract notice in their instruments transposing the Defence Directive. § 11(1) of the German VSVgV, § 23(1) of the Austrian BVergGVS, Regulation 24 of the Irish ACRDSR and Regulation 18 UK DSPCR do provide for the negotiated procedure with prior publication of a contract notice. This was to be expected considering the advantages of the procedure in general and in the defence and security sectors in particular discussed above. § 11(3) of the German VSVgV, § 89(3) of the Austrian BVergGVS, Regulation 18(4) United Kingdom DSPCR and Regulation 24(3) of the Irish ACRDSR allow to conduct the negotiated procedure with prior publication of a contract notice in phases during which the number of tenderers can gradually be reduced on the basis of the published award criteria.

5 Competitive dialogue

Similar to the 2004 and 2014 Public Sector Directive but different from Utilities Directive 2004/17/EC (but see Article 48 Directive 2014/25/EU), the Defence Directive provides for the competitive dialogue. The competitive dialogue is a highly complex procurement procedure which cannot be discussed comprehensively within the limits of this chapter.[108] The competitive dialogue shares many features with the negotiated procedure with prior publication of a contract notice but negotiations are more strictly regulated. The four national legislators discussed in this book have all included the competitive dialogue in their instruments transposing the Defence Directive.[109]

As in the other procedures, the competitive dialogue requires the publication of a contract notice in the OJ and, as in the negotiated procedure with prior publication of a contract notice, this shall set out their needs and requirements.[110] Detailed technical specifications are not required from the beginning

---

[108] On the competitive dialogue in the Public Sector Directive see Trepte, *Public Procurement in the EU, supra* note 4, at 404–9; Bovis, *EC Public Procurement, supra* note 4, at 171–3 and 239–43; and in great detail: Arrowsmith, *The Law of Public and Utilities Procurement, supra* note 22, ch. 10; and Michael Burnett and Martin Oder, *Competitive Dialogue – A Practical Guide* (Maastricht: European Institute of Public Administration, 2009), at 197. On a very extensive analysis of the competitive dialogue in the United Kingdom, apart from France the country using this procedure the most: Richard Craven, *Procurement Procedures under the Private Finance Initiative: The Operation of the New Legal Framework*, PhD thesis, University of Nottingham (2011), on file, and Sue Arrowsmith and Steen Treumer (eds.), *Competitive Dialogue in EU Procurement* (Cambridge University Press, 2012).

[109] §§ 11(1) and 13 of the German VSVgV, §§ 23(1) and 28 of the Austrian BVergGVS, Regulation 25 of the Irish ACRDSR and Regulation 27 UK DSPCR.

[110] Art. 27(2) Defence Directive.

of the process. As in the restricted procedure and the negotiated procedure with prior publication of a contract notice, interested bidders can send a request to participate within 37 days from the date on which the contract notice is sent.[111] There is also a shortlisting process which is based on objective and regulated criteria and only the shortlisted operators, a minimum of three,[112] will be invited to bid. Economic operators who did not request to participate may not be invited to bid and neither are those who do not have the required capabilities.[113] The essence of what follows is stipulated in Article 27(3) Defence Directive:

> Contracting authorities/entities shall open with the candidates selected in accordance with the relevant provisions of Articles 38 to 46, a dialogue, the aim of which shall be to identify and define the means best suited to satisfying their needs. They may discuss all aspects of the contract with the chosen candidates during this dialogue.

The reference to Articles 38–46 refers to the rules on qualification discussed in chapter 8.[114] This is a specific reference not made in Article 26(1) Defence Directive, but otherwise there is little difference to the negotiated procedure with prior publication of a contract notice. This already begs the question of why the legislator included both procedures, which will be discussed further below. The negotiated procedure with prior publication of a contract notice would have been sufficient. After all, the competitive dialogue is little more than the codification of the United Kingdom practice with the negotiated procedure for the award of PPPs/PFIs before 2004.[115] Since the two procedures are so similar, the equal treatment rule in Article 27(3) subparagraph 2 Defence Directive has almost the same wording as that in Article 26(2) Defence Directive. Moreover, the possibility for the procedure to take place in successive stages in Article 27(4) Defence Directive discussed above closely resembles that in Article 26(3) Defence Directive.

However, this is where the considerable similarities of the competitive dialogue with the negotiated procedure with prior publication of a contract notice end. What follows in Article 27 Defence Directive are rules on the competitive dialogue which cannot be found in Article 26 Defence Directive on the negotiated procedure with prior publication of a contract notice. These include a rule on not revealing confidential information to competitors in Article 27(3) subparagraph 3 Defence Directive; on declaring the dialogue concluded and asking for final tenders in Article 27(6) Defence Directive; on the clarification, specifying and fine-tuning of tenders and additional

---

[111] Art. 33(2) Defence Directive.   [112] Art. 38(3) Defence Directive.
[113] Art. 44(3) subpara. 3 Public Sector Directive 2004/18/EC. This rule is the same according to Art. 38(4) Defence Directive.
[114] At 382–400.
[115] Thanks to Pedro Telles for pointing this out to me when commenting on an earlier version of this chapter.

information in Article 27(7) Defence Directive; and on clarifications asked from the tender who submitted the most economically advantageous tender in Article 27(7) subparagraph 2 Defence Directive. Moreover, according to Article 27(1) subparagraph 2 Defence Directive the contract can only be based on the award criterion of the economically most advantageous tender and according to Article 27(8) Defence Directive contracting entities may specify prices or payments to the participants of the dialogue.

It is submitted that it is a moot point whether these additional requirements make the competitive dialogue a procedure that is significantly different to the negotiated procedure with prior publication of a contract notice. It has been argued that when comparing Articles 26 and 27 Defence Directive, there is not much more formalisation in the competitive dialogue, with the notable exception, however, of the formal closure of the dialogue and best and final offer stage.[116] Kennedy-Loest and Pourbaix called it "less flexible, and often lengthier and more costly".[117] This could be simply because the competitive dialogue is badly used. In the United Kingdom it has been deemed "best practice" to choose the preferred bidder as soon as possible and discuss the details of the contract with him or her.[118] However, this causes the contracting authority to lose any leverage over the tenderer due to competition. Without competition, the tenderer has all the incentives for delaying signing the contract until it claws back whatever has been agreed before. Reasons given by contracting authorities for accepting changes at this stage include the likelihood of challenge, the possibility of rewinding the process, the legal risks involved in rewinding process, the possibility of delay and political embarrassment and the personal relationship with bidder teams.[119] However, these considerations demonstrate the weak negotiating position of the contracting authority and why no changes should be accepted at this stage. Due diligences should be carried out before the final terms are agreed as they can have considerable influence on the final contract.[120] The practice in Spain is to discuss everything during the dialogue stage and not (only) with the preferred bidder. The end results are shorter procedures where the preferred bidder cannot claw back any concessions.

Heuninckx pointed out that the negotiated procedure with prior publication of a contract notice is less formalised and thus more open to abuse.[121] Anyway it can safely be said that the competitive dialogue is at least slightly more formalised. A crucial difference of the competitive dialogue from the negotiated

---

[116] Thanks to B. Heuninckx for pointing this out to me.
[117] Kennedy-Loest and Pourbaix, "The New Defence Procurement Directive", *supra* note 46, at 403.
[118] S. Arrowsmith and S. Treumer, "Competitive Dialogue in EU Law: A Critical Review" in Arrowsmith and Treumer (eds.), *Competitive Dialogue in EU Procurement, supra* note 108, at 115.
[119] Ibid., at 118–19.   [120] Thanks to Pedro Telles for discussing this point with me.
[121] Heuninckx, "Trick or Treat?", *supra* note 39, at 15.

procedure with prior publication of a contract notice is that the latter is freely available whereas the competitive dialogue is limited to cases of "particularly complex contracts".[122] This limitation of the competitive dialogue is even stronger in the wording of some of the national legislation transposing the Defence Directive, for example § 11(1) of the German VSVgV which limits its use – and that of the negotiated procedure without prior publication of a contract notice discussed below – to "justified exceptional cases".[123] In contrast, the transposition in § 28(1) of the Austrian BVergGVS, Regulation 19 of the United Kingdom DSPCR and Regulation 25 of the Irish ACRDSR are closer to the limitation to "particularly complex contracts". This is not such a crucial limitation in practice as the competitive dialogue is lengthy and costly and thus unlikely to be used unless the complexity of the contract justifies the effort. However, the contrast to the 2004 Public Sector Directive reveals an inconsistency in the coexistence of competitive dialogue and negotiated procedure with prior publication of a contract notice in the Defence Directive.[124] In the old Public Sector Directive the same "light" limitation to particularly complex contracts applies to the competitive dialogue[125] while at the same time the negotiated procedure with prior publication of a contract notice is limited to expressly stipulated situations or grounds. Its use needs to be justified. This limitation of the negotiated procedure with prior publication of a contract notice makes the competitive dialogue, which is lengthy and costly but at the same time only attached to the "light" limitation of complex contracts, an attractive option, at least for really complex contracts in which complexity justifies the cost, time and effort involved and no justification for the use of the other procedure is available.[126] As Burnett put it, the "key question" is "why use competitive dialogue when there is unrestricted choice of the negotiated procedure with prior publication?"[127] The negotiated procedure with prior publication of a contract notice is very flexible, in fact so flexible it could be conducted in exactly the same way with the same stages as the competitive dialogue, but without any "complex contracts" limitation and without being bound by the Directive to follow rules and limitations such as Article 27(1) subparagraph 2, (3)

[122] Art. 27(1) subpara. 1 Defence Directive.
[123] German original: "In begründeten Einzelfällen ist ein Verhandlungsverfahren ohne Teilnahmewettbewerb oder ein wettbewerblicher Dialog zulässig [translation of the author]."
[124] Heuninckx, "Trick or Treat?", *supra* note 39, at 17–18; Kennedy-Loest and Pourbaix, "The New Defence Procurement Directive", *supra* note 46, at 403.
[125] Art. 29 (1) subpara. 1 Public Sector Directive 2004/18/EC.
[126] See Art. 30(1)(a)–(d) Public Sector Directive 2004/18/EC for the "cases justifying use of the negotiated procedure with prior publication of a contract notice".
[127] M. Burnett (EIPA), in his presentation "Use of Negotiated Procedures and Competitive Dialogue in the Defence and Security Sectors" at the seminar "The European Defence and Security Procurement Directive and Challenges for its Implementation", European Institute of Public Administration (EIPA), Maastricht, 21 June 2010 (slide 32, on file).

subparagraph 2, (6), (7) subparagraph 2 and (8) Defence Directive. From the perspective of the Internal Market the competitive dialogue should be the preferred procedure since due to its additional limitations and requirements it is less susceptible to abuse.

If then the competitive dialogue accommodates the need for negotiation while at the same time being more resistant to abuse, the legislator should perhaps have regulated the relationship between the two procedures the other way round: allowing the free use of the competitive dialogue and limiting the use of the negotiated procedure with prior publication of a contract notice to exceptional situations.[128] The need for the coexistence of both procedures in the Defence Directive is also doubtful. The competitive dialogue was not included in the Utilities Directive where the use of negotiated procedure with prior publication of a contract notice is also freely available, without the need to justify its use. The restricted use of the former and the free use of the latter might make the competitive dialogue redundant in practice.[129] However, it should also be pointed out that, beyond France and the United Kingdom, the competitive dialogue is only used to a very limited extent anyway,[130] showing unease with this complex procedure. On the other hand, the complexity of many high-end armaments projects discussed in chapter 1[131] might make it particularly suited for the defence and security sectors in the future. The EU legislator did not want the procedure designed for particularly complex contracts left out of a sector, particularly defence, characterised by many of these particularly complex contracts.[132] At time of writing it is too early to say whether it will be used in practice. Overall, it is submitted that the competitive dialogue is not necessary in a Defence Directive allowing the free use of the negotiate procedure with prior publication of a contract notice, since the latter allows sufficient flexibility and even allows conducting procurement by using exactly the same stages as in the competitive dialogue. It should therefore be deleted in the revision

---

[128] Ibid., at 16.

[129] Kennedy-Loest and Pourbaix, "The New Defence Procurement Directive", *supra* note 46, at 403; Heuninckx, "Trick or Treat?", *supra* note 39, at 16. Burnett (2010 presentation), *supra* note 121, reports that 80% of competitive dialogues were conducted in France and the United Kingdom, with only few in Denmark and Sweden and for example none in Greece (notes of the author on file).

[130] As pointed out by Vierlich-Jürcke, "Specificities of the Defence Procurement Directive", *supra* note 54 (notes of the author, on file).

[131] At 49–58.

[132] Recital 48, without naming the competitive dialogue, is the most specific recital for this procedure for "particularly complex projects" where the "use of the restricted procedure and the negotiated procedure with the publication of a contract notice would not be feasible" and "It is therefore necessary to provide for a flexible procedure ensuring competition between economic operators and allowing the contracting authorities/ entities to discuss all aspects of the contract with each candidate."

of the Defence Directive as too many procedures can make the instrument too complex.

6 Negotiated procedure without prior publication of a contract notice

Similar to the old and new Public Sector and Utilities Directives, Article 25 subparagraph 4 Defence Directive provides for the negotiated procedure without prior publication of a contract notice. As the name indicates, there is no obligation to publish a contract notice and there are generally only very few procedural requirements. The contracting authority or entity may simply start unstructured negotiations with only one provider, although it may also do so with more than one provider or follow a more structured approach. However, Article 28(1) Defence Directive requires the publication of a contract *award* notice according to Article 30(3) which must include a justification for the use of the procedure based on one of the situations expressly provided in Article 28 Defence Directive discussed below. Similar to the other procedures of the Defence Directive discussed above, the negotiated procedure without prior publication of a contract notice is based on the same procedure in the old Public Sector and Utilities Directives.[133] As in the latter Directives, the procedure will normally be used when the provider is already known to the contracting entity and the negotiations are only needed to settle the precise terms and conditions of the eventual contract,[134] including for example the price and delivery date. As this procedure is often conducted with only one provider it is called "single-source" in other regimes, for example the 2012 UNCITRAL Model Law on Procurement.[135] However, as outlined above, the negotiated procedure without prior publication of a contract notice under the three EU procurement Directives does not have to be single-source. If there is a choice between more than one provider they will be contacted more or less informally, depending on the national rules, to start these negotiations.[136]

This procedure offers the lowest level of competition and transparency and the highest level of flexibility. In fact, it could be argued the procedural requirements are so limited that the award of a contract on the basis of the negotiated procedure without publication of a contract notice is very close to exemption of the contract from the Directive on the basis of one of the exclusions discussed in chapter 6 or from the TFEU on the basis of one of the derogations discussed in

---

[133] See Arts. 28 and 31 Public Sector Directive 2004/18/EC.
[134] Trybus, *European Defence Procurement Law, supra* note 20, at 54.
[135] Arts. 27(1)(j), 30(5) and 34(3) UNCITRAL Model Law on Procurement, *supra* note 17.
[136] Trybus, *European Defence Procurement Law, supra* note 20, at 54. This variation is closer to "competitive negotiations" in Arts. 27(1)(h), 30(4), and 34(3) UNCITRAL Model Law on Procurement, ibid.

chapters 2 and 3. Moreover, due to the lack of competition there is a danger of discrimination on grounds of nationality, especially in the defence sector where there will often be only one national supplier, as discussed in chapter 1.[137] Furthermore, due to the lack of transparency there is a danger of corruption. In 2006 Wilson, Scott and Pyman[138] found, based on data for the world market rather than specifically for the EU, that governments award about half or more of their defence procurement requirements to a single supplier. This figure reflects the close relationship and unique position of some companies in the market and opens the process to possible misconduct. It also shows the importance of the negotiated procedure without prior call for tender in practice as the only procedure that allows this practice inside the field of application of the Defence Directive.

Therefore, the use of this procedure is limited according to Article 25 sub-paragraph 4 Defence Directive to "specific circumstances referred to expressly in Article 28". These situations or cases are a central issue.[139] All circumstances have to be interpreted strictly[140] and the contracting authority has the burden of proof to show that the requirements of a ground for the use of the negotiated procedure without prior publication of a contract notice have been met.[141] This strict interpretation and burden-of-proof requirement also apply in the context of the derogations and exclusions discussed in chapters 2, 3 and 6. This shows the close relationship of exclusions and the grounds allowing the use of the negotiated procedure without prior publication of a contract notice. The narrow and strict interpretation, the requirements and the close supervision of the use of these grounds are completely justified. Use of the procedure comes close to not having to apply the Directive and the grounds justifying its use are the door through which to leave this regime of competitive procedures almost as much as the exclusions are doors through which to leave the application of the regime as a whole. Both exclusions and grounds can develop into loopholes which could undermine the functioning of the Directive.

On the other hand it needs to be remembered that contracts awarded on the basis of the negotiated procedure without prior publication of a contract notice are still awarded on the basis of the Defence Directive and thus, amongst other factors, will still be subject to several procedural requirements,

---

[137] At 33.
[138] R. Wilson, D. Scott and M. Pyman, "The Extent of Single Sourcing and Attendant Corruption Risk in Defence Procurement: A First Look" at the conference "Public Procurement: Global Revolution III", Public Procurement Research Group, University of Nottingham, 19–20 June 2006 (on file).
[139] Trybus, *European Defence Procurement Law, supra* note 20, at 54.
[140] Case 199/85, *Commission v. Italy* [1987] ECR 1039 at para. 14; Case C-71/92, *Commission v. Spain* [1993] ECR I-5923, at para. 36; Case C-328/92, *Commission v. Spain* [1994] ECR I-1569, at para. 15.
[141] Cases 199/85 and C-328/94, ibid.

including the obligation to publish a contract award notice containing the justification for the use of the procedure and the review and remedies system discussed in chapter 10. Moreover, the legislator also used the grounds justifying the use of this least competitive procedure to adapt to the needs of the defence and security sectors. As discussed below, it did so by increasing flexibility in the grounds transferred from the old Public Sector and Utilities Directives and by introducing new and specific grounds. Making the transferred grounds more flexible and introducing additional grounds both render the Defence Directive more flexible than the other procurement Directives and also shift the emphasis of procedures in the Defence Directive from formal tendering to negotiation. In addition to the free use of the negotiated procedure with prior publication of a contract notice, the negotiated procedure without prior publication of a contract notice is available in more cases or situations.

6.1 Situations not specific to the Defence Directive

Article 28 Defence Directive contains situations allowing the use of the nego-tiated procedure without prior publication of a contract notice which are also contained in the old Public Sector Directive. This includes, according to Article 28(1) for works, supplies and services, the following cases: (a) after an unsuc-cessful competitive tender, (b) after receiving only irregular tenders, (c) in cases of extreme urgency and (d) when for technical or intellectual property rights there is only one operator. There are certain differences in these situations in the Defence Directive compared to the similar situations in Public Sector Directive 2004/18/EC which are connected to the different catalogues of available proce-dures in the two Directives.

The EU procurement Directives allow the use of the least competitive procedure when a more competitive procedure has already been conducted without leading to a satisfactory result. This situation of an unsuccessful competitive procedure still gives competition a chance but balances this with the need to complete the procurement and to achieve the primary objective of any procurement law which is to allow the contracting entity to procure what it needs to operate. Article 28(1)(a) Defence Directive refers to an unsuccessful restricted procedure, negotiated procedure with prior publication of a contract notice or competitive dialogue, whereas Article 31(1)(a) Public Sector Directive 2004/18/EC refers to an unsuccessful open or restricted procedure. This differ-ence is only logical since the Defence Directive does not provide the open procedure and allows the free use of the negotiated procedure with prior publication of a contract notice. Thus this situation or ground allowing the use of the least competitive procedure has been adapted to the emphasis of the Defence Directive on less competitive procedures.

The Public Sector and Defence Directives also allow the use of the least competitive procedure in another case when a more competitive procedure has already been conducted without leading to a satisfactory result. This situation of an unsuccessful competitive procedure where only irregular tenders were received also still gives competition a chance but balances this with the need to complete the procurement and to achieve the primary objective of any procurement law which is to allow the contracting entity to procure what it needs to operate. However, there is a crucial difference between the roles of this ground in the two Directives. Article 28(1)(b) Defence Directive on irregular tenders is a situation justifying the use of the negotiated procedure without prior publication of a contract notice whereas Article 30(1)(a) Public Sector Directive 2004/18/EC justifies only the use of the negotiated procedure *with* prior publication of a contract notice, which is free to use without justification in the Defence Directive. This "upgrade" from a situation allowing the non-competitive rather than the competitive version of the negotiated procedure represents an increase in flexibility and a decrease in competition. However, it is only logical as the catalogue of available procedures is different with fewer competitive procedures on offer in the context of the Defence Directive. Consequently, the Utilities Directive 2004/17/EC does not contain this situation at all.[142]

Cases of extreme urgency can also justify the use of the least competitive procedure. The relevant ground of Article 28(1)(d) Defence Directive for these cases of extreme urgency is very similar to its almost equivalent in Article 31(1)(c) Public Sector Directive 2004/18/EC. However, the former refers to the restricted procedure and the negotiated procedure with prior publication of a contract notice when addressing the time limits which are too strict to comply with, whereas the latter also includes the open procedure. This is only a reflection of the different procedures provided in the two Directives. Similarly, the situation in Article 40(3)(d) Utilities Directive 2004/17/EC refers to the open, restricted and negotiated procedure with prior publication of a contract notice. In contrast to the Public Sector Directive, even the accelerated versions of the restricted procedure and negotiated procedure with prior publication of a contract notice must be too strict to comply with in the extreme emergency situation. Allowing the use of the negotiated procedure without prior publication of a contract notice is a necessary provision for the Defence Directive, also in relation to the objectives of the instrument. These situations can be very close to national security situations allowing derogation from EU Internal Market law as a whole on the basis of Articles 346 and even 347 TFEU. The use of the negotiated procedure without prior publication of a contract notice rather than derogation still keeps the procurement inside the Directive and TFEU, with limited, but still considerable, procedural requirements including the review and remedies procedures discussed in chapter 10. Thus, rather than the objective of competition, those of transparency and accountability are still present in this procedure. As with some of the defence and security-specific situations discussed below, the extreme

---

[142] See Art. 40 Utilities Directive 2004/17/EC.

urgency situation and ground are crucial to keep the threshold high for pro-portionately invoking, in particular, Article 346 TFEU. The contracting author-ity facing an extreme urgency situation may use the least competitive procedure rather than having to derogate from the Directive and Treaty.

For various reasons normally connected to intellectual property, there will often be only one operator who can legally provide the good, service or work in question. Article 28(1)(e) Defence Directive on "only one operator" has almost the same wording as its near equivalents in Article 31(1)(b) Public Sector Directive 2004/18/EC and Article 40(3)(c) Utilities Directive 2004/17/EC, with the exception of "or artistic [reasons]" which do not feature in the Defence Directive. The reason for this deletion of artistic reasons is not quite clear, especially as it also applies to works contracts where such reasons might apply even in a Defence Directive.

Moreover, for services and supplies, Article 28(2)(b) Defence Directive con-tains a situation for research and development products. With regards to supplies this is very similar to Article 31(2)(a) Public Sector Directive 2004/18/EC. There is no such ground in Article 40(3) Utilities Directive 2004/17/EC. Since the situation in the Defence Directive only refers to "products" it is not quite clear why, unlike its near equivalent in the old Public Sector Directive, it is grouped under para-graph (2) of Article 28 which refers to both supply and services contracts. It should have been grouped under paragraph (3) which only refers to supplies.

Furthermore, for supplies, Article 28(3) Defence Directive provides for situations for (a) "additional deliveries", (b) the "commodity market" and (c) "advantageous terms". The latter have their equivalents in Article 31(2)(b) and 31(2)(c) Public Sector Directive 2004/18/EC.

Additional deliveries can be awarded on the basis of the least competitive procedure as the initial contract had already been procured on the basis of a competitive procedure or its procurement on the basis of negotiation justified for another reason. Thus competition was accommodated in the initial con-tract award and the costs of a new procedure outweigh the benefits. The additional deliveries situation in Article 28(3)(a) Defence Directive differs from Article 31(2)(b) Public Sector Directive 2004/18/EC in that recurrent contracts may not generally exceed three years whereas in the Defence Directive this time limit is five years. Moreover, these five years might even be exceeded in "exceptional circumstances determined by taking into account the expected service life of any delivered items, installations or systems, and the technical difficulties which a change of supplier may cause". This increased flexibility of five years instead of three years in the old Public Sector Directive is due to the long in-service life of military equipment discussed in chapter 1,[143] but open to abuse if not applied strictly.[144]

For works and services Article 28(4) Defence Directive adds situations related to (a) additional works and services and (b) "repetition". Article 28(4)(a)

---

[143] At 52–3.   [144] Heuninckx, "Trick or Treat?", *supra* note 39, at 17.

Defence Directive has an equivalent in Article 31(4)(a) Public Sector Directive 2004/18/EC. Article 28(4)(b) Defence Directive contains a specific nuance since, in contrast to Article 31(4)(b) of the old Public Sector Directive, the procedure may be used for five years rather than three.[145] Moreover, these three years can even be exceeded. Similar to the similar situation relating to supplies in Article 28(3)(a) Defence Directive discussed above, this increase from three to five years is due to the long in-service life of military equipment but open to abuse if not applied strictly.[146] The increase to five years is also one of many aspects of the increased flexibility which is a characteristic of the Defence Directive and the topic of this chapter on procedures.

Thus the Defence Directive allows for the use of the negotiated procedure without prior publication of a contract notice in all the cases also provided in Public Sector Directive 2004/18/EC. Moreover, some of these situations, notably Article 28(1)(c) and (4)(b) Defence Directive, are wider than their near equivalents in the old Public Sector Directive, increasing flexibility and taking the long life cycle of defence equipment into account, thereby already representing adaptations to the defence and security sectors.

The four national legislators discussed in this book have all included the situations and ground for the use of the negotiated procedure without publication of a contract notice outlined in this section in their instruments transposing the Defence Directive.[147] This was to be expected since the situations are already part of the transposing legislations of the old Public Sector Directive and they provide the national contracting authorities and entities with welcome flexibility and clarity.

6.2 Situations specific to the Defence Directive

Article 28 Defence Directive contains a number of additional and defence and security-specific situations in which the negotiated procedure without prior publication of a contract notice can be used. These additional grounds for the use of the least competitive procedure represent an increase in flexibility in the Defence Directive in comparison with the old Public Sector Directive but also the old Utilities Directive which does not contain these grounds either. Flexibility is increased because the contracting authority or entity may, but does not have to, use the competitive procedure without prior publication of a contract notice. The additional grounds relate to urgency resulting from a crisis, research and development services and armed forces deployed abroad.

---

[145] See Art. 31(4)(b) Public Sector Directive 2004/18/EC.
[146] Heuninckx, "Trick or Treat?", *supra* note 39, at 17.
[147] § 12 of the German VSVgV, § 25 of the Austrian BVergGVS, Regulation 27 of the Irish ACRDSR and Regulation 16 UK DSPCR.

6.2.1 Urgency resulting from a crisis

Situations allowing the use of the negotiated procedures which relate to urgency are accommodated in all procurement Directives, as can be seen in the ground in Article 28(1)(d) Defence Directive or Article 31(1)(c) Public Sector Directive 2004/18/EC discussed above. An additional specific ground relating to urgency resulting from a crisis is stipulated in Article 28(1)(c) Defence Directive as follows:

> (c) when the periods laid down for the restricted procedure and negotiated procedure with publication of a contract notice, including the shortened periods referred to in Article 33(7), are incompatible with the urgency resulting from a crisis. This may apply for instance in the cases referred to in point (d) of the second paragraph of Article 23 . . .

Again, urgency of different kinds and for different reasons is accommodated in all the procurement Directives. As with the other Directives, this accommodation of urgency starts with a move from the regular procedures to their accelerated versions. This is also reflected in the reference to Article 33(7) Defence Directive in this ground. In the case of the Defence Directive these are the accelerated versions of the restricted procedure and of the negotiated procedure *with* prior publication of a contract notice. As there is no open procedure in the Defence Directive, there is no reference to its accelerated version here either. If accelerated procedures are not sufficient to respond to the urgency situation in question, a less competitive procedure can be used to increase flexibility and speed, which in the case of the Defence Directive is the negotiated procedure without publication of a contract notice. If this use of a less competitive procedure is not sufficient to respond to the urgency situation in question either, then derogation from the TFEU and, through its Article 2, the Defence Directive, on the basis of one of the security exemptions in Articles 36, 51, 52, 62 and 346 TFEU discussed in chapters 2 and 3, remains the only option. Moreover, within its limited field of application, the extreme crisis derogation in Article 347 TFEU, also briefly discussed in chapter 3, could be used in extreme cases. However, the use of the negotiated procedure without publication of a contract notice involves only very few procedural requirements and is therefore very close to derogation from the regime. The approach of the Defence Directive is to accommodate these situations as far as possible "inside" the instrument thereby making derogation unnecessary through flexibility. This follows the tradition of the old Public Sector and Utilities Directives. Derogation is not pre-empted by this accommodation as a Directive cannot prevent Member States from using Treaty derogations, but it can make derogation less necessary and thus more difficult to justify if challenged by the Commission or in the ECJ. The availability of this least competitive procedure in urgency situations will be taken into account when assessing the proportionality of derogation. The line or order of thought of a contracting officer of committee in an urgency situation should therefore be: (1) negotiated procedure with prior publication of a contract notice if possible, (2) accelerated version of that procedure if possible, (3) negotiated procedure without prior publication of a contract notice if possible and finally (4) derogation.

According to Recital 54 of the Defence Directive, the crisis leading to the urgency may result from the armed forces of the Member States having to intervene in crisis situations abroad, such as in the context of a peacekeeping operation. Moreover, it may arise on the territories of the Member States, when their security forces have to respond to a terrorist attack.[148] The reference to the security-of-supply requirement in Article 23(d) Defence Directive[149] is only intended as an example of a situation and requirement to which Article 28(1)(c) applies. According to Recital 54 this would apply at the start as well as during such a crisis. However, even with this relatively wide definition of crisis, the existence of a crisis is still the most important limitation of the ground. Procurement for the German forces in Afghanistan, for example, which have been deployed in the context of a peacekeeping mission for over ten years, cannot be conducted on the basis of the negotiated procedure without publication of a contract notice justified by this urgency due to a crisis ground. The crisis must lead to a degree of urgency that makes it impossible to abide by the time limits of even the accelerated version of the negotiated procedure with prior publication of a contract notice. However, the *Bundeswehr* mission in Afghanistan might use one of the other grounds discussed below instead and the interpretation of Article 28(1)(c) Defence Directive is supported by the existence of another ground referring to peacekeeping operations in Article 28(5) Defence Directive discussed under the next heading below. That ground only applies to air and maritime transport services to be procured as part of such operations, not to all procurement conducted in such a context. This narrow scope of Article 28(5) reinforces the interpretation that the ground in Article 28(1)(c) does not cover all procurement in the context of a peacekeeping operation such as Afghanistan, Mali or Kosovo. In contrast, necessary procurement for the response to a sudden terrorist attack on any Member State would be covered by this ground.

In contrast to the extreme urgency ground in Article 28(1)(d), the urgency resulting from a crisis according to Article 28(1)(c) Defence Directive can be due to events that were foreseeable by the contracting authorities or entities in question. Thus an important limitation of the earlier ground does not apply to the latter, thereby widening its scope. Moreover, the requirement of the extreme urgency ground that the circumstances invoked to justify extreme urgency

---

[148] Recital 53–4 Defence Directive.

[149] Art. 23(d) Defence Directive: "a commitment from the tenderer to establish and/or maintain the capacity required to meet additional needs required by the contracting authority/entity as a result of a crisis, according to terms and conditions to be agreed".

must not in any event be attributable to the contracting authority or entity does not apply to the urgency resulting from a crisis ground either. The lack of this limitation does again widen the defence-specific ground in comparison with the general extreme urgency ground. However the limited situations of crisis in which the ground can be used put this wider scope into perspective. Heuninckx interprets this situation as a response of the legislator to "very practical operational problems of defence and security procurement", which are unlikely to lead to many abuses.[150] The present author considers this to be a convincing assessment.

6.2.2 Armed forces deployed abroad

Article 28(5) Defence Directive contains a very defence-specific situation for armed forces deployed abroad:

> (5) for contracts related to the provision of air and maritime transport services for the armed forces or security forces of a Member State deployed or to be deployed abroad, when the contracting authority/entity has to procure such services from economic operators that guarantee the validity of their tenders only for such short periods that the time-limit for the restricted procedure or the negotiated procedure with publication of a contract notice, including the shortened time-limits as referred to in Article 33(7), cannot be complied with.

Similar to the exclusion in Article 13(d) Defence Directive discussed in chapter 6,[151] the deployment of forces abroad led to an adaptation of the Defence Directive in comparison to the old Public Sector Directive. However, in comparison to the exclusion in Article 13(d) the situation described in Article 28(5) and developed in Recital 54 Defence Directive is narrower. It only refers specifically to air and maritime transport services. The deployment has to be "abroad", although according to the wording of Article 28(5) itself it is not limited to deployments in third countries. In other words, the deployment could be in another Member State. However, apart from the fact that such a deployment in another Member State is highly unlikely, the reference to peacekeeping operations in Recital 54 could be interpreted as a limitation to the deployments in the context of peacekeeping and other "Petersberg" tasks in the context of the CSDP, NATO or the UN.[152] This would limit the situations to deployments in third countries. Moreover, the very nature of "air and maritime transport services" suggests a deployment far away from Europe.

It is submitted that the insertion of this defence and security-specific situation was appropriate to respond to a "very practical operational

---

[150] Heuninckx, "Trick or Treat?", *supra* note 39, at 17.   [151] At 288–92.
[152] See also ch. 1 at 44–5.

problem".[153] Moreover, it was necessary since none of the situations allowing the use of the negotiated procedure without prior contract notice in the old Public Sector Directive would have applied to this particular case. Heuninckx predicts that it will not lead to many abuses.[154]

The "urgency resulting from a crisis" and "armed forces deployed abroad" grounds are remarkable since these are situations allowing the use of the negotiated procedure without prior publication of a contract notice, *inside* the Directive, rather than exceptions taking it *outside* the instrument. Both situations take secondary EU Internal Market law deep into military operations and very close to situations where national security derogations can apply. These grounds are in themselves an indicator on the specific extension of EU procurement law into defence procurement. The Defence Directive does not itself extend EU procurement law into defence procurement since the old Public Sector Directive applied to defence procurement, but subject to national security derogations. By making these situations a justification for the least competitive procedure they raise the bar for a Member State to proportionately derogate from the Directive and Treaty as their national security concerns are already recognised and accommodated by allowing the use of the non-competitive procedure. The consequence is that, while the possibility of legal derogation from the Directive and Treaty still exists, it would be harder for a Member State to justify derogation as a proportionate measure even in such clearly military situations. In this context these "military" grounds are to be read in conjunction with free use of the negotiated procedure with prior publication of a contract notice discussed above in this chapter, the exceptions discussed in chapter 6, security-of-supply and information adaptations throughout the procedure discussed in chapter 8 and the review and remedies system discussed in chapter 10.

6.2.3 Research and development services

Article 28(2)(a) Defence Directive contains another additional and defence and security-specific ground for the use of the negotiated procedure without a prior contract notice for supply and services contracts "for research and development services other than those referred to in Article 13". First, this ground is different to the other research and development ground under Article 28(2)(b) Defence Directive or Article 31(2)(a) Public Sector Directive 2004/18/EC discussed above. Secondly, the words "other than those referred to in Article 13" refer to research and development conducted in the context of a cooperative programme and thus excluded from the scope of the Defence Directive on the basis of Article 13(c) Defence Directive as discussed in chapter 6.[155] What are left of the ground in Article 28(2)(a) Defence Directive are research and development phases of contracts awarded outside cooperative programmes by only one Member State.

---

[153] Heuninckx, "Trick or Treat?", *supra* note 39, at 17.   [154] Ibid.   [155] At 283–8.

According to the Commission's Guidance Note *Research and Development*, Article 28(2)(a) Defence Directive applies only to contracts which are wholly remunerated by the contracting authority or entity and where the benefits, especially intellectual property rights and other rights of use, accrue exclusively to the contracting authority or entity.[156] The Guidance Note also specifically addresses the follow-on contracts for the production phase of a research contract excluded by Article 13(c) Defence Directive or subject to the research ground for the use of negotiated procedure without publication of a contract notice according to Article 28(2)(a) Defence Directive. These follow-on contracts have to be awarded on the basis of the other procedures of the Directive,[157] in other words on the basis of the restricted procedure, competitive dialogue or negotiated procedure with prior publication of a contract notice, unless one of the other grounds in Article 28 Defence Directive justifies the use of the negotiated procedure without publication of a contract notice.

The four national legislators discussed in this book have all included the additional defence and security-specific situations and grounds for the use of the negotiated procedure without publication of a contract notice outlined in this section in their instruments transposing the Defence Directive.[158] This was to be expected since the situations provide the national contracting authorities and entities with welcome flexibility and clarity.

6.2.4 Summary

The negotiated procedure *without* prior call for tender is limited to regulated situations, the list of which is longer than those in the other Directives and contains a number of military and security-specific situations. Moreover, one of the grounds is more flexible than in the old Public Sector Directive. Article 28 Defence Directive contains the situations of the old Public Sector Directive and a number of additional defence-specific situations, namely on research and development and for forces deployed or to be deployed abroad. The approach of adding a limited number of military-specific situations and nuances to the old

---

[156] Guidance Note *R&D*, http://ec.europa.eu/internal_market/publicprocurement/docs/defence/guide-research_en.pdf [accessed 7 October 2013], at 5.

[157] Ibid. at 5 and 6.

[158] § 12(1) 1. b) aa) and § 12(1) 1. d) and § 12(1) 4. of the German VSVgV; § 25(3), (6) and (13) of the Austrian BVergGVS; Regulation 27(1)(c), (2)(b) and (8) of the Irish ACRDSR; and Regulation 16(a)(iii), (c)(i) and (e) of the United Kingdom DSPCR. In Austria and Ireland there is an express reference to the provisions transposing Art. 13 Defence Directive. In Germany and the United Kingdom there is no such reference, but § 1 VSVgV in conjunction with § 100c GWB for the former and Regulation 7(1)(c) DSPCR for the latter exclude collaborative programmes. Consequently Regulation 27(1)(c) DSPCR is limited to "research and development services to which these Regulations apply". There is no such half-sentence in the German law.

Public Sector Directive situations is appropriate[159] since it adds flexibility but still limits the procedure to certain prescribed situations.

6.3 Control mechanism

According to Article 37(1)(d) Defence Directive, "[f]or every contract ... the contracting authorities/entities shall draw up a written report to confirm that the selection procedure was undertaken in a transparent and non-discriminatory manner, which shall include", inter alia "in the case of a negotiated procedure without prior publication of a contract notice, the circumstances referred to in Article 28 which justify the use of this procedure". According to Article 37(3) Defence Directive that "report, or the main features of it, shall be communicated to the Commission, if it so requests". Transposing this report mechanism, in the United Kingdom, for example, the Cabinet Office or Ministry of Defence will collect that report;[160] in Germany, the Ministry of Economy;[161] in Ireland[162] and Austria,[163] the contracting authority itself. This report mechanism also applies to other aspects of various award procedures. However, with respect to the use of the negotiated procedure without prior publication of a contract notice, this is remarkable since the use of this procedure comes so close to derogation – and for derogation on the basis of, inter alia, Article 346 TFEU or if a contract is subject to one of the exemptions discussed in chapter 6, there is no possibility for the Commission to request such a report. With respect to Article 346 TFEU there could not be such a requirement in a Directive since that would represent a limitation through a procedural requirement in secondary legislation and procedural requirements would have to be provided in the Treaty itself, which indeed they are in Article 348 TFEU. However, the EDA discussed in chapter 5 could introduce such a system on a voluntary, not legally binding, basis. The Directive's reporting system highlights a crucial difference between the use of the least competitive procedure and derogation, even when they are otherwise very close: inside the Directive all of its other requirements, including reporting obligations, apply.

7 Other procedures in the Defence Directive

Framework agreements and electronic auctions are purchasing techniques that were developed in the context of the old Public Sector and Utilities Directives. They were also included in the Defence Directive.

---

[159] Kiltie (Ministry of Defence), "Implementing and Applying Directive 2009/81/EC in the UK", *supra* note 49, reports that the United Kingdom Ministry of Defence considers this to be "well done" in the Directive, the situations are "clear and all welcome" – "very, very welcome" (notes of the author, on file).

[160] Regulation 48 DSPCR.   [161] § 44 VSVgV.   [162] Regulation 40 ACRDSR.

[163] § 112 BVergGVS.

7.1 Framework agreements

Article 29 Defence Directive provides for framework agreements, in which one or several economic operators are selected for an agreement concerning a particular type of supply, service or work to be procured during a limited period in the future and on the basis of terms laid down by the contracting entity. During the lifetime of the framework agreement all relevant individual contracts, also called "call-offs", are awarded to either the only private party or to one of the selected operators party to the agreement on the basis of the same, if often more precisely formulated, terms. Framework agreements limit competition as only parties to the agreement may be awarded contracts, especially when they are concluded with only one private operator.[164] Framework agreements will not only be used for the purchase of office equipment or spare parts, but also for routine repair and maintenance services for equipment or buildings.[165] In the context of defence and security procurement they could be used for maintenance of vehicles or planes or the purchase of ammunition. Not all purchases would be too complex for framework agreements. However, the contracts suitable for the use of framework agreements in the defence sector will be limited.

The advantages of framework agreements are a higher level of security of supply,[166] because a number of qualified and known providers have already committed themselves to possible contracts, and faster delivery when the individual contracts are "called up" – for example, qualification and general competitiveness but also security clearances and exports licences, discussed further in chapter 8,[167] can be checked when the framework agreement is awarded. These advantages make framework agreements interesting for defence and security procurement.

The rules regarding framework agreements in Article 29(1), (2) subparagraphs 1–3 and 6, and (3)–(4) Defence Directive were taken from Article 33 Public Sector Directive 2004/18/EC word for word. There are a few differences. The longer the framework agreement, the better for security of supply, and possibly the worse for competition. However, if the same number of economic operators qualified for a framework agreement that would have been selected for tender in a restricted procedure, there could be added competition, as during the duration of the framework agreement the contracting entity could have several smaller "call-offs" instead of only one large contract.[168] On the other hand,

---

[164] Trepte, *Public Procurement in the EU, supra* note 4, at 212.   [165] Ibid., at 208.

[166] In the precise definition of the concept of security of supply see ch. 8, at 359–61.

[167] At 368–79.

[168] Thanks to Pedro Telles for pointing this out to me while commenting on an earlier draft of this chapter.

economic operators can go bankrupt or merge during the life cycle of a framework agreement thereby reducing competition[169] and possibly compromising security of supply. In contrast to the old Public Sector Directive, which in its Article 32(2) subparagraph 4 allows durations of up to four years, Article 29(2) subparagraph 3 Defence Directive allows durations for up to seven years. Further adaptations were made with respect to the exceptional circumstances which allow an even longer duration and the award notice which has to be published in the OJ in Article 32(3) Defence Directive and which must contain a justification for the longer duration according to Article 32(2) subparagraph 5 Defence Directive.[170] The Commission's Guidance Note *Security of Supply*[171] does not address framework agreements. However, it can safely be said that the longer standard duration of seven years represents an adaptation facilitating security of supply since the legislator appears to assume that the longer the duration, the longer the contracting authority can rely on a provider or a pool of providers for which all security-of-supply issues have been checked. However, again, since economic operators can go bankrupt or merge during the lifetime of a framework agreement this is not so certain. Nevertheless, in many if not most cases the longer duration of the framework agreement will lead to added security of supply.

The procurement procedure to be used for the award of the initial framework agreement as well as the call-up contracts based on the framework agreement has to be one of the procedures provided by the Defence Directive. In most if not all cases the restricted procedure will be used since the use of the negotiated procedures or the competitive dialogue would be inappropriate for framework agreements.[172] Moreover, as explained above, the Defence Directive does not provide for the open procedure. This leaves the restricted procedure as the only appropriate procedure for the award of the initial framework agreement. It is not clear whether this effect of the non-inclusion of the open procedure in the Defence Directive was an accident or intended by the legislator. The inclusion of the open procedure as an option advocated above could have enhanced the use of framework agreements in the context of the Defence Directive. However, framework agreements work perfectly well when awarded using the restricted procedure.

---

[169] Ibid.

[170] On framework agreements in the Public Sector Directive: Trepte, *Public Procurement in the EU*, *supra* note 4, at 208–12; Bovis, *EC Public Procurement*, *supra* note 4, at 251–3 and 320–2; and in great detail: Arrowsmith, *The Law of Public and Utilities Procurement*, *supra* note 22, ch. 11.

[171] http://ec.europa.eu/internal_market/publicprocurement/docs/defence/guide-sos_en.pdf [accessed 8 October 2013].

[172] Trepte, *Public Procurement in the EU*, *supra* note 4, at 437.

7.2 Electronic auctions

The Defence Directive provides for electronic auctions in its Article 48. According to Article 1(11) Defence Directive,

> "Electronic auction" means a repetitive process involving an electronic device for the presentation of new prices, revised downwards, and/or new values concerning certain elements of tenders, which occurs after an initial full evaluation of the tenders, enabling them to be ranked using automatic evaluation methods.[173]

According to Article 48(2) Defence Directive electronic auctions can be held in the context of restricted procedures, negotiated procedures with prior publication of a contract notice or framework agreements. Again, the open procedure cannot be used since it is not provided in the Directive. Since electronic auctions require the specifications (see below) to "be established with precision" as stipulated in Article 48(2) Defence Directive, they are less relevant for the procurement of armaments. However, relevant contracts are not entirely unthinkable for war material of a more off-the-shelf nature, such as, for example, certain small arms or ammunition. As they can be used in case of open, restricted or negotiated procedures, electronic auctions could be described as versions of these procedures rather than a procedure in its own right. Economic operators submit bids which are then evaluated. Then they are simultaneously invited by electronic means to submit new prices in successive phases. There are several ways to "close" the economic auction and decide on the award. The objective is to drive prices down.[174]

7.3 Dynamic purchasing systems

Dynamic purchasing systems are a hybrid electronic procedure for commonly used purchases[175] not included in the Defence Directive. This is a consequence of the fact that dynamic purchasing systems have to be based on the open procedure; they are "a new mechanism for the electronic application of the open procedure" as Trepte put it.[176] As discussed above, the Defence Directive does not provide for the open procedure and therefore its electronic variations have

---

[173] See also Arts. 1(7) and 1(6) of the old Public Sector and Utilities Directive respectively.

[174] On electronic auctions in the old Public Sector Directive: Trepte, *Public Procurement in the EU, supra* note 4, at 415–26; Arrowsmith, *The Law of Public and Utilities Procurement, supra* note 22, at 1186–207; and Bovis, *EC Public Procurement, supra* note 4, at 256–9 and 323–5.

[175] On dynamic purchasing systems in the old Public Sector Directive: Trepte, *Public Procurement in the EU, supra* note 4, at 409–15; Bovis, *EC Public Procurement, supra* note 4, at 253–6 and 320–3; and in great detail: Arrowsmith, *The Law of Public and Utilities Procurement, supra* note 22, at 1207–21.

[176] Trepte, *Public Procurement in the EU, supra* note 4, at 410.

to be excluded as well. Two points have to be mentioned in the context of leaving dynamic purchasing systems out of the Defence Directive. First, the type of off-the-shelf purchases dynamic purchasing systems are designed for have only a limited relevance in the context of defence and security procurement anyway. However, there are some contracts for which they could be used. Secondly, for simple off-the-shelf purchases of a civil nature, such as office supplies, cleaning services or computer maintenance, contracting entities in the field of defence and security still have to comply with the Public Sector and Utilities Directive where dynamic purchasing systems can be used.

8 Cooperative programmes based on research and development (R&D)

In addition to not providing the open procedure and dynamic purchasing systems discussed above, a number of other procedures are also absent from the Defence Directive. However, not all possible procedures shall be discussed in this section of the chapter. The 2011 UNCITRAL Model Law on Public Procurement, for example, now has ten main procedures on offer.[177] However, procedures relating to contracts which are excluded from the Defence Directive on the basis of one of the exemptions discussed in chapter 6 while at the same time frequently occurring in practice shall be discussed. In this context the exclusion in Article 13(c) Defence Directive deserves attention. As discussed in chapter 6,[178] this excludes

> contracts awarded in the framework of a cooperative programme based on research and development, conducted jointly by at least two Member States for the development of a new product and, where applicable, the later phases of all or part of the life-cycle of this product.

These are large collaborative programmes, such as the "Eurofighter/Typhoon" aircraft between two or more Member States which, as discussed in chapter 1,[179] are a regular occurrence for the development of new equipment.[180]

---

[177] See the list in Art. 27(1) UNCITRAL Model Law on Public Procurement, *supra* note 17: (a) Open tendering; (b) Restricted tendering; (c) Request for quotations; (d) Request for proposals without negotiation; (e) Two-stage tendering; (f) Request for proposals with dialogue; (g) Request for proposals with consecutive negotiations; (h) Competitive negotiations; (i) Electronic reverse auction; and (j) Single-source procurement. However, this is a Model Law and States using it for devising their national procurement law should choose only of a few of these procedures, not all.

[178] At 283–8.   [179] At 53–4.

[180] Either through OCCAR, EDA or NATO logistics organisations (NSPA), or by using the so-called "lead national concept", examples: Jaguar (lead national France), Bréguet Atlantique (lead national France), BVRAAM/Meteor (lead national United Kingdom), F-16 MNFP (lead national USA), F-35 JSF/FJCA (lead national USA). See the presentation by B. Heuninckx, "Collaborative Defence Procurement" at the seminar "European Defence

Collaborative projects cover the most expensive, high-profile and technologically advanced defence projects. The high costs both in relation to the R&D and
the production phases incur a high level of public investment for which the
investing government wants a return in the form of industrial participation of
its national industry. This will make it difficult to award such a contract on the
basis of the competitive procurement procedures, although not impossible.
Moreover, the high-technology character of these projects brings with it all
the problems of R&D procurement discussed in chapter 1: the necessity of
public investment in R&D and the difficulty of separating the R&D from the
production phase.[181] The Member States involved in the collaborative project
will procure their needs with respect to the piece of equipment produced at
the end of the project from the consortium involved in the project. In fact, a
guarantee to that effect is required to convince the relevant defence industries
to participate in the project in the first place. Thus with regards to the Member
States participating in the collaborative project there will be direct awards rather
than awards following a competitive procurement procedure. These combined
difficulties and the lack of procurement regulation led to unregulated ad hoc
arrangements with mixed results. European collaborative defence projects
are often inefficient, expensive and take more time than planned.[182] The cost
increases in times of austerity and budget cuts and the time overruns in times
where many military capability gaps have to be closed actually make a reform of
European collaborative projects necessary. This could be conducted through the
structures discussed in chapter 5. However, in the context of this chapter it
should be discussed how these now excluded projects could be regulated inside
the Directive and the Internal Market. Inspiration for such a Defence Directive
procedure for collaborative projects involving R&D is provided by the
European Space Agency (ESA) Procurement rules (section 8.1 below),[183] the
Defence Directive itself (section 8.2 below) and the new Public Sector Directive
2014/24/EU (section 8.3 below).[184]

8.1 European Space Agency

The European Space Agency (ESA) is also procuring costly equipment, such as
satellites, involving R&D in the context of collaborative projects involving more

---

and Security Procurement", European Institute of Public Administration (EIPA),
Maastricht, 19 January 2012 (slide 12, on file).
[181] At 53–4.
[182] See on this topic B. Heuninckx, "A Primer on Collaborative Defence Procurement in
Europe: Troubles, Achievements and Prospects" (2008) 17 *Public Procurement Law
Review* 123–45 and in great detail in *The Law of Collaborative Defence Procurement
Through International Organisations in the European Union*, PhD thesis, University of
Nottingham (2011) (on file).
[183] At 352–4.   [184] *Supra* note 7.

than one Member State. While these projects do not always share the national security implications of defence procurement, they essentially share the industrial, financial and general political and economic context of defence collaboration discussed above. A discussion of the ESA procurement regime as a model for defence procurement in the EU would require a separate monograph.[185] The essential question for the purposes of this chapter is how a procedure, and ideally a competitive procedure, can be used in the collaboration and R&D context addressed in the exclusion in Article 13(c) Defence Directive. The basic ESA response to the "collaboration dilemma" is addressed in Article VII of the ESA Convention as follows:

> The industrial policy which [ESA] is to elaborate and apply ... shall be designed in particular to: ...
>
> C. ensure that all Member States participate in an equitable manner, *having regard to their financial contribution*, in implementing the European space programme and in the associated development of space technology; in particular the Agency shall for the execution of the programmes grant preference to the fullest extent possible to industry in all Member States, which shall be given the maximum opportunity to participate in the work of technological interest undertaken for the Agency;
>
> D. exploit the advantages of free competitive bidding, *except where this should be incompatible with other defined objectives of industrial policy.*
> [emphasis added]

This establishes the principle of fair returns in ESA procurement which needs to be reconciled as far as possible with competitive bidding. However, the latter is a secondary objective in relation to the former. "Fair returns" is seen as an evolving concept and more complex than giving every Member State's industry precisely the share of the contract that equals their public financial contribution to the project.[186] Various ways to reconcile the needs of fair returns and

---

[185] The author discussed, *inter alia*, the then ESA rules as a model for European defence procurement regulation in *European Defence Procurement Law, supra* note 20.

[186] "From the outset, the ESA (and its preceding organisations) applied a principle of 'fair return' which has been constantly evolving. The main rule adopted by the Agency since its Council at Ministerial level in March 1997 is that the ratio between the share of a country in the weighted value of contracts, and its share in the contribution paid to the Agency, must be of X% (e.g. 0.98%) by the end of a given period. That ratio is called the industrial return coefficient. The achievement of geographical return continues to be looked upon globally over determined periods. Nevertheless, particular geographical return constraints may be imposed on optional programmes and on mandatory activities, to ensure that they cannot contribute to an unbalancing of the overall return situation. ESA devotes much time and effort in trying to meet all these requirements while still maintaining technical excellence and economy." See "Industrial Policy and Geographical Distribution", www.esa.int/About_Us/Industry/Industry_how_to_do_business/Industrial_policy_and_geographical_distribution [accessed 8 October 2013].

competitive procedures can be considered. For example, fair returns can be looked at from the perspective of a longer period, requiring a balance over various projects over a year or more. Alternatively, the supply chain of sub-contractors can be brought into view. For example, in a project financed by Member States A and B with equal shares (50:50), a Member State A prime contractor with a predominantly Member State B supply chain, for example, can compete with a Member State B prime contractor with a predominantly Member State A supply chain. Various other constellations involving more than one Member State are possible. The negotiated procedure with prior publication of a contract notice described above could be used, possibly adapting it by allowing a minimum of two rather than three tenderers. The price of being successful in the competition is then to be awarded the prime contract, while either way the funding countries' industries receive a fair return on their investments. It is submitted that the subcontracting regime of the Defence Directive discussed in chapter 9 would only need minor adaptations. Moreover, competition and fair returns could further be reconciled by requiring parts of the subcontracts to be awarded on a competitive basis, but possibly bids could only come from a Member State the contribution of which would still have to be balanced. The adaptations to the rules on specifications, qualification and award criteria discussed in chapter 8, however, would have to be considerable.

Moreover and more importantly, the essence of these adaptations would be to limit competitions or parts of them to economic operators based in certain Member States. This would clearly constitute discrimination on grounds of nationality and would therefore be in violation of the free movement of goods and services regimes of the Internal Market and the general principle of non-discrimination of the TFEU as discussed in chapter 2. In other words, it would be completely contrary to – and therefore very difficult to reconcile with – the basic approach of the Defence Directive and the Internal Market as a whole. This contradiction led to the exclusion in Article 13(c) Defence Directive and is a strong argument to regulate such a procedure not in the Defence Directive but in the context of EDA, perhaps in a revised Code of Conduct.[187] This would be possible also because of the express exclusion. However, Article 13(c) projects are the most expensive and technologically and militarily interesting projects and their exclusion from the regime of the Directive is disappointing. Perhaps the inclusion of these projects in a special regime of the Defence Directive, inside the Internal Market, could be considered in the long term. The most realistic and therefore constructive way forward is probably to develop such an Article 13(c) regime in the context of EDA.

---

[187] See ch. 5 at 191–216.

8.2 The Defence Directive

The use of one of the procedures of the Defence Directive discussed above, including the negotiated procedure without prior publication of a contract notice, cannot be reconciled with a need for fair returns in the context of collaborative R&D programmes now excluded in Article 13(c) Defence Directive. This is due to the fact already discussed in the context of the previous heading above: this would involve favouring economic operators on the basis of the Member States in which they are registered and that represents discrimination on grounds of nationality.

8.3 Public Sector Directive 2014/24/EU: innovation partnerships

The new Public Sector Directive 2014/24/EU contains several innovations which in the course of the review of the Defence Directive might also be inserted into the latter. For the purposes of the dilemma of collaborative R&D, the new innovation partnership procedure in Article 31 Public Sector Directive 2014/24/EU, which is specifically designed to enable research and innovation,[188] appears promising. However, the "procedure has several flaws"[189] and Apostol argued that defence should be excluded from innovation partnerships.[190] Moreover, the "new" procedure allows "any economic operator [to] submit a request to participate" in an innovation partnership according to Article 31(1) Directive 2014/24/EU and prescribes the use of what closely resembles the negotiated procedure with prior publication of a contract notice in the new Directive, to choose the "partner". As already pointed out above, the need for fair returns for the public financial investment in the project for the industry of the respective Member State cannot be accommodated in such a procedure.[191] As the innovation partnership is the only "new" procedure in the new Directive 2014/24/EU, there is no model to procure collaborative R&D projects in it. Finally, as explained above, the Defence Directive allows the free

---

[188] See also Recital 49 Public Sector Directive 2014/24/EU, *supra* note 7.

[189] According to Luke Butler, "Fostering Innovation", paper delivered at the "6th European Public Procurement Law Network Meeting", Aix-en-Provence, 5 July 2013 (on file), the procedure is poorly drafted, appears to be drafted "last minute" and is full of uncertainties.

[190] A. R. Apostol, "Pre-commercial Procurement in Support of Innovation: Regulatory Effectiveness?" (2012) 20 *Public Procurement Law Review* 213–35.

[191] Recital 47 Public Sector Directive 2014/24/EU, *supra* note 7, refers to Commission Communication "Pre-commercial Procurement: Driving Innovation to Ensure Sustainable High Quality Public Services in Europe (Communication)", COM (2007) 799 final, which is intended to subject the procurement of such contracts to a procedure that is compliant with the TFEU. However, that does not allow accommodating fair returns, which cannot be reconciled with the Internal Market. Moreover, pre-commercial procurement allows the purchase of pre-commercial pre-products but not of a "first product" which is commercially viable.

use of the negotiated procedure with prior publication of a contract notice the successor of which in the new Directive 2014/24/EU is also to be used for the stages of the innovation partnership.[192] Thus the inclusion of the new procedure in the Defence Directive would not result in more flexibility and contracting entities could already conduct "competitive negotiations" based on the model in Article 31 Directive 2014/24/EU.

9 Conclusions

Similar to the old and new Public Sector and Utilities Directives, the Defence Directive provides a number of procedures for contracts within its scope. These prescribe a sequence of stages that have to be followed, starting with publication of the contract in the OJ of the EU. Furthermore, there are additional publication requirements, especially regarding the eventual award, which safeguard the transparency requirements of EU law. Moreover, these procedures are characterised by competition. An exception is the negotiated procedure without prior publication of a contract notice, which is limited to situations regulated in the Directives, also in the Defence Directive. However, the most competitive "open procedure" of the other Directives has not been included, which has consequences for other procedures such as framework agreements. Moreover, there is a preference for negotiated procedures enshrined in the free use of the negotiated procedure with prior publication of a contract notice, the inclusion of the competitive dialogue and adapted and additional circumstances allowing the use of the negotiated procedure without prior publication of a contract notice. The preference for the negotiated procedures is intended to accommodate the specific needs of defence and security procurement, also in response to the requests of stakeholders expressed during the consultation mentioned above. This is the core element of the adaptation of the rules on procedures in the original Public Sector Directive in the Defence Directive: flexibility through increased access to negotiation. Collaborative procurement involving R&D has not been addressed in one of the procedures but excluded, as discussed in chapter 6. The end result of these adaptations is not entirely convincing. Some aspects should be reconsidered in the revision of the Defence Directive. The instrument should include the open procedure and delete the competitive dialogue. Finally, collaborative contracts involving R&D may perhaps not be accommodated inside the Defence Directive but an EDA Code of Conduct could introduce a procedure which reconciles competition and fair returns.

2011–13 figures published by the Commission in July 2013 on publication and competition since the transposition of the Defence Directive in the Member States indicate that the negotiated procedure without publication of a contract

---

[192] Art. 31 Public Sector Directive 2014/24/EU.

notice is used frequently and that many contracts are awarded on the basis of procedures not "foreseen in the [Defence] Directive."[193] Thus prima facie the flexibility provided by the procedures of the Defence Directive discussed in this chapter does not appear to be sufficient. However, the Defence Directive might arguably need more time to change not only the habits of the contracting authorities but also those of the European defence companies.[194]

---

[193] Commission Staff Working Document on Defence SWD (2013) 279 final accompanying COM (2013) 542 final, at 43–5.

[194] Ibid., at 44–5.

Security of supply and security of information

Description in the specifications, contract conditions, qualification and award criteria

1 Introduction

After it is determined that a contracting entity and the contract are within the scope of the Defence Directive as discussed in chapter 6, and after the appropriate procedure has been chosen as discussed in chapter 7, a number of requirements regarding the different stages of a procurement procedure have to be considered. This refers mainly to the procurement phase in the strict sense, from the publication of the contract notice to the conclusion or making of the eventual contract. First, there are rules on the precise description or definition of the good, service or work in question, the so-called (technical) specifications. Secondly, there are related rules on the rejection of bids that are not compliant with the contract requirements. Thirdly, there are rules on the qualification of the economic operators bidding for contracts, an issue of particular importance in defence and security procurement since the reliability of suppliers and providers is crucial for the security interests at stake. Fourthly, there are rules on the criteria that determine who is awarded the contract. However, some of these rules have an effect on the other two phases of the procurement process, before and after the procurement phase in the strict sense. Contract conditions are very closely connected to specifications. This made it necessary to regulate this issue relating to the final "post-procurement" contract management phase after the conclusion or making of the contract in the EU procurement Directives. The rules on specifications also affect to a limited extent the "pre-procurement" determination of what to buy, which is largely outside the ambit of the procurement Directives and the TFEU.

The rules of the Defence Directive on specifications, contract conditions, compliance, qualification and award criteria are based on those of Public Sector Directive 2004/18/EC. However, the rules of the earlier differ in a number of points as the Defence Directive was adapted to take the specific characteristics of the defence and security sectors into account. The 2007 Commission Staff Working Document with the Impact Assessment for the Defence Directive summarised the aim of these adaptions:

The general impacts of the new rules depend on their ability to maximise transparency, non-discrimination and equality of treatment without impacting negatively on Member States' security. If the rules focus on security safeguards at the cost of the implementation of Treaty principles, Member States may use them and reduce the recourse to the exemption, but the positive impacts on openness and transparency would be very limited. If, by contrast, the new rules fully implement Treaty principles at the cost of security interests, Member States will not apply them and continue to use the exemption. In both these cases, the impact of the new rules would be close to zero.[1]

There are two crucial requirements that guided the adaptations: security of supply and security of information. The adaptations are designed to allow defence and security procurement to be conducted within the regime of the Defence Directive and the TFEU, without Member States having to derogate from EU law on the basis of Article 346 TFEU and the other security exemptions discussed in chapters 2 and 3. If the needs of security of supply and security of information are sufficiently accommodated in the Defence Directive, the instrument will limit the use of the exemptions and defence and security procurement will be practiced inside the Internal Market.

1.1 Security of Supply

Security of supply is not defined as such in the Defence Directive. However, the Commission's Guidance Note *Security of Supply* defines the notion in "general terms" as

> a guarantee of supply of goods and services sufficient for a Member State to discharge its defence and security commitments in accordance with its foreign and security policy requirements.[2]

In footnote 1 the Guidance Note refers to the *Letter of Intent (LoI) Framework Agreement*[3] and *Implementing Arrangement*[4] discussed in chapter 5.[5] This

---

[1] Commission Staff Working Document – Impact Assessment SEC (2007) 1598 final, http://ec.europa.eu/internal_market/publicprocurement/docs/defence/impact_assessment_en.pdf [accessed 15 November 2013], at 44 (hereinafter "2007 Staff Working Document").

[2] Commission Guidance Note *Security of Supply*, at http://ec.europa.eu/internal_market/publicprocurement/docs/defence/guide-sos_en.pdf [accessed 10 October 2013], at 1.

[3] *Framework Agreement between the French Republic, the Federal Republic of Germany, the Italian Republic, the Kingdom of Spain, the Kingdom of Sweden, and the United Kingdom of Great Britain and Northern Ireland Concerning Measures to Facilitate the Restructuring and Operation of the European Defence Industry*, Farnborough, 27 July 2000 (United Kingdom) Treaty Series, No. 33 (2001), Cm. 5185.

[4] Ibid., Part 2, Arts. 4–11 of the Agreement. According to its Art. 1(c) one of the objectives of the Agreement is to "(c) contribute to achieve security of supply for Defence Articles and Defence Services for the Parties …"

[5] See ch. 5 at 225–31.

suggests that the definition is at least inspired by these LoI documents.[6] For the purposes of the definition of the Defence Directive it is the Commission's understanding of the notion which is important anyway, not whether that notion was inspired by the definition of another organisation. The definition is further developed in the Guidance Note *Security of Supply*:

> This includes the ability of Member States to use their armed forces with appropriate national control and, if necessary, without third party constraints. Such a broad concept can cover a wide range of different industrial, technological, legal and political aspects.[7]

The basic concern behind the notion of security of supply in the Defence Directive and in other relevant international agreements is that both initially and during the often long life cycle of a contract, both in peacetime and in times of crisis and war, a Member State needs to be sure that the goods, works and services it needs to operate its armed forces and other security activities will be supplied and provided. This is essential for an efficient national defence and security policy and therefore national security. They need a "guarantee", "control" and "no third-party constraints". Otherwise the effective use of the armed forces and other security activities can be compromised or completely undermined. Security of supply can be affected, inter alia, by unreliable economic operators, either as prime contractors or anywhere in the supply chain, or by disrupted transport or other communications. These dangers can occur in both domestic contracts as well as contracts with suppliers from another Member State or a third country. However, they might well be more significant in a non-domestic context since the government has less control over the factors affecting security of supply, such as the management of economic operators or transport links. The 2007 Commission Staff Working Document calls this the industrial dimension of security of supply.[8] Moreover, additional threats to security of supply exist in the non-domestic context. First, defence and security transfers are subject to licensing (authorisation) requirements of the national authorities in the country of production. This connects the accommodation of security-of-supply requirements in the Defence Directive to the other instrument of the "Defence Package", the Intra-Community Transfers (ICT) Directive discussed in chapter 4.[9] This will be discussed below. However, many products or operators in the supply chain are third countries outside the EU. Secondly, defence and security transfers can be subject to other legal

---

[6] *Supra* note 1, at 17, footnote 31.

[7] Guidance Note *Security of Supply*, *supra* note 2, at 1.

[8] 2007 Commission Staff Working Document, supra note 1, at 17 and 45–6.

[9] At 147–60. This connection is also highlighted again in the 2013 Commission Communication "Towards a more Competitive and Efficient Defence and Security Sector: A New Deal for European Defence", COM (2013) 542 final, at 11.

and political constraints affecting security of supply. Again the 2007 Commission Staff Working Document calls this the industrial dimension of security of supply.[10] This will also be discussed below.

As highlighted several times before in this book, the Defence Directive aims to provide a tailor-made framework for defence and security procurement thereby significantly limiting the use of Article 346 TFEU in practice. This objective will not be met if security-of-supply requirements are not sufficiently accommodated in the new instrument. While the Directive does not define security of supply, it does recognise the importance of the notion in its Recitals 9 and 44. More importantly a number of provisions taken from the old Public Sector Directive on contract conditions, selection criteria and award criteria were adapted to take security-of-supply concerns into account.

1.2 Security of Information

Security of information is not defined as such in the Defence Directive either. However, the Commission's Guidance Note *Security of Information* makes clear that this notion refers to "[t]he ability and the reliability of economic operators to protect classified information".[11] As security of information is concerned with the "ability and reliability of economic operators" it mainly affects the qualification and selection of tenderers. However, it also affects the rules on contract conditions and to a more limited extent on award criteria. Finally, the publication of the contract can be affected. Classified information is defined in Article 1(8) Defence Directive as

> any information or material, regardless of the form, nature or mode of transmission thereof, to which a certain level of security classification or protection has been attributed, and which, in the interests of national security and in accordance with the laws, regulations or administrative provisions in force in the Member State concerned, requires protection against any misappropriation, destruction, removal, disclosure, loss or access by any unauthorised individual, or any other type of compromise.

The Guidance Note rightly considers security of information to be a "particularly important feature" of the Defence Directive because of "the sensitive nature of many defence and security procurements".[12] The security of classified information needs to be safeguarded throughout the life cycle of the contract and even after its performance.[13] However, as will be explained further below, in the absence of an EU security-of-information regime, the Member States decide

---

[10] 2007 Commission Staff Working Document, *supra* note 1, at 17–18 and 44–5.
[11] Commission's Guidance Note *Security of Information*, http://ec.europa.eu/internal_market/publicprocurement/docs/defence/guide-soi_en.pdf [accessed 10 October 2013], at 1.
[12] Ibid.   [13] 2007 Commission Staff Working Document, *supra* note 1, at 47–8.

on the information to be classified, on the level of confidentiality and grant the necessary security clearances, which are not automatically recognised by other Member States. In contrast to the licences for intra-Community transfers mentioned above, there is no EU Directive on this issue.

This chapter provides a critical analysis of those rules of the Defence Directive regulating the different stages of a procurement procedure that were adapted from Public Sector Directive 2004/18/EC. All these adaptations were motivated by the need to take security of supply and security-of-information considerations into account. First, the chapter will consider the rules on technical specifications on contract documentation and the closely related rules on contract conditions (section 2 below). Secondly, the rules on qualification and selection will be discussed (section 3 below). Finally, the chapter will analyse the rules on award criteria (section 4 below). It will be shown that in addition to the limitation of scope discussed in chapter 6 and the greater flexibility in the procurement procedures discussed in chapter 7, the framing of the "technical" rules to accommodate security-of-supply and security-of-information concerns represent the third important theme in the adaptations to the rules of Public Sector Directive 2004/18/EC aiming at providing an instrument for defence and security procurement: description.

2 Contract notice, technical specifications and contract conditions

As with the 2004 and 2014 Public Sector and Utilities Directives, under the Defence Directive the public procurement procedure begins with the publication of a contract notice in Tenders Electronic Daily (TED), the electronic version of the Supplement to the Official Journal of the EU.[14] This requirement is in itself a significant innovation with respect to armaments contracts since, as discussed in the introduction to this book,[15] before the Directive only very few such contracts were advertised on TED. Under the former EDA Code of Conduct discussed in chapter 5[16] some were advertised on the EDA portal EBB[17] and before that there were only national bulletins as part of the WEAG/WEAO regime.[18] Most importantly many contracts were not subject to any contract notice in any publication. Under the Defence Directive all covered defence and security

---

[14] Art. 30(2) Defence Directive.   [15] At 1–2.   [16] At 191–8.

[17] www.eda.europa.eu/ebbweb/ [accessed in September 2012, but no longer online in October 2013, see ch. 5]. See also the figures in the Commission Staff Working Document SWD (2013) 279 final accompanying COM (2013) 542 final, at 41–3.

[18] On the WEAG/WEAO regime see M. Trybus, *European Defence Procurement Law: International and National Procurement Systems as Models for a Liberalised Defence Procurement Market in Europe* (The Hague: Kluwer Law International, 1999), ch. 2, "A Critical Analysis of the European Defence Equipment Market", at 31–44. See also ch. 5 of this book at 233–7.

contracts have to be advertised in one "place" which is the same "place" as the contracts covered by the Public Sector and Utilities Directives. The publication of the contract notice represents the borderline between the public procurement phase in the strict sense (the "*how* to buy phase) and the pre-procurement phase in which the contracting authority or the governmental or parliamentary bodies it serves determine the subject matter of the contract ("*what* to buy" phase). The "how to buy phase" is regulated by the TFEU and the Directives including the Defence Directive. The "what to buy phase" might be regulated by national laws but not by EU law. The "second" public procurement phase ends with the conclusion or making of the contract, after which the "third" post-procurement phase, the contract management phase ("after purchase"), begins, which can last for years and in the case of armaments projects decades. The latter phase is affected by EU law to only a very limited extent, which shall be explained below. Thus the contract notice starts the procurement phase but is also closely connected to both the pre-procurement and the post-procurement phases. First, the contract notice is to a certain extent the end result of the pre-procurement phase determining the subject matter of the contract. Up to this point the process is not regulated by EU law including the Defence Directive and the contracting entity may accommodate all kinds of objectives including security of supply and security of information. Secondly, contract conditions affecting the post-procurement phase determine the subject matter of the contract as well and therefore already have to be mentioned in the contract documentation. Thus the contract notice is a crucial stage of any procurement procedure connected to all three phases of the procurement process.

Adequate information on the subject matter of the contract, at least a general description of the product, work or service, including the contract performance conditions and award criteria, has to be provided in the contract notice to enable economic operators to decide if they are interested to bid or to send a request to participate. Annex IV to the Defence Directive provides a full list of the information to be included. In the context of the Defence Directive this should also include the main features of the security-of-supply[19] and security-of-information[20] requirements. The information does not have to be comprehensive for all the procedures discussed in chapter 7 since it may be complemented in the contract documents sent at a later stage. Apart from the requirement to include security-of-supply and security-of-information requirements in the contract notice and contract documents, information that may also be included in the contexts of the other procurement Directives, there are no major differences to the rules of the 2004 and 2014 Public Sector and Utilities Directives.

---

[19] Guidance Note *Security of Supply, supra* note 2, at 5.
[20] Guidance Note *Security of Information, supra* note 11, at 6–7.

The 2007 Commission Staff Working Document had considered limitations on publication requirements to safeguard security of information.[21] However, the non-publication of contracts containing confidential information was considered as too detrimental for transparency. Moreover, this would not sufficiently safeguard the confidentiality of this information after the publication,[22] for example during negotiations. Thus it was considered preferable to allow certain technical specifications only to be released to the successful bidder, "if information is so sensitive that limiting its dissemination as much as possible is necessary to the protection of Member State's security interests".[23] When the equipment must be integrated into an existing weapons system, the contracting authority may limit information to the technical specifications of that equipment and release the information on system integration only to the successful bidder. This limitation was considered to strike the right balance between the need to safeguard security of information and ensuring equal treatment and the right level of transparency.[24] It is submitted that these practices would be compatible with the requirements on contract notices in Article 30(2) Defence Directive and its Annex IV, provided they do not limit competition, are explained to the economic operators and are proportionate. However, in appropriate cases this would probably also have been possible under Article 35(2) Public Sector Directive 2004/18/EC. Information in contract award notices and framework agreements can be withheld also for defence and security interests according to Article 30(3) subparagraph 3 Defence Directive,[25] but that would also have been possible under Article 35(4) subparagraph 5 Public Sector Directive 2004/18/EC on which it was based; it was included in the notion of "public interest". Hence the reference is merely descriptive rather than adding substance in comparison to the original public sector provision. However, as with the other descriptions discussed in other parts of this chapter, this clarifies that defence and security considerations can be taken into account in this context, thereby reducing litigation risks and encouraging the use of the provision.

2.1 Technical specifications

The finalisation of technical specifications is an important stage of open and restricted procedures very closely connected to the determination of the subject matter of the contract and the publication of the contract notice. The procurement rules on technical specifications defining the good, work or service to be procured are mainly intended to prevent "product definitions" to be abused in order to reduce the pool of possible bidders and to lead to discrimination of

---

[21] 2007 Commission Staff Working Document, *supra* note 1, at 46–7.   [22] Ibid., at 46.
[23] Ibid.   [24] Ibid.   [25] See also Recital 56 Defence Directive.

tenderers because of their nationality.[26] After all, it is easy to tailor technical specifications for a particular provider. Article 18 Defence Directive on technical specifications closely resembles the rules of Public Sector Directive 2004/18/EC,[27] apart from the addition of "defence standards[28] . . . and defence materiel specifications similar to those standards", which is appropriate. The importance of standards was highlighted in chapter 4.[29] The 2007 Staff Working Document emphasised the "plethora of standards" used in defence contracting – national, NATO and multilateral[30] – leading to "hierarchies of standards", which differ significantly between Member States. Some Member States, France for example, give priority to defence standards whereas others, such as the United Kingdom, give priority to European standards.[31] This means that the impact of Article 18 Defence Directive will also differ from one Member State to the other, as some Member States already follow the hierarchy taken over from Public Sector Directive 2004/18/EC. It should be emphasised, however, that due to the absence of the open procedure and the reduced importance of the restricted procedure in the Defence Directive discussed in chapter 6,[32] the rules on specifications, which only apply to these two procedures, are of less importance in comparison to the 2004 and 2014 Public Sector Directives where only these two procedures are freely available. However, even in the negotiated procedures and the competitive dialogue parts of the contract, for example, certain components can be subject to standards.

---

[26] On the rules of 2004 Utilities Directive and 2004 Public Sector Directive see Christopher Bovis, *EC Public Procurement: Case Law and Regulation* (Oxford University Press, 2007), at 220–3 and 397–9; technical specifications are also frequently the subject of court decisions, see Case 45/87, *Commission* v. *Ireland* ("Dundalk") [1988] ECR 4929 and Case C-359/93, *Commission* v. *The Netherlands* ("UNIX") [1995] ECR I-157.

[27] Art. 23 Public Sector Directive 2004/18/EC.

[28] Defence standards are defined in Point 3 of Annex III Defence Directive as: "a technical specification the observance of which is not compulsory and which is approved by a standardisation body specialising in the production of technical specifications for repeated or continuous application in the field of defence . . ."

[29] At 166–9.

[30] The 2007 Staff Working Document, *supra* note 1, at 20 mentions national standards maintained by ministries of defence and national standardisation bodies and in footnote 37 use the United Kingdom as an example for memberships in multilateral networks: the American, British, Canadian and Australian Armies' Standardisation Program (ABCA). These ABCA standards were formerly called ABCA Quadripartite Standardization Agreements (OSTAGs) and the ABCA Advisory Publications were formerly called ABCA Quadripartite Allied Publications (QUAPS). The importance of common European defence standards is also highlighted in COM (2013) 542 final, at 12. They should remain voluntary and avoid duplication with NATO efforts.

[31] 2007 Staff Working Document, ibid., at 21 footnotes 39 and 40.

[32] Due to the free use of the negotiated procedure with prior call for tender which becomes the least competitive but freely available procedure and thus the default procedure, the default procedure of the Public Sector Directive being the restricted procedure, see ch. 7 at 322–31.

2.2 Contract performance conditions

Contracting authorities and entities can meet their objectives not only during the procurement procedure in the strict sense, from the contract notice to the award or conclusion of the contract, but also by imposing contract performance conditions on their private sector contractors.[33] The objectives pursued through contract performance conditions can be aimed at value for money, but also of a social, environmental or industrial policy nature.[34] Moreover, for the purposes of the Defence Directive they can include security-of-supply and security-of-information objectives. Contractual conditions will only be in operation after the conclusion or making of the contract,[35] during the post-procurement contract management phase. Trepte differentiates between two levels in which contract performance conditions operate. First, they can be used as a "mechanism to ensure statutory compliance" with legislation which is applicable anyway.[36] Secondly, contract performance conditions can be used to ensure compliance with existing legislation but from bidders not subject to it, most importantly because they are based in another jurisdiction, or to ensure compliance with standards and requirements not enshrined in legislation.[37] It is at this second level where contract performance conditions can be problematic. First, after all, the Defence Directive aims to facilitate an Internal Market for the relevant goods, works and services. For an economic operator from one Member State the contract performance conditions of a contracting authority or entity in another Member State can be a barrier to trade when he or she would otherwise not be subject to these conditions. Secondly, even an economic operator situated in the same Member State as the contracting authority or entity might be facing new conditions not previously subject to legislation, which might be problematic in a national constitutional rather than an

---

[33] Peter Trepte, *Public Procurement in the EU* (Oxford University Press, 2007), at 299.

[34] On secondary objectives in public procurement see C. McCrudden, "Social Policy Issues in Public Procurement: A Legal Overview" in Sue Arrowsmith and Arwel Davies (eds.), *Public Procurement: Global Revolution* (The Hague: Kluwer, 1998), ch. 12; P. Kunzlik, "Environmental Issues in International Procurement" in Arrowsmith and Davies, ibid., ch. 11; Christopher McCrudden, *Buying Social Justice* (Oxford University Press, 2007); N. Brunn and B. Bercusson, "Labour Law Aspects of Public Procurement in the EU" in Ruth Nielsen and Steen Treumer (eds.), *The New Public Procurement Directives* (Copenhagen: Djøf Publishing, 2005), at 97; P. Kunzlik, "Green Procurement under the New Regime" in Nielsen and Treumer, ibid., at 117; Roberto Carnata and Martin Trybus (eds.) *The Law of Social and Green Procurement in Europe* (Copenhagen: Djøf Publishing, 2010); Sue Arrowsmith and Peter Kunzlik, *Social and Environmental Policies in EC Public Procurement Law* (Cambridge University Press, 2009).

[35] See the discussion in R. Caranta, "Sustainable Public Procurement in the EU" in Caranta and Trybus, *The Law of Social and Green Procurement in Europe*, supra note 34, at 46–8.

[36] Trepte, *Public Procurement in the EU*, supra note 33, at 300.   [37] Ibid.

Internal Market context.[38] This is due to the fact that contract conditions are normally outside parliamentary and often judicial control.[39] On the other hand, it might be difficult to accommodate many of the relevant policy objectives at any other stage of the procurement cycle, especially during the procurement phase in the strict sense. Moreover, contract performance conditions might be a particularly efficient instrument to facilitate the policy objectives as they can be enforced throughout the life time of the contract and the contractor can prepare for them already at an early stage, provided they are also communicated early. To a certain extent both the Internal Market and the constitutional concerns can be addressed when contract performance conditions are regulated by the EU legislator in the procurement Directives. Thus regulated, they are harmonised in the Internal Market and subject to legislative and judicial control. The regulation of certain contract performance conditions in the EU procurement Directives is a relatively new technique only really used since the 2004 reform of the Public Sector and Utilities Directives. That reform was based on the relevant ECJ case law preceding it,[40] which remains instructive.

Similar to Article 26 Public Sector Directive 2004/18/EC and Article 38 Utilities Directive 2004/17/EC, Article 20 Defence Directive allows contract performance conditions, as long as these comply with EU law and are indicated in the contract documentation.[41] The requirement of compatibility with EU law means mainly, as emphasised in Recital 41 Defence Directive, that contract conditions must not be directly or indirectly discriminatory.[42] The requirement of the contract conditions to be communicated at the beginning of the procurement procedure partly explains their close connection to the specifications regulating the very beginning of the procurement procedure. In addition to the reference to environmental and social considerations made in all Directives, Article 20 Defence Directive also provides:

> These conditions may, in particular, concern subcontracting or seek to ensure the security of classified information and the security of supply required by the contracting authority/entity, in accordance with Articles 21, 22 and 23 . . .

---

[38] T. Daintith, "Regulation by Contract: the New Prerogative" (1979) 32 *Current Legal Problems* 41 as cited Trepte, *Public Procurement in the EU, supra* note 33, at 301.

[39] Ibid.

[40] The leading cases are Case 31/87, *Gebroeders Beentjes BV* v. *The Netherlands* [1988] ECR 4635 and Case C-225/98, *Commission* v. *France* ("Nord-Pas-de-Calais") [2000] ECR I-7445.

[41] Contract notices, contract documents, descriptive documents or supporting documents, see Arts. 20, 22 and 23 Defence Directive.

[42] Recital 41 Defence Directive reads: "Contract performance conditions are compatible with this Directive provided that they are not directly or indirectly discriminatory and are indicated in the contract notice or the contract documents."

In its Articles 21–3 the Defence Directive provides many contract performance conditions, especially concerning security of information and security of supply. Article 21 Defence Directive addresses subcontracting, which shall not be further discussed in this chapter on security of supply and information but in chapter 9 on offsets and subcontracting.[43] Contract conditions can be used to ensure security of information and supply in addition to qualification discussed under section 3 below. Contract conditions concern the contract whereas qualification concerns the bidder.

2.2.1 Security of supply

Regarding security of supply, Article 23 Defence Directive allows requirements concerning the transfer, export and transit of products; requirements regarding security of supply in crisis situations, when there are additional needs, for spare parts; and information obligations regarding possible changes of the production site or in the supply chain.

According to Article 23 subparagraph 1 Defence Directive contracting authorities and entities shall specify their security-of-supply requirements in the contract documentation, a requirement repeating that in Article 20 Defence Directive. Article 23 subparagraph 2 Defence Directive then "contains a non-exhaustive list of particulars" in the form of documentation, certification, information or other specific commitments.[44] It should be emphasised that the contracting entities have to reject bids which are not compliant with all requirements including those on security of supply. However, the tenderer can be given the opportunity to further clarify and explain the tender to avoid such a rejection in accordance with the principles developed in the context of the old Public Sector and Utilities Directives.[45]

2.2.1.1 Export, transfer and transit of goods associated with the contract

Article 23 subparagraph 2(a) Defence Directive provides that the following requirement may be included in the contract documentation:

> certification or documentation demonstrating to the satisfaction of the contracting authority/entity that the tenderer will be able to honour its obligations regarding the export, transfer and transit of goods associated with the contract, including any supporting documentation received from the Member State(s) concerned . . .

This requirement is particularly crucial in the context of the objectives of the Defence Directive. The licensing requirements addressed here apply "by

---

[43] At 428–52.   [44] Guidance Note *Security of Supply*, *supra* note 2, at 9.

[45] See the statement of the European Commission to this effect, [1994] OJ L111/114. See also the case law discussed by Trepte, *Public Procurement in the EU*, *supra* note 33, at 309–17.

definition"[46] to cross-border movements of goods which the Directive aims to facilitate. The risk against which the contracting authority or entity wants to protect itself is the possible "refusal, withdrawal, or delay of relevant exports and transfer authorisations but also possible conditions linked to these authorisations".[47] The realisation of any of these risks would obviously compromise security of supply.

There is a very clear connection of this contract performance condition to the Intra-Community Transfers (ICT) Directive 2009/43/EC[48] discussed in chapter 4,[49] the other Directive of the "Defence Package". Under the old regime of predominantly individual licences the bid would usually occur before a licence has been granted. After the regime of the ICT Directive is transposed and used in all Member States, which according to its Article 18 had to occur from 30 June 2012, the regime of general licences instead of individual licences might change this. Under a general licence the risk, against which the requirements in Article 23 subparagraph 2(a) Defence Directive represent a safeguard, no longer applies as the general licence will have been granted before the tender is prepared and any adverse effect on security of supply through licensing requirement is thus addressed. However, while this deals with many cases, not all equipment will be subject to a general licence and therefore these safeguards will still be needed for these cases. The Guidance Note *Security of Supply* provides a non-exhaustive list of examples of the requirements that can be included,[50] including evidence showing their planning and resources for obtaining any necessary licences and evidence improving the licensing process,[51] but also examples for requirements that cannot be included.[52] The crucial point under an individual licences regime is that the economic operator does

---

[46] Guidance Note *Security of Supply, supra* note 2, at 10.   [47] Ibid.

[48] Directive 2009/43/EC of the European Parliament and of the Council of 6 May 2009 simplifying terms and conditions of transfers of defence-related products within the Community, OJ [2009] L-146/1.

[49] At 147–60.

[50] Guidance Note *Security of Supply, supra* note 2, at 10, para. 30: "For this purpose, tenderers could furnish, for example: – a record of past transfers of the same equipment to the same or other Member States (to illustrate that the relevant authorities do not normally refuse such transfer licences), or . . . any documents obtained from national authorities through explanatory enquiries or other official contacts."

[51] Ibid., at 11, para. 31: "This could include requirements for the contractor to: – Notify all licensing requirements or other transfer restrictions applicable to the products to be delivered and to any parts, sub-systems thereof, in particular if these have to be provided from third countries . . . Notify the contracting authority of export-controlled content; . . . Institute timely action to obtain export licences; . . . Liaise fully with the contracting authority and/or other relevant authorities on the export licensing process to ensure that all requirements are met; . . . Ensure that contractual requirements are passed down to any subcontractor who may have to apply for export/transfer licences."

[52] Guidance Note *Security of Supply, supra* note 2, at 10, para. 29; at 11, paras. 33 and 34.

not have to provide a guarantee that the licence will be granted. Such a requirement would be objectionable as ultimately discriminatory, because the economic operator simply cannot provide a guarantee for the behaviour of its
national licensing authorities and a domestic operator would not have to
provide such a guarantee. What is required is that the economic operator
shows that he or she has done, or rather will do, everything necessary to acquire
the necessary licences. A sloppy economic operator – who does not stay on top
of the application process for licences and does not keep the contracting
authority or entity informed – compromises security of supply.

The 2007 Commission Staff Working Document reveals that three "sub-
options" to address the intra-Community part of the "political dimension" of
security of supply had been considered.[53] Sub-option (a) would have assumed
the de facto free circulation of defence goods on the basis that only very few
intra-Community transfer licences are ever refused.[54] However, this was considered too optimistic as refusals are still possible. A refusal therefore represents
a risk for security of supply which needs to be addressed in the Defence
Directive if its objective to reduce the use of Article 346 TFEU can be met.
Sub-option (b) would have allowed contracting authorities to ask for all necessary licences for the main delivery and all future deliveries as a contract
condition.[55] This would have of course served the security-of-supply requirements of the contracting authorities best. However, tenderers from other
Member States would have found obtaining all these licences for the initial
delivery and all future additional deliveries "extremely difficult" to an extent
that would have been "a constraint" that would "excessively weigh on tenderers
and favour national suppliers" thereby leaving "the way open to significant
discrimination".[56] Thus the sub-option (c) which became Article 23 subparagraph 2(a) Defence Directive was chosen to balance the Internal Market and
security interests involved, as a compromise.[57] Moreover, this would have been
consistent with the new ICT Directive which simplifies the ability of economic
operators to provide evidence for their ability of meet transfer obligations.

2.2.1.2 Restrictions on disclosure, transfer or use   Article 23 subparagraph
2(b) Defence Directive then provides for the possibility of including the following requirement in the contract documentation:

> the indication of any restriction on the contracting authority/entity regard-
> ing disclosure, transfer or use of the products and services or any result of

---

[53] *Supra* note 1, at 44–5.

[54] Ibid., at 44, citing the 2005 UNISYS Study *Intra-Community Transfers of Defence Products*
(Brussels: Unisys Belgium for the European Commission, 2005), www.edis.sk/ekes/
en_3_final_report.pdf.

[55] 2007 Staff Working Document, *supra* note 1, at 45.   [56] Ibid.

[57] 2007 Staff Working Document, *supra* note 1, at 45.

those products and services, which would result from export control or security arrangements . . .

According to the Guidance Note *Security of Supply* this requirement relates to "so called 'black boxes' and 'anti-tamper devices'" which are components and subsystems forming an integral part of the equipment to be purchased but cannot be accessed or modified by the supplier or purchaser.[58] Moreover, it relates to equipment covered by "export control regimes or special end-use monitoring such as ITAR" where special authorisation from the United States for exports to other countries including transfers to other Member States is required.[59] As with letter (a) discussed above, the risk addressed is that of the refusal, withdrawal or delay of any necessary authorisation. The required disclosure shall allow the contracting authority to react to the risk, also by "maintaining the possibility to award in competition contracts for downstream equipment support".[60] The tenderer merely has to inform the contracting authority comprehensively about any relevant restrictions. Letters (a) and (b) are closely connected and the latter complements the former. Therefore contracting authorities can combine the two requirements.[61]

2.2.1.3 Organisation of the supply chain   Article 23 subparagraph 2(c) Defence Directive provides for another requirement relating to the supply chain:

> certification or documentation demonstrating that the organisation and location of the tenderer's supply chain will allow it to comply with the requirements of the contracting authority/entity concerning security of supply set out in the contract documents, and a commitment to ensure that possible changes in its supply chain during the execution of the contract will not affect adversely compliance with these requirements . . .

A more in-depth analysis of subcontracting and the supply chain is provided in chapter 9 on offsets and subcontracting.[62] The risks addressed in this requirement are disruptions in, for example, transportation or through problems with licensing, not in relation to the tenderer bidding for the prime contract but in relation to all the subcontractors in the supply chain. These disruptions can affect security of supply as much as in relation to the prime contractor and the contracting authority might have even less control. This supply chain can include subcontractors from Member States other than that of the prime contractor and from third countries outside the EU. Therefore letter (c) allows contracting authorities to include requirements relating to the stability and reliability of the supply chain.

---

[58] Guidance Note *Security of Supply, supra* note 2, at 12.   [59] Ibid.
[60] Guidance Note *Security of Supply, supra* note 1, at 12, para. 35.   [61] Ibid., at para. 36.
[62] At 428–52.

The Guidance Note *Security of Supply* differentiates between requirements relating to the time of the tender on the one hand and requirements relating to "future changes in the supply chain"[63] on the other hand. Requirements regarding future changes in the supply chain represent a more general commitment to meet security-of-supply requirements throughout the possibly very long life cycle of the contract. This is also connected to the subcontracting regime of the Defence Directive discussed in chapter 9[64] when subcontracts are awarded on the basis of a competitive procedure. According to the Guidance Note *Security of Supply* both obligations – subcontracting on a competitive basis and meeting security-of-supply requirements throughout the execution of the contract – need to be reconciled in these cases.[65] In this context, as will be discussed in chapter 9, Article 53(2) Defence Directive allows refraining from subcontracting when it cannot be assured that security-of-supply requirements can be met.[66]

Moreover, in the context of requirements relating to the time of the tender the Guidance Note *Security of Supply* differentiates between, first, supply chains including only operators from EU Member States and, secondly, those which include operators from third countries outside the EU. However, this should possibly be further differentiated because a supply chain with providers only from the Member State of the prime contractor implies even fewer security-of-supply risks than a chain with operators from more than one Member State, at least in relation to authorisations. With regards to supply chains with operators from more than one Member State, the Guidance Note emphasises the principle of non-discrimination on grounds of nationality. This allows only requirements based on "objective and performance-based considerations". Geography can be taken into account in relation to transportation (distances and delivery) but not in relation to national territory.[67] It is submitted that as these supply chains operate in an Internal Market context all the requirements would have to meet the requirements of EU Internal Market law as discussed in chapter 2, including proportionality.

With regards to supply chains which include operators from third countries outside the EU, the Internal Market context does not apply directly. Here the Guidance Note *Security of Supply* suggests requirements such as only including "reliable sub-contractors from allied countries" or "to avoid sub-contractors which have to comply with specific control regimes in third countries". The earlier example would exclude operators from Syria or North Korea, for example, and would therefore not be very relevant in practice. The second example would be more problematic since this could include operators from the United States which will often be part of the supply chains of prime contract tenderers

---

[63] Guidance Note *Security of Supply*, supra note 2, at 13, para. 37.   [64] At 428–52.

[65] Guidance Note *Security of Supply*, supra note 2, at 12, para. 40.

[66] Ibid., at 14, para. 40.   [67] Guidance Note *Security of Supply*, supra note 2, para. 38.

from EU Member States. All these conditions have to be "appropriate and proportionate", with regards to the prime contract bidder from the EU, not with regards to the third-country operator in the supply chain.

2.2.1.4 Additional needs resulting from a crisis Article 23 subparagraph 2(d) and (e) Defence Directive provide for two possible requirements regarding additional needs resulting from a crisis. Article 23 subparagraph 2(d) Defence Directive allows requiring:

> a commitment from the tenderer to establish and/or maintain the capacity required to meet additional needs required by the contracting authority/entity as a result of a crisis, according to terms and conditions to be agreed . . .

Then Article 23 subparagraph 2(e) Defence Directive allows requiring:

> any supporting documentation received from the tenderer's national authorities regarding the fulfilment of additional needs required by the contracting authority/entity as a result of a crisis . . .

These requirements are aimed as safeguards against risks related to additional needs not part of the original contract arising in a crisis situation. The term "crisis" is defined in Article 1(10) Defence Directive.[68] The definition was included on the initiative of the Rapporteur in the European Parliament Alexander Count Lambsdorff.[69] According to the Guidance Note *Security of Supply* this contract performance condition is less relevant since these requirements concern the conditions of the contract after it has been awarded and not a situation that would allow derogation from the Directive.[70] The precise terms and conditions regarding such additional needs will only be agreed at a later stage when the crisis actually occurs as only then can the contracting authority determine what these needs are and the provider can know how to satisfy them.[71] The Guidance Note also offers an alternative here with options and/or conditional orders in the contract, possibly by also already agreeing on prices and delivery conditions, which would have

---

[68] Art. 1(10) Defence Directive reads: "'Crisis' means any situation in a Member State or third country in which a harmful event has occurred which clearly exceeds the dimensions of harmful events in everyday life and which substantially endangers or restricts the life and health of people, or has a substantial impact on property values, or requires measures in order to supply the population with necessities; a crisis shall also be deemed to have arisen if the occurrence of such a harmful event is deemed to be impending; armed conflicts and wars shall be regarded as crises for the purposes of this Directive . . ."

[69] According to N. Spiegel (European Commission), "Directive 2009/81/EC: Defence Specificities" at the seminar "The European Defence and Security Procurement Directive and the Challenges for its Implementation", European Institute of Public Administration (EIPA), Maastricht, 21 June 2010 (notes of the author, on file).

[70] Guidance Note *Security of Supply, supra* note 2, at 14, para. 40.   [71] Ibid., at para. 41.

to be paid for. The documentation referred to in letter (e) would usually be based on security-of-supply arrangements made in the context of the Letter of Intent or EDA frameworks discussed in chapter 5.[72] These would establish prioritisation systems or general commitments.[73] A problem is that in the event of a crisis situation more than one contracting authority which the economic operator has a contract with might have additional needs. Therefore there is a danger that the contractor is overwhelmed by additional needs caused by a crisis. This problem needs to be addressed in these arrangements.

The requirements in letters (d) and (e) can be affected by licensing obligations that tenderers from other Member States have to face and this could lead to discrimination. On the one hand, for national security reasons the contracting authority of Member State A needs to be sure that additional needs arising out of a crisis situation are satisfied by a bidder from Member State B. On the other hand, and also for national security reasons, Member State B cannot be limited in its competence to decide on individual licences at the time of the actual crisis. This danger of discrimination is addressed in Article 23 subparagraph 3 Defence Directive which prohibits a requirement obliging the tenderer to obtain at the time of the original tender a commitment from "its" Member State to grant such a licence when the additional needs arise. This is in line with the competence of the Member States to grant licences which is unaffected by both the Defence and the ICT Directives. This is also in line with the very nature of contract performance conditions as binding contractors and not the Member States in which they are based.

These requirements are quite specific to the defence and security context and especially military procurement. They need to be included in the Directive as the crisis situations accommodated in them affect national security interests in a way that would otherwise justify derogation from the Directive and Treaty on the basis of Article 346(1)(b) TFEU. It should be pointed out as well that if these contract conditions are adequately drafted and applied they can still be used in the context of competitive procedures. Crisis situations can also justify the use of the negotiated procedure without prior publication of a contract notice on the basis of Article 28(1)(c) Defence Directive, as discussed in chapter 7.[74] However the use of this non-competitive procedure is very close to procurement outside the Directive. Thus for the purpose of meeting the competition and Internal Market objectives of the Defence Directive, the accommodation of these additional needs in a crisis situation in contract conditions is preferable to derogation or the use of the non-competitive procedure.

---

[72] At 225–31 and 186–222.
[73] Guidance Note *Security of Supply, supra* note 2, at 14, para. 42.   [74] At 342–4.

2.2.1.5 Maintenance, modernisation and adaptation   Article 23 subparagraph 2(f) Defence Directive allows contracting authorities and entities to require:

> a commitment from the tenderer to carry out the maintenance, modernisation or adaptation of the supplies covered by the contract . . .

According to the Guidance Note *Security of Supply* this concerns follow-on work.[75] The risk against which this commitment is directed is that important maintenance, modernisation and adaptations needed for the operability of the equipment in question are not carried out thus compromising the utility of the equipment and therefore national security. As explained in chapter 1, security and especially military equipment often have a very long life cycle.[76] This can make it necessary to cover the future maintenance, modernisation and adaptation in the initial supply contract. Maintenance commitments have to be differentiated from "after-sales service and technical assistance" which are considerations which can be taken into account when determining the economically most advantageous tender at the award stage of the procurement procedure discussed in section 4 below, under all of the procurement Directives.[77] Maintenance, modernisation and adaptation will normally concern needs arising in the future, in the case of modernisation and adaptation possibly years after the contract has been awarded. Under the 2004 Public Sector Directive these needs would have to be satisfied in the context of a new contract to be awarded at that point in the future when the need arises, possibly on the basis of a negotiated procedure without prior publication of a contract notice. As discussed in chapter 1,[78] in the context of defence and security, industrial capacities are limited. Thus there is a danger that when the need for modernisation or adaptation arises at some point in the future there will be only one possible economic operator able to fulfil these needs, the supplier of the original equipment. Moreover, there is a danger that this provider might not be willing to satisfy these needs. Against this background it is appropriate to include future modernisation and adaptation in the contract to ensure that these needs are satisfied. This also enhances competition as future modernisation and adaptation can be addressed at the procurement stage when there are still competitors and not possibly years later when only the successful bidder of that contract can offer modernisation and adaptation and the negotiated procedure without prior publication of a contract notice might have to be used.[79]

---

[75] Guidance Note *Security of Supply*, *supra* note 2, at 15, para. 43.   [76] At 52–3.

[77] See Art. 53(1)(a) Public Sector Directive 2004/18/EC or Art. 47(1)(a) Defence Directive.

[78] At 21–7.

[79] As follow-on work or because there is only one possible provider or after an unsuccessful restricted procedure or negotiated procedure with prior call for tender, see ch. 7 at 340 for details.

Maintenance is slightly different from modernisation and adaptation as maintenance needs will arise much sooner than modernisation and adaptation needs, often from the very beginning of the contract performance phase. Moreover, maintenance concerns a service which is often carried out in-house or could be made the subject of a separate contract with another provider. However, while the inclusion of maintenance in this contract performance condition is not entirely convincing, the national security dimension of having operational equipment is a strong argument for it. As explained in chapter 1, up-to-date and fully operational equipment is crucial for military success and often also in other security contexts, for example police work.[80] This gives this particular commitment a national security dimension which needed to be accommodated in the Defence Directive.

In the Guidance Note *Security of Supply* the Commission points out that "it is advisable to specify such a commitment with more detailed stipulations on the nature and content of the maintenance, modernisation, and adaptation to be performed, including, if possible, at least a general agreement on prices".[81] This would make the commitment more useful in practice and reduce the legal risk which modifications of substantial contract terms at a later stage entail.

2.2.1.6 Industrial changes Article 23 subparagraph 2(g) Defence Directive provides for another possible contract performance condition:

> a commitment from the tenderer to inform the contracting authority/entity in due time of any change in its organisation, supply chain or industrial strategy that may affect its obligations to that authority/entity . . .

This commitment concerns changes of the economic operator's organisation, supply chain or industrial strategy and is intended as a safeguard against the risk of being taken by surprise by business decisions affecting security of supply.[82] Fulfilling the commitment will give the contracting authority time to address these changes. With regards to changes in the supply chain, letters (g) and (c) have to be read together. This contract condition only entails an information commitment in contrast to the performance commitments amounting to what could be a separate contract in, for example, Article 23 subparagraph 2(f) Defence Directive.

2.2.1.7 Ceasing of production A last commitment regarding security of supply is stipulated in Article 23 subparagraph 2(h) Defence Directive which allows contracting authorities and entities requiring

---

[80] At 50. [81] Guidance Note *Security of Supply*, *supra* note 2, at 15, para. 43.
[82] Ibid., para. 44.

a commitment from the tenderer to provide the contracting authority/ entity, according to terms and conditions to be agreed, with all specific means necessary for the production of spare parts, components, assemblies and special testing equipment, including technical drawings, licences and instructions for use, in the event that it is no longer able to provide these supplies.

This commitment is intended as a safeguard against the "risk resulting from the ceasing of production of military or security equipment".[83] This might be due to bankruptcy or a business decision. On the basis of the commitment the contracting authority could take over the production of the product in question if the economic operator ceased production; the production would become "in-house". The specific terms and conditions of this transfer would probably be only agreed at the point in time when production ceased and not at the time of the initial contract.

2.2.1.8 Conclusions on contract conditions concerning security of supply
The contract performance conditions relating to security of supply can be differentiated into four different groups according to the significance and the implications of the requirements they impose. Article 23 subparagraph 2(b) and (g) Defence Directive are merely information commitments to the contracting authority. They represent relatively "light" commitments and are well justified and proportionate in view of the national security concerns they aim to address.

Article 23 subparagraph 2(a), (c) first part, and (e) Defence Directive go beyond that in requiring certification and documentation. However, they also represent relatively "light" commitments and are well justified and proportionate in view of the national security concerns they aim to address.

Article 23 subparagraph 2(d) and (f) Defence Directive on capacity to meet additional needs as a result of a crisis and on maintenance, modernisation and adaptation represent considerably "heavier" commitments as they extend the subject matter of the supply contract beyond the initial piece or pieces of equipment to be procured to include follow-on supplies and services which could also be the subject of separate contracts. This is mainly intended to address defence-specific national security concerns and/or the long life cycle of defence and security equipment. *Prima facie*, there is a danger that these conditions compromise competition as the relevant goods and services are not subjected to new procurement procedures. However, due to the long life cycle of the relevant types of equipment and the limited industrial capacities to produce and adapt them, there might actually be more competition when these additional needs and services are integrated in and procured with the original supply contract, provided there are several competitors. The alternative might often be

---

[83] Guidance Note *Security of Supply, supra* note 2, at 16, para. 45.

an award by negotiated procedure without prior publication of a contract notice, in other words single-source procurement from the (original) supplier of the equipment.

Article 23 subparagraph 2(h) Defence Directive is potentially the "heaviest" contract condition as it essentially entails the transfer of considerable assets and intellectual property to the contracting authority. On the other hand the condition covers a case when the contractor itself will no longer be interested in producing the equipment in question. Moreover, it should be taken into account that a contracting authority or entity will normally have little interest in taking over a production capacity as an in-house capacity. Only in very rare and extreme cases, if that, will such a transfer really take place in practice. The national security implications of a production capacity for a piece of equipment which the armed forces still have to or want to use make Article 23 subparagraph 2(h) Defence Directive a proportionate and justified contract condition. In view of the Internal Market and constitutional implications of contract conditions discussed above, especially this potentially very "heavy" condition should be specifically stipulated in the Defence Directive.

Many of the requirements, such as those stipulated in Article 23 subparagraph 2 Defence Directive, are also allowed and customary within the scope of the 2004 and 2014 Public Sector and Utilities Directives. These rules simply provide an Internal Market regime for problems and requirements previously subject to national rules. Heuninckx criticised the lack of practical enforceability of some of these requirements, to which the tenderer commits himself at the time of the tender on the basis of the evidence available at that time.[84] Considering the long life cycle of defence equipment, such a contractual commitment might be difficult to live up to. Moreover, how can a contractual commitment of the tenderer ensure security of supply when this is disturbed by a conflict or embargo,[85] events over which the tenderer has no influence? In such a case the contractor could and probably would claim *force majeure* thereby making all the security of supply-related contract performance conditions discussed above ineffective.[86] Bowsher explained that some of the evidence required in the contract conditions where certification and documentation is required in Article 23 subparagraph 2(a), (c) and (e) Defence Directive might be difficult to acquire when other contracting authorities are reluctant to provide this information.[87] A binding commitment of all Member States "not to prevent the transfer of

---

[84] B. Heuninckx, "The EU Defence and Security Procurement Directive: Trick or Treat?" (2011) 20 *Public Procurement Law Review* 9–28, at 24–5.

[85] Ibid.   [86] Heuninckx, "Trick or Treat?", *supra* note 84, at 24.

[87] M. Bowsher, "How to Meet the Security of Supply Criteria and Avoid Disqualification of Your Bid" at the "C5 EU Defence and Security Procurement Conference", Brussels, 17 November 2009, as cited by Heuninckx, "Trick or Treat?", *supra* note 84 at 24.

defence ... supplies and services within the EU under any circumstances",[88] which does not (yet) exist,[89] would be more efficient in practice.[90]

2.2.2 Security of information

As explained above, security-of-information concerns the protection of classified information. Apart from a general power of contracting entities to impose requirements on prime contractors and subcontractors aimed at protecting classified information throughout the tendering and contracting phases in Article 7 Defence Directive,[91] Article 22 Defence Directive allows requirements to secure the protection of classified information on the required security level through contract performance conditions.[92] These performance conditions include a commitment to safeguard confidentiality (section 2.2.2.1 below) and information on subcontractors (section 2.2.2.2 below).

2.2.2.1 Commitment to safeguard confidentiality Article 22 subparagraph 2(a) and (b) Defence Directive provide for two requirements regarding the safeguarding of confidentiality. Article 22 subparagraph 2(a) Defence Directive provides that contracting authorities and entities may require

> a commitment from the tenderer and the subcontractors already identified to appropriately safeguard the confidentiality of all classified information in their possession or coming to their notice throughout the duration of the contract and after termination or conclusion of the contract, in accordance with the relevant laws, regulations and administrative provisions ...

Moreover, Article 22 subparagraph 2(b) Defence Directive provides that contracting authorities and entities may require

> a commitment from the tenderer to obtain the commitment provided in point (a) from other subcontractors to which it will subcontract during the execution of the contract ...

---

[88] Heuninckx, "Trick or Treat?", *supra* note 84, at 25.   [89] Recital 9 Defence Directive.

[90] The other Directive of the Defence Package, Directive 2009/43/EC simplifying terms on conditions of transfers of defence-related products within the Community, *supra* note 43, which is according to Heuninckx, "Trick or Treat?", *supra* note 84, at 25, "a good first step in that direction". There is no "licence-free room in Europe" and a licence requirement is a risk for security of supply and thus for the Internal Market for all goods and services subject to them, as emphasised by Spiegel (European Commission, June 2010), *supra* note 69 (notes of the author, on file).

[91] See T. Briggs, "The New Defence Procurement Directive" (2009) 18 *Public Procurement Law Review* NA129, at NA133.

[92] In principle these requirements are also applicable to subcontractors. See Art. 22(b)-(d) Defence Directive.

According to the Guidance Note *Security of Information* letter (b) allows the verification through security clearances of the tenderer's "general ability to safeguard classified information at the required level".[93] Letter (a) allows the contracting authority to get a firm commitment from the prime contractor and subcontractors which is underpinned by security clearances to use his or her ability to protect the concrete information received in the context of the contract. The two commitments, so the Guidance Note says, provide "a useful complement to the selection criterion in Article 42(1)(j)" Defence Directive discussed below (section 4 below). Articles 42(1)(j) and 22(2)(a) and (b) Defence Directive form a "coherent system that allows the contracting authority/entity to ensure firstly that only reliable operators possessing the necessary abilities are invited to tender and secondly that they undertake to ensure adequate protection of classified information".[94]

2.2.2.2 Information on subcontractors

Article 22 subparagraph 2(c) and (d) Defence Directive provide for two requirements for the protection of classified information which concern subcontractors. Article 22 subparagraph 2(c) Defence Directive provides that contracting authorities and entities may require

> sufficient information on subcontractors already identified to enable the contracting authority/entity to determine that each of them possesses the capabilities required to appropriately safeguard the confidentiality of the classified information to which they have access or which they are required to produce when carrying out their subcontracting activities . . .

Moreover, Article 22 subparagraph 2(d) Defence Directive provides that contracting authorities and entities may require

> a commitment from the tenderer to provide the information required under point (c) on any new subcontractor before awarding a subcontract.

According to the Guidance Note *Security of Information*, this information will consist of certificates from the national or designated security authority of the tenderer for the prime contract that all the subcontractors in the relevant supply chain "hold national clearances at the necessary security level".[95] The relevant information can then be checked with these authorities. This inclusion of the subcontractors in the verification of reliability is necessary and sensible. As mentioned in chapter 1[96] and discussed in greater detail in the following chapter 9,[97] defence and security contracts often have longer supply chains of subcontractors. These subcontractors pose confidentiality risks as much as the

---

[93] Guidance Note *Security of Information, supra* note 11, at 8, para. 17.   [94] Ibid.
[95] Ibid.   [96] At 27 and 57.   [97] At 428–52.

prime contractor and security-of-information requirements are not satisfied if only applied to the prime contractor.

2.2.3 Description

The security-of-supply and security-of-information rules on contract performance conditions are also allowed and customary within the scope of the old Public Sector[98] and Utilities Directives. It is not necessary for them to be expressly stipulated in the Defence Directive for them to be legally used. The added value of expressly stipulating them in the Defence Directive, of "description", is that there is no doubt about them being in compliance with EU law, thus reducing litigation risks and encouraging their use by contracting officers.

2.3 National transposition

The rules on specifications in Article 18 Defence Directive have been transposed in Austria in §§ 67–8 and 81–3 BVergGVS,[99] in Germany in § 15 VSVgV,[100] in Ireland in Regulation 16 ACRDSR,[101] and in the United Kingdom in Regulation 12 DSPCR.[102] The general provision on contract conditions in Article 20 Defence Directive has been transposed in Austria in §§ 68(5) and 84 BVergGVS, in Germany mostly in § 16 VSVgV (but other rules are important as well), in Ireland in Regulation 18 ACRDSR and in the United Kingdom in Regulation 16 DSPCR. The rules on security of supply in Article 23 Defence Directive have been transposed in Austria in § 70 BVergGVS, in Germany in § 8 VSVgV, in Ireland in Regulation 21 ACRDSR and in the United Kingdom in Regulation 39 DSPCR. Finally, the rules on security of information in Article 22 Defence Directive have been transposed in Austria in § 69 BVergGVS, in Germany in § 7 VSVgV, in Ireland in Regulation 20 ACRDSR and in the United Kingdom in Regulation 38 DSPCR. Transposition in Ireland and the United Kingdom follows the wording of the Directive very closely. The rules in Austria and Germany, while at times deviating slightly from the

---

[98] See Case C-324/93, *R* v. *Secretary of State for the Home Department, ex parte Evans Medical Ltd* [1996] ECR I-1631, [1996] 1 CMLR 53.

[99] Bundesgesetz über die Vergabe von Aufträgen im Verteidigungs- und Sicherheitsbereich (Bundesvergabegesetz Verteidigung und Sicherheit 2012 – BVergGVS 2012), BGBl. I Nr. 10/2012.

[100] Vergabeverordnung für die Bereiche Verteidigung und Sicherheit – VSVgV, BGBl. I S.1509/2012.

[101] European Union (Award of Contracts Relating to Defence and Security) Regulations 2012, S.I. No. 62 of 2012 (hereinafter ACRDSR).

[102] United Kingdom Defence and Security Public Contracts Regulations 2011, SI 2011/1848 (hereinafter DSPCR).

wording and order of the Directive are also compliant with the rules outlined above.

3 Qualification of bidders

Procurement qualification rules address the need to procure from reliable, appropriately trained, capable, experienced and trustworthy economic operators.[103] According to the case law of the ECJ developed in the context of the old Public Sector and Utilities Directives, qualitative selection criteria have to be clearly distinguished from the award criteria discussed in section 4 below: the earlier concern the quality of the bidder not the product or service subject to the tender.[104] The objective is to protect contracting authorities and entities from unreliable suppliers and providers who will not deliver in the end. Therefore the objective is ultimately to ensure the fulfilment of the primary objective of procurement: to provide the contracting entity with what it needs to operate. This objective is compromised or undermined if the company in question or companies in its supply chain go bankrupt or run into difficulties with the authorities of the country in which they are situated for criminal, tax or other reasons. Not having the technical capacity, the organisation or the skilled manpower to fulfil the eventual contract is at least equally problematic. The financial and technical capacity of possible contract partners has to be ensured. These concerns are related to security of supply. Security of information can also be made the subject of qualification requirements, which aim to ensure that bidders are capable and willing to safeguard the necessary confidentiality and secrecy of many of the contracts in question, especially in the military field.

In the defence and security procurement context, the reliability and trustworthiness of bidders is particularly important, especially if now and in future bidders from other Member States, of which the contracting authorities might not have any previous experience, are to have a realistic chance to be awarded contracts. Qualification requirements concern reliability and trustworthiness of bidders (a) at the time of tendering (present) and (b) for the entire contract management phase after the contract is concluded (future). In order to make

---

[103] On the rules of the 2004 Utilities Directive and Public Sector Directive see Trepte, *Public Procurement in the EU, supra* note 33, at 335–53; Bovis, *EC Public Procurement, supra* note 21, at 224–33 and 399–416; qualification is also frequently the subject of court decisions, see Case 76/81, *Transporoute et Travaux SA* v. *Minister of Public Works* [1982] ECR 417; Case C-389/92, *Ballast Nedam Group NV* v. *Belgian State* [1994] ECR I-1289; Case C-225/98, *Commission* v. *France* ("Nord-Pas-de-Calais") [2000] ECR I-7445; Joined Cases 27–29/86, *CEI and Bellini* [1987] ECR 3347.

[104] Especially Case C-532/06, *Lianakis* [2008] ECR I-251, at paras. 25–32 as cited by Guidance Note *Security of Supply, supra* note 2, at 6, footnote 9.

this prediction on the contract management phase (c) the track record of the companies on reliability and trustworthiness, in other words the past, can be evaluated.

The relevance of security of supply and security of information in the context of qualification is explicitly recognised in Recital 67 Defence Directive. The Guidance Note *Security of Supply* and the Guidance Note *Security of Information* distinguish for qualification or qualitative selection in the context of security of supply and information between three steps. First, economic operators not suitable for participating in a procurement procedure are excluded (section 3.1 below). Secondly, the economic and financial standing and the technical and professional capacity of the economic operators is assessed (section 3.2 below). Thirdly, as discussed in chapter 7,[105] only a limited number of the qualified tenderers are often invited to bid in restricted procedures or to negotiate. For that purpose a ranking is established on the basis of the qualitative selection criteria (section 3.3 below). The Member States have transposed these qualification rules without significant changes (section 3.4 below). The discussion in this section will show that the legislator has mostly used the technique of description when adapting the original rules of Public Sector Directive 2004/18/EC in the Defence Directive, while in some cases substantial additions have occurred.

3.1 Exclusion of unsuitable candidates

First, economic operators not suitable for participating in a procurement procedure are excluded. In cases of conviction by final judgment for certain offences in Article 39(1) Defence Directive, namely participation in a criminal organisation, corruption, offences concerning professional conduct, not paying social security contributions, not paying taxes and misrepresentation in supplying information, exclusion is mandatory. However, the second paragraph of the provision leaves a margin of discretion to the contracting authorities and entities.[106] Apart from all the exclusion criteria in Article 39(1) and (2) (a)–(b) and (f)–(g) Defence Directive[107] which also apply in the context of the old Public Sector Directive,[108] there are a number of criteria specific to the Defence Directive. The following discussion will focus on these defence-specific criteria, as they represent adaptations of Public Sector Directive 2004/18/EC.

---

[105] At 318–20, 323 and 332.

[106] Guidance Note *Security of Information, supra* note 11, at 3, para. 7.

[107] Art. 39(1)(a) participation in a criminal organisation, (b) corruption, (c) conviction of any offence concerning professional conduct, (f) not paying social security contributions, (g) not paying taxes and (h) misrepresentation in supplying information.

[108] Art. 45 (1) and (2) Public Sector Directive 2004/18/EC.

3.1.1 Professional conduct

Article 39(2)(c) Defence Directive does not provide a defence and security-specific criterion as such. It provides that an economic operator may be excluded if he or she

> has been convicted by a judgment which has the force of *res judicata* in accordance with the legal provisions of the country of any offence concerning its professional conduct, such as, for example, infringement of existing legislation on the export of defence and/or security equipment . . .

Article 39(2)(c) Defence Directive is based on Article 45(2)(c) Public Sector Directive 2004/18/EC, and the defence and security-specific security-of-supply aspect after the words "such as" is only an "example". This means that the text of the former is exactly the same as that of the latter with the only difference that a security-of-supply-specific example is described, which, as with the other example of description provided with regards to contract performance conditions discussed in section 3.2 above, adds no substance to the criterion. This assessment is supported by the fact that neither the Guidance Note *Security of Supply* nor the Guidance Note *Security of Information* address letter (c) whereas letter (d), discussed under the next heading below, is addressed in both. Describing a defence-specific example only gives this exclusion criterion a defence "look", although there is the added value that there is no doubt about the described examples of being in compliance with EU law, thus reducing litigation risks and encouraging their use by contracting officers.

3.1.2 Grave professional misconduct

Article 39(2)(d) Defence Directive appears to provide for a security-of-supply and security-of-information criterion specific to the Defence Directive. It allows an economic operator to be excluded if he or she

> has been guilty of grave professional misconduct proven by any means which the contracting authority/entity can supply, such as a breach of obligations regarding security of information or security of supply during a previous contract . . .

According to the Guidance Note *Security of Supply* and the Guidance Note *Security of Information*, this refers to the breach of obligations related to security of supply and security of information during past contracts, including breaches in the context of contracts with other contracting authorities or entities located in any Member State.[109] A conviction by final judgment is not required here but the Guidance Notes provide that the use of the "rather strong

---

[109] Guidance Note *Security of Supply*, *supra* note 2, at 7, para. 19; Guidance Note *Security of Information*, *supra* note 11, at 3, para. 8.

terms" of "has been guilty" and "proven" in Article 39(2)(d) Defence Directive require "objective and verifiable information" for exclusion on this basis.[110] While this cannot be exhaustively discussed in this chapter, this might become the subject of case law regarding what exactly is required here. However, this might take some time.[111] Article 39(2)(d) Defence Directive is based on Article 45(2)(d) Public Sector Directive 2004/18/EC, and the defence and security-specific security-of-supply and security-of-information aspect after the words "such as" suggests that the latter is only a descriptive example which would also be included if the text were exactly the same as in the old Public Sector Directive. The limited added value of the additional descriptive text of Article 39(2)(d) Defence Directive is to specifically address security of supply and security of information thereby avoiding any doubt about misconduct in this context being included and by alerting contracting officers to the importance of checking this issue in the context of qualification. Therefore, although it does not add much substance to the criterion in comparison with Public Sector Directive 2004/18/EC, the fact that an economic operator can be explicitly excluded for the breach of security-of-information and supply obligations in previous contracts can be seen as an innovation of the Defence Directive.[112]

In the recent judgment of *Forposta*[113] the ECJ decided that Article 45(2)(d) Public Sector Directive 2004/18/EC

> must be interpreted as precluding national legislation which provides that a situation of grave professional misconduct, which leads to the automatic exclusion of the economic operator at issue from a procedure for the award of a public contract in progress, arises where the contracting authority concerned has annulled, terminated or renounced a public contract with that same economic operator owing to circumstances for which that operator is responsible, where the annulment, termination or renouncement occurred in the three-year period before the procedure was initiated and the value of the non-performed part of the contract amounted to at least 5% of the contract's value.

This suggests a relatively narrow understanding of grave professional misconduct as a ground of exclusion. It could be asked whether *Forposta* contributes to the interpretation of Article 39(2)(d) Defence Directive. How far does the latter

---

[110] Ibid.

[111] K. Vierlich-Jürcke (European Commission, 2012) "Specificities of the Defence Procurement Directive" at the seminar "European Defence and Security Procurement" at the EIPA, Maastricht, 19 January 2012 (notes of the author, on file).

[112] Heuninckx, "Trick or Treat?", *supra* note 84, at 22 calls this with respect to security of information "[t]he only real innovation".

[113] Case C-465/11, *Forposta* v. *Poczta Polska*, judgment of 13 December 2012, nyr. Thanks to Michael Steinicke for pointing this case out to me when commenting on an earlier draft of this chapter.

provision differ from Article 45(2)(d) Public Sector Directive 2004/18/EC? The Polish provision on non-fulfilment of previous contracts could have been based on issues of security of supply.[114] *Forposta* was decided after the Commission Guidance Notes were published and could therefore not be addressed there. It is argued that the additional express references to security of supply in Article 39(2)(d) Defence Directive and the importance of that consideration for national security could lead to a different interpretation in a contract covered by the Defence Directive. The national Polish provision which was rejected as allowing exclusion for grave professional misconduct in *Forposta* might well be possible under the Defence Directive. If so, then the express stipulation of the security-of-supply and -information considerations would be more than description and have an impact on the substance of the provision. However, this is not clear and would ultimately require an ECJ judgment based on the Defence Directive. Based on the wording of Article 39(2)(d) Defence Directive the security references have to be interpreted as merely descriptive.

3.1.3 Risks to the security of the Member State

Article 39(2)(e) Defence Directive provides for another and clearly defence and security-specific criterion in the context of qualitative selection. It allows exclusion of an economic operator who

> has been found, on the basis of any means of evidence, including protected data sources, not to possess the reliability necessary to exclude risks to the security of the Member State.

This criterion has no equivalent in Public Sector Directive 2004/18/EC. According to the Guidance Note *Security of Supply* the criterion "addresses the link between Security of Supply and the reliability of the candidate or tenderer that appears also in recital 67".[115] This reference to Recital 67 Defence Directive is also contained in the Guidance Note *Security of Information* which also refers to Recital 65 as confirmation that "the reliability of economic operators may also depend on factors other than their ability to protect classified information".[116]

A crucial feature of the exclusion criterion is that the contracting authority or entity may prove the lack of reliability affecting national security "on the basis of any means of evidence, including protected data sources". This deviates from the rules on sufficient evidence for a lack of reliability in Article 39(3) and (4) Defence Directive and Article 45(3) and (4) Public Sector Directive 2004/18/EC. The Guidance Note *Security of Supply* and the Guidance Note *Security of Information* explain the special evidence rule in Article 39(2)(e) Defence Directive with

---

[114] Ibid. [115] Guidance Note *Security of Supply*, *supra* note 2, at 7, para. 20.
[116] Guidance Note *Security of Information*, *supra* note 11, at 3–4, para. 9.

reference to "the particular sensitivity of certain defence and security contracts" and cite Recital 65 Defence Directive:[117]

> it should ... be possible to exclude economic operators if the contracting authority/entity has information, where applicable provided by protected sources, establishing that they are not sufficiently reliable so as to exclude risks to the security of the Member State. Such risks could derive from certain features of the products supplied, or from the shareholding structure of the candidate.

The Guidance Note *Security of Information* also emphasises that letter (e) and Recital 65 imply that there could be cases where contracting authorities and entities question the reliability of economic operators as a minimum requirement leading to exclusion even when they have the necessary security clearances from their national authorities.[118] Such cases would "go well beyond purely legal or normal procurement issues ... so that protected data sources are an important and possibly the only way to establish that security risk for the Member State can be excluded".[119]

However, the use of protected data sources as a means of evidence for a decision as significant as exclusion is problematic. First, a bidder will rightly perceive exclusion as affecting him or her more negatively than even not being awarded the contract at the end of the procurement procedure. This perception will be worse when the evidence on which this decision is based is not even accessible to him or her. The lack of transparency can, rightly or wrongly, give an impression of arbitrariness with negative effects on the Internal Market objectives of the Directive and the willingness of the affected bidder and economic operators in general to participate in procurement procedures for future contracts. Moreover, there is a danger of abuse. Possible abuses will also be difficult to detect and prove in the context of the review proceedings discussed in chapter 10 or in the context of proceedings in the ECJ. The Guidance Note *Security of Supply* assumes that "the use of protected data sources as a means of evidence will certainly be limited to very exceptional cases" and both the Guidance Note *Security of Supply* and the Guidance Note *Security of Information* emphasise that Article 39(2)(e) Defence Directive "does not give unlimited discretion to contracting authorities/entities".[120] There has to be a risk to national security and the contracting authority or entity must be able to "demonstrate, if necessary in special review procedures, that there are objective and verifiable elements indicating a lack of reliability that causes risks to the security of the State", if a bidder is to be excluded.[121] Moreover, the

---

[117] Ibid.   [118] Guidance Note *Security of Information*, *supra* note 11, at 4, para. 9.
[119] Ibid.
[120] Guidance Note *Security of Supply*, *supra* note 2, at 7, para. 20; Guidance Note *Security of Information*, *supra* note 11, at 4, para. 9.
[121] Ibid.

alternative to the exclusion of a particular bidder for national security reasons, even when based on evidence contained in protected data, needs to be considered. The respective national security concerns might lead to derogation from the Defence Directive as a whole on the basis of Article 346(1)(b) TFEU if the exclusion of a bidder, the inclusion of which in the procurement procedure raises national security concerns, is not possible inside the Directive. Therefore it is argued that the Defence Directive is accommodating a defence and security-specific scenario and thus only follows its general approach of adapting the rules of Public Sector Directive 2004/18/EC to the defence and security sectors. Derogation from the Directive would be considerably more detrimental to its objectives and ultimately an affected bidder. The procedure would still be conducted on the basis of the Directive even when a bidder would be excluded for national security reasons. Allowing protected data sources as evidence for the exclusion of bidders is also an adaptation to the defence and security sector where such data is much more common than otherwise in the public sector.

According to the case law of the ECJ the list of grounds for exclusion of candidates in Article 45 Public Sector Directive 2004/18/EC is exhaustive.[122] This also applies to Article 39(1) and (2) Defence Directive.[123] Thus the national security ground in Article 39(2)(e) had to be provided in the Defence Directive to allow for the exclusion of a bidder. In the previous regime in which Public Sector Directive 2004/18/EC could be used, similar national security considerations would not have allowed exclusion due to the lack of a national security exclusion ground in Article 45 Public Sector Directive 2004/18/EC. This would probably have led to derogation from the Directive on the basis of Article 346(1)(b) TFEU or another security exemption. Therefore the national security ground in Article 39(2)(e) Defence Directive is more than description: it adds a substantive ground for exclusion which is not provided in Public Sector Directive 2004/18/EC.

3.2 Economic and financial standing and technical and professional capacity

Secondly, minimum requirements regarding the economic and financial standing and the technical and professional capacity of the economic operators are assessed. The assessment criteria in Article 42(2)(a), (b), (d)–(g) and (j) Defence Directive – namely previous contracts over the last five years, technicians and technical bodies involved, checks carried out on production capacities or technical capacity, educational and professional qualifications of staff involved, environmental management measures, average annual manpower and samples

---

[122] Case C-213/07, *Michaniki AE* [2008] ECR I-9999, at para. 43 as cited by the Guidance Note *Security of Information, supra* note 11, at 3, footnote 3.
[123] Guidance Note *Security of Supply, supra* note 2, at 7, para. 21.

and certificates for products[124] – also apply in the context of the old Public Sector Directive.[125] All these criteria are useful and to varying degrees tested in the context of the old Public Sector and Utilities Directives and it was sensible and necessary to insert them in the Defence Directive as well. Moreover, more importantly for the purposes of this chapter and book, there are a number of criteria specific or adapted to the defence and security sectors in the Defence Directive. Article 42(2)(j) Defence Directive covers assessment criteria which are specific to security of information and shall be discussed further below. According to the Guidance Note *Security of Supply* Article 42(2)(c) and (h) Defence Directive are particularly important for security of supply and they are also the letters or points that differ most from their equivalents in Public Sector Directive 2004/18/EC.

3.2.1 Study and research facilities

Article 42(1)(c) Defence Directive allows the assessment of

> technical facilities and measures used by the economic operator to ensure quality and the undertaking's study and research facilities, as well as internal rules regarding intellectual property . . .

Although this assessment criterion was taken from Article 48(2)(c) Public Sector Directive 2004/18/EC, the last half-sentence on internal intellectual property rules was added and is therefore specific to the Defence Directive. This specificity to the Defence Directive is supported by the fact that, similar to Article 48(2)(c) of the old Public Sector Directive 2004/18/EC, the equivalent provision in Annex XIV of the new Public Sector Directive 2014/24/EU does not contain the half-sentence on intellectual property either.[126] Moreover, it is not merely a description but adaptation of the original Public Sector rule by addition, actually adding substance. Recital 44 Defence Directive explains that the notion of "internal rules" refers to the relationship between parent company and a subsidiary and that those rules can affect security of supply if they regulate intellectual property rights. The Guidance Note *Security of Supply* provides an example in a selection criterion which requires the bidder to have "IP management standards ensuring a specific level of protection".[127] One possible scenario affecting security of supply could be when intellectual property rights are only

---

[124] Art. 42(1)(a) previous contracts over the last five years, (b) technicians and technical bodies involved, (d) checks carried out on production capacities or technical capacity, (e) educational and professional qualifications of staff involved, (f) environmental management measures, (g) average annual manpower and (i) samples and certificates for products.

[125] Art. 48(2) Public Sector Directive 2004/18/EC.

[126] Directive 2014/24/EU Annex XII Means of Proof of Selection Criteria, Part II letter (c) reads: "a description of the technical facilities and measures used by the economic operator for ensuring quality and the undertaking's study and research facilities".

[127] Guidance Note *Security of Supply, supra* note 2, at 8, para. 23.

held by the parent company or a subsidiary and, depending on who is the contract partner, either is prevented from delivering the respective good or service due to limitations related to these rights.

3.2.2 Geographical location of sources

Article 42(2)(h) Defence Directive provides for another assessment criterion:

> the tools, material, technical equipment, staff numbers and know-how and/ or sources of supply – with an indication of the geographical location when it is outside the territory of the Union – which the economic operator has at its disposal to perform the contract, cope with any additional needs required by the contracting authority/entity as a result of a crisis or carry out the maintenance, modernisation or adaptation of the supplies covered by the contract . . .

Again, the assessment criterion was taken from Public Sector Directive 2004/18/ EC, Article 48(2)(h), but significantly extended in the Defence Directive. It is therefore specific to the Defence Directive. This specificity to the Defence Directive is supported by the fact that, similar to Article 48(2)(h) Public Sector Directive 2004/18/EC, the equivalent provision in Annex XII to the new Public Sector Directive 2014/24/EU does not contain these additional parts either.[128] Especially noteworthy is the explicit reference to "indication of the geographical location when it is outside the territory of the Union". According to the Guidance Note *Security of Supply*, this allows taking into account an economic operator's location in a third country outside the EU in the assessment of its capability to perform the contract.[129] Therefore contracting authorities and entities considering that the geographical location of a candidate in a third country outside the EU could compromise the ability of that candidate to comply with the requirements of the authority or entity, in particular those related to security of supply, may exclude that candidate.[130] Moreover, if the operator who is awarded the prime contract has to award subcontracts on a competitive basis according to Title III Defence Directive as discussed in chapter 9,[131] subcontractors can also be excluded if their third-country location can compromise security of supply.[132] The location in a third-country outside the EU of parts of the supply chain of a prime contractor located inside the EU is covered by the assessment criterion in letter (h) anyway. The Guidance Note *Security of Supply* merely emphasises that such exclusion must be decided on a case-by-case basis, related to the subject matter of the contract, and that it must

---

[128] Directive 2014/24/EU Annex XII Means of Proof of Selection Criteria, Part II letter (i) reads: "a statement of the tools, plant or technical equipment available to the service provider or contractor for carrying out the contract".

[129] Guidance Note *Security of Supply*, *supra* note 2, at 8, para. 24.   [130] Ibid.

[131] At 428–52.   [132] Guidance Note *Security of Supply*, *supra* note 2, at 8, para. 24.

be proportionate. The Defence Directive aims to establish an Internal Market in defence and security procurement. Therefore it cannot accommodate geographical location in a Member State other than that of the contracting authority or entity as an assessment criterion. If such a location compromises security of supply, which can be the case, then the Member State can derogate from the Directive and the TFEU on the basis of Article 346(1)(b) or even Article 36 TFEU.[133] Location of sources in a third country outside the EU as an assessment and even exclusion criterion can be accommodated inside the regime of the Defence Directive since this relates to sources outside the Internal Market. With respect to allied countries such as the USA, Canada or Turkey, all the authorisation issues discussed above, which might be addressed to an extent that security-of-supply concerns can be excluded, will be important. With respect to non-allied countries outside the EU, for example Russia, China or Brazil, this might be more difficult.

The reference to being able to cope with additional needs as a result of a crisis was also added to the text of Article 48(2)(h) taken from Public Sector Directive 2004/18/EC. The Guidance Note *Security of Supply* does not specifically address this aspect of the assessment criterion. However, the addition of this national security-specific aspect of the assessment criterion is not surprising and considered necessary. Similar to the additional national security exclusion ground discussed above, this will allow addressing the national security needs in a crisis situation inside the Defence Directive without having to derogate from the Directive and the TFEU on the basis of Article 346(1)(b) or even Article 347 TFEU. Using the Defence Directive in anticipation of or even during a crisis situation would really put the instrument to the test. If the legitimate exclusion of a bidder on the basis of Article 42(2)(h) Defence Directive in such a situation can keep a contract award inside the regime of the Directive, then the provision was adequately adapted to the needs of the defence and security sectors.

Finally, the reference to "maintenance, modernisation or adaptation of the supplies covered by the contract" was also added to the text of Article 48(2)(h) taken from Public Sector Directive 2004/18/EC. This aspect of the assessment criterion, which is limited to supplies, addresses security-of-supply concerns related to the long life cycle of defence and security equipment, discussed in chapter 1,[134] which does not only require maintenance but also modernisation and adaptation. Again, it is necessary to accommodate the long life cycle of defence equipment and the national security consequences of it becoming

---

[133] See ch. 2 at 36–82 on Case 72/83, *Campus Oil Limited* v. *Minister for Industry and Energy* [1984] ECR 2727 in which security of supply of petrol justified derogation from the then EEC Treaty on the basis of public security.
[134] At 52–3.

dysfunctional, outdated or insufficiently adapted, to keep contracts in the context of which this could be important inside the regime of the Directive.

The additional references to security-of-supply considerations in Article 48(2)(h) Defence Directive are merely descriptive rather than adding substance to the original Public Sector provision. The described security-of-supply considerations could have already been taken into account for relevant contracts as they would be objective and proportionate, at least in a defence and security context.

3.2.3 Classified information and security clearances

As discussed in chapter 1[135] and in the context of contract performance conditions in section 2.2.2.2 above, secrecy is a prominent special characteristic and requirement of defence and security procurement. Therefore the ability of bidders to handle confidential or classified information can also be an important requirement in the context of qualitative selection. Article 42(1)(j) Defence Directive allows contracting entities to require,

> in the case of contracts involving, entailing and/or containing classified information, evidence of the ability to process, store and transmit such information at the level of protection required by the contracting authority/entity.

There is no equivalent to this provision in the 2004 or 2014 Public Sector Directive. Therefore this requirement is specific to the Defence Directive. The Guidance Note *Security of Information* considers this letter to be "particularly important" in the context of security of information, also citing Recital 68 Defence Directive.[136] This ability is normally ensured through security clearances which are issued by designated national security authorities to economic operators located in the respective Member State on the basis of the national rules of that Member State. Therefore Article 43(1)(j) Defence Directive continues:

> In the absence of harmonisation at Community level of national security clearance systems, Member States may provide that this evidence has to comply with the relevant provisions of their respective national laws on security clearance.

Article 22 subparagraph 3 Defence Directive on contract performance conditions discussed above contains exactly the same sentence. The Guidance Note

---

[135] At 43–4.

[136] Recital 68 Defence Directive reads: "In the absence of a Community regime as regards the security of information, it is for the contracting authorities/entities or Member States to define the level of technical capacity which is required in this regard for participation in an award procedure and to assess whether candidates have achieved the required security level."

Security of Information explains that the only evidence for the ability of an economic operator to handle classified information at the required level of protection is a facility security clearance (FSC) granted by the operator's own national designated security authorities under their relevant national rules. These facility security clearances are issued only for contracts involving classified information at the level of "confidential" or above. Economic operators do not themselves possess a copy of this security clearance. Only a statement that they hold such a clearance or that they are prepared to take the necessary security measures to obtain such a clearance can therefore be required from the candidates. The contracting authorities or entities shall then contact the competent national designated security authorities to obtain confirmation that the candidate holds a facility security clearance at the required level or, where appropriate, to request that the security clearance procedure for the candidate is initiated.[137] This at least partly addresses the problem that obtaining these clearances might take time and involves costs. The requirement for an economic operator from one Member State to obtain a security clearance of another Member State to bid for a contract there could compromise the market access of these economic operators and thus the objectives of the Directive in practice.

Articles 22 subparagraph 3 and 43(1)(j) and Recitals 42 and 68 Defence Directive highlight the lack of harmonisation of national security clearance systems in the EU. It is submitted that this repeated mentioning of the absence of an EU-side regime on security clearances suggests a certain lack of satisfaction of the drafters and legislator with this situation. However, Member States are currently not prepared to introduce harmonisation on this matter.[138] It is submitted this leaves a gap and that harmonisation in the form of an EU "Security Clearances Directive" would be useful for the removal of administrative barriers to an Internal Market for defence and security supplies and therefore the overall effectiveness of the Defence Directive.[139] This is also argued by the Commission in the third element of the Defence Package, the Communication "A Strategy for a Stronger and More Competitive European Defence Industry", which clearly envisages the adoption of such a regime.[140] Bialos, Fisher and Koehl have also interpreted the Defence Directive as recommending the introduction of an EU regime harmonising security clearances and security-of-information requirements in general to facilitate EU defence integration and suggest that such a

---

[137] Guidance Note *Security of Information, supra* note 11, at 5, para. 12.   [138] Ibid.

[139] Also arguing for such a regime: Heuninckx, "Trick or Treat?", *supra* note 84, at 22.

[140] COM (2007) 764 final, at 6–7: "Starting in 2008 the Commission will investigate, in close cooperation with Member States, possibilities for an EU system on security of information that would allow exchange of sensitive information between Member States and European companies. This exercise will consider the potential scope, contents and form of such a system."

measure is currently considered or even prepared in the EU.[141] If such harmonisation existed, all bidders for prime contracts and all subcontractors of such
prime contractors operating in one of the Member States of the EU would have
security clearances in the Member State in which they are operating. These
security clearances would be the same as in any other Member State as they
would be based on national legislation based on an EU Directive. No additional
security clearances would be required when bidding for a contract in another
Member State. Heuninckx argues that such an EU system of security clearances
would be particularly needed in the non-military security sectors which are
also included in the scope of the Defence Directive.[142] In these sectors EU
Member State practices are "much less coherent than in the military field".[143]
In the military sectors a longer practice and the relevant initiatives of especially
the Letter of Intent organisation discussed in chapter 5[144] have already led to a
certain degree of coherence. However, while the Letter of Intent initiatives on
security clearances are better than nothing and have made, and will make, a useful
contribution, they only apply to the six Member States participating in the
organisation. Moreover, as argued in chapter 5,[145] intergovernmental arrangements outside the EU cannot be a substitute for legally binding Internal Market
rules on a supranational basis. Finally, the efficient operation of the Defence
Directive as an Internal Market instrument to a certain extent also depends on
security clearances and therefore requires a legally binding Internal Market
instrument.

The absence of an EU regime on security clearances raises the question of the
mutual recognition of security clearances between Member States. Recital 43
Defence Directive provides:

> it is for the contracting authorities/entities or Member States ... to deter-
> mine whether they consider security clearances issued in accordance with
> the national law of another Member State as equivalent to those issued by
> their own competent authorities.

In the absence of harmonisation, mutual recognition is often the only way to
overcome barriers to trade. Article 22 subparagraph 3 Defence Directive also
suggests and encourages the mutual recognition of security clearances.
However, the subparagraph emphasises that even if mutual recognition is
applied the Member States retain the right to make investigations of their
own. Overall, it merely provides and defines a "weak obligation of considering
mutual recognition".[146] Article 42(1)(j) Defence Directive provides:

---

[141] Jeffrey P. Bialos, Catherine E. Fisher and Stuart L. Koehl, *Fortresses & Icebergs: The Evolution
of the Transatlantic Defense Market and the Implications for U.S. National Security Policy*,
2 vols. (Baltimore and Washington DC: Centre for Transatlantic Relations, The Johns
Hopkins University and the US Department of Defense, 2009), I, at 224.

[142] Heuninckx, "Trick or Treat?", *supra* note 84, at 22.   [143] Ibid.   [144] At 225–31.

[145] At 225–31.   [146] Heuninckx, "Trick or Treat?", *supra* note 84, at 22.

Member States shall recognise security clearances which they consider equivalent to those issued in accordance with their national law, notwithstanding the possibility to conduct and take into account further investigations of their own, if considered necessary . . .

Moreover, Recital 68 provides:

even where such agreements exist, the capacities of economic operators from other Member States as regards security of information can be verified, and such verification should be carried out in accordance with the principles of non-discrimination, equal treatment and proportionality . . .

As pointed out by the Guidance Note *Security of Information*, this verification can normally only be performed by the national designated security authority of the Member State in which the economic operator is located.[147] Accordingly, Article 42(1)(j) subparagraph 4 Defence Directive provides:

the contracting authority/entity may ask the national security authority of the candidate's Member State or the security authority designated by that Member State to check the conformity of the premises and facilities that may be used, the industrial and administrative procedures that will be followed, the methods for managing information and/or the situation of staff likely to be employed to carry out the contract.

Article 42(1)(j) subparagraph 3 Defence Directive then provides:

the contracting authority/entity may, where appropriate, grant candidates which do not yet hold security clearance additional time to obtain such clearance. In this case, it shall indicate this possibility and the time-limit in the contract notice . . .

The Guidance Note *Security of Information* encourages contracting authorities and entities to make use of this possibility "[i]n order to improve market access for newcomers and to broaden the defence and security supplier base to include non-established players".[148] Thus bidders have to comply with national rules on security clearances, based on a "basic principle" of mutual recognition of security clearances,[149] but with the final decision and power to make additional investigations left to Member States.[150]

---

[147] Guidance Note *Security of Information*, *supra* note 11, at 5, para. 12.   [148] Ibid.

[149] Heuninckx, "Trick or Treat?", *supra* note 84, at 21. See Art. 42(j) Defence Directive. Additional time may be given to bidders to obtain security clearances which they do not have. The national security authority of the Member State of the bidder may be asked to check their premises and facilities.

[150] See last paragraph of Art. 22 Defence Directive. See also the last part of Recital 68 to the Defence Directive: "the capacities of economic operators from other Member States as regards security of information can be verified, and such verification should be carried out in accordance with the principles of non-discrimination, equal treatment and proportionality".

Member States have bilateral agreements and some but not all include mutual recognition.[151] However, only comprehensive bilateral agreements of every single Member State with all of the other 27 Member States could substitute an EU harmonising measure on security clearances. The Member States participating in the Letter of Intent organisation discussed in chapter 5 – namely France, Germany, Italy, Sweden, Spain and the United Kingdom – have adopted detailed rules recognising security clearances issued by each participating nation without regard to the used standards.[152] Bialos, Fisher and Koehl reported that EU officials would base an EU harmonising measure on the Letter of Intent Agreement and praise this as "yet another area where the Letter of Intent arrangements are having a real effect and being adopted EU wide".[153] Article 1(e) Letter of Intent Agreement does indeed contain the following objective:

> facilitate exchanges of Classified Information between the Parties or their defence industry under security provisions, which do not undermine the security of such Classified Information . . .

The detailed rules on classified information in Part 4 (Articles 19–27) Letter of Intent Agreement[154] contain many detailed measures to facilitate the handling of classified information between the participating nations but no multilateral agreement for the mutual recognition of security clearances between them. The objective of one of the subcommittees under Spanish chairmanship is "to adapt procedures relating to security clearances, transmission of classified information and visits, to facilitate industrial cooperation without undermining the security of classified information and material".[155] While the work of the Letter of Intent nations and the Subcommittee on Security of Information addresses many of the relevant detailed problems and makes a contribution to overcoming security clearances as a barrier to trade, this regime is also problematic. First, the regime does not include all Member States but only applies to six participating nations. Secondly, in contrast to the Defence Directive, the Letter of Intent regime is not part of EU law and therefore it does not have the effect and enforceability of EU Internal Market law. Thirdly, it does not contain

---

[151] See Recital 68 to the Defence Directive and B. Schmitt and N. Spiegel (the drafters of the Defence Directive) in their presentation "The Specificities of the European Defence and Security Procurement Directive" at the seminar "European Defence Procurement and Other Defence Market Initiatives", at the EIPA, Maastricht, 15 November 2010 (notes of the author, on file). See also Guidance Note *Security of Information, supra* note 11, at 5, para. 12.

[152] http://archives.sipri.org/contents/expcon/indrest05.html [accessed 11 October 2013].

[153] Bialos, Fisher and Koehl, *Fortresses & Icebergs, supra* note 141, at 224.

[154] http://archives.sipri.org/contents/expcon/indrest05.html [accessed 11 October 2013].

[155] On the details of the work of Subcommittee 3 see the website of the United Kingdom Ministry of Defence: www.mod.uk/DefenceInternet/AboutDefence/WhatWeDo/Legal/LetterofIntent/Subcommittee3SecurityOfInformation.htm [accessed 11 October 2013].

legally binding obligations regarding the recognition of security clearances, only a number of facilitating measures. Fourth and most importantly and just like the relevant rules of the Defence Directive, the Letter of Intent regime is still based on national security clearances and the details of their application can differ considerably. Thus the Letter of Intent has not established a regime of the recognition of security clearances between the participating nations.

There were efforts to achieve more general mutual recognition in the context of the EU but nothing could be achieved due to national sovereignty concerns.[156] While this might lead to problems, if for example national security clearances are not equivalent, the fact that Member States cannot always ask for their own national security clearance is already a step in the right direction. After all, inter alia, time delays in obtaining national security clearances could be a potential for discrimination and therefore litigation. It is submitted that there would be obvious advantages of an EU-wide security clearance, possibly through the EDA, or harmonisation on the matter to avoid such discrimination.

The rules on security clearances in the Defence Directive add substance in comparison to the Public Sector Directive; they are not merely descriptive.

3.2.4 Security of supply and information as technical capacity criteria

Apart from accommodating security of supply and information in the contract award conditions, they feature prominently as factors of technical capacity, as minimum qualification criteria. The 2007 Commission Staff Working Document had identified this as the best option to balance national security with Internal Market interests.[157] Other options had been carefully considered as well. The option to include security of supply as a generic selection criterion, as an "open" clause allowing contracting authorities to request "evidence of the capacity to provide security of supply", was dismissed as not clear and transparent enough and possibly compromising equal treatment as such a criterion would not be very objective.[158] The favoured option to include security of supply as a technical capacity criterion had to include guarantees for the future, as the long life cycle of defence equipment mentioned in chapter 1[159] made it necessary to go beyond the performance of the initial contract and include in-service support and possible additional needs. This was also expressed by Member States during the consultation process.[160] Only then would the national security interests of the Member States be sufficiently accommodated.

---

[156] Schmitt and Spiegel, "The Specificities of the European Defence and Security Procurement Directive", *supra* note 151.
[157] 2007 Commission Staff Working Document, *supra* note 1, at 48 for security of information and at 46 for security of supply.
[158] Ibid., at 45.   [159] At 52–3.
[160] 2007 Commission Staff Working Document, *supra* note 1, at 46.

Thus it is submitted that the approach of the Defence Directive, which includes guarantees for the future, is a necessary response to the long life cycles of defence and security equipment and the relevant national security interests. The approach promotes the use of the Defence Directive by addressing the problems inside the Directive and thereby limiting the need to invoke the derogation in Article 346 TFEU to address these considerations. Relevant contracts are thus more likely to stay inside the Internal Market.

Similar considerations guided the drafters of the Defence Directive with respect to security of information. The option to include it as a generic selection criterion, as an "open" clause allowing contracting authorities to request "evidence of the capacity to provide security of information", was dismissed for the same reason as for security of supply outlined above.[161] The option to consider security of information as a selection criterion with mutual recognition of security clearances does not take account of the fact that only National Security Authorities can grant those clearances; there is no Internal Market regime for security clearances nor can Member States be forced to recognise these clearances.[162] The option to take the bilateral agreements existing between many Member States into account could lead to discrimination, as economic operators from Member States which are parties to such agreements would be favoured.[163] The chosen option of accommodating security of information as one aspect of technical capacity allows protecting national security while at the same time allowing transparency and avoiding the risk of discrimination. This approach still takes advantage of the existing bilateral agreements between Member States as, due to the fact that such agreements exist between most Member States with a defence industrial base, this "would de facto be more reliable than any other type of evidence".[164] Thus, also with respect to security of information, the chosen option takes account of the realities of the European armaments market and the national security interests of the Member States expressed during the consultation. It is therefore the option best to avoid derogation from the Directive on the basis of Article 346 TFEU.

3.3 Invitation to bid or negotiate: selection

Thirdly, according to Article 39(1) Defence Directive, the qualification criteria in Articles 41–6 Defence Directive are also the selection criteria[165] for candidates to be invited to tender in the restricted procedure, the negotiated procedure with prior publication of a contract notice and the competitive dialogue,

---

[161] Ibid., at 47.   [162] Ibid.   [163] Ibid.
[164] 2007 Commission Staff Working Document, *supra* note 1, at 48.
[165] "Selection" could also be called "pre-selection" to distinguish it from the actual award of the contract discussed under the next heading. It could also be called "shortlisting", although this is a slightly colloquial term not used in the Directives.

which as discussed in chapter 7 are the relevant procedures of the Defence Directive.[166] Also, because the negotiated procedure with prior publication of a contract notice is the default procedure of the Defence Directive, this selection represents an important stage of the procedure in practice. There are no significant differences to the similar rules of the old Public Sector Directive, apart from the additional qualification criteria and the fact that in restricted procedures the number of economic operators selected to tender may be limited to three rather than five.[167] For that purpose a ranking is established on the basis of the qualitative selection criteria of economic and financial standing and the technical and professional capacity discussed in section 3.2 above. In contrast to the second stage of qualitative selection discussed in that section in which minimum levels are assessed, *degrees* of economic and financial standing and the technical and professional capacity beyond minimum levels leading to exclusion are considered at this third and last stage. However, the last step is different in nature and purpose, since here not all the operators who are suitable and meet the qualitative criteria according to technical capacity and economic and financial standing are selected. The purpose is not qualification as such, as that needs to be checked in the context of the two previous stages. The purpose is rather to limit the number of candidates without reference to the subject matter of the contract and on the basis of qualitative criteria after it has been established that the minimum qualitative criteria have been met. While in the first two steps the narrowing of the field is only a side-effect of ensuring reliability, in the third step this is the main purpose of the exercise. However, in contrast to the award stage discussed in section 4 below, what is assessed is not the tender but the tenderer.

A candidate can prove his or her ability to process, store and transmit classified information, which is an assessment criterion but also a selection criterion in competitive procedures under Article 42(1)(j) Defence Directive, if the necessary security clearances have been granted by the national authority of the Member State of establishment. This makes it difficult to take this ability into account in a ranking, as the question is merely whether these security clearances are recognised or not.[168] Recognition will normally be automatic if there is a bilateral agreement between the Member States of the contracting authority or entity and the candidate. Without such a bilateral agreement there is no obligation to recognise security clearances.

Selection criteria other than those of the Public Sector and Defence Directive discussed in this chapter are thinkable, ranging from the drawing of lots to selecting the economic operator which is "likely to create the best competitive

---

[166] See on the rules in the Public Sector Directive (Art. 44) and Sue Arrowsmith, *The Law of Public and Utilities Procurement*, 2nd edn (London: Sweet & Maxwell, 2005), at 462–76.

[167] Five according to Art. 44(3) 3rd sentence Public Sector Directive 2004/18/EC.

[168] Guidance Note *Security of Information*, *supra* note 11, at 6, para. 21.

situation". This raises the question of whether the Defence Directive should have included additional selection criteria.[169] However, it is argued that the legislator has used an appropriate technique of adapting the rules of the 2004 Public Sector Directive by adding a few defence and security-specific criteria, as discussed in sections 3.2.1–3.2.3 above, in the Defence Directive. Moreover it is arguable that these "additional" criteria could also be used under the 2004 Public Sector Directive, and that they are merely descriptive. Additional criteria would, first, have to meet the requirement of being non-discriminatory and objective anyway, a significant limitation which already excludes techniques such as drawing lots. Secondly, the use of the "established" Public Sector criteria builds on a base of experience with them. Finally, the legislator did try to adapt the criteria of Public Sector Directive 2004/18/EC to the defence and security context. Overall it is therefore argued that no other selection criteria should have been included.

3.4 National transposition

The rules on exclusion in Article 39 Defence Directive have been transposed in Austria in § 57 BVergGVS, in Germany in § 24 VSVgV, in Ireland in Regulation 42 ACRDSR and in the United Kingdom in Regulation 23 DSPCR. The provision on economic and financial standing in Article 41 Defence Directive has been transposed in Austria in § 63 BVergGVS, in Germany in § 26 VSVgV, in Ireland in Regulation 44 ACRDSR and in the United Kingdom in Regulation 24 DSPCR. The rules on technical and professional ability in Article 42 Defence Directive have been transposed in Austria in § 64 BVergGVS, in Germany in § 27 VSVgV, in Ireland in Regulation 43 ACRDSR and in the United Kingdom in Regulation 25 DSPCR. Transposition in all these Member States follows the wording of the Directive very closely.

4 Award criteria

Similar to the respective provisions in the 2004 and 2014 Public Sector Directive and the Utilities Directive, Article 47 Defence Directive provides for the lowest price and the economically most advantageous tender as award criteria to determine the winner of competitive procurement procedures.[170] Recital 69 Defence Directive emphasises that the criteria have to be objective and must

---

[169] Thanks to Michael Steinicke for raising this issue when commenting on an earlier version of this chapter.

[170] On the rules of the 2004 Utilities and Public Sector Directives see Trepte, *supra* note 28, at 462–80; Bovis, *EC Public Procurement, supra* note 26, at 263–4 and 429–42; award criteria are also frequently the subject of court decisions, see Case C-324/93, *Evans Medical, supra* note 98; Case C-513/99, *Concordia Bus Finland* [2002] ECR I-7213; Case C-324/03, *Contse* [2005] ECR I-9315.

comply with the principles of transparency, non-discrimination and equal treatment. The criterion of lowest price is only suitable for simple "off the shelf" acquisitions[171] and is normally only used in open and restricted procedures. As discussed in chapter 7, the Defence Directive does not provide for the open procedure, and the free use of the negotiated procedure with prior publication of a contract notice reduces the importance of the restricted procedure.[172] Moreover, due to the complexity of most of the defence and security contracts covered by the Defence Directive, this criterion will be of only minor importance.[173]

The criterion of the economically most advantageous tender allows taking account of a multitude of economic (sub-)criteria which are connected to the subject matter of the contract, such as quality, delivery date, after-sales service etc. The presence of this second award criterion in the existing Directives made an adaptation to the characteristics of defence and security relatively easy.

According to Article 47(1)(a) Defence Directive, "security of supply" and "interoperability and operational characteristics" can expressly be taken into account as sub-criteria. Security of supply had already been a legitimate sub-criterion when determining the economically most advantageous offer under Public Sector Directive 2004/18/EC.[174] Moreover, the list of sub-criteria stipulated in Article 47 Defence Directive is not exhaustive anyway. As long as the requirements of non-discrimination, transparency and link to the subject matter of the contract[175] are respected, many other sub-criteria can be taken into account. Moreover, the award criteria must not give the contracting authority or entity unrestricted freedom of choice for the award of the contract,[176] must be expressed in concrete and measurable requirements that allow the information provided by the tenderers to be effectively verified,[177] must comply with the relevant fundamental principles of EU law and especially non-discrimination[178] and be aimed at determining the economically most advantageous tender rather than the ability of the tenderer to

---

[171] See ch. 1 at 50–1.   [172] At 312–18 and 322–31.

[173] Guidance Note *Security of Supply*, *supra* note 2, at 17, para. 47.

[174] Case C-324/93, *Evans Medical*, *supra* note 98, at paras. 44 to 45: "the reliability of supplies can in principle, number amongst the award criteria used to determine the most economically advantageous tender". See also Case C-448/01, *EVN Wienstrom* [2003] ECR I-14523 at para 70: "reliability of suppliers is one of the criteria which may be taken into account . . . in order to determine the most economically advantageous tender".

[175] Guidance Note *Security of Supply*, *supra* note 2, at 17, para. 49.

[176] Case C-513/99, *Concordia Bus Finland*, *supra* note 170, at para. 61 as cited by the Guidance Note *Security of Supply*, *supra* note 2 at 17, para. 49.

[177] Case C-448/01, *EVN AG and Wienstrom*, *supra* note 174, at para. 52 as cited by the Guidance Note *Security of Supply*, *supra* note 2, at 18, para. 49.

[178] Case C-513/99, *Concordia Bus Finland*, *supra* note 170, at para. 61 as cited by the Guidance Note *Security of Supply*, *supra* note 2, at 18, para. 49.

perform the contract.[179] These requirements apply equally and have been developed by the ECJ in the context of the old Public Sector and Utilities Directives. However, the relevant ECJ judgments of *Evans Medical* and *EVN Wienstrom* left a gap by failing to specify what requirements define security of supply, thereby leaving much discretion to the Member States.[180] With Article 23 Defence Directive and the Commission's Guidance Note *Security of Supply*[181] some guidance to address that gap[182] and to "channel" Member State discretion[183] is now provided.

Security of information is not expressly mentioned as a sub-criterion in the text of the Defence Directive or the Commission's Guidance Note *Security of Information*.[184] It has been argued that it may be considered when determining the economically most advantageous offer, for example when the measures of the bidder for the protection of sensitive information in the context of the execution of the contract are assessed.[185] However, security of information is better accommodated as a qualification and selection criterion and contract performance condition.[186]

The award of the contract is a rather late stage to take security of supply and security of information into account. It could be argued that the nature of both these considerations make it necessary to ensure them at an earlier stage, with the contract performance conditions and as part of the qualification and selection process. The 2007 Commission Staff Working Document does not consider security of supply and information as factors at the award stage either.[187] Moreover, the use of security of supply and information as sub-criteria to determine the economically most advantageous tender suggests that these are relative concepts, that tenderers can offer higher or lower levels of security of supply and security of information that can be measured and compared. Alternatively this could mean that the contract performance conditions and qualification criteria ensure a certain absolute and minimum level of

---

[179] Case C-532/06, *Lianakis, supra* note 104, at paras. 26–30 and Case C-199/07, *Commission v. Greece* [2009] ECR I-10669, at paras. 51–5, as cited by the Guidance Note *Security of Supply, supra* note 2, at 18, para. 49.

[180] Heuninckx, "Trick or Treat?", *supra* note 84, at 23.

[181] *Supra* note 2 at 16–18. Some Member States have provided additional guidance documents; see, for example, the United Kingdom Ministry of Defence Guidance on the UK Defence and Security Public Contracts Regulations 2011 (MoD, 21 August 2011), at www.gov.uk/government/uploads/system/uploads/attachment_data/file/27662/dspcr_chapter12_securitysupply_update1.pdf [accessed 28 April 2014].

[182] Vierlich-Jürcke (European Commission, 2012), *supra* note 111; Spiegel (European Commission), *supra* note 69 (both notes of the author, on file).

[183] Heuninckx, "Trick or Treat?", *supra* note 84, at 23.   [184] *Supra* note 11.

[185] C. Kennedy-Loest and N. Pourbaix, "The New Defence Procurement Directive" (2010) 11 *ERA Forum* 399, at 405.

[186] See the discussion in sections 3.1 and 2.2.2. above.

[187] 2007 Commission Staff Working Document, *supra* note 1, at 44–8.

security of supply and information and that a relative concept of security of supply and information only applies during the award stage. The danger of blurring the distinction between selection and award criteria exists in the context of the Defence Directive as much as in the context of the other procurement Directives. The relative weighting given to security of supply and information, between tenderers who are at that stage already meeting the minimum requirements on the basis of the contract performance conditions and the qualification process, entails a danger of discrimination on grounds of nationality since a domestic provider with a domestic supply chain will normally offer a higher level of security of supply and possibly information than a provider from another Member State with a nationally diverse supply chain. The Guidance Note *Security of Supply* recognises this danger when it repeats the requirement of non-discrimination in the context of its discussion of award criteria.[188] This danger and the importance of ensuring a certain level of security of supply and information at earlier stages of the procurement procedure should limit their use as award sub-criteria. Only differences above a minimum and absolute level of security of supply and information are to be taken into account at the award stage.

The rules on exclusion in Article 39 Defence Directive have been transposed in Austria in § 106(1) BVergGVS, in Germany in § 34(2) VSVgV, in Ireland in Regulation 55 ACRDSR and in the United Kingdom in Regulation 31(1) DSPCR. While transposition in these Member States follows the wording of the Defence Directive very closely, Germany did not include the lowest price as an award criterion. This reinforces the point made above, that this criterion is only of limited utility in defence and security procurement.

5 Conclusions

The Defence Directive is intended as a legal instrument specifically designed for defence and security procurement. For that purpose the provisions of Public Sector Directive 2004/18/EC were adapted to the requirements of security of supply and security of information. The objective of these adaptations is to limit the use of the exemptions in Article 346 TFEU and the free movement regimes, discussed in chapter 3 and 2 respectively, by providing a tailor-made Directive which makes the use of these derogations unnecessary in practice. Both the Guidance Note *Security of Supply* and the Guidance Note *Security of Information* acknowledge that the Defence Directive does not limit the derogations in the Treaty. They can still be invoked if and when the adapted rules are not sufficient to safeguard security of supply or security of information or another national or public security consideration. However, as explained in chapters 2 and 3, the derogations not only have to be specifically invoked on a

---

[188] Guidance Note *Security of Supply*, *supra* note 2, at 16, para. 47; at 18, para. 49.

case-by-case basis and the conditions justifying their use explained and proved. The use of these exemptions is also subject to judicial review and a proportionality test. This means that the proportionality of derogation will be more difficult to argue and thus derogation more difficult to justify when the legislator provided a procurement regime that accommodated security-of-supply and security-of-information requirements inside the regime of the Directive and the Internal Market of the TFEU. The argument that the use of the allegedly unsuitable 2004 Public Sector Directive would compromise security of supply and security of information is no longer available as neither that instrument nor its 2014 successor apply to the relevant contracts any more.

Security of supply and security of information were taken into account in the rules at various stages of the procurement process under the Defence Directive. This includes the rules on specifications, contract performance conditions, qualification and selection and award criteria. The rules on specifications in the strict sense are not significantly adapted. However, due to the absence of an open procedure and the reduced importance of the restricted procedure due to the free use of the negotiated procedure with prior publication of a contract notice explained in chapter 7, these rules are less important than in the 2004 and 2014 Public Sector Directives anyway. Moreover, a distinct feature of the Defence Directive in comparison to the old and new Public Sector Directives is the importance of detailed contract performance conditions. These relate mainly to security of supply but also to security of information. These contract performance conditions are very closely linked to the specifications as they define the contract as much as or even more than the materials to be used or other features of the product or service. Moreover, in negotiated procedures including the competitive dialogue there are no detailed specifications as such but the contract performance conditions will apply nevertheless. Consequently and in line with the other procurement Directives and the relevant ECJ case law these conditions need to be communicated at the beginning of the procurement procedure. Moreover, as the reliability of economic operators has a national security and public security dimension, security of supply and security of information led to a qualification regime in the Defence Directive which is considerably more extensive when compared to the old and new Public Sector Directives. The importance of the qualification regime is enhanced by the fact that the qualification criteria are also the selection criteria for the restricted procedure, the negotiated procedure and the competitive dialogue. In comparison, the adaptations of the award criteria regime of the Defence Directive were relatively limited. Both the rules on contract performance conditions and qualification/selection are connected to two "regimes" outside the Defence Directive: a regime on intra-Community transfers which does exist with the ICT Directive and a "regime" on security clearances which does not exist. The smooth operation of the transfer licensing regime of the ICT Directive would have a positive impact on the security of supply of defence goods from other Member States and therefore on the effectiveness of the

Defence Directive in creating an Internal Market for these goods. If this is not the case during the first years of the operation of the transposed Directives of the Defence Package, the relevant rules of both instruments need to be revisited. The absence of a similar regime for security clearances could well have a negative impact on security of information with regards to economic operators from other Member States and therefore on the effectiveness of the Defence Directive in allowing market access to economic operators from other Member States.

An important feature of the Defence Directive has to be highlighted with respect to its security of supply and security of information adapted rules. As explained in chapter 6, the instrument applies to armaments in the sense of Article 346 TFEU and to certain sensitive security supplies, services and works to which Article 346 TFEU does not apply. The discussion of intra-Community transfers and security clearances applies only or mainly to the former and not to the latter. With regards to security supplies, services and works not covered by Article 346 TFEU, the public security exemptions of the free movement regimes of the Internal Market are the only basis that could justify exemption. In the context of these exemptions, judicial review is more intense; the proportionality test is applied, which is well developed in the case law of the ECJ. As contracting authorities and entities do not only benefit from the increased flexibility of the procedures discussed in chapter 7 but also from many of the rules discussed in this chapter, it will be more difficult for them to derogate from the rules of the Defence Directive. Moreover, far fewer of the exemptions discussed in chapter 6 are relevant for these non-military security contracts. Thus the Defence Directive might become more relevant for these non-military security contracts than for the procurement of armaments in the sense of Article 346 TFEU.

While some of the adaptations to the rules of the original Public Sector Directive 2004/18/EC in the Defence Directive add substance, most of the additions are adaptations in the form of description. The relevant security-of-supply and security-of-information considerations could also be taken into account, but they were not expressly stipulated in the Directive. The added value of this description in the Defence Directive is that there is no doubt about them being in compliance with EU law, thus reducing litigation risks and encouraging their use by contracting officers. Description is an important technique of adaptation in the Defence Directive which, in addition to the techniques of limitation discussed in chapter 6, the flexibility discussed in chapter 7 and the substitution in chapter 9, contributed to transform the original Public Sector Directive 2004/18/EC into an instrument more suitable for defence and security procurement.

9

Addressing the structure of the European defence industries

Substituting offsets with subcontracts?

1 Introduction

After a discussion of the adaptations to the personal and material scope of the Defence Directive in chapter 6 (limitation), its procedures in chapter 7 (flexibility) and the accommodation of security of supply and information throughout the procurement process in chapter 8 (description), this chapter will discuss the crucial offset and subcontracting regimes of the Defence Directive. This will introduce a fourth technique the EU legislator used to adapt the rules of the original Public Sector Directive 2004/18/EC to defence and security requirements: substitution. However, it will be explained that, in contrast to the limitation, flexibility and description techniques responding to the strategic defence and security needs of the contracting entities, substitution is mainly a response to the structure of the European defence industries.

The chapter will first introduce the phenomena of offsets and subcontracts in defence procurement to provide the background for how they are addressed in the Defence Directive. Secondly, the legality of offsets in Internal Market law will be discussed as an important part of that background. Thirdly, the chapter will analyse the position of offsets under the regime of the Defence Directive. Fourthly, the subcontracting regime of the Defence Directive will be introduced. It will be argued that while not expressly mentioning offsets, the Defence Directive essentially offers its subcontracting regime in substitution for offsets, which are assumed to be very difficult to justify under EU law.

2 Offsets and subcontracts in defence procurement

As mentioned in chapter 1,[1] offsets[2] are a regular occurrence in defence procurement, whenever contracts are awarded to economic operators from a

---

[1] At 54–7.

[2] Related terms describing offsets are: industrial compensation, industrial cooperation, industrial and regional benefits, balances, *juste retour* (English: fair returns) or equilibrium.

country other than that of the contracting entity.[3] As part of the contract with the non-domestic economic operator, "compensation" for the taxpayer's money of the country awarding the contract is required from the economy of the country of the successful bidder. The German Defence and Security Industries Association *BDSV* provided the following definition of offsets:

> Offsets are understood to be some form of industrial compensation when buying defence technology products and/or relevant services, both in transactions between national governments and between the industry and a national government . . . offset can be used as a synonym for any kind of compensation claimed.[4]

Offsets can take various forms but according to the 2007 European Defence Agency (EDA) *Study on the Effects of Offsets on the Development of a European Defence Industry and Market*[5] they can be divided into three main categories: direct (military) offsets, indirect military offsets and indirect civil offsets. Direct and indirect military offset requirements favour the defence industries of the awarding country, for example through the establishment of (job-creating) production sites in the awarding country, or through "sub-contracting, licensing, technology transfer, investment and joint ventures between the seller and the purchasing country".[6] Direct military offsets only require compensation for the original defence procurement contract for which they are agreed. In contrast, indirect military offsets are independent from the performance of the original defence procurement contract but still require compensation in the form of contracts with the defence industries of the awarding state of the original contract. Finally, indirect offsets to the civilian industries (indirect civil offsets) are completely independent from both the original contract and the defence industrial sector of the awarding state. According to the 2007 figures of the 2007 *EDA Offsets Study* the overall distribution in the participating Member States according to type was: direct offsets 40 per cent, indirect military offsets 35 per cent and civil indirect offsets 25 per cent.[7] Georgopoulos has convincingly argued that due to the fact that modern defence systems contain technology which is used in both civil and military sectors, the distinction between indirect civil offsets and indirect military offsets will be especially difficult in

---

[3] For a detailed analysis of offsets see Stephen Martin (ed.), *The Economics of Offsets: Defence Procurement and Countertrade* (London: Routledge, 1996); Jürgen Brauer and Paul Dunne (eds.), *Arms Trade and Economic Development: Theory, Policy and Cases in Arms Trade Offsets* (London: Routledge, 2004).

[4] *Bundesverband der Deutschen Sicherheits- und Verteidigungsindustrie* (BDSV), www.bdsv. eu/en/Issues/Offsets_compensation_benefits.htm [accessed 16 July 2013].

[5] E. Anders Erikson *et al.*, *Study on the Effects of Offsets on the Development of a European Defence Industry and Market* (Brussels: SCS Henley on Thames and FOI Stockholm, for the EDA, 2007), hereinafter *"EDA Offsets Study"*, at 3.

[6] Ibid. [7] According to the 2007 figures, ibid., at 4.

practice.[8] The significance of this difficulty for the legal analysis will be addressed below. However, while the above classification into three categories will be used in this chapter, many other classifications of offsets are thinkable,[9] and as Heuninckx pointed out, "the types of offsets are only limited by the imagination of the parties concerned".[10]

An offset arrangement is often a contract separate from the initial procurement contract[11] but that separate contract is a condition for the latter.[12] However, it can also simply be an annex to the procurement contract.[13] The offset can amount to more than 100 per cent of the value of the initial contract.[14] Offset practices vary considerably between EU Member States. Some Member States, notably France and Germany, do not require them at all,[15] in others they

---

[8]   A. Georgopoulos, "Revisiting Offset Practices in European Defence Procurement: The European Defence Agency's Code of Conduct on Offsets" (2011) 20 *Public Procurement Law Review* 29–42.

[9]   See, for example, T. Taylor, "Using Procurement Offsets as an Economic Development Strategy" in Brauer and Dunne, *Arms Trade and Economic Development, supra* note 3, and S. Markowski and P. Hall, "Mandatory Defence Offsets – Conceptual Foundations" in Brauer and Dunne, ibid.

[10]   B. Heuninckx, "Security of Supply and Offsets in Defence Procurement: What's New in the EU?", (2014) 22 *Public Procurement Law Review* 33–49.

[11]   BDSV, *supra* note 4: "Offsetting consists of a defined obligation on the part of the supplier that is laid down as fringe benefits in an offset agreement which is associated with the supply contract, but is an independent agreement."

[12]   "Offsets function as a condition of the sale of defence articles to the purchasing foreign government, whereby that foreign government or its economy recoups some portion of the acquisition's value." Source: Bureau of Industry & Security, US Department of Commerce, 14 *Offsets in Defense Trade* (2009), at i.

[13]   Thanks to B. Heuninckx for pointing this out to me.

[14]   According to the 2007 figures of a 2008 EDA Study, *Study on the Effects of Offsets, supra* note 5, at 4, the underlying contract volume for offsets in the then 24 participating Member States was €4.2 billion. At an average offset percentage of 135% (!), this made an offset volume of €5.6 billion. According to the Commission Staff Working Document – Impact Assessment SEC (2007) 1598 final, http://ec.europa.eu/internal_market/publicprocurement/docs/defence/impact_assessment_en.pdf [accessed 15 November 2013], at 44 (hereinafter "2007 Commission Staff Working Document"), at 23 the minimum volume of offsets requirements is 8–100% but can reach 200%.

[15]   However, this statement on the absence of offsets from French practice needs to be seen in context. Comparable to the USA, France does not require offsets because it has a large defence industry and usually purchases its major weapon systems from its domestic industry, so offsets are not really necessary there. In addition, France (like the US) does not support offset requirements from other countries because of its large domestic industry, which is required to provide offsets when exporting. Germany clearly rejects offsets as inefficient (see the very clear position expressed at: www.eda.europa.eu/offsets/viewpolicy.aspx?CountryID=DE [accessed 16 July 2013]), but for collaborative procurement they support fair returns. However, when not purchasing from its domestic industry, almost all of Germany's major weapon systems purchases are conducted through collaborative programmes, for which they strongly push for their fair returns compensation. Thus in fact

are a legal requirement, for example as an award criterion.[16] This can mean that the offset contract has nothing to do with the subject matter of the original defence contract and that the qualification of the economic operator or the quality of the bid become minor considerations. Many Member States support considerable offset administrations, traditionally as part of their ministries for economy but more recently in their ministries of defence. This reorganisation is possibly motivated by the wish to hide the economic rather than defence rationale for offsets. However, it cannot be emphasised enough that offsets rarely serve national security but normally economic interests.[17] It would not be too much of an oversimplification to say that Member States with a defence industrial base will not use offsets because they award contracts to their own domestic industries anyway and that only countries without a domestic defence industrial base use offsets. Offsets have been called "a strange animal" and "an idiosyncrasy of defence procurements".[18]

Normally the awarding defence procurement authority implements the offset requirements through contractual obligations in the original defence procurement contract. These contractual obligations require offset contracts with the dedicated offsets administration of the awarding state and with the companies in the awarding state. The eventual contracts with the companies are regularly private law contracts and their compliance with the offset require-ments will be determined by a national offsets administration. Offset require-ments are also often considered as an award sub-criterion. Thus in procurement terms, offset requirements are contract performance conditions[19] or award sub-criteria.[20] In the first case a bidder not meeting the required offset conditions will be rejected and in the second case the chances of a bidder offering no or less attractive offsets will be reduced in comparison to a bidder who does offer them. The award of contracts on the basis of the EU public procurement Directives is affected twice. First, the award of the original con-tract imposing the offset requirements is directly affected by the contract performance conditions or sub-award criteria. Secondly, the award of the offset contract or contracts is affected because either that contract would otherwise

the official position of these two countries regarding offsets is not necessarily so open. Thanks to B. Heuninckx for pointing this out to me.

[16] France and Germany do not accept offsets as a matter of policy, but see the previous footnote. The United Kingdom, Italy, Sweden and the Netherlands (net EU exporters with transatlantic imports) use indirect military offsets. Finland, Poland, Portugal, Greece and Spain (big importers with some exports) use different kinds of offsets, mainly direct. The Member States without defence industries use indirect civil offsets. See the *EDA Study on Offsets, supra* note 5, at 4.

[17] See the 2007 Commission Staff Working Document, *supra* note 14, at 48 and D. Eisenhut, "Offsets in Defence Procurement: A Strange Animal – at the Brink of Extinction?" (2013) 38 *European Law Review* 393–403.

[18] Eisenhut, "Offsets in Defence Procurement", supra note 17, at 393.

[19] Discussed in chapter 8, at 366–82.   [20] Discussed in chapter 8, at 400–3.

be awarded to another bidder or not be awarded at all. The two sides of this double effect have to be evaluated separately. However, it is the effect on the original contract which is the main concern in the context of this discussion of offsets under the Defence Directive.

As explained in chapter 1[21] and discussed in chapter 8,[22] subcontracts can be and are a feature in both the military defence sectors and the non-military sectors as much as in contracts covered by the Utilities and Public Sector Directives. The more complex the contract the more extensive the supply chain of subcontracts. Subcontracts and offsets are closely connected. As will be explained below, the Defence Directive facilitates the earlier and implicitly prohibits the latter.[23] Other than winning the prime contract and without the Member State in which the contracting authority or entity is situated derogating from the Defence Directive and the TFEU on the basis of Article 346 TFEU, the industries of the awarding country can only participate through subcontracts – and only if they represent the economically most advantageous tender. The subcontracting regime of the Defence Directive is intended as a substitute for the "now" almost prohibited offsets.[24] This chapter will first discuss offsets under the TFEU and Defence Directive and, secondly, the subcontracting regime of the Defence Directive before highlighting the connection between the two. It will be argued that it is not clear whether the subcontracting regime of the Defence Directive can be considered a sufficient substitute for offsets.

3 Offsets in EU Internal Market law and the Defence Directive

To address the question of the legality of offsets under EU law, the following sections of this chapter will first discuss the legality of offsets under primary EU law determined by the TFEU. Secondly, the extent to which offsets can be

---

[21] At 27 and 57.   [22] At 371–3 and 380–1.

[23] See Guidance Note *Offsets*, http://ec.europa.eu/internal_market/publicprocurement/docs/defence/guide-offsets_en.pdf [accessed 16 July 2013], at 1: "Since [offsets] violate basic rules and principles of primary EU law, the Directive cannot allow, tolerate or regulate them. At the same time, the Directive takes into account security-related justifications for offsets and offers, via its provisions on … sub-contracting, a non-discriminatory alternative which allows Member States to protect legitimate security interests and to drive competition into the supply chain of successful tenderers without infringing EU law."

[24] See Guidance Note *Subcontracting*, http://ec.europa.eu/internal_market/publicprocurement/docs/defence/guide-subcontracting_en.pdf [accessed 16 July 2013], at 1: "Many Member States have traditionally requested (sub)-contracting to their local defence companies as compensation for buying military equipment from suppliers abroad. Offset arrangements have thus been used to give local industries access to other defence markets via the supply chain of foreign prime contractors. This practice, however, goes against the principle of non-discrimination and the basic freedoms of the Internal Market. Consequently, the Directive does not allow this practice, but fosters market access for SMEs throughout the entire European Union via competition in the supply chain."

compliant with secondary EU law determined by the Defence Directive will be considered. Thirdly, the position of the Commission in a number of soft law instruments[25] shall be addressed. Finally, the impact of the interpretation of the TFEU, the Defence Directive, the Commission soft law instruments and the *EDA Code of Conduct on Offsets*[26] discussed in chapter 5[27] on the laws and practices of the Member States regarding offsets will be discussed. It will be shown that based on an overall hostile position of the EU to offsets, they currently appear to be phased out by several Member States with regards to contracts awarded inside the EU.

3.1 Offsets under the TFEU[28]

The TFEU[29] does not expressly mention offsets. Nevertheless, it is submitted that offsets clearly represent violations of the core free movement of goods and services regimes in Articles 34 and 56 TFEU of the EU Internal Market discussed in chapter 2,[30] unless justified by Articles 36, 52 or 346 TFEU.[31]

With regards to the procurement of supplies, an offset requirement imposed by a contracting authority by law, practice or on an ad hoc basis would represent a measure having equivalent effect to a quantitative restriction under Article 34 TFEU as it would be a measure imposed by Member States that could at least potentially and at least indirectly hinder intra-Union trade.[32] The economic operator from another Member State would not get access to the respective market or contract without him or her, or his or her Member State, arranging for costly and possibly unwanted purchases from economic operators in the Member State of the contracting authority.[33] Such an offset requirement would represent a considerable barrier to the free movement of goods. If the offset requirement is an obligation, in the form of a contract performance condition or required for all contracts by law, the restraint on the free movement of goods

---

[25] See the Guidance Notes mentioned *supra* note 23 and ibid.

[26] www.eda.europa.eu/docs/default-source/documents/The_Code_of_Conduct_on_Offsets. pdf [accessed 22 July 2013].

[27] At 198–204.

[28] This section of the chapter draws on the discussion of the same issue in the *EDA Offsets Study*, *supra* note 5, at 24–6, which was written by the author.

[29] Neither did the EEC or EC Treaties in their Rome, Maastricht, Amsterdam, or Nice versions.

[30] At 63–70.

[31] It is less clear whether offsets violate the State aid provisions of the TFEU discussed in chapter 4, at 176–82 see T. Eilmansberger, "Gegengeschäfte und Gemeinschaftsrecht" (2003) 17 *Wirtschaftsrechtliche Blätter: Zeitschrift für österreichisches und europäisches Wirtschaftsrecht* 501–10, at 506–7.

[32] Case 8/74, *Procureur du Roi v. Dassonville* [1974] ECR 837, at para. 5.

[33] See the 2007 *EDA Offset Study*, *supra* note 5, from 42 on the additional costs of offset arrangements.

is actual and direct. If there is no obligatory offset requirement but the offered offset increases the chances of being awarded the contract, when offsets are taken into account as award sub-criteria or as selection criteria, the restraint on the free movement of goods is actual and indirect.[34] In all these cases the requirements of the *Dassonville* definition of a measure having equivalent effect to a quantitative definition would be met and the measures would thereby be prohibited by Article 34 TFEU.[35]

Similarly, in a services or works contract offset requirements represent a barrier to the free movement of services and therefore violate Article 56 TFEU.[36] In essence the imposed or induced offset requirement represents an additional burden on the bidder from another Member State compared to a bidder from the awarding state. The domestic bidder would normally procure the goods and services he needs for the performance of the contract, but cannot provide himself domestically, inside the country of both that bidder and the awarding authority. Without the offset requirement or award sub-criterion or selection criterion, the bidder from another Member State would normally also source domestically or commercially from the economically most advantageous providers, regardless of where they are situated or registered. The requirement to source in the awarding state will often already limit sources and competition and make the relevant goods and services more expensive. This can already be considered an additional burden. However, even if hypothetically these goods and services can be sourced at competitive prices and conditions in the award-ing state, the onerous, lengthy, complicated and normally very costly obligation to arrange and offer an offset scheme represents a considerable additional burden in itself. This will make the sale of the good or service subject to the original contract less attractive[37] and it is widely recognised in the industry that this will have a significantly inflating impact on the price, often 30 per cent and in isolated cases 100 per cent, even when the contracting authority usually requests the offsets not to have such an impact.[38]

---

[34] Case 249/81, *Buy Irish* [1982] ECR 4005, at paras. 27 and 28 or Case 103/84, *Commission* v. *Italy* [1986] ECR 1759, at para. 24 as cited by Eisenhut, *supra* note 17, at 397.

[35] See ch. 2, at 63–7.   [36] Case C-3/95, *Reisebüro Broede* [1996] ECR I-6511, at para. 25.

[37] Eisenhut, "Offsets in Defence Procurement", *supra* note 17, at 397.

[38] Eilmansberger, "Gegengeschäfte und Gemeinschaftsrecht", *supra* note 31, at 508. While the reasons for the price increases cannot be determined for sure, a combination of shorter production runs, duplicate investments, higher manufacturing costs in the receiving country, higher sales price from the contractor in order to compensate for lost work or licence fees that can amount to 10% of the sales price, see Heuninckx, *supra* note 10. For some examples of these cost increases see Aris Georgopoulos, "European Defence Procurement Integration: Proposals for Action Within the European Union", PhD Thesis, University of Nottingham (2004), at 282–3, footnote 705; W. Struys, "Offsets and Weapons Procurement" in Martin, *The Economics of Offsets: Defence Procurement and Countertrade*, *supra* note 3, at 99; Nicholas Antonakis, "Offset Benefits in Greek Defence Procurement Policy" in Martin,

These offset requirements would represent blatantly discriminatory measures as they would only be applied to bidders from other Member States and by their very nature not to bidders in the Member State of the contracting authority.[39] Thus offset requirements could not, even when proportionate, be justified or considered outside the scope of the prohibitions in Articles 34 and 56 TFEU on the basis of mandatory requirements or overriding public interest grounds.[40] Furthermore, it is difficult for such offset requirements to be justified as proportionate measures taken to safeguard one of the public interests, including public security, recognised in Articles 36 and 52 TFEU and discussed in chapter 2,[41] which can justify even blatantly discriminatory measures. This is because for the measures to be justified thus, they must not be based on economic considerations.[42] Most offsets, however, are motivated by economic considerations, save for some extreme and defence-specific situations which can be covered by the armaments exemption in Article 346(1)(b) TFEU discussed in chapter 3 but normally not by the public interest justifications of the Internal Market regimes discussed in chapter 2. There could be offset requirements that are unrelated to the 1958 list of goods, but that could be justified on the grounds of public security or protection of health. Such a case where Article 36 or 52 TFEU could apply can be imagined. For example the procurement of vaccines against dangerous diseases, whereby the contracting authority or entity requires offsets to domestic companies to sustain a production facility located in the territory of the Member State to guarantee security of supply in case of epidemics, could be justified on public health grounds.[43] However, the public health requirement could also be met if a non-domestic company established

---

ibid., at 167. Moreover, it appears that the impact of most offsets in terms of job creation or diversion, technology transfer and international competitiveness is, despite the large sums involved, much smaller than expected, see Stephen Martin and Keith Hartley, "The UK Experience with Offsets" in Martin, ibid., at 354.

[39] Eisenhut, "Offsets in Defence Procurement", *supra* note 17, at 397.

[40] Case 120/78, *REWE – Zentrale AG* v. *Bundesmonopolverwaltung für Branntwein* ("Cassis de Dijon") [1979] ECR 649, [1979] 3 CMLR 494. While the ECJ has been putting less emphasis on discrimination and considered mandatory requirements or overriding public interest grounds in the context of discriminatory measures, for example in Case C-120/95, *Decker* [1995] ECR I-1831, the Court will revert to its old jurisprudence in cases of blatant discrimination, see, for example, in a services case: Case C-224/97, *Erich Ciola* v. *Land Vorarlberg* [1999] ECR I-2530. It is submitted that offset requirements would be such blatantly discriminatory measures in the context of which the ECJ would not consider *Cassis*-type overriding public interest grounds but only justification on the basis of Arts. 36 or 52 TFEU.

[41] At 70–82.

[42] Inter alia, Case 72/83, *Campus Oil Limited* v. *Minister for Industry and Energy* [1984] ECR 2727.

[43] Thanks to B. Heuninckx for providing this example when commenting on an earlier draft of this chapter.

a production site on the territory of the awarding Member State. Moreover, the example also shows how exceptional, narrow and thus unlikely such a situation is.

Finally, offset requirements can violate the equally fundamental freedom of establishment and other crucial principles of the EU Internal Market law and most notably the general prohibition of discrimination on grounds of nationality.[44] Offsets are requirements for bidders from other Member States and do not apply to domestic bidders. Therefore, at least with regards to non-military contracts not covered by Article 346 TFEU, offsets are almost illegal under the TFEU.

It is submitted that the legality of offset arrangements is not argued by anybody with regards to non-military procurement or procurement by utilities, which, as discussed in chapter 6,[45] are also covered by the Defence Directive. Consequently the public security exemptions of the free movement regimes on goods and services in Articles 36 and 52 TFEU discussed in chapter 2[46] have so far not been used to derogate from the Treaty to arrange offsets. However, offsets are an issue in relation to armaments procurement.[47] Armaments are subject to the special exemption of Article 346(1)(b) TFEU. As discussed in chapter 3, this provision represents a possibility for Member States to derogate from the application of the Treaty and can justify Member State measures taken for national security reasons in connection with armaments.[48] The use of the derogation is subject to control mechanisms through the European Commission, other Member States and the ECJ. In the judgment of *Spanish Weapons* the ECJ clarified that this provision does not represent an automatic or categorical exclusion of armaments from the application of the Treaty.[49] As a derogation it needs to be narrowly defined,[50] Member States need to specifically invoke and substantiate the exemption and prove that a situation justifying its use actually exists. Therefore the judgment in *Spanish Weapons* clarified the narrow interpretation of Article 346(1)(b) TFEU, an interpretation reiterated in the Interpretative Communication of the Commission[51] and later confirmed

---

[44] See also ch. 2 at 63–70.   [45] At 253–5.   [46] At 70–82.

[47] There have been arrangement similar to offsets in some larger non-military projects, such as the construction of nuclear plants, oil platforms, or shipbuilding, see Thorsten Iske, *Verbundgeschäfte* (Frankfurt am Main: Lang, 1986), at 79 as cited by Eilmansberger, "Gegengeschäfte und Gemeinschaftsrecht", *supra* note 31, at 503.

[48] Ch. 3 at 87–128.

[49] Case C-414/97, *Commission* v. *Spain* [1999] ECR I-5585, [2000] 2 CMLR 4.

[50] Case 222/84, *Marguerite Johnston* v. *Chief Constable of the Royal Ulster Constabulary* [1986] ECR 1651, [1986] 3 CMLR 240, at para. 26. See also Case 13/68, *SpA Salgoil* v. *Italian Ministry of Foreign Trade* [1968] ECR 453, at 463, [1969] CMLR 181, at 192 and Case 7/68, *Commission* v. *Italy* [1968] ECR 633, at 644.

[51] "Interpretative Communication [of the Commission] on the Application of Art. 296 of the Treaty in the Field of Defence Procurement", COM (2006) 779 final, 7 December 2006.

in the *Agusta*,[52] *Weapons Exports*[53] and *Finnish Turntables*[54] judgments of the ECJ. Thus Article 346(1)(b) TFEU can allow the use of offsets in relation to contracts regarding war material, but only if this is a necessary measure for the protection of the essential security interests of the Member State in question. However, according to the interpretation of Article 346(1)(b) TFEU clarified in *Spanish Weapons* these provisions do not represent automatic or categorical exemptions from the regimes of the Defence Directive and TFEU. The lawfulness of offsets needs to be decided on a case-by-case basis. Hence a general practice of requiring offsets for armaments contracts without appreciation of the individual case is unlawful under EU Internal Market law. Moreover, it is generally difficult to justify any type of offset on the basis of Article 346(1)(b) TFEU since Member States not only have to prove that the offset would promote their essential national security interests, not their economic interests; they also have to prove that the offset is necessary to address these essential security interests, leaving them no other choice than requiring the offset to safeguard their essential national security interest. In addition, Article 346(1)(b) TFEU, which provides that "such measures shall not adversely affect the conditions of competition in the common market regarding products which are not intended for specifically military purposes", will make it impossible to justify indirect civil offsets since they necessarily affect competition regarding products which are not covered by Article 346(1)(b) TFEU.[55] In summary, it is very difficult to justify offsets in defence procurement on the basis of Article 346(1)(b) TFEU.[56] Offset arrangements violate the TFEU, unless this is justified as a necessary measure to safeguard essential national security interests. The fact that offsets have been so frequently used between Member States was only possible due to the sensitivity of defence procurement and an essentially inaccurate interpretation of Article 346(1)(b) TFEU. As derogation based on the armaments exemption is only possible on a case-by-case basis, abstract offset legislation requiring offsets for all defence contracts is a violation of the

---

[52] Case C-337/05, *Commission v. Italy* [2008] ECR I-2173 and C-157/06, *Commission v. Italy* [2008] ECR I-7313. See ch. 3 at 96–101.

[53] Case C-284/05, *Commission v. Finland* [2009] ECR I-11705; Case C-294/05, *Commission v. Sweden* [2009] ECR I-11777; Case 387/05, *Commission v. Italy* [2009] ECR I-11831; Case C-409/05, *Commission v. Greece* [2009] ECR I-11859; Case C-461/05, *Commission v. Denmark* [2009] ECR I-11887; Case C-38/06, *Commission v. Portugal* [2010] ECR I-1569; Case C-239/06, *Commission v. Italy* [2009] ECR I-11913. See ch. 3 at 109–25.

[54] Case C-615/10, *Insinööritoimisto InsTiimi Oy*, nyr, 7 June 2012.

[55] COM (2006) 779 final: "Indirect non-military offsets, for example, which do not serve specific security interests but general economic interests, are not covered by Article [346 TFEU], even if they are related to a defence procurement contract exempted on the basis of that Article." The "spill-over" into civil markets is also highlighted in the 2007 Commission Staff Working Document, *supra* note 15, at 26.

[56] Eisenhut, "Offsets in Defence Procurement", *supra* note 17, at 400–2.

Treaty.[57] Offset requirements can only be justified as imperative measures to safeguard national security interests in the light of each individual case.

However, as pointed out above the TFEU does not expressly prohibit offsets and the ECJ has not yet ruled against offsets either. Thus, at least in theory, direct and indirect military offsets can be legal in certain exceptional situations. A scenario where offsets could be justified is a contract in which the Republic of Cyprus aimed to ensure its air defence by anti-aircraft missiles, as Cyprus has no combat aircraft. There is an at least theoretical possibility that Cyprus could be subjected to an effective blockade enforced by Turkey. If Cyprus bought anti-aircraft missiles, it could require offsets to build these missiles on Cypriot territory in order to have the capacity to fulfil the additional demands of (1) resisting an invasion, (2) resisting air attack, even (3) in case of a blockade.[58] In this scenario the offset could be a proportionate measure to safeguard a national security interest, more specifically a strategic security of supply need, for a contract on an item on the 1958 list and possibly justified by Article 346(1)(b) TFEU. Following the line of argument of Advocate General Slynn in *Campus Oil* in relation to what is now the exemption in Article 36 TFEU[59] discussed in chapter 2, comparisons with the Republic of Ireland can be made. Cyprus is also situated on a relatively isolated island without neighbours and without allies due to its neutral status. Most significantly, however, the potential military threat posed by the much larger neighbour Turkey and manifest in the 1974 invasion of the island and the continued occupation of the northern part[60] by Turkish troops, would make this a strong case for an offset justified by Article 346(1)(b) TFEU. On the other hand, the possibility of a contract requirement for a non-domestic company rather than a Cypriot company to establish the required production site in Cyprus could question the proportionality of the offset requirement to satisfy the strategic security of supply need. However, as convincingly argued by Heuninckx, domestic companies can be more efficiently controlled by the State in which they are registered, and can therefore be expected to give sufficient priority to the national requirements and to invest the funds necessary to keep, and upgrade as necessary, the resources needed

---

[57] Abstract offset legislation merely prepared for cases in which offsets might be justified would not in itself be violating the Treaty.

[58] Thanks to B. Heuninckx for providing this scenario when commenting on an earlier draft of this chapter. The consolidation of a domestic defence industrial capability has frequently been the subject of offsets, see Katia G. Vlachos, *Safeguarding European Competitiveness – Strategies for the Future European Arms Production and Procurement*, Occasional Paper No. 4 (Paris: Institute for Security Studies of the Western European Union, 1998), ch. 2.1; Antonakis, "European Defence Procurement Integration", *supra* note 38, at 163.

[59] See Advocate General Slynn in Case 72/83, *Campus Oil Limited* v. *Minister for Industry and Energy* [1984] ECR 2727, at 2764, and the arguments of the Irish Government, at 2735. See ch. 2, at 79–80 and note 83.

[60] The "Turkish Republic of Northern Cyprus" is only recognised by Turkey itself.

to support the equipment of the armed forces over time.[61] Overall, even in this extreme example it would not be entirely clear whether it could be justified by Article 346 TFEU and this also shows how narrow the room for offsets is under the TFEU.[62]

Indirect civil offsets can never be justified on the basis of Article 346(1)(b) TFEU because by their very nature they "adversely affect the conditions of competition in the internal market regarding products which are not intended specifically for military purposes" in the sense of Article 346(1)(b) second sentence TFEU.[63]

Direct military offsets are most likely to be justifiable under Article 346(1)(b) TFEU because of their direct relation and impact on the individual procurement contract in question. Eisenhut provided examples. The necessity for national security reasons to have ballistic calculations for missiles performed on the territory of the country to ascertain confidentiality and to preserve the ability to decide autonomously on modifications and updates of these calculations is one of these examples. Another example might be to request service parts of a highly sensitive contract performed nationally to remain autarkic in the maintenance of such weapons systems.[64] However, the considerations of security of supply and information behind these examples can arguably be accommodated without offsets, inside the Defence Directive, through contracts performance conditions or minimum qualification criteria, as discussed in chapter 8.[65] Article 346(1)(b) TFEU can only justify the use of direct military offsets under special circumstances in the context of highly sensitive military contracts and with detailed justification. It is submitted that this would only be possible in very extreme and exceptional circumstances, so rare and unlikely that it could be said that even direct military offsets are almost never legal under Article 346 TFEU.

Similarly to direct military offsets, indirect military offsets can be justified on the basis of Article 346(1)(b) TFEU. Depending on the individual case this might be more difficult than for direct military offsets, but there might be cases where an indirect military offset is justified whereas direct military offsets might not. The crucial standard is the case-by-case assessment of the proportionality of the measure discussed in chapter 3 and above. The stronger the national

---

[61] Heuninckx, "Security of Supply and Offsets in Defence Procurement: What's New in the EU?", *supra* note 10, at 43.

[62] Perhaps a similar scenario could be imagined in Finland in relation to a Russian "threat", on the Spanish Canary Islands, Greek islands close to the Turkish coast, or Malta. However, it is argued that due to NATO membership (Spain), an until recently peaceful Russian neighbour (Finland) or a lack of any immediate threat from Northern Africa (Malta) the case would not be as strong as in the Cyprus scenario discussed above.

[63] Eisenhut, "Offsets in Defence Procurement", *supra* note 17, at 400–2. Eilmansberger, "Gegengeschäfte und Gemeinschaftsrecht", *supra* note 31, at 504–5.

[64] Eisenhut, "Offsets in Defence Procurement", *supra* note 17, at 402.

[65] At 366–82 and 382–400.

security requirement of the case, the more likely is the proportionality of the measure. Depending on the individual case, the national security needs are stronger in a *direct* rather than in an *indirect* military offset. Moreover, even if the preservation of a particular defence industrial capability can be recognised as a national security interest, the individual offset requirement needs to be necessary for the preservation of that capability. This would question the use of the armaments exemption if it can be demonstrated that the capability could be preserved by other means. More importantly, *Spanish Weapons* clarified that economic or financial considerations may under no circumstances be "essential security interests" in the sense of the derogation.[66]

Overall, while in theory certain military offsets might be justifiable on the basis of Article 346(1)(b) TFEU, it is submitted that in practice the possibility is highly unlikely to exist for the Member States in mainland Europe in times of peace. It is a dangerous weapon to be locked away in a remote and safe vault only to be taken out under exceptional circumstances. The EU legislator and the Member States should look for other ways to address the structure of the European defence industries. These shall be discussed below.

3.2 Offsets and the Defence Directive

Similar to the TFEU, the Defence Directive does not expressly mention offsets either.[67] Eisenhut explained that the Commission's initial intention to ban "or at least strictly limit" offsets in the Defence Directive met strong opposition, especially from smaller Member States concerned about their defence companies which depend on these arrangements.[68] Since this opposition might have delayed or even derailed the Defence Directive as a whole, its final draft did not contain a ban or even a mention of offsets. This is confirmed by the 2007 Commission Staff Working Document which argues for the option of not mentioning offsets in the Directive:

> since offsets are a problem by itself which goes far beyond the current initiative ... Expecting EC rules to solve the offset problem would thus be mistaken and could endanger the initiative (given the sensitivity of the issue).[69]

The Working Document also discussed the prohibition of offsets as an option. However, this was considered misleading as implying that offsets "were allowed for contracts exempted from the Defence Directive under Article [346 TFEU]".[70] However, this is not convincing: a practice prohibited by a secondary EU law instrument does not imply that this practice is allowed under

---

[66] C-414/97, *supra* note 49, at para. 22.
[67] This was also noticed by Eisenhut, "Offsets in Defence Procurement", *supra* note 17, at 396.
[68] Ibid.   [69] 2007 Commission Staff Working Document, *supra* note 14, at 48.   [70] Ibid.

primary EU law, quite the opposite. Moreover, a contract subject to Article 346 TFEU is also exempt from the Treaty, not just the Directive. In other words, if it is possible in a given situation to derogate from EU law on the basis of Article 346 TFEU, then EU law no longer applies to the measure taken by the Member State in response to that national security situation, even if that measure is an offset. While, as argued below, invoking Article 346 TFEU to justify an offset would be very difficult in practice, its prohibition in the Defence Directive would not mislead contracting authorities about the legality of offsets if Article 346 TFEU is successfully invoked; Article 346 TFEU would still have to meet all of its requirements on a case-by-case basis. Thus it is more plausible that it was the opposition from smaller Member States which prevented the prohibition of offsets in the Defence Directive, as outlined above. As discussed in chapter 1,[71] politicians can gain points through offsets, companies are awarded contracts they might otherwise not have been awarded and many civil servants and public employees work in the national offset administrations. The smaller Member States without defence industrial capabilities have no chance of being awarded prime contracts and demand a return on the taxpayer's money they spend on such a contract. It is unlikely that these interested parties would have accepted or would accept the banning of offsets without opposition. While the Commission as initiator of legislation might be able to resist such opposition, the lobbying and political pressure had an effect on some governments in the Council. There is no information on whether it would also have had an effect on the European Parliament since the drafts of the Defence Directive which Strasbourg-Brussels decided on never mentioned offsets.

Nobody ever suggested that offsets could be legal under the 2004 or 2014 Public Sector or Utilities Directives, and the contracting entities on the national, regional and municipality level (and the utilities) in the Member States do not require offsets in their supply, services and works contracts. Even so, similar to the Defence Directive, offsets are not expressly prohibited in the old or new Public Sector and Utilities Directives. However, offsets in the civil sectors are thinkable, as their express prohibition in Article XVI(1) of the WTO Government Procurement Agreement shows.[72] Nevertheless, in the EU offsets are clearly limited to armaments procurement.

There are parts of the Defence Directive that could be interpreted as references to offsets. According to Recital 45 Defence Directive, "no performance conditions may pertain to requirements other than those relating to the performance of the contract itself". This could be interpreted as implicitly restricting indirect offsets because, with the exception of direct military offsets,

---

[71] At 54–7.

[72] There have been arrangement similar to offsets in some larger non-military projects, such as the construction of nuclear plants, oil platforms, or shipbuilding, see Iske, *Verbundgeschäfte*, *supra* note 47, at 79.

offsets are performance conditions which do not relate "to the performance of the contract itself".[73] However, clearly this does not represent an express reference to offsets.

According to Article 4 Defence Directive, "Contracting authorities/entities shall treat economic operators equally and in a non-discriminatory manner and shall act in a transparent way." This could also be interpreted as implicitly addressing offsets as they do make a distinction between domestic and foreign bidders.[74] However, again, this is not an express reference and therefore offsets are not expressly prohibited by the Directive.[75]

As explained in the previous three chapters, the Defence Directive is a Public Sector Directive adapted to defence and security requirements to reduce the invocation of the Treaty's security derogations and in particular of Article 346 TFEU in practice. However, a closer look at the specific rules of the Defence Directive, and in particular those on the selection of suppliers and service providers discussed in chapter 7 and the evaluation of tenders discussed in chapter 8, reveals that they do not allow taking offsets into account. Most notably contracts should be awarded on the basis of objective criteria which ensure compliance with the principles of transparency, non-discrimination and equal treatment and which guarantee that tenders are assessed in conditions of effective competition. As a result, it is appropriate to allow the application of two award criteria only: the lowest price and the most economically advantageous tender. While the rules on the latter accommodate economic considerations other than price, such as quality, delivery time and after-sale service, they do not allow taking offsets into account. This assessment is confirmed by the fact that some defence and security-specific sub-criteria such as security of supply are expressly stipulated in Article 47(1)(a) Defence Directive.[76] If security of supply is expressly mentioned then offsets could have been expressly mentioned as well.

While offsets are not expressly banned or limited in the Defence Directive, they are not expressly allowed in the Directive either. Not even the "ambiguous wording" of Article 20 Defence Directive can be interpreted as allowing them. While permitting the laying down of "special conditions relating to the performance of a contract" in the first sentence of the provision, this does not amount to an express legitimisation of offsets since they are simply not mentioned. Moreover, the wording does not allow this interpretation because

---

[73] Eisenhut, "Offsets in Defence Procurement", *supra* note 17, at 396.   [74] Ibid.

[75] In contrast, the Government Procurement Agreement (GPA) of the World Trade Organisation WTO expressly rules out offsets. According to Art. XVI(1) GPA entities shall not, in the qualification and selection of suppliers, products or services or in the evaluation of tenders and award of contracts, impose, seek or consider offsets. However, armaments are subject to a more extensive armament exemption in Art. XXIII GPA. See the discussion in ch. 3 at 114–15.

[76] See ch. 8, at 400–3.

these conditions have to be compatible with EU law, which offsets almost never are, as discussed above. The first sentence of Article 20 Defence Directive was not adapted and is identical to Article 26 Public Sector Directive 2004/18/EC. This word-for-word adoption of the original first sentence of Article 26 suggests that it is to be applied in the same way as in the context of the old Public Sector Directive. Only the second sentence of Article 20 Defence Directive contains an adaptation to defence and security needs in the form of description:

> These conditions may, in particular, concern subcontracting or seek to ensure the security of classified information and the security of supply required by the contracting authority/entity, in accordance with Articles 21, 22 and 23 . . .

As explained in chapter 8, description does not add substance in comparison to Article 26 Public Sector Directive 2004/18/EC, but simply expressly allows taking considerations into account that are allowed but not stipulated in the original provision.[77] However, the provision was adapted and that adaptation did not include a reference to offsets, an "omission" to be interpreted as reflecting the will of the legislator. Overall, Article 20 Defence Directive clearly neither expressly nor impliedly allows offsets.

It is argued that the fact that offsets are not mentioned could be interpreted as implying that they are not to be taken into account. On the other hand, the position of the Commission on the illegality of offsets is clear, as later set out in the Guidance Notes and discussed below. No previous draft of the Defence Directive in the public domain mentioned offsets. Thus, leaving the word offsets completely out of the Directive has to be assumed to have been intentional. However, this deliberate ignoring of the phenomenon in the text of the Directive is only partly due to the "obvious" illegality of offsets. Their obvious illegality makes it perhaps unnecessary to mention them in the 2004 and 2014 Public Sector and Utilities Directives. However, in the armaments sector offsets are so common that their illegality should ideally be addressed in the Defence Directive, which has armaments contracts at its core. In fact, it is submitted here that an express ban on offsets is something to be considered in the context of a revision of the Directive. The fact that offsets are not addressed is rather due to political tactics, as discussed at the beginning of this section. Thus the fact that offsets are not listed as award sub-criteria is as much a reflection of this political background as of the fact that the Commission considers them to be illegal.

---

[77] See also M. Trybus, "The Tailor-made EU Defence and Security Procurement Directive: Limitation, Flexibility, Descriptiveness, and Substitution" (2013) 38 *European Law Review* 3, at 21–5.

3.3 Commission Guidance Notes

While the TFEU and the Defence Directive do not expressly mention offsets, a number of soft law instruments issued by the Commission in the context of the transposition process of the Defence Directive *do* mention them. Most importantly, the Commission issued an entire Guidance Note *Offsets* which clearly sets out:

> offset requirements are restrictive measures which go against the basic principles of the Treaty, because they discriminate against economic operators, goods and services from other Member States and impede the free movement of goods and services. *Since they violate basic rules and principles of primary EU law, the Directive cannot allow, tolerate or regulate them.* [emphasis added][78]

This wording could not be clearer. Another Commission guidance note, the Guidance Note *Subcontracting* is equally clear about the illegality of offsets under EU law:

> Offset arrangements have thus been used to give local industries access to other defence markets via the supply chain of foreign prime contractors. *This practice, however, goes against the principle of non-discrimination and the basic freedoms of the Internal Market.* Consequently, *the Directive does not allow this practice.* [emphasis added][79]

Furthermore, the Guidance Note *Offsets* is detailing which specific actions are thereby prohibited:

> contracting authorities/entities may not require or induce, by whatever means, candidates, tenderers or successful tenderers to commit themselves to:
>
> - purchase goods or services from economic operators located in a specific Member State;
> - award sub-contracts to operators located in a specific Member State;
> - make investments in a specific Member State;
> - generate value on the territory of a specific Member State.
>
> This applies to all kind of works, supplies, services and investments, whether they are military, security-related or civil in nature or purpose, and irrespective of whether they are directly or indirectly related to the subject-matter of the procurement contract in question. Furthermore, tenderers, candidates and successful tenderers may not be required to mobilise other undertakings, be

---

[78] *Supra* note 23, at 1 para. 3 and at 5 para. 18. See also the 2007 Commission Staff Working Document, *supra* note 15, at 48: "since offsets usually entail discrimination by their very nature, they stay in direct contrasts to the Treaty (EC primary law). Consequently, public procurement rules (EC secondary law) cannot allow or regulate them."

[79] *Supra* note 24, at 1 para. 3.

they related to them or not, to make such purchases, subcontracting or investments.[80]

This means that all types of offsets are included in this assessment, including the three main types identified in the 2007 *EDA Offsets Study*: direct military offsets, indirect military offsets and civil offsets.

Further proof of the Commission's actual position on offsets is their intention to ensure the "phase-out" of offsets in the 2012 "Progress Report on the Implementation of the Defence Directive"[81] and their infringement proceedings against the Czech Republic and Greece for using offsets in defence procurement in 2010.[82] Moreover, in the 2012 Progress Report the Commission announced that they intend to use infringement proceedings against Member States using offsets more often in the future.[83]

It is submitted that according to the Commission in these Guidance Notes and other sources, offsets cannot be arranged inside the Directive or Treaty.[84] However, as neither the Commission's Guidance Note *Offsets* nor the Guidance Note *Subcontracting* nor, for example, the 2012 Progress Report are legally binding, there is no express ban on offsets in the legislation.

The practice of not addressing an issue as significant as a ban on offsets in the legislation – which involves the Council and the European Parliament and may involve the ECJ through an action of annulment – and then making it the subject of soft law instruments such as the Guidance Notes, which are Commission instruments that do not involve Council, European Parliament, and possibly the ECJ, might be considered problematic from a constitutional

---

[80] Guidance Note *Offsets*, *supra* note 23, at 5–6 para. 19.

[81] "Report from the Commission to the European Parliament and the Council on Transposition of Directive 2009/81/EC on Defence and Security Procurement", COM (2012) 565 final, at 1: "In particular it will take action to accomplish the phasing out of offsets which diverge from the basic principles of the Treaty." At 8–9: "Such offset requirements are restrictive measures which go against the basic principles of the Treaty. They discriminate against economic operators, goods and services from other Member States, and they impede the free movement of goods and services."

[82] As reported by Eisenhut, "Offsets in Defence Procurement", *supra* note 17, at 3–4, footnote 132.

[83] 2012 Progress Report, *supra* note 81, 9: "The Commission will now monitor whether these changes will bring about a change in practice. It is convinced that a rapid phasing out of the discriminatory practice of offsets is necessary to create a truly European Defence Equipment Market. The Commission will, therefore, take appropriate action where this is not the case. It will also do so where Member States continue to have offset rules that are clearly incompatible with EU law."

[84] This is confirmed by one of the drafters of the Defence Directive: B. Schmitt, "Defence Procurement and Offsets, Clarifying the Legality of Offsets and its Scope for Application" at the "C5 EU Defence and Security Procurement Conference", Brussels, 18 November 2009 as cited by B. Heuninckx, "The EU Defence and Security Procurement Directive: Trick or Treat?" (2011) 20 *Public Procurement Law Review* 9 at 25, footnote 146.

point of view. This is not only due to the fact that the Guidance Notes are only available in English, whereas legislation has to be translated into all EU languages. Democracy, the rule of law and the role of the Member States could be affected. The legislator in the Council effectively rejected the ban on offsets and yet the Commission is taking action, most notably in the Guidance Notes, on which the other institutions and the Member States have no direct influence. However, a number of considerations put these "constitutional concerns" into perspective. As outlined above, the Commission did try to ban offsets in the Defence Directive.[85] Moreover, the compliance of offsets with the TFEU, discussed above, is the crucial issue. As most offsets violate the TFEU the legislator cannot allow them in the Defence Directive and the Guidance Notes are merely *stating* a law that already applies rather than *making* law. As Eisenhut puts it, the Defence Directive "did not change the legal framework under which offsets have to be assessed".[86] As a consequence there would be no constitutional concerns. Most importantly a secondary law Directive cannot change a primary law Treaty provision and Article 346 TFEU remains in place and may at least in theory justify offsets.

Due to the opposition of some Member States against expressly banning offsets in the Directive, the Commission has found a sensible and pragmatic approach by using Guidance Notes to highlight the difficulty of reconciling offsets with the Internal Market and the Defence Directive and to initiate infringements proceedings if necessary. However, it is submitted that an express ban on offsets in the Defence Directive should be considered in the context of the revision of the instrument over the next years. First, the Guidance Notes clearly and correctly state that offsets cannot be reconciled with the Defence Directive for contracts within its scope. Normally Article 346 TFEU has to be invoked to derogate from the Directive and Treaty to allow offsets. Thus an express ban on offsets would not change their legality under the Defence Directive. It would, however, create clarity to stop offsets. Due to the opposition to the banning of offsets discussed above, it will not be possible to abolish them; the best scenario is their gradual phasing out. Thus, commencing with the 2011 *EDA Code of Conduct on Offsets*[87] mentioned in chapter 5[88] and below, the current approach through Guidance Notes without an express ban in the Defence Directive could be a second phase of that phasing-out process. As discussed below, there are signs that this phasing-out is well on the way,

---

[85] See Eisenhut, "Offsets in Defence Procurement", *supra* note 17, at 396 and the discussion at the beginning of the section on the Defence Directive above.

[86] Ibid.

[87] www.eda.europa.eu/docs/default-source/documents/The_Code_of_Conduct_on_Offsets. pdf [accessed 27 August 2013]. On the code: A. Georgopoulos, "Revisiting Offset Practices in European Defence Procurement: The European Defence Agency's Code of Conduct on Offsets" (2011) 20 *Public Procurement Law Review* 29–42.

[88] At 198–204.

although with considerable differences between the Member States. As a possible result of the first or a later revision of the Defence Directive, a third phase with an express ban on offsets in that Directive could complete the phasing out of offsets.

3.4 National laws of the Member States

The selection of national laws and regulations of the Member States transposing the Defence Directive discussed throughout Part II of this book do not mention offsets. The Austrian Federal Procurement Defence and Security Act 2011 (BVergGVS),[89] the German Competition Act as amended in December 2011 (GWB) and the Defence and Security Procurement Regulation 2011 (VgVVS),[90] the Irish European Union (Award of Contracts Relating to Defence and Security) Regulations 2012 (ACRDSR)[91] and the United Kingdom Defence and Security Public Contracts Regulations 2011 (DSPCR)[92] do not mention offsets. This is a consequence of the fact that offsets are not expressly mentioned, let alone prohibited, in the Defence Directive. The Guidance Notes discussed above did not lead to national provisions on offsets in the laws and regulations transposing the Defence Directive. It is not surprising that the national legislators did not introduce a controversial prohibition if that is not expressly required in the original Directive, especially when they cannot be sure not to be the only one to limit their defence procurement officers in this way. This does not of course challenge the position of the Commission regarding offsets expressed especially in the Guidance Note *Offsets* but also the Guidance Note *Subcontracting*. However, not mentioning offsets in the national legislation does not confirm the Commission's position either. The Austrian, German, Irish and British legislators could have expressly mentioned offsets and thus clarified the situation for their respective jurisdictions. This was not necessarily done deliberately. National legislators are under an obligation to transpose Directives, not Guidance Notes. If the EU legislator wants offsets to be expressly addressed in the national defence and security procurement legislation, offsets should be addressed in the EU legislation first.

However, while the Defence Directive did not lead to offsets being prohibited in the transposing legislation, there appears to have been an effect on the offset

---

[89] Austria: Bundesgesetz über die Vergabe von Aufträgen im Verteidigungs- und Sicherheitsbereich (Bundesvergabegesetz Verteidigung und Sicherheit 2012 – BVergGVS 2012), BGBl. I Nr. 10/2012.

[90] Germany: Gesetz gegen Wettbewerbsbeschränkungen, of 15 July 2005, BGBl. I S. 2114; 2009 I S, 3850, as last amended by Art.1 and Art. 4(2) of the Law of 5 December 2012, BGBl. I S. 2403.

[91] Republic of Ireland: European Union (Award of Contracts Relating to Defence and Security) Regulations 2012, SI No. 62 of 2012.

[92] United Kingdom: Defence and Security Public Contracts Regulations 2011, SI 2011/1848.

laws and regulations of the 18 Member States which were using offsets before the transposition of the Defence Directive. According to the 2012 Progress Report:

> The Commission has ... been in close contact with the 18 Member States concerned, helping them to abolish or revise their offset rules. As a result, *most* of these Member States have either abolished the respective rules *or revised* their legislation. In this case, offsets are no longer required systematically but solely in exceptional cases where the conditions of Article 346 TFEU are met. Major legal changes have, therefore, been implemented.

Thus it appears that – even without an impact on national defence procurement legislation itself – there has been an impact on offset regulations and thus *potentially* on the relevant practice based on these regulations. The second phase of the phasing out of offsets described under the previous heading above could already have started. However, the statement above contains a number of important limitations. First, only "most" but not all of the 18 relevant Member States have altered their offset regulations. Moreover, it is not revealed how many and which Member States have done so, although it is submitted that the use of the word "most" implies a majority of the 18. Thus some Member States have not (yet) changed their offset rules. Secondly, not all of the Member States which have altered their offset rules have abolished their rules; some have only "revised" them. However, there is some detail as to these revisions as offsets are no longer required systematically but only exceptionally, specifically when the conditions of Article 346 TFEU are met. Nevertheless, this also represents a third limitation, since the occurrence of offsets in practice will depend on the interpretation of Article 346 TFEU discussed at length in chapter 3 and above in section 3.1 of this chapter.

Fourthly and finally, since the Defence Directive does not expressly prohibit offsets, the described impact on the offset rules of some Member States cannot exclusively be claimed as an achievement of the Commission or the Internal Market legislator. The statement from the 2012 Progress Report does not claim this either – it simply states that "major legal changes have been implemented". Limiting and phasing out offsets, however, has been the business of the 2011 *EDA Code of Conduct on Offsets* mentioned in chapter 5 and under the previous section above. The Code aims to make offsets more transparent, reducing their size and generally and gradually reducing their use in practice. While this Code does not prohibit offsets, it requires a 100 per cent cap,[93] considers offsets to be limited to cases where Article 346 TFEU applies[94] and requires transparency of all relevant offset rules.[95] The required transparency of the rules should allow a

---

[93] EDA *Code of Conduct on Offsets*, *supra* note 87, at 4: "Offsets, both required and accepted, will not exceed the value of the procurement contract."
[94] EDA *Code of Conduct on Offsets*, ibid., at 2.   [95] Ibid., at 3.

comparison of the 100 per cent cap on offsets before and after the Code. According to the EDA Offset Portal[96] in 2013 a certain change to the situation described in the 2007 EDA *Offset Study*[97] can be detected.

However, not having an official policy does not necessarily mean that offsets will never be required, even on a case-by-case basis.[98] With this reservation the EU and EEA Member States should currently – post implementation of the Defence Directive – be subdivided into five broad groups with regards to offsets. First, Cyprus, Germany, Greece, Ireland and the United Kingdom explicitly state that no offsets will be asked for, although as mentioned above Germany may ask for offsets in collaborative programmes. Secondly, France,[99] Latvia and Malta do not have an official offset policy and therefore are not entirely clear as to their use on a case-by-case basis. Thirdly, the Czech Republic and Sweden clearly state that offsets could be asked for on a case-by-case basis. Fourthly, Austria, Belgium and Norway have a policy of asking for offsets. Fifthly and finally, the offset policies of Bulgaria, Estonia, Finland, Hungary, Italy, Lithuania, Luxembourg, Netherlands, Poland, Portugal, Slovakia, Slovenia and Spain were under review in 2013 and therefore uncertain. On the basis of the interpretation of Article 346(1)(b) TFEU in relation to offsets discussed above, which requires offsets to be a proportionate measure to be taken on a case-by-case basis, it can be said that only the "abstract" policies of Austria, Belgium and Norway, as expressed in the *EDA Offset Portal*, appear in violation of the TFEU.

On the *EDA Offset Portal* Greece refers to the Directive as the reason for not having an offset policy (any more). Austria and Norway have the 100 per cent cap on offsets, indicating an *EDA Code of Conduct on Offsets* motivation. However, Austria refers to the Defence Directive, Article 346 TFEU and even the Commission's Guidance Note *Offsets* as the legal background of their policy. The United Kingdom reports that their offset policy is now "abolished completely". Cyprus and Ireland state that they do not require offsets in defence procurement, but Latvia states that it has no official offset policy. However, the latter does not necessarily mean that it will not require offsets on a case-by-case basis (like the Czech Republic), only that there is no official overarching policy. These references suggest an impact of the Defence Directive and even the Guidance Note *Offsets* on national offset policies, even when in November 2013 this impact appeared to be still ongoing in several Member States. However, it is submitted that the *EDA Code of Conduct on Offsets* had already paved the way for this impact, especially with regards to transparency and the 100 per cent cap. The step from a 100 per cent cap to phasing out is easier than

---

[96] www.eda.europa.eu/offsets/ [accessed 21 November 2013]. [97] *Supra* note 5.
[98] I have benefited enormously from discussions with B. Heuninckx when writing this crucial paragraph.
[99] As discussed above, France's position is that it does not have an offset policy. This does not necessarily mean it would never ask for offsets on a case-by-case basis.

from a 200 per cent level. Thus Internal Market and CFSP instruments have reinforced each other's impact on offsets, rather than being simply competing or even contradictory frameworks.

As the Defence Directive is not explicit on offsets whereas the Commission's position is clear, the resulting grey zone might lead to a final battle in the ECJ.[100] As discussed above, offsets cannot be reconciled with the Defence Directive and are difficult to justify on the basis of Article 346 TFEU as they often, if not always, meet economic and financial requirements rather than respond to national security considerations. They violate the EU Internal Market and procurement regime, since they make an open, transparent and competitive procurement procedure without discrimination very difficult or entirely impossible. The EU legislator should use a future revision of the Defence Directive to include an express ban in the instrument in order to create a maximum of clarity and uniformity regarding offsets in the EU.

4 The subcontracting regime of the Defence Directive

As mentioned in chapter 1,[101] for any larger civil or defence contract, successful bidders will often have a supply chain of subcontractors. This is because most companies are not able to produce every single component of their products or to provide all services themselves but need to procure them from specialised providers. In the consultation process leading to the adoption of the Defence Directive, stakeholders suggested the adoption of "[c]lauses to ensure adequate competition throughout the supply chain, in particular to improve market access for SMEs".[102] However, in the Green Paper[103] triggering the consultation process, the Commission had not specifically addressed subcontracting. This suggests that the idea for a subcontracting regime in the Defence Directive is at least to an extent a result of the consultation process. In contrast, the Green Paper had specifically addressed the issue of offsets,[104] an issue the stakeholders only mentioned in passing in their response.[105] This shows the sensitivity of offsets, which, as explained above, are not even mentioned in the later Defence Directive. Moreover, since the supply chain is mentioned in the context of necessary adaptation to the rule of the old Public Sector Directive, this can be interpreted as a hint at the connection of offsets and subcontracting, which will be discussed further below.

---

[100] Although this may take some time, see K. Vierlich-Jürcke (European Commission, 2012), "Subcontracting and Remedies in the Field of Defence and Security Procurement" at the "Seminar on European Defence and Security Procurement", European Institute of Public Administration (EIPA), Maastricht, 19 January 2012 (notes of the author, on file).
[101] At 27 and 57.   [102] COM (2005) 626 final, at 7.   [103] COM (2004) 608 final.
[104] Ibid., see Question 11, at 11.   [105] COM (2005) 626 final, at 9.

Thus, in contrast to the Public Sector Directive 2004/18/EC,[106] the Utilities Directive 2004/17/EC[107] and the new 2014 Directives[108] which mostly leave the supply chain to be organised by successful tenderers, under the Defence Directive contracting authorities may require that parts of a main contract be awarded as subcontracts to third parties. This is intended to drive competition into the supply chain and to open opportunities to small and medium-sized enterprises (SMEs).[109] Therefore the more detailed subcontracting regime of the Defence Directive is both economically and politically motivated.[110] Subcontracting opportunities also provide a "second chance" to the domestic industries of the contracting Member State and, with respect to Member States with limited industrial capabilities, a first realistic chance. In other words, there are more companies in more Member States capable of bidding for subcontracts on components of a large contract than companies able to bid for the prime contract. Indeed, the market for subcontracts is often bigger than that for prime contracts. Therefore there is more potential for competition and its benefits.

As mentioned in chapter 5,[111] between 2006 and 2013 subcontracting was the subject of a non-binding *EDA Code of Best Practice in the Supply Chain* ("EDA Supply Chain Code")[112] which also aimed to drive competition and opportunities for SMEs into the supply chain.[113] As also explained in chapter 5, this Code is currently under revision and might not be replaced by a new code in the future. As the *Code of Conduct on Defence Procurement* and the *Code of Conduct on Offsets*, the EDA Supply Chain Code was part of the intergovernmental EDA and therefore CFSP/CSDP framework. Therefore it was outside EU Internal Market law, not legally binding, voluntary and did not include all

---

[106] See Art. 25 Public Sector Directive 2004/18/EC. There are also a number of specific obligations for subcontracting by concessionaires in Arts. 60 and 62-5.

[107] See Art. 37 Utilities Directive 2004/17/EC.

[108] See Art. 71 Public Sector Directive 2014/24/EU. The main innovation is the possibility of direct payments to subcontractors in Art. 71(3).

[109] Guidance Note *Subcontracting, supra* note 24, at 1; see also the Implementation Report, *supra* note 81, at 6.

[110] Ibid.   [111] At 204-7.

[112] http://data.grip.org/documents/200909141545.pdf [accessed 22 July 2013]: "The Code of Best Practice in the Supply Chain was agreed by EDA's Member States subscribing to the Regime on Defence Procurement (sMS) and approved by the Association of Defence & Aerospace Industries of Europe (ASD) on 27 April 2006. It is an indispensable element of the Regime on the Defence Procurement, working in parallel and in complementarity with the Code of Conduct (CoC). Its implementation tool is the Electronic Bulletin Board (EBB). It is a voluntary code to be used not only when Article 346 of the TEC is invoked, but for any defence-related procurement requirements, assuming that it makes both technical and financial sense for the contractor. The [Supply Chain Code] is to be complementary to national procedures with such procedures taking precedence where they exist. No legal commitment is involved or implied nor is there a transfer of risk involved or implied by the [Supply Chain Code]."

[113] Para. 2 EDA Supply Chain Code, ibid.

Member States since Denmark decided not to participate. The application of this Code would (now) be limited to cases when Article 346 TFEU can be invoked. According to the EDA, the Code was "to be used *not* only when Article 346 of the TFEU [was] invoked, but for any defence-related subcontracts, assuming that it makes both technical and financial sense for the contractor [emphasis added]".[114] This reads like a challenge to the subcontracting regime of the Defence Directive and would be a problem if there had been a conflict between the two frameworks. However, the EDA continues to emphasise that "[t]he [EDA Supply Chain Code was] complementary to similar national procedures with such procedures taking precedence where they exist. No legal commitment was involved or implied". While the notion of "national procedures" cannot be interpreted as to include the Defence Directive, it does include national procedures of the Member States which are now almost all based on the Directive. Thus these procedures would have prevailed in case of conflict. However, first, the new subcontracting regime of the Defence Directive shares certain crucial features with that of the EDA Supply Chain Code, which had been in operation for a certain period of time. These features include the general objectives of competition and transparency at subcontract level and the publication of subcontract opportunities.[115] Secondly, the EDA Code represented the subcontracting regime applicable when for whatever reason Article 346 TFEU was invoked. Nevertheless, for the analysis of the subcontracting rules of the Defence Directive the differences between the frameworks are to be highlighted. These include that Title III Defence Directive is legally binding and far more detailed.[116]

4.1 Options for subcontracting

Article 21 Defence Directive provides four options for subcontracting requirements, explained further in Title III[117] and a Commission Guidance Note *Subcontracting*.[118] These options differ with regards to the scope and extent of the requirements applicable to subcontracting. As part of the "toolbox" approach of the Defence Directive, not all four options have to be transposed into national law, thereby allowing for flexibility and the accommodation of

[114] www.eda.europa.eu/projects/projects-search/code-of-best-practice-in-the-supply-chain [accessed 25 April 2013, with the date 12 September 2012].

[115] Paras. 2, 5 and 11 EDA Supply Chain Code, *supra* note 112.

[116] B. Heuninckx, "Towards a Coherent European Defence Procurement Regime? European Defence Agency and European Commission Initiatives" (2008) 17 *Public Procurement Law Review* 1–20, at 9 calls it "very general" and "a document [which] still leaves a wide scope of flexibility to all parties involved". See also A. Georgopoulos, "European Defence Agency: The New Code of Best Practice in the Supply Chain" (2006) 15 *Public Procurement Law Review* NA145.

[117] Arts. 50–4 Defence Directive.   [118] *Supra* note 24.

differences in the industrial structure and national preferences. In contrast, the other procurement Directives provide only one "option" which has to be transposed. The EDA Supply Chain Code was much less detailed and vague and did not contain comparable options.

4.1.1 Option A: the prime contractor is free to choose subcontractors

"Option A" only prohibits discrimination on grounds of nationality and leaves the prime contractor to choose the subcontractors. This is regulated in Article 21(1) Defence Directive:

> 1. The successful tenderer shall be free to select its subcontractors for all subcontracts that are not covered by the requirement referred to in paragraphs 3 and 4, and shall in particular not be required to discriminate against potential subcontractors on grounds of nationality.

The relatively limited requirements for this option are then summarised in Article 21(2) Defence Directive:

> 2. The contracting authority/entity may ask or may be required by a Member State to ask the tenderer:
> – to indicate in its tender any share of the contract it may intend to subcontract to third parties and any proposed subcontractor, as well as the subject-matter of the subcontracts for which they are proposed; and/or,
> – to indicate any change occurring at the level of subcontractors during the execution of the contract . . .

This is elaborated further in the Guidance Note *Subcontracting*:

> 11. The first option for the contracting authority, described in Article 21(1) and (2), is to leave it up to the successful tenderer to determine a) which share of the main contract, b) which part(s) of the main contract and c) to whom he wants to sub-contract. The contracting authority would basically accept the tenderer's sub-contracting proposal, subject to a possible verification of its selection criteria, in accordance with Article 21(5). The Directive's provisions relating to this option must be transposed, but Member States can either leave it up to their contracting authorities to use them or require them to do so.[119]

This Option A equates to that in Article 25 Public Sector Directive 2004/18/EC, Article 37 Utilities Directive 2004/17/EC and Article 71 of new Directive 2014/24/EU and is therefore not an innovation of the Defence Directive. The only adaptation is the requirement in Article 21(2) second hyphen "to indicate any change occurring at the level of subcontractors during the execution of the contract". Since all Member States have to transpose this paragraph it is, strictly speaking, not an option for national legislators. It can be understood as an

---

[119] Ibid.

option for contracting authorities since at least options A and B have to be transposed. However, in their transposition into national law Member States may either require or only allow the use of "Option" A. Depending on the transposition it is then of course an option or an obligation for the contracting authorities.

The transposing legislations of the four Member States discussed in this book all include this Option A. § 73(1) BVergGVS (Austria), Regulation 19(1) ACRDSR (Ireland), § 9(2) VSVgV 2012 (Germany)[120] and Regulation 37(1) United Kingdom DSPCR transpose Article 21(1) Defence Directive almost word for word. Then § 73(4) BVergGVS, Regulation 19(2) of the Irish Regulation, Regulation 37(2) of the United Kingdom Regulation and § 9(1) VSVgV transpose Article 21(2) Defence Directive word for word. The contracting authority "may ask [tenderers] to indicate" in Ireland or "may require" tenderers to provide in the United Kingdom – whereas in Germany it "may require [tenderers] to indicate" and in Austria "is required to ask [tenderers] to indicate"[121] – the information on subcontracts stipulated in Article 20(2) Defence Directive. The transposition of this option was not difficult since it is in line with the approach of previous Directives. Again, this option is not an innovation of the Defence Directive or adaptation of the original Public Sector Directive 2004/18/EC.

4.1.2 Option B: awarding subcontracts on the basis of competitive procedures

As in Option A, in Option B the prime contractor decides what share and which parts of the contract are subcontracted and has to indicate that share, the subject matter of the subcontract and the identity of the subcontractor in the tender. This is regulated in Article 21(2) and (3) Defence Directive. However, crucially Article 21(3) provides:

> 3. The contracting authority/entity may oblige or may be required by a Member State to oblige the successful tenderer to apply the provisions set out in Title III to all or certain subcontracts which the successful tenderer intends to award to third parties.

This is further elaborated in the Guidance Note *Subcontracting*:

> 13. In this case, the contracting authority must indicate in the contract notice that it may use this option (depending on the tender). The tenderers

---

[120] Vergabeverordnung für die Bereiche Verteidigung und Sicherheit zur Umsetzung der Richtlinie 2009/81/EG des Europäischen Parlaments und des Rates vom 13. Juli 2009 über die Koordinierung der Verfahren zur Vergabe bestimmter Bau-, Liefer- und Dienstleistungsaufträge in den Bereichen Verteidigung und Sicherheit und zur Änderung der Richtlinien 2004/17/EG und 2004/18/EG (Vergabeverordnung Verteidigung und Sicherheit – VSVgV) [2012] BGBl. I S. 1509.

[121] Translations of the author.

first state, in their tenders, their intentions for subcontracting (how much, which parts, and the proposed subcontractors). The contracting authority then tells the tenderers which of the intended subcontracts it requires to be awarded in accordance with Title III. The successful tenderer is obliged to award the subcontracts concerned in accordance with the transparent and non-discriminatory procedures of Title III. The Directive's provisions relating to this option must be transposed, but Member States can either leave it up to their contracting authorities to use them or require them to do so.[122]

The crucial difference from Option A discussed above is that the subcontracts have to be awarded on the basis of the competitive and transparent procedures of Title III. These procedures will be discussed further in section 4.2 below. Suffice it to say here that, depending on the value of the subcontract and other circumstances, that can involve the publication of a subcontract notice in the OJ and the award of the contract on the basis of the same procedures as the prime contract. The private prime contractors have to follow public procurement law when subcontracting, a significant innovation of the Defence Directive also featuring in Options C and D discussed below.

Again, since all Member States have to transpose this paragraph it is, strictly speaking, not an option for the Member States and consequently the transposing legislations of the four Member States discussed in this book all include this Option B. As indicated above, § 73(4) BVergGVS (Austria), Regulation 19(2) ACRDSR (Ireland), § 9(1) VSVgV (Germany) and Regulation 37(2) United Kingdom DSPCR transpose Article 21(2) Defence Directive. Moreover, § 74(1) BVergGVS, Regulation 19(3) of the Irish Regulation, Regulation 37(3) of the United Kingdom Regulation and § 9(1) of the German VSVgV transpose Article 21(3) Defence Directive. All transposing provisions, including those of 17 other Member States, leave to the contracting authorities the decision on whether to ask tenderers to apply the provisions of Title III Defence Directive rather than requiring contracting authorities to do so.[123] Requiring contracting authorities to ask tenderers to apply the provisions of Title III Defence Directive would also have been possible under Article 21(3) Defence Directive. Apparently in October 2012 only one Member State had omitted to transpose Article 21(3) Defence Directive.[124]

Option B is an innovation of the Defence Directive. Moreover, Option B is potentially the most important aspect of the innovative subcontracting regime of the Defence Directive since it is the only innovative subcontracting option which all Member States have to transpose into their national laws. If Options C and D are transposed in all Member States they will be equally important. However, as will be explained further below, some Member States such as the United Kingdom have not transposed Options C and D. This perfectly legal

---

[122] *Supra* note 24, at 4.   [123] Transposition Report, *supra* note 81, at 7.   [124] Ibid.

"omission" makes Option B particularly important for these Member States, since it is the only Option that differs from the other procurement Directives.

4.1.3 Option C: awarding minimum percentage of subcontracts on the basis of competitive procedures

In Option C, contained in Article 21(4) Defence Directive, the contracting authority requires the prime contractor to award a minimum percentage of the contract as subcontracts on the basis of competitive procedures contained in Title III Defence Directive. Further details are provided in the Guidance Note *Subcontracting*:

> In this case, the contracting authority must specify the minimal percentage of the value of the main contract it wants to be subcontracted (for example 15–20 % or 25–30 %) and ask the selected tenderers to indicate in their tenders which parts of their offer they intend to subcontract to fulfil this requirement. Hence, the contracting authority determines the minimal percentage of the main contract to be subcontracted while the successful tenderer decides which parts are to be subcontracted. All subcontracts concerned by this provision must be awarded in a transparent and non-discriminatory procedure under the rules laid down in Title III.[125]

The minimum percentage set by the contracting authority may be exceeded. This is clarified by Article 21(4) Defence Directive:

> Tenderers may propose to subcontract a share of the total value which is above the range required by the contracting authority/entity. . . . The contracting authority/entity may ask or may be required by a Member State to ask tenderers also to specify which part or parts of their offer they intend to subcontract beyond the required percentage, as well as the subcontractors they have already identified.

The crucial difference between subcontracts subject to the minimum percentage set by the contracting authority on the one hand, and subcontracts exceeding that minimum percentage on the other hand, is that the former have to be awarded on the basis of competitive procedures and the rules in Title III Defence Directive and the latter do not. The treatment of contracts exceeding the minimum percentage set by the contracting authority also constitute the difference between Option C and Option D discussed below: in Option D these subcontracts also have to be awarded on the basis of Title III.

Option C is not only an option for contracting authorities and entities but also for the Member States since they do not have to transpose it. See the Guidance Note *Subcontracting*:

---

[125] *Supra* note 24, at 4.

The Directive's provisions relating to this option do not have to be trans-posed. If a Member State decides to do so, then again it can either leave it up to the contracting authorities to use these provisions or it can require them to do so.[126]

This includes both an option and a "sub-option", as if a Member State trans-poses Option C, it may require its use in the legislation or leave the decision to use the Option to the contracting authorities. The transposing legislations of three of the four Member States discussed in this book include this option: § 74(2) and (3) BVergGVS (Austria), Regulation 19(4)–(9) ACRDSR (Ireland) and § 9(3) VSVgV (Germany). The United Kingdom did not transpose this option in its 2011 Regulations. This impression from the text of the Regulations is confirmed by guidance provided by the Ministry of Defence which explains that tenderers have (only) two options.[127] This decision of the British legislator shall be discussed further below. According to the Transposition Report of October 2012 one other Member State did not provide Option C either.[128]

Liebmann calls Option C an "appropriate addition".[129] The crucial substantive difference from Option B is that a minimum percentage of the prime contract has to be subcontracted. This reduces the control of the prime contractor over subcontracting. Moreover, while Option B only drives competition into the supply chain, in line with the general competition objective of all EU procure-ment Directives, Option C is clearly identifiable as accommodating a policy of industrial participation, as the contracting authority or the legislator determine the share of the prime contract to be subcontracted. This makes Option C more attractive for Member States with an industrial base mainly suitable for subcon-tracts rather than prime contracts and less attractive for Member States with an industrial base capable of managing prime contracts. It is more acceptable for a Member State to impose requirements and therefore an administrative burden on prime contractors to open opportunities for subcontractors when the prime contractors are all in other Member States. Option C is less attractive for the latter because it reduces the control of the prime contractors. This is possibly why Austria and Ireland, with their limited defence and security industrial base, have transposed the option, whereas the United Kingdom, with its large defence contractors, has not. However, this limited implementation of options is also in line with the traditional minimal approach to the transposition of most if not all

---

[126] Ibid., at 5.
[127] Ministry of Defence, *Guidance Defence and Security Public Contracts Regulations 2011: Chapter 13 – Subcontracting under the DSPCR*, London: 2012, www.gov.uk/government/uploads/system/uploads/attachment_data/file/27663/dspcr_c13_mandating_subcontracting_3rd_parties_apr12.pdf [accessed 20 November 2013], at para. 18.
[128] Transposition Report, *supra* note 81, at 7.
[129] H. Liebmann, § 74, in Michael Fruhmann and Hanno Liebmann, *BVergGVS 2012: Bundesvergabegesetz Vergabe und Sicherheit 2012* (Vienna: Manz, 2012), at 246.

Directives in Britain. Nevertheless the presence of prime contractor potential in the United Kingdom makes Options C and D less attractive. Germany has transposed Option C because although it has large defence contractors it is also committed to policies promoting SMEs.

4.1.4 Option D: requirement of minimal percentage to be subcontracted and competition for subcontract beyond the minimal percentage

In Option D the provisions of Article 21(3) and (4) Defence Directive are combined. As in Option C, the contracting authority can require a share of the prime contract of up to 30 per cent to be subcontracted, ask for the relevant parts to be identified in the tender and to be awarded on the basis of a competitive procedure. Option D is further elaborated in the Guidance Note *Subcontracting*:

> 19. In this case, the contracting authority would specify in the contract notice the minimal percentage of the main contract it wants to be subcontracted, and it would ask the selected tenderers to specify in their tenders (1) which parts of their offer they intend to subcontract to fulfil the minimal percentage requirement, and (2) which parts of their offer they intend to subcontract beyond the required percentage. Based on the tender, the contracting authority/entity would then require that some or all of the proposed subcontracts beyond the required percentage be awarded in a transparent and non-discriminatory procedure. However, the tenderer remains free to decide which parts he wants to subcontract (to meet the minimal percentage or beyond). In any case, all subcontracts which are imposed by contracting authorities must be awarded by the successful tenderer in accordance with Title III.

Thus the crucial difference from Option C is that in Option D there is no difference between the subcontracts subject to the minimum percentage set by the contracting authority and the subcontracts exceeding that minimum percentage. Both have to be awarded on the basis of competitive procedures and the rules in Title III Defence Directive. In comparison to Option C, the control of the prime contractor over the "if" of subcontracting above the minimum percentage is not further reduced. However, it is further reduced with regards to the "how" of subcontracting as subcontracts beyond the minimum threshold also have to be awarded on the basis of Title III. This might discourage prime contractors from subcontracting beyond the minimum percentage. Thus, while Option D would still serve the Internal Market and competition objectives, it might lead to fewer opportunities for SMEs in practice. On the other hand, subcontracting is often simply a necessity and not a choice as the prime contractor cannot provide the relevant goods or services him or herself.

Moreover, Option D is obviously providing a maximum of transparency and competition in subcontracting since the rules of Title III do not only apply to the minimum percentage but also beyond that. Finally, it needs to be kept in mind that for the Member States and ultimately the contracting authorities, Options C and D are options and therefore suggestions, not obligations they have to follow.

Similar to Option C, Option D is also optional with regards to transposition: Member States do not have to transpose it.[130] Austria has introduced Option D, however, as the use of the word "may" in § 74(2) BVergGVS indicates Austria has introduced it as an option for contracting authorities and entities, not an obligation imposed by the BVergGVS. This is also the case for § 9 of the German VSVgV[131] and Regulation 19(4)–(6) of the Irish ACRDSR.[132] So far only the United Kingdom and one other Member State has not implemented Option D.[133]

Overall, the EU legislator has provided a flexible set of two options which have to be transposed and two options which do not. This can lead to a Member State transposing (1) Options A and B, (2) A–C or (3) A–D. Moreover, the decision to use competitive procedures for subcontracting can be left to the contracting authority or required in the Member State legislation. As discussed above, Member States appear to have left the decision to contracting authorities. With respect to the procurement units of the ministries of defence this gives the latter rather than the national legislators the discretion to require competitive subcontracting and to what percentage of the prime contract. This is important since the governments of the Member

---

[130] See also the Guidance Note *Subcontracting, supra* note 24: "Not all of the Directive's provisions related to this option have to be transposed. If a Member State decides to transpose them all, it can then again either leave it up to the contracting authorities to use them or it can require them to do so."

[131] See www.forum-vergabe.de/fileadmin/user_upload/Rechtsvorschriften/VSVgV_25.07.2012_f%C3%BCr_PDF.pdf [accessed 6 February 2014].

[132] Out of the 15 Member States which had notified their formally completed transposition to the Commission in January 2012 most had implemented this Option C and the following Option D, but not as an obligation: the contracting entities can choose between Options A–D: Vierlich-Jürcke, "Subcontracting and Remedies in the Field of Defence and Security Procurement", *supra* note 100.

[133] Transposition Report, *supra* note 81, at 7; David Kiltie (United Kingdom Ministry of Defence, 2012), "Implementing and Applying Directive 2009/81/EC in the UK" at the seminar "European Defence and Security Procurement", EIPA, Maastricht, 20 January 2012 (notes of the author, on file). Belgium also intends to not transpose Options C and D. Baudouin Heuninckx (University of Nottingham), "Implementing and Applying Directive 2009/81/EC in Belgium" at the "Seminar on European Defence and Security Procurement", European Institute of Public Administration (EIPA), Maastricht, 20 January 2012.

States will in future to a large extent be deprived of the offset instrument to favour their national industries.

4.2 Subcontracting requirements in the prime contract award procedure

The regime on subcontracting is divided into rules applying to subcontracting as such (when the prime contract has been awarded) on the one hand and rules applying to the original prime contract (in view of later subcontracting) on the other hand. The rules on the original prime contract are contained in Article 21 Defence Directive. These rules aim to achieve transparency and to be practical at the same time.[134] Article 21(6) requires contracting authorities and entities to publish all their subcontracting requirements in the contract notice, including for all options:

- the selection criteria regarding the personal situation of subcontractors that may lead the contracting authority/entity to reject potential subcontractors, and the required information proving that these subcontractors do not fall within the cases justifying rejection, and
- the information and documentation required for assessing the minimum economic and technical capacities of subcontractors.[135]

Article 21(5) clarifies that the rejection of a subcontractor may only be based on criteria applied for the selection of tenderers for the main contract. This will be discussed under qualification of subcontractors below.

These additional requirements regarding the contract notice differ depending on the option used. For Options A and B the notice must include information on "any share of the contract [the prime contractor] intends to subcontract to third parties, the subject-matter of the subcontracts it intends to award, and the identity of the proposed subcontractors, if these are already known".[136] For Option C, the notice must include information on "which part or parts of its offer it intends to subcontract to fulfil the minimal percentage requirement, and if the tenderer intends to subcontract beyond the minimal percentage: the subject-matter of the subcontracts beyond the minimal percentage and the identity of the proposed subcontractors, if these are already known".[137] For Option D all these additional information requirements for Options A, B and C have to be fulfilled.

Apart from transparency and practicability, the rules also have to accommodate one of the main concerns of the Defence Directive: security of information. This was discussed also in relation to subcontracts in chapter 8.[138] According to

---

[134] Guidance Note *Subcontracting, supra* note 24, at 6, para. 20.   [135] Ibid., at para. 23.
[136] Ibid., at 7, para. 24.   [137] Ibid., at para. 25.   [138] At 380–1.

Article 22(c) and (d) contracting authorities and entities can require prime contract tenderers to provide:

> sufficient information on subcontractors already identified to enable the contracting authority/entity to determine that each of them possesses the capabilities required to appropriately safeguard the confidentiality of the classified information to which they have access or which they are required to produce when carrying out their subcontracting activities . . .

Moreover, they can require "a commitment from the tenderer to provide the same information in due course with respect to any new subcontractor".

As discussed in chapter 8,[139] according to the Guidance Note *Security of Information*, this information will consist of certificates from the national or designated security authority of the tenderer for the prime contract that all the subcontractors in the relevant supply chain "hold national clearances at the necessary security level".[140] The relevant information can then be checked with these authorities. This inclusion of the subcontractors in the verification of reliability is necessary and sensible. Defence and security contracts often have long supply chains of subcontractors which pose confidentiality risks as much as the prime contractor. Security-of-information requirements are not satisfied if only applied to the prime contractor. The Guidance Note *Subcontracting* clarifies regarding the practical implementation of these requirements:

> In practice, this information will normally consist of statements of the proposed subcontractors that they hold the relevant security clearances (statements to be verified by the contracting authorities/entities at the competent National Security Authorities).[141]

This is in line with security-of-information requirements for prime contractors discussed in chapter 8.[142]

When examining the bids in the context of all four options the contracting authority or entity will also check compliance with the information requirements on subcontracting outlined above. However, beyond that, the examination of the tenders differs depending on the option used. In Option A the contracting authority or entity can only reject individual subcontracts according to Article 21(5) Defence Directive. In Option B the prime contractor can be required to procure all or parts of the subcontracts on the basis of the procedures in Title III. As discussed under the next heading below, this represents an extensive intervention of the contracting authority or entity in the award of subcontracts by the prime contractor. The same can be said about Option D. In Option C the prime contractor specifies which subcontracts are to be awarded on the basis of Title III within the context of a minimum percentage required by the contracting

---

[139] At 380-1. [140] Guidance Note *Subcontracting, supra* note 24, at 8, para. 18.
[141] Ibid., at 7, para. 26. [142] At 379–81 and 392–8.

authority or entity. Consequently the latter can only examine the application of Title III to subcontracts beyond that percentage.[143]

4.3 Title III: rules applicable to subcontracting

Title III of the Defence Directive contains detailed rules applicable to subcontracting, separated into two chapters. The more important Chapter I[144] addresses subcontracts awarded by successful tenderers which are *not* contracting authorities or entities. It provides rules on scope in Article 50, on principles in Article 51, on thresholds and rules on advertising in Article 52 and on criteria for the qualitative selection of subcontractors in Article 53 Defence Directive. This regime is a novelty as there is no comparable regime in any of the other 2004 or 2014 procurement Directives. The EDA Supply Chain Code also contained rules on scope and principles and, incidentally, on advertising and the qualification of subcontractors. However, these rules were less detailed and vague, as will be explained below.

4.3.1 Scope

Article 50(1) on scope clarifies, in conjunction with Article 21(3) and (4) Defence Directive, that the rules in Chapter I of Title III Defence Directive only apply to the Options B–D outlined above. This limits the requirements of Option A to an absolute minimum not exceeding the equivalent regimes of the 2004 and 2014 Public Sector and Utilities Directives.

However, the scope of the regime is not determined by the value thresholds of the Directive discussed in chapter 6.[145] While according to Article 52(1) Defence Directive the more detailed requirements of that Article only apply to subcontracts above the value thresholds of Article 8 Defence Directive, the principles of Article 51 apply to all subcontracts. These principles, which will be discussed below, are those provided by the ECJ as emanating from the TFEU for contracts below the thresholds. Thus there is – within the scope of Options B–D – a more detailed subcontracting regime for subcontracts above the value thresholds on the one hand and a lighter "principle-based" subcontracting regime for subcontracts below these thresholds on the other hand.

Article 50(2) subparagraph 1 Defence Directive differentiates between "third parties" to whom the subcontracting regime applies on the one hand and companies of bidding consortia on the other hand. The latter are considered

---

[143] Guidance Note *Subcontracting, supra* note 24, at 8, para. 32.

[144] Chapter II regulates "Subcontracts awarded by successful tenderers which are contracting authorities/entities" and consist of only one article, Art. 54, according to which Titles I and II of the Defence Directive have to be applied when awarding subcontracts. In other words the subcontract has to be awarded on the basis of these same rules as a prime contract, not the regime of Title III.

[145] At 269–72.

part of the prime contractor. For these prime level consortium companies Article 50(2) subparagraph 2 Defence Directive imposes an obligation to exhaustively list all companies of the consortium in the tender and a related obligation to update such a list "following any change in the relationship between the undertakings".

4.3.2 Principles

Article 51 Defence Directive requires successful tenderers for prime contracts to conduct their subcontracting activities on the basis of the principles of transparency, equal treatment and non-discrimination. This implies that it is prohibited to use subcontracts to ensure offsets when the subcontracting provisions of Title III apply, as this practice would be discriminatory.[146] The 2004 Public Sector and Utilities Directives do not contain a comparable provision for subcontracting. However, they contain an article containing these principles for the award of prime contracts.[147] Article 71(1) of the new Public Sector Directive 20014/24/EU extends the prime contract principles in its Article 18 to subcontracts. Thus in the Defence Directive (and now also in the new Public Sector Directive 2014/24/EU) the "long-established" prime contract principles are expressly extended to subcontracting. This is remarkable because the procurement Directives regulate the award of contracts by public bodies (2004/18/EC and 2014/24/EU) and certain utilities (2004/17/EC and 2014/25/EU), not – with the exception of the special case of private utilities – private companies. By extending the principles developed for public bodies and utilities to the private economic operators being awarded the principal contracts, the Defence Directive regulates private companies. This takes some discretion and decision-making power from these private companies and transfers it to the contracting authorities and entities and the EU and Member State legislators who regulate them. With regards to regulation, the main power rests with the Member States because, of the four options on subcontracting provided in the Defence Directive, only Options A and B have to be transposed; Options C and D are optional. Moreover, the transposition of the Defence Directive in the four Member States investigated in this book has shown that the national legislators have ultimately transferred this power to the contracting authority: as discussed above, Austria, Germany, Ireland, the United Kingdom and 18 other Member States all left the decision on the use of the Options to the contracting entities rather than requiring them to do so in their national legislations.[148] Therefore, it is the contracting

---

[146] Thanks to B. Heuninckx for drawing my attention to this point when commenting on an earlier draft of this chapter.

[147] See Arts. 2 Public Sector Directive 2004/18/EC, 10 Utilities Directive 2004/17/EC or Art. 18 Directive 2014/24/EU and Art. 36 Directive 2014/25/EU. Art. 4 Defence Directive also contains such a provision.

[148] Austria in § 74 BVergVS, Germany in § 9 (3) VSVgV, Ireland in Regulation 19 (2)–(4) ACRDSR and the United Kingdom in Regulation 37(2) and (3) DSPCR leave the decision

authorities that ended up in charge of the decision on which option of subcontracting to use. A certain reservation to this submission applies to the United Kingdom and one further Member State where the legislator decided not to include Options C and D.[149]

Article 51 is reiterated by Article 52(7) and (8) Defence Directive which require the application of the TFEU competition and transparency principles for contracts below the thresholds of Article 8 Defence Directive.[150] This is developed further in the Guidance Note *Subcontracting*:

> According to ECJ case-law, this may imply an obligation to ensure an adequate degree of publication if the subcontract in question might be of interest for economic operators from other Member States.[151]

The Commission basically assumes that the principles listed in the Defence Directive have a similar scope and impose similar obligations to those of the TFEU. This is probably accurate. However, the argument could be made that the principles of the Directive, although similar to those of the TFEU, do not necessarily carry the same scope and/or obligations, because they are imposed on private parties by secondary legislation rather than on Member States by the TFEU.[152]

The principles in Article 51 Defence Directive alone also put an additional burden on the successful prime contract tenderers; as the Guidance Notes suggest, the principles of transparency and non-discrimination will often require some publication and a competitive procedure.[153] Costs may increase and it will take more time and administrative effort to organise the supply chain. It could also be argued that, although a competition may lead to additional administrative costs for the prime contractor, introducing competition in the supply chain could bring costs down if, rather than "use the supplier we have always used", the prime contractor conducts a competition.[154] However, the

about which Option to use to the contracting authorities and entities. See also the Transposition Report, *supra* note 81, at 7.

[149] Ibid., not naming the United Kingdom or the other Member State.

[150] See ch. 6 at 269–72.

[151] *Supra* note 24, at 10 citing: "judgment of 15 May 2008 in Cases C-147/06 and C-148/06 SECAP, paras. 18 to 35; Commission Interpretative Communication on the Community law applicable to contract awards not or not fully subject to the provisions of the Public Procurement Directives. 2006 OJ C-179/2; judgment of 20 May 2010 in Case T-258/06 Germany v Commission, paras. 68–100".

[152] I benefited from discussions with B. Heuninckx on this point when he commented on an earlier draft of this chapter.

[153] This is recognised in the (UK) Ministry of Defence, *Guidance Defence and Security Public Contracts Regulations 2011: Chapter 13 – Subcontracting under the DSPCR, supra* note 127, at para. 24: "Procurers also need to take account the additional bureaucracy and costs associated with requiring successful tenderers to place subcontracts . . ."

[154] I benefited from discussions with B. Heuninckx on this point when he commented on an earlier draft of this chapter.

Article 51 requirements do not apply in the context of the other procurement Directives and Option A of the Defence Directive. This issue of additional burden for prime contractors will be discussed further below.

The principles in Article 51 Defence Directive are those provided by the case law of the ECJ for principal contracts outside the scope of the procurement Directives. This case law was discussed in chapter 2.[155] As outlined above, these principles apply to all subcontracts awarded in the contexts of Options B–D. However, as especially the more detailed requirements of Article 52 Defence Directive discussed below only apply to subcontracts above the value thresholds, the principles in Article 51 are more important for subcontracts below the thresholds. Moreover, it should be pointed out that as subcontracts by their nature only concern parts of a principal contract, they are more likely to be below these thresholds than prime contracts are. This also makes the TFEU-based principles potentially more important for subcontracts than for prime contracts. For example, the rules on advertising in Article 52, discussed next, only apply to contracts above the thresholds of the Defence Directive.[156] Beyond the principles, however, Member States have flexibility regarding the regulation of subcontracting below the thresholds, including the option not to regulate it at all beyond the transposition of Article 51 Defence Directive.

The four Member States investigated in this book transposed the principles in Article 51 Defence Directive almost word for word: Austria in § 116(2) BVergGVS, Germany in § 38(1) sentence 2 VSVgV, Ireland in Regulation 60 ACRDSR and the United Kingdom in Regulation 41 DSPCR. All these Member States therefore require successful tenderers to comply with the Treaty principles of non-discrimination and transparency when subcontracting below the

---

[155] Case 76/81, *Transporoute et Travaux SA* v. *Ministère des travaux publics* [1982] ECR 417; Case 263/85, *Commission* v. *Italy* [1991] ECR I-2457; Case 45/87, *Commission* v. *Ireland* ("Dundalk") [1988] ECR 4929; Case C-3/88, *Commission* v. *Italy* ("Re Data Processing") [1989] ECR 4035, [1991] CMLR 115; Case C-21/88, *Du Pont de Nemours Italiana* v. *Unita Sanitaria Locale No. 2 di Carrara* [1990] ECR 889; Case C-113/89, *Rush Portuguesa* v. *Office national d'immigration* [1990] ECR I-1417; Case C-243/89, *Commission* v. *Denmark* ("Storebaelt") [1993] ECR I-3353; C-360/89, *Commission* v. *Italy* [1992] ECR I-3401; Case C-272/91, *Commission* v. *Italy* ("Lottomatica") [1992] ECR I-3929; Case C-87/94, *Commission* v. *Belgium* ("Walloon Buses") [1996] ECR I-2043; Case C-359/93, *Commission* v. *The Netherlands* ("UNIX") [1995] ECR I-157; Case C-275/98, *Unitron Scandinavia* [1999] ECR I-8291; Case C-324/98, *Telaustria* [2000] ECR I-10745; Case C-470/99, *Universale Bau AG* [2002] ECR I-11617; Case C-59/00, *Bent Mousten Vestergaard* v. *Spøttrup Boligselskab* [2001] ECR I-9505; Case C-358/00, *Buchhändler Vereinigung* [2002] ECR I-4685; Case C-231/03, *Coname* [2005] ECR I-7287; Case C-234/03, *Contse and others* [2005] ECR I-9315; Case C-264/03, *Commission* v. *France* [2005] ECR I-8831; Case C-358/03, *Parking Brixen* [2004] ECR I-12055; Case C-535/03, *Commission* v. *Italy* [2006] ECR I-2689. See also: "Commission Interpretative Communication on the Community Law Applicable to Contracts Not or Not Fully Subject to the Provisions of the Public Procurement Directives", *supra* note 51.
[156] Art. 8 Defence Directive, see ch. 6 at 269–72.

thresholds.[157] However, this recognition of the application of TFEU principles to subcontracts below the thresholds does not extend to the availability of the review and remedies discussed in the next chapter 10.[158] Further detailed regulation of contracts below the thresholds was not provided in Germany, the United Kingdom and Ireland. The regime for contracts below the thresholds in §§ 30–4 of the Austrian BVergGVS was not extended to subcontracts below the thresholds, although contracting entities may voluntarily use these provisions. The problem might be that the EU and national regimes for subcontracts below the thresholds now share all the uncertainties of prime contracts below the thresholds. This might lead to Options B–D not being used in practice due to these uncertainties and the litigation risk involved. This problem could be made worse by the fact that the private prime contractors will often not have much experience in competitive procurement procedures, especially when they are SMEs. On the other hand the abilities of SMEs, especially to adapt to new challenges, should never be underestimated.

With regards to these principles there might have been a conflict between Title III Defence Directive and the EDA Supply Chain Code. On the one hand, principles rather than detailed rules were the dominant feature of the latter and competition and transparency are parts of those principles.[159] On the other hand, the principle of non-discrimination was not expressly stipulated and is unlikely to have been included in the notions of "fairness" and "openness" in Paragraph 8 EDA Supply Chain Code. The Code was a part of the EDA regime that authorises the use of offsets. Thus a generic principle requiring subcontracting under the regime to be non-discriminatory would be a contradiction as offsets necessarily involve discrimination in favour of companies from the State of the contracting authority.[160] Therefore it is more likely that the principle of non-discrimination was deliberately left out of the text of the Code. As the Code should apply to cases where Article 346 TFEU can be invoked, its more limited principles should also apply to subcontracts awarded in such a situation. Whether the national security considerations leading Member States to invoke Article 346 TFEU will allow subcontracting on the basis of even these more

---

[157] For the United Kingdom, for example, this is confirmed in Ministry of Defence, *Guidance Defence and Security Public Contracts Regulations 2011: Chapter 13 – Subcontracting under the DSPCR, supra* note 127, at para. 63 under the heading "Subcontracts below the threshold": "Successful tenderers still have to adhere to the principles of the TFEU regarding transparency and competition when awarding subcontracts."

[158] See the Guidance Note *Subcontracting, supra* note 24, para. 41 at 12. With regards to Austria, for example, see: Liebmann, § 116, in Fruhmann and Liebmann, *Bundesvergabegesetz Verteidigung und Sicherheit 2012, supra* note 129, at 326.

[159] See especially paras. 5 and 8 EDA Supply Chain Code.

[160] I benefited from discussions with B. Heuninckx, on this point when he commented on an earlier draft of this chapter.

limited principles will depend on the individual case. However, it can be doubted whether this will always be possible.

4.3.3 Thresholds and advertising

Article 52 Defence Directive on thresholds and rules on advertising is the most detailed and extensive provision of Title III. Article 52(1) clarifies that its requirements only apply to subcontracts exceeding the value thresholds of Article 8 Defence Directive discussed in chapter 6.[161] Below these thresholds only the principles stipulated in Article 51 discussed above apply. Article 52(2) requires the publication of contract notices according to the standard rules for prime contracts: Annex V and Article 32(2)–(5) Defence Directive. The Guidance Note *Subcontracting* especially highlights the requirements in Article 53 Defence Directive:

> the criteria for qualitative selection prescribed by the contracting authority/ entity, as well as any other criteria [the successful tenderer] will apply for the qualitative selection of subcontractors.[162]

This only excludes cases in which the negotiated procedure without publication of a contract notice according to Article 28 can be used (Article 52(4) Defence Directive).[163] The Guidance Note *Subcontracting* argues:

> In such a case, even a contracting authority/entity would be entitled to award a contract without advertising; the same must apply to a successful tenderer.[164]

However, for these contracts and contracts outside the scope of the Defence Directive, prime contractors may still publish subcontract notices according to Article 50(5), most importantly to avoid the longer period of the remedy of ineffectiveness for direct illegal awards discussed in the next chapter 10.[165]

Beyond the requirement to publish a subcontract notice in the OJ and to respect the basic principles when awarding subcontracts, the successful prime contract tenderers retain considerable flexibility.[166] They may use any of the procedures provided in the Defence Directive discussed in chapter 7, namely the restricted procedure, the negotiated procedure with prior publication of a contract notice or competitive dialogue. The negotiated procedure without a prior publication of a contract notice could also be used, if one of the situations allowing its use stipulated in Article 28 Defence Directive and discussed in chapter 7[167] apply,[168] although the publication requirements for subcontracts do not apply, as explained above. They may also use the open procedure not

---

[161] At 269–72.   [162] Guidance Note *Subcontracting, supra* note 24, at 9, para. 34.
[163] Discussed in ch. 7 at 338–47.   [164] *Supra* note 24, at 9.   [165] At 477–81.
[166] Guidance Note *Subcontracting, supra* note 24, at 9, para. 33.   [167] At 338–47.
[168] Guidance Note *Subcontracting, supra* note 24, at 9, para. 35.

provided in the Defence Directive for prime contracts or any other procedure meeting the basic requirements. In Austria, the special regime for contracts below the thresholds in §§ 30–4 BVergGVS might also be used for subcontracting. The four Member States discussed in this book have all implemented Article 52 Defence Directive, almost word for word.[169]

4.3.4 Framework agreements

As outlined above, the prime contractor might use any procurement procedure meeting the basic requirements of transparency, competition, equal treatment and non-discrimination for the award of subcontracts, including framework agreements. Framework agreements were only briefly discussed in chapter 7 on flexibility and procedures.[170] This is because for most prime contracts to be awarded under the Defence Directive this will not be a suitable procedure since the contracts will be too complex. However, there will be contracts such as ammunition purchases, the resupply of spare parts for military equipment and maintenance service procurement where framework agreements can be a suitable method of procurement. For subcontracts, which only cover fragments of a prime contract and which more often can be of a simpler nature, framework contracts are more important. The Guidance Note *Subcontracting* also emphasises the importance of framework agreements as a method facilitating SMEs' participation in the market:

> give sub-suppliers – in particular SMEs – an opportunity to build up cross-border business relationships and to become part of the supply chain of big system integrators from other Member States. They can therefore be an important instrument for opening up established supply chains.

This explains the prominence of framework agreements in the subcontracting regime of the Defence Directive: as explained in chapter 1,[171] SMEs can be found in all Member States and not only in the big six who have a larger defence industrial base.[172] Thus the subcontracting regime in general and the framework agreement regime for subcontracts in particular are consequences of the necessity of accommodating the 22 Member States with limited or no defence industries. Their defence companies, niche companies and "civilian" companies, are to be integrated into the EU defence market through subcontracting. This does not exclude some defence companies in these 22 Member States from winning prime contracts. Neither does it exclude SMEs in the "big six" Member States from winning subcontracts. Subcontracting – particularly through framework agreements – gives the industries of most, if not all, Member

---

[169] Austria in §§ 117–118 BVergGVS, Germany in § 39 VgVVS, in Ireland in Regulation 60 ACRDSR and the United Kingdom in Regulation 42 DSPCR.

[170] At 348–9.   [171] At 27.

[172] France, Germany, Italy, Spain, Sweden and the United Kingdom, see ch. 1 at 22–5.

States a chance in the EU Internal Market for defence and security goods and services.

Article 52(6) Defence Directive sets out a subcontracting regime based on framework agreements for Options B, C and D. According to Article 52(6) subparagraph 1 these framework agreements have to be concluded in compliance with the rules of Title III Defence Directive. Article 52(6) subparagraph 2 requires the award of subcontracts based on such a framework agreement within the limits of the terms laid down in the framework agreement. Only economic operators originally party to the framework agreement can be awarded a subcontract consistent with its terms. According to Article 52(6) subparagraph 3 a framework agreement may not exceed seven years:

> except in exceptional circumstances determined by taking into account the expected service life of any delivered items, installations or systems, and the technical difficulties which a change of supplier may cause.

This is in line with the duration of framework agreements on the prime contract level in Article 29(2) subparagraph 4 Defence Directive which, as discussed in chapter 7,[173] is longer than in the other procurement Directives.[174] It is argued here that this longer duration is appropriate for the same reasons as on the prime contract level.[175] Finally, Article 52(6) subparagraph 4 stipulates the general rule "that framework agreements may not be used improperly or in such a way as to prevent, restrict or distort competition". This is meant as a warning.[176] The four Member States investigated in this book have all transposed Article 52(6) Defence Directive, almost word for word.[177]

4.3.5 Qualitative selection

Qualification on the prime contract level was discussed in the previous chapter 8.[178] Article 53 Defence Directive contains requirements regarding the qualification of subcontractors. According to Article 53 subparagraph 1 the prime contractor has to indicate the criteria for qualitative selection prescribed by the contracting authority or entity and "any other criteria it will apply for the qualitative selection of subcontractors" in the subcontract notice. These criteria must be "objective, non-discriminatory and consistent with the criteria applied by the contracting authority/entity for the selection of the tenderers for the main contract". Moreover, "the capabilities required must be directly related to the subject of the subcontract, and the levels of ability required must be commensurate with it". These qualification rules are consistent with those

---

[173] At 348–9.
[174] 4 years in Art. 33(1) subpara. 3 of the new Public Sector Directive 2014/24/EU.
[175] At 348–9.   [176] Guidance Note *Subcontracting, supra* note 24, at 10, para. 37.
[177] Austria in § 120 BVergGVS, Germany in § 41 VSVgV, in Ireland in Regulation 61(6)–(10) ACRDSR and the United Kingdom in Regulation 42(5)–(8) DSPCR.
[178] At 382–400.

applying to prime contractors under the Defence Directive discussed in chapter 8 and with the similar rules in the other procurement Directives. However, the Guidance Note *Subcontracting* highlights under "rejection of subcontractors" certain limitations for subcontracts:

> In practice, the selection criteria used to reject subcontractors will be a subset of the selection criteria used in the award of the main contract since *not all of the original selection criteria may be relevant for a particular proposed subcontractor or its activity* [emphasis added].[179]

This suggests that while no criteria can be used for the selection of subcontracts that have not been used for the selection of the prime contract, not all the criteria used for the latter have to be used in the context of the selection of subcontractors for the same prime contract. This is a welcome clarification. The four Member States investigated in this book have implemented Article 53 subparagraph 1 Defence Directive, almost word for word.[180] This suggests that these Member States did not consider the provision problematic.

4.3.6 Exception clause

According to Article 53 subparagraph 2 Defence Directive prime contractors who can prove that no subcontractors participating in the competition or their tenders meet the criteria indicated in the subcontract notice and "thereby would prevent the successful tenderer from fulfilling the requirements set out in the main contract" must not be required to subcontract. This exception clause is explained in the Guidance Note *Subcontracting*:

> This concerns, in particular, cases where none of the participating undertakings would meet the selection criteria prescribed by the contracting authority/entity, or where none of the submitted bids would comply with mandatory requirements in the main contract, such as security-of-supply requirements. If the successful tenderer has provided the contracting authority/entity with the appropriate evidence, he is relieved of the obligation to subcontract and can decide freely whether to supply the required elements by his own means or to conclude a subcontract without observing the rules set out in Title III.[181]

It is noticeable that the prominence of security of supply in this context is stipulated not in the text of the Defence Directive but only in the Guidance Note *Subcontracting*. However, this does not represent a substantive difference since security-of-supply requirements would be included in the notion of "mandatory requirements of the main contract". The mentioning of security of supply

---

[179] Guidance Note *Subcontracting*, *supra* note 24, at 11, para. 40.
[180] Austria in § 119 BVergGVS, Germany in § 40(1) VSVgV, in Ireland in Regulation 62(1)–(3) ACRDSR and the United Kingdom in Regulation 44(1) and (2) DSPCR.
[181] *Supra* note 24, at 10.

suggests that in the opinion of the Commission security-of-supply problems in the supply chain might be a prominent if not the most important case in which exception from the obligation to subcontract might be justified. Such security-of-supply problems can arise, for example, if there are problems with the licences for intra-Community transfers of sensitive goods.[182] This would make the "exception clause"[183] a defence-specific provision reflecting security-of-supply concerns. However, exception is allowed beyond security-of-supply scenarios. Moreover, for many goods and services in the supply chain there will be no security-of-supply concerns, most importantly because the goods and services are of a "civil" nature and thus not subject to licensing requirements.

Certain safeguards are built in to prevent abuse of the exception clause by prime contractors. According to Article 53 subparagraph 2 Defence Directive they have to prove the situation "to the satisfaction" of the contracting authority or entity. Moreover, according to the Guidance Note *Subcontracting* they have to provide the contracting authority or entity "with the appropriate evidence".[184] This clarifies that the contracting authority or entity has a wide discretion in its decision to "relieve" the prime contractor of its subcontracting obligations. It is not exactly clear what will constitute appropriate evidence. However, case law might develop in the context of review proceedings also covering the decision of a contracting authority or entity to relieve a prime contractor of its subcontracting obligations. According to Article 55(1) Defence Directive review proceedings can only be launched against contracting authorities or entities and therefore subcontractors cannot launch review proceedings against prime contractors.[185] However, the decision to relieve a prime contractor of his or her subcontracting obligations under Article 53 subparagraph 2 Defence Directive is taken by the contracting authority or entity and it is therefore submitted that a subcontractor could challenge that decision to achieve its set-aside by a review body. The general possibility for subcontractors to launch review proceedings against the contracting authority or entity is also recognised in the Guidance Note *Subcontracting*.[186]

According to the Guidance Note *Subcontracting*[187] when the contracting authority or entity relieves the prime contractor from its subcontracting obligations in the context of the exception clause, the latter "can decide freely whether to supply the required elements by his own means or to conclude a subcontract without observing the rules set out in Title III".[188] The fact that this discretion is given to the prime contractor is understandable with regards to subcontracting that involves companies from other Member States, which

---

[182] See the discussion of the relevant EU regime on intra-Union transfers in ch. 5 at 147–60.
[183] This is an expression of the Guidance Note *Subcontracting*, *supra* note 24, at 10, para. 38, not Art. 53 subpara. 2 Defence Directive.
[184] Ibid.   [185] Guidance Note *Subcontracting*, *supra* note 24, at 12, para. 41.
[186] Ibid., at para. 42.   [187] Ibid.   [188] Ibid.

might cause, for example, security-of-supply problems due to licensing requirements. However, the subcontracting regime of the Defence Directive is not only
an approach to address the varying defence industrial capabilities of the
Member States. It is also a regime to facilitate the participation of SMEs in
procurement. There will often be SMEs in the market without, for example,
security-of-supply issues due to licensing requirements, most importantly
because they are situated in the contracting Member State. However, the
exception clause only covers cases in which no subcontractor could be found
by using a competitive procedure. Therefore it is ultimately sensible to give this
discretion to the prime contractor, a discretion that includes the possibility of
directly awarding a subcontract.

At the prime contract level, the situation addressed in this "exception
clause"[189] is accommodated by allowing the contracting authority or entity to
use the negotiated procedure without prior publication of a contract notice[190]
discussed in chapter 7.[191] "Exception" from the requirement to subcontract is
a slightly more drastic consequence than allowing the use of the negotiated
procedure without prior publication of a contract notice. However, as discussed
in chapter 7 the use of this procedure is very close to procurement outside the
Directive as only very limited requirements apply. Moreover, Article 52(4)
Defence Directive does not even require a subcontract notice in cases where
the negotiated procedure without prior publication of a contract notice can be
used. Thus it is only a sensible overall approach in the subcontracting regime of
the Directive not to impose it when competition cannot be achieved.

Of the four Member States investigated in this book, they have all implemented Title III of the Defence Directive, almost word for word.[192] This
suggests that these Member States did not consider the provision problematic.

4.3.7 Award criteria

The Defence Directive does not address award criteria, discussed with regards
to prime contracts in chapter 8,[193] in the context of subcontracting. Only
the basic principles outlined above, most importantly transparency and
non-discrimination, apply. According to the Guidance Note *Subcontracting*,
"[a]part from these requirements, it is left to the successful tenderer to define
the award criteria". It is interesting that the Directive regulates the criteria for
quantitative selection of subcontractors, but not the award criteria.[194] However,

---

[189] This is an expression of the Guidance Note *Subcontracting*, ibid, at 10 para. 38, not of Art.
53 subpara. 2 Defence Directive.
[190] See, inter alia, Art. 28(1) Defence Directive.   [191] At 338–47.
[192] Austria in § 121 BVergGVS, Germany in § 40(2) VSVgV, in Ireland in Regulation 62(4)
ACRDSR and the United Kingdom in Regulation 44(3) DSPCR.
[193] At 400–3.
[194] I benefited from discussions with B. Heuninckx, on this point when he commented on an
earlier draft of this chapter.

a number of considerations put this flexibility into perspective. First, the award criteria would still have to be in compliance with the clearly stipulated principles.[195] Consequently, discriminatory award criteria, for example, would clearly not be lawful under the Directive. Secondly, not regulating the award criteria further is compliant with the approach of Title III Defence Directive to introduce a subcontracting regime which is as flexible as possible, although it can arguably not be described as "light touch". Thirdly, it is questionable whether award criteria can be found which would still comply with the basic principles of transparency and non-discrimination other than the lowest price and economically most advantageous tender stipulated in the procurement Directives for prime contractors. Finally, if such additional award criteria could be found they could be found by the national legislators transposing the Defence Directive. However, neither §§ 116–22 of the Austrian BVergGVS, §§ 38–41 of the German VSVgV, Regulations 59–62 of the Irish ACRDSR nor Regulations 40–5 of the British DSPCR contain rules on award criteria. Thus within the limits of the principles, the contracting authorities of these Member States are free to define their award criteria in the context of subcontracting.

4.3.8 Subcontracts awarded by prime contractors which are contracting authorities or entities

Chapter II of Title III regulates subcontracts awarded by prime contractors which are contracting authorities or entities. The only Article 54 on "Rules to be applied" stipulates that these prime contractors "shall comply with the provisions on main contracts laid down in Titles I and II when they award subcontracts". Hence they are treated like prime contractors.

4.4 The new Public Sector Directive 2014/24/EU

The new Public Sector Directive 2014/24/EU contains a number of provisions favouring SMEs which are relevant for subcontracting and are likely to ultimately be inserted into the Defence Directive in the course of a revision of the instrument. These include the simplification of information obligations, mainly through a "European Single Procurement Document" (ESPD);[196] the division of contracts into lots and an obligation to provide an explanation if that is not done;[197] limitations on requirements for

---

[195] This, but no award criteria, is pointed out in para. 57 of the very detailed Guidance of the British MOD, www.gov.uk/government/uploads/system/uploads/attachment_data/file/27663/dspcr_c13_mandating_subcontracting_3rd_parties_apr12.pdf [accessed on 18 July 2013].

[196] Art. 59 Public Sector Directive 2014/24/EU. This provision may also benefit prime contractors.

[197] Art. 46 Public Sector Directive 2014/24/EU. This provision may also benefit prime contractors.

participation;[198] and direct payments of subcontractors.[199] While a thorough discussion of these innovations would go beyond the aim of this chapter, Article 71(3) of the new Directive 2014/24/EU stipulates that Member States can provide that subcontractors may request for direct payment by the contracting authority of supplies, works and services provided to the main contractor in the context of the contract performance. This offers subcontractors, which are often SMEs, an efficient way of protecting their interest in being paid. It is submitted that this provision should and will be inserted into the Defence Directive as well.

5 Conclusions

The subcontracting regime of the Defence Directive is the result of a compromise between the six Member States with developed defence industries, which include prime contracting capabilities,[200] and the rest who have mainly subcontracting capabilities.[201] Their insertion was a request of the latter,[202] who want opportunities for their industries at least as subcontractors. The rules faced some criticism since they not only reduce the share of the prime contractor but also impose a considerable burden on them when subcontracting.[203] However, while some requirements are imposed by Option B, this is more of an issue with Options C and D, which might be the reason why so far no Member State has transposed them as obligations and the United Kingdom did not transpose these options at all. Moreover, Heuninckx suggests that these obligations "embody good commercial practice".[204] The award of subcontracts on a competitive and transparent basis not only facilitates an internal subcontracting market based on non-discrimination but may also promote value for money. The legislator simply transferred the principles of its regime for the award of prime contracts to the subcontracting level. Nevertheless, the objective of accommodating the diverse defence industrial structures of the EU Member States discussed in chapter 1, most of which do not have a defence industrial

---

[198] Art. 58 Public Sector Directive 2014/24/EU. This provision may also benefit prime contractors.

[199] Art. 71(3) Public Sector Directive 2014/24/EU.

[200] France, Germany, Italy, Spain, Sweden and the United Kingdom.

[201] C. Kennedy-Loest and N. Pourbaix, "The New Defence Procurement Directive" (2010) 11 ERA Forum 399, at 409. See also Guidance Note Subcontracting, supra note 24, at 1: "[Subcontracting] is important ... politically, since the defence industrial base of many Member States consists mainly of small and medium-sized enterprises (SMEs)."

[202] B. Schmitt (European Commission), "Directive on Defence and Security Procurement" at the "European Defence Procurement Seminar", European Institute of Public Administration, Maastricht, 11 May 2009 as cited by B. Heuninckx, "The EU Defence and Security Procurement Directive: Trick or Treat?", supra note 84, at 19.

[203] Kennedy-Loest and Pourbaix, "The New Defence Procurement Directive", supra note 201; Heuninckx, "Trick or Treat?", supra note 84, at 19.

[204] Heuninckx, supra note 84, at 20.

base that includes prime contractors, was the main motivator for the regime in Article 21 and Title III of the Defence Directive. Closely connected to this objective is the need to accommodate the presence of SMEs in all 28 Member States. These are only "mentioned in passing" in the 2004 Public Sector and Utilities Directive and even the new Public Sector Directive 2014/24/EU inserts only minor innovations regarding SMEs. The main message of the subcontracting regime is that the Defence Directive is not only an instrument for the prime contractors in France, Germany, Italy, Sweden, Spain and the United Kingdom but also for subcontractors in all 28 Member States. While the new Public Sector Directive shows that more could be done, the subcontracting regime of the Defence Directive is the most extensive so far and a substantial innovation of the instrument, a "cornerstone of the Commission's policy".[205]

Subcontracts and offsets are closely connected. The Defence Directive facilitates the earlier and implicitly almost prohibits the latter. The Guidance Note *Offsets* makes this connection very clear:

> Since [offsets] violate basic rules and principles of primary EU law, the Directive cannot allow, tolerate or regulate them. At the same time, the Directive takes into account security-related justifications for offsets and offers, via its provisions on . . . sub-contracting, a non-discriminatory alternative which allows Member States to protect legitimate security interests and to drive competition into the supply chain of successful tenderers without infringing EU law.[206]

Similarly the Guidance Note *Subcontracting* explains:

> Many Member States have traditionally requested (sub)-contracting to their local defence companies as compensation for buying military equipment from suppliers abroad. Offset arrangements have thus been used to give local industries access to other defence markets via the supply chain of foreign prime contractors. This practice, however, goes against the principle of non-discrimination and the basic freedoms of the Internal Market. Consequently, the Directive does not allow this practice, but fosters market access for SMEs throughout the entire European Union via competition in the supply chain.[207]

---

[205] Transposition Review, *supra* note 81, at 6. See also the importance attributed to SME and subcontracting in the 2013 Commission Communication "Towards a more Competitive and Efficient Defence and Security Sector: A New Deal for European Defence", COM (2013) 542 final, at 9 and 14–15 and the accompanying Staff Working Document SWD (2013) 279 final, at 46, 52, and especially 53–5 which appear to imply that some of the innovations of the new Public Sector Directive 2014/24/EU mentioned above are now considered for the Defence Directive.

[206] See Guidance Note *Offsets*, *supra* note 23, at 1.

[207] See Guidance Note *Subcontracting*, *supra* note 24, at 1.

The substitution of offsets with subcontracts also addresses the fact that offsets advantage large prime contractors who have the capacity and networks to arrange offset deals, as highlighted in the 2007 Commission Staff Working Document.[208] Thus not only the subcontracting regime but also the phasing out of offsets favours SMEs.

Other than winning the prime contract, without derogating from the Defence Directive and the TFEU, the industries of the awarding country can only participate through subcontracts and only if they best meet the award criteria specified by the prime contractor. The subcontracting regime is intended as a substitute for the now almost prohibited offsets. Whether the prohibition of offsets can be implemented also through subcontracting depends on many factors: the strong offset lobby in the industries and the administration, the use of enforcement proceedings by the Commission and of the new remedies system described in chapter 10 by aggrieved bidders or the development of offsets with third countries and especially with the USA.[209] The EDA does not believe that it will be easy to remove offsets very soon.[210]

---

[208] *Supra* note 14, at 26.

[209] See Jeff P. Bialos, Christine. E. Fisher and Stuart L. Koehl, *Fortresses & Icebergs: The Evolution of the Transatlantic Defense Market and the Implications for U.S. National Security Policy*, 2 vols. (Baltimore and Washington DC: Centre for Transatlantic Relations, The Johns Hopkins University and the US Department of Defense, 2009), I, at 215. COM (2013) 542 final, *supra* note 205, at 10, does not just reiterate the Commission's position on offsets discussed in this chapter but also threatens that the Commission "will in particular mobilise its policies against offsets".

[210] www.eda.europa.eu/migrate-pages/Otheractivities/CoCOffsets [accessed 22 July 2013]. See the sources cited by Heuninckx, "Trick or Treat?", *supra* note 84, at 26 who argue that "the security of supply and subcontracting provisions of the Directive were adequate non-discriminatory alternatives to offsets" (footnote 151), but that offsets "will in any case survive under another name" (footnote 152).

10

The "hidden Remedies Directive"

Review and remedies in the Defence Directive

1 Introduction[*]

Contrary to the public and utilities sectors where public procurement review and remedies are regulated in a separate Public Sector Remedies Directive[1] and a Utilities Remedies Directive[2] respectively, the public procurement review and remedies system of the Defence Directive is covered in its Title IV. Thus what could have been a separate "Defence and Security Remedies Directive" is "hidden" in, or is an integral part of, the Defence Directive 2009/81/EC. Remedies do not feature in the name of the instrument. This has to do with the fact that it was inserted at a late stage, as discussed below. Title IV of the Defence Directive is based on the Public Sector Remedies Directive, with certain adaptations.

This final chapter will discuss this review and remedies system of the Defence Directive for aggrieved bidders in the national courts and procurement review bodies of the Member States. The general techniques the EU legislator used to adapt the substantive rules of the 2004 Public Sector Directive in the Defence Directive discussed in the previous four chapters will be referred to. As in these other chapters, this will, first, facilitate the understanding of the Defence Directive as a Public Sector Directive and Public Sector Remedies Directive adapted to defence and security requirements, a nature also applicable to the review and remedies system of the Defence Directive. Thus the Defence Directive and more specifically its Title IV also represents a Public Sector Remedies Directive adapted to defence and security requirements. Moreover, some adaptations to the substantive parts of the Defence Directive will impact

---

[*] An earlier version of this chapter was published as "The Hidden Remedies Directive: Review and Remedies under the EU Defence and Security Remedies Directive" (2013) 22 *Public Procurement Law Review* 135–55. Thanks to Tony Arnull (University of Birmingham) and an anonymous referee for comments on an earlier draft of that article.
[1] Public Sector Procurement Remedies Directive 89/665/EEC [1989] OJ L395/33 as amended especially by Directive 2007/66/EC [2007] OJ L335/31.
[2] Utilities Procurement Remedies Directive 92/13/EEC [1992] OJ L76/14 as amended especially by Directive 2007/66/EC.

on the scope of the remedies system and the substantive problems featuring in review proceedings. Most importantly, the adaptations to the review and remedies system itself will be discussed. This will include an analysis of the rules on the relevant defence and security procurement review bodies of the Member States and the adaptations to the remedies which can be awarded by these public procurement review bodies. Overall the analysis will focus on those features of the review and remedies system that have been adapted to create a "suitable" procurement review and remedies system for defence and security procurement. It will be argued that the review and remedies system is "suitable" if it takes defence and security interests sufficiently into account to avoid or at least reduce the cases in which Member States invoke the security exemptions in the Treaty and most notably Article 346(1)(b) TFEU for national and public security reasons. However, in addition to their defence and security objectives, the rules on review and remedies have to meet fundamental rights standards and generate trust among bidders and respect for the substantive rules among contracting officers. These requirements will also be discussed, where appropriate.

2 The need for review and remedies

It is widely accepted that the substantive rules of the procurement Directives on specifications, publication, qualification, award criteria etc. require an enforcement system. Otherwise there is a danger that these procedural rules are not taken seriously and thus less likely to be followed in practice.[3] The lack of a comprehensive enforcement system has always been considered one of the main reasons for the lack of liberalisation of defence procurement in Europe.[4] A crucial aspect of this enforcement system is conducted by the Commission against Member States on the basis of Articles 258 or 348 TFEU.[5] As discussed in chapters 2 and 3, relevant judgments with defence and security aspects have been rare but did occur.[6] However, it can be assumed that there have been many such cases that were resolved before they went to the ECJ.

---

[3] Sue Arrowsmith, John Linarelli and Don Wallace Jr, *Regulating Public Procurement* (The Hague: Kluwer Law International, 2000), at 749; Peter Trepte, *Public Procurement in the EU: A Practitioner's Guide*, 2nd edn (Oxford University Press, 2007), at 531; Christopher Bovis, *EC Public Procurement: Case Law and Regulation* (Oxford University Press, 2006), at 481.

[4] See T. Stormanns, "Europe's Defence Industry: Single Market, Yes – But How?" (1992) *EC Public Contract Law* 75; A. Cox, "The Future of European Defence Policy: The Case for a Centralised Procurement Agency" (1994) 3 *Public Procurement Law Review* 65, 82 and 85.

[5] Strictly speaking, Member States can bring enforcement action as well, but this does not occur very often in practice. A recent example is Case C-364/10 *Hungary* v. *Slovak Republic*, judgment of 16 October 2012, nyr, which is only the fourth judgment ever under Art. 259 TFEU.

[6] See the Agusta case law: Case C-337/05 *Commission* v. *Italy* [2008] ECR I-2173 and Case C-157/06 *Commission* v. *Italy* [2008] ECR I-7313. See the case notes of M. Trybus, (2009) 46

The enforcement of procurement law "from above" through the Commission is insufficient to ensure compliance with the substantive procurement rules.[7] Thus the Public Sector and Utilities Remedies Directives allow for enforcement "from below". The review and remedies system provided in these Directives allows aggrieved bidders to initiate review proceedings against contracting entities in courts of law or special procurement review chambers of the Member States in which the respective contracting authority or entity is situated. The Remedies Directives require the establishment of such review bodies with the power to award rapid and effective remedies.[8] There are remedies before and after the conclusion or making[9] of the contract. To comply with the requirements of these Remedies Directives the Member States created special procurement review chambers,[10] allocated the competence for procurement cases to existing courts[11] or combined both.[12]

Under the Remedies Directives, the most important remedies before the conclusion of the contract allow procurement decisions to be set aside during an ongoing procurement procedure, also in the form of interim relief. Relevant decisions include discriminatory specifications, unlawful disqualifications and even the award decision itself. After such a judgment or order, the procurement procedure has to be recommenced or moved back to the stage when the violation of procurement law occurred. After the conclusion of the contract

---

Common Market Law Review 973–90; P. McGowan, (2009) 18 *Public Procurement Law Review* NA59; B. Heuninckx, (2008) 17 *Public Procurement Law Review* NA187.

[7] The resources of the Commission for the investigation and litigation of violations of EU law are limited.

[8] Art. 1 Directive 89/665/EEC and Art. 1 Directive 92/13/EEC.

[9] Contract "conclusion" is a term used in the Directives, probably originating from the French word. In English law the term "making" of the contract is used. In order to avoid a constant repetition of both terms, the "European" term "conclusion" will be used, although the English law term should generally be used when writing in the English language because the term "conclusion" could be confused with the English law term "discharge".

[10] For example, in Slovenia; see M. Trybus, P. Blomberg and P.-N. Gorecki, *Public Procurement Remedies Systems in the European Union* (Paris: OECD/SIGMA, 2007), www.oecd-ilibrary.org/docserver/download/5kml60q9vklt.pdf?expires=1363952857&id=id&accname=guest&checksum=3A7D7C8ED03598C570D27A051ED16261, at 102.

[11] For example, France or the United Kingdom. On France see F. Lichère and N. Gabayet, "Enforcement of the Public Procurement Rules in France" in Steen Treumer and François Lichère (eds.), *Enforcement of the EU Public Procurement Rules* (Copenhagen: Djøf Publishing, 2011), at 299–328 and Trybus, Blomberg and Gorecki, *Public Procurement Remedies Systems in the European Union*, supra note 10, at 62. On the United Kingdom, see M. Trybus, "An Overview of the United Kingdom Public Procurement Review and Remedies System with an Emphasis on England and Wales" in Treumer and Lichère, at 201–34 and Trybus, Blomberg, and Gorecki, *Public Procurement Remedies Systems in the European Union*, supra note 10 at 107.

[12] For example, Germany. On Germany see: M. Burgi, "EU Procurement Rules – A Report about the German Remedies System" in Treumer and Lichère, *Enforcement of the EU Public Procurement Rules*, supra note 11, at 105–54 and Trybus, Blomberg, and Gorecki, *Public Procurement Remedies Systems in the European Union*, supra note 10, at 67.

these remedies are no longer available. What remains then are only damages and the recently introduced remedy of "ineffectiveness", allowing the annulment of the contract, which shall be discussed below. However, it is the remedies available before the conclusion of the contract which are really interesting for aggrieved bidders. Only then can they hope for a second chance to be awarded the actual contract. The importance of pre-conclusion remedies led to the introduction of the "*Alcatel*" clause, named after the relevant judgment of the ECJ.[13] This requires a standstill period of on average ten days between the communication of the award decision to all bidders and the actual conclusion of the contract. This standstill clause facilitates an effective review system in practice, as before there was often not enough time to initiate proceedings in the procurement review bodies. In some Member States, such as the United Kingdom, the number of procurement review proceedings appears to have increased after the introduction of *Alcatel*.[14] A small number of cases are also affected by a general unwillingness of parties to enforce their rights in procurement cases due to fear of damaging their relationship with the procurement authority, of "biting the hand that feeds"; of the difficulty in proving any wrongdoing;[15] and of the cost of litigation.[16]

2.1 The "hidden" Remedies Directive

The first drafts of the Defence Directive did not contain rules on review and remedies. This complied with the tradition of the other procurement Directives:

---

[13] Case C-81/98, *Alcatel Austria AG and others, Siemens AG Österreich, Sag-Schrack Anlagentechnik AG* v. *Bundesministerium für Wissenschaft und Verkehr* [1999] ECR I-1477.

[14] This impression emerges from the increased number of United Kingdom and Scotland judgments published in the law reports and discussed in law journals and especially the *Public Procurement Law Review* or the websites of the leading law firms. See "Public Procurement Litigation in the New Remedies Era", http://publicsector.practicallaw.com/blog/publicsector/plc/?p=264; M. Clough, "Win Some, Lose Some: New Procurement Litigation Risks", www.whoswholegal.com/news/features/article/28529/win-some-lose-some-new-procurement-litigation-risks/; and S. Arrowsmith, "New Remedies for Tenderers May Mean Greater Risks in the Public Procurement Process", www.procurementblog.com/tag/sue-arrowsmith/. It also appears that more litigation is threatened or started rather than followed through to a final judgment. Thanks to Sue Arrowsmith for pointing this out to me. However, no conclusive empirical research into procurement litigation in the United Kingdom after *Alcatel* – to see whether there is a statistically relevant increase – has yet been conducted.

[15] For the time before *Alcatel* see *The Wood Review: Investigating UK Business Experiences in Competing for Public Contracts in Other EU Countries*, HM Treasury and the Department of Trade and Industry (2004), see www.bipsolutions.com/docstore/pdf/8756.pdf [accessed 22 April 2014].

[16] The costs were identified as a deterrent to litigation by D. Pachnou, "Bidder Remedies to Enforce the EC procurement rules in England and Wales" (2003) 12 *Public Procurement Law Review* 35.

the Public Sector Directive and Utilities Directive do not contain such rules either; these are provided in the additional and specific Remedies Directives 665/89/EEC and 92/13/EC. A similar "Defence and Security Procurement Remedies Directive" was planned afterwards.[17] It was only the European Parliament that in the course of its discussions as part of the co-decision procedure and especially its Internal Market and Consumer Protection Committee (Rapporteur: Alexander Count Lambsdorff) achieved the amendment of the Directive to include review and remedies to ensure enforceability.[18] The majority of the rules of the amended Public Sector Remedies Directive 665/89/EEC were inserted in Title IV of the Defence Directive, including the rules on *Alcatel* and ineffectiveness: "the complete panoply of the *acquis* in the area of procurement remedies".[19] The Parliament move came as a surprise to the Commission but was not a problem in the end.[20] This only deviated from the traditional legislative approach but serves the Defence Directive objectives and saved the Commission some work. Unfortunately, this inclusion of review and remedies in Title IV "at the eleventh hour" meant that this aspect had not been taken into account in the consultation process preceding the Directive: the Commission asked no questions regarding review and remedies in the Green Paper Defence Procurement[21] and

[17] K. Vierlich-Jürcke (European Commission, 2012), "Subcontracting and Remedies in the Field of Defence and Security Procurement" at the "Seminar on European Defence and Security Procurement", European Institute of Public Administration (EIPA), Maastricht, 19 January 2012; B. Schmitt and N. Spiegel (European Commission, the drafters of the Defence Directive) in their presentation "The Specificities of the European Defence and Security Procurement Directive" at the seminar "European Defence Procurement and Other Defence Market Initiatives", at the EIPA, Maastricht, 15 November 2010. References to conference papers are from notes of the author (on file) unless stated otherwise.

[18] The author gave evidence to this Committee of the European Parliament in June 2008. See Notice to Members (IMCO/CM/05/2008) Subject: Summary of the IMCO mini-hearing on the defence package, *Rationalising the European defence market – risks and benefits IMCO Committee Meeting*, 2 June 2008, 15h00–18h30, 3, www.europarl.europa.eu/meetdocs/2004_2009/documents/cm/727/727589/727589en.pdf: "Prof. Trybus from Birmingham University focused on the impact of the proposal on the current legal framework. He concluded that the defence package would provide more coherence, compliance and clarity on the application of internal market rules. In particular he defended the inclusion of security goods in the scope of the defence procurement Directive, pleaded to keep the thresholds untouched, *and finally, to introduce legal remedies* [emphasis added]."

[19] A. Georgopoulos, "Defence and Security Procurement Directive: Remedies" at the (UK) "Procurement Lawyers Association Event on the Defence and Security Directive", London, 8 June 2011, www.procurementlawyers.org/training_and_events/past_events/pla_events/defence_and_security_directive.aspx [accessed 21 November 2013].

[20] Schmitt and Spiegel, "The Specificities of the European Defence and Security Procurement Directive", *supra* note 17.

[21] COM (2004) 608 final.

consequently received no relevant contributions from stakeholders.[22] However, the adoption of the review and remedies system of the Public Sector Remedies Directive for the field of application of the Defence Directive, subject to certain adaptations which will be discussed below, is significant. This will not only subject especially the armaments procurement authorities of the Member States to detailed substantive EU rules on public procurement but also to the risk of litigation and thus consequences for the completion and costs of their projects. There is a danger that some of these risks might lead Member States to invoke the defence and security exemptions in the Treaty and most notably Article 346(1)(b) TFEU discussed in chapter 3, if the review and remedies rules in Title IV Defence Directive were not adequately adapted to defence and security considerations.

2.2 Security derogations in the TFEU

It is against the background of the armaments derogation in Article 346(1)(b) TFEU, its interpretation and use in practice, discussed in chapter 3, that the adaptations in the Defence Directive were made. The national security considerations leading Member States to invoke the armaments exemption and also the other security exemptions were to be accommodated in the Directive by adapting some of the rules of Public Sector Directive 2004/18/EC, as discussed in the previous four chapters of this book. The main requirements of the defence and security sector to be accommodated through the adaptations are "security of supply" and "security of information". As explained in chapters 1 and 8, security of supply is a national security concern about supplies not being delivered[23] whereas security of information is a national security concern about the confidentiality of sensitive information not being safeguarded.[24] The requirements of the procurement Directives can conflict with these concerns. In the context of review and remedies, the delay caused by the set-aside of a procurement decision or even the annulment of a contract can easily have an impact on the timely delivery of equipment or services and therefore security of supply. The publicity and access-to-documents requirements of due process can easily have an impact on confidentiality and therefore security of information.

---

[22] The Green Paper started a consultation process leading to the Defence Directive the results of which were published a year later in the Communication on the results of the consultation, COM (2005) 626 final. The otherwise rather comprehensive 2007 Commission Staff Working Document – Impact Assessment SEC (2007) 1598 final, at http://ec.europa.eu/ internal_market/publicprocurement/docs/defence/impact_assessment_en.pdf [accessed 15 November 2013], does not address review and remedies either.

[23] Commission's Guidance Note *Security of Supply*, http://ec.europa.eu/internal_market/ publicprocurement/docs/defence/guide-sos_en.pdf [accessed 21 November 2013], at 1.

[24] Commission's Guidance Note *Security of Information*, http://ec.europa.eu/internal_market/ publicprocurement/docs/defence/guide-soi_en.pdf [accessed 21 November 2013], at 1.

The notion that Title IV Defence Directive "introduced" a review and remedies system to defence and security contracts is not entirely accurate. Before the Defence Directive, the Public Sector Remedies Directive applied to defence and security contracts, "subject to Article 346 TFEU".[25] However, in practice the application of the Public Sector Remedies Directive was determined by the extensive interpretation of Article 346 TFEU discussed in detail in chapter 3. Thus in practice defence and security contracts were not subject to review proceedings on the basis of the Public Sector Remedies Directive.

An example from a Member State might facilitate the understanding of the change brought by Title IV Defence Directive. In Germany, as discussed further below, in line with all other procurement review cases, proceedings under the Defence Directive now have to be initiated in the Procurement Review Chambers and the State Courts of Appeal. Before the transposition of the Defence Directive, armaments contracts were outside the jurisdiction of these procurement review bodies and for a while the jurisdiction of the administrative courts was discussed.[26] Thus in Germany armaments contracts were in practice not reviewed at all, irrespective of the interpretation of Article 346 TFEU discussed in chapter 3. The transposition of the Defence Directive clearly changes this, although Article 346 TFEU remains in place. Therefore speaking of the "introduction" of a review and remedies system through Title IV Defence Directive is not entirely inaccurate. The German Parliament speaks of an "extension" of the review and remedies system, which is an accurate expression since before the transposition of the Defence Directive, the remedies available for public sector and utility contracts did not extend to armaments contracts.[27] The situation in the United Kingdom and the Republic of Ireland was comparable. In Austria even the word "extension" is not accurate since the remedies for public sector and utility contracts in the BVergG 2006 did apply to armaments contracts. Thus the BVergGVS 2011 simply reinstates the "*status quo ante*".[28]

---

[25] Art. 10 Public Sector Directive 2004/18/EC before the amendment through Art. 71 Defence Directive.

[26] See the administrative court judgments VG Koblenz, decision of 31 January 2005, 6 L 2617/ 04.KO and OVG Koblenz, decision of 25 May 2005, 7 B 10356/05.OVG discussed by H.-J. Prieß and F.-J. Hölzl, "Trust Is Good – Control Even Better: German Higher Administrative Court Reviews Military Procurement Decision" (2005) 14 *Public Procurement Law Review* NA128–35.

[27] German: "Ausweitung des Rechtsschutzes", see http://dip21.bundestag.de/dip21/btd/17/ 072/1707275.pdf [accessed 21 November 2013].

[28] Bundesgesetz über die Vergabe von Aufträgen in Verteidigungs- und Sicherheitsbereich (*Bundesvergabegesetz*, 2012), BGBL. I NC 10/2012. See H. Liebmann, § 135, in Michael Fruhmann and Hanno Liebmann, *BVergGVS 2012: Bundesvergabegesetz Vergabe und Sicherheit 2012* (Vienna: MANZ, 2012), at 372.

3 Adapting Public Sector Directive 2004/18/EC

In the previous four chapters of this book it was argued that the EU legislator used four main techniques to adapt certain provisions of the original Public Sector Directive to defence and security needs in the Defence Directive. These techniques are limitation, flexibility, description and substitution and they have a direct or indirect impact on the review and remedies system in Title IV of the Defence Directive.

3.1 Limitation

As discussed in chapter 6, adaptation by "limitation" refers to the fact that in comparison to the scope of the old and new Public Sector Directive, the material scope of the Defence Directive is more limited. The personal scope, the contracting entities to which the Defence Directive applies, is more extensive than that of the Public Sector Directives. It is equivalent to that of the 2004 Public Sector Directive *and* the 2004 Utilities Directive taken together.[29] However, the material scope, the contracts to which the Defence Directive applies, is more limited than that of the Public Sector Directives. First, the Defence Directive only applies to certain types of contracts in the defence and security fields.[30] Secondly, the potential number of contracts below the thresholds is higher than those of the 2004 Public Sector Directive since the thresholds of the Defence Directive are actually the higher ones of the 2004 Utilities Directive.[31] However, this ultimately depends on the average value of defence contracts compared to the other sectors. While the high costs of most high-end defence equipment will have contract values of millions and beyond, there are supplies such as ammunition and services such as vehicle

---

[29] The abstract definition for the covered contracting entities for the Defence Directive is contained in its Art. 1(17), which defines contracting entities as "contracting authorities as referred to in Article 1(9) [2004 Public Sector Directive] and contracting entities referred to in Article 2 [2004 Utilities Directive]". See ch. 6 at 248–60.

[30] According to its Art. 2 the Defence Directive applies only to military equipment, sensitive equipment, works, supplies and services directly related to military and sensitive equipment and finally works and services for specifically military purposes. See ch. 6 at 260–7.

[31] Art. 8 Defence Directive provides for thresholds of €414,000 for supply and service contracts and €5,186,000 for works contracts. The threshold for works contracts equals that in the old and new Public Sector Directives. In contrast, the value thresholds for supplies and services are considerably higher with respect to central government (€134,000) and other contracting entities (€207,000). See Art. 4 of Regulation 1336/2013/EU and Art. 4 Directive 2014/24/EU. Before 2012, in accordance with the then Art. 3 of Regulation 1177/2009/EC on the application thresholds of the procurement Directives, the following changes were incorporated in respect of the original wording of the Defence Directive: Art. 8(a) was amended so that the threshold in Euros for supplies and services contracts was modified from €412,000 to €387,000; Art. 8(b) was amended so that the threshold in Euros for works contracts was modified from €5,150,000 to €4,845,000. Hence in 2011 the thresholds were actually increased to €400,000 for supplies and services and €5,000,000 for works. Similarly in 2013 they were increased again to €414,000 and €5,186,000 respectively. See ch. 6 at 269–72.

maintenance which are of a lower contract value. Furthermore, the application of the Defence Directive to security contracts of non-defence authorities such as the police and even utilities will mean that thresholds do matter for contracts within the material scope of the Defence Directive, regarding the procurement of, for example, airport security equipment or handguns. Finally, in addition to all the exceptions of the old and new Public Sector Directives, the Defence Directive contains a number of additional defence and security-specific exemptions, most notably on collaborative projects and government-to-government purchases.[32]

All these limitations do not only affect the substantive rules of the Defence Directive but also limit its review and remedies regime. If a contract is outside the scope of the Defence Directive, an aggrieved bidder does not have access to the review and remedies in its Title IV either. The limitation of the material scope of the Directive is also a limitation of the application of the review and remedies regime. This follows the blueprint of the public sector and utilities regimes since the scope of the Public Sector Remedies Directive is determined by that of the Public Sector Directive and the scope of the Utilities Remedies Directive is determined by that of the Utilities Directive. An interesting difference between the review and remedies systems of the United Kingdom, Germany and Ireland on the one hand and Austria on the other hand should be mentioned here. In Austria the public procurement remedies system applies to contracts above and below the thresholds.[33] This "mirror principle" is not required by EU law but by Austrian constitutional law. In contrast, in the other three Member States discussed in this book, the procurement remedies system only applies to contracts above the thresholds. These different approaches to the treatment of the thresholds of the Directives also apply in the context of the Defence Directive and its review and remedies system. In Austria there will be access to review, but not in Ireland, Germany and Britain.

---

[32] The exclusions in Art. 13(a)–(d) and (f) are specific to the Defence Directive. Exclusion (a) is on "contracts for which the application of the rules of this Directive would oblige a Member State to supply information the disclosure of which it considers contrary to the essential interests of its security"; exclusion (b) is on "contracts for the purposes of intelligence activities"; exclusion (c) is on "contracts awarded in the framework of a cooperative programme based on research and development, conducted jointly by at least two Member States for the development of a new product and, where applicable, the later phases of all or part of the life-cycle of this product"; exclusion (d) is on "contracts awarded in a third country, including for civil purchases, carried out when forces are deployed outside the territory of the Union where operational needs require them to be concluded with economic operators located in the area of operations"; and exclusion (f) is on "contracts awarded by a government to another government relating to: (i) the supply of military equipment or sensitive equipment, (ii) works and services directly linked to such equipment, or (iii) works and services specifically for military purposes, or sensitive works and sensitive services". See ch. 6 at 276–301.

[33] See H. Liebmann, *supra* note 28, 374 explaining that for contracts above the thresholds proceedings at the *Bundesvergabeamt* have to be initiated within 10 days and within 7 days for contracts below the thresholds.

Moreover, while the Defence Directive aims to reduce the cases in which the armaments exemption in Article 346(1)(b) TFEU is used in practice by providing a tailor-made instrument for the defence and security sectors, the Treaty derogation itself remains unchanged. This means that the Member States still have the possibility of derogating from the TFEU for national security reasons in relation to armaments contracts. This does not limit the scope of the Defence Directive further in comparison to that of the old and new Public Sector Directives but represents a possible limitation that is more relevant in the context of the application of the former, an instrument specifically designed for defence and security contracts. Moreover, beyond this aspect of limiting the scope of the Defence Directive as a whole, it is not unlikely that national security considerations might lead to the use of Article 346(1)(b) TFEU exactly because they conflict with the operation of the review and remedies system in Title IV. This may happen if review would compromise security of information because the confidentiality of sensitive information would be compromised. Moreover, this could happen if review would compromise security of supply because it would affect the timely delivery of the supplies or services. However, this would depend on the extent to which these national security considerations were taken into account when adapting the rules of the Public Sector Remedies Directive in Title IV or the extent to which this adaptation was not even necessary because the rules already accommodated considerations such as security of supply and information. This will be discussed below.

3.2 Flexibility

As discussed in chapter 7, adaptation by "flexibility" refers to the adapted choice of procurement procedures under the Defence Directive in comparison to that of the 2004 Public Sector Directive. First, in contrast to not only the old and new Public Sector and Utilities Directives but most procurement laws, the open procedure is not available at all,[34] although this limitation of choice is not in itself a feature of flexibility as less choice means less not more flexibility. Secondly, and more importantly, similar to the old and new Utilities Directive but different from the old and new Public Sector Directives, there is a free choice between the restricted procedure and the negotiated procedure with prior publication of a contract notice.[35] This reduces the importance of the restricted procedure and makes the negotiated procedure with competition the *de facto* default procedure

---

[34] Art. 25 Defence Directive "choice of procedures" does not mention the open procedure, nor is it mentioned anywhere else in the provisions of the Directive or its preamble. See also B. Heuninckx, "The EU Defence and Security Procurement Directive: Trick or Treat?" (2011) 20 *Public Procurement Law Review* 9, at 14 and C. Kennedy-Loest and N. Pourbaix, "The New Defence Procurement Directive" (2010) 11 *ERA Forum* 399, at 403.

[35] Art. 25 subpara. 2 Defence Directive.

of the Defence Directive.[36] Finally, a number of additional grounds justifying the use of the negotiated procedure without prior publication of a contract notice were inserted, all of them related to the defence and security context.[37]

The effect of these adaptations on the review and remedies system is less direct than that of limitation discussed above. However, the substantive reasons related to procedures leading to procurement review proceedings are likely to be different with a different choice of procedures. The technique of adaptation through increased flexibility does not feature in the review and remedies regime in Title IV.

3.3 Description

As discussed in chapter 8, adaptation by "description" does not involve a substantive change to the relevant rules but the insertion of expressly described requirements and conditions which are also legally possible but not expressly stipulated in the Public Sector Directive. The substantive rules affected by description are those on specifications, contract conditions, qualification and award criteria. Description aims to accommodate the security-of-supply and security-of-information considerations. Security of supply can be affected, for example, by transfer licences, which as discussed in chapter 4 are a feature of the European defence and security market. Security of information can be affected if, at the different stages of the procurement procedure normally requiring publicity and transparency, the need to protect confidential information is not safeguarded, as discussed in chapter 8. The rules on different stages of the procurement procedure were adapted to address these concerns. The results are expressly stipulated and thus described defence and security-specific standards,[38] contract performance conditions, qualification criteria and award sub-criteria in the Defence Directive.[39] This raises awareness amongst contracting

---

[36] Heuninckx, "Trick or Treat?", supra note 34, at 14: "the 'standard' procedure". The differentiation of *de facto* and *de jure* is also an expression on B. Heuninckx communicated to the author when discussing an earlier draft of his article "The Tailor-made EU Defence and Security Procurement Directive: Limitation, Flexibility, Description, and Substitution" (2013) 39 *European Law Review* 3–29.

[37] Art. 28(1)(c) Defence Directive "urgency resulting from a crisis", (2)(a) "research and development services" and especially (5) "armed forces deployed abroad". See also Recital 58. The accelerated versions of the restricted procedure and the negotiated procedure with publication are also limited to a situation of "urgency", see Art. 33(7) Defence Directive.

[38] Defence standards are defined in Point 3 Annex III Defence Directive.

[39] The main relevant adaptations through description in the Defence Directive are the addition of defence standards in Art. 18, the requirements regarding security of information in Art. 7, contract conditions to secure classified information in Art. 22, contract conditions to ensure security of supply in Art. 23, the possibility of excluding at the qualification stage a bidder with a negative history regarding security of supply and

officers to use them and offers possibilities to accommodate security of supply and information inside the Directive. Moreover, it is clear that these requirements are in compliance with the Directive. The requirements do not add substance but are merely descriptive and many other requirements can be added in practice, provided they are in compliance with EU law.

As with adaptation through flexibility, the effect of description on the review and remedies system in Title IV Defence Directive is indirect. The use of expressly stipulated and described contract performance conditions and qualification and award criteria could lead to less litigation as their legality is clear from the text of the Defence Directive. However, this is far from certain as this effect would depend on the quality of drafting and relevance of these requirements and it is too early to assess this. Standards, qualification, contract performance conditions and award criteria have of course frequently been subject to procurement review proceedings. In theory, the better the quality of drafting, including detail, and the higher the relevance of these requirements, the less room is left for litigation. It will be shown below that the technique of adaptation through description also features in the review and remedies regime in Title IV.

3.4 Substitution

As discussed in chapter 9, adaptation by "substitution" refers to how offsets and subcontracting are addressed in the Defence Directive. In contrast to the old and new Public Sector Directives which mostly leaves this supply chain to be organised by the successful tenderer,[40] under the Defence Directive contracting authorities may require parts of a prime contract to be awarded as subcontracts to third parties. This is intended to drive competition into the supply chain and to open opportunities to SMEs. Article 21 Defence Directive provides four options for subcontracting requirements explained further in Title III[41] and the Commission's Guidance Note *Subcontracting*.[42] Subcontracts and offsets are closely connected, not least because they are both about industrial participation. The Defence Directive facilitates the former and implicitly (almost) prohibits the latter.[43] Other than winning the prime contract and without derogating from the Defence Directive and the TFEU, the industries of the contracting Member State can only participate through subcontracts; and only if they represent the economically most advantageous tender. Therefore it

---

information in Art. 39, defence and security-specific requirements regarding technical capacity in Art. 42 and security of supply and information as sub-award criteria in Art. 47.

[40] See Art. 25 Public Sector Directive 2004/18/EC.   [41] Arts. 50–4 Defence Directive.

[42] http://ec.europa.eu/internal_market/publicprocurement/rules/defence_procurement/index_en.htm [accessed 21 November 2013].

[43] Ibid., 1.

represents a fourth technique of adapting the rules of the 2004 Public Sector Directive in the Defence Directive: substitution (for offsets). Rather than only implicitly banning offsets, to which there was no alternative, the legislator offered something instead. The subcontracting regime is intended as a substitute for the "now" almost prohibited offsets.[44]

The substitution described above will only have an indirect effect on the operation of the national review and remedies systems under Title IV Defence Directive. As offsets cannot be accommodated in the Directive, the armaments exemption in Article 346(1)(b) TFEU would have to be used by Member States who wish to use offsets for national security reasons to derogate from the Directive and the TFEU. This derogation could then be the subject of enforcement action against these Member States on the basis of Articles 258 or 348 TFEU if the Commission questions the necessity of the use of Article 346 TFEU. Subcontracting, however, could be the subject of litigation in the procurement review bodies of the Member States. As with description discussed above, the stipulation of a more detailed subcontracting regime might reduce the need for litigation. On the other hand, provided the substitution described above is implemented in practice, the then increased importance of subcontracting might well make it a judicial battleground. The technique of substitution does not feature in Title IV Defence Directive.

4 Adapting the Public Sector Remedies Directive

As already mentioned above, the rules of the review and remedies regime in Title IV Defence Directive were based on those in the amended Public Sector Remedies Directive. Some of these rules were adapted to meet the specific needs of the defence and security sectors and thus to limit Member State recourse to the defence and security derogations discussed in chapters 2 and 3, especially Article 346(1)(b) TFEU. Adaptations in a system of judicial review to accommodate security interests may raise fundamental rights and rule-of-law issues if they lead to disproportionate limitations of access to justice. Therefore it is submitted the adaptations do not only have to be adequate to accommodate defence and security concerns and thus to allow the effective operation of a review and remedies system inside the regime of the Defence Directive and TFEU. Rather, the adapted system also has to meet the fundamental rights and rule-of-law standards of the EU and the national legal orders of the Member States it has to be transposed into. In order to discuss whether these standards are met, the adaptations are measured against the EU Charter on Fundamental Rights,[45] since the Treaty of Lisbon part of primary EU law.[46] The right to effective judicial protection in Article 47 of the Charter, especially, is a crucial

---

[44] Ibid.   [45] Charter on Fundamental Rights of the European Union, OJ [2010] C-83/389.
[46] Art. 6(1) TEU (Lisbon).

benchmark in this context.[47] The Charter was drafted on the basis of the fundamental rights and their limitations contained in the constitutional laws of the Member States and the European Convention on Human Rights, and also recognised by the ECJ as general principles of EU law.[48] Thus the Charter represents an adequate standard for the analysis of a review system required by a Directive and thus to be transposed into the national legal orders of the Member States; it reflects the fundamental rights standards of the Treaties, the Member States and the ECJ.[49] However, in addition to accommodating defence and security considerations in compliance with fundamental rights standards, the adaptations have to lead to a review and remedies system which generates trust among bidders and respect for the substantive rules among contracting officers. This section of the chapter will discuss the adaptations to defence and security needs in the review and remedies system in Title IV of the Defence Directive itself and whether the balancing act between the different objectives and standards was successful. There are three noteworthy adaptations in Title IV, namely those regarding the procurement review bodies, interlocutory procedures and ineffectiveness.

4.1 Review bodies

A crucial question to be addressed in any public procurement review and remedies system is which bodies – courts of law or special procurement review bodies – have jurisdiction for public procurement review proceedings. The relevant rules in Title IV Defence Directive[50] are almost equal to those in the amended Public Sector

---

[47] On Art. 47 of the Charter in EU law see Case C-317/08, *Rosalba Alassini* v. *Telecom Italia SpA*; Case C-318/08, *Filomena Califano* v. *Wind SpA*; Case C-319/08, *Lucia Anna Giorgia Iacono* v. *Telecom Italia SpA*; Case C-320/08, *Multiservice Srl* v. *Telecom Italia SpA* [2010] ECR I-2213; and Case C-279/09, *DEB Deutsche Energiehandels- und Beratungsgesellschaft mbH* v. *Germany* [2010] ECR I-13849,

[48] See A. Arnull, "From Charter to Constitution and Beyond: Fundamental Rights in the New European Union" [2003] *Public Law* 704; and "The European Court of Justice after Lisbon" in Martin Trybus and Luca Rubini (eds.), *The Treaty of Lisbon and the Future of European Law and Policy* (Cheltenham: Edward Elgar, 2012) 34; H. Raulus, "The Charter of Fundamental Rights as a Set of Constitutional Principles", 181; M. Borowski, "The Charter of Fundamental Rights in the Treaty on European Union", 200; W. Weiß, "EU Human Rights Protection after Lisbon", 220.

[49] That principle of effective judicial protection in Art. 47 of the Charter is also a general principle of EU law stemming from the constitutional traditions common to the Member States, which has been enshrined in Arts. 6 and 13 of the European Convention for the Protection of Human Rights and Fundamental Freedoms. See the relevant case law in Case 222/84, *Marguerite Johnston* v. *Chief Constable of the Royal Ulster Constabulary* [1986] ECR 1651, [1986] 3 CMLR 240, paras. 18 and 19; Case 222/86, *Heylens and others* [1987] ECR 4097, para. 14; Case C-424/99, *Commission* v. *Austria* [2001] ECR I-9285, para. 45; Case C-59/00 P, *UPA* [2002] ECR I-6677, para. 39; Case C-467/01, *Eribrand* [2003] ECR I-6471, para. 61.

[50] Especially Art. 56(2)–(3), (6), and (8)–(9) Defence Directive.

Remedies Directive.[51] However, according to Article 56(10) Defence Directive the relevant review bodies of the Member States have to take the defence interests of the Member States in general and security of information in particular into account. This adaptation addresses directly the defence and security concerns in the relevant derogations of the Treaty, especially Article 346 TFEU.

To accommodate these purposes the Member States can opt for the establishment of special defence and security procurement review bodies when transposing the Defence Directive, as provided in its Article 56(10) subparagraph 2:

> Member States may decide that a specific body has sole jurisdiction for the review of contracts in the fields of defence and security.

This would involve the establishment of new and separate national defence and security procurement courts, tribunals or review chambers, in addition to those hearing cases under the public sector and utilities regimes. The alternative would be to simply extend the jurisdiction of the existing procurement review bodies to the scope of the Defence Directive, with certain adjustments to safeguard confidentiality and national security. Prima facie, the assumption of Article 56(10) subparagraph 2 Defence Directive appears to be that not only the confidentiality of sensitive information but national security interests in general are better safeguarded in a separate defence and security review body. However, it is submitted that this first appearance of paragraph (10) is deceiving. The use of the word "may" in subparagraph 2 clearly only introduces specific review bodies with "sole jurisdiction" as an *option* without indicating any preference of the EU legislator. It simply recognises that certain Member States might consider this necessary and expressly stipulates special review bodies as a possibility when transposing Title IV of the Defence Directive. A Member State might consider a specific review body necessary because certain requirements for transparency and public access to official documents, rooted in constitutional law or the law regulating the court procedure of existing procurement review bodies, are difficult to reconcile with special confidentiality requirements of defence contracting thus making it necessary to separate review under the Defence Directive from the existing court system. However, it is possible to reconcile both interests without creating new review bodies. An example in the TFEU is the review of decisions of Member States to derogate from the Treaty, inter alia on the basis of the armaments exemption in Article 346(1)(b) TFEU discussed in chapter 3.[52] Article 348 subparagraph 2 TFEU allows the ECJ to hear such a case *in camera*, clearly due to the national security and especially confidentiality aspects of such cases. Another example from the context of the transposition of the Defence Directive is Germany where, in the transposition

---

[51] Especially Art. 2(2)–(3), (6), and (8)–(9) Public Sector Remedies Directive 89/665/EEC as amended.
[52] At 88–128.

of the Defence Directive, the jurisdiction of the existing procurement review chambers has been extended to contracts covered by the Directive and confidentiality requirements for these chambers were introduced with this transposition,[53] as will be discussed further below.

Article 56(10) subparagraph 2 Defence Directive suggests the option of specific review bodies only for confidentiality and other national security reasons. However, further advantages could be considered. There could be, for example, a higher level of specialisation as defence and security experts from the military or the police could be involved as lay judges acting in concert with fully qualified judges. Moreover, possible previous experience could be taken into account when recruiting the fully qualified judges. Finally, specialisation could develop over time when the specialised court has gathered some experience with review cases. However, most of these advantages could also be accommodated if the Member States opted for extending their existing public procurement review system to defence and security contracts. For example, the German first-instance procurement review chambers (*Vergabekammern*) on the federal and state levels use lay judges in concert with full-time judges[54] and the second-instance state courts of appeal (*Oberlandesgerichte*) have specialised divisions dealing only with procurement cases.[55]

Furthermore, the advantages of specialised review bodies have to be balanced against possible negative implications. Specialised defence and security procurement review bodies did not exist in any Member State prior to the Defence Directive and would have to be newly established. Such a move could obviously have financial, organisational, legal and even constitutional implications which might make this not the most attractive option. New judges, support staff, equipment and perhaps even a building would have to be found or reallocated. Thus it is perhaps not surprising that it appears that the Member States have not taken advantage of this option.[56] In Germany, for example, review proceedings will have to be initiated in the procurement review chambers of the 16 German

---

[53] See § 110a GWB (see ch. 9 note 90 and discussed below).

[54] § 105 (2) GWB: "The public procurement tribunals shall take their decisions through a chairman and two associate members of whom one shall serve in an honorary capacity. The chairman and the full-time associate member shall be civil servants appointed for life with the qualification to serve in the higher administrative service, or comparably expert employees. Either the chairman or the full-time associate member shall be qualified to serve as a judge; generally this should be the chairman. The associate members should have in-depth knowledge of the practice of awarding public contracts, and honorary associate members should also have several years of practical experience in the field of the awarding of public contracts."

[55] § 116 (3) GWB: "The immediate complaint shall be decided exclusively by the Court of Appeal having jurisdiction at the seat of the public procurement tribunal. *An award division shall be set up at every Court of Appeal.*"

[56] "Report from the Commission to the European Parliament and the Council on Transposition of Directive 2009/81/EC on Defence and Security Procurement", COM

States (*Länder*) or the procurement review chambers of the Federal Competition Agency (*Bundeskartellamt*) in Bonn[57] and on appeal in the state courts of appeal, for federal cases the *Oberlandesgericht* Düsseldorf, just as for all other contracts. Similarly in France, the administrative courts (*tribunaux administratifs*), the administrative courts of appeal (*cours administratives d'appel*), and the *Conseil d'Etat* will also hear actions against defence contracts,[58] as will the High Court, the Court of Appeal and the Supreme Court in the United Kingdom.[59] In Ireland the High Court will also hear cases on defence and security contracts,[60] in addition to all other cases, as will the *Bundesvergabeamt* and *Verwaltungsgerichtshof* in Austria.[61] Thus in addition to the disadvantages of separate review bodies high-lighted above, the Commission might be right in arguing that the transposing national legislators "did not share some of the concerns voiced in the legislative process".[62] At least any security concerns must have been considered less significant than the costs.

As separate review bodies were not established in any Member State, there are no fundamental rights implications of extending the jurisdiction of existing tribunals. However, even the establishment of new review bodies would not have represented a fundamental rights issue per se. The "use" of existing tribunals is likely to generate trust in and respect for the system. Possible suspicions among bidders are avoided and contracting officers will probably not expect special treatment by a special court, although this is far from certain.

4.2 Security in the review bodies

If the existing procurement review bodies are charged with deciding cases under the Defence Directive, various measures to adapt to the often sensitive character of the cases can be provided. The public could be excluded, security clearances for the members (judges) of these bodies required, access to classified information be limited. However, it appears that most Member States refrained from introducing special rules on security clearances for the members of their procurement review bodies. The Commission might be right in interpreting

---

(2012) 565 final (from 2 October 2012), at 8: "It seems that no Member State has used the option to endow a specific body with jurisdiction."

[57] §§ 104(1) and 116 GWB as amended in December 2011.

[58] Arts. L22 and L23 Code des tribunaux administratifs et des cours administratives d'appel.

[59] Regulation 52(2) Defence and Security Public Contracts Regulations 2011 (DSPCR), SI 2011/1848: "Proceedings for that purpose must be started in England and Wales and in Northern Ireland in the High Court or in Scotland in either the Sheriff Court or the Court of Session, and Regulations 53 to 65 apply to such proceedings."

[60] See Regulation 64 European Union (Award of Contracts Relating to Defence and Security) Regulations (ACRDSR), SI 620/2012.

[61] § 135 BVergGVS 2012, referring to the review and remedies system of the BVergG 2006.

[62] Transposition Report, *supra* note 56, at 8.

this as another indication that many national legislators did not share some of the concerns voiced in the EU legislative process.[63] In the context of security in the review bodies, however, the last subparagraph of Article 56(10) Defence Directive, a provision not to be found in the Public Sector Remedies Directive, is to be discussed:

> Member States shall determine how review bodies are to reconcile the confidentiality of classified information with respect for the rights of the defence, and, in the case of a judicial review . . ., shall do so in such a way that the procedure complies, as a whole, with the right to a fair trial.

This might well become a challenge for the review bodies and a topic for academic discourse. The problem is that this subparagraph might lead to problems with the rights in the EU Charter on Fundamental Rights. Article 47 of the EU Charter on "Right to an effective remedy and to a fair trial" provides:

> Everyone whose rights and freedoms guaranteed by the law of the Union are violated has the right to an effective remedy before a tribunal in compliance with the conditions laid down in this Article.
>
> Everyone is entitled to a fair and public hearing within a reasonable time by an independent and impartial tribunal previously established by law. Everyone shall have the possibility of being advised, defended and represented.

Article 47 of the Charter is relevant[64] since Article 56(10) last subparagraph Defence Directive might allow confidentiality and security-of-information concerns more generally to limit the rights of defence and to a fair trial. Most importantly this will apply when confidentiality requirements conflict with the rights of the bidder and his legal representatives to have access to documents which they would have in review proceedings under the Public Sector and Utilities Remedies Directives but not under the Defence Directive due to its Article 56(10).

Thus it appears to be possible for the rights of the defence and to a fair trial to be affected for the sake of confidentiality. However, this limitation of the rights in Article 47 of the Charter might be legal under the Charter. Article 52(1) of the Charter on the "Scope of guaranteed rights" provides:

> 1. Any limitation on the exercise of the rights and freedoms recognised by this Charter must be provided for by law and respect the essence of those rights and freedoms. Subject to the principle of proportionality, limitations

---

[63] Ibid.

[64] Art. 48(2) of the Charter on "presumption of innocence and right of defence" (which reads: "Respect for the rights of the defence of anyone who has been charged shall be guaranteed") is less relevant here since in the context of public procurement review proceedings no bidder is charged and therefore needs the protection of this article. On the contrary, the bidder is the applicant and the contracting authority or entity the defendant.

may be made only if they are necessary and genuinely meet objectives of general interest recognised by the Union or the need to protect the rights and freedoms of others.

Therefore the interest of confidentiality accommodated in Article 56(10) Defence Directive must (1) be an objective in the general interest recognised by the Union, (2) the limitation must have been introduced to genuinely meet this objective, (3) the limitation must be proportionate (necessary) and (4) the limitation must respect the essence of the rights of the defence and a fair trial.

It is submitted that confidentiality in the context of defence and security procurement and therefore also review proceedings under Title IV Defence Directive is an objective in the general interest recognised by the Union. Most importantly, Article 346(1)(a) TFEU,[65] discussed in chapter 3,[66] addresses confidentiality directly. Moreover, it is submitted that confidentiality in the context of armaments procurement is "recognised" in Article 346(1)(b) TFEU as security of information is one of the main aspects of national security in the context of armaments trade and procurement. After all, security of information is one of the interests the Defence Directive aims to accommodate inside its field of application to limit the necessity to invoke Article 346 TFEU. Furthermore, confidentiality is a part of public security which is recognised in the Internal Market public security exemptions, such as Articles 36 and 52 TFEU discussed in chapter 2.[67] Finally, security of information is recognised in the Defence Directive itself, most importantly in its Article 23 but also in Article 56(10). It is also submitted that the limitation in Article 56(10) last subparagraph Defence Directive was introduced to genuinely meet this objective.

Furthermore it is argued, that the limitation in Article 56(10) last subparagraph Defence Directive is proportionate. The provision itself requires the confidentiality of confidential information rights to be reconciled with the rights to defence and to a fair trial. First, the limitation of access to information is obviously an adequate measure to safeguard the confidentiality of classified information. Secondly, this limitation can be necessary when no other measure could be taken which would provide equal protection for classified information but would be less detrimental to the rights of defence and to a fair trial. Finally, the essence of the rights of the defence and to a fair trial is not affected by the limitation in the last subparagraph of Article 56(10) Defence Directive.

An analysis of relevant provisions transposing Title IV Defence Directive into the national laws of the Member States might also shed some light on the question of whether the adaptation of the court proceedings to confidentiality considerations can be reconciled with the rights to defence and to a fair trial. In

---

[65] Art. 346(1)(a) TFEU reads: "The provisions of the Treaties shall not preclude the application of the following rules: (a) no Member State shall be obliged to supply information the disclosure of which it considers contrary to the essential interests of its security ..."
[66] At 128–33. [67] At 70–82.

Germany, for example, the new § 110a of the Competition Act GWB which represents a relevant part of the German transposition of the Defence Directive reads:

> Storage of confidential documents (1) The Procurement Review Chamber ensures the confidentiality of classified items and other confidential information contained in the documents submitted by the parties. (2) The members of the Procurement Review Chamber are obliged to secrecy; the stipulation of reasons for their decisions must not convey the type and contents of classified documents, files, electronic documents, or information.[68]

First, both paragraphs of § 110a GWB contain a general obligation to safeguard the secrecy and confidentiality of classified information. There is no reason to question the adequacy and necessity and therefore proportionality of this obligation. The requirement in the second half of § 110a GWB, that "the stipulation of reasons for their decisions must not convey the type and contents of classified documents, files, electronic documents, or information", is slightly more problematic. This is because it suggests that the applicant will not learn about the full basis for the decision. However, this does not necessarily mean that the applicant does not have access to this information in the course of the proceedings, if that can be reconciled with its confidentiality. This would allow the applicant as a party of the proceedings to understand the eventual decision without all the information leading to the decision being explained in the decision itself. The decisions of the review bodies, however, have to be published and this requirement cannot easily be reconciled with the confidentiality requirements of classified information. Thus it is submitted that this limitation is adequate and necessary since no measure which would be less detrimental to the rights of defence and to a fair trial is available. Overall, it is argued, it is possible to reconcile the protection of the confidentiality of classified information in defence and procurement review proceedings with the right to a fair trial and to a defence without violating the Charter of Fundamental Rights, the ECHR or the constitutions or human rights acts of the Member States.

Since the adaptation is only minor and proportionate it is unlikely to undermine the trust of bidders in the review system or affect the respect of contracting officers for the Defence Directive.

4.3 Interlocutory proceedings

Interlocutory proceedings play an important role in public procurement review proceedings because they allow the influencing of ongoing procurement procedures before the conclusion of the contract. The review body grants interim relief, often suspending the procurement procedure, pending a final decision.

---

[68] Translation of the author.

This is done on the basis of a prima facie assessment balancing the interests of the bidder with those of the contracting entity. If the latter is a public body its interests are public interests. Interlocutory proceedings are crucial for the effectiveness of a review system, which is arguably its most important objective. However, suspension means delay of the project and that can have security-of-supply implications when the supply or service is not operational at the time envisaged. In the context of these interlocutory proceedings, the Defence Directive therefore contains an adaptation expressly stipulating that the review body has to take the defence and security interests of the Member State into account when balancing interests. Article 56(5) Defence Directive provides:

> Member States may provide that the body responsible for review procedures may take into account the probable consequences of interim measures for all interests likely to be harmed, as well as the public interest, *in particular defence and/or security interests*, and may decide not to grant such measures when their negative consequences could exceed their benefits.
>
> A decision not to grant interim measures shall not prejudice any other claim of the person seeking such measures. [emphasis added]

As in Article 60(3) Defence Directive on ineffectiveness discussed below, there is no definition or description of the relevant "defence and security interests" and the Commission should probably have added a "Guidance Note *Review and Remedies*" to its catalogue of guidance notes[69] to clarify at least these important notions. A document published by the British Ministry of Defence,[70] however, lists relevant defence[71] and security interests.[72] This guidance covers both interlocutory proceedings and situations in which a review body might refrain from declaring a contract ineffective. Failing a Commission Guidance Note on remedies, this British guidance could be used by other Member States as well.

However, the adaptation in Article 56(5) Defence Directive is of limited significance. The public interest also has to be taken into account under the Public Sector Remedies Directive. Defence and security interests are only

---

[69] See these guidance notes: http://ec.europa.eu/internal_market/publicprocurement/rules/defence_procurement/ [accessed 21 November 2013].

[70] Ministry of Defence/Finance, The Defence and Security Public Contract Regulations Chapter 17 – Legal Review, Remedies and Ineffectiveness, Version 2.0 dated 23/02/2012, paras. 37–40, www.gov.uk/government/uploads/system/uploads/attachment_data/file/27668/dspcr_chapter17_legal_review_rem.pdf [accessed 21 November 2013].

[71] Ibid.: "(1) effective conduct of military operations; (2) safety of members of our Armed Forces or our Allies; (3) operational sovereignty of our Armed Forces; or (4) key defence industrial or technical capabilities regarded as essential for national security reasons."

[72] *Supra* note 70: "(1) effective conduct of security or police operations; (2) safety of members of our security agencies and police forces; (3) ability of our security agencies and police forces to conduct future operations as required by the Government; or (4) key security industrial or technical capabilities regarded as essential for national security reasons."

special aspects of the public interest which can be considered in decisions on applications for interim measures under the Public Sector Remedies Directive. Therefore expressly stipulating defence and security interests in the rules on interlocutory proceedings is merely descriptive. It does not add to the substance of the provision when compared to Article 2(5) Public Sector Remedies Directive. This is in line with the description technique of adapting substantive provisions taken from the Public Sector Directive 2004/18/EC in the Defence Directive outlined above and discussed in great detail in chapter 8. This point is confirmed in some of the transposing national legislation, such as Regulation 57 (2) of the United Kingdom DSPCR 2011 which provides:

> When deciding whether to make an order under paragraph (1), the Court must take into account the probable consequences of interim measures for all interests likely to be harmed, as well as the public interest, and in particular defence or security interests.

The use of the words "in particular", taken from Article 56(5) Defence Directive, expresses the merely descriptive nature stipulating defence and security interests. § 137 of the Austrian BVergGVS 2011 does not amend the relevant § 329(1) BVergG 2006.[73] Therefore neither the relevant Austrian procurement law, nor Regulation 71(4) of the Irish ACRDSC 2012 expressly mention defence and security interests.[74] Thus in Austria and Ireland the description of defence and security interests provided in Article 56(5) Defence Directive was not even considered necessary when transposing the Directive, thereby emphasising the merely descriptive character of the adaptation. § 115(2) sentence 2 (second half-sentence) of the German GWB, amended in 2011 in the context of the trans-position of the Defence Directive provides that, in defence and security contracts,

> defence and security interests have to be taken into account *in addition* to [the public interest in an economically efficient performance of the tasks of the contracting entity].[75]

The use of the words "in addition" suggests that the stipulated defence and security interests are not merely descriptive but that they can only be taken into account since the transposition of the Defence Directive. However, it is sub-mitted that this first impression is inaccurate. The "public interest in a rapid

---

[73] www.jusline.at/Bundesvergabegesetz_2006_(BVergG2006).html [accessed 22 July 2013].

[74] Regulation 71(4) reads: "When considering whether to make an interim or interlocutory order, the Court may take into account the probable consequences of interim measures for all interests likely to be harmed, as well as the public interest, and may decide not to make such an order when its negative consequences could exceed its benefits."

[75] Edited translation of the author with emphasis by the author.

completion of the procurement procedure and the negative impact of a delay"[76] in § 115(1) GWB did not exclude defence and security considerations; a "delay" can have a negative impact on defence and security and defence and security are also considerations of the "public interest in the rapid completion of the procurement procedure". Hence, similar to Article 56(5) Defence Directive and Regulation 57(2) of the United Kingdom DSPCR, the defence and security interests in § 115(2) sentence 2 GWB are only descriptive.

The "added value" of this description is that the judges are made aware of these particular interests. Moreover, in practice the defendant contracting authorities could be prevented from reverting to security derogations such as Article 346 TFEU in more cases because defence and security interests can sufficiently be taken into account in interlocutory proceedings and therefore inside the Defence Directive and EU Internal Market law. As the express stipulation of defence and security interests is only descriptive, there are neither fundamental rights concerns nor reasons to assume that the trust of bidders in and the respect of contracting officers for this part of the review and remedies system were negatively affected. Therefore it is argued that the EU legislator did not have any alternative and balanced the different requirements well.

4.4 Ineffectiveness

The reform of the Public Sector and Utilities Remedies Directives in 2007[77] brought the new remedy of "ineffectiveness". This breaks with the principle of the sanctity of contracts and allows aggrieved economic operators during a period of 30 days or six months after the conclusion of a contract to seek its annulment by a review body. In the Directives this rather radical remedy is limited to mainly two[78] equally radical violations of procurement law. The first concerns the violation of the important *Alcatel* clause for a standstill between award and conclusion.[79] The second concerns the quite frequent case in which a contract is awarded without following any procurement procedure, completely ignoring the requirements of procurement law, so-called "direct illegal awards".[80] This can happen out of defiance or ignorance or because exceptions

---

[76] Translation of the author.   [77] Directive 2007/66/EC.

[78] Art. 2a(1)(c) Public Sector Remedies Directive contains a third violation and reads: "in the cases referred to in the second subparagraph of Article 2b(c) of this Directive, if Member States have invoked the derogation from the standstill period for contracts based on a framework agreement and a dynamic purchasing system." See the almost identical Art. 60(1)(c) Defence Directive.

[79] Art. 2a(1)(b) Public Sector Remedies Directive. See the almost identical Art. 60(1)(b) Defence Directive.

[80] Art. 2a(1)(a) Public Sector Remedies Directive. See the almost identical Art. 60(1)(a) Defence Directive.

are interpreted wrongly. At least in theory this case is of particular importance for the defence sector, which so far has been determined by widely interpreted exceptions and which in practice was not conducted on the basis of the procurement Directives and the transposing national laws. As there is now a clear procurement legal framework in the form of the Defence Directive, the illegal avoidance of this instrument brings with it the risk of ineffectiveness.[81]

A third violation of procurement law that may lead to ineffectiveness was added by case law. According to the *Pressetext* case law, amendments to a public contract constitute a new award when they are materially different from the original contract and demonstrate the intention of the parties to renegotiate the essential terms of that contract.[82] If changes to a lawfully concluded contract create a materially different contract[83] then that new contract has to be awarded on the basis of a new procedure. If the contracting authority does initiate a new procurement procedure for a new contract, this contract can also be subject to ineffectiveness. The situation is similar to, and arguably only a variation of, a direct illegal award. Thus the case law extends ineffectiveness to these cases of substantial modifications which have to be newly awarded.[84] This situation can also be relevant in the context of defence and security contracts. In particular, the long life cycle of many defence contracts discussed in chapter 1[85] can make substantial modifications necessary. Contracting authorities have to consider carefully whether new procurement procedures have to be initiated.

The rules on ineffectiveness were also adapted in Article 60(3) Defence Directive, allowing review bodies *not* to annul the contract if

---

[81] The remedy has been adapted, see below.

[82] Case C-454/06, *Pressetext Nachrichtenagentur GmbH* v. *Austria (federal level), APA-OTS Originaltext-Service GmbH and APA Austria Presse Agentur registrierte Genossenschaft mit beschränkter Haftung* [2008] ECR I-4401.

[83] *Pressetext*, ibid., provides an illustrative list of such substantial modifications: An amendment may be regarded as *material* when: (a) it introduces conditions which, had they been part of the initial award procedure, would have allowed for the admission of tenderers other than those initially admitted, or for the acceptance of a tender other than the one initially accepted; (b) it extends the contract's scope to encompass services not initially covered; or (c) it changes the economic balance in favour of the contractor in a manner not provided for in the initial contract. See the codification in Art. 72 of the new Public Sector Directive.

[84] This was the message of the presentations of Professor Sue Arrowsmith, Nico Spiegel (European Commission, one of the drafters of the Defence Directive), and Michael Bowsher QC in Workshop A3 on "Changes to Concluded Contracts" at the conference "Public Procurement: Global Revolution VI", in Nottingham, 25 June 2013. In 2011 such a case was decided by the High Court of England and Wales: *Alstom Transport* v. *Eurostar International Limited and Siemens plc* [2011] EWHC 1828 (Ch). This decision was taken on the basis of Regulation 45J of the United Kingdom Utilities Contract Regulations 2006. However, the application was not successful not least because there was no new contract.

[85] At 52–3.

reasons relating to a general interest, *first and foremost* in connection with defence and/or security interests, require that the effects of the contract should be maintained . . .

The criticism of the lack of a definition of "defence and/or security interests" expressed in the context of interlocutory proceedings above applies equally to this provision. A Commission Guidance Note would have been useful.

Comparable to Article 2d(3) Public Sector Remedies Directive, Article 60(3) Defence Directive limits the economic interests to be taken into account in this context. However, in addition,

> *In any event*, a contract may not be considered ineffective if the consequences of this ineffectiveness would *seriously* endanger the very existence of a *wider* defence or security programme which is essential for a Member State's security interests.

> [emphasis added]

This subparagraph accommodates the strategic importance of large defence industrial programmes. The opening words "in any event" suggests that in this particular situation the limitations on economic interests being taken into account, such as that they may not be directly linked to the contract concerned, do not apply. This appears to be mitigated by limiting expressions: the danger must be serious and the relevant programme must be "wider". Thus the review bodies will have to take degrees of danger and the size of the programme into account – a potentially difficult task. Again, a Commission Guidance Note on remedies could have been useful here.[86]

Article 60(3) Defence Directive is comparable to the rule in Article 2d(3) Public Sector Remedies Directive. The additional defence and security references were probably inserted in response to pressure of the governments of the Member States.[87] The rule allows flexibility in the face of the consequences of the annulment of a concluded contract by a review body. The procurement procedure would have to be repeated, the deployment of the respective equipment could be delayed and the mission of the relevant forces could be negatively affected. On the other hand, the radical remedy of ineffectiveness is only available in two or three cases of radical violations of the procurement rules. It would be a rather odd situation if a strategically important contract would be awarded, for example, in violation of the *Alcatel* standstill clause and would

---

[86] The United Kingdom Ministry of Defence guidance mentioned above, *supra* note 70, at para. 39, is not helpful on this issue either.

[87] During the hearing of the Internal Market and Consumer Protection Committee of the European Parliament referred to above, *supra* note 30 (at which the author was present) and at which the review and remedies system of the Defence Directive were a major topic, a representative of the French government (at the time holding the presidency of the EU) addressed ineffectiveness as a crucial problem.

then escape its annulment because of its defence implications. Although "alternative penalties" would have to be imposed by the review body in such a case,[88] these would only be disproportionately mild sanctions against a relatively drastic violation of the procurement rules. In contrast, a case in which the procurement rules as a whole were ignored, by accident or deliberately, is more likely. In a case where this happens accidentally, alternative penalties could be an adequate instrument. In a case where this happens deliberately, the envisaged alternative penalties are too mild a sanction. Higher penalty fines, however, might be a way to address this defect to an extent.

The question is whether the defence and security adaptations in Article 60(3) Defence Directive are merely descriptive or add substance to the original rule in the Public Sector Remedies Directive. Similar to the treatment of defence and security interests in the context of interlocutory proceedings, there is no reason to assume that defence and security interests cannot be taken into account as part of the wider notion of "reasons relating to a general interest" in Article 2d(3) Public Sector Remedies Directive. The example provided by the then United Kingdom Office of Government Commerce for a relevant scenario in the context of the implementation of Directive 2007/66/EC was also from the military context.[89] Hence expressly stipulating them could be interpreted as merely descriptive and not adding substance to the original rule in the Public Sector Remedies Directive. However, the use of the words "first and foremost" might make the review bodies more willing to maintain a contract where the general interest considerations are specifically related to defence or security. "Civilian" scenarios leading to a contract being maintained are not expressly mentioned in either Directive and the review bodies might be less likely to declare a contract ineffective in those scenarios than in a situation where this would affect defence and security interests. Therefore the defence and security references in Article 60(3) Defence Directive are descriptive but nevertheless meet their objectives. They not only alert the review bodies to the possibility of not declaring the contract ineffective for defence and security reasons but also give these considerations a "privileged" status as "first among equals". The "privileging" description of these interests in Article 60(3) is also a message to the Member States as it might contribute to reducing cases in which they invoke security exemptions such as Article 346 TFEU to avoid ineffectiveness. Defence and security interests are accommodated *inside* the rules on ineffectiveness. However, as

---

[88] Last subparagraph of Art. 60(3) Defence Directive. Alternative penalties according to Art. 60(2) Defence Directive are fines and shortening of the duration of the contract.

[89] "For example, the ineffectiveness of a contract for essential medical supplies to troops in a war-zone could have disastrous consequences for any injured troops, which would not be in the general interest." *Implementation of the Remedies Directive: OGC Guidance on the 2009 amending regulations Part 3: The new remedies rules*, at 15, para. 60, http://webarchive.nationalarchives.gov.uk/20110601212617/http:/www.ogc.gov.uk/documents/Remedies_Guidance_Part_3_Remedies_Rules(1).pdf [accessed 21 November 2013].

the adaptations are merely descriptive they do not raise fundamental rights concerns. Even if the "privileged" description discussed in this paragraph was interpreted as going beyond mere description, the possible effect on fundamental rights would stay within the limits set by Article 52(1) of the EU Charter on Fundamental Rights, for the same reasons discussed in the context of interlocutory proceedings in section 4.3 above. Whether the adaptation could undermine the trust of bidders in and the respect of contracting officers for the review system depends on how the review bodies apply Article 60(3) Defence Directive in practice. It is too early to gather the necessary data to make an assessment on this question. However, it is submitted that the notion of defence and security interests in Article 60(3) Defence Directive is too narrow to feature very often in practice.

An extreme case is thinkable in which a review body declares a contract ineffective disagreeing with the contracting authority about the existence of an Article 60(3) Defence Directive situation. In this case the Member State could still invoke a security exemption such as Article 346 TFEU to avoid ineffectiveness. This could lead to enforcement action in the ECJ where the assessment of the review body might have an impact.

The Member States, with the exception of only two, appear to have transposed the special rules on the possibility of refraining from declaring a contract ineffective in certain situations relating to defence and security word for word, or very closely.[90] Examples are Regulation 73(5)–(7) of the Irish ACDSR, § 137(8) of the Austrian BVergGVS and Regulation 61 of the United Kingdom DSPCR. In sharp contrast, the relevant § 101b of the German GWB was not amended with the transposition of the Defence Directive in December 2011, showing that the German legislator considered the adaptation in Article 60(3) to be only descriptive.

5 Conclusions

Title IV Defence Directive represents a crucial aspect of the regulation of defence and security procurement introduced by the Directive. Procurement review proceedings are the latest stage at which lawyers, as judges and advocates, may become parts of the procurement process. The availability of a procurement review procedure creates a litigation risk for the relevant contracting entities. Review is connected to possible delays of the affected project, additional costs and consequences for the careers of the responsible procurement officers. This has an intended effect on the use of the procurement rules in practice and may also reduce incompetence and corruption in defence and

---

[90] Transposition Report, *supra* note 56, at 8.

security procurement, where it exists. While it is still early to predict the impact of the Defence Directive, practising lawyers predict an increase in litigation, with variations depending on the Member State.[91]

In addition to the defence and security objectives of the adaptations and to the question of whether they meet fundamental rights and rule-of-law standards, the resulting review and remedies rules should generate trust in the review system among bidders and respect for the substantive rules among contracting officers. Title IV Defence Directive introduces a system heavily based on the public sector review and remedies regime to defence and security procurement. This includes the basic rules that remedies must be rapid and effective, that there must be independent review and at least a second-instance judicial review. Moreover, it includes the full range of remedies that can be awarded in the context of these review proceedings, ranging from the set-aside of decisions taken by the contracting authority or entity up to and including the award decision before the conclusion of the contract and damages and ineffectiveness after conclusion. The adaptations to these rules have been described as "only a few minor differences" by Heuninckx[92] and in the same vein as "only minor adaptations" by Spiegel.[93] The fact that only half of the Member States included a review and remedies part in their instruments transposing the Defence Directive, whereas the other half merely adapted parts of their general procurement review and remedies system,[94] shows that at least the latter half of the Member States also see the adaptations as only limited.[95] If the adaptations are only minor, then the standing of the public sector review system it was based on might give an indication of the future standing of the defence and security review system. The "civilian" review and remedies system that was adapted is, by and large, generating a certain level of trust among bidders. This is documented by the number of review proceedings initiated, although these numbers

---

[91] J. Jenkins, "Remedies: Scope, Risks, and Trends" and H.-J. Prieß (both Freshfields Bruckhaus Deringer), "Remedies – A US Challenging Culture? A German Perspective", Seminar: "The New Defence Procurement Directive", International Chamber of Commerce (ICC), Paris, 11 February 2011: http://iccwbo.org/policy/law/id41387/index.html [accessed 21 November 2013]. In contrast, M. Sitsen (Orth Kluth Rechtsanwälte, Düsseldorf) does not expect many review proceedings for the otherwise arguably very litigious German jurisdiction: see his presentation "Rechtsschutzmöglichkeiten übergangener Bieter" at the Forum Vergabe conference "Vergaben im Bereich von Verteidigung und Sicherheit", University of the Federal Armed Forces, Munich-Neuiberg, 15 February 2012 (notes of the author, on file).

[92] Heuninckx, "Trick or Treat?", *supra* note 34, at 26.

[93] Schmitt and Spiegel, "The Specificities of the European Defence and Security Procurement Directive", *supra* note 17.

[94] Transposition Report, *supra* note 56, at 8.

[95] Although implementation through the instrument transposing the Defence Directive does not imply that the adaptations are seen as major.

vary from one Member State to another.[96] If bidders had no trust in the system they would not use it so frequently. Moreover, the existence of the remedies system and its frequent use generates a litigation risk which contracting officers ignore at their peril.

It is submitted that the Commission should have added a "Guidance Note Review and Remedies" to their extensive arsenal of guidance notes on the Defence Directive.[97] Topics to be covered in such a document could have included, inter alia, the Commission's interpretation of the circumstances affecting defence and security interests leading to procedures not being suspended in the context of interim relief or a contract being maintained in the context of ineffectiveness.[98] The guidance provided by the United Kingdom Ministry of Defence mentioned above[99] shows a need for such guidance. The review bodies may of course make references for a preliminary ruling to the ECJ under Article 267 TFEU if they need an interpretation of the Defence Directive. Some of this case load, however, could have been avoided and it is not too late: the Commission should issue a "Guidance Note Review and Remedies" as soon as possible.

It is submitted that this introduction of a slightly adapted public sector remedies system to defence and security contracts is possibly the most significant and bold feature of the Defence Directive overall.[100] However, the inclusion of a review and remedies system is a necessity, as with any procurement law, to ensure that the substantive rules are followed in practice. This point is potentially reinforced in the defence and security sectors, and especially the armaments sector, where in many Member States the operation of a transparent and competitive procurement system is a novelty. However, the importance of the introduction of a review and remedies system in its Title IV is at the same time diminished by the limited scope of the Defence Directive as a whole, which was discussed in detail in chapter 6. Nevertheless, an important change has occurred and the review and remedies system for armaments is here to stay. In contrast, thresholds and exceptions can change as the system evolves over time.

---

[96] In Germany, for example, in 2009, 1,275 proceedings were initiated in the 24 Procurement Review Chambers, see Burgi, "A Report about the German Remedies System", *supra* note 12, at 119. On the figures in Denmark see S. Treumer, "Enforcement of the EU Public Procurement Rules in Danish Regulation and Practice" in S. Treumer and F. Lichère (eds.), *Enforcement of the EU Public Procurement Rules*, supra note 11, 255 at 296; on the lower but rising number of cases in the United Kingdom see Trybus, "An Overview of the United Kingdom Public Procurement Review and Remedies System with an Emphasis on England and Wales" in Treumer and Lichère, ibid., at 232.

[97] *Supra* note 69.   [98] See above in sections 4.3 and 4.4 respectively.

[99] *Supra* note 70.

[100] M. Fruhmann, "Der Begutachtungsentwurf für ein BVergGVS" (2011) *Zeitschrift für Vergaberecht und Bauvertragsrecht* 353 considers the inclusion of review and remedies a "fundamental ... reform"; Liebmann, *supra* note 28, § 135, at 373 calls it the "actual quantum leap".

Conclusions and recommendations

The legal context of defence and security procurement in the EU has clearly changed. With Defence Directive 2009/81/EC the legislator has produced a "tailor-made" instrument for the procurement of armaments and other sensitive goods, works and services. The "cloth" of Public Sector Directive 2004/18/EC was used as raw material and tailored to adapt it to the special requirements of defence and security. The objective was to reduce the need to derogate from the Internal Market on the basis of Article 346 TFEU and other security exemptions in defence and security procurement by providing a Directive adapted to defence and security concerns.

Part I of this book discussed the economic and political but most importantly the legal context of the Defence Directive, including its legal base in the EU Internal Market, the national security exemptions the use of which the Directive aims to reduce, other relevant regimes of EU Internal Market law affecting the defence and security industries and defence market regimes outside the Internal Market and even the EU. The discussion of this background was necessary to provide an understanding of the environment which the Defence Directive aims to change and to accommodate. Moreover, this context explains the challenges the instrument is and will be facing. Finally, most of the issues discussed in the five chapters of Part I explain many of the detailed rules of the Defence Directive discussed in Part II.

Part II discussed the contents of the Defence Directive and the four main techniques used by the EU legislator to adapt the rules of the original Public Sector Directive 2004/18/EC: limitation, flexibility, description and substitution.

Chapter 6 discussed the scope and coverage and thus the limitation of the Defence Directive, which applies to a considerable part but not all of the defence and security procurement of the Member States. On the one hand it applies not only to armaments, but also to related and sensitive goods, works and services. Moreover, it applies not only to ministries of defence but to any public body or utility procuring relevant goods, services or works. On the other hand, a large part of the relevant contracts are outside the scope of the instrument. First, while the overall aim of the Defence Directive is to limit the use of Article 346 and the public security exemptions of the TFEU, these derogations remain in force and can be invoked to take contracts outside the Directive and the Internal

Market on a case-by-case basis. Secondly, a set of value thresholds exclude a number of contracts without any need for justification. Thirdly, a long list of exclusions exempt a significant part of the European armaments market from the scope of the Defence Directive. In particular, the exemption of large collaborative projects involving R&D represents a significant limitation. The share of defence contracts actually subject to the Defence Directive might be only around 10 per cent and the more significant impact of the instrument might be felt in the markets of sensitive goods, works and services rather than in armaments procurement, markets which initially were merely an "appendix" to defence. This leaves room for frameworks outside the Internal Market, such as the EDA, OCCAR and Letter of Intent. However, scope will have to be discussed in the context of a possible revision of the new Directive. This should include an Annex to the Defence Directive listing relevant contracting authorities, taking utilities out of the scope of the Defence Directive, the deletion of redundant exclusions and a re-evaluation of the exclusion of cooperative programmes involving R&D and safeguards regarding the inclusion of new products in the government-to-government exclusion. The comparison with the Public Sector Directive 2004/18/EC reveals that the rules on the material scope of the Defence Directive, especially the defence-specific exemptions but also changes to other exemptions, have been adapted to take defence and security into account. The scope was adapted through its limitation.

Chapter 7 discussed the procedures and flexibility of the Defence Directive. Similar to the 2004 and 2014 Public Sector and Utilities Directives, the Defence Directive provides a number of procedures for contracts within its scope. Most of these procedures are characterised by competition. An exception is the negotiated procedure without prior publication of a contract notice, which is limited to situations regulated in the procurement Directives, including the Defence Directive. However, the most competitive "open procedure" of the other procurement Directives has not been included, which has consequences for other procedures such as framework agreements. Moreover, there is a preference for negotiated procedures enshrined most importantly in the free use of the negotiated procedure with prior publication of a contract notice, the inclusion of the competitive dialogue and adapted and additional circumstances allowing the use of the negotiated procedure without prior publication of a contract notice. The preference for the negotiated procedures is intended to accommodate the specific need of defence and security procurement for flexibility, also in response to the requests of stakeholders expressed during the consultation mentioned above. This is the core element of the adaptation of the rules on procedures in the original Public Sector Directive 2004/18/EC in the Defence Directive: flexibility through increased access to negotiation. The end result of these adaptations is not entirely convincing. Some aspects should be reconsidered in the revision of the Defence Directive. The instrument should include the open procedure and delete the competitive dialogue. Finally, rather than excluding collaborative contracts involving R&D from any regulation, a new procedure, which accommodates competition and addresses fair returns, could at least be part of an intergovernmental EDA regime.

Chapter 8 discussed the accommodation of security of supply and information in the Directive, which were taken into account in the rules on various stages of the procurement process under the Defence Directive. This includes the rules on specifications, contract performance conditions, qualification and selection and award criteria. The rules on specifications in the strict sense are not significantly adapted. However, due to the absence of an open procedure and the reduced importance of the restricted procedure due to the free use of the negotiated procedure with prior publication of a contract notice explained in Chapter 7, these rules are less important than in the 2004 or 2014 Public Sector Directive anyway. Moreover, a distinct feature of the Defence Directive in comparison to the Public Sector Directive 2004/18/EC is the importance of detailed rules on contract performance conditions. These relate mainly to security of supply but also to security of information. These contract performance conditions are very closely linked to specifications as they define the contract as much as or even more than the specification of the materials to be used or other features of the product or service. Moreover, in negotiated procedures, there are no specifications as such but the contract performance conditions will apply nevertheless. Consequently and in line with the other procurement Directives and the relevant ECJ case law, these conditions need to be communicated at the beginning of the procurement procedure. Moreover, as the reliability of economic operators has a national security and public security dimension, security of supply and security of information led to a qualification regime in the Defence Directive which is considerably more extensive when compared to 2004 Public Sector Directive. The importance of the qualification regime is enhanced by the fact that the qualification criteria are also the selection criteria for the restricted procedure, the negotiated procedure with prior publication of a contract notice and the competitive dialogue. In comparison, the adaptations of the award criteria regime of the Defence Directive were relatively limited. Both the rules on contract performance conditions and qualification/selection are connected to two "regimes" outside the Defence Directive: a regime on intra-Community transfers which does exist with the ICT Directive discussed in chapter 4 and a "regime" on security clearances which does not exist. The smooth operation of the transfer licensing regime of the ICT Directive would have a positive impact on the security of supply of defence goods from other Member States and therefore on the effectiveness of the Defence Directive in creating an Internal Market for these goods. If this is not the case during the first years of the operation of the transposed Directives of the Defence Package, the relevant rules of both instruments need to be revisited. The absence of a similar regime for security clearances could well have a negative impact on security of information with regards to economic operators from other Member States and therefore on the effectiveness of the

Defence Directive in allowing market access to economic operators from other Member States. While some of the adaptations to the rules of the original Public Sector Directive in the Defence Directive add substance, most of the additions are adaptations in the form of description. The relevant security-of-supply and security-of-information considerations could also be taken into account under the old Public Sector Directive 2004/18/EC, but they were not expressly stipulated in the Directive. The added value of this description in the Defence Directive is that there is no doubt about them being in compliance with EU law, thus reducing litigation risks and encouraging their use by contracting officers. Description is an important technique of adaptation in the Defence Directive which – in addition to the techniques of limitation discussed in chapter 6, the flexibility discussed in chapter 7 and the substitution in the following chapter 9 – contributed to transform the original Public Sector Directive 2004/18/EC into an instrument more suitable for defence and security procurement.

Chapter 9 discussed offsets and subcontracting under the Defence Directive. Subcontracts and offsets are closely connected. The Defence Directive facilitates the earlier and implicitly almost prohibits the latter. The subcontracting regime of the Defence Directive is the result of a compromise between the six Member States with developed defence industries, which include prime contracting capabilities, and the rest who have mainly subcontracting capabilities. Their insertion was a request of the latter, who want opportunities for their industries at least as subcontractors. The rules faced some criticism since they not only reduce the share of the prime contractor but also impose a considerable burden on them when subcontracting. However, while Option B already imposes some requirements, this is mainly the case in the context of Options C and D, which might be the reason why so far no Member State has transposed them as obligations and the United Kingdom did not transpose these options at all. The award of subcontracts on a competitive and transparent basis not only facilitates an Internal subcontracting Market based on non-discrimination but may also promote value for money. The legislator simply transferred the principles of its regime for the award of prime contracts to the subcontracting level. Nevertheless, accommodating the diverse defence industrial structures of the EU Member States, in which most of them do not have a defence industrial base that includes prime contractors, was the main motivator for the subcontracting regime in the Defence Directive. The main message of the subcontracting regime is that the Defence Directive is not only an instrument for the prime contractors in France, Germany, Italy, Sweden, Spain and the United Kingdom but also for subcontractors in all 28 Member States. While more could be done, the subcontracting regime of the Defence Directive is the most extensive so far and a substantial innovation of the instrument. Other than winning the prime contract, without violations of the Defence Directive and the TFEU the industries of the awarding country can only participate through subcontracts, and only if they best meet the award criteria specified by the prime contractor.

The subcontracting regime is intended as a substitute for the "now" almost prohibited offsets. Whether the "prohibition" or rather the phasing out of offsets can be implemented also through subcontracting depends on many factors: the strong offset lobby in the industries and the administration, the use of enforcement proceedings by the Commission and of the new remedies system described in chapter 10 by aggrieved bidders or the development of offsets with third countries and especially with the USA.

Chapter 10 discussed the review and remedies regime in Title IV Defence Directive which represents a crucial aspect of the regulation of defence and security procurement introduced by the Directive. The availability of a procurement review procedure creates a litigation risk for the relevant contracting authorities and entities. Review is connected to possible delays of the affected project, additional costs and consequences for the careers of the responsible procurement officers. This has an intended effect on the use of the procurement rules in practice and may also reduce incompetence and corruption in defence and security procurement, where it exists. While it is still too early to predict the impact of the Defence Directive, practising lawyers predict an increase in litigation, with variations depending on the Member State. In addition to the defence and security objectives of the adaptations and to the question whether they meet fundamental rights and rule of law standards, the resulting review and remedies rules should generate trust in the review system among bidders and respect for the substantive rules among contracting officers. Title IV Defence Directive introduces to defence and security procurement a system heavily based on the public sector review and remedies regime. This includes the basic rules that remedies must be rapid and effective, that there must be independent review and at least as a second-instance judicial review. Moreover, it includes the full range of remedies that can be awarded in the context of these review proceedings, ranging from the set-aside of decisions taken by the contracting authority or entity up to and including the award decision before the conclusion of the contract and damages and ineffectiveness after conclusion. It is submitted that the Commission should have added a "Guidance Note *Review and Remedies*" to their extensive arsenal of guidance notes on the Defence Directive. Topics to be covered in such a document could have included, inter alia, the Commission's interpretation of the circumstances affecting defence and security interests leading to procedures not being suspended in the context of interim relief or a contract being maintained in the context of ineffectiveness. It is submitted that this introduction of a slightly adapted public sector remedies system to defence and security contracts is possibly the most significant and bold feature of the Defence Directive overall. However, the inclusion of a system of review and remedies is a necessity, as with any procurement law, to ensure that the substantive rules are followed in practice. This point is potentially reinforced in the defence and security sectors, and especially the armaments sector, where in many Member States the operation of a transparent and competitive procurement system is a novelty. However, the importance of the introduction of a review and remedies system in its Title IV is at the same time diminished by the limited scope of the Defence Directive as a whole, which was discussed in detail in chapter 6. Nevertheless, an important change has occurred and the review and remedies system for armaments is here to stay. In contrast, thresholds and exceptions can change as the system evolves over time.

Overall, the EU legislator has made every effort to provide an instrument adapted for defence and security procurement and, while Directive 2009/81/EC could be improved and goes too far in some of the adaptations to the characteristics of the defence sector, it does represent a more suitable instrument for defence and security procurement inside the Internal Market than the Public Sector Directive 2004/18/EC which applied before the introduction of the Defence Directive. Several suggestions regarding individual features of the context and provision of the Defence Directive were made throughout this book:

1 The now rather dated Commission Interpretative Communication on the application of Article 296 [now 346] of the Treaty in the field of defence procurement, COM (2006) 779 final should be replaced by an updated version. This new instrument should especially take the introduction and transposition of the Defence Directive and the ICT Directive and the latest ECJ case law in the *Agusta* cases, the *Military Exports* cases and *Finnish Turntables* into account and thus provide a more precise Communication.

2 The 1958 list of armaments based on what is now Article 346(2) TFEU should be officially published in the OJ. The half-secrecy of the list undermines the rule of law and transparency and serves no legitimate purpose.

3 A harmonising regime of security clearances including all EU Member States should be introduced. This can be based on the relevant Letter of Intent regime but should at least be introduced on an intergovernmental basis by the EDA. However, an EU Internal Market Directive on security clearances could be the end result.

4 A reformed defence procurement regime of the EDA, replacing the now suspended EDA Procurement Code, possibly again in the form of a Code of Conduct, should be limited to areas excluded from the Defence Directive, most importantly collaborative projects involving research and development.

5 A special Annex to the Defence Directive itself should provide a non-exhaustive illustrative list of contracting authorities to which it applies.

6 Utilities should be removed from the personal scope of the Defence Directive and subjected to an adapted regime of the Utilities Directive (new Directive 2014/25/EU) instead. This would also allow bringing the thresholds of the Defence Directive in line with those of the Public Sector Directive (now Directive 2014/24/EU).

7 The exclusion of collaborative projects involving research and development leaves this arguably most important part of defence procurement largely

unregulated. These projects could be addressed on an intergovernmental basis in the context of the EDA (see point 4 above). Their complete exclusion from any regime is not convincing. Regulation in an intergovernmental Code of Conduct is more likely than in a Directive, at least in the medium term. A competitive negotiated procedure and an adapted subcontracting regime could be features of such a Code. A considerable obstacle is that projects are managed by different organisational structures, which would first have to merge or coordinate their activities more. This ongoing merger of some of these structures was discussed in chapter 5.

8 The inclusion of newly purchased equipment in the exclusion of government-to-government contracts is problematic, in particular when a Member State government is buying from a third country government and there is competition for the equipment in question in the EU Internal Market. Practice over the coming years will show if the inclusion of new equipment from third countries will develop into a loophole. Therefore this will have to be closely observed. If this proves to be the case, the Commission could propose a change of the text of the Directive, for example by adding the words "delivered from existing stocks" to Article 13(f) or by regulating the case in which there is competition for the good in question in the Internal Market in greater detail. Alternatively they could change the wording of its Guidance Notes to regulate the inclusion of new items in the scope of the exemption, at least when they are bought from a third-country government and there is competition for the items in the Internal Market. As a second alternative, a revised Commission Guidance Note *Defence-Specific Exclusions* should address the case of a Member State government buying new equipment as part of a government-to-government arrangement with a third-country government when there is competition for the equipment in the Internal Market.

9 The Defence Directive should provide an open procedure based on the open procedure in the 2004 and 2014 Public Sector and Utilities Directives.

10 The free use of the negotiated procedure with prior publication of a contract notice is not entirely convincing when coexisting with the competitive dialogue. The negotiated procedure with prior publication of a contract notice is flexible enough to be conducted exactly like a competitive dialogue. The latter is therefore redundant and should be deleted.

11 Offsets should be expressly addressed in the Defence Directive.

12 A "Commission Guidance Note *Review and Remedies*" should be added to the current selection of Commission Guidance Notes to clarify a number of points in relation to the remedies system for aggrieved bidders discussed in chapter 10.

The Defence Directive is intended as a legal instrument specifically designed for defence and security procurement. For that purpose the provisions of the Public Sector Directive 2004/18/EC were adapted to the requirements of complexity, security of supply and security of information; the scope was reduced especially through adapted and additional exemptions; and a detailed subcontracting regime as well as a slightly adapted review and remedies regime were added. The objective of these adaptations is to limit the use of the exemptions in Article 346 TFEU and the free movement regimes, by providing a tailor-made Directive which makes the use of these derogations unnecessary in practice. The Defence Directive does not limit the derogations in the Treaty. They can still be invoked if and when the adapted rules are not sufficient to safeguard security of supply or information or other national or public security consideration. However, the derogations not only have to be specifically invoked on a case-by-case basis and the conditions justifying their use explained and proved. The use of these exemptions is also subject to judicial review and a proportionality test. This means that the proportionality of derogation will be more difficult to argue and thus derogation more difficult to justify when the legislator has provided a procurement regime that accommodated complexity and security-of-supply and security-of-information requirements inside the regime of the Directive and the Internal Market of the TFEU. The argument that the use of the allegedly unsuitable Public Sector Directive 2004/18/EC would compromise security of supply and security of information and would not accommodate the complexity of many defence and security projects is no longer available as that instrument or its successor Directive 2014/24/EC does not apply to the relevant contracts anymore.

It is too early to comment on the success of the new instrument. This is also confirmed by data published by the Commission in July 2013.[1] The Defence Directive was finally implemented in all of the then 27 Member States in March 2013 (plus Croatia with accession in July 2013) and the number of published contracts appears to have increased in several Member States. However, this increase has not occurred in all Member States and increased publication did not necessarily lead to cross-border contract awards or the use of competitive procedures. An assessment of the impact of the Defence Directive would require a few years of its use in practice. Moreover, the Directive will not suffice on its own. Other barriers to trade in arms will have to be addressed, inter alia the lack of an EU-wide security-of-information framework and State ownership and aid to the defence industries. Furthermore, the relevant trade relations with third countries, especially the USA, require attention. Further research is therefore needed, inter alia, on the procurement practice of the Member States on the basis of the Defence Directive and its impact on transatlantic trade. Moreover, many of the reforms of the new Public Sector Directive 2014/24/EU will have to be considered for the Defence Directive as well. The possible review of the

---

[1] Commission Staff Working Document SWD (2013) 279 final accompanying the Communication "A New Deal for European Defence: Towards a More Competitive and Efficient Defence and Security Sector", COM (2013) 542 final, at 43–6.

Defence Directive, which has to be completed by 2016, will consider these reforms and possibly some of the recommendations made above.

The legislative achievement of the Defence Directive is considerable: the Internal Market finally applies in a sector which has traditionally excluded it in practice. This book has shown that with the Defence Directive defence and security procurement has evolved to a distinct regime of EU procurement law, from contracts largely unregulated by EU law in practice, to a regime sharing substantial similarities with the public sector and utilities regimes.

BIBLIOGRAPHY

Aalto, Erkki, "Towards a Common Defence? Legal Foundations after the Treaty of Lisbon" in Martin Trybus and Luca Rubini (eds.), *The Treaty of Lisbon and the Future of European Law and Policy* (Cheltenham: Edward Elgar, 2012).

Alcaro, Riccardo and Erik Jones, *European Security and the Future of Transatlantic Relations* (Rome: Nuova Cultura, 2011).

Andersson, Jan Joel, *Cold War Dinosaurs or High-tech Arms Providers? The West European Land Armaments Industry at the Turn of the Millennium*, Occasional Paper 23 (Paris: Institute for Security Studies of the European Union, 2001).

Apostol, Anca Ramona, "Pre-commercial Procurement in Support of Innovation: Regulatory Effectiveness?" (2012) 6 *Public Procurement Law Review* 213–25.

Argent, Pierre d', "Les Enseignements du COCOM" (1993) 26 *Revue belge de droit international* 147–64.

Arnull, Anthony, *The European Court of Justice* (Oxford University Press, 2006).

"From Charter to Constitution and Beyond: Fundamental Rights in the New European Union" in Martin Trybus and Luca Rubini (eds.), *The Treaty of Lisbon and the Future of European Law and Policy* (Cheltenham: Edward Elgar, 2012).

"The European Court of Justice after Lisbon" in Martin Trybus and Luca Rubini (eds.), *The Treaty of Lisbon and the Future of European Law and Policy* (Cheltenham. Edward Elgar, 2012).

Arrowsmith, Sue, *The Law of Public and Utilities Procurement*, 2nd edn (London: Sweet & Maxwell, 2005).

Arrowsmith, Sue and Arwel P. Davies (eds.), *Public Procurement: Global Revolution* (The Hague: Kluwer Law International, 1998).

Arrowsmith, Sue and Peter Kunzlik, *Social and Environmental Policies in EC Procurement Law New Directives and New Directions* (Cambridge University Press, 2009).

Arrowsmith, Sue, John Linarelli and Don Wallace Jr, *Regulating Public Procurement: National and International Perspectives* (The Hague: Kluwer Law International, 2000).

Bacon, Kelyn (ed.), *European Union Law of State Aid*, 2nd edn (Oxford University Press, 2013).

Barnard, Catherine, *The Law of the Single European Market: Unpacking the Premises* (Oxford: Hart Publishing: 2002).

Bercusson, Brian and Niklas Bruun, "Labour Law Aspects of Public Procurement in the EU" in Ruth Nielsen and Steen Treumer (eds.), *The New EU Public Procurement Directives* (Copenhagen: Djøf, 2005).

Bialos, Jeffrey P., Christine E. Fisher and Stuart L. Koehl, *Fortresses and Icebergs: The Evolution of the Transatlantic Defense Market and the Implications for U.S. National Security Policy*, 2 vols. (Washington DC: Center for Transatlantic Relations, Paul H. Nitze School of Advanced International Studies, Johns Hopkins University, 2009).

Borowski, Martin, "The Charter of Fundamental Rights in the Treaty on European Union" in Martin Trybus and Luca Rubini (eds.), *The Treaty of Lisbon and the Future of European Law and Policy* (Cheltenham: Edward Elgar, 2012).

Bothe, Michael, "The Arms Trade: Comparative Aspects of Law" (1993) 26 *Revue belge de droit international* 20–42.

Bovis, Christopher, *EC Public Procurement: Case Law and Regulation* (Oxford University Press, 2006).

Brauer, Jürgen, "An Economic Perspective on Mercenaries, Military Companies, and the Privatisation of Force" (1999) 13 *Cambridge Review of International Affairs* 130–46.

Brauer, Jürgen and Paul Dunn, *Arms Trade and Economic Development: Theory, Policy and Cases in Arms Trade Offsets* (London: Routledge, 2004).

Braun, Peter, "A Matter of Principle(s) – The Treatment of Contracts Falling Outside the Scope of the European Public Procurement Directives" (2000) 9 *Public Procurement Law Review* 39–48.

Briggs, Tim, "The New Defence Procurement Directive" (2009) 4 *Public Procurement Law Review* 129–35.

Broberg, Morten P., *The European Commission's Jurisdiction to Scrutinise Mergers* (The Hague: Kluwer Law International, 1998).

Búrca, Gráinne de, "The Principle of Proportionality and Its Application in EC Law" (1993) 13 *Yearbook of European Law* 105–50.

Burgi, Martin, "A Report about the German Remedies System" in Steen Treumer and François Lichère, *Enforcement of the EU Public Procurement Rules* (Copenhagen: Djøf Publishing, 2011).

Burnett, Michael and Martin Oder, *Competitive Dialogue: a Practical Guide* (Maastricht: European Institute of Public Administration, 2009).

Comba, Mario and Steen Treumer (eds.), *The In-house Providing in European Law* (Copenhagen: Djøf, 2010).

Courades Allebeck, A. "The European Community: From the EC to the European Union" in Herbert Wulf (ed.), *Arms Industry Limited* (Oxford University Press, 1993).

Cox, Andrew, "The Future of European Defence Policy: The Case of a Centralised Procurement Agency" (1994) 3 *Public Procurement Law Review* 65–86.

Craig, Paul, *EU Administrative Law* (Oxford University Press, 2006).

"The Lisbon Treaty: Process, Architecture, and Substance" (2008) 33 *European Law Review* 137.

Craig, Paul and Gráinne de Búrca, *EU Law: Text, Cases and Materials*, 5th edn (Oxford University Press, 2008).

Craig, Paul and Gráinne de Búrca (eds.), *The Evolution of EU Law*, 2nd rev. edn (Oxford University Press, 2011).

Craven, Richard, "Procurement Procedures under the Private Finance Initiative: The Operation of the New Legal Framework", PhD Thesis, University of Nottingham (2011).

Daintith, Terence, "Regulation by Contract: The New Prerogative" (1979) 32 *Current Legal Problems* 41–64.

Dodd, Tom, *European Defence Industrial and Armaments Co-operation*, Research Paper 97:15 (London: House of Commons, 1997).

Doern, Alix, "The Interaction between EC Rules on Public Procurement and State Aid" (2004) 3 *Public Procurement Law Review* 97–129.

Duke, Simon, "CESDP: Nice's Overtrumped Success?" (2001) 6 *European Foreign Affairs Review* 155–75.

Eekelen, Willem Frederik van, *The Parliamentary Dimension of Defence Procurement: Requirements, Production, Cooperation and Acquisition*, Occasional Paper 5 (Geneva: Geneva Centre for the Democratic Control Armed Forces, 2005).

Eikenberg, Katharina, "Article 296 (ex 223) E.C. and External Trade in Strategic Goods" (2000) 25 *European Law Review* 117–38.

Eilmansberger, Thomas, "Gegengeschäfte und Gemeinschaftsrecht" (2003) 17 *Wirtschaftsrechtliche Blätter Zeitschrifts für österreichisches und europäisches Wirtschaftsrecht* 501.

Eisenhut, Dominik, *Europäische Rüstungskooperation: Zwischen Binnenmarkt und zwischenstaatlicher Zusammenarbeit* (Baden-Baden: Nomos, 2010).

"Offsets in Defence Procurement: A Strange Animal at the Brink of Extinction?" (2013) 38 *European Law Review* 393–403.

Emiliou, Nicholas, "Strategic Export Controls, National Security and the Common Commercial Policy" (1996) 1 *European Foreign Affairs Review* 55–78.

"Restrictions on Strategic Exports, Dual-use Goods and the Common Commercial Policy" (1997) 22 *European Law Review* 68–75.

Franck, Thomas M., *Political Questions/Judicial Answers: Does the Rule of Law Apply to Foreign Affairs?* (Princeton University Press, 1992).

Fredland, Eric, "Outsourcing Military Force: A Transactions Cost Perspective on the Role of Military Companies" (2004) 15 *Defence and Peace Economics* 205–19.

Fruhmann, Michael and Hanno Liebmann, *BVergGVS 2012 Bundesvergabegesetz Verteidigung und Sicherheit 2012: Textausgabe mit Erläuterungen und Anmerkungen* (Vienna: Manz, 2012).

Georgopoulos, Aris, "Industrial and Market Issues in European Defence: The Commission Communication of 2003 on Harmonisation and Liberalisation of Defence Markets" (2003) 12 *Public Procurement Law Review* 82–9.

"European Defence Procurement Integration: Proposals for Action within the European Union", PhD Thesis, University of Nottingham (2004).

"The Commission's Green Paper on Defence Procurement" (2005) 14 *Public Procurement Law Review* CS34–8.

"The European Defence Agency's Code of Conduct for Armament Acquisitions: A Case of Paramnesia?" (2006) 15 *Public Procurement Law Review* 51–61.

"European Defence Agency: The New Code of Best Practice in the Supply Chain" (2006) 15 *Public Procurement Law Review* NA145–9.

"The Commission's Interpretative Communication on the Application of Article 296 EC in the Field of Defence Procurement" (2007) 16 *Public Procurement Law Review* NA43–52.

"The European Armaments Policy: A Conditio Sine Qua Non for the European Defence and Security Policy?" in Martin Trybus and Nigel D. White (eds.), *European Security Law* (Oxford University Press, 2007).

"Legislative Comment: The New Defence Procurement Directive Enters into Force" (2010) 19 *Public Procurement Law Review* NA1.

"Revisiting Offset Practices in European Defence Procurement: The European Defence Agency's Code of Conduct on Offsets" (2011) 20 *Public Procurement Law Review* 29–42.

Gilsdorf, Peter, "Les Reserves de sécurité du traité CEE, à la lumière du traité sur l'Union Europénne" (1994) 374 *Revue Du Marché Commun et l'Union Européenne* 17–25.

Gordon, Harvey, Shane Rimmer and Sue Arrowsmith, "The Economic Impact of the European Union Regime on Public Procurement: Lessons for the WTO" in Sue Arrowsmith and Arwel P. Davies (eds.), *Public Procurement: Global Revolution* (The Hague: Kluwer Law International, 1998).

Groeben, Hans von der, *et al.*, *Kommentar zum EWG-Vertrag* (Baden-Baden: Nomos, 1983).

Guay, Terrence and Robert Callum, "The Transformation and Future Prospects of Europe's Defence Industry" (2002) 78 *International Affairs* 757–76.

Gucht, Karel de and Stephan Keukeleire, "The European Security Architecture: The Role of the European Community in Shaping a New European Geopolitical Landscape" (1991) 44 *Studia Diplomatica* 29–90.

Gupta, Sanjeev, Luiz R. De Mello and Raju Sharan, *Corruption and Military Spending* (Washington DC: International Monetary Fund, Fiscal Affairs Department, 2000).

Haine, Jean-Yves (ed.), *From Laeken to Copenhagen: European Defence, Core Documents* (Paris: Institute for Security Studies, European Union, 2003).

Hartley, Keith, "Public Procurement and Competitiveness: A Community Market for Military Hardware and Technology?" (1987) 25 *Journal of Common Market Studies* 237–47.

"Competition in Defence Contracting in the United Kingdom" (1992) 1 *Public Procurement Law Review* 440.

"The Future of European Defence Policy: An Economic Perspective" (2003) 14 *Defence and Peace Economics* 107–15.

"The Economics of Military Outsourcing" (2004) 4 *Defence Studies* 199–206.

"Defence Industrial Policy in a Military Alliance" (2006) 43 *Journal of Peace Research* 473–89.

The Economics of Defence Policy: A New Perspective (Abingdon: Routledge, 2011).

Hartley, Keith, and Todd Sandler, *Handbook of Defense Economics* (North Holland: Elsevier, 2007).

Heijboer, Govert and Jan Telgen, "Choosing the Open or Restricted Procedure: A Big Deal or a Big Deal?" (2002) 2 *Journal of Public Procurement* 197.

Heuninckx, Baudouin, "Defence Procurement in the European Union: Time to Listen to the Wake-up Calls" (2006) 7 *Business Law International* 208.

"Towards a Coherent European Defence Procurement Regime? European Defence Agency and European Commission Initiatives" (2008) 17 *Public Procurement Law Review* 1–20.

"A Note on Commission v Italy (Case C-337/05) (Agusta Helicopters Case)" (2008) 17 *Public Procurement Law Review* 187–92.

"A Primer to Collaborative Defence Procurement in Europe: Troubles, Achievements and Prospects" (2008) 17 *Public Procurement Law Review* 123–45.

"Defence Procurement: The Most Effective Way to Grant Illegal State Aid and Get Away with It. . . or Is It?" (2009) 46 *Common Market Law Review* 191–211.

"Lurking at the Boundaries: Applicability of EU Law to Defence and Security Procurement" (2010) 19 *Public Procurement Law Review* 91–118.

"The EU Defence and Security Procurement Directive: Trick or Treat?" (2011) 20 *Public Procurement Law Review* 9–28.

"The Law of Collaborative Defence Procurement through International Organisations in the European Union", PhD Thesis, University of Nottingham (2011).

"Security of Supply and Offsets in Defence Procurement: What's New in the EU?" (2014) 22 *Public Procurement Law Review* 33–49.

Hillger, Jens, "The Award of a Contract as State Aid Within the Meaning of Article 87(1) EC" (2003) 12 *Public Procurement Law Review* 109.

Hordijk, E. Peter and Maarten Meulenbelt, "A Bridge Too Far: Why the European Commission's Attempts to Construct an Obligation to Tender outside the Scope of the Public Procurement Directives Should Be Dismissed" (2005) 14 *Public Procurement Law Review* 123–30.

Hummer, Waldemar and Wolfgang Wessel, "Artikel 223" in Eberhard Grabitz (ed.), *Kommentar zum EWG-Vertrag* (Munich: C. H. Beck, 1997).

Jones, Seth G., "The Rise of a European Defense" (2006) 121 *Political Science Quarterly* 241–67.

The Rise of European Security Cooperation (Cambridge University Press, 2007).

Jürg, Martin Gabriel, "The Integration of European Security: a Functionalist Analysis" (1995) 50 *Aussenwirtschaft* 135–59.

Kapteyn, Paul Joan George, *Kapteyn & VerLoren van Themaat: The Law of the European Union and the European Communities with Reference to Changes to Be Made by the Lisbon Treaty* (The Hague: Kluwer Law International, 2009).

Kaufman, Allen, *In the Procurement Officer We Trust: Constitutional Norms, Air Force Procurement and Industrial Organization, 1938–1948* (Cambridge, MA: Defense and Arms Control Studies Program, Center for International Studies, Massachusetts Institute of Technology, 1996).

Kennedy-Loest, Ciara and Nicolas Pourbaix, "The New EU Defence Procurement Directive" (2010) 11 *ERA-Forum* 399–410.

Keohane, Daniel C., *Europe's New Defence Agency* (London: Centre for European Reform, 2004).

"Towards a European Defence Market" in Daniel Keohane (ed.), *Towards a European Defence Market* (Paris: Institute for Security Studies of the European Union, 2008).

Keohane, Daniel C. (ed.), *Towards a European Defence Market* (Paris: Institute for Security Studies of the European Union, 2008).

Klepsch, Egon A., *Future Arms Procurement (The Klepsch Report) USA-Europe Arms Procurement* (London; New York: Brassey's, Crane Russak, 1979).

Koutrakos, Panos, "Community Law and Equal Treatment in the Armed Forces" (2000) 25 *European Law Review* 433–42.

"Inter-pillar Approaches to the European Security and Defence Policy: The Economic Aspects of Security" in Vincent Kronenberger (ed.), *The European Union and the International Legal Order: Discord or Harmony* (The Hague: T. M. C. Asser Press, 2001).

Trade, Foreign Policy and Defence in EU Constitutional Law: The Legal Regulation of Sanctions, Exports of Dual-use Goods and Armaments (Oxford: Hart Publishing, 2001).

The EU Common Security and Defence Policy (Oxford University Press, 2013).

Kronenberger, Vincent (ed.), *The European Union and the International Legal Order: Disorder or Harmony* (The Hague: TMC Asser Press, 2001).

Küchle, Hartmut, *Rüstungsindustrie im Umbruch: Strategien deutscher Unternehmen und Ansätze einer europäischen Neuordnung* (Baden-Baden: Nomos Verlagsgesellschaft, 2001).

The Cost of Non-Europe in the Area of Security and Defence (Bonn International Center for Conversion for the European Parliament, 2006).

Kunzlik, Peter, "Environmental Issues in International Procurement" in Sue Arrowsmith and Arwel P. Davies (eds.), *Public Procurement: Global Revolution* (The Hague: Kluwer Law International, 1998).

"'Green Procurement' under the New Regime" in Ruth Nielsen and Steen Treumer (eds.), *The New EU Public Procurement Directives* (Copenhagen: Djøf, 2005).

Larrabee, F. Stephen, *NATO and the Challenges of Austerity* (Santa Monica: Rand, 2012).

Lenaerts, Koenraad *et al.* (eds.), *Procedural Law of the European Union* (London: Sweet & Maxwell, 2006).

Lhoest, Olivier, "La Production et la commerce des armes, et l'article 223 du traité constituant la Communauté Européene" (1993) 1 *Revue Belge de Droit International* 176–207.

Lichère, François and Nicholas Gabayet, "Enforcement of the Public Procurement Rules in France" in Steen Treumer and François Lichère, *Enforcement of the EU Public Procurement Rules* (Copenhagen: Djøf Publishing, 2011).

Lorell, Mark A., *Cheaper, Faster, Better?: Commercial Approaches to Weapons Acquisition* (Santa Monica: Rand, 2000).

Lovering, John, "Military Expenditure and the Restructuring of Capitalism: The Military Industry in Britain" (1990) 14 *Cambridge Journal of Economics* 453–67.

McCrudden, Christopher, "Social Policy Issues in Public Procurement: A Legal Overview" in Sue Arrowsmith and Arwel P. Davies (eds.), *Public Procurement: Global Revolution* (The Hague: Kluwer Law International, 1998).

Buying Social Justice (Oxford University Press, 2007).

Martin, Stephen, *The Economics of Offsets: Defence Procurement and Countertrade* (Amsterdam: Harwood Academic, 1996).

Mezzadri, Sandra, *L'Ouverture des marchés de la défense: enjeux et modalités,* Occasional Paper 12 (Paris: Institute for Security Studies of the Western European Union, 2000).

Missiroli, Antonio, *From Copenhagen to Brussels: European Defence: Core Documents,* Chaillot Paper 67 (Paris: Institute for Security Studies, European Union, 2003).

Neuman, Stephanie, *Defense Industries and Dependency: Current and Future Trends in the Global Defense Sector* (Zurich: ISN, 2006).

Nielson, Ruth and Steen Teurmer (eds.), *The New EU Public Procurement Directives* (Copenhagen: Djøf Publishing, 2005).

Noguellou, Rozen, "Scope and Coverage of the EU Procurement Directives" in Martin Trybus, Roberto Caranta and Gunilla Edelstam (eds.), *EU Law of Public Contract Law* (Brussels: Bruylant, 2014).

Ohlhoff, Stefan and Hannes L. Schloemann, "'Constitutionalization' and Dispute Settlement in the WTO: National Security as an Issue of Competence" (1999) 93 *American Journal of International Law* 424–51.

Oliver, Peter, *Free Movement of Goods in the European Community: Under Articles 28 to 30 of the EC Treaty* (London: Sweet & Maxwell, 2003).

Pachnou, Despina, "Bidder Remedies to Enforce the EC Procurement Rules in England and Wales" (2003) 12 *Public Procurement Law Review* 35.

Parker, David and Keith Hartley, "Transaction Costs, Relational Contracting and Public Private Partnerships: A Case Study of UK Defence" (2003) 9 *Journal of Purchasing and Supply Management* 97–108.

Pelkmans, Jan, "The New Approach to Technical Harmonisation and Standardization" (1987) 25 *Journal of Common Market Studies* 249–69.

Pourbaix, Nicholas, "The Future Scope of Application of Article 346 TFEU" (2011) 20 *Public Procurement Law Review* 1–8.

Priess, Hans-Joachim and Franz Josef Hoelzl, "Trust is Good – Control is Better: German Higher Administrative Court Reviews Military Procurement Decision" (2005) 14 *Public Procurement Law Review* NA 128–35.

Raulus, Helena, "The Charter of Fundamental Rights as a Set of Constitutional Principles" in Martin Trybus and Luca Rubini (eds.), *The Treaty of Lisbon and the Future of European Law and Policy* (Cheltenham: Edward Elgar, 2012).

Salmon, Trevor C. and Alistair J. K. Shepherd, *Toward a European Army: A Military Power in the Making?* (Boulder: Lynne Rienner Publishers, 2003).

Schake, Kori, *Constructive Duplication: Reducing EU Reliance on US Military Assets*, Working Paper (London: Centre for European Reform, 2002).

Schmitt, Burkard, *European Armaments Cooperation: Core Documents*, Chaillot Paper 58 (Paris: Institute for Security Studies of the European Union, 2003).

Defence Procurement in the European Union: The Current Debate: Report of an EUISS Task Force (Paris: Institute for Security Studies of the European Union, 2005).

Schwarze, Jürgen, *European Administrative Law* (London: Sweet and Maxwell, 1992).

Sempere, Carlos M., *A Survey of the European Security Market* (Berlin: Deutsches Institut für Wirtschaft, 2011).

Shearer, David, "Private Military Force and Challenges for the Future" (1999) 13 *Cambridge Review of International Affairs* 80–94.

Snell, Jukka, *Goods and Services in EC Law: A Study of the Relationship Between the Freedoms* (Oxford University Press, 2002).

Stormanns, Thomas, "Europe's Defence Industry: Single Market, Yes But How?" (1992) *EC Public Contract Law* 74.

Trepte, Peter Armin, *Public Procurement in the EU: A Practitioner's Guide* (Oxford University Press, 2007).

Treumer, Steen "Enforcement of EU Public Procurement Rules in Danish Law and Practice" in Steen Treumer and François Lichère (eds.), *Enforcement of the EU Public Procurement Rules* (Copenhagen: Djøf Publishing, 2011).

Treumer, Steen and François Lichère (eds.), *Enforcement of the EU Public Procurement Rules* (Copenhagen: Djøf Publishing, 2011).

Tridimas, Takis, *The General Principles of EU Law* (Oxford University Press, 2006).

Tridimas, Takis and Paolisa Nebbia (eds.), *European Union Law for the Twenty-first Century: Rethinking the New Legal Order. Internal Market and Free Movement Community Policies* (Oxford: Hart Publishing, 2004).

Trybus, Martin, "The Challenges Facing the European Defence-related Industry – Commission Communication COM (96) 08" (1996) 4 *Public Procurement Law Review* CS98–102.

European Defence Procurement Regulation: International and National Procurement Systems as Models for a Liberalised Defence Procurement Market in Europe, PhD Thesis, University of Wales (1998).

"European Defence Procurement: Towards a Comprehensive Approach" (1998) 4 *European Public Law* 111–33.

European Defence Procurement Law: International and National Procurement Systems as Models for a Liberalised Defence Procurement Market in Europe (The Hague: Kluwer Law International, 1999).

"On the Application of the E.C. Treaty to Armaments" (2000) 25 *European Law Review* 663–8.

"The Recent Judgment in Commission v. Spain and the Procurement of Hard Defence Material" (2000) 4 *Public Procurement Law Review* NA99–103.

"The EC Treaty as an Instrument of European Defence Integration: Judicial Scrutiny of Defence and Security Exceptions" (2002) 39 *Common Market Law Review* 1347–72.

"The List of Hard Defence Products under Article 296 EC" (2003) 2 *Public Procurement Law Review* NA15–21.

"Sisters in Arms: Female Soldiers and Sex Equality in the Armed Forces" (2003) 9 *European Law Journal* 631–58.

"Defence Procurement: The New Public Sector Directive and Beyond" (2004) 2 *Public Procurement Law Review* 198–210.

European Union Law and Defence Integration (Oxford: Hart, 2005).

"With or Without the EU Constitutional Treaty: Towards a Common Security and Defence Policy?" (2006) 3 *European Law Review* 145–66.

"The Morning after the Deadline: The State of Implementation of the New EC Public Procurement Directives in the Member States on 1st Feb. 2006" (2006) 15 *Public Procurement Law Review* NA82–90.

"The New European Defence Agency: A Contribution to a Common European Security and Defence Policy and a Challenge to the Community Acquis?" (2006) 43 *Common Market Law Review* 667–703.

"Case Comment on C-337/05 and C-157/06" (2009) 46 *Common Market Law Review* 973–90.

"An Overview of the United Kingdom Public Procurement Review and Remedies System with an Emphasis on England and Wales" in Steen Treumer and François Lichère (eds.), *Enforcement of the EU Public Procurement Rules* (Copenhagen: Djøf Publishing, 2011).

"The Hidden Remedies Directive: Review and Remedies under the Defence Directive" (2013) 22 *Public Procurement Law Review* 135–55.

"The Tailor-made EU Defence and Security Procurement Directive: Limitation, Flexibility, Descriptiveness and Substitution" (2013) 38 *European Law Review* 3–29.

Trybus, Martin and Luca Rubini (eds.), *The Treaty of Lisbon and the Future of European Law and Policy* (Cheltenham: Edward Elgar Publishing, 2012).

Trybus, Martin, Roberto Caranta and Gunilla Edelstam (eds.), *EU Public Contract Law: Public Procurement and Beyond* (Brussels: Bruylant, 2014).

Trybus, Martin and Nigel D. White (eds.), *European Security Law* (Oxford University Press, 2007).

Vestel, Pierre de, *Defence Markets and Industries in Europe: Time for Political Decisions?* (Paris: Institute for Security Studies of the Western European Union, 1995).

Vlachos, Katia G., *Safeguarding European Competitiveness: Strategies for the Future of European Arms Production and Procurement*, Occasional Paper 4 (Paris: Institute for Security Studies of the Western European Union, 1998).

Vredeling, Hendrik, *Towards a Stronger Europe* (Brussels: IEPG, 1986).

Walker, William and Philip Gummett, *Nationalism, Internationalism and the European Defence Market* (Paris: Institute for Security Studies of the Western European Union, 1993).

Walker, William and Susan Willett, "Restructuring the European Defence Industrial Base" (1993) 4 *Journal of Defence Economics* 141–60.

Weltzien, Kurt, "Avoiding the Procurement Rules by Awarding Contracts to an In-house Entity: The Scope of the Procurement Directives in the Classical Sector" (2005) 14 *Public Procurement Law Review* 237–55.

Weiss, Wolfgang, "EU Human Rights Protection after Lisbon" in Martin Trybus and Luca Rubini (eds.), *The Treaty of Lisbon and the Future of European Law and Policy* (Cheltenham: Edward Elgar, 2012).

Wessel, Ramses A., *The European Union's Foreign and Security Policy: a Legal Institutional Perspective* (The Hague: Kluwer Law International, 1999).

Wheaton, James B., "Defence Procurement and the European Community: The Legal Provisions" (1992) 1 *Public Procurement Law Review* 432.

Winter, Jan A., "Public Procurement in the EEC" (1991) 28 *Common Market Law Review* 741–82.

Wogau, Karl von and Barbara Rapp-Jung, "The Case for a European System Monitoring Foreign Investment in Defence and Security" (2008) 45 *Common Market Law Review* 47–68.

Wulf, Herbert, *Arms Industry Limited* (Oxford University Press, 1993).

INDEX

A400M transport aircraft, 53
abatements, mutual, for offsets, 202
abuse
   of dominant position, 170, 171, 173
   of security exemptions, 106,
      129–131, 238
   of subcontracting exception
      clause, 449
accelerated version
   of negotiated procedure with prior
      publication of contract notice, 326
   of restricted procedure, 321
access to documents. *See* security of
   information
acquis (communautaire), 194, 209,
   210, 459
Action Plan for the Defence-related
   Industry, 167
ad hoc basis, 53, 54, 188, 194, 219, 220,
   236, 352, 411
adaptation
   as contract performance condition.
      See maintenance, modernisation,
      and adaptation
   of Public Sector Directive for Defence
      Directive review and remedies,
      462–467
additional deliveries, use of negotiated
   procedure without prior
   publication for, 340–341
additional needs resulting from a crisis,
   contract performance conditions
   addressing, 373–374, 377
administrative courts, 461, 471
advantageous terms, use of negotiated
   procedure without prior
   publication for, 340

advertising. *See* publication of notice
Aérospatiale, 44, 171
Afghanistan, 44, 290, 291, 292, 343
aggrieved bidders, review and remedies
   system for. *See* litigation; remedies;
   review
Agusta Westland, 25
air and maritime transport operations,
   343, 344
air raid shelters, 266
aircraft, 23. *See also specific types*
   fighter, 25, 169, 170, 236, 270, 416
   leasing, 49
   military, 35, 91, 92, 93, 100, 101
   transport, 53, 95, 231
amendments to contract materially
   different from original contract, 478
Amsterdam Treaty, 107, 118, 234
Anglo-French Defence Treaty 2010,
   231, 233
anti-corruption, 3, 58
anti-tamper devices, 371
anti-trust law. *See* competition and
   competition law
Apostol, A. R., 355
appeals courts, 461, 470, 471
arbitration and conciliation services, 277
Area of Freedom, Security, and
   Justice, 71
armaments, defence exports of, 163–166
armaments exemption (Article 346(1)(b)
   TFEU), 87–128
   abuse of, 106, 238
   bilateral examinations, 122
   burden of proof, 119–120, 126
   case-by-case basis, derogation on,
      120–121, 128–129, 415, 419

armaments exemption (cont.)
  Commission's Interpretative
    Communication of 2006, 125–127,
    414, 489
  competition law and, 170
  confidentiality and, 473
  Defence Directive aiming to reduce
    recourse to, 72, 85
  dual use materials, 93, 94–95,
    96–101
  ECJ reluctance to interpret, 107
  EDA Procurement Codes and, 193,
    199, 209–213, 215–216, 221, 238,
    430, 444
  effect of, 104–125
  effet utile and proportionality, 117
  enforcement actions involving, 467
  exports, intended for, 88
  hard defence material, 89, 93, 95,
    103–104, 105, 106
  integration, European tendency
    toward, 48
  intensity of scrutiny, 110–113
  Internal Market and, 104–108
  interpretation of, 104–108, 127–128
  intra-Community transfers, 141–142
  items included on list, 90–94
  items not on list, 94–95
  judicial review, 100, 116, 119, 122
  list (of arms, munitions, and war
    material) of 1958, 88–104, 134
  markets affected and, 128, 129
  material scope of Defence Directive
    and, 263, 464
  merger control and, 174
  military use requirement, 96–103,
    128–133
  national security and, 41, 108–110
  necessity requirement, 108–110,
    114–116
  negotiated procedure without prior
    publication used instead of, 339
  notification, 121
  offsets under, 414–418, 467
  procedural requirements, 121–122
  proportionality test, 113–119
  provisions of, 87
  remedies, 122

review and remedies procedures
    adapted from, 460–461
  secrecy exemption, characteristics
    shared with, 133
  special review procedures, 117–119,
    153–156
  state aid and, 181
armaments, intra-Community transfers
    of, 140–156
  armaments exemption and, 141–142
  before ICT directive, 143–146
  under ICT Directive, 147–156. See
    also Intra-Community Transfers
    (ICT) Directive
  licences for. See licences
  national laws on, 143–146
  procurement, direct impact on,
    146–147
armaments or defence market (military)
  "Big Six" and "other" Member States,
    division into, 24
  differentiated from security market,
    18, 21, 60
  duplication, 33–35
  high costs, problem of, 35–37
  importance for European economy, 18
  limited capabilities of all Member
    States, 24
  monopolies and duopolies, 33
  monopsony, 31–32
  primary economic characteristics of,
    27–39
  prime contractors in, 22–25
  protectionism, 28–31
  subcontractors in, 27
armaments, trade in, 138
  defence exports, 163–166
  intra-Community transfers. See
    armaments, intra-Community
    transfers of
  market. See armaments or defence
    market
  TFEU exemption for. See armaments
    exemption
armed forces
  as contracting authorities for
    purposes of Defence Directive,
    249–251
  deployed abroad, 288–292, 344–345

interoperability in cooperation
between, 44–45
multinational, 44
non-military, 264
stationing of, 274–275
arms embargoes, 164
Arrowsmith, Sue, 324, 329–330
artillery, 23, 90, 92
auctions, electronic, 350
Australia, defence exports to, 162
Australia Group, 161
Austria
offsets, 427
review and remedies in, 461, 463, 471,
476, 481
transposition of Defence Directive in.
See transposition of Defence
Directive
autarky, 39, 41
authorisation
defence exports of armaments, 164
defence exports of dual-use goods, 162
global export, 162
individual export, 162
intra-Community trade of dual-use
goods, 159
national general export, 162
obligation of prior, 149
awards. *See* contract awards and award
criteria

B-2 Spirit, 35
bacteriological goods and services, 195
BAe Systems, 25, 34, 38
balances. *See* offsets
bankruptcy, 349, 377, 382
Belgium
in armaments or defence market, 24
bilateral initiatives with Netherlands
and Luxembourg, 231
defence budget cuts, 19
OCCAR and, 235
offsets, 427
Berlin-Plus Agreement, 49
Bialos, Jeffrey P., 396
bid invitation, 398–400
bidders. *See also* contract performance
conditions; non-discrimination
principle; qualification of bidders;

selection criteria for bidders;
technical specifications
equal treatment of, 1, 196, 213, 323,
332, 401, 441–445
ranking of, 399
reliability of, 11, 42, 43, 358, 360,
361, 372, 380, 382, 383, 386, 404,
439, 486
"Big Six" Member States in defence
market, 24
bilateral examinations of armaments
exemptions, 122
bilateral initiatives (defence integration),
231–232
biological weapons or agents, 90,
161, 195
black boxes, 371
Blair, Tony, 186
border protection, 252, 264, 267, 279,
281, 306, 309
Bowsher, Michael, 378
Bribe Payer's Index, 58
budget (pre-procurement) phase,
358, 363
Bulgaria
defence budget cuts, 19
joining NATO and EU, 46
offsets, 427
Búrca, Gráinne de, 76, 77, 78, 110
burden of proof
armaments exemption, 119–120,
126
negotiated procedure without prior
publication and, 337
Burnett, Michael, 334
Butler, Luke, 303
Buy-American
Internal Market agenda of Defence
Directive and, 29
tendency of Member States toward, 29
Buy-European
Defence Directive encouraging, 30
resistance of Member States to, 29

call-offs, 348, 349
Canada
defence exports to, 162
geographical location of sources
(qualification of bidders), 391

capital and payments, free movement of, 71
capital injection, 37, 176
case-by-case basis, TFEU derogations applied on, 120–121, 128–129, 133, 304, 415, 419
CCP (Common Commercial Policy), 163
ceasing of production, as contract performance condition, 376–377
CEN (European Committee for Standardisation), 167
CENELEC (European Committee for Electrotechnical Standardisation), 167
Central European Pipeline Management Agency (CEPMA), 239
central purchasing bodies, 255–259
centralised European defence agency proposals, 35, 59
CEPMA (Central European Pipeline Management Agency), 239
CERTIDER (Register of the Certified Defence-related Enterprises), 152
certificates and certification
  contract performance conditions requiring, 377
  end-user certificates, 140, 164
  under ICT Directive, 151–152, 156
  of subcontractors, 439
CFSP. See Common Foreign and Security Policy
The Challenges Facing the European Defence-related Industry (1996), 167, 221
charges having equivalent effect to a customs duty, 64, 70
Charter of Fundamental Rights of the European Union, 467, 472–473, 474
chemical weapons and agents, 90, 159, 161, 195
Chief Executive (of EDA), 187–189
Chirac, Jacques, 186
civil goods, services, and works, 2, 18, 41, 98, 289–291
civil offsets, indirect, 55, 407, 415, 417
civil protection, 264
classified information, 43–44, 263–264, 361, 379, 380, 392–397, 399

cleaning services, 266, 290, 306, 351
clearances. See security clearances
COCOM (Coordinating Committee on Multilateral Export Control), 161
co-decision, 83, 459
Cold War end and defence budget reductions, 19
collaboration, 53–54
  EDA collaborative projects and joint research programmes, 53, 218–220, 351
  ESA procurement procedures and, 352–354
  LoI and joint research programmes, 228–229
  material scope exclusion of cooperative programmes, 283–288
  OCCAR management of collaborative projects, 53, 219, 223–224, 351
  procurement procedures for co-operative R&D-based programmes, 351–356
  in R&D, 53, 283–288
  regulation, need for, 489
combat effectiveness (interoperability), 44–45, 217, 401
Commission. See European Commission
commodity market, use of negotiated procedure without prior publication for, 340
Common Commercial Policy (CCP), 163
common European interest
  LoI areas of, 225, 226
Common Foreign and Security Policy (CFSP)
  Common Positions in context of, 163
  CSDP as part of, 185
  defence exports of armaments, 165
  EDA and, 221–222
  integration, European tendency toward, 46
common law jurisdictions, 6
Common Military List
  defined, 164
  ICT Directive and, 154–155

intra-Community transfers of dual-use goods, 159
material scope of Defence Directive and, 262
Common Position, concept of, 163
Common Security and Defence Policy (CSDP), 185
armed forces deployed in third countries, 288, 292, 344
CFSP, as part of, 185
ECAP as part of, 186
EDA as main element of, 186, 221–222
integration, European tendency toward, 46
interoperability issues, 44–45
national sovereignty and, 40
Communication of December 2005 (European Commission), 212, 221
competence
of Member States in field of foreign policy, 163
of Member States in field of intra-Community transfers, 148, 153
shared, 62
Communication Implementing European Union Strategy on Defence-related Industries (1997), 167
competition and competition law, 1, 169–171. See also mergers and merger control; protectionism
abuse of dominant position, 170, 171, 173
armaments exemption and, 170
cross-border competition, 199, 200
Defence Directive and, 171
defence industries, relevance to, 169–170
distortion of competition, 37, 85, 124, 161, 169, 171, 172, 176, 182, 447
minimum percentage of subcontracts awarded on basis of competitive procedures (Option C), 434–436
minimum percentage of work subcontracted and competition for subcontracting beyond minimal percentage (Option D), 436–438
monopolies, 33, 171, 173

monopsony, 31–32
procurement procedures, range of competitiveness of, 311, 314, 319, 327, 329, 336
state aid affecting, 176
subcontracts awarded on basis of competitive procedures (Option B), 432–434
take-overs, 172, 175
competitive dialogue, 331–336
additional requirements of, 332
characteristics of, 331–332
flexibility of, 334
negotiated procedure with prior publication of contract notice compared, 331–336, 490
state aid and, 178, 180
complexity of defence contracting, 326
compliance
of bids and tenders, 197, 313, 319
contract performance conditions as mechanism of, 366
in EDA Procurement Codes award criteria, 197
conciliation and arbitration services, 277
conferred powers, principle of, 82
confidentiality
armaments exemption and, 473
commitment to safeguard, as contract performance condition, 379–380
review and remedies, 60, 471–474
conflicts, law of, 273
Conseil d'Etat (France), 471
Constitutional Treaty, 107, 186
consumer protection, 13, 66, 69, 166, 459
contract awards and award criteria, 400–403
award without any procurement procedure (direct illegal awards), 477
economically most advantageous tender, 400, 401
EDA Procurement Codes criteria and procedures, 196–198
interoperability and operational characteristics, 401
lowest price, 400

contract awards and award criteria
(cont.)
  notice required in negotiated
    procedure without prior
    publication of contract notice,
    336
  offsets and, 420
  Public Sector and Utilities Directives
    on, 400, 402
  qualifications of bidders
    distinguished, 382, 383, 403
  security-of-information and security-
    of-supply issues, 400–403
  standstill period, 179, 302, 458,
    477, 479
  subcontracts, 450–451
  transparency, non-discrimination,
    and equal treatment principles,
    401, 403
  transposition of, 403, 405
contract management (post-
  procurement) phase, 311, 358, 363,
  366, 382
contract performance conditions,
  366–382
  certification and documentation
    requirements, 377
  confidentiality, commitment to
    safeguard, 379–380
  crisis situations, additional needs
    resulting from, 373–374, 377
  Defence Directive provisions, 367–368
  disclosure, transfer, and use
    restrictions, 370–371
  export, transfer, and transit of goods,
    368–370
  express stipulation in Defence
    Directive not required, 381
  industrial changes, 376
  information commitments, 377
  maintenance, modernisation,
    and adaptation requirements,
    375–376, 377
  production requirements, 376–377,
    378
  in Public Sector Directive, 378, 381
  in published contract notice, 362–364
  security of information and, 366,
    379–381
  security of supply, ensuring, 366,
    368–379
  subcontractor information, 380–381
  supply chain organisation, 371–373
  in Utilities Directive, 367,
    378, 381
contracting entities or authorities
  covered by Defence Directive. See
    personal scope
  EDA as, 220
  list, lack of, 259–260, 489
  as prime contractors in award of
    subcontracts, 451
  security clearances and, 392–397
contracts. See also qualification of
    bidders; subcontractors and
    subcontracting; technological and
    contractual context
  amendments materially different
    from original contract, 478
  call-offs, 348, 349
  cost plus, 179, 180
  defined, 248
  of employment, 277
  fixed price, 179
  for follow-on work, 195, 346,
    375, 377
  government-to-government,
    292–299, 490
  in-house, 268–269
  invitation to bid or negotiate for,
    398–400
  nature of contexts covered by
    Defence Directive, 59
  notice, publication of, 362–364, 438,
    445–446
  offsets implemented through
    contractual obligations in, 409
  offsets separate from, 408
  pricing structure, 179
  sanctity of, 477
  secrecy exemption and notice
    requirements, 128, 129
  selling-on, 295
  sensitive, 263–264
  stages of making, 358–359
  subcontracting requirements in
    prime contract, 438–440
  target cost incentive, 179, 180

control mechanism (for procedures), 347
cooperation. *See* collaboration
Coordinating Committee on Multilateral Export Control (COCOM), 161
corruption
  anti-corruption, 3, 58
  negotiated procedure without prior publication and, 337
  problem of, 57, 58
cost-plus contracts, 179, 180
costs
  high costs, as economic problem in armaments market, 35–37
  of licensing, 141–142
  pricing structure of normal commercial transactions, 179
  transaction costs, of restricted procedure, 315, 320
Council of the European Union, 83
counter-intelligence, 281
courts, administrative, 461, 471
courts of appeal, 461, 470, 471
coverage. *See* scope
Cox, Andrew, 35
Craig, Paul, 78
criminal convictions as mandatory grounds for exclusion of bidders, 382, 383
criminal organisations, 20, 219, 279, 281, 382, 383
crisis management missions, 264
crisis situations
  contract performance conditions regarding additional needs resulting from, 373–374, 377
  defined, 373
  exemption (Article 347 TFEU) for, 133–134, 342
  negotiated procedure without prior publication used for urgency resulting from, 342–344
cross-border business relationships, 446
cross-border competition, 199, 200
cross-border mergers, 173, 174
cross-border movement of goods, 369
cross-border procurement, 173
cross-border share-holdings, 173

cross-subsidisation, 179, 182
cryptography and cryptographical equipment, 159, 195
CSDP. *See* Common Security and Defence Policy
customs duties, 64, 70, 139
customs services, 264
Cyprus, and offsets, 416, 417, 427
Czech Republic
  in armaments or defence market, 24
  joining NATO and EU, 46
  offsets, 427

damages, 458
default procedures
  negotiated procedure with prior publication as default Defence Directive procedure, 327
  open procedure as default procedure in older public directives, 313
defence derogations from TFEU, 7, 85–135. *See also* armaments exemption; secrecy exemption
  case-by-case basis, applied on, 120–121, 128–129, 133, 304, 415, 419
  crisis situations exemption (article 347 TFEU), 133–134, 342
  ECJ on, 86
  ICT Directive subject to, 154
  interoperability and, 45
  material scope of Defence Directive and, 267, 303–305
  national security and, 42
  negotiated procedure without prior publication used instead of, 339
  public security exemption compared, 85, 87, 111
  review and remedies for Defence Directive derived from, 460–461
Defence Directive (EU Defence and Security Procurement Directive 2009/81/EC), 1–14, 17–60, 484–492
  aims of, i, 12, 72, 85, 147, 148, 490
  changes wrought by, 4
  comparative analysis of Public Sector Directive and, 5

Defence Directive (cont.)
competition law and, 171
contract notice, publication of,
362–364
on contract performance conditions,
367–368. *See also* contract
performance conditions
crisis situations exemption limited
by, 134
defence derogations from TFEU and,
7, 85–135. *See also* defence
derogations from TFEU
differentiated from Public Sector
Directive, 87
economic context, 18–39. *See also*
economic context
EDA Procurement Codes,
compatibility with, 209–216
entry into force, 3
European armaments law and policy
beyond Internal Market and, 8,
185–241. *See also specific
organisations and initiatives*
Internal Market context, 8,
136–184. *See also* Internal Market
interpretation of, 5
legal basis for, 7, 61–84, 484. *See also*
legal basis for Defence Directive
OCCAR and, 224–225
offsets, 11, 54–57, 410–428,
487–488. *See also* offsets
political/military context, 39–49. *See
also* political/military context
political will of Member States
regarding, 13
principles in TFEU and, 442
procurement procedures, 10,
310–356, 485–486. *See also*
procurement procedures
public procurement law in EU,
purpose and aims of, 1
Public Sector Directive, based on,
4, 484
review and remedies, 12, 455–483,
488–489. *See also* review and
remedies
safeguard clause, 301
scope of, 10, 245–309, 484–485. *See
also* scope of Defence Directive

security of supply and information,
11, 358–405, 486–487. *See also*
security of information; security of
supply
special contexts, importance of
considering, 59
subcontracting, 11, 428–452,
487–488. *See also* subcontractors
and subcontracting
success of, 491
on technical specifications,
364–365. *See also* technical
specifications
technological and contractual
context, 49–58. *See also*
technological and contractual
context
thresholds, 269–272
transposition in Member States, 6,
14. *See also* transposition of
Defence Directive
defence economic problem, 36
defence electronics, 23, 36
defence exemptions and exclusions. *See*
exemptions, exceptions, and
exclusions
defence exports, 160–166
of armaments, 163–166
armaments exemption and, 103–104
control regimes, 161
defined, 138
differentiation from intra-Community
transfers, 149
of dual-use goods, 161–163
EU Code of Conduct on, 162
importance of, 160
national laws for, 144
protectionism in, 160
defence industries, monitoring of, 137,
152, 182, 184, 207
defence market. *See* armaments or
defence market
Defence Package, 3, 8, 39, 43, 47, 48,
59, 127, 137, 142–143, 147, 156,
169, 175, 177, 184, 230–231,
237, 360, 369, 393, 403, 405,
459, 486
defence procurement
benefits of integrating, 2

differentiation of armaments market and security market, 18, 21. *See also* armaments or defence market; security market

economic context for. *See* economic context

importance in European economy, 2

inefficiency in Europe, 38–39

political/military context for. *See* political/military context

procedures for. *See* procurement procedures

regulation by Defence Directive. *See* Defence Directive

research prior to regulation of, 4

technological and contractual context. *See* technological and contractual context

unregulated status prior to Defence Directive, 1

delay of exports, 369, 371

demand for defence and security goods and services, 18–21

democracy/democratic deficit, 77, 190, 424

Denmark
in armaments or defence market, 24
CFSP and, 18
defence budget cuts, 19
EDA collaborations and, 220
EDA Procurement Codes and, 191, 192

deployability, 197

derogations from Treaty. *See* defence derogations from TFEU

description and descriptiveness, 381, 402, 464, 465–466

Dini, Lamberto, 107

direct illegal awards, 477

direct military offsets, 55, 407, 417

disclosure of information, restrictions on, 370–371

disposal phase/service contract, 52–53

distortion of competition, 37, 85, 124, 161, 169, 171, 172, 176, 182, 447

documentation requirements, as contract performance conditions, 377

dominant market position, 170, 171, 173

dual-use goods
armaments exemption not applicable to, 93, 94–95, 96–101
customs duties, 139
as defence exports, 161–163
defined, 157
intra-Community transfers of, 156–160
public security exemption for, 156
regulation of, 158–160
state aid and, 182
trade in, 138

duopolies, 33

duplication, 33–35, 58, 230–231, 232. *See also* fragmentation

dynamic purchasing systems, 350–351

EADS (European Aeronautic Defence and Space Company), 25, 38

EBB (European Bulletin Board), 196, 211–216, 257, 271, 298, 362

ECAP (European Capabilities and Armaments Policy), 186, 189, 190, 221

ECDP (European Capabilities Development Plan), 217

ECHR (European Convention on Human Rights), 468–474

ECJ. *See* European Court of Justice

economic context, 18–39
"Big Six" and "other" Member States, division of markets between, 24, 26
demand for defence and security goods and services, 18–21
differentiating armaments market from security market, 18, 21, 60. *See also* armaments or defence market; security market
duplication, 33–35, 58
high costs, problem of, 35–37
inefficiency of defence procurement in Europe, 38–39, 58
monopolies and duopolies, 33
monopsony, 31–32
primary economic characteristics of defence procurement, 27–39
protectionist tendencies, 28–31
R&D, financing, 50

economic context (cont.)
 state ownership and control issues,
  37–38
 structure of defence and security
  industries, 21–27
economic crisis of 2008, 19
economic and financial standing of
 bidders, 388–398, 399
economic operators. *See* bidders
economically most advantageous
 tender, as contract award criterion,
 400, 401
economies of learning, difficulty of
 achieving, 59
economies of scale
 collaboration as means of
  achieving, 54
 difficulty of achieving, 59
EDA. *See* European Defence
 Agency
EDA Codes for Procurement and the
 Supply Chain (EDA Procurement
 Codes), 5, 191–216
 aims and objectives, 191
 armaments exemption and, 193,
  199, 209–213, 215–216, 221, 238,
  430, 444
 award procedures and criteria,
  196–198
 compatibility with Defence Directive,
  207–209
 contract notice, publication of, 362
 enforcement and remedies, 207–209
 establishment of, 191
 exemptions from scope of, 194–195
 offsets, 198–204, 424, 426, 427
 scope of, 193–195
 subcontracting in, 198, 204–207, 429,
  440, 444
 suspension of, 214, 238
 thresholds, 270
 voluntary and nonbinding nature of,
  192–193
EDA Offset Portal, 427
EDA Procurement Gateway, 215
EDC (European Defence Community)
 and EDC Treaty, 106, 221
EDEM (European Defence Equipment
 Market), 187, 224

EDIG (European Defence Industries
 Group), 141
EDITB (European Defence Industrial
 and Technological Base), 187,
 203, 284
EDSTAR (European Defence
 Standards Reference System),
 168–169
EEA (European Economic Area), 14, 32,
 142, 190, 207, 427
EEC (European Economic
 Community), 106
effet utile, 117
Eisenhut, Dominik, 417, 418
electronic auctions, 350
employment
 contracts, 277
 in the defence sector, 2, 32, 36, 39,
  54, 160
 free movement of workers, 68, 71
end-user certificates, 140, 164
enforcement. *See also* review and
 remedies
 armaments exemption and, 467
 EDA Procurement Codes, 207–209
 importance of, 456–458
engines, 23
equal treatment principle, 1, 196, 213,
 323, 332, 401, 441–445
equilibrium. *See* offsets
equivalent effect
 charges having equivalent effect to a
  customs duty, 64, 70
 measure having equivalent effect to
  quantitative restriction, 65, 66, 71,
  79, 139, 141, 411
ESA (European Space Agency),
 352–354
ESDP (European Security and Defence
 Policy), 86, 158
ESS (European Security Strategy), 35
essential interests of security, 73, 87,
 109, 114, 116, 128, 129, 277, 278,
 463, 473
establishment, freedom of, 67–70,
 414
Estonia
 joining NATO and EU, 46
 offsets, 427

ETSI (European Telecommunications Institute), 167
EU. *See* European Union
Eurocopter SA, 171
Eurofighter/Typhoon aircraft, 25, 53, 169, 218, 283, 338, 351
EUROPA (European Memorandum of Understanding of Research Organisation, Programmes and Activities), 229, 233, 234
European Aeronautic Defence and Space Company (EADS), 25, 38
European Armaments Cooperation Strategy, 217
European Bulletin Board (EBB), 196, 211–216, 257, 271, 298, 362
European Capabilities and Armaments Policy (ECAP), 186, 189, 190, 221
European Capabilities Development Plan (ECDP), 217
European Commission
  on armaments and "Community" law, 221
  armaments exemption, 2006 interpretative communication on, 125–127, 414, 489
  EDA Procurement Codes and, 190, 211, 212
  enforcement of procurement law by, 456–458
  Guidance Notes, 12, 247, 422–425, 483, 490
  Internal Market initiatives. *See* Internal Market
  on offsets, 422–425
  on scope of Defence Directive, 12, 247
  secrecy exemption and, 130
  voting rights, 188, 190, 216
European Committee for Electrotechnical Standardisation (CENELEC), 167
European Committee for Standardisation (CEN), 167
European Convention (Constitutional), 107, 186
European Convention on Human Rights (ECHR), 468–474
European Council

EDA Council Decision, 186–187, 189–190, 209
offset ban necessarily involving, 423
European Court of Justice (ECJ). *See also separate table of case law*
  armaments exemption, reluctance to interpret, 107
  on contract award criteria, 402
  on defence derogations from TFEU, 86
  on defence exports, 163
  EDA and, 190, 212
  EDA Procurement Codes and, 194, 196
  on free movement of goods, 66
  on free movement of services and freedom of establishment, 69
  integration, European tendency toward, 48
  offsets and, 416, 423, 428
  on proportionality, 76–81
  on public security exemption, 72
  on qualification of bidders, 382, 383–388
  safeguard clause and, 302
European Defence Agency (EDA), 186–222. *See also* EDA Codes for Procurement and the Supply Chain
  as central purchasing body within personal scope of Defence Directive, 256–258
  collaborative projects and joint research programmes, 53, 218–220, 351
  as contracting entity, 220
  CSDP, as main element of, 186, 221–222
  development of policies by, 189–191
  ECAP, 186, 189, 190, 221
  EDA Offset Portal, 427
  EDA Procurement Gateway, 215
  ESA, procurement procedures for collaborative R&D programmes in, 354
  establishment and aims, 185, 186–187
  external fragmentation between other institutions and, 232–237

European Defence Agency (cont.)
fragmentation, overcoming, 232–234,
235–237
internal fragmentation between
Internal Market initiatives and,
234
judicial review and, 190, 192, 207
licences not addressed by, 146
LoI and, 227–231, 232–234
material scope of Defence Directive
and, 273, 276
national capability commitments,
evaluation of, 217–218
OCCAR and, 219, 225, 232–234
on offset phase-out, 454
organisational structure, 187–189
participation, flexibility regarding, 236
Point of Contact, 207
pooling and sharing, Code of
Conduct on, 218
pressing operational urgency, 195
Procurement Regulations, 220
Procurement Rules and Rules for
Financial Contributions for the
Operational Budget of the
EDA, 220
reformed procurement regime, need
for, 489
R&T Projects User Guide, 220
scope of, 247
subscribing Member States, 191
tasks of, 189
WEAG and WEAO activities
transferred to, 233–237
European Defence Community (EDC)
and EDC Treaty, 106, 221
European Defence Equipment Market
(EDEM), 187, 224
European Defence-Industrial and
Market Issues: Towards an EU
Defence Equipment Policy
(European Commission), 137, 168
European Defence Industrial and
Technological Base (EDITB), 187,
203, 284
European Defence Industries Group
(EDIG), 141
European Defence Standards Reference
System (EDSTAR), 168–169

European Economic Area (EEA), 14, 32,
142, 190, 207, 427
European Economic Community
(EEC), 106
European Internal Market and
Consumer Protection Committee,
13, 459, 479
European Joint Action, 86, 158,
186–222, 235, 236
European Memorandum of
Understanding of Research
Organisation, Programmes and
Activities (EUROPA), 229, 233, 234
European Monetary Union, 19
European Parliament, 13, 83, 190, 419,
423, 459
European Procurement Gateway (of
EDA), 215
European public bodies, 255–256, 258
European Security and Defence Policy
(ESDP), 86, 158
European Security Strategy (ESS), 35
European Space Agency (ESA), 352–354
European Steering Board (of EDA),
187–189
European Telecommunications
Institute (ETSI), 167
European Treaty. See TFEU
European Union (EU). See also specific
EU Directives, e.g. Defence
Directive
Charter of Fundamental Rights, 467,
472–473, 474
Code of Conduct on Arms Exports,
162, 163, 165
Military Committee, 46, 188
Military Staff, 46
NATO, possible competition with, 46
Political and Security Committee,
46, 188
primary EU law, 17, 247, 262, 279,
304, 410, 418, 422, 424, 453, 467
secondary EU law, 17, 61, 63, 66, 68,
82, 109, 118, 123, 128, 134, 137,
163, 241, 247, 262, 279, 280, 345,
410, 418, 422, 424, 442
three-Pillar structure, abolition of, 46
Eurozone, 19, 40
ex-ante control, 149–150

ex ante licences, 140
exemptions, exceptions, and
    exclusions. *See also* armaments
    exemption; public security
    exemption
    automatic or categorical, 105, 107,
        142, 181, 210, 303
    case-by-case, 120–121, 128–129, 133,
        304, 415, 419
    from EDA Procurement Codes scope,
        194–195
    from material scope of Defence
        Directive, 267–307. *See also*
        material scope
    subcontracting, exception clause for,
        448–450
    unsuitable bidders, exclusion of, 382,
        383–388
existing stocks, 293, 299, 378, 490
exports. *See also* defence exports
    armaments exemption and
        armaments intended for export,
        103–104
    authorisation for defence exports, 162
    contract performance conditions
        regarding, 368–370
    defined, 158
    delay of, 369, 371
    goods, free movement of, 63–67
    limitations under ICT Directive,
        152–153
    LoI on export procedures and
        transfers, 227–228
    monopsony and policies
        regarding, 31
    public security exemptions regarding,
        70–82
    re-exports, 147, 148, 158
    refusal of, 164, 369, 371
    withdrawal of, 369, 371
extraterritorial deployment of armed
    forces, 288–292

F-22 Raptor, 35
fair return principle, 51, 54, 220, 223,
    353–354, 355. *See also* offsets
Farnborough Agreement (LoI), 226
Federal Competition Agency
    (Germany), 471

field of application
    list of 1958, for armaments exemption,
        91, 104
    proportionality and, 66
    scope of Defence Directive,
        Commission Guidance Note on,
        12, 247
    secrecy exemption, 133
fighter aircraft, 25, 169, 170, 236, 270,
    416. *See also specific types*
financial and economic standing of
    bidders, 388–398, 399
Finland
    in armaments or defence market, 24
    offsets, 409, 417, 427
first-instance review, 99, 111, 177, 470
First Pillar (of the EU), 137, 238
Fisher, Catherine E., 396
fixed price contracts, 179
flexibility
    of participation in EDA, 236
    procurement procedure issues, 323,
        328, 330, 334, 336, 464–465,
        485–486
    of review and remedies, 464–465
follow-on work, 195, 346, 375, 377
force majeure, 299, 378
forces. *See* armed forces
foreign sales. *See also* defence exports
    monopsony, 31
    state aid for, 177
fragmentation, 232
    duplication and inconsistency,
        problem of, 33–35, 58, 230–231,
        232
    external, 233–237
    internal, 237–239
    overcoming, 232–234
framework agreements
    LoI FA (Framework Agreement)
        Treaty (2000), 226
    as procurement procedure,
        348–349
    subcontracting, 446–447
Framework Arrangement for Security of
    Supply between subscribing
    Member States in Circumstances
    of Operational Urgency (EDA,
    2006), 197

France
  in armaments or defence market,
    23, 24
  bilateral Defence Treaty with the
    United Kingdom (2010), 231, 233
  defence budget cuts, 19
  as defence exporter, 160, 161
  LoI, participation in, 396. *See also*
    Letter of Intent
  monopoly of Eurocopter SA
    encouraged by, 171
  as nuclear power, 23, 231, 233
  offsets, 56, 408, 409, 427
  review and remedies in, 471
  in security market, 26
  standards, hierarchy of, 365
  state aid in, 176
  state ownership and control of national
    defence industries in, 37, 38
Franco-German Armaments
  Cooperation, 222, 231
free movement
  of capital and payments, 71
  of goods, 63–67, 139, 411–412
  public security exemption to, 70–82
  of services, 67–70, 411–412
  of workers, 68, 71
freedom of establishment, 67–70, 414
freedom of price contractor to choose
  subcontractors (Option A), 431–432
Freedom, Security, and Justice, Area
  of, 71
fundamental rights, 467, 471,
  472–473, 482

G-18 Globemaster II, 35
Gabriel, J. M., 47
General Agreement on Tariffs and
  Trade (GATT), 114–115, 130, 134
General Agreement on Trade in Services
  (GATS), 114, 134
general licences, 145, 150–151, 162
geographical location of sources
  (qualification of bidders), 390–392
Georgopoulos, Aris, 55, 111, 193, 208,
  245, 407
German Military Exports cases, 121,
  131–133
Germany

in armaments or defence market,
  23, 24
as defence exporter, 160, 161
European and US troops stationed
  in, 274
Federal Competition Agency, 471
Franco-German Armaments
  Cooperation, 222, 231
land systems in, 34
LoI, participation in, 396. *See also*
  Letter of Intent
monopoly of Eurocopter SA
  encouraged by, 171
monopsony and export policies, 31
offsets, 56, 408, 409, 427
proportionality test adopted from
  German public law, 76, 78
review and remedies in, 461, 463, 471,
  474, 476, 481
in security market, 26
state ownership and control of national
  defence industries in, 37, 38
transposition of Defence Directive in.
  See transposition of Defence
  Directive
unification of, 46
global economic crisis of 2008, 19
global export authorisation, 162
global licences, 145
Global Project Licences (GPLs), 228
golden shares, 38
goods
  cross-border movement of, 369
  free movement of, 63–67, 139, 411–412
government contracting authorities,
  249–252
Government Procurement Agreement
  (GPA), WTO, 420
government-to-government contracts,
  292–299, 490
GPA (Government Procurement
  Agreement), WTO, 420
grave professional misconduct, 384–386
Greece
  defence budget cuts, 19
  offsets, 409, 417, 427
Green Paper on Defence Procurement
  (2004), 12, 125, 127, 168, 212, 221,
  317, 328, 428, 459

Gripen fighter aircraft, 25, 169
guarantees, 37, 176
Gucht, Karel de, 47

hard defence material, 89, 93, 95,
    103–104, 105, 106, 193
harmonisation
    EDA Procurement Codes and, 191
    ICT Directive promoting, 155
    military requirements, LoI on
        harmonisation of, 230
    of national security clearances,
        489
    standardisation and, 166–169
Hartley, Keith, 35, 36
Heuninckx, Baudouin, 92, 98, 100,
    178–179, 180, 210, 217, 300–303,
    317, 333, 344, 378, 379, 394, 408,
    416, 482
"hidden" Remedies Directive, 455,
    458–460
High Court (England and Wales,
    Northern Ireland, Republic of
    Ireland), 471
High Representative for Foreign Affairs
    and Security Policy, 187
high technology, 21, 51, 54, 286, 352
human rights, 467, 474
Hungary
    joining NATO and EU, 46
    offsets, 427

ICT Directive. See Intra-Community
    Transfers (ICT) Directive
IEPG (Independent European
    Programme Group), 194
Implementing the European Union
    Strategy on Defence-related
    Industries, 221
in camera hearings and rulings, 85, 100,
    130, 469
in-house contracts, 268–269
in-service support phase/contract,
    52–53
Independent European Programme
    Group (IEPG), 194
independent review, 482
indirect civil offsets, 55, 407,
    415, 417

indirect military offsets, 55, 407,
    415, 417
individual export authorisation, 162
individual licences, 145, 150–151
industrial changes, as contract
    performance condition, 376
industrial compensation/cooperation/
    participation. See offsets;
    subcontractors and subcontracting
industrial and regional benefits. See
    offsets
ineffectiveness (as remedy), 458,
    477–481
inefficiency of defence procurement in
    Europe, 38–39, 58
information. See also security of
    information
    classified, 43–44, 263–264, 361, 379,
        380, 392–397, 399
    contract performance conditions,
        as information commitments, 377
    disclosure restrictions, 370–371
    on subcontractors, as contract
        performance condition,
        380–381
information asymmetries, 329
Ingels, H., 156
innovation partnerships, 355–356
integration of European defence and
    security, trend toward, 45–49
intellectual property (IP)
    management standards of bidders,
        389–390
    negotiated procedure without prior
        publication and, 326
intelligence
    civilian intelligence agencies, 267
    counter-intelligence, 281
    material scope exclusion
        of intelligence activities, 281–283,
            304
    services, 57, 267, 277, 281
    specific functions (military, security,
        criminal, or external), 282
intensity of scrutiny
    armaments exemption, 110–113
    public security exemption, 76–77, 78,
        81–82
    secrecy exemption, 131–133

inter-pillar approach, 158, 165
interest rates, 37, 176
intergovernmental bodies, 190–191,
    256, 258
interim relief, 457
interlocutory proceedings, 474–477
internal disturbances, serious, affecting
    the maintenance of law and
    order, 133
Internal Market, 8, 136–184. *See also*
    competition and competition law;
    defence exports; intra-Community
    transfers; Intra-Community
    Transfers (ICT) Directive; mergers
    and merger control; state aid
armaments exemption and,
    104–108
benefits of establishing, 59
customs duties, 64, 139
fragmentation between EDA and
    armaments policy initiatives of,
    237–239
interoperability and, 44–45
as legal basis for Defence Directive,
    61–63, 82
protectionism and, 30
R&D (research and development),
    183
SMEs (small and medium-sized
    enterprises, 183
standardisation, 166–169
TFEU establishing, 62–63
trade in armaments and dual-use
    goods, 138. *See also* armaments,
    trade in; dual-use goods
international arrangements
defence exports, authorisation
    of, 162
ICT Directive not affecting, 153
material scope exception for
    contracts awarded under,
    272–276
on stationing of troops, 274–275
international security and peace,
    obligations accepted for the
    purpose of maintaining, 134
international tension, serious,
    constituting a threat of war, 134
interoperability, 44–45, 217, 401

intra-Community transfers,
    139–160. *See also* armaments,
    intra-Community transfers of
customs duties on, 139
defence exports differentiated
    from, 149
defined, 138, 139
of dual-use goods, 156–160
judicial review, 156
LoI and, 145, 228
public security, affecting, 139
Intra-Community Transfers of Defence
    Products (2005), 141, 142, 144,
    147, 154
Intra-Community Transfers (ICT)
    Directive
armaments, 147–156
certification under, 151–152, 156
competence of Member States and,
    148, 153
contract performance conditions and,
    369–370
defence derogations from TFEU,
    subject to, 154
"Defence Package", as part of,
    142–143
definition of transfer for purposes
    of, 148
ex-ante control, objective of
    replacing, 149–150
export limitations, 152–153
goods listed in annex to, 154–155
harmonisation promoted by, 155
importance of, 136, 138
Internal Market agenda of Defence
    Directive and, 30
international agreements not affected
    by, 153
licensing as sole application of, 148
limitations of, 153–156
security of supply in, 360
simplification as aim of, 148
transposition of, 142, 155
types of licences under, 150–151
invitation to bid or negotiate, 398–400
IP. *See* intellectual property
Iraqi armed forces, 50
Ireland
Cyprus compared, 416

offsets, 427
review and remedies in, 461, 463, 471, 476, 481
transposition of Defence Directive in. *See* transposition of Defence Directive
irregular tenders, 338, 351
Italy
in armaments or defence market, 23, 24
as defence exporter, 160
LoI, participation in, 396. *See also* Letter of Intent
offsets, 409, 427
security market, absence from, 26
ITAR, 371

Jacobs, Francis, Advocate General, 67, 86, 124, 158
Japan, defence exports to, 162
Joint Action, 86, 158, 186–222, 235, 236
joint research programmes. *See* collaboration
joint ventures, 172
Jones, Seth G., 47
judges, 99, 470, 471–474, 477, 481
judicial control of ECAP and EDA, 191
judicial review
armaments exemption, 100, 116, 119, 122
EDA and, 190, 192, 207
intra-Community transfers, 156
in at least second instance, 482, 488
legal basis for Defence Directive and, 62, 75, 84, 87
Public Sector Remedies Directive, adaptation of, 467
security of supply and information, 404, 405
judicial scrutiny, 79, 104, 122
juste retour (fair return principle), 51, 54, 220, 223, 353–354, 355

Kennedy-Loest, Ciara, 333
Keukeleire, Stephan, 47
Koehl, Stuart L., 396
Koutrakos, Panos, 111

Lambsdorff, Alexander Count, 13, 373, 459
land systems, 34
Latvia
joining NATO and EU, 46
offsets, 427
law of conflicts, 273
law and order, serious internal disturbances affecting maintenance of, 133
Le Touquet summit (2003), 186
lead national concept, 53, 283, 351
legal basis for Defence Directive, 7, 61–84, 484. *See also* proportionality; public security exemption
establishment, freedom of, 67–70
goods, free movement of, 63–67
Internal Market regime as, 61–63, 82
non-discrimination principle, 70
services, free movement of, 67–70
TFEU foundations, 61, 82–83
legitimate interests, 174, 175
Leopard 2, 36
Letter of Intent (LoI), 185, 225–231
assimilation to EDA, 232–234, 235–237
as central purchasing body within personal scope of Defence Directive, 258–259
common European interests, areas of, 225, 226
duplication and overlap with other institutions, 230–231
EDA and, 227–230, 232–234
FA (Framework Agreement Treaty, 2000), 226
initial LoI of 1998, 225
intra-Community transfers and, 145, 228
material scope of Defence Directive and, 273
security clearances, 394, 396–397
on security of supply, 359
tasks and functions, 227–230
level playing field, 38, 177, 199, 200, 205
lex specialis, 134, 305, 308
liberalised defence market, 35, 59, 65, 119, 170, 224

licences
  ex ante, 140
  fees, 144, 412
  general, 145, 150–151, 162
  general export authorisation of defence
    exports of dual-use goods, 162
  global, 145, 150–151
  GPLs (Global Project Licences)
    (LoI), 228
  ICT Directive, as sole application
    of, 148
  ICT Directive, types of licences
    under, 150–151
  impact and costs of, 141–142
  individual, 145, 150–151
  LoI and, 145
  under national law, before ICT
    Directive, 144
  number of applications for, 140
  OGELs (Open General Export
    Licences), 145
  procurement, direct impact on,
    146–147
Liebmann, Hanno, 435
life cycle, 52–53
  contract performance specifications
    and, 377
  high costs associated with, 35
  ineffectiveness as remedy and, 478
  R&D and, 50, 52–53
limitations of scope. See scope
Lisbon Treaty. See also TFEU
list of 1958
  for armaments exemption, 88–104,
    134
  material scope of Defence Directive
    and, 261
  need to publish, 101, 489
  offsets and, 413, 416
List, Common Military. See Common
    Military List
Lithuania
  joining NATO and EU, 46
  offsets, 427
litigation. See also judicial review; review
    and remedies
  costs of, 458
  decreasing, 466, 467
  increasing, 458, 482, 488

risks of, 320, 364, 381, 384,
    397, 405, 444, 460, 481, 483,
    487, 488
local contracting authorities, 249–252
logistics, 53, 239, 288, 289, 351
LoI. See Letter of Intent
lowest price, as contract award
    criterion, 400
Luxembourg
  bilateral initiatives with Belgium, 231
  OCCAR and, 235
  offsets, 427

Maastricht Treaty, 46, 107, 118, 235
maintenance of law and order, serious
    internal disturbances affecting, 133
maintenance, modernisation, and
    adaptation
  contract performance conditions,
    375–376, 377
  qualification of bidders, 389–390
maintenance and repair, 149, 151, 190,
    265, 270, 348
Malta, and offsets, 417, 427
mandatory requirements, 66, 69, 71
marine systems, 33, 34
maritime and air transport operations,
    343, 344
market access, 10, 29, 167, 171, 232,
    246, 330, 393, 395, 403,
    405, 428
material scope
  armaments exemption and, 263, 464
  armed forces deployed outside EU
    territory, exclusion of contracts
    involving, 288–292
  broad nature of, 261
  contracts outside Ministry of
    Defence and armed forces covered
    by, 266–267
  cooperative programmes, exclusion
    of, 283–288
  covered contracts, 260–267
  defined, 246
  derogation from, 267, 303–305
  exemptions and exclusions, 267–307
  government-to-government
    contracts exclusion, 292–299, 490
  in-house contracts, 268–269

intelligence activities, exclusion of, 281–283
international arrangements, exclusion of contracts awarded under, 272–276
limitation, for review and remedies purposes, 462–464
list of 1958 and, 261
military equipment, 261–263
new equipment exemption, 295
Public Sector Directive and, 261, 266–267, 276, 277, 290, 305–307, 462–464
R&D exclusions, 283–288, 299–301
safeguard clause and, 301
secrecy exclusion, 278–280
sensitive contracts, 263–264
specific defence and security-related exemptions, 276–301
surplus equipment exemption, 294
TFEU and, 267, 303–305
thresholds, 269–272
transposition of, 267
typology of exceptions, 272
Utilities Directive and, 261, 267, 277, 290, 307, 462–464
works, supplies, and services directly related to military equipment, 265–266
materially different from original contract, amendments as, 478
MBB, 171
MBDA, 25
measure having equivalent effect to quantitative restriction, 65, 66, 71, 79, 139, 141, 411
Memoranda of Understanding, 202, 229, 233, 273
mergers and merger control, 172–176
armaments exemption and secrecy exemption, subject to, 174
cross-border mergers, 173, 174
defence company mergers, 170
economic operators, mergers of, 349
limited national defence industrial capabilities leading to, 24
regulation of mergers, 172, 173–175
state ownership and control of national defence industries and, 38

trans-border mergers, 172
Meteor air-to-air missile, 53
methods of procurement. See procurement procedures
Military Committee, EU, 46, 188
military context. See political/military context
military defence market. See armaments or defence market (military)
military equipment, under material scope of Defence Directive, 261–263
Military Exports cases, 109, 110, 111, 112, 113, 115, 116, 117, 118, 120, 121, 124, 125, 126, 127, 128–129, 131–133, 139, 142, 146, 163, 165, 181, 210, 489
military forces. See armed forces
military security. See security
Military Staff, EU, 46
ministries of defence, 249–251
Missile Technology Control Regime, 161
missiles, 23, 36, 53, 90, 161, 170, 416, 417
modernisation. See maintenance, modernisation, and adaptation
Mölling, Christian, 155
monitoring of defence industries, 137, 152, 182, 184, 207
monopolies, 33, 171, 173
monopsony, 31–32
MTCR technology, 159
multinational forces, 44
mutual abatements, for offsets, 202
mutual recognition of security clearances, 394–397

NAHEMA (NATO Helicopter for the 1990s (NH90) Design and Development, Production and Logistics Management Agency), 186, 239
NAMA (NATO Airlift Management Agency), 239
NAMSA (NATO Maintenance and Supply Agency), 239
national capability commitments, EDA evaluation of, 217–218
national champions, 32

national general export authorisation, 162
national security
    armaments exemption and, 41,
        108–110
    as characteristic of defence
        procurement, 41–45
    crisis situations exemption and,
        133–134
    exemptions due to. See defence
        derogations from TFEU
    extraordinary and compelling
        reasons of, 195
    judicial scrutiny, 79, 104, 122
    public security and, 41, 73
    review and remedies and need to
        safeguard, 60
national security clearances. See security
    clearances
national sovereignty, 39, 40–41
national transposition. See entries at
    transposition
nationality, prohibition of
    discrimination on grounds of. See
    non-discrimination principle
NATO. See North Atlantic Treaty
    Organization
necessity
    armaments exemption and, 108–110,
        114–116
    proportionality and, 76, 77, 114–116
negotiated procedure with prior
    publication of contract notice,
        322–331
    accelerated version of, 326
    characteristics of, 322–323
    competitive dialogue compared,
        331–336, 490
    competitiveness of, 327, 329
    complexity of defence contracting,
        suitability for, 326
    as default Defence Directive
        procedure, 327
    disadvantages of, 328
    flexibility of, 323, 328, 330
    free use of, in Defence Directive, 324,
        325, 326, 330
    in Public Sector Directive, 322, 324,
        325, 328, 334
    security of information and, 326

security of supply and, 326
standardisation and, 167
state aid and, 178, 180
transparency of, 326, 327
in Utilities Directive, 322, 324, 328
negotiated procedure without prior
    publication of contract notice,
        336–347
    for additional deliveries, 340–341
    for advantageous terms, 340
    or armed forces deployed abroad,
        344–345
    burden of proof requirements, 337
    characteristics of, 336–338
    for commodity market, 340
    contract award notice required
        by, 336
    control mechanisms, 347
    crisis, urgency resulting from,
        342–344
    in extreme urgency, 339–340
    intellectual property, 340
    irregular tenders, after receiving,
        338, 351
    limitations on use of, 337
    list of cases justifying, 325
    in Public Sector Directive, 336,
        338–341
    R&D products and services, 340,
        345–346
    in situations not specific to Defence
        Directive, 338–341
    in situations specific to Defence
        Directive, 341–347
    standardisation and, 167
    state aid, 178, 179
    strict interpretation regarding, 337
    unsuccessful competitive tender,
        following, 338–341
    in Utilities Directive, 336, 339, 340
negotiation or bid invitation, 398–400
Netherlands
    in armaments or defence market, 24
    bilateral initiatives with Belgium, 231
    as defence exporter, 161
    monopsony and export policies, 31
    OCCAR and, 235
    offsets, 409, 427
    in security market, 26

NETMA (NATO Eurofighter and
Tornado Management Agency),
53, 186, 239
neutrality, 6, 45, 79, 80, 122, 416
new Directives for Public Sector
and Utilities, 5, 355–356, 431,
451, 453
new equipment, government-to-
government contracts for, 295, 490
New Zealand, defence exports to, 162
NH90 helicopter, 231, 239
Nice Treaty, 107, 118, 186, 235, 238
non-discrimination principle, 1
contract award criteria, 401, 403
ESA, procurement procedures for
collaborative R&D programmes
in, 350
as legal basis for Defence Directive, 70
negotiated procedure without prior
publication and, 337
offsets and, 413, 414
public procurement law generally, as
aim of, 1
security clearances, 397
subcontracting process and,
441–445, 452
technical specifications and, 364
"Non-Europe in defence", 44–45
non-military forces, 264
non-military security market. See
security market
normal commercial transaction,
177–181
North Atlantic Treaty Organization
(NATO), 239–240
armaments exemption and, 108
armed forces deployed in third
countries and, 288, 344
CEPMA (Central Europe Pipeline
Management Agency), 239
EU, possible competition with, 46
integration, European move toward,
45–49
interoperability, importance of, 44–45
material scope of Defence Directive
and, 273, 275–276, 288
NAHEMA (NATO Helicopter for the
1990s (NH90) Design and
Development, Production and

Logistics Management Agency),
186, 239
NAMA (NATO Airlift Management
Agency), 239
NAMSA (NATO Maintenance and
Supply Agency), 239
national sovereignty and, 40
NETMA (NATO Eurofighter and
Tornado Management Agency),
53, 186, 239
NSPA (NATO Support Agency), 186,
239–240, 351
production logistics organisations, 53
scope of, 247
Norway
defence exports to, 162
EDA collaborations and, 220
EDA Procurement Codes and, 191
offsets, 427
notice, publication of. See publication of
notice
NSG technology, 159
NSPA (NATO Support Agency), 186,
239–240, 351
nuclear powers, 23, 231, 233
Nuclear Supplier's Group, 161
nuclear technology and weapons, 157,
195, 232, 233, 414, 419

obligation of prior authorisation, 149
OCCAR. See Organisation For Joint
Armaments Procurement
off-the-shelf purchases, 50–51,
351, 401
office equipment and supplies, 266, 351
Office of Government Commerce
(United Kingdom), 480
officers' casino, 266
Official Journal of the European
Union (OJ), 1, 3, 92, 165, 166, 213,
257, 271, 298, 312, 318, 322–323,
331, 349, 356, 433,
445, 489
offsets, 11, 54–57, 410–428, 487–488
Commission Guidance Notes on,
422–425
contract award criteria and, 420
in Defence Directive, 418–421
in defence procurement, 406–410

offsets (cont.)
defined, 54, 55, 407, 408
direct military, 55, 407, 417
EDA Procurement Codes and, 198–204, 424, 426
implementation of, 56
indirect civil, 55, 407, 415, 417
indirect military, 55, 407, 415, 417
legality of, 410–428, 453–454
mutual abatements, 202
national laws of Member States and transposition of Defence Directive, 425–428
need for direct address by Defence Directive, 490
original contract, implemented through contractual obligations in, 409
original contract, separate from, 408
outright ban, problems with, 423
Public Sector and Utilities Directives and, 419, 421
review and remedies, 466–467
as separate contracts, 55
SMEs favoured by phase-out of, 454
subcontracts closely related to, 410, 428, 453–454, 466
in TFEU, 411–418
with third countries, 454
typology of, 407
variations between Member States regarding, 408
OGELs (Open General Export Licences), 145
OJ (Official Journal of the European Union), 1, 3, 92, 165, 166, 213, 257, 271, 298, 312, 318, 322–323, 331, 349, 356, 433, 445, 489
Open General Export Licences (OGELs), 145
open procedure, 312–318
advantages of, 314
characteristics of, 312–314
competition, encouraging, 314
as default or normal procedure in older public directives, 313
disadvantages of, 314–317

missing from Defence Directive, 317–318, 490
in Public Sector Directive, 312–313
state aid, 178
transparency of, 314, 316
in Utilities Directive, 313
operational requirements, 189, 289
options for subcontracting. See subcontractors and subcontracting
ordinary legislative procedure, 71, 83
Organisation for Joint Armaments Procurement (OCCAR), 185, 222–225
aims and objectives, 222
assimilation to EDA, 232–234, 235–237
bilateral initiative, starting as, 231
as central purchasing body within personal scope of Defence Directive, 258–259
collaborative projects, management of, 53, 219, 223–224, 351
Defence Directive and, 224–225
EDA and, 219, 225, 232–234
licences not addressed by, 146
material scope of Defence Directive and, 273, 276, 288
scope of, 247
tasks and functions, 223
Organisation For Security and Cooperation in Europe (OSCE), 162
organisation of supply chain, 371–373
organised crime, 20, 219, 279, 281, 382, 383
OSCE (Organisation For Security and Cooperation in Europe), 162
overriding public interest grounds, 66, 69, 71

P-8A Poseidon, 35
Parliament (EU), 13, 83, 190, 419, 423, 459
Parliamentary control of ECAP and EDA, 191
participation in EDA, flexibility of, 236
peace and international security, obligations accepted for the purpose of maintaining, 134

peacekeeping operations, 288–292, 343, 344
peer pressure, 164, 192, 207, 208
Pelkmans, Jan, 166
penalties, 153, 479, 480
personal scope, 248–260
  Annex III and Annex IV of Public Sector Directive, use of, 249–252
  Annex IV listing covered entities, Defence Directive's lack of, 259–260, 489
  armed forces, 249–251
  central purchasing bodies, 255–259
  defined, 246, 248
  EDA, status of, 256–258
  European public bodies, 255–256, 258
  LoI, status of, 258–259
  Ministries of Defence, 249–251
  OCCAR, status of, 258–259
  public law, bodies governed by, 252–253
  state, regional, or local government authorities, 249–252
  utilities, 253–255, 489
Petersberg tasks, 344
PFI (Private Finance Initiative; United Kingdom), 329–330, 332
Pillar structure of EU, abolition of, 46
Point of Contact (EDA), 207
Poland
  in armaments or defence market, 24
  Buy-American tendency in, 29
  joining NATO and EU, 46
  OCCAR and, 235
  offsets, 409, 427
  state aid in, 176
  state ownership and control of national defence industries in, 37
POLARM, 225
police and security forces, 20, 36, 51, 53, 59, 73, 252, 264, 267, 279, 281, 306, 309, 376, 462, 470, 475
political/military context, 39–49
  autarky, 39, 41
  cooperation with other forces, need for interoperability in, 44–45
  information, security of, 43–44

integration, trend toward, 45–49
national security issues, 41–45
national sovereignty issues, 40–41
supply, security of, 42–43
Political and Security Committee, EU, 46, 188
pooling and sharing, EDA Code of Conduct on, 218
Portugal
  offsets, 409, 427
  state ownership and control of national defence industries in, 37
post procurement (contract management) phase, 311, 358, 363, 366, 382
Pourbaix, Nicolas, 113, 114, 117, 333
PPPs (public–private partnerships), 57–58, 329–330, 332
PQQ (Pre-Qualification Questionnaire), 320
pre-emption, 63
pre-procurement phase, 358, 363
Pre-Qualification Questionnaire (PQQ), 320
pre-selection, 315, 319, 320, 398
pressing operational urgency (EDA), 195
prices and pricing. *See* costs
primary EU law, 17, 247, 262, 279, 304, 410, 418, 422, 424, 453, 467
prime contractors
  in armaments or defence market (military), 22–25
  contracting entities or authorities as, in award of subcontracts, 451
  in security market (non-military), 26–27
  subcontracting by. *See* subcontractors and subcontracting
prime contracts. *See entries at* contract
Private Finance Initiative (PFI; United Kingdom), 329–330, 332
procurement procedures, 10, 310–356, 485–486. *See also* competitive dialogue; *entries at* negotiated procedure; open procedure; restricted procedure
  collaborative R&D-based projects, 351–356

procurement procedures (cont.)
  competitiveness of, 311, 314, 319,
    327, 329, 336
  contract award without using (direct
    illegal awards), 477
  contracting stages, 358–359
  control mechanism, 347
  dynamic purchasing systems,
    350–351
  EDA Procurement Codes award
    procedures and criteria, 196–198
  electronic auctions, 350
  flexibility/choice issues, 323, 328, 330,
    334, 336, 464–465, 485–486
  framework agreements, 348–349
  for innovation partnerships, 355–356
  LoI on export procedures and
    transfers, 227–228
  Public Sector Directive provisions, 311
  subcontracting options, 430–438
  transposition of, 312, 317–318, 331,
    334, 341, 347
  typology of, 311
  UNCITRAL Model Law, 336, 351
  Utilities Directive provisions, 311,
    464, 465–466
Procurement Remedies Directives, 5
procurement review proceedings. See
  review and remedies
production phase
  collaboration and, 53
  contract performance conditions
    related to, 376–377, 378
  separating R&D from, 52
professional conduct of potential
  bidders, 384–386
professional rules justified by the
  common good, 69
professional and technical capacity of
  bidders, 323, 332, 388–398, 399
Progress Report on the Implementation
  of the Defence Directive
  (Commission, 2012), 423, 426
prohibition of discrimination on
  grounds of nationality. See
  non-discrimination principle
project-by-project basis, 194, 228
proportionality, 76–79. See also
  intensity of scrutiny

armaments exemption and, 113–119
free movement of goods and services
  and freedom of establishment,
  exemptions for, 66, 69
necessity and, 76, 77, 114–116
public security exemption and, 71,
  76–81
secrecy exemption and, 131–133
strictu sensu, 76, 78
suitability, 76–77
protectionism
  customs duties as, 139
  in defence exports, 160
  in economic context, 28–31
  in political/military context, 39
  TFEU prohibiting, 134
public health, offsets justified on
  grounds of, 413
public law, bodies governed by, 252–253
public–private partnerships (PPPs),
  57–58, 329–330, 332
public procurement law in EU, purpose
  and aims of, 1
Public Sector Directive (2004/18/EC)
  Annex III list of bodies governed by
    public law, 252
  Annex IV list of central government
    authorities, 249–252
  application to defence and security
    procurement before Defence
    Directive, 12
  comparative analysis of Defence
    Directive and, 5
  competitive dialogue and, 334
  on contract awards and award
    criteria, 400, 402
  contract notice, publication of,
    362–364
  on contract performance
    conditions, 367
  contract performance conditions in,
    378, 381
  contracting stages and, 358
  Defence Directive based on, 4, 484
  differences between Defence
    Directive and, 87
  draft for new directive, 5, 355–356,
    431, 451, 453
  dynamic purchasing systems, 351

exemptions, 71
framework agreements in, 348, 349
in-house contracts in, 268
material scope and, 261, 266–267,
    276, 277, 290, 305–307, 462–464
negotiated procedure with prior
    publication in, 322, 324, 325,
    328, 334
negotiated procedure without prior
    publication in, 336, 338–341
offsets and, 419, 421
open procedure in, 178, 312–313
procurement procedures allowed
    by, 311
on qualification of bidders, 389
restricted procedure in, 318, 321,
    322
review and remedies, adaptation for
    purposes of, 462–467
scope of, 245, 247, 463
standards, hierarchy of, 365
subcontracting and, 428, 429,
    431, 441
thresholds, 270
Public Sector Remedies Directive, 5,
    455, 457, 460, 461, 463, 464,
    467–481
public security
    defining, 72–73
    intra-Community transfers
        affecting, 139
    merger regulation, derogation
        of, 175
    national security and, 41, 73
    offsets, legality of, 413
public security exemption, 70–82
    defence derogations from TFEU
        compared, 85, 87, 111
    defining public security for purposes
        of, 72–73
    for dual-use goods, 156
    narrow interpretation of, 73–76
    offsets and, 414
    proportionality test, 71, 76–81
publication of List of 1958, 101, 489
publication of notice, 362–364, 438,
    445–446. See also negotiated
    procedure with prior publication of
    contract notice; negotiated

procedure without prior
    publication of contract notice
    on EBB, 196, 211–216, 257, 271,
        298, 362
    in OJ, 1, 3, 92, 165, 166, 213, 257, 271,
        298, 312, 318, 322–323, 331, 349,
        356, 433, 445
    Public Sector Directive on, 362–364
    security of information and,
        362–364
    security of supply and, 362–364
    subcontracting, 445–446
    Utilities Directive on, 362–364
publicly owned companies. See state aid;
    state ownership and control
Pyman, Mark, 337

qualification of bidders, 382–400
    classified information, 392–397, 399
    contract award criteria distinguished,
        382, 383, 403
    economic and financial standing,
        388–389, 399
    exclusion of unsuitable candidates,
        382, 383–388
    geographical location of sources,
        390–392
    grave professional misconduct,
        384–386
    intellectual property management
        standards, 389–390
    maintenance, modernisation, and
        adaptation, 389–390
    mandatory grounds for exclusion,
        382, 383
    professional conduct, breaches of,
        384–386
    professional and technical capacity,
        323, 332, 388–398, 399
    Public Sector Directive on, 389
    rankings based on, 399
    security clearances, 392–397, 399
    security risks, 386–388
    selection criteria, qualification criteria
        as, 398–400
    study, technical, and research
        facilities, 389–390
    transposition of, 400
    Utilities Directive on, 389

qualitative selection of subcontractors,
    447–448
quantitative restrictions on
    imports, 65

R&D. *See* research and development
radiological goods and services, 195
Rafale fighter aircraft, 25, 169
ranking of bidders, 399
re-exports, 147, 148, 158
reasonableness of prices, 179
red tape, 140, 141, 155, 184
regional contracting authorities,
    249–252
Register of the Certified Defence-related
    Enterprises (CERTIDER), 152
regulator capture, 329
reliability (of bidders), 11, 42, 43, 358,
    360, 361, 372, 380, 382, 383, 386,
    404, 439, 486. *See also* qualification
    of bidders
remedies. *See* review and remedies
repair. *See entries at* maintenance
Report on the Transposition of
    Directive 2009/43/EC (2009),
    142
request to participate, 319, 320, 321,
    323, 326, 332, 355, 363
request for proposals, 351
request for quotations, 351
research and development (R&D),
    50–52
  collaboration in, 53, 218–220,
      283–288, 351–356
  defined, 283
  EDA and collaborative procurement
      programmes, 218–220
  financing, 50
  Internal Market and, 183
  life cycle and, 50, 52–53
  LoI and joint research programmes,
      228–229
  material scope exclusions, 283–288,
      299–301
  negotiated procedure without prior
      publication for, 340,
      345–346
  off-the-shelf purchases and, 50–51
  procurement involving, 51–52

procurement procedures for
    cooperative programmes based on,
    351–356
qualification of bidders based on
    study, technical, and research
    facilities, 389–390
separation from production phase, 52
standarisation and, 169
state aid for, 177
restricted procedure, 318–322
  accelerated version of, 321
  advantages of, 319
  characteristics of, 318–319
  disadvantages of, 320–321
  number of economic operators
      invited in, 321
  in Public Sector Directive, 318,
      321, 322
  state aid and, 178, 180
restrictions on disclosure, transfer, or
    use, 370–371
review and remedies, 12, 455–483,
    488–489. *See also* judicial review
  administrative courts, 461, 471
  armaments exemption, 122
  in camera hearings and rulings, 85,
      100, 130, 469
  confidentiality issues, 60, 471–474
  courts of appeal, 461, 470, 471
  damages, 458
  defence derogations from TFEU,
      derived from, 460–461
  description, adaptation by, 464,
      465–466
  EDA Procurement Codes, 207–209
  flexibility of, 464–465
  Guidance Note, need for, 483, 490
  "hidden" Remedies Directive in
      Defence Directive, 455, 458–460
  independent review, 482
  ineffectiveness, 458, 477–481
  interim relief, 457
  interlocutory proceedings, 474–477
  limitation of material scope, 462–464
  national security, need to safeguard, 60
  need for, 456–458
  offsets and subcontracting, 454,
      466–467
  penalties, 153, 479, 480

Public Sector Directive, adaptation of, 462–467

Public Sector Remedies Directive, 5, 455, 457, 460, 461, 463, 464, 467–481

review chambers or review bodies, 457, 468–474

second instance review, 470, 482, 488

security in review bodies, 471–474

security of supply and information, 460, 471–474

set-asides, 457

special review procedures for armaments exemption, 117–119

Utilities Remedies Directive, 5, 455, 457, 463, 477

risk

of litigation, 320, 364, 381, 384, 397, 405, 444, 460, 481, 483, 487, 488

real, specific, and serious (to security of Member State), 81–82

Romania

in armaments or defence market, 24

EDA Procurement Codes and, 191, 192

joining of NATO and EU, 46

Rome, Treaty of, 88

Ruiz-Jarabo Colomer, Advocate General, 124, 153

rule of law principle, 76, 78, 101, 113, 190, 424, 467, 482, 488, 489

safeguard clause, 301

Safran, 25

sanctity of contracts, 477

Schengen Zone and national sovereignty, 40

Schwarze, Jürgen, 72

scope

of EDA Procurement Codes, 193–195

of other legal frameworks relevant to Defence Directive, 247

of Public Sector Directive, 245, 247, 463

of Public Sector Remedies Directive, 463

of Utilities Directive, 247, 253–255, 463

of Utilities Remedies Directive, 463

scope of Defence Directive, 10, 245–309, 484–485. See also material scope; personal scope

importance of, 246

Public Sector Directive and, 245, 247

rules and guidance on, 247–248

subcontracting, 440–441

transposition of, 259–260, 267, 307–308

Scott, D., 337

scrutiny

intensity of. See intensity of scrutiny

judicial, 79, 104, 122

second instance review, 470, 482, 488

Second Pillar (of the EU), 46, 221, 238. See also Common Foreign and Security Policy

secondary EU law, 17, 61, 63, 66, 68, 82, 109, 118, 123, 128, 134, 137, 163, 241, 247, 262, 279, 280, 345, 410, 418, 422, 424, 442

secrecy exclusion from material scope of Defence Directive, 278–280

secrecy exemption (Article 346(1)(a) TFEU), 128–133

abuse, potential for, 129–131

armaments exemption, characteristics shared with, 133

case-by-case basis, 133

intensity of scrutiny and proportionality test, 131–133

material scope exclusion in Defence Directive and, 278–280

merger control and, 174

negotiated procedure without prior publication used instead of, 339

provisions of, 128–129

sectoral activities, 253

security. See also national security; public security

area of freedom, security, and justice, 71

derogations of TFEU for reasons of. See defence derogations from TFEU

essential interests of, 73, 87, 109, 114, 116, 128, 129, 277, 278, 463, 473

security clearances
  harmonisation of, 489
  mutual recognition of, 394–397
  qualification of bidders, 392–397, 399
  subcontractors, 439
security exemptions. *See* defence
    derogations from TFEU; public
    security exemption
security of information, 11, 358–405,
    486–487
  classified information, 43–44,
    263–264, 361, 379, 380,
    392–397, 399
  contract awards and award criteria,
    400–403
  contract notice, publication of,
    362–364
  contract performance conditions and,
    366, 379–381
  contracting stages dependent on,
    358–359
  defined, 361–362
  in negotiated procedure with prior
    publication of contract notice, 326
  OCCAR and, 228
  in political/military context, 43–44
  qualification of bidders and. *See*
    qualification of bidders
  review and remedies, 460, 471–474
  subcontracting requirements,
    438–439
  as technical capacity criterion,
    397–398
  technical specifications and, 364–365
security market (non-military)
  "Big Six" and "other" Member States,
    division of between, 26
  differentiated from armaments
    market, 18, 21, 60
  importance to European economy, 20
  monopsony not an issue in, 32
  prime contractors in, 26–27
  subcontractors in, 27
security risks, potential bidders as,
    386–388
security of supply, 11, 358–405, 486–487
  contract awards and award criteria,
    400–403

contract notice, publication of,
    362–364
contract performance conditions
  ensuring, 366, 367–368
contracting stages dependent on,
    358–359
defined, 359–361
EDA and, 197
framework agreements and, 348
in ICT Directive, 360
Internal Market and, 146–147
LoI on, 359
in negotiated procedure with prior
    publication of contract notice, 326
OCCAR and, 227, 275
in political/military context, 42–43
qualification of bidders and. *See*
    qualification of bidders
review and remedies, 460
subcontracting and, 448
as technical capacity criterion,
    397–398
technical specifications and, 364–365
selection criteria for bidders
  pre-selection, 315, 319, 320, 398
  qualification criteria as, 398–400. *See
    also* qualification of bidders
  subcontractors, qualitative selection
    of, 447–448
selling-on contracts, 295
sensitive contracts, 263–264
sensitive equipment, works, and
    services, 263
serious internal disturbances affecting
    the maintenance of law and
    order, 133
serious international tension
    constituting a threat of war, 134
services, free movement of, 67–70,
    411–412
set-asides, 457
shared competence, 62
sharing and pooling, EDA Code of
    Conduct on, 218
ships and shipbuilding, 23, 25, 34, 91,
    92, 100, 169, 170, 265, 270
shortlisting, 319, 320, 323, 332,
    398

single source procurement procedure.
See negotiated procedure without
prior publication of contract notice
SIPRI (Stockholm International Peace
Research Institute), 160
Slovakia
joining NATO and EU, 46
offsets, 427
Slovenia, offsets in, 427
Slynn, Sir Gordon, Advocate
General, 416
small arms, 23, 36, 51, 53, 100, 350
small and medium-sized enterprises
(SMEs)
EDA Procurement Codes on
subcontracting and, 205
framework agreements and, 446
Internal Market and, 183, 184
life cycle, contracting separate parts
of, 52
offsets, favoured by phase-out of, 454
in security market, 26
subcontracting and, 428, 429,
436–437, 446, 450, 453, 466
thresholds and, 272
SMEs. *See* small and medium-sized
enterprises
soft defence material, 95
soft law, 216, 256, 411–412, 422, 423
soft loans, 37, 176
sovereignty, national, 39, 40–41
Soviet Union
dissolution of, 45
end of Cold War and defence budget
reductions, 19
Spain
in armaments or defence market,
23, 24
defence budget cuts, 19
as defence exporter, 160
LoI, participation in, 396. *See also*
Letter of Intent
offsets, 409, 417, 427
procurement procedures in, 316
in security market, 26
special review procedures for
armaments exemption, 117–119,
122–125
Spiegel, Nico, 482

stakeholders, 4, 5, 12, 61, 125, 168,
185, 212, 317, 327, 328, 356, 428,
460, 485
standardisation, 166–169, 196,
365
standstill period, 179, 302, 458,
477, 479
state aid, 176–182
armaments exemption and, 181
competition affected by, 176
cross-subsidisation problem,
179, 182
defence sector practices in EU,
176–181
dual-use goods, 182
legality under TFEU, 181–182
"normal commercial transaction"
and, 177–181
as public ownership, 176
as support, 176
state contracting authorities,
249–252
state ownership and control
economic consequences of,
37–38
political/military context for, 39
state sovereignty, 39, 40–41
stationing of troops, 274–275
stealth technology, 159
Stockholm International Peace
Research Institute (SIPRI), 160
strategic assets, 175
A Strategy for a Stronger and More
Competitive European Defence
Industry (European Commission,
2007), 106, 137, 141, 168, 169, 175,
177, 393
study, technical, and research facilities,
389–390
subassemblies, 261
subcontractors and subcontracting, 11,
428–452, 487–488
in armaments or defence market
(military), 27
awards and award criteria, 450–451
competitive procedures, awarded
on basis of (Option B), 432–434,
438, 439, 440, 441, 443,
444, 452

subcontractors and subcontracting
(cont.)
  competitive procedures, minimum
    percentage of subcontracts
    awarded on basis of (Option C),
    434–436, 438, 439, 440, 441, 443,
    444, 452
  contracting authorities or entities as
    prime contractors, 451
  in defence procurement, 406, 410
  EDA Procurement Codes and, 198,
    204–207, 429, 440, 444
  equal treatment principle, 441–445
  exception clause, 448–450
  framework agreements for, 446–447
  freedom of price contractor to choose
    subcontractors (Option A),
    431–432, 438, 439, 441
  geographical location of sources, 390
  importance of Defence Directive
    regime on, 452–453
  information on subcontractors, as
    contract performance condition,
    380–381
  minimum percentage of work
    subcontracted and competition for
    subcontracting beyond minimal
    percentage (Option D), 436–438,
    439, 440, 441, 443, 444, 452
  new Directives on, 451, 453
  non-discrimination principle,
    441–445, 452
  notice, publication of, 445–446
  offsets closely related to, 410, 428,
    453–454, 466
  options for, 430–438
  prime contract, subcontracting
    requirements in, 438–440
  Public Sector Directive and, 428, 429,
    431, 441, 453
  qualitative selection of, 447–448
  review and remedies, 466–467
  scope rules, 440–441
  security clearances, 439
  security-of-information
    requirements, 438–439
  security of supply and, 448
  SMEs and, 428, 429, 436–437, 446,
    450, 453, 466
  thresholds, 440, 443, 445–446
  Title III Defence Directive rules
    applicable to, 440–451
  transparency requirements, 438,
    441–445, 452
  transposition of rules on, 430, 432,
    433, 434–436, 437, 441, 443, 448,
    450, 451
  Utilities Directive and, 429, 431,
    441, 453
subscribing Member States (EDA), 191
substitution, 406, 410, 466–467. *See also*
  offsets; subcontractors and
  subcontracting
sunrise and sunset industries, 182
supplementary goods and services, 195
supply chains, 428. *See also*
  subcontractors and subcontracting
  EDA Code of Best Practice on. *See*
    EDA Codes of Conduct for
    Procurement and the Supply
    Chain
  length of, 57
  organisation of, 371–373
supply, security of. *See* security of supply
supranationality and supranational
  institutions, 190–191, 192, 193,
  210, 218, 221, 224, 229, 348, 394
Supreme Court (United Kingdom), 471
surplus equipment, 292–299
suspension of EDA Procurement Codes,
  214, 238
Sweden
  in armaments or defence market,
    23, 24
  LoI, participation in, 396. *See also*
    Letter of Intent
  offsets, 409, 427
  in security market, 26
Switzerland
  defence exports to, 162
  EDA and, 220

take-overs, 172, 175
target cost incentive contracts, 179, 180
tax exemption, relief, deferral, or
  cancellation, 37, 176
TDCs (Transnational Defence
  Companies), 227

technical information, LoI on treatment of, 229

technical or intellectual property rights. *See* intellectual property

technical and professional capacity of bidders, 323, 332, 388–398, 399

technical specifications, 364–365
  Internal Market and, 166, 168, 169
  national transposition of, 381–382
  OCCAR and, 223
  procurement procedures and, 29, 318, 319, 320, 322, 323, 325, 326, 331
  in published contract notice, 362–364
  security of supply and information, 364–365

technical, study, and research facilities of bidders, 389–390

technological and contractual context, 49–58. *See also* life cycle; offsets; research and development
  collaboration, 53–54
  corruption, 57, 58
  off-the-shelf purchases, 50–51
  production cycle separated from R&D, 52
  public–private partnerships, 57–58
  supply chains, length of, 57

Tenders Electronic Daily (TED), 362

tenders and tendering, 313
  irregular tenders, 338, 351
  two-stage tendering, 351
  unsuccessful competitive tender, 338–339

terrorism, 20, 188, 219, 279, 281

testing, of proportionality. *See* proportionality

TFEU. *See also* defence derogations from TFEU
  competition law in, 169–171
  Internal Market established by, 62–63
  legal basis for Defence Directive in, 61, 82–83
  material scope of Defence Directive and, 267, 303–305
  offsets under, 411–418
  principles in Defence Directive and, 442

protectionist measures prohibited by, 134

scope of, 247

state aid, legality of, 181–182

Thales, 25

Thessaloniki meeting of European Council (2003), 186

third countries. *See also specific third countries*
  armed forces deployed in, 288–292, 344–345
  defence exports to. *See* defence exports
  defined, 273
  geographical location of sources (qualification of bidders), 390–392
  government-to-government contracts, 292–299
  ICT Directive limitations on exports to, 152–153
  material scope exception for contracts awarded under international arrangements, 272–276
  offsets with, 454
  stationing of troops, 274–275
  two different groups of, 162

three-Pillar structure of EU, abolition of, 46

thresholds, 269–272, 440, 443, 445–446, 462

Thyssen Krupp Maritime Systems, 34

TI (Transparency International), 58

Towards an EU Defence Equipment Policy, 221

trade in armaments and dual-use goods, 138. *See also* armaments, trade in; dual-use goods

training, 329

trans-border mergers, 172

transaction costs, of restricted procedure, 315, 320

Transnational Defence Companies (TDCs), 227

transparency, 1
  in Afghan market, 292
  of competitive dialogue procedure, 331
  contract awards and award criteria, 401
  EDA Procurement Codes and, 196, 213

transparency (cont.)
List of 1958, publication of, 101
of negotiated procedure with prior
publication, 326, 327
of negotiated procedure without prior
publication, 336
of open procedure, 314, 316
of restricted procedure, 319, 320
state aid and, 177
subcontracting process and, 438,
441–445, 452
Transparency International (TI), 58
transport aircraft, 53, 95, 231
transposition of Defence Directive,
6, 14
on contract award criteria, 403, 405
on contract performance conditions,
381–382
ineffectiveness, as remedy, 481
offsets, 425–428
procurement procedures, 312,
317–318, 331, 334, 341, 347
on qualification of bidders, 400
scope, 259–260, 267, 307–308
on security of supply and
information, 381–382
on subcontracting, 430, 432, 433,
434–436, 437, 441, 443, 448,
450, 451
on technical specifications, 381–382
transposition of ICT Directive, 142, 155
Transposition Report of Defence
Directive (European Commission,
2012), 149, 154, 155, 214, 261
Trepte, Peter Armin, 329, 350, 366
tribunaux administratifs (France), 471
troops. See armed forces
Trybus, Martin
European Defence Procurement Law
(1999), 4, 136
European Union Law and Defence
Integration (2005), 4, 136
as witness at IMCO hearing on
Defence Package, 459
Turkey
geographical location of sources
(qualification of bidders), 391
hypothetical offsets cases involving,
416, 417

OCCAR and, 235
two-stage tendering, 351
Typhoon. See Eurofighter/Typhoon
aircraft

UNCITRAL (United Nations
Commission for International
Trade Law), Model Law on
Procurement, 336, 351
uniforms, 266, 306
United Kingdom
in armaments or defence market,
23, 24
bilateral Defence Treaty with France
(2010), 231, 233
competitive market for national
defence industries in, 38
defence budget cuts, 19
as defence exporter, 160, 161
on EDA Procurement Codes
(2004), 212
land systems in, 34
LoI, participation in, 396. See also
Letter of Intent
monopsony and export policies, 31
as nuclear power, 23, 231, 233
Office of Government Commerce, 480
offsets, 409, 427
OGELs (Open General Export
Licences) in, 145
PFI (Private Finance Initiative),
329, 330, 332
procurement procedures in, 315, 320,
324, 332, 333
public–private partnerships in,
57, 58
review and remedies in, 458, 461, 463,
471, 475, 476, 481, 483
in security market, 26
standards, hierarchy of, 365
state aid in, 176
transposition of Defence Directive in.
See transposition of Defence
Directive
United Nations
armed forces deployed in third
countries and, 288, 344
Charter requirements and national
sovereignty, 40

defence exports, authorisation of, 162
interoperability for acting in concert
with, 44–45
United Nations Commission for
International Trade Law
(UNCITRAL), Model Law on
Procurement, 336, 351
United States. *See also* Buy-American
access to market, 29
defence equipment market in,
33–35, 108
defence exports to, 162
geographical location of sources
(qualification of bidders), 391
Germany, troops stationed in, 274
offsets, 408, 454
protectionism and defence
exports, 160
unipolar world order and trend toward
European integration, 45, 47
unsuccessful competitive tender,
allowance of negotiated procedure
without prior publication after,
338–339
urgency
extreme, 339–340
resulting from a crisis, 342–344
utilities
as contracting authorities, 253–255
personal scope, inclusion in,
253–255, 489
Utilities Directive, 5
on contract awards and award
criteria, 400, 402
contract notice, publication of,
362–364
on contract performance conditions,
367, 378, 381
draft for new directive, 451
dynamic purchasing systems, 351
exemptions, 71
material scope and, 261, 267, 277,
290, 307, 462–464
negotiated procedure with prior
publication in, 322, 324, 328

negotiated procedure without prior
publication in, 336, 339, 340
offsets and, 419, 421
open procedure in, 178, 313
procurement procedures allowed by,
311, 464, 465–466
on qualification of bidders, 389
scope of, 247, 253–255, 463
subcontracting and, 429, 431, 441
Utilities Remedies Directive, 5, 455, 457,
463, 477

value for money, 1, 14, 30, 171, 292,
300–303, 314, 366, 452
value thresholds, 269–272, 440, 443,
445–446, 462
Verloren van Themaat, Pieter, Advocate
General, 80
Vosper Thornycraft, 34

war
crisis situations exemption in event
of, 134
serious international tension
constituting a threat of, 134
war material, list of 1958, 88–104,
134
Warsaw Pact, 45
Wassenaar Arrangement, 161
Western European Armaments
Group (WEAG), 194, 218,
233–237, 362
Western European Armaments
Organisation (WEAO),
233–237, 362
Western European Union (WEU), 225,
233–237
Wilson, R., 337
withdrawal of exports, 369, 371
workers, free movement of, 68, 71
World Bank, 247, 273
World Trade Organization (WTO)
GATS, 114, 134
GATT, 114–115, 130, 134
GPA, 420